ENCYCLOPEDIA OF AMERICAN HISTORY

Revolution and New Nation
1761 to 1812

VOLUME III

ENCYCLOPEDIA OF AMERICAN HISTORY

ENCYCLOPEDIA OF AMERICAN HISTORY

Revolution and New Nation
1761 to 1812

VOLUME III

Paul A. Gilje, Editor
Gary B. Nash, General Editor

Facts On File, Inc.

Encyclopedia of American History:
Revolution and New Nation (1761 to 1812)

Copyright © 2003 by Paul A. Gilje
Maps on pages 47, 58, 83, 95, 112, 128, 152, 158, 174, 196, 211, 219, 220, 244, 257,
262, 274, 288, 306, 318, 319, 348, 357 and 389 Copyright © 2003 by Facts On File, Inc.

Editorial Director: Laurie E. Likoff
Editor in Chief: Owen Lancer
Chief Copy Editor: Michael G. Laraque
Associate Editor: Dorothy Cummings
Production Director: Olivia McKean
Production Associates: Rachel L. Berlin and Theresa Montoya
Art Director: Cathy Rincon
Interior Designer: Joan M. Toro
Desktop Designers: Erika K. Arroyo and David C. Strelecky
Maps and Illustrations: Dale E. Williams and Jeremy Eagle

Facts On File, Inc.
132 West 31st Street
New York NY 10001

Library of Congress Cataloging-in-Publication Data

Encyclopedia of American history / Gary B. Nash, general editor.
p.   cm.
Includes bibliographical references and indexes.
Contents: v. 1. Three worlds meet — v. 2. Colonization and settlement —
v. 3. Revolution and new nation — v. 4. Expansion and reform — v. 5. Civil War
and Reconstruction — v. 6. The development of the industrial United States —
v. 7. The emergence of modern America — v. 8. The Great Depression
and World War II — v. 9. Postwar United States — v. 10. Contemporary
United States. — v. 11 Comprehensive index
ISBN 0-8160-4371-X (set)   ISBN 0-8160-4363-9 (v. 3)
1. United States—History—Encyclopedias. I. Nash, Gary B.
E174 .E53 2002
973′.03—dc21   2001051278

Contents

List of Entries

About the Editors

General Editor: Gary B. Nash received a Ph.D from Princeton University. He is currently director of the National Center for History in the Schools at the University of California, Los Angeles, where he teaches American history of the colonial and Revolutionary era. He is a published author of college and precollegiate history texts. Among his best-selling works is *The American People: Creating a Nation and Society* (Addison Wesley, Longman), now in its fifth edition.

Nash is an elected member of the Society of American Historians, American Academy of Arts and Sciences, and the American Philosophical Society. He has served as past president of the Organization of American Historians, 1994–95, and was a founding member of the National Council for History Education, 1990.

Volume Editor: Paul A. Gilje, University of Oklahoma, holds a Ph.D from Brown University. He is the author of several books, including *Rioting in America* (Indiana University Press, 1996) and *The Road to Mobocracy: Popular Disorder in New York City, 1763–1834* (University of North Carolina Press, 1987).

Foreword

The Encyclopedia of American History series is designed as a handy reference to the most important individuals, events, and topics in U.S. history. In 10 volumes, the encyclopedia covers the period from the 15th century, when European explorers first made their way across the Atlantic Ocean to the Americas, to the present day. The encyclopedia is written for precollegiate as well as college students, for parents of young learners in the schools, and for the general public. The volume editors are distinguished historians of American history. In writing individual entries, each editor has drawn upon the expertise of scores of specialists. This ensures the scholarly quality of the entire series. Articles contributed by the various volume editors are uncredited.

This 10-volume encyclopedia of "American history" is broadly conceived to include the historical experience of the various peoples of North America. Thus, in the first volume, many essays treat the history of a great range of indigenous people before contact with Europeans. In the same vein, readers will find essays in the first several volumes that sketch Spanish, Dutch, and French explorers and colonizers who opened up territories for European settlement that later would become part of the United States. The venues and cast of characters in the American historical drama are thus widened beyond traditional encyclopedias.

In creating the eras of American history that define the chronological limits of each volume, and in addressing major topics in each era, the encyclopedia follows the architecture of *The National Standards for United States History, Revised Edition* (Los Angeles: National Center for History in the Schools, 1996). Mandated by the U.S. Congress, the national standards for U.S. history have been widely used by states and school districts in organizing curricular frameworks and have been followed by many other curriculum-building efforts.

Entries are cross-referenced, when appropriate, with *See also* citations at the end of articles. At the end of most entries, a listing of articles and books allows readers to turn to specialized sources and historical accounts. In each volume, an array of maps provide geographical context, while numerous illustrations help vivify the material covered in the text. A time line is included to provide students with a chronological reference to major events occurring in the given era. The selection of historical documents in the back of each volume gives students experience with the raw documents that historians use when researching history. A comprehensive index to each volume also facilitates the reader's access to particular information.

In each volume, long entries are provided for major categories of American historical experience. These categories may include: African Americans, agriculture, art and architecture, business, economy, education, family life, foreign policy, immigration, labor, Native Americans, politics, population, religion, urbanization, and women. By following these essays from volume to volume, the reader can access what might be called a mini-history of each broad topic, for example, family life, immigration, or religion.

— Gary B. Nash
University of California, Los Angeles

Introduction

The American Revolution was one of the most dramatic and important eras of our history. It was during this period that a group of relatively unconnected colonies revolted against the king of England, proclaimed their independence, and reformulated politics. In the process, Americans not only molded representative government within the states but also created a new nation. This story has larger-than-life characters—George Washington, Thomas Jefferson, John Adams, and James Madison, to name just a few. At the same time, there were others who made sacrifices and left an indelible mark on what it means to be an American. Without the men who lived and died aboard the *Jersey* prison ship, without the Native Americans who fought with and against the British, and without the slaves who seized upon the ideal of liberty in the Age of Revolution, our history would have been very different. In relating how colonial America became a vibrant and expanding republic, this volume does more than tell the story of the victors.

The word *patriots* for supporters of revolution has been avoided, and it is not assumed that the advocates of the Constitution were right in attacking the Articles of Confederation. Loyalists were as concerned with liberty as revolutionaries, and the anti-Federalists sought to protect the republic as well as the Federalists. Within this volume the reader will find entries on the founding fathers alongside entries that reveal the range of voices—Native American, African-American, European-American, male and female—of the people who made the American nation.

—Paul A. Gilje
University of Oklahoma

ENTRIES
A TO Z

Adams, Abigail (1744–1818)

Abigail Adams is best remembered as the wife of one president and the mother of another. She was born on November 11, 1744, in Weymouth, Massachusetts, the daughter of William Smith, a Congregationalist minister, and his wife Elizabeth Quincy. She did not receive any formal schooling and was educated at home. Despite this, she was an avid reader and letter-writer throughout her life. When she was 15 years old, Abigail Smith met JOHN ADAMS, a lawyer nine years her senior from nearby Braintree (now Quincy), Massachusetts. After a long courtship they married in 1764, when Abigail was 19. It was a happy marriage that lasted 54 years until Abigail's death in 1818.

John and Abigail Adams were separated for many years during their marriage because of John's activities in support of the Revolution, first as congressman in Philadelphia between 1774 and 1777 and later when he served abroad as a diplomat between 1778 and 1788. During the latter years of John Adams's tenure as a diplomat, Abigail joined him in France and Britain. During their years apart Abigail raised four children: Abigail, John Quincy, Charles, and Thomas Boylston. Another child died in infancy.

Owing to their separation, Abigail and John Adams carried on an extensive correspondence that provides an invaluable insight into how one famous couple coped with the domestic challenges posed by the Revolution. In her letters Abigail did not simply discuss domestic matters; she also expressed political opinions—for example, condemning slavery and advocating improved education for women. When Congress declared independence in 1776, Abigail famously cautioned John and other congressmen to "remember the ladies." She made this request in the context of criticizing the legal authority of husbands over wives in America. Abigail recognized that if Congress declared independence, then it would be necessary to rewrite the laws in America, and she saw an opportunity to ameliorate the legal restrictions on women. Her comment has been portrayed as one of the first statements of feminist thinking in America, although this interpretation is tempered by the fact that her sentiments were expressed in the form of a request in a private letter.

Abigail Adams was a close friend and political confidant and adviser to her husband. In her later years she was a staunch supporter of the political aspirations of her eldest son, John Quincy Adams, who was elected president in 1824. Abigail Adams died on October 28, 1818.

See also WOMEN'S RIGHTS AND STATUS.

Further reading: Charles W Akers, *Abigail Adams: An American Woman* (Boston: Little, Brown, 1980); Edith B. Gelles, *Portia: The World of Abigail Adams* (Bloomington: Indiana University Press, 1992).

— Francis D. Cogliano

Adams, John (1735–1826)

Revolutionary leader, born October 30, 1735, in Braintree (now Quincy), Massachusetts, John Adams was descended from a family that enjoyed local prominence. His father was a farmer who had held office as a selectman and militia officer. In 1751 John Adams gained admission to Harvard College and became the first of his family to attend college. When he graduated from Harvard in 1755, he accepted a position as a teacher in Worcester, Massachusetts. The life of a provincial schoolmaster did not appeal to Adams, and he began to read law with James Putnam, a prominent Worcester lawyer. In 1758 he returned to Braintree with an eye to practicing law and gaining admission to the Boston bar. During the years when he established his legal practice, Adams began to court Abigail Smith, the daughter of a minister, William Smith, from neighboring Weymouth. They were married on October 25, 1764. John and ABIGAIL ADAMS enjoyed a long, loving, and happy marriage that lasted for 54 years until Abigail's death in 1818.

Adams's legal work frequently took him to Boston, where he became involved in the movement against British

John Adams, second president of the United States. Painting by E. Savage in 1800 *(Library of Congress)*

rule. In 1765 he penned a series of anonymous articles for the *Boston Gazette* in opposition to the STAMP ACT (1765). In these articles, which were collected and published as *A Dissertation on Canon and Feudal Law,* Adams traced the origin and rise of freedom. Britons derived their rights, he argued, from God, not from the Crown or Parliament. In the same year he opposed the Stamp Act more explicitly when he drafted the Braintree Instructions, in which he asserted the act was unconstitutional because Americans had not given their consent to it. Through these writings Adams established himself as an articulate and intelligent critic of British imperial regulations. As a lawyer Adams was committed to the rule of law. He demonstrated this in 1770 when he agreed to defend the British soldiers tried for murder as a result of the so-called BOSTON MASSACRE (March 5, 1770). Adams, along with JOSIAH QUINCY, secured acquittals for the accused soldiers except for two who were convicted of a lesser charge of manslaughter. Adams was criticized by radical voices in the Boston press for his role in the trial. His defense of the soldiers revealed a willingness to take stands and to challenge popular sentiment, traits that would characterize Adams's later public career. In the wake of the adoption of the COERCIVE ACTS (1774) in the aftermath of the BOSTON TEA PARTY (December 16, 1773), Adams concluded that reconciliation between Britain and the colonies was unlikely. Thus in

1774, when he was elected to represent Massachusetts in the FIRST CONTINENTAL CONGRESS (1774), Adams went to Philadelphia as one of the foremost radicals in the revolutionary movement.

Between 1774 and 1777 Adams served in the first and SECOND CONTINENTAL CONGRESS (1775) in Philadelphia. This was probably the most productive and important period in the long public career of John Adams. In 1775 he published a series of newspaper essays under the pseudonym 'Novanglus' (New Englander) in which he argued that Parliament could only regulate the external TRADE of the colonies and, therefore, its revenue acts were illegal. He contended that Americans had sought to preserve the British constitution and that it was the British government that was acting in an unconstitutional manner. When fighting broke out in the spring of 1775 Adams worked tirelessly within Congress. He made crucial contributions to the war effort as chair of the Board of War and Ordnance. In June 1775 he successfully advocated the appointment of the Virginian GEORGE WASHINGTON as the commander in chief of the rebel forces. Washington's appointment indicated that the rebellion would be an intercolonial effort rather than a New England affair. Adams was also an early and forceful advocate of the creation of a navy to challenge British dominance at sea. By the time Adams left Congress in 1777, he had served on 90 congressional committees, more than anyone else, chairing 25 of them. His myriad efforts led the New York congressman JOHN JAY to describe Adams as "the first man in the House." Adams also contributed to the debate over independence. In January 1776 he published a pamphlet, *Thoughts on Government,* that set out a design as to how the colonies could govern themselves if independent, recommending republican legislative and executive forms for the state governments. In May 1776 Adams helped to draft the resolutions debated by Congress that would declare the colonies independent. In June he served on the committee that assisted THOMAS JEFFERSON in drafting the DECLARATION OF INDEPENDENCE, and on July 1 he delivered a crucial speech in favor of independence that helped to sway moderate congressmen in favor of the Declaration.

Adams spent most of the decade from 1778 to 1788 abroad on diplomatic missions on behalf of the fledgling United States in France, the Netherlands, and Britain. As a diplomat he secured loans from the Dutch to help finance the REVOLUTIONARY WAR (1775–83); chaired the American commission that agreed to the TREATY OF PARIS (1783), which won the independence of the United States on generally favorable terms; and served as the first American ambassador to Britain between 1785 and 1788. Despite these achievements Adams found his years as a diplomat trying. For much of his time abroad he was isolated from Abigail and their children. Combative, blunt, and sometimes abrasive, Adams was ill-suited for diplomacy. Soon after his arrival in France he fell out with BENJAMIN FRANKLIN and offended his French hosts.

During Adams's service abroad, significant constitutional developments occurred in the United States, including the ratification of the ARTICLES OF CONFEDERATION and the writing and ratification of the United States Constitution. Adams contributed indirectly to the federal constitution. In 1779 he was the major author of a draft constitution for Massachusetts, which was eventually adopted in 1780. That constitution created a strong executive, judiciary, and a bicameral legislature (as well as a bill of rights) and served as one of JAMES MADISON's models when drafting the federal constitution. Adams also contributed to the debate over the federal constitution when he published *Defense of the Constitutions of the Government of the United States* in three volumes in 1787 and 1788. The work—a wide-ranging (and occasionally rambling) commentary on the history, structure, and functioning of political systems—presented Adams's arguments in favor of a centralized bicameral system such as the one he had designed for Massachusetts. The *Defense of Constitutions* signaled that Adams, the radical of 1776, was by 1788 more closely identified with the conservative wing of the revolutionary movement. As early as 1770, when he defended the British soldiers accused in the Boston Massacre, Adams had expressed skepticism about placing too much faith in the will of the common people. He believed that the public, whose will must be consulted in a republic, could also be fickle, passionate, and unstable. By 1788 he feared, as did many supporters of the constitution, that excessive democracy constituted as much a threat to American liberty as royal tyranny did in 1776 and parliamentary high-handedness had in 1765. Adams's concern about popular upheaval was confirmed by the outbreak of the FRENCH REVOLUTION (1789–1815). In response to civil disorder in Europe and North America, Adams published a series of essays that appeared as a book in 1791, *Discourses on Davila*, which reflected his increasingly conservative views on politics.

Owing to his conservative outlook, Adams was associated with the FEDERALIST PARTY (though he was not close to the party's leader, ALEXANDER HAMILTON). In 1789 Adams was elected vice president to serve under George Washington. Although he described the vice presidency as "the most insignificant office that ever the invention of man contrived," Adams served two terms as Washington's deputy. This period witnessed the emergence of sharp partisan divisions between the Federalists led by Washington and Hamilton and the DEMOCRATIC-REPUBLICANS led by Jefferson and Madison. In the first openly contested presidential election in 1796, Adams narrowly defeated Jefferson by a vote of 71 to 68 in the Electoral College.

The most urgent issue confronting Adams when he became president concerned American relations with France. Britain and France had been at war since 1793. Although the United States pursued a policy of neutrality, JAY'S TREATY (1794) had established a close trading relationship between Britain and the United States. The French interpreted Adams's victory as an endorsement of the Federalists' pro-British policy. In 1796 the French began seizing American ships and in early 1797 expelled the American ambassador at Versailles. The two nations engaged in an undeclared naval war (the QUASI WAR, 1798–1800), and both sides felt that an open declaration of war was inevitable. Indeed, there was tremendous clamor in the United States for war with France in 1798. In anticipation of war, Congress appropriated money to strengthen the nation's defenses and adopted a series of bills known as the ALIEN AND SEDITION ACTS (1798) to stifle IMMIGRATION and internal dissent. Despite a brief surge in his own popularity and the pressure to declare war, Adams hesitated. Always one who preferred to be right rather than popular, Adams pursued long and complex negotiations with the French and succeeded in preventing an open breach between the two former allies. However, his policy alienated many within his own party, especially Alexander Hamilton, who strongly supported a war with France.

Adams stood for reelection in 1800 without the full support of his party. Alexander Hamilton schemed against Adams, splitting the Federalist vote. In the controversial ELECTION OF 1800, Adams finished third in the Electoral College behind Jefferson and AARON BURR. Repudiated by the public and his party, Adams was bitterly disappointed. One of his last official acts was to fill a large number of lifetime judgeships with Federalist jurists. These were the so-called midnight judges, whose appointments angered the Democratic-Republicans because they were made after the election. Adams departed WASHINGTON, D.C., without attending the inauguration of his old friend, colleague, and successor Thomas Jefferson.

Thirty-six years after the Stamp Act crisis, John Adams left public life in 1801. He spent the next 25 years writing newspaper articles reviewing the AMERICAN REVOLUTION and his presidency. In 1812 his wife Abigail mediated the rebirth of the friendship between Adams and Jefferson. The long correspondence carried on by these elder statesmen remains a monument in the history of American letters. Adams lived to see his oldest son John Quincy Adams elected president in 1824. He died on July 4, 1826, the 50th anniversary of the Declaration of Independence. His last words were "Thomas Jefferson still survives." Jefferson had died several hours earlier on the same day.

See also JUDICIARY ACT OF 1801; POLITICAL PARTIES; REPUBLICANISM.

Further reading: Lester J. Cappon, ed., *The Adams-Jefferson Letters*, 2 vols. (Chapel Hill: University of North Carolina Press, 1959); Joseph J. Ellis, *Passionate Sage: The Character and Legacy of John Adams* (New York: W. W. Norton, 1993); John Ferling, *John Adams: A Life* (New York: Henry Holt, 1996); David G. McCullough, *John Adams* (New York: Simon & Schuster, 2001); Peter Shaw *The Character of John Adams* (Chapel Hill: University of North Carolina Press, 1976).

— Francis D. Cogliano

Adams, Samuel (1722–1803)

During the decade from 1765 to 1775, when Boston was at the center of the RESISTANCE MOVEMENT (1764–75) against British rule, Samuel Adams was the town's most important political leader. Born in Boston on September 27, 1722, Adams was the son of a merchant. After graduating from Harvard College in 1740, Adams endeavored, unsuccessfully, to establish himself as a brewer and newspaper publisher. Between 1756 and 1765 Adams served as a tax collector in Boston, where he proved no more suc-

Samuel Adams. Painting by John Singleton Copley
(Hulton/Archive)

cessful at collecting taxes than he had at publishing or brewing. Indeed, the Boston Town Meeting found him to be more than £10,000 in arrears in his collections.

Despite, or perhaps because of, his laxness as a tax collector, Adams was elected to the Massachusetts assembly, the Great and General Court, in 1765, where he served as the assembly's clerk until 1780. In this capacity Adams played a prominent role in coordinating the assembly's opposition to British taxation from 1765 to 1775. Adams was also active in several organizations including the LOYAL NINE, the North End Caucus, and most importantly, the SONS OF LIBERTY. He also served as the chair of the Boston Town Meeting. Through his participation in these groups, Adams emerged as the most important popular political leader in Boston prior to the REVOLUTIONARY WAR (1775–83). He was a vocal critic of British taxation and contended that Parliament, along with its few American allies, sought to enslave Americans and take away their liberties. Adams was a very effective political leader, protest-organizer, and propagandist, writing newspaper articles that were critical of the British taxation policies. He also organized numerous popular demonstrations and protests. For example, he led the successful movement to demand the removal of British troops from Boston after the BOSTON MASSACRE (March 5, 1770). In 1772 he created the Boston COMMITTEE OF CORRESPONDENCE, which helped to coordinate anti-British resistance throughout Massachusetts and, eventually, across the colonies. He also chaired the extralegal meetings that preceded the BOSTON TEA PARTY (December 16, 1773). In 1774, through the Committee of Correspondence, he led the call for a CONTINENTAL CONGRESS to coordinate American resistance to the COERCIVE ACTS (1774). During the decade between the STAMP ACT (1765) and the outbreak of war at LEXINGTON (April 19, 1775), Adams was at the forefront of the revolutionary movement in Massachusetts and North America.

Adams made his greatest contribution to the revolutionary movement prior to the Revolutionary War. Nonetheless he continued to play an important role in Massachusetts politics and the revolutionary movement. Between 1774 and 1781 he represented Massachusetts in the Continental Congress. He proved to be a stalwart in that body, serving on numerous committees that helped to manage the war effort. Back in Massachusetts he served on the committee that drafted the state's new constitution in 1780 (largely the handiwork of his distant cousin, JOHN ADAMS), and he campaigned for the successful ratification of that document. Although his political influence had waned during the post-war period, Adams remained politically active during the 1780s and 1790s. He served in the Massachusetts senate and attended the Massachusetts convention that considered the ratification of the proposed federal constitution. Always wary of centralized power,

Adams had been a moderate ANTI-FEDERALIST. A series of popular demonstrations combined with an intense campaign within the convention convinced Adams and Governor JOHN HANCOCK to give the document their reluctant support, which proved instrumental in the convention's decision to endorse it. Adams served as lieutenant governor of Massachusetts under Hancock from 1789 to 1793 and as governor from 1793 to 1797. Because of his populist inclinations and suspicion of centralized power, Adams was never really accepted by the FEDERALIST PARTY who came to dominate Massachusetts politics during the 1790s. In the ELECTION OF 1800 he supported the Republican THOMAS JEFFERSON against his Federalist kinsman, John Adams. Samuel Adams died on October 2, 1803.

Further reading: Pauline Maier, *The Old Revolutionaries: Political Lives in the Age of Samuel Adams* (New York: Knopf, 1980); John C. Miller, *Sam Adams: Pioneer in Propaganda* (Boston: Little, Brown, 1936).

— Francis D. Cogliano

African Americans

African-American life and identity underwent significant changes during the late 18th and early 19th centuries. In 1750 SLAVERY was legal in all British North American colonies, and well over 90 percent of African-descended people remained in bondage. The international SLAVE TRADE operated throughout the 1700s: In the 1750s alone, 53,000 Africans per year were transported to the Americas. Before the AMERICAN REVOLUTION, ANTISLAVERY AND ABOLITION sentiment touched few slaveholding white colonials. By the early 1800s, however, the situation had changed: Every northern state moved to abolish slavery between 1777 and 1804; the slave trade was banned in the United States beginning in 1808; free black populations grew and prospered, particularly in northern urban locales such as Boston, Philadelphia, and New York City; and an abolitionist movement took shape, putting issues such as stopping the domestic slave trade before state and federal politicians. At the same time, slavery expanded both geographically and demographically, and slaveholders gained constitutional protections that secured bondage in the South. Even in the emancipating North, free black communities experienced pervasive racism in the form of discriminatory customs as well as laws restricting movement and access to the vote. In short, African-American history up to the 1820s was marked by hope, liberation, disappointment, brutality via continued enslavement, and, perhaps above all, continued black activism.

Hope came from the ideals of the American Revolution. The focus on liberty and human rights prompted many Americans to question the institution of slavery.

Pennsylvania QUAKERS had initiated the first colonial attack on bondage in the late 1750s by declaring that all members of the Society of Friends must relinquish slavery. The American Revolution brought this religious antislavery sentiment into the mainstream of political and social debate. White colonists opposing the British proclaimed that they were fighting against their own enslavement. THOMAS JEFFERSON stated, "I tremble for my country when I recall that God is just." Fellow Virginian ARTHUR LEE wrote in 1767 that "as freedom is unquestionably the birth-right of all mankind, of Africans as well as Europeans, to keep the former in a State of slavery is a constant violation of that right, and therefore to Justice." American statesmen, religious figures, and others attacked the overseas slave trade as inhumane.

African Americans joined in the call for the end of slavery. The language of liberty arguing against imperial regulation could as well be applied to the condition of enslaved African Americans. In 1774 Caesar Sarter, a free African American, wrote an essay published in a Massachusetts newspaper explicitly connecting the plight of slaves to the rhetoric used by revolutionary WHIGS. He wrote, "that as *Slavery* is the greatest, and consequently most to be dreaded, of all temporal calamities: so its opposite, *Liberty*, is the greatest temporal good." Addressing himself to the revolutionary leaders, he therefore asked for the liberty of "oppressed Africans" so that "may you with confidence and consistency of conduct, look to Heaven for a blessing on your endeavours to knock the shackles with which your task masters are hampering you, from your own feet." The African-American poet PHILLIS WHEATLEY wrote that "In every human breast God has implanted a Principle, which we call love of freedom; it is impatient of Oppression, and pants for Deliverance" and "the same principle lives in us."

Liberation came to many African Americans in a variety of ways. African Americans attacked bondage: Tens of thousands of slaves, largely in the southern colonies, fled during the REVOLUTIONARY WAR (1775–83). In November 1775 Virginia's royal governor, JOHN MURRAY, LORD DUNMORE, promised American slaves freedom if they fled from their masters. Throughout the war the British continued to attract runaways, recruiting them into the army and offering protection. At the end of the war, thousands of African Americans evacuated with the British army, some to settle in CANADA, others migrating to the WEST INDIES. Unfortunately, the British commitment to the African Americans was limited. While some achieved freedom, others were abandoned in the United States to be reenslaved, and still others were forced into slavery in British colonies. Many faced poverty and racism after the war. One group that confronted these problems in Canada later decided to join the British colony in Sierra Leone in Africa.

While many African Americans sought liberty with the British, others seized upon the American cause. One of the earliest martyrs of the RESISTANCE MOVEMENT (1764–75) against imperial regulation was CRISPUS ATTUCKS, a half-Indian and half-African American who was killed in the BOSTON MASSACRE (March 5, 1770). African Americans fought in the Revolutionary War for the United States. Many served on privateers and in the CONTINENTAL NAVY, since these services accepted men regardless of race. At the beginning of the war a few African Americans fought in the army, only to find limitations placed on their service by the CONTINENTAL CONGRESS and state assemblies. As the war continued, however, several states, desperate for recruits of any race, allowed African Americans to serve in their units. Such men were often promised freedom in exchange for their service.

Liberation for slaves also came from the antislavery ideals that prompted many state legislatures to allow for manumission of slaves by owners and the creation of gradual abolition laws. Hundreds of masters freed thousands of slaves during the late 1770s and 1780s. Virginia, the nation's largest slaveholding state, altered its laws so that masters would no longer need the special permission of the legislature to manumit blacks. Nevertheless, no southern states voted to emancipate slaves, although such legislation was passed in Pennsylvania in 1780, in Connecticut and Rhode Island in 1784, in New York in 1799, and in New Jersey in 1804.

Hope also arose from the development of vibrant free-black communities. Between the 1790s and 1820s, the population of free blacks nearly quadrupled, growing from roughly 70,000 to well over 200,000 30 years before the Civil War. In the South, the presence of free African Americans, mainly in the cities, provided a tantalizing vision of freedom for those who were still enslaved. Equally important, some of these free African Americans obtained property and became leaders of their community. In northern urban centers, the explosion of black populations proved most significant: Between 1790 and 1820, Philadelphia's African-American population increased by over 400 percent; New York City's by over 200 percent; and Boston's over 100 percent. Beyond these numbers, free blacks developed a host of autonomous community institutions in the early national period: churches, associations, insurance societies, libraries, and schools. In Philadelphia, RICHARD ALLEN and ABSALOM JONES formed the Free African Society in 1787 as a black mutual-aid organization. By the early 1790s, Allen and Jones had led an exodus of black parishioners from a segregated white church to establish the African Methodist Episcopal Church and the African Episcopal Church in Philadelphia. In Boston, PRINCE HALL used his masonic lodge as a community organizing center and activist base. Hall also opened a school for African-American children in his own home after the state assembly delayed starting one. In both cities, free black institutions such as churches, lodges, and debating clubs sponsored the publication of protest pamphlets.

Disappointment came from several sources. During the years of the early republic, southerners soon abandoned any serious discussion of the contradiction between American slavery and American freedom. Politically and constitutionally, American slaveholders received significant new protections to human property during the 1780s and 1790s. While the NORTHWEST ORDINANCE of 1787 prohibited slavery's expansion into the territories north of the Ohio River, another proposed ordinance from 1784 had already failed to limit bondage in the Southwest. This earlier measure would prove significant during Thomas Jefferson's presidency, when the LOUISIANA PURCHASE (1803) opened sugar plantations of Louisiana and other valuable land to migrating slaveholders. By 1810 the Louisiana Territory contained about 35,000 slaves. The United States Constitution enshrined slave property by counting the enslaved population in the apportionment of votes for Congress and the Electoral College (each slave equivalent to three-fifths of a European American), by guaranteeing masters the return of fugitive slaves, and by delaying any consideration of a slave-trading ban until the congressional session of 1807.

Political and social developments further abetted slavery. Congress in 1790 and 1799 refused to hear abolitionist and free black petitions against the domestic and overseas slave trades. Furthermore, Congress passed fugitive slave legislation in 1793 that made the return of escaped slaves the law of the land. Several new slave states entered the union between 1790 and 1820: Kentucky and Tennessee in the 1790s, and Alabama, Mississippi, and Louisiana in the early 1800s. Slaveholders harnessed new technology in the form of the cotton gin at the close of the 18th century to rejuvenate bondage. Moreover, slaveholders in South Carolina and Georgia began articulating publicly that slavery was a positive good in American culture. In 1790 there were more than 700,000 slaves, and slave territory was confined largely to the Atlantic seaboard; by the 1820s, the number of slaves exceeded 1.5 million, and slavery had spread to the interior of the nation.

Within the South, the decline in the supply of new slaves from Africa resulted in some key developments for African Americans. The limited number of imported slaves—limited by the upheaval of revolution, state law, and federal fiat after 1808—led to the further elaboration of a separate African-American culture. Crucial to this development was the spread of Christianity among slaves, which African Americans molded to their own purposes. White masters hoped the Bible would teach their slaves to be obedient and refrain from challenging earthly authority.

Instead, slaves seized upon the ideal of Christian equality and identified with the stories of the Egyptian bondage of Israel, with its assurance of deliverance to the promised land. Christianity proved a recruiting ground for black leaders, and African Americans who became preachers—even those who were slaves—often became the spokespeople for their communities.

Another outgrowth of the decline in the importation of new slaves was a greater balance between male and female African Americans, allowing slaves to form more-permanent relationships, have children, and sustain family ties. The ability to form families—even within the context of slavery—provided the foundation for a truly African-American culture. However, while black men and women experienced a greater degree of stability in their relationships, American law did not recognize slave marriage. Masters retained ultimate power over slaves, at times sexually exploiting their property and, more frequently, separating family members through sale and migration. In fact, because of the geographical expansion of slavery, many African Americans had the wrenching experience of being forced to move to new locations in the West.

In the North, where slavery was gradually edging toward abolition in the early 19th century, racial injustice continued. The African Americans who had achieved freedom were not considered equal by most European Americans. A few African Americans became businessmen and artisans, but most were relegated to less-skilled labor and to specific, poorly paid professions. While the creation of African American churches represented a major achievement and reflected a new sense of group identity, it also was a response to the racial prejudice African Americans discovered in mainstream churches. White Americans resisted giving any political voice to African Americans and sought to limit their right to vote. In the early 19th century the African-American community in the North was increasingly subjected to mob attacks. In short, racism permeated northern as well as southern society.

The continuance of slavery and racial injustice thus became the defining issue of black life throughout the early American republic. Pamphlets from the early 1800s by such writers as William Hamilton of New York City, Russell Parrott and JAMES FORTEN of Philadelphia, and Nathaniel Paul of Albany underscored the discrepancy between American liberty (in theory) and American racial oppression. Some enslaved people chose outright rebellion as the means of gaining freedom. In 1800 Virginia's Gabriel Prosser planned a revolution outside of Richmond that would have routed bondage and demanded black equality. It was foiled by a massive rainstorm and informers. Other slave rebellions occurred in 1794 (Southampton, Virginia) and in 1811 (near Natchez, Mississippi). These actions were not simply isolated cases but, rather, the extreme end of a spectrum of resistance to oppression among enslaved blacks.

See also BENJAMIN BANNEKER; GABRIEL'S REBELLION; HAITI; SALLY HEMMINGS; RACE AND RACIAL CONFLICT.

Further reading: Ira Berlin, *Many Thousands Gone: The First Two Centuries of Slavery in North America* (Cambridge, Mass.: Harvard University Press, 1998); Sylvia Frey, *Water from the Rock: Black Resistance in a Revolutionary Age* (Princeton, N.J.: Princeton University Press, 1991); James Horton and Lois Horton, *In Hope of Liberty: Culture, Community and Protest among Northern Free Blacks 1700–1860* (New York: Oxford University Press, 1997); Gary B. Nash, *Race and Revolution* (Madison, Wis.: Madison House, 1990); Richard Newman, Patrick Rael, and Philip Lapsanky, eds., *Pamphlets of Protest: An Anthology of Early African-American Protest Writing* (New York; Routledge, 2001); Benjamin Quarles, *The Negro in the American Revolution* (Chapel Hill: University of North Carolina Press, 1961).

— Richard Newman

agriculture

Between 1754 and 1820 agriculture remained the most important sector of the American ECONOMY. There were, however, regional differences, and the upheaval of revolution and war created some problems.

The southern colonies were the most profitable part of the British empire in North America because of their agricultural products. Although tobacco exhausted the soil and often experienced suppressed prices, it provided income to the Crown and made fortunes for many British merchants. A crop that demanded intensive work, tobacco was heavily dependent on the labor of slaves. South Carolina produced rice and indigo and also relied upon SLAVERY. The imperial crisis and the REVOLUTIONARY WAR (1775–83) disrupted exports of these cash crops. After the war there were changes. Tobacco lost ground as more Chesapeake planters turned to wheat and other grains. The invention of ELI WHITNEY's cotton gin in 1793 transformed southern agriculture by making it possible to grow short-staple cotton profitably. The gin efficiently separated the seeds from the cotton. South Carolina, and then a growing belt of states just to its west (Alabama, Mississippi, and Tennessee) produced more and more cotton. In 1791 about 2 million pounds of cotton was grown in the United States; by 1820 the cotton crop had increased to more than 127 million pounds. By that time, cotton had expanded to one-third of all exports from the United States.

The colonies north of the Mason-Dixon line also depended heavily upon agriculture, but none ever produced a single cash crop equivalent to tobacco, rice, or cotton. Instead, the North produced a variety of food-stuffs based on grains and livestock. Fishing and lumber were also important. Northern states exported their produce to the WEST INDIES, Europe, and even the South. War disrupted this production, as it did further south, but created less havoc because of a greater degree of self-sufficiency. But no farm was ever entirely self-sufficient, and all farmers depended to some extent on the market. That reliance increased in the 1790s and early 1800s. In particular the wars in Europe and the West Indies after 1793 increased the value of agricultural food exports. The opening of the Ohio Valley for settlement and the securing of the Mississippi River and New Orleans as outlets contributed to the expansion of grain and livestock production into new areas.

Although slaves and hired labor worked on some farms, most farmers relied on family labor. As northern states emancipated their slaves, the region—including the area north of the Ohio River—relied more extensively on free labor. Women did not usually labor in the fields, centering their activities instead in the barnyard and household. In these areas they were crucial to the productivity and profitability of agricultural enterprise. Often, the special labor of women in the churning of butter or production of homespun, and, in New England, even the making of brooms, added vital capital to the farm family.

See also LABOR AND LABOR MOVEMENTS; POPULATION TRENDS; RURAL LIFE; WOMEN'S RIGHTS AND STATUS.

Further reading: John J. McCusker and Russell R. Menard, *The Economy of British America, 1607–1789* (Chapel Hill: University of North Carolina Press, 1985); Douglass C. North, *The Economic Growth of the United States, 1790–1860* (Englewood Cliffs, N.J.: Prentice Hall, 1961).

Alamance, Battle of (May 16, 1771)

In response to Regulator RIOTS (see NORTH CAROLINA REGULATION) at the Superior Court in Hillsborough in September 1770, the North Carolina assembly passed the notorious Johnston Act, which turned rebellious farmers into outlaws and provided the governor with the authorization and funds he needed to suppress the farmers with military force. Early in May 1771, Governor William Tryon arrived with his militia troops in the Piedmont region. Officers and "gentlemen volunteers," many of them leading WHIGS who would achieve military honor in the REVOLUTIONARY WAR (1775–83), comprised nearly 10 percent of the army. The troops, only half the number the governor had hoped for, had been difficult to raise, since many ordinary North Carolinians sympathized with the backcountry

Regulators. On May 16, 1771, the governor and his troops met upwards of 2,000 defiant farmers on a field near Alamance Creek some 20 miles from Hillsborough. After two hours of fighting, in which the Regulators initially had the upper hand, the governor's forces emerged victorious. As many as 20 Regulators were killed in battle, along with about nine militia men. More than 150 men were wounded, many seriously. The next day, the governor ordered an outlawed Regulator who had been captured during the battle executed without trial. Thereafter the governor led the troops on a destructive rampage through the Piedmont region. In mid-June, six more Regulators were hanged after a hasty trial.

The Battle of Alamance has been hailed as the first battle of the Revolutionary War. Yet Regulators were not fighting to gain independence from Britain but, rather, to liberate themselves from oppressive local and colonial authorities. The battle and its repressive aftermath decisively ended the collective struggle of free Piedmont inhabitants for independence through social justice. While individual farmers remained defiant well into the Revolutionary War, the Regulation was crushed as an organized movement.

Further reading: Marjoleine Kars, *Breaking Loose Together: The Regulator Rebellion in Pre-Revolutionary North Carolina* (Chapel Hill: University of North Carolina Press, 2002); Wayne E. Lee, *Crowds and Soldiers in Revolutionary North Carolina: The Culture of Violence in Riot and War* (Gainesville, Fla.: University Press of Florida, 2001).

— Marjoleine Kars

Alaska

The first European to lead an expedition to Alaska was Vitus Bering, a Dane sailing for the Russian Empire. As a result of Bering's explorations in 1741–42, the Russians laid claim to the area. However, Russian settlement was initially sporadic and driven by private individuals in search of furs. Grigory Ivanovich Shelikhov, who headed the largest fur company trading in Alaska, established the first permanent Russian settlement in North America on Kodiak Island in 1784. In 1797 Shelikhov's son-in-law, Nikolay Petrovich Rezanov, consolidated all the fur trading companies operating in Alaska and in 1799 obtained an imperial charter for the Russian American Fur Company, modeled after the British East India Company. Rezanov visited Alaska in 1805–06 and traveled to CALIFORNIA to establish trade contacts with the Spanish. The success of the Russian enterprise was largely due to the management of Aleksandr Andreyevich Baronov, who had been appointed by Shelikhov to take control of Alaskan affairs in 1790. Baronov became the dominant presence in Russian America for almost two decades and established the town of New Archangel at Sitka in 1804. Recognizing his need for supplies, Baronov opened trading relations with the British and Americans, even though this action was technically illegal. He also established a base at Fort Ross in California and purchased supplies from the Spanish. During the early 19th century, the company made huge profits, in part by using American ships to bring furs to China. Baronov died in 1819, on his way back to Russia after being forced out of power by company officials.

Russian relations with NATIVE AMERICANS were mixed. The Aleut were subdued in the 18th century and provided much of the labor in building Russian settlements. The Tlingit were more hostile and wiped out some outposts. New Archangel struggled for survival in its first years because settlers could not hunt and fish for fear of Tlingit attack. The Russian church sent missionaries to Alaska in 1794, but they had a limited impact on the natives.

Further reading: Claus M. Naske and Herman Slotnick, *Alaska: A History of the 49th State* (Norman: University of Oklahoma Press, 1979); S. Frederick Starr, ed., *Russia's American Colony* (Durham, N.C.: Duke University Press, 1987).

Alien and Sedition Acts (1798)

The FEDERALIST PARTY passed the Alien and Sedition Acts to suppress political opposition during the QUASI WAR (1798–1800) with France. After the French began to seize American shipping and stumbled into the diplomatic fiasco of the XYZ AFFAIR (1797), the threat of war strengthened the hand of the Federalists in dealing with the DEMOCRATIC-REPUBLICANS (Jeffersonians). Not only did the Federalists push legislation that expanded the army and navy and increased taxes, but they also sought the means to stifle political opposition. The Alien and Sedition Acts, passed in June and July 1798, were intended to further the Federalist political agenda. Federalists believed that the majority of immigrants, many of whom were from Ireland, were pro-French and pro-Republican. Any restrictions they could place on immigrants, therefore, would aid their cause.

There were three Alien Acts. The first of these, called the Naturalization Act, was passed on June 18 and changed the process of allowing immigrants to become citizens. Previous legislation in 1795 allowed an immigrant to become a citizen after five years of residence, having declared his intent to do so three years before becoming a citizen. This act increased the residence requirement to 14 years, with a five-year lag time between declaring intent

and citizenship. The idea was to restrict immigrant citizenship to limit the impact of these voters at the polls. Oddly, the measure actually convinced many immigrants to seek citizenship before the law came into effect, thus strengthening the Democratic-Republican vote in the crucial ELECTION OF 1800. The second measure, called the Alien Act, was passed on June 25, 1798, and empowered the president to deport any alien he deemed a threat to the country. This law was set to expire after two years and was never used by President JOHN ADAMS. The third part of this legislation was the Alien Enemies Act, passed July 6, 1798. It declared that any person born in a country at war with the United States, or that invaded the United States, was liable to being "apprehended, restrained, secured, and removed, as enemy aliens." Since the United States never declared war against France, this measure was not used at this time.

Perhaps the most controversial law was the Sedition Act of July 14, 1798. It made it unlawful to combine with others to oppose measures of the government, and, more significantly, it stated that "if any person shall write, print, utter, or publish . . . Any false, scandalous, and malicious writing or writings against the government of the United States . . . with the intent to defame said government," they could be brought to trial by the federal government and could be assessed up to $2,000 in fines and sentenced to two years in prison. This law has sometimes been held as a violation of civil liberties and contrary to the First Amendment guarantee of freedom of speech and the press. However, it merely put into writing what was common-law practice in England and America at the time. It actually protected some rights, since it stipulated that "the truth of the matter contained in the publication" could be used as defense in any criminal trial resulting from the law. The law was set to expire at the end of the Adams administration in March 1801. The Federalists used this law to prosecute several Democratic-Republican editors and politicians. Congressman MATTHEW LYON was convicted for sedition and sentenced to four months in prison and given a $1,000 fine.

Democratic-Republican leaders believed that these laws were unwarranted and outrageous. Vice President THOMAS JEFFERSON and Congressman JAMES MADISON wrote the VIRGINIA AND KENTUCKY RESOLUTIONS (1798) in response to these laws. Once Jefferson was elected, the two laws that had time limits were not renewed. The Alien Enemies Act was irrelevant as long as the country was not at war. The Republicans repealed the Naturalization Act shortly after Jefferson's election, reinstating the previous rule of the five-year residence period before qualifying for citizenship.

See also IMMIGRATION; POLITICAL PARTIES.

Further reading: James Morton Smith, *Freedom's Fetters: The Alien and Sedition Laws and American Civil Liberties* (Ithaca, N.Y.: Cornell University Press, 1956).

Allen, Ethan (1737–1789)

Ethan Allen was an American revolutionary, famous for helping lead the effort to establish the State of Vermont. Born in Connecticut, Allen had moved to what is now Vermont by 1769. He quickly became a leader of the movement to attach the area to New Hampshire. At that time the region of the Green Mountains was claimed by both New York and New Hampshire. The colony of New York had the better claim, and the Crown decided in its favor when the case finally came to its attention. But many of the settlers in the area, like Allen, came from New England and opposed the large land grants issued to big landlords in New York. Allen became a leader of the GREEN MOUNTAIN BOYS, organized in 1770. This group forcefully opposed efforts by New York authorities to establish law and order in the region. The Green Mountain Boys compelled New York sheriffs to leave the area and tore down the houses of settlers with deeds from New York. Eventually, New York authorities offered as much as £100 for the capture of Allen, who led many of the "mobs" and who was also pursuing his own land schemes under New Hampshire claims.

Against this background, news of the battles of LEXINGTON AND CONCORD (April 19, 1775) arrived. Allen and the Green Mountain Boys saw the rebellion against the British as an opportunity to solidify their position in Vermont. When he received instructions from Connecticut, he led a contingent of Green Mountain Boys and joined BENEDICT ARNOLD in the capture of the British outpost of FORT TICONDEROGA at dawn on May 10, 1775. This action was crucial to the opening phases of the war. Artillery from the fort would eventually be taken to Boston and placed on DORCHESTER HEIGHTS (March 4–5, 1776), forcing the British to evacuate. Moreover, with Ticonderoga in rebel hands, the path was open for American forces to march into CANADA. In an effort to export the rebellion to the St. Lawrence Valley, two armies moved north. One under the command of Benedict Arnold crossed the Maine wilderness in late fall and the beginning of winter 1775; the other headed along Lake Champlain toward Montreal, under General Richard Montgomery. Allen joined Montgomery, who ordered him to reconnoiter near Montreal in September 1775. Allen, thinking that the Canadian city would be easy pickings, decided to try to capture it with a small force. Montreal was not Fort Ticonderoga. Allen quickly found himself in an untenable situation and was compelled to surrender. Montgomery later captured Montreal. Arnold's depleted force arrived before Quebec in November, and

the Americans failed to capture the city in an assault during a snow storm on December 31. The entire Canadian expedition ended in failure, with many men killed and thousands captured. Ethan Allen remained a prisoner of war for two years, enduring extremely harsh treatment, and was transferred across the Atlantic and back again before he was finally exchanged in September 1778.

Broken in mind, body, and spirit by his imprisonment and by the news of his son's death, Allen wrote *A Narrative of Col. Ethan Allen's Captivity*, published in 1779 and reprinted many times. The book became an important statement of the sacrifices that patriots suffered in the American cause. It also helped to resuscitate his waning reputation and enabled him to identify himself with Vermont's ongoing struggle to establish itself as a state. In 1780 Allen even opened negotiations with the British to see if they would accept Vermont as a separate province, but those negotiations came to naught. Allen devoted the rest of his life to his own land investments and Vermont business. Between 1780 and 1784 he wrote a deist tract, *Reason the Only Oracle of God,* published in November 1785, about the same time he retired from public life. Allen died a few years later in 1789.

See also DEISM; LAND RIOTS.

Further reading: Michael A. Bellesiles, *Revolutionary Outlaws: Ethan Allen and the Struggle for Independence on the Early American Frontier* (Charlottesville: University Press of Virginia, 1993).

Allen, Richard (1760–1831)

Richard Allen was one of the preeminent leaders of the free AFRICAN-AMERICAN community during the early republic. Born a slave in Philadelphia, he grew up in that city and in nearby Delaware. At about age 17, shortly after much of his family had been sold to cover the debts of their master, Allen had a religious experience and began practicing METHODISM. He quickly gained a reputation for his piety and ability to preach to others. When he was about 20, Allen's master also became a Methodist. At this time Methodists often opposed SLAVERY as a violation of the equality of humans before God. His new master offered Allen the opportunity to earn his way to freedom. During the next few years Allen rode the Methodist circuit throughout much of the United States and earned his living, when not preaching, by hauling wood and making shoes. By 1786 Allen had stopped his wanderings and centered his ministry in the area around Philadelphia. There he preached to mixed audiences of both whites and blacks. But his preaching attracted more and more African Americans, who soon outnumbered whites when he conducted services. This led to racial tension, as some of the whites insulted the blacks, insisting that they stay in the gallery. Eventually there came a call for a separate African-American congregation, with Allen at its head in 1794. Other black congregations soon formed throughout the region. In 1816 these black congregations broke from the white-dominated Methodist church entirely, forming the African Methodist Episcopal Church, for which Allen served as the first bishop.

Allen was more than a religious leader. He sought to gain respectability for himself and his people by acquiring property and achieving modest entrepreneurial success. In 1787 he was one of the founders of what was probably the first African-American voluntary society—the Free African Society. He vocally supported the abolition of slavery in all of the United States. He also was one of the organizers of African Americans in Philadelphia during the great yellow fever epidemic of 1793 (see DISEASE AND EPIDEMICS), when the city was virtually paralyzed by the disease. Believing that African Americans were immune to yellow fever (they are not entirely), BENJAMIN RUSH appealed to Allen and others to help nurse the sick and bury the dead. Allen and ABSALOM JONES, in the hope that this benevolent role would raise African Americans in the estimation of whites, convinced many Philadelphia blacks to provide assistance during the crisis. Allen spent his life working for the cause of RELIGION and for his fellow African Americans. He died in 1831.

Further reading: Gary B. Nash, *Forging Freedom: The Formation of Philadelphia's Black Community, 1720–1840* (Cambridge, Mass.: Harvard University Press, 1988).

— Richard Newman

American Philosophical Society

The present American Philosophical Society, still housed at its original location at Fifth and Chestnut Streets in downtown Philadelphia next to Independence Hall, came into being in 1769 when two competing learned societies merged. One, proposed in 1743 by BENJAMIN FRANKLIN, planned to unite in "one society . . . ingenious men" with a view to "Promoting Useful Knowledge among the British Plantations of America." It failed to materialize, but in 1768 the American Philosophical Society became the new name of Franklin's Junto, a discussion club Franklin began as a young man that expanded its interests to include scientific experiments. The second association was the Medical Society—composed of the physicians who taught at the Pennsylvania College of Medicine—which was founded in 1767 and principally organized by Dr. John Morgan. The new society numbered 251 members: 144 Pennsylvanians, 90 from other colonies, and 17 foreigners, including such world-renowned scientists as the Swede Carl Linnaeus and the Frenchmen Antoine Laurent Lavoisier and the marquis de Condorcet.

The society consciously modeled itself on the British Royal Society, where papers from throughout the world explaining scientific and practical discoveries and exploring intellectual topics were presented and discussed. The *Transactions of the American Philosophical Society*—first published in 1771 and today the oldest continuously published scholarly journal in the Western Hemisphere—was modeled on a similar British publication and was beautifully printed by William Bradford of Philadelphia. Copies were sold immediately throughout the colonies and distributed to libraries and universities in Europe. Despite the political split developing in the colonies that became the AMERICAN REVOLUTION, learned members with different political views—such as Franklin and Charles Thomson ("the Samuel Adams of Philadelphia") on the one hand and LOYALIST leaders of the rival Proprietary faction on the other—were admitted based on merit. Members included botanist John Bartram, College of Pennsylvania president William Smith, former governor James Hamilton, and composer Francis Hopkinson. Only Governor John Penn, a bitter enemy of Franklin, balked: "I shall never be a patron of a Society that has for its President such a ——— as Franklin." Despite Penn, the society soon realized its goal of becoming the principal colonial body supporting and disseminating knowledge.

The society's first major projects supported local clockmaker and astronomer DAVID RITTENHOUSE. With the society's financial help he designed the first moving and accurate scale model of the solar system, the orrery that is still on display at the University of Pennsylvania Museum. Next, Rittenhouse was one of several Americans who observed the 1769 transit of the planet Venus from different locations. This was the first intercolonial scientific endeavor and was also coordinated with similar observations by scientists of many nationalities throughout the world.

The society was a Pennsylvania-wide as well worldwide body. The Juliana Library Company in Lancaster worked closely with the society, encouraging William Henry, manufacturer of the Pennsylvania Rifle, to continue his experiments with steam, resulting in the invention of a system for heating houses and an unsuccessful steamboat. Agricultural experiments by Dr. Bodo Otto in Bethlehem also received society support. The society's interests in the exploration of the western Illinois country (where many of the members held interests as land speculators) led to the opening of a public museum where people could examine exotic species of flora and fauna, scientific instruments, and medical curiosities. A canal, planned by Thomas Gilpin with the society's support, to connect the Delaware River with Chesapeake Bay received endorsement from the

Pennsylvania Assembly and was actually begun in 1771, before the REVOLUTIONARY WAR (1775–83) intervened and put the society's activities on hold for the duration of the conflict.

The American Philosophical Society paradoxically stands as a representative of both colonial British and American nationalism. Modeled on the leading British scientific association, it marked the coming of age of colonials proud of their British connection and anxious to be recognized as equals by their overseas counterparts. However, the naming of the Rittenhouse Planetarium after the earl of Orrery—whose experiments in mapping the planets followed Rittenhouse's—showed, in the scientific realm, the failure of American attempts to be recognized as equals of the British in the political sphere. After the Revolutionary War, the society then became, as it remains today, a center that supports and brings together Americans engaged in all sorts of "useful and scientific" pursuits. Its magnificent library embodies this continuity with the colonial period: It features the original journals of Meriwether Lewis and William Clark (see LEWIS AND CLARK EXPEDITION), original photographs of the first atomic bomb, and original images of Neil Armstrong walking on the Moon.

Further reading: Edward C. Carter III, *One Grand Pursuit: A Brief History of the American Philosophical Society's First 250 Years, 1743–1993* (Philadelphia: American Philosophical Society, 1993).

— William Pencak

American Revolution

There are at least three ways of defining the American Revolution. First, and on the most fundamental level, the American Revolution can be defined as the movement that led to independence from Great Britain. Second, this definition can be expanded to include the creation of a new form of republican government. Finally, the American Revolution can also be described as a series of political, social, and cultural transformations that totally altered the American world.

The movement toward independence can be divided into two parts. First is the RESISTANCE MOVEMENT (1764–75) that began in reaction to imperial regulation. After the French and Indian War (1754–63), Great Britain passed a series of regulations intended to rationalize their overseas empire and to raise revenue for the defense of that empire. Colonists objected to these efforts. This resistance did not lead inevitably to independence. In fact, most colonists believed that they were merely asserting their rights as Englishmen when they opposed imperial regulation. Yet in the process of opposing laws like the STAMP ACT (1765), the TOWNSHEND DUTIES (1767), and

the TEA ACT (1773), a pattern of conflict, mistrust, and misunderstanding developed that led the colonies and Great Britain to the precipice of war by 1775. The war that broke out in April 1775, which in turn led to the DECLARATION OF INDEPENDENCE (1776), forms the second part of this definition of the American Revolution. Without the armed conflict, independence would have been impossible. Only after the defeat of its armies did Great Britain at last acquiesce in the independence of its former North American colonies.

The second definition of the American Revolution picks up the story during the REVOLUTIONARY WAR (1775–83) and carries it through to the writing and ratification of the United States Constitution (1787–88). During the war, it became obvious to the revolutionary leaders that some form of government must be created to replace the one being overthrown. On the local level, each state wrote or adopted its own constitution. This process was extremely important to the revolutionaries, since at that time (before 1787) they had only the vaguest notion of a national form of government. What counted was the state constitutions. Each state experimented with a slightly different form of government in an effort to meet the republican (see REPUBLICANISM) ideal of balanced government that would protect the public welfare. The government of the United States under the ARTICLES OF CONFEDERATION was intended as a limited form of alliance that would bind otherwise independent states to one another. The creation of the United States Constitution therefore represented a radical break from the previous form of government. It not only created a truly national government, it also placed tremendous power in the executive while limiting democratic input on several levels. The president of the United States became commander in chief of the armed forces, had vast appointive powers, and could veto legislation (this veto could only be overridden by two-thirds of both houses of legislature).

The third definition of the American Revolution is more difficult to delineate and more difficult to date. Many historians now view the entire period running from 1760 to 1830 as the era of the American Revolution. These historians claim that the political transformations and debates—beginning with the resistance movement and the creation of a republican form of government—continued through the decades of the 1790s and early 1800s as Americans sought to stabilize their republican experiment and delineate a democratic political system. For these historians, the ultimate political end of the revolution comes with the rewriting of state constitutions in the 1820s and 1830s, which opened up the political process to all adult white men in American society.

Other historians push their definition of the revolution even further and talk about a profound social and cultural change. For these scholars, the colonial world was marked by a social hierarchy cemented by the bonds of deference and paternalism. In such a world, no person was independent; each individual was bound and dependent upon another within a social structure that reached to the colonial governor and eventually to the king. The American Revolution overthrew this hierarchical world. The key to this revolution was THOMAS JEFFERSON's phrase "we hold these truths to be self-evident, that all men are created equal." The rise of the ideal of equality, however, did not emerge magically overnight. Instead, the triumph of this ideal took decades to unravel. Some men sought to slow or prevent the full implications of the ideal from taking force. From this perspective, even the Constitution of 1787 was an effort to limit the impact of equality. Likewise, the FEDERALIST PARTY program of the 1790s sought to reinstall a hierarchical ideal in politics. These efforts failed. In the triumph of Thomas Jefferson during the ELECTION OF 1800, and again in the victory of Andrew Jackson in 1828, the common man became paramount. The ideal became the independent man—independent from those above and below him and capable of making his own decisions regardless of his economic or social standing. This success encompassed the political, social, and cultural world.

See also CONSTITUTIONAL CONVENTION; CONSTITUTIONS, STATE; WHIGS.

Further reading: Francis D. Cogliano, *Revolutionary America, 1763–1815: A Political History* (London: Routlege, 2000); Robert Middlekauff, *The Glorious Cause: The American Revolution, 1763–1789* (New York: Oxford University Press, 1982); Gordon S. Wood, *The Radicalism of the American Revolution* (New York: Knopf, 1992).

Ames, Fisher (1758–1808)

Fisher Ames became one of the leading spokesmen for the FEDERALIST PARTY in the 1790s, noted for his wit and biting pen. Ames was born in Massachusetts and entered Harvard when he was only 12 years of age. He started studying law in 1779 and was admitted to the bar in 1781. Although he was an excellent lawyer, he never really enjoyed practicing law. However, he loved politics, and the political arena quickly became a showplace for his talents.

His politics were conservative: He opposed price-fixing during the REVOLUTIONARY WAR (1775–83), decried SHAYS'S REBELLION (1786–87), and supported the Federal Constitution of 1787. He feared that the democratic impulses of the age would lead to anarchy and strove to assert the power of government in support of order. Having gained notoriety in his "Camillus" essays in defense of the Constitution, he was elected to the First Congress, defeating SAMUEL ADAMS. He was reelected three times and served in the House of Representatives until 1797. During

his years in Congress he became one of the leaders of the Federalist Party, supporting ALEXANDER HAMILTON's program, and opposing THOMAS JEFFERSON and the DEMOCRATIC-REPUBLICANS. He favored the policies of Boston merchants who wanted to maintain strong TRADE connections with Great Britain. He was known for his writing and speaking abilities. One of his speeches in 1794 gained so much notoriety among opponents that he was burned in effigy in Charleston, South Carolina. During the debates over the pro-British JAY'S TREATY (1794), which he favored, he gave what some scholars call one of the greatest speeches ever uttered in the halls of Congress. Although he retired from Congress in 1796, returning to his home in Dedham, Massachusetts, he still wrote essays attacking Jefferson's party. He believed that the United States should be a Roman Republic led by a natural elite, individuals like himself. He feared democracy, viewed the FRENCH REVOLUTION (1789–1815) as anathema, and saw the followers of Jefferson as Jacobins ready to turn the guillotine upon their opponents. Jefferson's win in the ELECTION OF 1800 was a hard blow, and in the ensuing years he wrote bitterly about the government's policies and encouraged Federalists to take control of their state governments. The Federalist Party lost an important political spokesman when he died on July 4, 1808. His funeral, which included a huge procession in Boston, not only was a testament to his popularity, but also a massive demonstration of political support for the Federalist Party.

See also POLITICAL PARTIES; REPUBLICANISM.

Further reading: Winfred E. A. Bernhard, *Fisher Ames, Federalist and Statesman, 1758–1808* (Chapel Hill, N.C.: University of North Carolina Press, 1965).

Andre, John (1750–1780)

John Andre was a British officer and is best known for his role in aiding BENEDICT ARNOLD's treason. Arriving in the colonies in 1774, he saw firsthand the movement toward the open break with Great Britain. Stationed at Quebec in 1775, he was captured by the CONTINENTAL ARMY during its invasion of CANADA in 1775. He remained a prisoner of war until late 1776 when he was exchanged. He then saw service in the campaign that led to the capture of Philadelphia in 1777. During the British occupation of Philadelphia in 1777–78, Andre organized several entertainments for his fellow officers and the local LOYALIST elite. He continued these activities in New York after his arrival in 1778 and was particularly noted for his role in theatrical productions. But Andre was no lightweight fop.

Born of Huguenot parents, Andre was a talented, educated, and sophisticated officer who spoke French, German, and English fluently. He served on the general staff of

General Charles Grey and was involved in several important campaigns between 1778 and 1780. When Grey went back to Great Britain, Andre transferred to General HENRY CLINTON's staff. He quickly became Clinton's most trusted officer, responsible for many of the day-to-day duties of the staff office. Clinton showed further confidence in Andre by having him run the British army's intelligence in New York. It was in this role that he first made contact with Benedict Arnold and opened negotiations for the surrender of West Point. With Clinton's permission, Andre traveled through the American lines for a meeting with Arnold on the night of September 21, 1780. After they met, it was too late for Andre to return to the British ship in the Hudson that had taken him to the rendezvous. He went into hiding during the day, intending to make his way back to the British lines the next night. It was during this interlude that he took off his uniform and put on civilian clothes (up until this point he had worn an overcoat to hide the uniform). Unfortunately for Andre, on September 23 he ran into three American militiamen near Tarrytown, New York. Once captured, he did not hide his true identity, nor did he provide any information on the people who helped him. He did carry incriminating papers, and when Arnold found out about Andre's capture, he immediately left West Point and went over to the British. At his court-martial on September 28, Andre did not attempt to defend himself, freely admitting the clandestine nature of his mission. He was quickly sentenced to hang. Clinton desperately sought to exchange Andre for any prisoner then held by the British. GEORGE WASHINGTON, however, insisted that he would take only one man for Major Andre—Benedict Arnold. Clinton could not allow that exchange, and Andre was executed as a spy on October 2, 1780. After the war, Americans romanticized the dashing Major Andre in books and plays, contrasting his honesty and loyalty to country to the perfidy of the treasonous Benedict Arnold.

Further reading: James Thomas Flexner, *The Traitor and the Spy* (New York: Harcourt Brace, 1953).

Annapolis Convention (1786)

The Annapolis Convention is notable as the event leading to the CONSTITUTIONAL CONVENTION in Philadelphia in 1787. Delegates from five states, including Delaware, New Jersey, New York, Pennsylvania, and Virginia, met in Annapolis to consider a federal plan for regulating commerce. Because of the lack of attendance, the delegates soon decided to call a new convention to meet the next year with the broad purpose of amending the ARTICLES OF CONFEDERATION.

An earlier conference at Mount Vernon, Virginia, in 1785 had successfully resolved a number of disputes concerning the navigation of Chesapeake Bay, thus illustrating the advantages of independent state action. The success of this conference led to Virginia's invitation to the states to meet at Annapolis in 1786, with the purpose of creating a more uniform standard for dealing with interstate commerce. The government under the Articles of Confederation did not have the power to regulate commerce, which often led to difficulties between states. Disputes between Maryland and Virginia over navigation of the Potomac River were the immediate catalyst of the Annapolis Convention. However, discussions were brief and futile, as the delegates soon decided that because of such low attendance and the complexities of commerce, there was little they could accomplish. ALEXANDER HAMILTON was key in convincing his colleagues that the issues they were concerned with required revision of other political and economic practices. After only two days of discussion, the delegates to the Annapolis Convention issued a report, written primarily by Hamilton, requesting the states to select delegates to send to a convention in Philadelphia the next year to revise the Articles. They expressed their opinion that the situation of the United States was delicate and critical, requiring the attention of all members of the Confederacy. The delegates stated that the Philadelphia convention should create "provisions as shall appear to them necessary to render the constitution adequate to the exigencies of the Union." The report was completed on September 11, 1786, and copies of the report were submitted to Congress and to all the state legislatures. The legislatures were asked to send their delegates to Philadelphia in May 1787. This action was technically unconstitutional but soon gained the support of the CONTINENTAL CONGRESS. On the suggestion of the Annapolis Convention, delegates from 12 states met in Philadelphia at the Constitutional Convention, which eventually produced the Constitution of the United States.

Further reading: Merrill Jensen, *The New Nation: A History of the United States during the Confederation* (New York: Knopf, 1950).

— Crystal Williams

anti-Federalists

Anti-Federalists were those who did not support the ratification of the Constitution. Although they were ultimately defeated, they were successful in creating pressure to have a BILL OF RIGHTS included as amendments to the Constitution, and their ideals had a significant impact on early American political theory. Prominent anti-Federalists included PATRICK HENRY, James Monroe, and SAMUEL ADAMS. Many of the anti-Federalists were older and had already formed their political ideals, often based in the

COMMONWEALTHMEN tradition before the REVOLUTIONARY WAR (1775–83). Another group who joined the anti-Federalist ranks in large numbers were farmers, who saw a strong government as merely an instrument of taxation. However, anti-Federalists came from every social and economic station.

The debate between the FEDERALISTS and anti-Federalists is often cast in terms of economic self-interest, but the disagreement was also one of contrasting ideologies. It is also important to note that the anti-Federalist program was more than just a negative campaign against the Constitution. The anti-Federalists had a different conception of what a republic should look like, but their beliefs were not necessarily less valid than the Federalists' view. The theories of the anti-Federalists were heavily influenced by Montesquieu's writings and REPUBLICANISM. The anti-Federalists believed that the greatest threat to the liberty of the people and the safety of the republic came from the risk of the government becoming too powerful. To the anti-Federalists, tyranny was much more to be feared than placing too much power in the hands of the people. They believed that the Constitution was a tool of a select few to oppress the masses, and the secretive manner in which the Constitution was created only heightened their suspicions of a conspiracy. Anti-Federalists also subscribed to the notion that a republic could not be successful in a large area and would only work in a local setting in which the people had common needs and goals. Therefore, they attacked the idea that the national government could possibly represent the interests of all of the United States's 6 million white inhabitants. The virtue of the people would not be enough to sustain the republic, and the government would have to resort to coercion to impose its will on the people. In keeping with their republican ideology, anti-Federalists looked to historical examples to confirm their fears. If the American people were not vigilant, corruption would set in and a despotic government would take power, destroying the republic. The ultimate goal of the anti-Federalists was always the preservation of the republic, through the maintenance of state sovereignty and limitations on federal power. Much like the Federalists, the anti-Federalists were active in publishing pamphlets to promote their point of view concerning the Constitution. Perhaps the most popular of these pamphlets was *Letters of a Federal Farmer*, which listed the rights that anti-Federalists felt should be protected by the Constitution.

In some states, anti-Federalist sentiment was strong, and the Constitution was barely ratified. For example, it passed by only 19 votes in Massachusetts and three votes in New York. After it began to appear that the Constitution would be ratified, the main goal of the anti-Federalists became ensuring the inclusion of a bill of rights in the Constitution. They hoped this bill of rights could at least provide some protection from tyranny. Although the anti-Federalists were unable to stop the ratification of the Constitution and maintain the ARTICLES OF CONFEDERATION, they forced the Federalists to defend their position and promoted the passage of a bill of rights. Many of the anti-Federalists would eventually become members of the DEMOCRATIC-REPUBLICAN PARTY.

See also STATE'S RIGHTS.

Further reading: Saul Cornell, *The Other Founders: Anti-federalism and the Dissenting Tradition in America, 1788–1828* (Chapel Hill: University of North Carolina Press, 1999); Jackson Turner Main, *The Antifederalists: Critics of the Constitution, 1781–1788* (Chapel Hill: University of North Carolina Press, 1961); Robert Allen Rutland, *The Ordeal of the Constitution: The Antifederalists and the Ratification Struggle of 1787–1788* (Norman: University of Oklahoma Press, 1966); Gordon S. Wood, *The Creation of the American Republic, 1776–1787* (Chapel Hill: University of North Carolina Press, 1969).

— Crystal Williams

antislavery and abolition

Antislavery became an increasingly important movement during the REVOLUTIONARY WAR (1775–83) and the years of the early republic. THOMAS JEFFERSON represented a moderate stand: SLAVERY violated religious doctrine and natural law, Jefferson believed, but it remained perhaps a too-sensitive issue (and too economically vital to masters) to eradicate altogether. Some Americans, however, began to advocate a means to end slavery, even if it was only piecemeal. Many AFRICAN AMERICANS seized opportunities to obtain freedom and advocated ending slavery as quickly as possible.

QUAKERS, led by John Woolman and Anthony Benezet, established the first formal antislavery movement in America during the 1750s. The Society of Friends in Pennsylvania considered slavery a violation of religious principles and therefore created an internal antislavery policy: Slaveholders must relinquish their bondsmen or leave the society. Quakers subsequently became leading voices against bondage during the American revolutionary era. They also set a precedent for other religious groups. Although every religious sect sanctioned slavery prior to 1770, METHODISTS, BAPTISTS, and Anglicans all began debating members' slaveholding practices by the 1780s. In Virginia and Maryland, which contained large slave populations, guilty masters began manumitting slaves in greater numbers than ever. Virginia altered its emancipation policy to accommodate this trend: Masters no longer needed to petition the general assembly to liberate the enslaved. However, nei-

Logo for an early abolition society *(New York Public Library)*

ther Methodists nor Baptists in the South adopted Quaker-style prohibitions on slaveholding.

Northern Quakers and their allies established the world's first abolition societies in the 1770s and 1780s: The Pennsylvania Abolition Society began in 1775, the New York Manumission Society in 1784. These groups petitioned governments to adopt gradual abolition laws that would slowly end slavery in the new American nation. Pennsylvania adopted the world's first emancipation act in 1780. It required all masters to register bondsmen born after the act with a state official; male slaves would then be freed at the age of 28. Between 1780 and 1804, every northern state would adopt similar laws. (Vermont banned slavery in its 1777 constitution, and Massachusetts ended slavery by a judicial decree in 1783 after an enslaved person, Quok Walker, sued for his freedom.)

The ideals of the AMERICAN REVOLUTION further encouraged antislavery. As colonists began to protest what they perceived to be Britain's political and economic oppression, they found slavery to be an apt metaphor for their servile condition. Colonial activists began arguing that freedom was the end of just society and all civil governments. In making such arguments about political slavery and human rights, American revolutionaries prompted widespread consideration of antislavery itself. During the 1760s, and 1770s, pamphlets, newspaper essays, and speeches criticized the SLAVE TRADE as inhumane and slavery as unjust. JAMES OTIS questioned slavery in his *Rights of the British Colonies* (1764) by declaring that the "Colonists are by the law of nature free born, as indeed all men are, white or black." He wondered, "Can any logical inference in favour of slavery be drawn from a flat nose, a long or short face?" In 1773, BENJAMIN RUSH called slavery "a national crime" that would lead to "a national punishment." THOMAS PAINE, who had just arrived in North America in 1774, began his revolutionary career with an attack on slavery. Southerners like Thomas Jefferson, JAMES MADISON, and GEORGE MASON not only expressed guilt at owning slaves, but believed that slavery would gradually disappear once Americans ended the slave trade. Believing slavery an evil, GEORGE WASHINGTON created provisions for the future emancipation of his slaves.

In the new American nation, debate persisted over antislavery's place in a country dedicated to freedom. Luther Martin, who was attorney general of Maryland, believed "that *slavery is inconsistent* with the *genius of republicanism* and has a tendency to *destroy* those *principles* on which it is *supported,* as it *lessens the sense* of the *equal rights of mankind,* and habituates us to *tyranny* and *oppression.*" In 1784 the CONTINENTAL CONGRESS considered, but did not adopt, an ordinance prohibiting slavery's expansion into future southwestern territories. In 1787 the Continental Congress passed the NORTHWEST ORDINANCES, which prohibited bondage from taking root north of the Ohio River. In 1787 the CONSTITUTIONAL CONVENTION, meeting in Philadelphia to revise the ARTICLES OF CONFEDERATION, debated several clauses relating to slavery and antislavery measures and established the three-fifths clause (the counting of three-fifths of the enslaved population to determine representation in federal elections), a guarantee of the return of fugitive slaves, and a future date for congressional consideration of ending the overseas slave trade (1808). All states, at least for a while, enacted state statutes to end the slave trade before that date.

First-generation abolitionists tried to keep antislavery momentum going during the early republic. Hoping to gradually end slavery at the state level, to stop the overseas slave trade at the federal level, and to encourage political leaders to debate emancipation as a national goal, early abolitionists were led by groups in Pennsylvania and New York (although abolition societies appeared in most northern states before 1800, and, for very brief periods, in Maryland and Virginia). These early reformers petitioned Congress on such issues several times between the 1790s and 1820s, but they never pushed for immediate emancipation nationally. Their most radical proposal was to abolish the slave trade, and perhaps even slavery itself, in the federally controlled District of Columbia. Early abolitionists in Pennsylvania and New York also distinguished themselves by representing kidnaped blacks and occasionally fugitive slaves in courts of law, and they helped liberate hundreds of slaves in negotiations with masters. But the effect was piecemeal; bondage persisted. According to the first federal census of 1790, 700,000 slaves lived in America and only 63,000 free blacks. Although the number of free blacks grew to 250,000 by 1830, the number of slaves nearly tripled to 2 million. In short, after successes during the revolutionary era, when masters liberated slaves in relatively large numbers and every northern state began the process of abolition, antislavery efforts stalled by the early 1800s.

Perhaps the most consistent antislavery advocates were free African Americans. The growth of this group came from several sources. During the Revolutionary War, many slaves had taken advantage of bounties, been given offers of freedom from both sides in the conflict, or simply ran away. Manumissions in the North and South freed many others during the war and in the years after the peace. And the legal efforts abolishing slavery in the North all but ended the institution in that region by 1830. Although free African Americans were not formally permitted to join early abolitionist organizations, they served as important community contacts and teachers for white reform groups such as the Pennsylvania Abolition Society. Increasingly angered by white abolitionists' racism, African-American reformers created a parallel antislavery movement during the early republic. Coming primarily from northern urban centers, a generation of black activists publicized their antislavery views beginning in the 1780s and 1790s: RICHARD ALLEN and JAMES FORTEN of Philadelphia, PRINCE HALL of Boston, and Peter Williams and William Hamilton of New York City. These men created independent institutions dedicated to community uplift and racial justice. From the pulpit and lectern, black leaders denounced the slave trade, domestic slavery, and racism in areas where gradual abolition laws had already taken effect. Many of these speeches were published as protest pamphlets, and they were a critical part of early efforts to influence the general public to accept African Americans as equals and to establish antislavery policies at both the state and federal levels.

The many pamphlets and speeches prepared by black activists during the early republic formed a distinct brand of antislavery, one that diverged from the conservative, legalistic tactics of early white abolition groups and that would become a seminal influence on radical abolitionists emerging after 1830 (such as William Lloyd Garrison). Richard Allen and ABSALOM JONES published the first copyrighted African-American pamphlet in 1794, "A Narrative of the Proceedings of the Black People during the Late Awful Calamity in Philadelphia." The pamphlet took Philadelphia's leaders to task for accusing black relief workers of pillaging homes during the city's yellow fever epidemic of 1793. Allen and Jones noted that black citizens aided white Philadelphians in disproportionate numbers and deserved only commendations. They went on to address the underlying issue: the continuance of slavery. This institution, they claimed, mocked egalitarian creeds and religious principles. Equally important, it denied African Americans the full measure of American justice and left them open to the most flagrant abuses imaginable. Remove the stain of slavery, Allen and Jones argued, and African Americans would become valuable citizens in their own right. Before the slave narrative tradition became a central part of abolitionist activism in the antebellum era, pamphlets such as those published by Allen and Jones were an important means of transmitting African-American antislavery ideas.

This public protest became particularly important during the 1810s and 1820s. Not only had slavery expanded south into FLORIDA, Alabama, and Mississippi and west into Missouri, but the American Colonization Society (ACS) emerged in 1816 with a plan to export free black activists. While some members of the ACS claimed to be antislavery advocates (and while some slaveholders feared the organization as a Trojan horse of antislavery itself), the group was dominated by slaveholders and many northern antiabolitionists. Early abolition groups refused to publicly condemn the ACS because it had a prominent membership, including figures such as Henry Clay and James Madison. Free black activists did not hesitate to attack the group, however, becoming the most significant sector of society to oppose colonization consistently before 1830. African-American anticolonization documents would become a wellstone of future antislavery activists: William Lloyd Garrison republished many of them in his 1832 pamphlet, "Thoughts on African Colonization," to ignite the new brand of antislavery.

See also RACE AND RACIAL CONFLICT.

Further reading: Ira Berlin, *Many Thousands Gone: The First Two Centuries of Slavery in North America* (Cambridge, Mass.: Harvard University Press, 1998); David Brion Davis, *The Problem of Slavery in the Age of Revolution, 1770–1823* (Ithaca, N.Y.: Cornell University Press, 1975); Gary B. Nash, *Race and Revolution* (Madison, Wis.: Madison House, 1990).

— Richard Newman

architecture

The diverse traditions of American architecture underwent dramatic change during the late 18th and early 19th centuries. Population grew, cities expanded, and new ideas about public and private life gained currency. During this period architectural fashions shifted, housing standards improved substantially for some Americans, public buildings diversified and proliferated, and a new type of building designer—the professional architect—gained prominence.

The most readily discernible change in Anglo-American architecture during the period 1754–1820 is that of architectural style. The mid-18th century saw the growing popularity of "Georgian" architecture. First introduced into the American colonies about 1700 and embraced by the very wealthy, the Georgian style represented the extension of ideas spreading in Europe since the Renaissance. Georgian houses were characterized by a new attention to bilateral symmetry: two windows on either side of an entrance and five windows across the second floor. These houses typically extended two rooms deep with a central hallway; kitchen and work areas were placed in a rear wing. The central hallway, which allowed people to move through the house without intruding into individual rooms, increased personal privacy while also separating work spaces from those for entertainment. The Georgian style of architecture also showcased decorative details borrowed from architectural publications of the period known as "patternbooks." Most popular was the practice of accentuating entrances with classical ornaments such as pilasters (flat columns applied to a building's surface) or pediments (triangular decorative elements of applied molding). Windows, too, were often topped with pediments and contained many panes of glass in upper and lower window sashes. In New England, a good example of Georgian domestic architecture is the Vassal-Craigie-Longfellow House in Cambridge, Massachusetts (1759). Mount Airy in Richmond County, Virginia (1754–64), and the Corbitt-Sharp House, in Odessa, Delaware (1771–72), are also typical examples.

In the decades following the REVOLUTIONARY WAR (1775–83) and lasting well into the 19th century, the Georgian style was replaced by a variant of classical architecture known as "neoclassical" or "federal." This style of architecture used a refined classical vocabulary that emphasized thinness, verticality, and delicacy. Particularly popular in East Coast seaport towns, such as Salem, Massachusetts; Newport, Rhode Island; Annapolis, Maryland, and Charleston, South Carolina, neoclassical buildings retained the Georgian style's emphasis on symmetry, but more often rose a full three stories in height with few horizontal breaks in the front facade. Windows of neoclassical houses sported larger and fewer panes of glass, while doorways surrounded by sidelights and fanlights further emphasized the lightness and transparency of the buildings. Surviving examples of neoclassical-style buildings include the HARRISON GRAY OTIS House in Boston (1805), the Octagon in WASHINGTON, D.C. (1799–1801), and the Nathaniel Russell House in Charleston, South Carolina (1809).

The changes taking place in domestic architecture from 1754 to 1820 are evident not only in changing architectural fashion but also in the increasing numbers and improving quality of houses for the "middling sort"—primarily yeoman farmers, craftspeople, and prosperous tradespeople. Prior to the mid-18th century, an affluent minority—both rural and urban—lived in substantial houses with a high degree of architectural finish, but the majority of people lived in one- or two-room houses, often with dirt floors, unglazed windows, and wooden chimneys. The very poor, including enslaved AFRICAN AMERICANS, ordinarily lived in spaces used for other purposes, such as garrets or agricultural buildings. Following the Revolutionary War, Anglo-Americans witnessed a "housing revolution": Domestic structures for the "middling sort" noticeably improved. While the gulf between the well-housed and poorly housed remained great, many more people lived in substantial, finely finished houses that adopted some elements of "gentility" or "refinement"—work spaces separated from entertainment spaces by new circulation patterns and increased attention to interior finishes, including wooden floors, plastered walls, and paint. In rural New England this late-18th-century "rebuilding" was manifest in large numbers of two-story houses (one room deep with interior chimneys) and two-story, side-hall houses with two rooms front to back. South of New York, the typical house was two-story, with a central passage flanked by single rooms. In German-speaking areas of western Maryland and the Shenandoah Valley, wealthy farmers slowly began to move away from the traditional Germanic three-room asymmetrical house to adopt these fashionable Anglo-American forms.

The "housing revolution" of the post-Revolutionary period and the influence of architectural fashion, however, did not directly affect many people living in North America. For NATIVE AMERICANS, this was a time of struggle to maintain their traditional livelihoods in the face of war and brutal resettlements. Architectural historians studying Native American building traditions have primarily concentrated on the period of first contact between Europeans and Native Americans, and they have not yet fully explored the subsequent periods when Native American communities were profoundly affected by centuries of European colonization. For most Native Americans, housing and sacred architecture constructed during this period reflected the fundamental shift from a migratory to a sedentary way of life and the adaptation of European building forms to traditional lifestyles. Often, however, Native American community members differed among themselves about appropriate housing forms. Prior to their forced relocation, some members of Creek, Cherokee, Choctaw, and Chickasaw communities, for instance, tried to "Americanize" by building southern-style plantation houses, while others continued living in structures organized around traditional "square grounds" or ceremonial courtyards.

The inhabitants of the Spanish Southwest, similarly, did not experience a "housing revolution" comparable to that of the British colonies. Spanish settlements in FLORIDA, Texas, Arizona, New Mexico, and CALIFORNIA were all outposts of a much larger colonization effort to the south and therefore did not attract the population of their British counterparts. Settlement in those areas followed the objectives laid out for town planning in the *Law of the Indies,* Spain's regulations for colonization in the New World, which specified that new towns be centered on a plaza bordered by government buildings, churches, and markets, all surrounded by a grid of streets. This intricate city planning was largely unnecessary for Spain's small FRONTIER communities, but towns were laid out as defensive plazas. Chimayo, in northern New Mexico, begun in

the mid-18th century, is the best surviving example of these walled towns. Most of the buildings constructed by the Spanish in the Southwest were made of adobe bricks or stone, blending Spanish and Native American building traditions. The Spanish goal of converting Native Americans to Catholicism was expressed in the construction of mission churches ranging from elaborate Spanish baroque structures like San Xavier del Bac in Tucson, Arizona (1795), to simple pueblo mission churches such as St. Francis of Assisi in Ranchos de Taos, New Mexico (1805–15).

In addition to changing architectural style and some advancement in housing standards, the 1754–1820 period was marked by a proliferation of public buildings which had begun just prior to the Revolutionary War. In New England towns, the primary public space during the 17th and early 18th centuries had been the meetinghouse or, in urban seaports, the townhouse. Both of these structures

This classic Georgian home was built about 1773 in Delaware. *(National Images of North American Living Research and Archival Center, Washington)*

served a wide variety of public functions. Similarly, in the mid-Atlantic region and the South, churches, courthouses, and some market houses accommodated all of a community's public activities. Beginning in the mid-18th century and accelerating through the 19th, civic functions began to split off from these multipurpose buildings, and many towns, small and large, began to support an array of purpose-built public structures: courthouses, market halls, town halls, customs houses, and BANKS. After the Revolutionary War, most of the new states also immediately began construction of buildings to house state government. Surviving examples of these new state capitols include the Virginia State Capitol in Richmond (1785–89) and the Massachusetts State House in Boston (1795–97).

The most significant public structure was the United States Capitol in WASHINGTON, D.C. Throughout the 19th century the Capitol underwent a number of design changes, including the addition of its well-known dome at mid-century, but the core structure had been completed by 1828. No fewer than six architects were involved in the Capitol's early design and construction. Particularly influential was the collaboration between President THOMAS JEFFERSON and the architect Benjamin Henry Latrobe, hired by Jefferson in 1803. Jefferson and Latrobe worked closely together to create a neoclassical building with unmistakably American symbols. Latrobe achieved this synthesis most famously in his design of interior columns capped with indigenous American plants such as corn and tobacco. In 1814 British troops burned the Capitol, leaving just the walls standing. Latrobe was hired to rebuild in 1815 but resigned in 1817, and President James Monroe hired Bostonian architect CHARLES BULFINCH to complete the structure.

The proliferation of public buildings and their increasing complexity of design highlights the prominence achieved by architects as professionals during this period. The building process in the 17th and 18th centuries had been dominated by trained craftsmen, both European and African American. In most cases, a master builder or "undertaker" would contract with a client to build a structure for a specific price. The design was normally spelled out in a building contract, with details to be worked out in consultation with the client during construction. In the late 18th century, however, some designers began to assume a new role in the building process. Referring to themselves as "architects" rather than builders, these designers looked to secure control over the entire construction project and began to view their work as a form of art rather than a craft. Architects such as Latrobe, Alexander Parris, Robert Mills, and William Strickland marketed their design services to clients by arguing that they alone had the education and expertise to create fashionable buildings.

Last, the early 19th century brought a new type of architecture to the North American landscape: factory buildings to house the New England textile industry. New England's abundant water power, shipping industry, and merchant capital made it the most attractive region for mechanized textile production, which began in 1793 with the construction of the Slater Mill in Pawtucket, Rhode Island. The new textile factory had to respond to distinct requirements: housing large pieces of machinery, accommodating the power-transmission system (consisting of water wheels, belts, pulleys, gears, and shafts), providing adequate natural light, and allowing for open interior spaces. Early mill builders resolved these problems by designing wood frame, two-to-three-story buildings with monitor roofs that admitted light through an extra band of windows set into the roof. Belfries added symbolic importance to mill buildings as well as providing factory owners a means of calling workers to the mill. Following the expansion of New England textile production as a result of the EMBARGO OF 1807 and the War of 1812 (1812–15), factory owners built larger buildings—60 feet in length, three to five stories high, made of brick or stone, and incorporating exterior stair towers. These mills, built in Slatersville, Rhode Island (1806–07 and later), and Waltham, Massachusetts (1816), provided the prototype for mill buildings constructed in places like Lowell, Massachusetts, during the second quarter of the 19th century.

See also CITIES AND URBAN LIFE; INDUSTRIAL REVOLUTION; RURAL LIFE.

Further reading: Edward A. Chappell, "Housing a Nation: The Transformation of Living Standards in Early America," in *Of Consuming Interests: The Style of Life in the Eighteenth Century,* eds. Cary Carson, Ronald Hoffman, and Peter J. Albert (Charlottesville: University Press of Virginia, 1994); Lois Craig, *The Federal Presence: Architecture, Politics, and Symbols in United States Government Buildings* (Cambridge, Mass.: MIT Press, 1976); Dora P. Crouch, Daniel J. Garr, and Axel I. Mundigo, *Spanish City Planning in North America* (Cambridge, Mass.: MIT Press, 1982); Gabrielle M. Lanier and Bernard L. Herman, *Everyday Architecture of the Mid-Atlantic: Looking at Buildings and Landscapes* (Baltimore: Johns Hopkins University Press, 1997); Peter Nabokov, *Native American Architecture* (New York: Oxford University Press, 1989); William H. Pierson, *American Buildings and Their Architects,* vol. 1, *The Colonial and Neoclassical Styles* (Garden City, N.Y.: Doubleday, 1970); Boyd C. Pratt and Chris Wilson, *The Architecture and Cultural Landscape of North Central New Mexico* (Newport, R.I.: The Vernacular Architecture Forum, 1991); Leland Roth, *A Concise History of American Architecture* (New York: Harper & Row, 1979).

— Martha J. McNamara

Arnold, Benedict (1741–1801)

Serving brilliantly, if contentiously, as an officer in the CONTINENTAL ARMY during the REVOLUTIONARY WAR (1775–83), Benedict Arnold is best known for betraying the American cause and joining the British in September 1780. Born to a respectable but not affluent family in Norwich, Connecticut, Arnold apprenticed as a druggist. As a young man he moved to New Haven, set up his own shop, and married Margaret Mansfield, the daughter of a prominent Connecticut official. Arnold expanded his business and became a colonial merchant of some property and standing by the eve of the AMERICAN REVOLUTION. He was an ardent supporter of the resistance to British imperial measures.

When news of LEXINGTON AND CONCORD (April 19, 1775) arrived, Arnold—a captain in the militia—volunteered to lead his company to Boston. Once he joined the forces surrounding the British in Boston, Arnold suggested that an attack on FORT TICONDEROGA on Lake Champlain would put much-needed gunpowder and artillery in the hands of the new Continental army. He headed west with his Connecticut troops. Upon hearing of ETHAN ALLEN's plan to accomplish the same end, he rushed ahead of his men and joined Allen shortly before the attack that brought the poorly defended British outpost into American hands. Both Allen and Arnold shared the credit for this victory on May 10, 1775. Arnold then led his own troops on a successful raid to the other side of Lake Champlain at St. John's, CANADA. Returning to Ticonderoga, Arnold quickly became involved in a series of disputes over responsibilities and his expenditures. Simultaneously he heard the news of his wife's death on June 19, 1775.

In September he was made a colonel in the Continental army, given command of 1,000 men, and ordered to invade Canada through the Maine wilderness. During this campaign his leadership and endurance skills came to the fore as he led his men on an impossible expedition. They started on September 19, 1775, and arrived before Quebec on November 8. By that time a quarter of the men had turned back, and the rest were tired, hungry, and sick. In December Arnold was reinforced by Americans under General Richard Montgomery, who had captured Montreal. Together the two men led an ill-fated attack on Quebec during a snowstorm on December 31. Montgomery was killed in the action and Arnold severely wounded. Congress appointed Arnold a brigadier general in January 1776, and he maintained the siege of Quebec after the defeat until the spring thaw brought British reinforcements. At this turn of events, Arnold retreated to Lake Champlain. During the summer of 1776 Arnold entered into a dispute over supplies captured in Canada that were lost or stolen during the retreat. During the fall of 1776 Arnold organized a small fleet to defend against a planned British invasion. On October 11, 1776, Arnold's fleet met a hastily assembled and larger British force on Lake Champlain at the BATTLE OF VALCOUR ISLAND. Although the British were ultimately successful in the battle, scuttling or destroying Arnold's entire fleet, the effort had stalled the British army and compelled the 12,000-man force to return to Canada.

During the winter of 1776–77 Arnold once again became embroiled in controversy. Congress promoted five junior officers over Arnold to major general. Both GEORGE WASHINGTON, who favored Arnold, and Arnold himself objected. Congress relented and finally promoted Arnold in May 1777, although it did not restore his seniority. Arnold was ready to resign when Washington asked him to join General HORATIO GATES in the defense of New York against the invading British from Canada. Arnold then led a successful relief column to Fort Stanwix, which was under siege from a combined British and Indian force invading from the Great Lakes. Although Arnold squabbled with Gates in the fall and did not have direct command, he played an instrumental role at the Battle of Bemis Heights, which led to Burgoyne's surrender at SARATOGA on October 17, 1777. Unfortunately Arnold was so seriously wounded that it became difficult for him to resume a field command. Washington made him military commandant of Philadelphia after the British evacuated the city the following spring. There, Arnold met and married his second wife Margaret Shippen. In Philadelphia, too, he spent extravagantly, ran into debt, and argued with other officers and local officials. Sometime in May 1779 Arnold opened communications with the British and supplied information to Major JOHN ANDRE, a member of General HENRY CLINTON's staff. His motivation for this treachery is not clear. Perhaps he became convinced of the hopelessness of the American cause and believed that he could lead the way to a reconciliation. Had he succeeded he might well have been considered a hero. Perhaps it was the money he spent in his high life in Philadelphia. Perhaps, too, he was persuaded by the LOYALIST sympathies of his wife and her family. Or he may have simply tired of the slights he had suffered and the contentiousness of the American officer corps. By the summer of 1780 he was ready for a dramatic gesture to change sides. At Arnold's request, Washington gave him the command of West Point. If the British captured this fortress they could control the Hudson and cut off New England from the rest of the new nation. Before Arnold could turn West Point over to the British, Major Andre (Arnold's main contact with the British) was captured. Upon hearing the news of Andre's capture, and having met with him a few days before and knowing that his own treachery would certainly soon be found out, Arnold fled to the British lines. His wife, who played an important role in the betrayal scheme, feigned surprise at this action.

Benedict Arnold, with view of Quebec, Canada in the background. Published by Thos. Hart, 1776, London *(Library of Congress)*

She returned to Philadelphia but was later allowed to join her husband in New York.

Although Arnold failed to deliver West Point, he issued an appeal to others to join him in switching sides. He also became a British officer. He engaged in two notorious raids that only further sullied his American reputation. In December 1780 Clinton sent Arnold to Virginia, where he captured Richmond and destroyed supplies intended for the Continental army. He remained in Virginia until June 1781. His second raid took place in September 1781 only a few miles from where he grew up in his home state in Connecticut. He burned New London, and troops under his command massacred the defenders of Fort Griswold. In December the Arnolds left New York and sailed to England. Although paid £6,000 for joining the British and given a pension in England and lands in Canada, Benedict Arnold's act of betrayal became infamous even in England. He asked to serve in the army during the 1790s in the wars against France, but he was never given an active commission. Benedict Arnold died in 1801; his wife died three years later.

Further reading: James Thomas Flexner, *The Traitor and the Spy* (New York: Harcourt, Brace, 1953); James Kirby Martin, *Benedict Arnold, Revolutionary Hero: An American Warrior Reconsidered* (New York: New York University Press, 1997); Willard Sterne Randall, *Benedict Arnold: Patriot and Traitor* (New York: William Morrow, 1990).

art

Two key developments emerged in American art in the closing years of the colonial period. First, there arose a core of portrait painters, some more skilled than others, who found patronage among the merchants and landed elite. Second, a select group of these individuals began to expand their horizons beyond portraiture. The AMERICAN REVOLUTION would have a profound effect on these developments and the American art world.

Colonial portrait painters could only succeed if they could find a market for their talents. The increased affluence of the colonial elite, and its desire to consume luxury items, provided just such a market. Whether in Virginia or Massachusetts, the colonial political and economic leaders wanted to adorn their homes with paintings of themselves and members of their families. However, no one locality provided enough work to steadily employ an artist. Painters like JOHN SINGLETON COPLEY and RALPH EARLE had to travel from community to community in search of new subjects willing to pay for a portrait. The best of the colonial painters decided that they needed to study in Europe. BENJAMIN WEST took the lead in the movement, traveling to Italy and France and settling in London in 1763. West established himself as one of Britain's premier painters, working in the neoclassical style. His *Death of General Wolfe* transformed the art world by not only depicting a recent historical event but also by placing his subjects in their modern clothing. After the success of this painting, it became appropriate to commemorate contemporary events with historical painting. Several American artists flocked to West's studio to learn from the master, including Copley, Earle, CHARLES WILLSON PEALE, GILBERT STUART, and JOHN TRUMBULL.

The REVOLUTIONARY WAR (1775–83) intruded upon these developments. In the upheaval of the war some artists became LOYALISTS while others supported the cause of independence. West, already well ensconced in cosmopolitan London and under royal patronage, developed his connections further, received a royal stipend, and painted extensively for GEORGE III. Copley had gone to Europe in 1774, was joined in England by his Loyalist family in 1775, and never returned to the United States. Earle also left America sometime around the beginning of the war, but his politics are more difficult to discern. By the 1780s, however, he was back in the United States and was again an itinerant painter. Trumbull was a supporter of independence, served in the CONTINENTAL ARMY as an officer, and was even arrested in London in 1780. Peale, who had left London in 1769, was an ardent revolutionary, participating in the radical politics of Pennsylvania.

The REPUBLICANISM of the American Revolution created an intellectual problem for many of these artists. Virtue and self-sacrifice seemed to work at cross-purposes with the self-adulation and luxury represented by a personal portrait. What could be more superfluous than a merchant seeking to immortalize his visage by paying to have his own picture painted? As John Adams explained, art had been "enlisted on the side of Despotism and Superstition throughout the ages." A society that valued the artist had vast differences in wealth, with "shoeless beggars and brilliant equipage" next to each other. For many Americans,

simple republican society with some claim on equality was not the appropriate setting for the artist.

While Loyalists like West and Copley may not have had to worry about this issue, revolutionary WHIGS like Trumbull and Peale did. To gain legitimacy in a republic, they decided not only to continue to paint portraits for money but also to turn their brushes to republican purposes. Trumbull used the historical style developed by West to create a visual chronicle of the American Revolution, painting between 250 and 300 historical scenes of crucial events, including the signing of the DECLARATION OF INDEPENDENCE (July 4, 1776) and great battles. Peale kept his hand mostly devoted to portraits, but he also created a gallery of American heroes with portraits of the founding fathers and heroes of the Revolutionary War to be viewed in a museum open to the public (for a fee).

Watson and the Shark by John Singleton Copley, 1778 *(National Gallery of Art)*

Despite their republican aspirations, the revolutionary artists of the period continued to struggle. Trumbull's historical paintings achieved some contemporary notice, but his involvement in business—and his decline in talent with age—limited his financial success. Peale's museum could not sustain an audience, and he ultimately had to turn to a more eclectic collection of curiosities to attract visitors.

Further reading: Neil Harris, *The Artist in American Society: The Formative Years, 1790–1860* (New York: George Braziller, 1966); Kenneth Silverman, *A Cultural History of the American Revolution* (New York: Columbia University Press, 1976).

Articles of Confederation

Proposed by the SECOND CONTINENTAL CONGRESS in 1777 and finally ratified by all the states in 1781, the Articles of Confederation were the first national constitution. Although many have written off the Articles of Confederation as a complete failure, their inherent weaknesses appear clearly only with the advantage of hindsight. In fact, the Articles created a stronger central government than many Americans expected or even desired at the time. The authors of the Articles saw the threat of too much government, or tyranny, as much more ominous than an excess of liberty, and thus sought intentionally to limit the powers of the national government. Furthermore, the Articles were successful in that they created a government that won the REVOLUTIONARY WAR (1775–83). There were other notable achievements under the Articles, including the land ordinances.

The Second Continental Congress drew up the Articles of Confederation to create a form of government for the revolting British colonies of North America. Having convened in May 1775, Congress had begun to operate as a government. In this time of war, the Congress was able to raise an army and establish diplomatic contacts. However, the powers of the Congress were not defined, and its members wanted to have a more legitimate form of government. As the war continued and independence appeared inevitable, it became clear that a more formal central government was needed. Congress organized a committee in June 1776 to draft a plan of perpetual union. The committee—chaired by JOHN DICKINSON of Pennsylvania—worked quickly and submitted its draft to Congress within a month. The Dickinson draft actually gave the government a great deal of power, with only one serious restriction: It could not impose taxes except in relation to the post office. However, as the delegates began to debate these proposals there was immediate disagreement over how strong the government should be. Some members still believed that the union should only be a loosely organized confedera-

tion of states. This group—believing that a large centralized government would be detrimental to the people's liberty and that power should be kept as close to the populace as possible—feared that a new oppressive central government was about to replace the one they had so recently left. Opponents of a strong central government held that they were not fighting a war just to exchange one form of tyranny for another. Because of this lingering fear, Dickinson's plan for the Articles of Confederation was weakened.

The fact that the states were able to organize collectively at all was quite an achievement. The colonies had been founded separately and developed in very distinct ways. Furthermore, there had been disputes among the colonies over rival land claims. Nevertheless, the government established by the Articles was not totally impotent and had considerable powers in foreign affairs and bor-

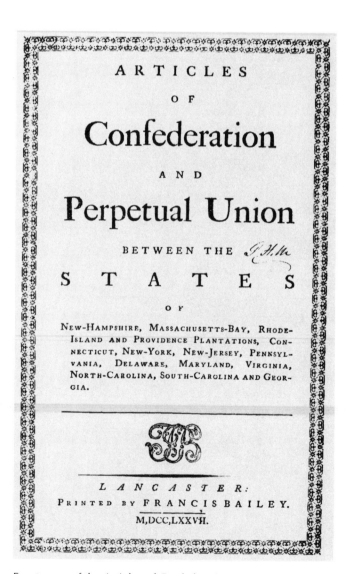

Front page of the Articles of Confederation *(National Archives)*

rowing money. However, the states maintained a final say on laws and the crucial power to tax. Resolutions passed by Congress did not have the force of law because Congress had no power of enforcement. It was up to the states to enforce these resolutions on a good-faith basis. Also, Congress could not raise troops or levy taxes. Instead, it had to ask the states to assist them in these efforts. Article 1 gave the confederacy the title of "The United States of America." Article 4 asserted that all free inhabitants of every state would be entitled to the "privileges and immunities" of every other state. This clause was the basis for national citizenship. Article 6 forbade individual states from making treaties or alliances with foreign powers. Article 9 gave the Congress sole authority to declare wars, reconcile boundary disputes between the states, manage Indian affairs, and regulate land and naval forces. The Articles were much like a treaty among sovereign states, as each state was given equal representation in Congress and amendments required consent of all states. Each state had one vote. Often, states would not vote at all because its delegation could not come to a consensus.

While the government had some powers, there were still many weaknesses in practice. The national government could not regulate commerce or levy taxes, so it was difficult to implement other measures that required funding. States often acted on their own in military affairs. Some states negotiated with foreign countries, and some formed their own armies and navies. Currency was another problem. In addition to the national paper bills, states printed their own paper and minted their own coins. The states retained many powers under the conditions of Article 2, which declared that each state would retain every "power, jurisdiction, and right which is not by this confederation expressly delegated to the United States in congress assembled." Finally, it was almost impossible to change the Articles because amendments required the approval of all 13 states.

The Articles were sent to the states for approval in 1777, but disputes over the lands west of the Appalachian Mountains delayed ratification until 1781. States such as Maryland, which had limited boundaries, refused to take any action until states with large western land claims (New York and Virginia) ceded their western territory to Congress. When the large states ceded these lands, Maryland finally agreed to ratify. While waiting for ratification, Congress continued to operate as the government of the United States, following the provisions of the unratified Articles.

Once the Articles were passed, problems quickly arose because it was difficult to get the states to agree on anything. Furthermore, the states frequently refused to comply with congressional requests for funds. Congress had no recourse other than simply encouraging cooperation. Congress also had a hard time supporting the CONTINEN-TAL ARMY and had to grant General GEORGE WASHINGTON extra powers to allow him to manage the war on his own. However, it is important to note that this weak structure is exactly what the framers of the Articles had in mind. The government under the Articles successfully guided the nation through war and passed the NORTHWEST ORDI-NANCES, which influenced westward settlement for the next century. During the 1780s some Americans began to argue for a stronger national government. These individuals eventually called for changes to the Articles and organized the ANNAPOLIS CONVENTION to meet in 1786. Although the Articles were soon replaced by the Constitution, they were important as the first government of the United States.

See also CONSTITUTIONAL CONVENTION; REPUBLICANISM.

Further reading: Merrill Jensen, *The Articles of Confederation: An Interpretation of the Social-Constitutional History of the American Revolution, 1774–1781* (Madison, Wis.: University of Wisconsin Press, 1940); Peter S. Onuf, *The Origins of the Federal Republic: Jurisdictional Controversies in the United States* (Philadelphia: University of Pennsylvania Press, 1983); Jack N. Rakove, *The Beginnings of National Politics: An Interpretive History of the Continental Congress* (New York: Knopf, 1979).

— Crystal Willams

artisans

Artisans composed the largest sector of the colonial and early national seaports (most notably Boston, New York, Philadelphia, Baltimore, and Charleston). They were skilled craftsmen who had learned their trades following an apprenticeship that might last from ages 13 to 21 under the tutelage of a master craftsman (though the period often became shorter in America). Apprenticeship was a legal contract requiring the apprentice to work for the master for a specified number of years in return for room, board, instruction in the trade, and rudimentary schooling. After completion of an apprenticeship, the craftsman advanced to journeyman standing.

Journeymen were essentially skilled wage laborers. They were called journeymen because many traveled from place to place, such as between major seaports and inland towns, looking for work. The amount of time a man would spend as a journeyman depended on talent and fortune. If he were highly skilled and could find capital to buy equipment and rent space, he could open his own store and become a master craftsman, hiring journeymen and apprentices.

Master craftsmen and journeymen were part of the middling classes of American urban society. They ranged from the lower end, most noticeably the shoemakers and tailors, to the upper ranks, such as the goldsmiths, silversmiths, and watchmakers, with the middle tier occupied by butchers, bakers, and cabinetmakers. A cabinetmaker could be quite poor, doing rudimentary repair work and making crude furniture, or—if he were one of the city's finest, such as New York's DUNCAN PHYFE—he could become quite prominent and hire many journeymen; Phyfe had 100.

From the mid-colonial period on, many artisans had achieved "freedom" of the city, an English right to practice their trade. This status entitled them to vote. In many colonial elections, artisans made the difference between competing factions. This central role brought artisans political awareness, as they were vigorously courted by individuals contending for office. During the RESISTANCE MOVEMENT (1764–75) to British imperial regulation, artisans played a prominent role, forming the core of the SONS OF LIBERTY, extralegal organizations that attempted to enforce anti-British boycotts of the dreaded STAMP ACT (1765) as well as limit imports and exports. Artisans made up the heart of the crowd that dumped the infamous tea into Boston Harbor during the BOSTON TEA PARTY (December 16, 1773).

As war broke out with Great Britain, artisans became active in the government of the cities, particularly in New York and Philadelphia. In New York they formed a Committee of Mechanics that demanded and achieved a share in the governance of the city after British control dissolved. While there were LOYALIST artisans, craftsmen tended to be radicals, asserting a greater political voice in government. In New York they opposed the merchants and demanded a declaration of independence. Paying close attention to the words of THOMAS PAINE, they also insisted that the new constitution of New York State be ratified by a popular vote of the people. In Philadelphia, however, after the QUAKER leadership abandoned politics, as did the proprietary faction (those who politically supported the colony's proprietary family—the Penns), a new group of leaders emerged that included prominent artisans.

During the 1790s artisans aligned themselves with the FEDERALIST PARTY as advocates of a strong central government that would be able to better assert American power. Such a government would also be able to enforce tariffs against British imports that threatened to undersell artisans. However, craftsmen were also backers of the FRENCH REVOLUTION (1789–1815), and many became members of the DEMOCRATIC-REPUBLICAN SOCIETIES. With the rise of the Jeffersonian DEMOCRATIC-REPUBLICANS, many artisans shifted to this party, particularly those in the less wealthy trades. They were attracted by the party's antideferential stance that treated them with respect as American citizens and repelled by Federalist tactics that at times attempted to coerce mechanics with threats regarding their employment. These low-paid artisans were a key element to the success of THOMAS JEFFERSON in the presidential ELECTION OF 1800.

In the early decades of the 19th century, artisans remained a pivotal electoral constituency in the nation's seaports, generally favoring the Jeffersonians. As the ECONOMY grew, and capital requirements for artisan professions increased, fewer journeymen became masters, especially in the largest trades: printing, shoemaking, cabinetmaking, tailoring, and construction (masons and carpenters). Journeymen in these trades, aware of the likely permanence of their standing, began to form trade societies that went beyond the traditional benevolent functions of education and welfare for the sick and aged and deceased. These new trade societies espoused walkouts as a tactic to compel masters to hire only society members and particularly not to hire semiskilled men who had never completed their apprenticeship. In so doing they became the embryonic start of the American labor movement.

See also INDUSTRIAL REVOLUTION; LABOR AND LABOR MOVEMENTS.

Further reading: Howard B. Rock, *Artisans of the New Republic: The Tradesmen of New York City in the Age of Jefferson* (New York: New York University Press, 1979); W.J. Rorabaugh, *The Craft Apprentice: From Franklin to the Machine Age in America* (New York: Oxford University Press, 1986).

— Howard B. Rock

Asbury, Francis (1745–1816)

Frances Asbury was the first METHODIST bishop in America. Born near Birmingham, England, Asbury grew up in a modest but religious family. He had a religious experience at age 14 but continued to serve as an apprentice to a trade until age 21. Before completing his apprenticeship, however, he began to attend prayer meetings and became something of a local religious preacher. During this time he was attracted to the growing Methodist movement. After he turned 21 he became a full-time preacher, traveling on the Methodist circuit in England. In 1771 he volunteered to go to America as a missionary. Upon his arrival in America, Asbury was just one of several missionaries sent by the Methodists. In 1772, however, John Wesley appointed him superintendent of the Methodists in America. Asbury pursued his own agenda, enforcing his ideas about discipline until June 1773, when Wesley ordered him to surrender his authority to Thomas Rankin. Asbury did not readily do so, and in March 1775 Wesley ordered Asbury to return home. Asbury did not obey this command, believing that he needed to be in America during the upheaval that was then breaking out in the colonies.

During the American REVOLUTIONARY WAR (1775–83) the Methodists were often identified as LOYALISTS. Rankin left for England. When Asbury, who sought to remain neutral, refused to take an oath of allegiance in Maryland, he had to seek refuge in Delaware. Before the end of the war, however, he sided with the independence cause. He also played a prominent role in mediating doctrinal disputes between northern and southern Methodists, emerging from the conflict as the virtual head of the American Methodists. In 1784 Wesley sent the Reverend Thomas Coke to America to jointly run the Methodist Church with Asbury. Asbury stalled by insisting that American conferees should make the appointments instead of Wesley. In December 1784 both Asbury and Coke were appointed joint superintendents by a Baltimore Conference. But Coke was not as active as Asbury, who started calling himself Bishop Asbury, and the Methodist organization fell largely on Asbury's shoulders.

Asbury's talents were organizational. He traveled incessantly, covering as many as 300,000 miles during his ministry, from one end of the country to the other. Only after 1800, when his illnesses began to seriously weaken him, did he surrender some control of the Methodist organization. He died in Virginia, on his way to a Baltimore conference, in 1816.

See also RELIGION; RELIGIOUS LIBERTY.

Francis Asbury, the first bishop of the Methodist Episcopal Church *(Library of Congress)*

Further reading: Herbert Asbury, *A Methodist Saint: The Life of Bishop Asbury* (New York: Knopf, 1927).

Association, the (October 20, 1774)

Sometimes known as the Continental Association, the Association agreement represented one of the most radical acts of the FIRST CONTINENTAL CONGRESS. Confronted with calls for action against the COERCIVE ACTS (1774), Congress drew up the Association as a means to establish nonimportation (to begin December 1, 1774), nonconsumption (to begin March 1, 1775), and nonexportation (to begin September 10, 1775) to bring economic pressure on Great Britain to repeal its repressive laws. Although the colonists had used similar measures in the controversy over the STAMP ACT (1765) and TOWNSHEND DUTIES (1767), never had the Americans taken such a bold and sweeping stand. Congress did more than simply vote on these economic sanctions in the Association; it also empowered local COMMITTEES OF CORRESPONDENCE to become committees of inspection to guarantee compliance with the boycott. These committees were to inspect customhouse papers and publish the names of any violators. All mercantile connections would be banned with those who ignored the Association's edicts. In essence, the Association advocated turning local government over to these committees, thus providing a mechanism to transfer power from the king to the people while still maintaining order. If the Association advocated economic coercion and provided a political tool for revolution, it also offered a republican vision of society. To sustain the resistance to imperial measures—and to demonstrate the virtue of the American people—the Association encouraged "frugality, economy, and industry" while it discountenanced and discouraged "every species of extravagance and dissipation, especially all horse-racing, and all kinds of gaming, cock-fighting, shews, plays, and expensive diversions and entertainments." It even advocated simpler dress during funerals. The Association thus represented not only a critical step toward revolution and breaking ties with Great Britain but also the creation of a new moral order.

See also REPUBLICANISM.

Further reading: Jack N. Rakove, *The Beginnings of National Politics: An Interpretive History of the Continental Congress* (New York: Knopf, 1979).

Attucks, Crispus (c. 1723–March 5, 1770)

Crispus Attucks, born of mixed-race heritage, was one of the civilians killed in the BOSTON MASSACRE (March 5, 1770). Since then, he has been held up as an example of a common man who died for the cause of American liberty.

Scholars do not know much about Attucks's life before that fateful evening when he was killed. He was probably part AFRICAN AMERICAN and part NATIVE AMERICAN, possibly with some European blood. In all likelihood he was born in Mashpee, a Natick Indian community near Framingham, Massachusetts. Despite converting to Christianity in the 17th century, the Indians of this community had been pushed to the economic and social periphery by the European American settlers. Many of the New England Christian Indians intermarried with the local and relatively small African-American population. They also frequently found themselves in a form of bondage, either as slaves or in long-term indentures. Attucks apparently was some sort of bond servant in 1750, a conclusion based on the discovery of a runaway ad with his name and description. Like many New England Indians and mixed-race men of his era, he probably also served on a whaler. At the time of the Boston Massacre, he was described as a sailor.

Unlike the great political leaders of the period, Attucks did not leave any written record of his ideas or commitment to the ideal of liberty. Scholars therefore have to surmise from Attucks's actions what brought him to King Street on the night of March 5, 1770. Men like Attucks had many grievances against British imperial policy. For decades they had been liable to IMPRESSMENT and resented this threat to their immediate liberty. Moreover, imperial regulations directly affected their livelihood, since work on the waterfront depended upon TRADE. Laws that limited trade therefore limited employment opportunities. Compounding these difficulties was the post-war recession that occurred after the French and Indian War (1754–63). The recession struck Boston particularly hard, leaving many workers unemployed and milling around the docks. Attucks and other waterfront workers also had more immediate concerns. The presence of British troops in the city made life more difficult for poor Bostonians, since off-duty soldiers competed for jobs along the wharfs and in workshops. In the days leading up to the riot on King Street, soldiers and common people in Boston clashed repeatedly in fights connected to this employment issue. Moreover, common folk had great confidence in the power of the mob. Sailors and other waterfront workers had repeatedly rioted against impressment and, starting in the 1760s, joined in disturbances against the STAMP ACT (1765) and customs regulations. Some of the participation in crowd action was merely an expression of rowdyism—the sheer joy of shouting in the street and disturbing the peace. Much of it, however, was connected to the real issues of the imperial crisis and unemployment. Moreover, those issues were given a larger meaning by the rhetoric of liberty used by the leaders of the RESISTANCE MOVEMENT (1764–75).

Although a few witnesses denied that Attucks was in the forefront of the crowd, most of the evidence indicates that Attucks was one of the leaders of the mob that confronted the soldiers on King Street on the night of March 5. His huge stature—he was six feet two inches (which was tall for the 18th century)—and the fact that he was killed by two bullets striking his breast support the idea that he was not a bystander. JOHN ADAMS vilified Attucks while defending the soldiers on trial for murder, declaring that it was due to his "mad behavior" that "the dreadful carnage of the night is chiefly ascribed."

Attucks was buried with three other victims of the "massacre" on March 8 in a huge ceremony. Subsequently, he has been honored as a hero of the revolution. In the 19th and 20th centuries, African Americans in particular took pride in his racial identity.

See also RIOTS.

Further reading: Dirk Hoerder, *Crowd Action in Revolutionary Massachusetts, 1765–1780* (New York: Academic Press, 1977); Hiller B. Zobel, *The Boston Massacre* (New York: Norton, 1970).

B

Bache, Benjamin Franklin (1769–1798)

Benjamin Franklin Bache was the leading journalist to support THOMAS JEFFERSON and the DEMOCRATIC-REPUBLICANS in the 1790s. Grandson of BENJAMIN FRANKLIN, his parents allowed him to accompany the famous statesman to France in 1777. Educated in France and Switzerland, young Bache returned with his grandfather to Philadelphia in 1785, completing his education at the College of Pennsylvania in 1787. Franklin launched the young man's career in the printing business and served as his nominal partner until his death in 1790.

Bache used the skills and inheritance he acquired from Franklin to set up a new newspaper, *The General Advertiser.* It quickly won the favor of Secretary of State Thomas Jefferson for its fine presentation of Congressional debates and local and foreign news, as well as its opposition to the FEDERALIST PARTY headed by ALEXANDER HAMILTON. For much of the 1790s, Bache was the chief competitor to John Fenno, whose *Gazette of the United States* presented the Federalist line. In 1794, Bache—a staunch supporter of the FRENCH REVOLUTION (1789–1815) and friend of numerous refugees in Philadelphia—changed the paper's name to the *Aurora,* since it would "diffuse light, dispel the shades of ignorance, and strengthen the fair fabric of freedom on its surest foundation, publicity and information."

Bache virulently opposed the administrations of Federalist presidents GEORGE WASHINGTON and JOHN ADAMS. Obtaining a copy of the 1794 JAY'S TREATY with Britain from an ally of Jefferson's, he rapidly printed and distributed it personally from Philadelphia to Boston, ensuring a public outcry against the agreement, which permitted the British navy to intercept American ships trading with France and its colonies.

In 1797 French foreign minister CHARLES MAURICE TALLEYRAND-PÉRIGORD (only recently a refugee in Philadelphia himself) refused to meet American envoys to repair damaged relations with France caused by the treaty with Britain, although he hinted that a $250,000 payment (to be handled by three unnamed individuals X, Y, and Z—hence the XYZ AFFAIR of 1797) might change his mind. The QUASI WAR (1798–1800) with France resulted, yet Bache continued to favor the French, even printing a long letter by Talleyrand in his newspaper defending French policy.

Efforts to silence Bache—including an indictment for treason—failed. Soon thereafter, Bache was one of 14 people arrested under the Sedition Act, passed in 1798 to squelch criticism of the federal government. From his jail cell, Bache continued to champion freedom of speech. He died while awaiting trial during one of Philadelphia's horrendous yellow fever epidemics, leaving a wife, Margaret, and four children.

The *Aurora,* with a circulation that had risen from an initial 400 to 1,700 subscribers by the time of his death, was the most prominent Jeffersonian organ in the nation. Margaret married her husband's assistant, WILLIAM DUANE, who continued his struggle. Margaret wrote his obituary, calling him "a man inflexible in virtue, unappalled by power or persecution, and who, in dying knew no anxieties but what were excited by his apprehensions for his country—and for his young family."

See also ALIEN AND SEDITION ACTS; DISEASE AND EPIDEMICS; JOURNALISM.

Further reading: Richard N. Rosenfeld, *American Aurora: A Democratic Republican Returns* (New York: St. Martin's Press, 1997).

— William Pencak

Backus, Isaac (1724–1806)

Isaac Backus was as an advocate of RELIGIOUS LIBERTY. Raised in an affluent Norwich, Connecticut, family, Backus experienced religious conversion in 1741 during the First Great Awakening. Inspired by the preaching of James Davenport and George Whitefield, he soon joined a New Light separatist church. At that time, state taxes in Connecticut and Massachusetts still supported the religious establishment of the Congregational Church. During the 1740s and 1750s, Backus began to accept the principle of adult baptism, which helped in elevating the BAPTIST Church to prominence. In 1756 he became a founding member and then pastor of a Baptist Church in Middleborough, Massachusetts. Backus committed the rest of his life to religious work, serving as the pastor of his Middleborough congregation for the next 50 years. He also frequently traveled thousands of miles each year as an itinerant, preaching and seeking converts to the Baptist Church.

Backus gained his greatest claim to fame as an advocate of religious liberty, seeking an end to the state-established church in New England. In pursuit of this goal, Backus petitioned both the state legislature and the CONTINENTAL CONGRESS for religious liberty. He also supported the independence movement during the REVOLUTIONARY WAR (1775–83) and even attended the Massachusetts ratification convention in 1788. Backus frequently engaged in newspaper and pamphlet controversy in his defense of religious liberty. Although his efforts were not entirely successful in his lifetime, he stands as an important spokesperson for an ideal that was incorporated into the First Amendment of the United States Constitution.

See also RELIGION.

Further reading: William G. McLoughlin, *Isaac Backus and the American Pietistic Tradition* (Boston: Little, Brown, 1967).

Bank of North America

The Bank of North America was the first real commercial BANK in the United States, beginning operations in 1782. The bank first received a charter to operate from the CONTINENTAL CONGRESS in 1781 and then from the Pennsylvania General Assembly in 1782. Under the direction of wealthy Philadelphians ROBERT MORRIS and Thomas Willing, it quickly became an important component of the Philadelphia mercantile community, the Pennsylvania state government, and the national government. The bank began conducting business in 1782 by taking over the operations of the Bank of Pennsylvania, which had been an exclusive tool of the Continental government since 1780. Soon, the bank was lending capital to the federal and state governments and beginning to lend money to merchants in Philadelphia. By 1784 it had become a powerful instrument of finance for Philadelphians involved in commerce. Its solid hard-money reserves helped to maintain its financial credibility and the value of its banknotes. Meanwhile, the bank aroused political controversy because of rural Pennsylvanians in the assembly, who viewed it as a corrupt institution that was too closely connected to the state

government. Morris himself served in the assembly and debated his rural colleagues in 1785 on the question of the bank's charter. The state revoked its charter in 1785, but the bank continued to operate under its federal charter before winning back its state charter in 1787.

The debate over the bank in the 1780s is important because it highlighted differing attitudes on the role of banks in the new nation and, in particular, exposed a regional schism surrounding state politics in Pennsylvania. The Bank of North America continued to operate as a lender and repository for the Philadelphia mercantile community throughout the years of the early republic and beyond.

Further reading: Belden L. Daniels, *Pennsylvania: Birthplace of Banking in America* (Harrisburg, Pa.: Pennsylvania Banker's Association, 1976); Bray Hammond, *Banks and Politics in America: From the Revolution to the Civil War* (Princeton, N.J.: Princeton University Press, 1957); George David Rappaport, *Stability and Change in Revolutionary Pennsylvania* (University Park: Pennsylvania State University Press, 1996).

— James R. Karmel

Bank of the United States (First) (1791–1811)

The controversial commercial Bank of the United States provided financial support to the federal government, lent resources for business interests, and helped stabilize the national ECONOMY from 1791 to 1811. The Bank of the United States began operations in 1791 after Congress approved a charter allowing it to operate for 20 years. The bank—based in Philadelphia with branches in eight major cities around the United States—was one component of the financial plan submitted by Secretary of the Treasury ALEXANDER HAMILTON during President GEORGE WASHINGTON's first term in office (1789–93). Hamilton modeled his plan on the Bank of England, which had proved to be a stabilizing force for the British economy since the mid-17th century. The bank issued currency, made payments on American debt abroad, provided a depository for government funds, and lent money to merchants. It also provided a mechanism to raise money for the federal government by selling government bonds. Holders of continental certificates could use these notes to buy shares in the new institution, and new bank stock was offered for sale to private investors. Three-fifths of the bank's capital stock was in the form of government securities while the government itself owned one-fifth of the original stock.

The bank became a divisive political issue in 1790 as the first two-party system emerged in national politics, pitting FEDERALIST PARTY against the DEMOCRATIC-

REPUBLICANS (Jeffersonians). Federalists supported the bank by accepting Hamilton's plans and theory that the bank could stabilize and support the American economy. They also suggested that it was constitutional, based on the power of Congress to manage national finances, raise government revenue, and create national institutions such as the military. Led by Secretary of State THOMAS JEFFERSON and Speaker of the House of Representatives JAMES MADISON, Democratic-Republicans argued unsuccessfully against chartering the bank on the basis that the bank was unconstitutional because Congress did not have the explicit power to charter CORPORATIONS. To Jeffersonians, it represented an abuse of federal power by overriding state legislative authority to charter a bank. Therefore, it was an issue that spurred latent ANTI-FEDERALIST sentiments wary of a powerful national government. Jeffersonians also believed that the bank would give financial speculators and merchants too much influence in the national government, to the detriment of farmers and other producers. A sectional dynamic also became manifest in Congress over the bank, with most of its support coming from New England and mid-Atlantic representatives, and southerners opposed.

The bank quickly established itself as an important component of the expanding economy in the early American republic. The bank followed a conservative lending policy to merchants while also lending steadily increasing amounts of money to the federal government. In time, the operations of the bank became integrated with government administration. In addition, the branch BANKS served as regulators of the local economies in which they operated, providing credit and exchange facilities for the state-chartered banks that started businesses in the period from 1791 to 1811. Throughout this period, the bank's managers strictly observed policies that preserved specie, or hard-money reserves, in the banks rather than extensively lend these resources out to other banks and individuals. An important feature of this policy was the curtailment of banknotes, or paper notes, used by the bank as currency. For example, in 1792 the bank had $976,910 in specie reserves and $1,689,486 in banknotes in circulation. In 1800 the bank had $5,671,949 in specie reserves and $5,469,063 in banknotes in circulation.

Political controversy and an evolving economy affected the bank in the latter years of its existence (1808–11). The growing numbers of state banks intensified pressure on the Bank of the United States to ease its lending policies. Meanwhile, many small farmers and producers around the nation never reconciled themselves to the constitutionality or financial necessity of the bank. This opposition contrasted with the position of President James Madison and many Jeffersonians in Congress who had come to accept and appreciate the bank's central and

First Bank of the United States *(New York Public Library)*

stabilizing role for the national economy. Under Secretary of the Treasury ALBERT GALLATIN, the Madison administration supported rechartering the bank in 1810–11. Local bankers and merchants in cities where the bank operated were among the strongest supporters of the bank. Their arguments now included the point that the national bank was necessary to regulate the expanding network of state banks around the nation. Opponents of recharter again tended to be farmers and producers, now acting with considerable force through state assemblies and congressional delegations. They emphasized STATE'S RIGHTS, constitutional issues, and a new objection to foreign ownership of the bank's stock. The bank lost its charter due to a split Congressional decision to postpone renewal in early 1811. In the Senate, Vice President GEORGE CLINTON cast a decisive vote against the bank in opposition to President Madison and Secretary Gallatin. Clinton, an old ANTI-FEDERALIST from New York, was characteristic of Jeffersonians who never did accept the bank. After unsuccessfully attempting to secure a charter from the state of Pennsylvania, the bank's trustees liquidated the bank's assets and it ceased to function by the end of 1811. In 1812, wealthy merchant STEPHEN GIRARD purchased the bank's building in Philadelphia and established his own private bank.

Further reading: Stuart Bruchey, *Enterprise The Dynamic Economy of a Free People* (Cambridge, Mass.: Harvard University Press, 1990); Bray Hammond, *Banks and Politics in America: From the Revolution to the Civil War* (Princeton, N.J.: Princeton University Press, 1957); John Thom Holdsworth and Davis Dewey, Jr., *The First and Second Banks of the United States* (Washington, D.C.: Government Printing Office, 1910).

— James R. Karmel

banks

Following the colonial period of financial dependence on Great Britain, banks began operations in the 1780s and steadily became an important, ubiquitous, and sometimes controversial component of the early American ECONOMY. Banks in colonial America existed mainly in the form of merchants' associations or colonial land offices that issued paper currency or bills of credit to farmers and others in selected colonies, such as Pennsylvania, Massachusetts, and Rhode Island. Also, many private individual lenders operated in the absence of real institutionalized banking. Between 1741 and 1773, Parliament passed a series of laws that first restricted and then secured the rights of the colonies to issue paper notes, thereby providing banking facilities for their growing numbers of entrepreneurial farmers, ARTISANS, and merchants. Fear of problems resulting from inordinate land speculation using paper money issued by colonial governments led to two restrictive acts from Parliament in 1741 and 1751. These officially banned the issuance of paper money or bills of credit by colonial authorities in New England. In 1764, the CURRENCY ACT banned the use of paper bills of credit as legal tender throughout the colonies, although it allowed for the issuance of paper money that was not used as legal tender. Finally, a 1773 act gave broad clearance to the colonies for the issuance of paper money in the absence of enough gold and silver currency (specie). However, the 1773 act probably came too late to ease the growing revolutionary viewpoint that banking restrictions were similar to other parliamentary actions by illegitimately suppressing independent American economic pursuits.

The first true American bank began in Philadelphia in 1780 as financier ROBERT MORRIS and other wealthy Philadelphians organized the Bank of Pennsylvania with private investment to raise revenue to support the CONTINENTAL ARMY. Through their collective efforts, the merchants managed to build credit and supply the army through the end of the war. Between 1780 and 1790, a few commercial banks started operations in Philadelphia, New York, Boston, and Baltimore. These began with Morris's BANK OF NORTH AMERICA in Philadelphia in 1782. Likewise, ALEXANDER HAMILTON organized the Bank of New York in 1784. These early banks existed largely to support the merchant communities of the port cities in which they operated. They lent money, provided other means of credit, sold stock, and issued paper banknotes for use mainly by merchants and others in the urban mercantile communities. At times, they proved more financially stable than the new state governments, with their paper notes relied upon more than those issued by the states. This reliability was probably due to the fact that they often had more specie in reserve and held less debt than many of the states. In Pennsylvania, the new bank aroused the suspicion of rural citizens who viewed it as a scheme for elite Philadelphians to monopolize the state's finances and control the state's political arena via politicians who were also involved in the bank. Significantly, the United States Constitution explicitly banned state governments from issuing paper money but was silent on the subject of banks doing so.

In 1791, Congress chartered the BANK OF THE UNITED STATES to provide revenue, a repository, credit, and financial stability to the new nation. The bank was signed into law by President GEORGE WASHINGTON and went into operation despite substantial objections raised on the basis that it was unconstitutional and biased towards elites. The bank stayed in operation for 20 years, providing a regulatory anchor for the growing number of state banks chartered in the same period.

From 1791 to 1811 the number of banks in the United States increased from five to 117, and their overall capital stock grew from $4,600,000 to $66,290,000. The increase in the number of state banks mirrored the expanding American economy, which grew in every respect in those years. Popular demand for capital increased as manufacturing and commerce expanded throughout the nation. New banks were often designed to support artisans, farmers, and mechanics through loan guarantees or long-term loans. Sometimes, the new banks became political entities, designated as either Jeffersonian (DEMOCRATIC-REPUBLICAN) or FEDERALIST. Political opponents of the Bank of the United States viewed the expanding state banking system as generally favorable because it gave Americans more financial opportunities while decreasing the power of the national bank to create and regulate lending policies.

Between 1811 and 1820 the number of banks around the nation expanded even more dramatically; by 1820 there were more than 300 state-chartered banks in the United States. Between 1807 and 1814, in the rural interior of the early republic, the disruption in commerce and the growth in manufacturing related to the War of 1812 (1812–15) had the effect of increasing public support for independent sources of capital. Regions such as the Ohio River Valley, central Pennsylvania, and rural New England experienced tremendous growth in the financial sector in these years. Typically, the new banks of this period had a substantial popular appeal. Laborers, women, AFRICAN AMERICANS, and Native Americans all became stockholders and customers in the new institutions. In some areas, such as New England, banks developed as money clubs administered by a select few, for their own benefit or for the benefit of their colleagues and families. The new banks issued millions of dollars in the form of banknotes, which became the standard form of currency used in local marketplaces. State legislatures utilized the new banks to develop transportation networks by mandating that banks invest in turnpike, bridge, and canal companies in exchange for charters.

In 1816, Congress chartered the Second Bank of the United States to once again serve the government and national economy as a funds repository, regulator, revenue generator, and exchange mechanism for smaller banks. Savings banks also originated in this era with the establishment of the three banks—designed solely for depositors to earn interest on savings—in Philadelphia, New York, and Boston between 1816 and 1819.

Many Americans involved with the new banks suffered during an economic downturn between 1818 and 1821, popularly known as the Panic of 1819. Upon beginning operations, the Second Bank of United States reinstituted the conservative lending practices of its predecessor, implementing policies designed to build up its specie reserves. This policy had the effect of causing specie to flow from small rural banks to larger urban banks, and eventually to the national bank; this process led to a devastating currency crisis by 1819, in which the banknotes issued by many of the new rural banks decreased precipitously in value. This depreciation, along with other factors, contributed substantially to a difficult recession in which many people lost jobs, endured mortgage foreclosures, and had savings wiped out. However, the recession eased by 1821, and Americans were once again experiencing economic prosperity, with banks at the forefront.

See also CORPORATIONS; TRADE.

Further reading: Bray Hammond, *Banks and Politics in America: From the Revolution to the Civil War* (Princeton, N.J.: Princeton University Press, 1957); Naomi Lamoreaux, *Insider Lending: Banks, Personal Connections, and Economic Development in Industrial New England* (Cambridge: Cambridge University Press, 1994); Edwin J. Perkins, *American Public Finance and Financial Services, 1700–1815* (Columbus: Ohio State University Press, 1994); Fritz Redlich, *The Molding of American Banking, Part I: Men and Ideas, 1781–1840* (New York: Johnson Reprint Corp, 1968); Gordon S. Wood, *The Radicalism of the American Revolution* (New York: Knopf, 1992).

— James R. Karmel

Banneker, Benjamin (1731–1806)

Born free in 1731 in Baltimore County, Maryland, Benjamin Banneker became one of the most famous AFRICAN AMERICANS of the late 18th and early 19th centuries. He rose from humble roots: Banneker's mother was a freeborn woman of mixed parentage (Banneker's free status flowed from his mother), his father a slave taken from African shores. Although he grew up in a rural environment of tobacco cultivation and farm labor in which the majority of African Americans were not only denied freedom but also education, Banneker attended a small country school and

displayed early talents in literature, statistics, and nature observation. As an adult, Banneker became a mathematician, surveyor (he was one of three men to survey the layout of WASHINGTON, D.C., in the 1790s), and astronomer. But he remains best-known for his almanacs, the first of which dates from 1791, the last from 1797. A calendar of astronomical calculations—"the rising and setting of the sun," as he put it, "the rising, setting and southing place of the moon," the dates of eclipses, and so forth—Banneker's almanac also contained miscellaneous poetry, prose, and other "interesting and entertaining" information.

Beyond its usefulness to farmers and a growing reading public (the almanac circulated in Pennsylvania, Delaware, Maryland, and Virginia), Banneker's publication bolstered early ANTISLAVERY thought and action. Its very production confounded the antiblack stereotypes of the late 18th century that served to rationalize the enslavement of people of African descent. THOMAS JEFFERSON often defended himself as a slaveholder by arguing that African Americans were inferior mental beings. Where is the proof that they can master the literary arts or scientific inquiry, he wondered in *Notes on the State of Virginia*

Benjamin Banneker *(Hulton/Archive)*

(1787). Just as other African-American writers of the revolutionary era and early republic (from PHILLIS WHEATLEY to RICHARD ALLEN) challenged this argument by producing pamphlets, poetry, and essays, so too Banneker hoped that his almanac would alter prevailing racial beliefs. In fact, Banneker wrote Thomas Jefferson a letter in August 1791, carefully but also adamantly challenging the latter's racial philosophies. "Now Sir," Banneker argued, "I apprehend you will readily embrace every opportunity to eradicate that train of absurd and false ideas and opinions which so generally prevail with respect to us, and that your sentiments are concurrent with mine, which are that one universal father hath given being to us all . . ." Jefferson replied to Banneker cordially that he hoped to see further proof of African-American achievement, and he forwarded Banneker's documents to the noted French philosopher and antislavery advocate, the marquis de Condorcet. Still, Jefferson remained steadfast in his belief that Banneker was an exception to his racial beliefs. Banneker may have outwitted Jefferson somewhat, however: The exchange between the two writers was published in both pamphlet and periodical form, and subsequent generations of activists and scholars have used it to reexamine Jefferson's racial attitudes as well as black challenges to them.

Banneker lived most of his entire life in Baltimore County, passing away in October 1806. Although an enigmatic figure—Banneker did not continue to press Jefferson publicly, nor did he produce any other explicit antislavery literature beyond that found in his almanacs—Banneker remains a celebrated figure in African-American history. In the early 1800s, for example, Baltimore blacks organized the Banneker Monument Committee to honor perhaps their most famous son. Modern memorials, scholarships, and schools continue to honor Banneker in this fashion.

Further reading: Silvio A. Bedini, *The Life of Benjamin Banneker* (New York: Scribner's, 1972).

— Richard Newman

Baptists

The first Baptists were radical Protestants who fled England to Holland in the early 1600s. This small group took seriously the doctrines of the Reformation, emphasizing an individual's complete reliance on the Bible and the belief that God could only be known through personal experience (hence, they believed in "adult baptism," or baptizing only those who had become true believers). Baptists challenged any connection between earthly authority (the state) and the church, arguing instead for the autonomy of each local congregation. Denying the legitimacy of any authority that ran counter to Christian teachings, early Baptists proved a political threat to the established churches, both in England and in colonial North America.

Baptists benefitted greatly from the religious fervor surrounding the First Great Awakening. Although many Baptist churches divided along the same lines as their Congregational and Presbyterian counterparts, the general upsurge in religiosity and desire for moral orthodoxy made Baptists appealing to many colonists. Following the Great Awakening, Baptists became a minor, yet important, presence throughout the colonies. The Great Awakening also spawned a group known as Separate Baptists, who preached the absolute separation of church and state. Separate Baptists were especially strong among small farmers in the western regions of the South. In states like Virginia, they challenged the leadership of wealthy, usually Anglican, planters in the east. In New England, the number of Baptists rose dramatically following the revivals of mid-century.

During the REVOLUTIONARY WAR (1775–83), Baptists capitalized on the backlash against the Anglican Church to gather more adherents. Emphasizing their long tradition of challenging church hierarchies, Baptists appealed to democratic Americans no longer willing to defer to the established church. The famous Baptist minister John Leland, a New Englander, moved to Virginia between 1777 and 1791 and encouraged his fellow ministers to bring down the Anglican establishment. In New England, Baptists struggled against efforts to strengthen the Congregational church. ISAAC BACKUS, a prominent minister in Massachusetts and Rhode Island, railed against Massachusetts's continued taxation to support Congregationalism. Joining with the DEMOCRATIC-REPUBLICAN PARTY (Jeffersonian), Baptists in Connecticut, New Hampshire, and Massachusetts were central participants in the battle to disestablish the church.

After the Revolutionary War, the tremendous growth of Baptist churches led to an effort to consolidate and rationalize the denomination. From local associations to state conventions and missionary societies, Baptists united around their common cause and shared values. It was not that there was no cooperation before. The Philadelphia Baptist Association was founded in 1707, and it played an important role in establishing Brown University in 1764. The Warren Association in Massachusetts and Rhode Island served as a common space to hash out disagreements among New England Baptists. Yet, the efforts to develop denominational institutions in the early decades of the 19th century convinced many Baptists that their leaders were moving away from the central creeds of the early church. These "hard shell" or "primitive" Baptists once again turned to absolute separation between earthly and church authority, and reiterated the autonomy of local congregations.

Although Baptists were a minor presence before the Revolutionary War, they grew tenfold during the three decades following independence. Their growth rate has continued steadily throughout American history. Today, Baptists are the largest Protestant denomination in the United States. Since their radical beginnings in the 17th century, Baptists had emphasized individual discipline combined with an absolute commitment to RELIGIOUS LIBERTY. During the early republic era, this combination proved to be a powerful draw for many Americans.

See also RELIGION.

Further reading: Samuel S. Hill, *One Name but Several Faces: Variety in Popular Christian Denominations in Southern History* (Athens, Ga.: University of Georgia Press, 1996); Rhys Isaac, *The Transformation of Virginia, 1740–1790* (Chapel Hill: University of North Carolina Press, 1982); Anne Devereaux Jordan and J. M. Stifle, *The Baptists* (New York: Hippocrene Books, 1990); William G. McLoughlin, *New England Dissent, 1630–1833: The Baptists and the Separation of Church and State,* 2 vols. (Cambridge, Mass.: Harvard University Press, 1971).

— Johann Neem

Barbary pirates

The Barbary pirates preyed upon the shipping interests of the new United States, resulting in several wars. The Barbary states consisted of Morocco, Algeria, Tunis, and Tripolitania (or Tripoli), small kingdoms in North Africa. The pirates gained treasure by capturing merchant ships in the Mediterranean and Atlantic Ocean and by collecting protection fees from countries trading in the area. The Barbary pirates had been molesting European commerce for centuries. The money they made from reselling goods and ransoming slaves provided a major source of revenue for the rulers of the Barbary states. The British could have defeated the pirates but chose instead to pay the tribute. Before the REVOLUTIONARY WAR (1775–83) the colonies were protected by the British flag.

After independence, the United States had to deal with the Barbary pirates on its own. In 1785, and again in 1794–95, Algeria was able to send its corsairs into the Atlantic because it was at peace with the European powers that had been blockading the Straits of Gibraltar. In 1785 the Algerians captured a few American vessels and held hostage about 20 American seamen. A weak Congress could do little to aid them. The United States reacted more rigorously in 1794–95 by beginning to build a fleet of frigates and negotiating a settlement—the payment of tribute for the release of over 100 hostages. During the same years, the United States government made treaties with other Barbary states, guaranteeing annual payments in exchange for immunity from attacks.

War broke out with Tripoli in 1801 when its leader increased his demands for tribute. The American government refused to pay any more, and Tripoli declared war on the United States on May 14. President THOMAS JEFFERSON responded by sending warships to blockade Tripoli in 1803. During the conflict the United States lost the frigate *Philadelphia* to Tripoli when it grounded and was unable to defend itself. Lieutenant Stephen Decatur led an expedition into Tripoli Harbor to burn the captured ship, instantly becoming a national hero. The blockade eventually proved successful and a peace treaty, signed on June 4, 1805, eliminated future tribute, while providing a $60,000 ransom for the officers and crew of the *Philadelphia.*

Problems arose again during the War of 1812 (1812–15) when the Algerians captured and ransomed several American merchant vessels. As soon as the war was over, the United States sent Commodore Decatur to the Mediterranean. Decatur quickly captured two Algerian ships and compelled the ruler of Algiers to sign a peace releasing the United States from all tribute. The American fleet then forced the other Barbary states to make similar treaties. The pirates continued to attack some European ships, but after 1830, when the French occupied Algeria, the depredations came to an end. The Tripoli War was important in the development of the United States. Not only did it contribute to a growing feeling of nationalism, but it also demonstrated that the United States was willing and able to protect its rights whenever necessary.

See also FOREIGN AFFAIRS.

Further reading: William M. Fowler Jr., *Jack Tars and Commodores: The American Navy, 1783–1815* (Boston: Houghton Mifflin, 1984); Glenn Tucker, *Dawn like Thunder: The Barbary Wars and the Birth of the U.S. Navy* (Indianapolis, Ind.: Bobbs-Merril, 1963).

— Crystal Williams

Barlow, Joel (1754–1812)

Joel Barlow had the good fortune to grow into maturity just as the REVOLUTIONARY WAR (1775–83) broke out. An enthusiastic supporter of the cause of independence, he spent part of his summer vacation from Yale fighting in the BATTLE OF LONG ISLAND (August 27–30, 1776). He graduated from Yale in 1778 and embarked on a variety of careers, including newspaper editor, storekeeper, and military chaplain in the CONTINENTAL ARMY. Barlow kept to this uncertain course in the years immediately after the war while also gaining some notoriety as an author and poet. As one of the CONNECTICUT WITS he coauthored "The Anarchiad," a satire that appeared in newspapers in 1786 and 1787, and an epic American poem called *The Vision of Columbus* in 1787.

Barlow traveled to Europe in 1788 as an agent for land speculators, but he failed in this business effort. He was in Europe during the outbreak of the FRENCH REVOLUTION (1789–1815). Between 1790 and 1792 he and his wife were in London, where he became involved in reform politics, befriending THOMAS PAINE and several English radicals. His publications led to his expulsion from England and honorary citizenship in France. Having moved to Paris, he managed to make a fortune in the 1790s. He became the American consul to Algiers in 1795 and negotiated treaties with that country, Tunis, and Tripoli. He returned to the United States in 1805 and retired. He also published a revised form of his epic poem, now called *The Columbiad,* which has since been often mocked because of its cumbersome verse. THOMAS JEFFERSON persuaded him to serve as the United States ambassador to France in 1811. In 1812 he traveled to Poland to complete negotiations with NAPOLEON BONAPARTE, who was then confronting his devastating defeat in Russia. Unable to meet Napoleon as the French army retreated in the winter of 1812, Barlow died in Poland on his way back to Paris.

See also BARBARY PIRATES; LITERATURE.

Further reading: Samuel Bernstein, *Joel Barlow: A Connecticut Yankee in an Age of Revolution* (New York: Rutledge, 1985); James Leslie Woodress, *A Yankee's Odyssey: The Life of Joel Barlow* (New York: Greenwood Press, 1968).

Barry, John (1745–1803)

John Barry was one of the leading naval officers in the REVOLUTIONARY WAR (1775–83) and the early years of the republic. Born in Ireland, and a Roman CATHOLIC, the young sailor settled in Philadelphia at the age of 15. While working his way to becoming a captain on merchant vessels before 1775, he developed strong connections with merchant ROBERT MORRIS. At the outbreak of the war he eagerly supported independence. Shortly after the founding of the American navy by the CONTINENTAL CONGRESS on October 13, 1775, John Barry was asked to supervise the outfitting of his old merchant vessel, the *Black Prince,* as the warship *Alfred.* However, he was not given its command. Instead he had to wait a few months longer before being named captain of the newly acquired *Lexington.* He sailed in that vessel in the spring of 1776 and had the distinction of captaining the first American warship to capture a British naval vessel, the HMS sloop *Edward,* on April 7, 1776. On returning to Philadelphia he was given command of a newly built frigate, the *Effingham,* but never sailed in her because of difficulties in outfitting the vessel, recruiting a crew, and a British assault on Philadelphia. Against his own judgment, he was ordered to scuttle the *Effingham* to prevent her from getting into the hands of the enemy.

During the British occupation of Philadelphia (1777–78), Barry commanded a small squadron on the Delaware to harass and interrupt British supplies and transport Continental soldiers across the river. In May 1778 Barry was ordered to Boston to take command of the *Raleigh.* When he set sail in that vessel in August, he quickly ran into a superior British force. Outgunned, he fought tenaciously, finally attempting to scuttle the vessel on a rocky island off the coast of Maine. Barry and most of the crew escaped, but the British managed to salvage the *Raleigh.* Unable to find another naval command, Barry took a leave of absence and captained a PRIVATEER on a successful cruise to the WEST INDIES. Upon his return, he was assigned to another ship under construction, but the project moved very slowly. In 1780 he accepted command of the *Alliance,* one of the few remaining ships in the American navy. In the *Alliance,* he crossed the Atlantic several times, including a voyage in 1782 when he transported the MARQUIS DE LAFAYETTE to France. He also fought the last naval battle of the war when he engaged and severely damaged the HMS *Sybil.* He was the only active captain in the American navy after the war, until Congress sold the *Alliance* in 1785.

After he left the navy he served as a merchant captain again for several years and even made a voyage to China in the new TRADE with the Far East. When the United States decided to build a navy in 1794, Barry again volunteered his services. President GEORGE WASHINGTON appointed Barry the first captain of this reconstituted navy, and he took command of the first frigate built for it, the *United States,* in 1797. At that time the United States government was involved in the QUASI WAR (1798–1800) with France. As senior officer, Barry was named commodore of the American naval forces in the West Indies. However, he did not take part in any head-to-head battles with French frigates. That distinction fell to Captain Thomas Truxton in the *Constellation.* In part because he failed to win a single ship in the Quasi War, Barry was criticized as a commanding officer of the fleet. When the United States and France came to an agreement, avoiding all-out war, and with the election of THOMAS JEFFERSON in 1800, the *United States* was laid up at the Washington naval yard, and Barry retired from the navy. He died in 1803.

Further reading: James C. Bradford, ed., *Command under Sail: Makers of the American Naval Tradition, 1775–1850* (Annapolis, Md.: Naval Institute Press, 1985).

Bartram, William (1739–1823)

The son of the famous botanist, John Bartram, William floundered in his early life, training as a merchant and trying his hand at farming, although he also had a gift as an artist and as a naturalist. Because of this talent he came under the sponsorship of Dr. John Frothergill in England, who underwrote in 1773–77 an expedition to what is now the southeastern United States. Bartram, who was a QUAKER, was charged with collecting seeds and specimens. He was also to make drawings of the flora and fauna. The REVOLUTIONARY WAR (1775–83) limited what Bartram could send back, but based on this trip Bartram wrote *Travels through North and South Carolina, Georgia, East and West Florida, the Cherokee Country, the Extensive Territories of the Muscogulges, or Creek Confederacy, and the Country of the Choctaws* in 1791. Within the decade, this work would be republished several times on both sides of the Atlantic and would be translated into German, Dutch, and French. It became the most important naturalist study of late 18th-century America, with ample illustrations of plants, birds, and wildlife. Bartram kept up an extensive correspondence, was elected to several learned societies, and published a number of papers as a naturalist. Bartram turned down a professorship at the University of Pennsyl-

William Bartram *(Library of Congress)*

vania in 1786, preferring to live as a bachelor with his brother at his father's famous botanic garden outside Philadelphia. When his brother died, he continued on at the garden in the household of a niece until he died in 1823.

See also SCIENCE.

Bernard, Francis (1712–1779)

Sir Francis Bernard was the governor of Massachusetts throughout most of the turbulent 1760s. He was born in England, went to Oxford, and became a lawyer in 1737. He might have lived in obscurity as a country lawyer in Lincolnshire had he not married Amelia Offley, a cousin of Lord Thomas Barrington. This noble was highly influential at court and served in the British government for most of the time from 1755 to 1778. Politics in England depended heavily on patronage, and Bernard, something of a social climber, soon became a client of Lord Barrington. In 1758 Barrington managed to get Bernard appointed as the governor of New Jersey. A talented bureaucrat and a careful politician, Bernard quickly won over the local leadership in that colony and thus became a successful governor. Barrington and other English officials took note of this success and transferred Bernard to the governorship of Massachusetts, one of the most populous and richest colonies. Unfortunately for Bernard, as he moved from Perth Amboy to Boston in 1760, the British empire was about to face its greatest challenge.

Interestingly, Bernard recognized that the British-colonial relationship was troubled, and soon after he arrived in Massachusetts, he worked out an elaborate plan to reorganize the North American empire. Bernard's advice was not acted upon, but it suggests that independence was not the only possibility available on the eve of the AMERICAN REVOLUTION. Bernard wanted to rewrite the colonial charters to create larger, more coherent colonies, especially in New England where there were many jurisdictions divided into small entities like Rhode Island and Connecticut. He also wanted to create an American nobility, which would form an upper house of legislature in each colony and help to stabilize a volatile social situation. He believed that the king in Parliament remained sovereign in the colonies, with the right of taxation. But he also advocated that the colonial assemblies be responsible for most taxes and that Parliament should be mainly concerned with TRADE regulations. Instead of acting on these recommendations, the British government began to pass a series of customs duties and laws—SUGAR ACT (1764), STAMP ACT and (1765), TOWNSHEND DUTIES (1767)—that made governing Massachusetts all but impossible. The successful governor of New Jersey struggled throughout the 1760s with a tide of events beyond his control. Although sympathetic to many colonial demands, Bernard witnessed outright flouting of customs regulations, the nullification of the Stamp Act through mob action, and the harassment of customs officials. Bernard struggled to keep up with events. The publication in 1769 of a series of letters he had sent home to officials in England complaining of colonial behavior made him extremely unpopular. At the request of the assembly he was recalled to England. There he was exonerated, but he did not return to the colonies. He was made a baronet, becoming Sir Francis Bernard of Needleham, Lincolnshire. He held some other government sinecures and received a pension. He died in relative isolation and retirement in 1779.

See also RESISTANCE MOVEMENT.

Further reading: Edmund S. Morgan and Helen M. Morgan, *The Stamp Act Crisis: Prologue to Revolution* (Chapel Hill: University of North Carolina Press, 1953).

Billings, William (1746–1800)

William Billings was the leading composer and singing teacher of his generation, and he helped define a distinct American MUSIC. Billings was born into a modest Boston family and was apprenticed as a tanner. Although he continued in the tanner trade off and on for the rest of his life, while in his early 20s he began to establish a reputation as a psalm singer and music teacher. He had opened his first singing school by 1769.

American music was undergoing an important transformation in the revolutionary era. Church music expanded beyond psalm singing and increasingly included more sacred songs, organ playing, and elaborate choral performances. Initially these changes were introduced based on English practices; Billings added a particular American cast to this development. In 1770, he published *The New England Psalm Singer: or American Chorister*. All of this collection, as the book proudly proclaimed, was American and written by Billings. The book contained music and songs for church performances as well as instructions on how to teach the music. Innovative in its approach and in its identity as American, the book was an instant success. Over the next couple of decades, Billings taught at singing schools throughout New England. He became an ardent supporter of the AMERICAN REVOLUTION and published another book, *The Singing Master's Assistant, or Key to Practical Music,* in 1778. This work featured many patriotic tunes, portraying the revolutionary movement as the work of God. If anything, this book was even more popular than *The New England Psalm Singer* and was sometimes called "Billing's Best." Billings continued to write and publish music in the 1780s and 1790s and remained the most popular and renowned American composer of sacred music during his lifetime. Despite this success, he seems to have struggled financially in his later years. After his death, his music declined in popularity as American musical tastes shifted in the 19th century.

Further reading: Kenneth Silverman, *The Cultural History of the American Revolution: Painting, Music, Literature, and Theatre in the Colonies and the United States from the Treaty of Paris to the Inauguration of George Washington, 1763–1789* (New York: Columbia University Press, 1976).

Bill of Rights

The Bill of Rights is the collective term given to the first 10 amendments to the United States Constitution. These amendments guarantee, among other things, the freedoms of speech, press, and RELIGION. The amendments were ratified in December 1791. Several states had made the inclusion of such amendments a condition of their ratification of the Constitution. The Bill of Rights was influenced by the bills of rights that had been added to many of the state constitutions, such as the Virginia Declaration of Rights. Although the FEDERALISTS believed that there were many problems inherent in including an explicit written bill of rights, they eventually agreed to give the issue consideration. Initially the Federalists were concerned that ANTI-FEDERALISTS would use the call for a bill of rights as an excuse to ask for serious changes to the Constitution itself. Many also saw the Bill of Rights as unnecessary because the federal government could only exert powers that were expressly delegated to it and thus did not pose a threat to individual liberties. Also, the Federalists believed that popular majorities posed a much greater threat to individuals than the powers of the government. However, Federalists capitulated in the interest of appeasing the opposition. In so doing, they hoped to build support for the new government and end talk of calling another CONSTITUTIONAL CONVENTION. One of the Federalists' main theoretical concerns was how to decide which rights deserved protecting to the exclusion of all the others. JAMES MADISON and others realized that it was impossible to enumerate all of the rights that needed protection. Because one of the goals of the Bill of Rights was to squelch resistance to the Constitution, some decisions were influenced by politics as much as principle.

Although Madison was among those who thought that a bill of rights was not necessary, he was the one person most responsible for the fact that they were added to the Constitution. Madison took on the work of deciding which rights should be included as amendments. From the variety of proposals offered by the states, Madison selected a set of specific propositions for Congress to consider. Although he considered over 200 amendments, he chose only 19 for further debate. After extensive deliberation, Congress accepted most of Madison's suggestions and ratified the first 10 amendments to the Constitution. Madison's careful wording of what would become the Ninth Amendment dealt with the concern that enumerating certain rights would cause others to not be protected.

The Bill of Rights had little impact on the immediate future of the United States and did not become particularly important until after the passage of the Fourteenth Amendment and its successive interpretations applied the protection of rights to state and local governments. However, the Bill of Rights has become the foundation for civil liberties in modern society and is especially important in protecting the rights of minority groups. For example, the First Amendment protection of free speech allows people to hold opinions that stray from the official or even popular opinion. One of the more controversial of the first 10 amendments has been the Second Amendment, which concerns the right to bear arms. However, it is important to note that many of the amendments do not expressly give people rights. Instead, they simply prevent the government from infringing on these rights, a provision embodied in the phrase "Congress shall make no law. . . ." The Third Amendment states that soldiers will not be quartered in private homes, while the Fourth Amendment protects against unreasonable search and seizure. There are also provisions for criminal issues. Speedy trials, trial by jury, and protection from cruel and unusual punishment are guaranteed by the Fifth, Sixth, and Seventh Amendments. The Fifth Amendment protects the individual against self-incrimination while also stating that no one can be deprived of "life, liberty, or property, without due process of law." Finally, the Tenth Amendment reserves to the people all rights not specifically allotted to the United States and not prohibited by the states. Overall, the effects of the Bill of Rights in practice have been subject to fluctuations in SUPREME COURT interpretation. The interpretation of these rights has often caused great public controversy. Some scholars attempt to discern the original intentions of the founders when deciding these debates. Others believe that the founders intended the Constitution to be a changeable document and that original meanings are irrelevant. Originally, Federalists were concerned that including a bill of rights was unwise and thought that the national government could do little to protect individual liberties; despite their reservations, the Bill of Rights has proved to be a success, protecting the privileges of the individual throughout American history.

See also REPUBLICANISM.

Further reading: Irving Brant, *The Bill of Rights: Its Origin and Meaning* (Indianapolis, Ind.: Bobbs-Merrill, 1965);

Leonard Williams Levy, *Constitutional Opinions: Aspects of the Bill of Rights* (New York: Oxford University Press, 1986); Robert A. Rutland, *The Birth of the Bill of Rights, 1776–1791* (Boston: Northeastern University Press, 1983).
— Crystal Williams

Blackstone, William (1723–1780)

Sir William Blackstone was the author of *Commentaries on the Laws of England,* the most influential legal text in the early republican United States. He was born in Cheapside, London, on July 10, 1723, and orphaned before the age of 12. At the age of 15, on the nomination of Sir Robert Walpole, he entered Pembroke College, Oxford, where his studies focused on the classics. In 1741 he commenced the study of law at the Middle Temple in London, one of several legal academies controlled by the practicing bar. After completing his legal studies, Blackstone was admitted to practice in 1746. His strength and interest lay more in legal education, however, and he was nominated for the professorship of civil law at Oxford in 1752. "Civil law" covered the laws of most of the nations of Europe, excluding England. Blackstone was passed over for this appointment, but supporters encouraged him to go to Oxford anyway and lecture on English law. At this time, no university in England offered training in English law. Blackstone's lectures were so popular, Oxford established a chair of English law in 1758 and appointed Blackstone its first holder. His success in this position led to the renewal of his law practice, his election to Parliament, and his eventual selection as justice of the Courts of King's Bench and Common Pleas.

Blackstone's fame in the United States rests on his written works. Blackstone's lectures had been copied by others and circulated, often for sale; to arrest this practice, Blackstone decided to publish them himself. The first volume, under the title *Commentaries on the Laws of England,* appeared in 1765. Three additional volumes appeared over the next four years. They were phenomenally successful. Eight editions appeared during Blackstone's lifetime, and the ninth was ready for publication at the time of his death on February 14, 1780. New editions continued to appear with the same frequency for the next 60 years in England, and for even longer in the United States. The reason for their success was their comprehensiveness and readability. Laypersons could pick up the *Commentaries* and gain a basic understanding of English law. While not without error, and while certainly subject to strong criticism (Jeremy Bentham called Blackstone's views on the law "nonsense on stilts"), the *Commentaries* stood for generations as the standard text on the law.

In the United States, the *Commentaries* had an even greater impact than in England. During the early republican period, very few institutions offered legal training.

Most would-be LAWYERS apprenticed themselves to a practicing lawyer for a time. To supplement this experience—to gain some knowledge of areas beyond the mentor's field of practice—would-be lawyers needed a textual guide, and that text was Blackstone. The widespread availability of the *Commentaries* led to a democratization of the legal profession in the United States. Anyone with access to the four volumes could hold himself out as a lawyer. This bothered many, including THOMAS JEFFERSON, who worried that a student found in Blackstone "a smattering of everything, and his indolence easily persuades him that if he understands that book he is master of the whole body of the law." The practice was, at the time, unstoppable, however, and the lawyer trained on Blackstone quickly became the norm. This circumstance was not without consequence to the development of thinking about legal issues. Blackstone was committed to the preservation of private property, and this commitment forms the major unifying theme of his *Commentaries*. To a great extent, the modern American commitment to private property descends from Sir William Blackstone and the thousands of early republican lawyers who were trained on the *Commentaries*.

Further reading: Daniel J. Boorstin, *The Mysterious Science of the Law: An Essay on Blackstone's Commentaries* (Cambridge, Mass.: Harvard University Press, 1941).

— Lindsay Robertson

Bland, Richard (1710–1776)

Educated at William and Mary and a member of the Virginia planter elite, Bland was an early advocate of popular rights in opposition to the royal governor and the king. Bland first became a member of the House of Burgesses in 1742 and remained so until 1775. At that time he was elected to Virginia's revolutionary convention and became a delegate to the FIRST CONTINENTAL CONGRESS. He was also elected to the SECOND CONTINENTAL CONGRESS, but only attended a few days. He was in the forefront in opposition to the imperial regulations of the 1760s and 1770s, being the first to sign the non-importation agreement in 1769, and serving on both the Virginia COMMITTEE OF CORRESPONDENCE set up in 1773 and the Virginia Committee of Safety organized in 1775. While advocating colonial rights, he hesitated to break entirely from Great Britain and the king.

Bland was known for his careful study of Virginia history and was considered by many to be one of the most scholarly members of his generation. THOMAS JEFFERSON referred to him as "the most learned and logical man of those who took prominent lead in public affairs, profound in constitutional lore." As early as 1753 he stood against royal prerogative, opposing the effort by the Virginia governor to gain additional revenue in the Pistole Fee controversy, a debate over the right of the royal governor to charge a fee for sealing land patents. Similarly, Bland helped to lead the opposition to the Anglican clergy when they complained against limits on their salaries imposed by the Two Penny Act (which allowed clergy salaries to be paid in money, rather than tobacco, thus effectively reducing salaries) in the early 1760s. While not a fiery speaker, he was a powerful writer. Perhaps his most noteworthy work was the pamphlet he published in 1764 concerning the Two Penny controversy, *The Colonel Dismounted* (Williamsburg, Virginia), in which he asserted that colonial Americans enjoyed the benefits of the English Constitution and that Virginians as Englishmen "are born free, are only subject to laws made with their own consent, and cannot be deprived of the benefit of these laws without a transgression of them." He also drew a distinction between issues concerning "internal" and "external" affairs that became important in the debates over the STAMP ACT in 1765 and 1766. Bland asserted that the Virginia legislature was responsible for all matters concerning internal affairs (laws within the colony) and that Parliament was responsible for the regulation of the empire and external affairs. In 1766 he pushed some of his ideas about colonial rights further in *An Inquiry into the Rights of the British Colonies* (Williamsburg, Virginia), declaring that, as Englishmen, colonists had rights that no power could infringe upon.

See also REPUBLICANISM.

Further reading: Bernard Bailyn and Jane E. Garrett, eds., *Pamphlets of the American Revolution, 1750–1776* (Cambridge, Mass.: Harvard University Press, 1965).

Blount, William (1749–1800)

William Blount was the first territorial governor of Tennessee, and he was the United States senator who triggered a political controversy in 1797 by supporting a planned pro-British invasion of Spanish North American possessions. Blount was born in North Carolina and worked as a paymaster for that state during the REVOLUTIONARY WAR (1775–83). During the 1780s he became an active politician, serving in both North Carolina's House of Commons (its lower house) and Senate. On four occasions he was elected speaker of the state House of Commons. He also represented North Carolina at the CONSTITUTIONAL CONVENTION in 1787, although he did not actively participate in the debates. He signed the Constitution at the end of the Convention, but his support seemed lukewarm. However, he voted for the Constitution during North Carolina's state ratification convention.

An ambitious man, Blount hoped to become a senator from North Carolina. When he was unsuccessful, he sought his fortune by turning west. North Carolina ceded its claims to the trans-Appalachian west in 1789, and in 1790 the United States government created a new territory in Tennessee. GEORGE WASHINGTON appointed Blount as the governor of this new territory. An able administrator, Blount did well as governor and as superintendent for Indian affairs in the Southern Department. He managed to appease the demands of the FRONTIER settlers, keep the peace with NATIVE AMERICANS and follow the directives from the national government. Simultaneously he advanced his own interests. This balancing act took a great deal of adroitness. In 1796 he was chosen as president of the Tennessee convention that applied for statehood and was rewarded for his services by being selected a United States senator from Tennessee.

Blount, however, was always after the main chance. In 1797 he was asked to support a wild scheme wherein a combined force of Native Americans and westerners would invade Spanish Louisiana and FLORIDA on behalf of the British government. Blount agreed to the scheme and even stated in writing that he would head the force himself. Apparently he anticipated a huge land grant and greater political power in a British-governed west. The plan never materialized, and British support was never very strong. However, Blount's letter of support fell into the hands of the newspapers, and copies came to the secretary of war and the secretary of state. Despite the pro-British aspect of the scheme, Blount was an avid Jeffersonian (DEMO-CRATIC-REPUBLICAN). The FEDERALIST PARTY in Congress cried for some action against a United States senator who was willing to lead an invasion of a neighboring country on behalf of another neighboring country. The Senate voted 25 to one to expel Blount from their chambers, and the House of Representatives clamored to impeach him. This controversy continued for almost two years and led to a debate over whether the Constitution allowed Congress to impeach a senator. Although Blount had briefly been held in custody, ultimately the impeachment was dismissed for lack of jurisdiction in 1799.

Oddly, Blount remained popular back in Tennessee. When he returned there in 1798, he was not only elected to the state senate but was chosen as that body's speaker. Only his early death in 1800 ended his political career.

Further reading: William H. Masterson, *William Blount* (Baton Rouge: Louisiana State University Press, 1954).

Blue Jacket (1740?–1808?)

Having earlier established a reputation as a warrior, Blue Jacket emerged in the 1790s as the foremost leader of the NATIVE AMERICANS resisting the American incursion on territory north of the Ohio River. Blue Jacket was a mem-ber of the Shawnee tribe who grew up in the region referred to as the old northwest. He was married twice, once to a European-American captive and a second time to the daughter of a French-Canadian trader and an Indian woman. These marriages provided him with strong family connections to CANADA and European Americans. He probably fought against the Virginians in LORD DUNMORE'S War (1774), and he fought with the British in the REVOLU-TIONARY WAR (1775–83). In the 1780s he opposed American settlement in Kentucky and the ceding of lands north of the Ohio.

During the 1790s Blue Jacket became the preeminent Native-American leader opposing American expansion in the northwest. In 1790 Blue Jacket orchestrated a multitribal movement that defeated General Josiah Harmar's invasion of Indian land in Ohio. Blue Jacket also led the forces that beat ARTHUR ST. CLAIR the following year, creating a major crisis for the United States government in its efforts to control the territory west of the Appalachians. Blue Jacket helped to organize an Indian congress at the Glaize, located in what is now northeastern Indiana, that attracted Native Americans from Canada to west of the Mississippi in the fall of 1792. This meeting endorsed the Shawnee demand for a limit to American settlement. After peace negotiations broke down in 1793, Blue Jacket worked to sustain the multitribal alliance to oppose American advances. However, when General ANTHONY WAYNE defeated Blue Jacket's forces at the BATTLE OF FALLEN TIMBERS (August 20, 1794), Blue Jacket decided to seek peace. Without the full support of the British, who had failed to protect the Indians after their defeat, Blue Jacket agreed to the TREATY OF GREENVILLE (1795), opening up most of Ohio to American settlement. Blue Jacket remained an important leader of his people and, in the years before his death, worked to support the developing multitribal confederacy under TECUMSEH.

Further reading: John Sugden, *Blue Jacket: Warrior of the Shawnees* (Lincoln: University of Nebraska Press, 2000).

Bonaparte, Napoleon (1769–1821)

Napoleon Bonaparte is one of the most famous men in history. Born in an impoverished petty noble family in Corsica, he rose to become emperor of the French by 1804. Napoleon conquered most of Europe. His invasion of Russia in 1812 ended in failure, and he was forced to abdicate in 1814 and live on the island of Elba in the Mediterranean. He returned to France in 1815, only to be defeated at Waterloo (1815) and forced into exile on St. Helena, an island in the middle of the South Atlantic Ocean. While his actions changed the course of European history, they also had a big impact on the United States.

Shortly after seizing power in France (1799), Napoleon began thinking of extending his empire into the Western Hemisphere. There were two key components to Napoleon's vision. First, he planned to subdue the rebellion in what was once the French colony on the island of Hispaniola, Saint-Domingue (HAITI). Second, Napoleon planned to reestablish a French colony on the mainland in the huge territory of Louisiana. Haiti had been in rebellion since 1792, and a vicious race war with the slaves there had caused countless French deaths. Napoleon sent his brother-in-law, Victor-Emmanuel Leclerc, and another army to Haiti in 1801. After reconquering Haiti, Leclerc and his army were to be sent to Louisiana, which had been retroceded to France by Spain in the Treaty of San Ildefonso in 1800. Disease and the opposition of the Haitians destroyed the French army and compelled Napoleon to change plans. Rather than establishing a French North American empire, Napoleon agreed to sell the entire Louisiana Territory to the United States in 1803.

Although Napoleon had agreed to the Peace of Amiens in 1802, war broke out anew against Britain and her allies in 1803. During the next decade Napoleon and French armies conquered most of Europe. With Europe divided into warring camps, American TRADE, which had thrived during the earlier wars between Revolutionary France and Great Britain, was caught in the middle. The British issued ORDERS IN COUNCIL (1807) outlawing trade with countries under the control of Napoleon (most of Europe by 1808), and Napoleon issued the Berlin (1806) and Milan (1807) Decrees prohibiting ships from stopping in English ports. Caught in this bind, the government of the United States attempted several measures—the EMBARGO OF 1807, the NON-INTERCOURSE ACT (1809), and MACON'S BILL NO. 2 (1810)—to compel both empires into lifting their restrictions on American trade. In 1810, Napoleon suggested that he might repeal the Berlin and Milan Decrees as they pertained to American shipping. The United States government thus decided to stop all trade with Great Britain, precipitating the crisis that brought on the War of 1812 (1812–15).

Although the United States went to war with Great Britain at the same time that Napoleon was at war with the British, the United States never signed a formal alliance with Napoleon. His defeat in 1814 and again in 1815 thus had little direct effect on the Anglo-American war. The ongoing struggle with Napoleon had meant that the American war remained a side conflict for the British during the years of 1812 to 1815. After Napoleon's first defeat in 1814, however, the British could devote more resources to the American war. His defeat also meant that some of the causes for the war—restrictions on trade and IMPRESSMENT of Americans into the British navy—were removed.

See also FRENCH REVOLUTION; LOUISIANA PURCHASE.

Further reading: Felix Markham, *Napoleon* (New York: New American Library, 1963).

Boone, Daniel (1734–1820)

Sometimes hailed as "the first white man of the West," Daniel Boone was really just one of many Americans who crossed the Appalachians in the late 18th century. Boone was born in a QUAKER family in Pennsylvania in 1734, moving with his parents to North Carolina as a young man. Here he served as a teamster and blacksmith in a North Carolina contingent attached to General Edward Braddock's army in its ill-fated march to western Pennsylvania in 1755. He escaped on a horse after the French and Indians attacked Braddock's forces just south of present-day Pittsburgh. The army experience, however, introduced Boone to stories about Kentucky. Boone married a neighbor girl in North Carolina in 1756, shortly after his return from the army. In 1767 he made his first visit to Kentucky, probably in the company of one or two other woodsmen. He returned to Kentucky via the Cumberland Gap with a slightly larger party in 1769, staying there until 1771. As an agent of the Transylvania Company, he headed for Kentucky in March 1775 and set up the community named Boonesborough. Later in the year he returned to North Carolina for his family and to get more settlers.

For over a decade thereafter, Boone worked to build a life in Kentucky. But success did not come easy for Boone. The REVOLUTIONARY WAR (1775–83) broke out and there were worries about hostilities with Indians. Boone was even captured by the Shawnee for several months. He served as a militia officer and continued his land speculation. The titles of the Transylvania Company were repudiated by the Virginia legislature, and when he went east with money to secure legal title for his neighbors and himself, he was robbed. He moved several times and had taken up many tracts of land, but all of the titles proved invalid. Finally, Boone gave up on Kentucky in 1788 and moved to what is now West Virginia. There he was elected to the Virginia assembly in 1791. Sometime in 1798 or 1799, when all of his holdings in Kentucky had been clearly lost, he moved to present-day Missouri, which was then in territory belonging to Spain. One of his sons preceded him. Again he ran into legal problems concerning land titles after the territory was transferred to the United States as part of the LOUISIANA PURCHASE (1803). Congress finally confirmed his title to the Missouri lands in 1814.

Although in many ways Boone's story is unexceptional and demonstrates the troubles confronted by many frontiersmen, his life assumed legendary proportions even before he died. John Filson's *The Discovery, Settlement, and Present State of Kentucke* (1784), supposedly written in Boone's own words (he was nearly illiterate), identified the frontiersman as the leader of the Kentucky settlement. Other books repeated the tale, and Lord Byron even devoted seven stanzas to Boone in a poem in 1821. George Caleb Bingham further immortalized Boone in his oil painting *Daniel Boone Escorting Settlers through the Cumberland Gap* (1851–52). The result is that even today Daniel Boone is identified with the westward movement and is known as America's first great frontiersman.

See also FRONTIER.

Further reading: John Mack Faragher, *Daniel Boone: The Life and Legend of an American Pioneer* (New York: Holt, 1992).

Boston Massacre (March 5, 1770)

The Boston Massacre refers to the killing of five Boston citizens by British soldiers on the evening of March 5, 1770. British troops fired on an unruly mob that had been heckling them and throwing snowballs and ice chunks. At the end of the mayhem, five men, including CRISPUS ATTUCKS, were dead or dying and six others were seriously wounded. The "massacre" was the result of many months of tension between the people of Boston and the soldiers, not only because of the military presence but also because the townspeople viewed the redcoats as threats to their jobs, homes, and families. This was not the first confrontation between the two groups, as many brawls had erupted on earlier occasions.

The problems began in 1768, when the commissioners of customs, who were appointed in Britain but were paid with what they collected in the colonies, requested military protection. This protection was necessary because the commissioners were met with a great deal of resistance, especially in Boston. The British government sent about 700 men to protect the customs collectors, and the people of Boston were outraged. Most of the troops were unable to find accommodations in town and so set up camp on the town common. Governor FRANCIS BERNARD had planned on housing the troops in local homes, but the city council would not allow it. The council stated that citizens did not have to provide quarters unless there were no barracks space. There was an installation in the harbor called Castle William, which had plenty of room for the soldiers. However, the governor opposed putting the troops in Castle William because he had hoped that housing them in the homes of townspeople would help quell resistance. The council refused to back down, so the governor was forced to find some empty buildings in the city for the troops.

Besides the fact that men of the town felt economically and socially threatened by the soldiers, the redcoats had also left a negative impression upon Americans during the French and Indian War (1754–63). The colonists were not interested in having these men, whom they believed to be vile and rude, anywhere near their families. Furthermore, they were insulted by the imposition of what they saw as an occupation force in peacetime.

Given these conditions, it took very little provocation to cause serious confrontations between the two groups. On March 5, a soldier of the 29th Regiment was on sentry duty in front of the Customs House, when a young man began to shout insults at him. The sentry used the butt of his rifle to rap the boy on the head. The boy then screamed and ran for help; someone rang the church bell; and soon a large unruly crowd had gathered in the street. Now facing an angry mob of around 400, the sentry called for assistance. Captain Thomas Preston of the 29th Regiment responded with six men. The crowd was led by a half African-American and half Indian man, Crispus Attucks, who has since gained legendary status in American history. The Bostonians began to throw snowballs and dangerous chunks of ice at the soldiers, daring the troops to fire. The soldiers loaded their guns, but the crowd refused to back down, taunting the soldiers and striking at them with clubs and other weapons. To this day, no one is sure who yelled "fire," but someone did, and the soldiers shot into the throng. Three men were killed instantly and two others were fatally wounded. Governor Bernard had been replaced by THOMAS HUTCHINSON who took swift action and arrested Captain Preston, the six soldiers, and four men who were alleged to have fired shots from inside the Customs House. All troops were immediately removed from Boston.

Two young LAWYERS, JOHN ADAMS and JOSIAH QUINCY, defended the soldiers at their trials, which occurred between October 24 and December 5, 1770. The prosecutors called witnesses to testify about the insolent behavior of the soldiers in the period leading up to the massacre, and they emphasized the troops' hatred for the citizens. However, the talented defense team reminded the jury that they should base their judgment solely on the evidence presented in court. None of the soldiers were allowed to testify on their own behalf. The local press described the crowd as much smaller, consisting of around 80 people and denied that the crowd had provoked the soldiers. Nevertheless, these statements were clearly contrary to the facts. Captain Preston and four other men were acquitted, but two of the soldiers were found guilty of manslaughter. However, they were released after being branded on the hand, having claimed the medieval relic of benefit of clergy.

Originally a provision to protect clergy in civil courts, benefit of clergy allowed a person convicted of certain crimes, such as manslaughter, to avoid execution by prov-

The Boston Massacre. Engraving by Paul Revere *(Library of Congress)*

ing clergy status by reading. By the 18th century this provision had been expanded to any and all who could read.

Some historians also believe that this was the first trial in which a judge used the term "reasonable doubt." Surprisingly, the outcome of the trials did not cause an uproar in the community. Although the Boston Massacre appears to be an episode that should have caused further resistance within the colonies, opposition to British policies diminished within the year. This restraint was partly due to the fact that there was convincing evidence that the crowd had attacked the soldiers first. The depression that had promoted a tumultuous atmosphere in 1770 had ended by the time the trials were over. Finally, the troops had been withdrawn, thus reducing the tension in the town. However, the implications of sending British warships and troops to Boston were not forgotten and were an important step in the progression toward revolution. Boston radicals such as SAMUEL ADAMS continued to use the "Massacre" as anti-British propaganda and organized memorial demonstrations for several years afterward.

See also GOLDEN HILL, BATTLE OF; RIOTS.

Further reading: Dirk Hoerder, *Crowd Action in Revolutionary Massachusetts, 1765–1780* (New York: Academic

Press, 1977); Hiller B. Zobel, *The Boston Massacre* (New York: W. W. Norton, 1970).

—Crystal Williams

Boston Tea Party (December 16, 1773)

The Boston Tea Party was an important protest of British tax policies that helped push the colonies closer to revolution, both because of the spirit of resistance it aroused among the colonists and because of the retaliation it would bring from England. The Boston Tea Party was preceded by Parliament's passage of the TEA ACT in early 1773. At this time, the East India Company was on the verge of bankruptcy and so asked the British government for assistance. In order to aid the company, the government granted it a monopoly on all tea exported to the colonies. Even more irksome to the colonists was an additional provision that allowed the East India Company to sell its tea directly to colonial merchants, thus bypassing the colonial wholesalers. Most of the tea consumed in the colonies was illegally smuggled Dutch tea. Because the East India Company would be selling tea directly through its agents, the price would be much lower than that paid for the smuggled tea. On the surface, this new plan seemed ideal for everyone: The colonists would be able to purchase inexpensive tea, the East India Company would be saved from bankruptcy, and the government would obtain some additional revenue from taxing the tea. However, the act aroused the colonial merchants who would no longer be able to profit from smuggling and who were also concerned about the issue of monopolies. The fear that Parliament might grant other monopolies pushed the conservative colonial merchants to side with the more radical colonists. Ignoring the benefit of cheaper tea, other colonists also protested the Tea Act because they felt it was an attempt by Parliament to demonstrate its taxing power. The Tea Act was clearly not a scheme by Parliament to force the colonists to drink taxed tea at a low price, but the colonists perceived it as such and acted on this interpretation.

In September 1773 the East India Company planned to ship 500,000 pounds of tea to merchants in Boston, New York, Philadelphia, and Charleston. By this time opposition had grown, and colonial merchants agreed not to sell the tea. The tea agents in New York, Philadelphia, and Charleston canceled their orders or resigned their positions as tea agents. In these cities, the shipments of tea were either returned to England or stored in warehouses. However, in Boston, most of the tea agents were friends or relatives of Governor THOMAS HUTCHINSON, who was sympathetic to the British and felt it was important to uphold the supremacy of the government. Opposition in the city was rampant, though, and was led by SAMUEL ADAMS, JOSIAH QUINCY, and JOHN HANCOCK in the form of the COMMITTEE OF CORRESPONDENCE and the SONS OF LIBERTY. When the first East India Company ship reached Boston with its cargo of tea in November 1773, these radical groups prevented the owner from unloading the tea. They quickly convinced the captains of these ships to leave without unloading the tea, but Governor Hutchinson would not give them clearance to do so. According to the law, the tea had to be unloaded within 20 days or it would be seized and sold to pay custom duties. The radicals did not want to see this happen either because they felt that this would still constitute payment of unconstitutional taxes. Ultimately, Hutchinson's refusal to allow the tea ships to return to England led to dramatic action. On the night of December 16, 1773, encouraged by several thousand townspeople, about 60 men disguised themselves as Mohawk Indians and boarded the three ships that were in Boston Harbor. With the aid of the ships' crews these quite unconvincing "Indians" broke open the chests of tea and threw about £10,000 worth of the East India Company's property into Boston Bay. The patriots took this radical step because they feared that if the tea were unloaded, most of the colonists would buy it at the cheaper price.

The Boston Tea Party was an effective piece of political theater, inspiring further action and revolutionary sentiment. Furthermore, it pushed the situation with Britain to the point of crisis. The British government had to deal with this action swiftly and decisively. The East India Company had operated completely within the bounds of law, and if the destruction of the tea went unpunished, Parliament would be admitting that it had lost control over the colonies. British officials condemned the Boston Tea Party as vandalism and passed the COERCIVE ACTS (1774), which practically eliminated self-government in Massachusetts and closed Boston's port until the colony paid for the tea. The news of the destruction of the tea promoted resistance in other colonies as well. In April 1774 one of the East India Company's ships attempted to land tea at New York. It was boarded by a mob in an occurrence similar to Boston's, and the tea it was carrying was destroyed. Other incidents occurred in cities such as Annapolis, Maryland. East India Company tea continued to be boycotted throughout the colonies.

See also RESISTANCE MOVEMENT.

Further reading: Benjamin Woods Labaree, *The Boston Tea Party* (New York: Oxford University Press, 1964); Alfred F. Young, *The Shoemaker and the Tea Party: Memory and the American Revolution* (Boston: Beacon Press, 1999).

— Crystal Williams

Boucher, Jonathan (1738–1804)

Compelled to leave the colonies in 1775, Jonathan Boucher was an important LOYALIST spokesman who advocated the divine origin of government and established authority. Boucher grew up relatively impoverished in England but managed to obtain some education. He came to Virginia in 1759 to tutor gentlemen's sons. He returned to England in 1762 to take Anglican orders, having been promised a parish in Virginia. As an Anglican priest he became a social climber, using connections with the Chesapeake gentry, including GEORGE WASHINGTON, to obtain a series of posts. He also continued to tutor the children of the wealthy, including John Parke Custis, MARTHA WASHINGTON's son by her previous marriage. Boucher moved to Maryland, was chaplain of the lower house of assembly in Annapolis, and took the desirable rectory of Queen Anne's Parish. He was also granted an honorary Master of Arts by King's College in New York for his support of an American episcopacy (he wanted the Anglican church to settle a bishop in the colonies—an unpopular position with many non-Anglicans in North America). He married a wealthy woman, bought a plantation on the Potomac, and by 1773 appeared successful and contented.

The imperial controversy, however, prevented his life from proceeding on a peaceful course. As many colonists formed committees of safety and advocated resistance to British imperial measures in 1774 and 1775, Boucher called for compliance with all authority. He had the audacity to announce his intention to preach against resistance to the British. A group of armed men refused to allow him to ascend the pulpit that day. Thereafter, he felt his life was in jeopardy and later reported that every time he preached he kept a pair of loaded pistols nearby. Efforts to publish his sermon, "On Civil Liberty, Passive Obedience, and Nonresistance," in 1775 were fruitless, since the advocates of resistance controlled the local presses. In this sermon Boucher said that it was God's will that every man should obey the constituted authority. He also argued that the notion of equality was both wrong and dangerous. He wrote, "Man differs from man in everything that can be supposed to lead to supremacy and subjection." He believed that "a musical instrument composed of chords, keys, or pipes all perfectly equal in size and power might as well be expected to produce harmony as a society composed of members all perfectly equal to be productive of order and peace. . . ." For such ideas, Boucher was put under surveillance by the committee of safety and burned in effigy by a mob. In September 1775 he and his wife sailed for England, where he was provided with another parish and a pension. His property in the colonies was confiscated by revolutionaries, although he did receive some compensation from the British government for his loss. He finally published his ideas on the revolution in 1797 in a book entitled *A View of the Causes and Consequences of the American Revolution.*

See also RESISTANCE MOVEMENT.

Further reading: Bernard Bailyn, *The Ideological Origins of the American Revolution* (Cambridge, Mass.: Harvard University Press, 1967).

Brackenridge, Hugh Henry (1748–1816)

Hugh Henry Brackenridge was an ardent supporter of the AMERICAN REVOLUTION and the author of one of the first novels written in the United States, *Modern Chivalry* (1792–1815). He was born in Scotland but immigrated to Pennsylvania with his family when he was five years old. Although he grew up relatively impoverished, he demonstrated an early capacity for learning. A neighboring clergyman taught him the classics, and he began teaching school at age 15 to earn money to further his education. Entering Princeton sometime around 1768, Brackenridge helped work his way through college by teaching in a grammar school. At Princeton he became friends with PHILIP FRENEAU and JAMES MADISON, sharing with them a love for literature and politics. Brackenridge and Freneau coauthored a commencement poem in 1771 called *The Rising Glory of America* (published in 1772), which was an early statement of American national feeling. He took a master's degree in divinity in 1774. During the REVOLUTIONARY WAR (1775–83) he served as a chaplain in the army and wrote several patriotic pieces extolling American valor.

His career took a new turn in 1778 when he left the ministry to set up a literary magazine. But his expectations, despite his own and Freneau's contributions, were met with failure, and the *United States Magazine* ceased publication after only a year. Brackenridge then studied law in Annapolis with SAMUEL CHASE and was admitted to the bar in 1780. With legal, literary, and educational credentials, Brackenridge decided to seek his fortune on the FRONTIER and moved to the newly settled community of Pittsburgh. There he found several outlets for his energy, being elected to the state legislature, starting a newspaper (the *Pittsburgh Gazette*) in 1786, opening a book store, helping to found the Pittsburgh Academy, and practicing law. Politics remained his true passion throughout the 1780s.

Brackenridge was typical of many leaders in the Revolutionary era. While a strong advocate of independence and republican values, he believed that the mass of people should naturally rely on the judgment of an educated elite. This natural aristocracy, like Brackenridge, did not have to be born into its social position. Rather, he saw leadership as an outgrowth of education and talent—just the path taken by men such as himself.

However, much to Brackenridge's chagrin, the voters did not necessarily agree with this position. In 1787 Brackenridge, reflecting his longstanding nationalism, supported the new document that his friend Madison and the others at the Philadelphia CONSTITUTIONAL CONVENTION had written. Most of the people in western Pennsylvania, on the other hand, feared a strong central government and opposed the Constitution. As a result, Brackenridge was defeated by an Irish immigrant for a seat at the state ratifying convention. (Despite western opposition, Pennsylvania quickly and easily ratified the Constitution.) This failure left Brackenridge both bitter and unpopular, forcing him to withdraw from politics and restore his declining law practice.

In 1794 he attempted to regain popularity by engaging in an awkward balancing act during the WHISKEY REBELLION. He sought to join and guide the rebellion while trying to mediate a settlement with the federal government. The result was that he narrowly escaped being charged with treason and did not add greatly to his popularity in western Pennsylvania. Nevertheless, he became the leader of the DEMOCRATIC-REPUBLICANS in western Pennsylvania in the late 1790s and was rewarded for his party loyalty by being appointed to the Pennsylvania Supreme Court in 1799.

Among Brackenridge's writings, two stand out as reflecting his odd mixture of democratic and elitist politics. In his *In Incidents of the Insurrection in Western Pennsylvania in 1794* (1795) Brackenridge tells the story of the Whiskey Rebellion from his perspective, emphasizing how he had only appeared to lead some aspects of the rebellion to minimize violence and defuse the situation. He strove to portray himself as both popular leader and supporter of the government. He offered a more powerful social criticism in *Modern Chivalry,* a book that he first published in 1792 and added several sections in subsequent printings until 1815. Patterning the book after Miguel de Cervantes's *Don Quixote,* his central character, Captain John Farrago, travels the American countryside with an ignorant sidekick, an Irishman named Teague O'Regan. Farrago is a natural aristocrat, like Brackenridge, who is not recognized for his talents, and the people are shown to be easily mislead. To demonstrate this popular ignorance, Teague is offered a variety of positions during their journeys, including congressman, minister, philosopher, Indian chief, and husband to a rich widow. When the captain finally allows Teague to take a position for which his ignorance should have disqualified him— an excise officer on the eve of the Whiskey Rebellion— the Irishman gets his just desserts by being tarred and feathered. Although satirizing the new democratic society of the early republic, Brackenridge also expressed faith that the United States could be saved when the public was educated and could make more intelligent decisions.

See also LITERATURE.

Further reading: Hugh Henry Brackenridge, *Incidents of the Insurrection,* ed. Daniel Marder (New Haven, Conn.: College and University Press, 1972); Hugh Henry Brackenridge, *Modern Chivalry,* ed. Lewis Leary (New Haven, Conn.: College and University Press, 1965).

Brandywine, Battle of (September 11, 1777)
Armies under General GEORGE WASHINGTON and General Sir WILLIAM HOWE clashed on Brandywine Creek, south of Philadelphia. This American defeat helped open the way for the conquest of Philadelphia.

With two humiliating setbacks for the king's forces at TRENTON (December 26, 1776) AND PRINCETON (January 3, 1777), New Jersey, the previous winter, Howe began a series of maneuvers in early June designed to lure the CONTINENTAL ARMY out of its winter quarters at MORRISTOWN,

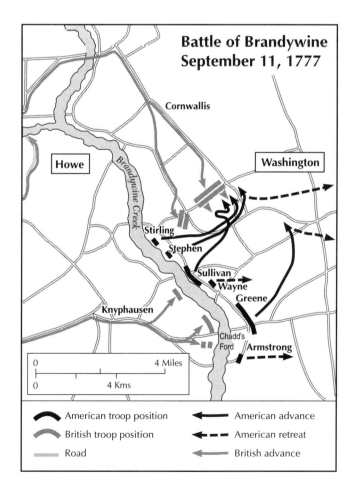

NEW JERSEY, and to confuse Washington as to the British general's ultimate goal. By the end of June, however, Howe was back where he started with little to show for his efforts. Then on July 23, he and his army—complete with baggage, artillery, horses, and provisions for a month—disappeared from New Jersey into the Atlantic aboard vessels in the fleet of his brother, RICHARD, Lord HOWE. Various sightings kept Washington guessing, wrongly in fact, as to Howe's objective and where to deploy his own troops. When the fleet appeared at Head of Elk, Maryland, Washington knew for certain that Philadelphia was the goal.

Howe could have spent about 10 days at sea and landed within 15 miles of his target, but poor information as to the navigability of the Delaware River prompted his move south to the Chesapeake Bay. After suffering a debilitating month at sea, Howe's men had a 50-mile march to the rebel capital. Washington and his men took positions along the eastern shore of the Brandywine, a creek of uneven depth that had several fords, or shallow areas, where crossing was possible. Howe, who had divided his army into two divisions under CHARLES, LORD CORNWALLIS and General William von Knyphausen, planned a flanking movement, a tactic that had been successful in other encounters with Washington. The American general, bracing instead for a frontal attack, then received conflicting reports as to the enemy's whereabouts. Hearing first that Howe was on the west bank, Washington ordered General JOHN SULLIVAN's division to cross over and attack. But soon a second dispatch from Sullivan arrived refuting that information, and Washington retracted his orders. Sullivan had not bothered to resolve the conflicting reports, and the British were indeed on the move. Howe, Cornwallis, and two-thirds of their forces had crossed the Brandywine and were coming at the right of the rebel line. By believing the second report, Washington unwittingly spared the almost certain annihilation of Sullivan's division and maintained the integrity of the American positions. When word arrived that the British were approaching, Washington sent the three divisions forming the right of the line to the Birmingham (Quaker) Meeting House to meet them. Washington initially remained at the center with General NATHANAEL GREENE's division while General ANTHONY WAYNE's forces were to stand on the left against Knyphausen at Chadd's Ford.

The battle opened late in the afternoon near the Meeting House, with Knyphausen beginning a bombardment of Wayne's position shortly thereafter. The terrain was uneven and the Americans were badly situated, with Sullivan's division separated from the other two. While attempting to close the gap, the British and their HESSIAN mercenaries bore down on the Americans with bayonets drawn, and the unnerved troops began to scatter. The outnumbered remnants of the three divisions rallied bravely but fell back

into the ranks of Greene's division that had moved north, with Washington, to assist them. The reorganized line held for a time but could not withstand the enemy's steady advance. Greene began a slow, fighting retreat, and when the sun finally set, he withdrew his entire division. The enemy, exhausted by the action and with night falling, did not follow. Wayne's forces were also no match for Knyphausen, and they, too, withdrew with the rest of the American forces toward Chester, Pennsylvania. Howe was the victor, and he marched into Philadelphia on September 26, 1777. But he had failed to deliver a crushing blow to Washington and the Continental army at Brandywine, and they escaped to fight another day.

See also REVOLUTIONARY WAR.

Further reading: Robert Middlekauf, *The Glorious Cause: The American Revolution, 1763–1789* (New York: Oxford University Press, 1982).

— Rita M. Broyles

Brant, Joseph (Thayendanegea) (1743–1807)

Joseph Brant led the Mohawk and many other IROQUOIS people through the difficult period from the start of the REVOLUTIONARY WAR (1775–83) until his death in 1807. Brant was born into an unimportant Mohawk family in the colony of New York. His sister's relationship with William Johnson (1715?–74), the British agent for the Mohawk, gave him his first opportunity for advancement. Johnson sent the young Brant to Reverend Wheelock's school in Lebanon, Connecticut, for an English-style education. There he learning to read, write, and speak English. He also learned other lessons about American society and left the stern discipline of the school after less than two years.

Brant accompanied some Iroquois war parties against the French during the closing days of the French and Indian War (1754–63). William Johnson's patronage and Brant's friendship with Guy Johnson, William's nephew, kept Brant close to the center of power in the Mohawk world. Soon his own abilities as a speaker and a leader brought him to the attention of his people. In the early days of the Revolutionary War, Brant sailed to England where he was presented to King GEORGE III and was well received by English society. His poise and bearing impressed many of those who met him.

Brant returned home in 1776 to find the colonists in full rebellion against the king. After personally witnessing the power and might of the British, he thought the colonists stood little chance of winning. His friend Guy Johnson inherited the late William Johnson's post as the Crown's agent to the Iroquois. Johnson fled the Mohawk Valley when the war started and took Brant's sister and her

Joseph Brant *(Library of Congress)*

family to CANADA to protect them from the revolutionary committees searching the New York backcountry for British sympathizers. Brant's loyalty fell to the British. He spent much effort to get his fellow Mohawks to side with the Crown against the revolutionaries.

Brant immediately organized a company of Iroquois warriors and American LOYALISTS to fight for the British. In 1777 the company traveled with Colonel Barry St. Leger's column as it marched through western New York on its way to meet with General JOHN BURGOYNE on the Hudson. Brant led the force that ambushed General Nicholas Herkimer's relief column as it attempted to reach the besieged Fort Stanwix at the Battle of Oriskany (August 6, 1777). The siege, however, fell apart after British forces received news of the approach of BENEDICT ARNOLD and another relief force. St. Leger withdrew to Canada, sealing the fate of Burgoyne at SARATOGA (October 17, 1777). At that point, Brant and his men cut loose from the main army to attack settlements and farms along the FRONTIER. He gained a reputation as a clever but bloody commander responsible for the deaths of many innocent civilians. The Americans responded with equally ferocious raids upon any NATIVE AMERICAN villages they could find, whether the inhabitants sympathized with the British or not. General JOHN SULLIVAN led troops from the CONTINENTAL ARMY through Iroquois territory (1779) and destroyed the Six Nations's ability to make war.

The war split the Iroquois into those who favored the Americans and those who supported Great Britain. When the war ended (1783), the United States controlled most of the land where the Iroquois lived. Brant moved to Grand River in Canada, where the British purchased land for a new home for the Iroquois. He spent the last years of his life struggling to reunite the Iroquois people under his leadership in Canada.

Further reading: Barbara Graymont, *The Iroquois in the American Revolution* (Syracuse, N.Y.: Syracuse University Press, 1972); Isabel Thompson Kelsay, *Joseph Brant, 1743–1807: A Man of Two Worlds* (Syracuse, N.Y.: Syracuse University Press, 1984).

— George Milne

Brown, Charles Brockden (1771–1810)

Charles Brockden Brown is known as the first American author who attempted to live by his pen alone. Born into a relatively affluent Philadelphia family, Brown was well-educated and trained for a law career in the late 1780s. He gave up law in 1793 to turn his attention to writing. Living mainly in New York City in the late 1790s, he published six novels between 1798 and 1801. He also edited a short-lived magazine called *The Monthly Magazine and American Review* (1799–1800). In 1800 he returned to Philadelphia and became a merchant, in partnership with his brothers. After some success, their business fell upon hard times, and Brown became a small trader for the remainder of his life, occasionally writing some essays and editing the *Literary Magazine and American Register* (1803–07) and the *American Register or General Repository of History, Politics, and Science* (1807–11).

Brown's novels reflected the influence of the romantic movement in America at this time and deal with both the supernatural and the psychology of his characters. They often revolve around issues of how and why people do evil in this world. Perhaps his most noted work is *Weiland* (1798), which centers on the mysterious death of one member of a family, occult RELIGION, and the practice of ventriloquism, a subject considered akin to the supernatural in the 1790s. Although his work is often characterized as Gothic, Brown set his stories within an American context and offered some interesting views of the world of the new republic. *Weiland* takes place in Philadelphia and its surrounding countryside. His books *Ormond* (1799) and *Arthur Mervyn* (published in two parts in 1799 and 1800) provide graphic descriptions of the horror of the yellow fever epidemics that struck Philadelphia and other port cities during the 1790s. Not only did he depict the physical devastation of the epidemics, but he also explored the mental anguish and psychic costs of DISEASE AND EPIDEMICS.

He placed another of his works, *Edgar Huntly* (1799), on the FRONTIER with NATIVE AMERICAN hostility as a background for his plot. Brown has been criticized for the similarity of his novels, his debt to English writer Charles Godwin, and his sometimes difficult and ponderous prose. More recently, several scholars have viewed Brown's achievement as more central to the development of American culture. In particular, scholars have looked at both his fiction and nonfiction to emphasize their role in the "reading revolution" of the early republic and their effort to probe "the limits of individualism."

See also LITERATURE.

Further reading: Cathy N. Davidson, *Revolution and the Word: The Rise of the Novel in America* (New York: Oxford University Press, 1986); Steven Watts, *The Romance of Real Life: Charles Brockden Brown and the Origins of American Culture* (Baltimore: Johns Hopkins University Press, 1994).

Bulfinch, Charles (1763–1844)

Charles Bulfinch brought the architectural style of neoclassicism to post-Revolutionary New England. Born into a wealthy Boston family, Bulfinch graduated from Harvard College in 1783. After college, like other elite young gentlemen of his time, he embarked on a tour of Europe. There he was impressed with a newly popular style of ARCHITECTURE that took its inspiration from the classical world of ancient Greece and Rome. Returning to Boston in 1787, Bulfinch married well-to-do Hannah Apthorp and began to design buildings as an intellectual and civic-minded pursuit. By the early 1790s, Bulfinch had provided plans for a number of Massachusetts meetinghouses and for the Connecticut state capital in Hartford, as well as houses for wealthy family friends.

In 1793–94, Bulfinch's construction of the Tontine Crescent, an elegant and expensive row of Boston townhouses, became a financial disaster and forced him to turn to architecture as a means of support rather than as a gentlemanly pursuit. His most important commission, the Massachusetts state house in Boston, quickly followed in 1795–97. Despite the popularity of his designs, the practice of architecture ultimately could not provide Bulfinch with any financial security. To supplement his income, he became chairman of Boston's board of selectmen and the town's superintendent of police. For almost 20 years, Bulfinch's service as both an architect and administrator enabled him to transform Boston's architecture through construction of nearly two dozen public buildings and approximately 30 houses. During this time, Bulfinch also designed public buildings and prominent residences in towns throughout Massachusetts.

On a tour of Boston in 1817, President James Monroe was delighted with Bulfinch's work and offered him a position as architect of the United States Capitol. Bulfinch accepted and moved to WASHINGTON, D.C., in 1818 to oversee construction of the partially completed building. In Washington, Bulfinch also designed the Federal Penitentiary and Unitarian Church before returning to Boston in 1830, where he died in 1844.

Further reading: Harold Kirker, *The Architecture of Charles Bulfinch* (Cambridge, Mass.: Harvard University Press, 1060); Harold Kirker and James Kirker, *Bulfinch's Boston, 1787–1817* (New York: Oxford University Press, 1964).

— Martha J. McNamara

Bunker Hill, Battle of (June 17, 1775)

The Battle of Bunker Hill is often considered the first major battle of the REVOLUTIONARY WAR (1775–83). After the BATTLES OF LEXINGTON AND CONCORD (April 19, 1775), the British army in Boston found itself besieged by an ad hoc army of New England militia that filled the surrounding countryside. Recognizing the need to occupy the nearby high ground—outside Charlestown, Bunker and Breed's Hills, and Dorchester Heights—to secure Boston Harbor, the British planned to move in mid-June. Reports of the British plan reached the American commanding officer, General Artemas Ward, who hesitantly decided to strike before the British. Both Bunker and Breed's Hills stood on the tadpolelike Charlestown Peninsula, connected to the mainland by a narrow neck. Any American forces on the peninsula could be subject to cannon fire on three sides from the British navy in the harbor. Likewise, an attack focused on the neck could cut the Americans off from reinforcements or retreat. Ward ordered Colonel William Prescott to fortify Bunker Hill on the night of June 16. Once the force of about 1,000 Americans reached the Charlestown Peninsula, however, General ISRAEL PUTNAM and Colonel Richard Gridley, chief engineer of the army, decided that Prescott should fortify the lower Breed's Hill that was closer to Boston. Putnam remained at Bunker Hill and began to entrench there. By morning, to the surprise of the British, Prescott had built a redoubt on Breed's Hill, and the entire Charlestown Peninsula was in the hands of the Americans.

The British reacted quickly. Warships soon began bombarding the American positions, and a force of over 2,000 regulars prepared to dislodge the Americans. Rather than placing his force behind the American redoubt, General WILLIAM HOWE, who had command of the British attack, opted for a frontal assault. There are several possible explanations for this tactic. Conventional military wisdom suggested that it was best not to place your soldiers between two lines of the enemy. Had the British attacked Breed's Hill from the rear, their own rear would have been subject to enemy fire. Second, the British believed that the American forces were untrained and unprepared to face professional soldiers. British officers argued that if they were to be successful in putting down a rebellion, they had to demonstrate the absolute superiority of their soldiers in battle. Finally, and connected to the second point, the British seriously underestimated their opponents. The result was a near disaster for the British. Three times the British regulars marched up the hill. Twice they were forced to retreat by withering fire from entrenched American troops. On the third assault the British overwhelmed the American forces on Breed's Hill, who were almost out of ammunition. The Americans fell back in partial disorder. The British, however, had become so disorganized that they had difficulty following up their victory, and the remaining Americans retreated from the peninsula. The British won a tactical victory by holding on to the contested ground, but they also suffered devastating casualties. The British sustained 226 dead and 828 wounded; the Americans, 140 killed and 271 wounded.

Bunker Hill, as the battle was called, quickly became an important symbol of American fortitude. Untrained Americans had stood against the best trained army in the world. While the American forces surrendered their ground, the Battle of Bunker Hill was considered an American triumph and became a rallying cry during the war. The British also took note of the action. Henceforth, the British paid more attention to their battle tactics and did not assume their opponent would run at the sight of redcoats and glistening bayonets. General Howe in his subsequent campaigns in 1776 and 1777 would also be much more cautious.

Further reading: Robert Middlekauf, *The Glorious Cause: The American Revolution, 1763–1789* (New York: Oxford University Press, 1982).

Burgoyne, John (1722–1794)
General John Burgoyne is most noted for his surrender at SARATOGA (October 17, 1777). He came from a military family in England and used his friendship with a schoolboy friend, James Stanley-Smith, Lord Strange, to advance his career. Burgoyne, however, alienated the powerful Stanley family by eloping with his friend's sister, Lady Charlotte Stanley, in 1743. Without the patronage leverage, and having accumulated gambling and other debts, Burgoyne sold his commission as a junior captain in 1745 and commenced a nine-year self-imposed exile on the continent. He and Lady Charlotte traveled in France and Italy. Burgoyne used

some of his time profitably by learning French and studying European military innovations, especially the use of light dragoons and light infantry. Reconciled with his father-in-law, the powerful Lord Derby, in 1756, he returned to England and reentered the army, quickly advancing through the ranks through purchase and promotion. He was elected to the House of Commons in 1761 and kept his seat in Parliament for most of the remainder of his life. He also wrote on subjects connected to the army, advocating treating soldiers like human beings who could think for themselves. This approach would gain him the nickname "Gentleman Johnny" from his men when he obtained his independent command during the REVOLUTIONARY WAR (1775–83).

Burgoyne was one of three generals sent to Boston in the spring of 1775 to help advise General THOMAS GAGE (the other two were Sir HENRY CLINTON and Sir WILLIAM HOWE). By the time they arrived, battles had been fought in LEXINGTON AND CONCORD (April 19, 1775) and the war had begun. Burgoyne saw a little action during the engagement at BUNKER HILL (June 17, 1775). In the spring of 1777, Burgoyne was appointed commander in chief of the army in CANADA that was to invade New York and sever New England from the rest of the colonies. His aim was to join with Colonel Barry St. Leger, approaching Albany

Sir John Burgoyne *(Library of Congress)*

from the Great Lakes, and then to connect with the forces of Sir William Howe centered on New York City.

Burgoyne's army of about 10,000 began its long thrust into the wilderness of New York in June 1777. His forces included some of the best regiments in the army, as well as 3,000 HESSIAN mercenaries. Burgoyne also had about 400 NATIVE AMERICAN allies at his disposal. Although the Indians proved of limited use during the campaign, they managed to antagonize many FRONTIER settlers by their depredations. Burgoyne's task should have been daunting. He had to take his army through 200 miles of rough territory, often constructing roads as he went along. That he was able to capture several American outposts, including FORT TICONDEROGA, and almost reach Albany is testimony to his leadership and the quality of the men under his command. However, the distance was too great, and the delays too many, for him to gain the ultimate prize. St. Leger was driven back from Fort Stanwix, and a raiding party to Vermont was beaten at the Battle of Bennington on August 16, 1777. Moreover, the plan of the larger campaign had never been fully agreed upon. Howe decided to focus most of his attention on capturing the rebel capital of Philadelphia. The small force left to General HENRY CLINTON in New York City was not strong enough to force its way up the Hudson, although late in the campaign Clinton tried to come to Burgoyne's assistance. The result was that the early fall found Burgoyne deep in enemy territory with a long line of supplies. His army had shrunk to about 5,000 through losses in battle and detachments to protect his line of communications. Canadians and Indians had also deserted. He was confronted with a combined Continental and militia army about four times the size of his own forces. The core of the CONTINENTAL ARMY had taken up defensive positions on Bemis Heights, commanding the path south along the Hudson. When efforts at dislodging the American army failed on September 18 and October 7, 1777, Burgoyne had little choice but to surrender his army on October 17, 1777, under the best terms possible.

According to the surrender agreement, the army was to be sent back to England under the promise that it would not fight in America again. These generous terms were not accepted by General GEORGE WASHINGTON and the CONTINENTAL CONGRESS. The army was held captive throughout the war. Burgoyne, however, was allowed to sail back to England in the spring of 1778. There he quickly became embroiled in controversy, as he sought to be exonerated for his defeat. The government did not support him in this effort, and he joined the parliamentary opposition. Although something of a flamboyant person—he had four children by a mistress late in life—Burgoyne was a popular officer with his men. Despite unflattering accounts in some histories, it is not true that Burgoyne slowed the army down with personal baggage and wine. Marching through 200 miles of northern New York was a logistical nightmare that would have slowed any army. His failure can be blamed on circumstances as much as anything else.

Further reading: Richard J. Hargrove, *General John Burgoyne* (Newark: University of Delaware Press, 1983); Max M. Mintz, *The Generals of Saratoga: John Burgoyne and Horatio Gates* (New Haven, Conn.: Yale University Press, 1990).

Burke, Edmund (1729–1797)

Edmund Burke was a British politician who supported the American colonists in their opposition to British imperial measures in the 1760s and 1770s but later criticized the FRENCH REVOLUTION (1789–1815). Burke was born in Ireland, attended Trinity College in Dublin, and trained as a lawyer. Giving up his legal practice sometime in the 1750s, Burke set out to become a man of letters. As a part of this effort he wrote several pamphlets and established a magazine called the *Annual Register* in 1758. Although his career took a variety of turns after 1760, he continued to be involved with the publication of the *Annual Register* into the 1780s. In 1765 he became the private secretary of Charles Watson-Wentworth, Lord Rockingham. When Rockingham became the first lord of the treasury (the chief minister in the British government) in the same year, Burke also entered the realm of politics.

As a supporter of Rockingham, Burke was given a seat in Parliament. Although the district he would represent changed a few times, Burke remained a member of Parliament for most of the rest of his life. He also became something of a spokesman for the Rockingham WHIGS, using his gifts as an orator and his command of the facts to quickly become a prominent member of Parliament. Rockingham's administration lasted only until July 1766, a turn of events that placed Burke among the opposition as Great Britain headed for a crisis with its North American colonies in the 1770s. In 1774 and 1775 Burke argued for a pragmatic position in the controversy. The Rockinghams had taken a similar line during their brief moment of power in 1765–66. They had repealed the STAMP ACT (1765) as an unwise measure but passed the DECLARATORY ACT (1766), asserting the right of Parliament to legislate for the colonies in all cases whatsoever. In the 1770s Burke did not contest that Parliament was sovereign and had the right to tax the colonies. He only believed that it was foolish and impolitic to push the point. He thought that the colonies were a great source of wealth for Britain through TRADE, even if no taxes were levied there. He wanted Parliament to repeal the TEA ACT (1773) and opposed the passage of the COERCIVE ACTS (1774). When Americans heard of these positions, they viewed Burke as a hero, a statesman, and a defender of rights. But Burke was less a defender of rights and more a pragmatic politician who wanted to preserve the empire. Burke also took a pro-American stand once hostilities broke out. He advocated an acceptance of the CONTINENTAL CONGRESS as a representative body for the colonies and held that only an American legislature should raise taxes in North America. His ideas were rejected by the majority in Parliament. By the time Rockingham regained political power in 1782, it was too late for anything but independence for the United States. Burke held a minor office briefly in the 1780s, but the Rockingham control did not last. During the 1780s, Burke is best known for his role in Parliament's investigation into the affairs of the British administration of India.

Although Burke was not given any major office even when his party held power, he gained his greatest fame after 1790 for his opposition to the French Revolution. In that year he published *Reflections on the Revolution in France,* which has been held up ever since as the epitome of the conservative approach to government and society. Burke argued that tradition and inherited institutions are the true bulwark of politics and society. Overthrowing the past, from this perspective, was innately bad. The French Revolution in 1790, which had not yet taken some of its most radical steps, threatened to overturn all that was good in the hope of replacing it with some unknown new future. For Burke this was anathema. Burke published his study at a time when many in Great Britain still had hope that the French Revolution would bring about a truly enlightened government. THOMAS PAINE wrote *The Rights of Man* in opposition to Burke's *Reflections.* When the French Revolution entered its radical phase, as mass executions followed more mass executions and as the French took their king to the guillotine in 1793, many Englishmen began to think that Burke was right in his *Reflections.* Burke retired from Parliament in 1794 and died three years later.

Further reading: George W. Fasel, *Edmund Burke* (Boston: Twayne, 1983).

Burr, Aaron (1756–1836)

Aaron Burr was an officer in the CONTINENTAL ARMY and was such an important politician that he was almost elected president. Yet he was also overly ambitious, engaged in a duel with ALEXANDER HAMILTON, and became involved in conspiracies to establish an independent country in the West.

Burr was born on February 6, 1756, in Newark, New Jersey, the son of Aaron Burr, second president of the College of New Jersey (now Princeton) and Ester Edwards. His mother was the daughter of the famous religious leader Jonathan Edwards. At the age of three Burr's parents died

Aaron Burr *(Library of Congress)*

and he was raised by an uncle, Timothy Edwards. At age 13 Burr enrolled at the College of New Jersey and graduated with distinction in 1772. In 1774 he began to study law, but the REVOLUTIONARY WAR (1775–83) erupted. Burr immediately joined the Continental army and served as a captain under BENEDICT ARNOLD in the Quebec invasion of 1775–76. Burr displayed great valor and leadership during the failed campaign, resulting in his promotion to major and appointment to GEORGE WASHINGTON's secretarial staff. However, Burr and Washington did not get along with each other, leading Burr to transfer to the staff of General ISRAEL PUTNAM, Washington's second in command. During the British siege of New York, Burr helped to rescue trapped soldiers at Brooklyn Heights, leading to his further promotion by the CONTINENTAL CONGRESS to lieutenant colonel. Burr fought at the BATTLE OF MONMOUTH (June 28, 1778) in New Jersey. During the battle, horrific heat and humidity killed many of Burr's men and exacerbated his bouts of illness. Given his poor health and his belief that this assignment held no promise of advancement, Burr resigned his commission in March 1779.

Burr resumed his legal studies in 1780 and soon began his political career. In 1782 he was admitted to the New York bar and married Theodosia Prevost, a woman 10 years older than he. (She would die in 1794 due to poor health.) The couple moved to New York City in 1783, where they had one child. Burr rose to prominence as a lawyer and competed with Alexander Hamilton for the city's best legal cases. He was elected to the state assembly in 1784, and in 1789 he was appointed the attorney general of New York by Governor GEORGE CLINTON. In 1791 Burr was selected to serve as a United States senator. He served one term in the Senate, during which he became a diehard DEMO-CRATIC-REPUBLICAN. As such, he ran in the 1796 presidential election as THOMAS JEFFERSON's vice president. The campaign was unsuccessful, but Burr used his rising reputation to build a following in New York. Known as the Burrites, this group of Democratic-Republicans helped win New York over to the Jeffersonians in 1800, which allowed Burr to reprise his role as Jefferson's running mate in the presidential ELECTION OF 1800. At that time, electors did not cast separate votes for the president and vice president. Each elector had two votes for president. Whoever won the most votes won the presidency. The individual with the next highest total became vice president. Jefferson and Burr received equal numbers of votes, and the decision was left to Congress. Burr did not concede to Jefferson. However, Burr lost the presidency on the 36th ballot and became vice president because Hamilton influenced the FEDERALIST PARTY in Congress to allow Jefferson to win.

Burr served only one term as vice president because of an ideological and personal rift between Burr and Jefferson. George Clinton was selected to replace Burr as the vice presidential candidate in 1804. Burr subsequently lost a bid for the New York governorship to the Jeffersonian candidate. During this election, Burr declined an offer from the Federalists for their support in exchange for Burr's promise to unite New York with the New England states in a secessionist plot. Hamilton also published letters denouncing Burr. Angry and seeking a retraction of Hamilton's negative opinions, Burr issued a challenge to Hamilton, who was unwilling to retract. This culminated in the famous Burr-Hamilton duel at Weehawken, New Jersey on July 11, 1804. Burr mortally wounded Hamilton, who died the next day. The outpouring of grief and anger—many northerners saw Burr as a murderer—forced him to flee to Philadelphia and the southern states to avoid warrants for his arrest.

During this flight, Burr sought support for a scheme he had plotted while still the vice president. He would lead an army and seize Spanish lands beyond the Mississippi to create a new nation. Burr also hoped to incorporate the Americans beyond the Appalachian Mountains into his scheme. His allies included the wealthy Harman Blenner-hassett as well as General JAMES WILKINSON, the ranking United States general who was secretly in the pay of the Spanish government. The plot ultimately failed in 1806 thanks to Wilkinson's betrayal. In 1807 Burr stood trial for treason but was acquitted. He spent the years 1808–12 in Europe attempting to interest the European powers in his plot, with no success. He returned to New York in 1812 and practiced law. Burr remarried in 1833 to Elizabeth Brown Jumel, a rich widow. He managed to squander her money and she filed for divorce. Burr died in 1836 on Staten Island.

Further reading: Thomas J. Fleming, *Duel: Alexander Hamilton, Aaron Burr, and the Future of America* (New York: Basic Books, 1999): Roger G. Kennedy, *Burr, Hamilton, and Jefferson: A Study in Character* (New York: Oxford University Press, 2000); Arnold A. Rogow, *A Fatal Friendship: Alexander Hamilton and Aaron Burr* (New York: Hill and Wang, 1998).

— Michael L. Cox

Bute, John Stuart, earl of (1713–1792)

The third earl of Bute, John Stuart is best known as the tutor of GEORGE III before he became king and as his chief minister briefly between 1762 and 1763. The earl of Bute taught George III languages and the usual kingly skills—riding, fencing, and etiquette—from 1755 to 1760. But he also spent a great deal of time with him examining European and British history, especially concerning the British Constitution. The first two Georges of the House of Hanover had been little more than German princes who had been elevated to the Crown of Great Britain. George III, who was only 22 when he ascended the throne in 1760, was more thoroughly British. Bute and George III read the works of the Viscount Bolingbroke, which held that the British Constitution was best protected by a patriot king who would not only reign but also govern. When George III became king, he decided to put these ideas into practice. He did not intend to become an absolute monarch, but as king he did believe that it was his constitutional right to select his chief advisors. This mind-set initiated a period of political instability in the British government that led to seven changes in administration in 10 years. It also led to inconsistencies in policy that had a devastating effect on British and colonial relations.

One of those seven administrations was organized under the earl of Bute, the king's teacher, friend, and adviser. Bute advised the king in a variety of official and unofficial capacities, forcing first William Pitt and then the Duke of Newcastle out of the government. Bute was appointed first lord of the treasury (the king's chief minister) on May 26, 1762. His most significant achievement was to end the Seven Years' War (called the French and Indian War in America, 1754–63). However, his political maneuvers, his influence over the king, and the terms of the peace were extremely unpopular. Moreover, there were many rumors that Bute was having an affair with the king's mother. The result was that it became very difficult for him to govern, and he was compelled to resign on April 8, 1763. However, many politicians continued to fear that Bute was still active behind the scenes, and he was compelled to withdraw completely from the king's household in 1765.

During Bute's administration, only one crucial decision was made concerning colonial affairs: to maintain an army in North America after the French and Indian War. But that decision contributed to the imperial crisis, provided a rationale for taxation, and offered an irritant to colonials, who detested British soldiers living in their midst. As in Great Britain, Bute was seen by the colonists as a symbol of the corruption of British government. During the STAMP ACT (1765) demonstrations, for example, some crowds marched through the streets displaying a boot as a mocking symbol of the man who was believed to be an evil influence on the king.

After 1765 Bute had little impact on British and imperial politics. Rumors persisted concerning his secret influence, however, contributing to a distrust of British politics on both sides of the Atlantic.

See also RESISTANCE MOVEMENT.

Further reading: James Lee McKelvey, *George III and Lord Bute: The Leicester House Years* (Durham, N.C.: Duke University Press, 1973).

C

California

Concerned that the English or the Russians might claim California, the Spanish government decided to colonize the region in the 1760s. Instrumental in this effort was José de Galvéz, who as inspector general of New Spain (Mexico) organized the first Californian settlements. Galvéz sent an expedition to Alta California, as the Spanish called the area, in 1769, thus establishing a precarious foothold and presidio at San Diego from which he went on to explore nearly to San Francisco Bay. Over the next few years Franciscan fathers built a series of missions and the Spanish founded three other presidios: Monterey (1770), San Francisco (1776), and Santa Barbara (1782). Although never more than a backwater FRONTIER of the Spanish American empire, by 1821 the Hispanic population of California reached about 3,200.

The early years of California were difficult for the colony, which remained dependent on supplies from Mexico. From 1774 to 1776, the Spanish sent out several reconnaissance parties to expand California's boundaries and to explore the possibility of land communication with Sonora in Mexico and the settlement at Santa Fe in New Mexico. Communication with New Mexico across the current state of Arizona appeared unfeasible. An overland trail was discovered to Sonora, but it required the construction of an outpost at the juncture of the Colorado and Gila Rivers. When the Yuma Indians destroyed that outpost in 1782, California again became almost entirely dependent on communication by sea. Spanish explorers also traveled in the Pacific as far north as ALASKA, establishing Spain's claim to the area of the current northwest United States and coastal British Columbia.

By the time of the Yuma revolt, California was becoming more self-sufficient, with expanding cattle herds and developing agriculture. In recognition of the growing importance of Alta California, the Spanish Crown ordered the provincial seat of government moved from Baja California to Monterey in 1776. The Franciscan missions con-tributed to this success by converting thousands of Indians to Christianity and then using NATIVE AMERICAN labor on the missions. As many as 23,000 Indians lived in the missions by 1821. However, runaways and high mortality constantly put a strain on the missions' native populations. Conditions for all of the California Indians deteriorated over the course of Spanish colonization, with the region's diverse native population declining from about 300,000 to 200,000 from 1769 to 1821.

Although never overly successful, Spanish California helped to forge the Hispanic culture of the Southwest sustained by Mexico until the region was conquered by the United States in the Mexican War (1846–48). Contact before 1820 with the United States was minimal; by that date a few American vessels had touched at the Californian shore as American merchants began to TRADE in the Pacific.

See also NEW SPAIN (MEXICO), NORTHERN FRONTIER OF.

Further reading: David J. Weber, *The Spanish Frontier in North America* (New Haven, Conn.: Yale University Press, 1992).

Camden, Battle of (August 16, 1780)

Three months after capturing CHARLESTON (May 12, 1780), with virtually the entire CONTINENTAL ARMY in the South, British forces under LORD CHARLES CORNWALLIS overwhelmed American troops at Camden, South Carolina, and brought about the fall from grace of HORATIO GATES, the hero of SARATOGA (October 17, 1777). After the surrender of Charleston, Congress had appointed Gates as head of the Southern Department. Unfortunately for the American cause, his tenure was riddled with poor decisions.

Upon assuming his command, Gates immediately targeted the British supply base at Camden, which was vital to their intended campaign to subjugate the Carolinas and

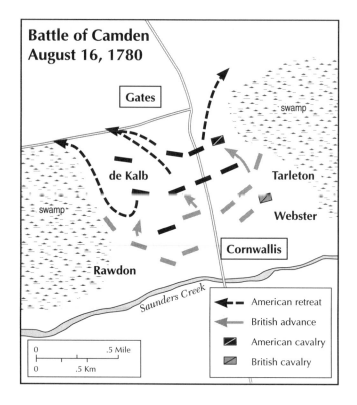

**Battle of Camden
August 16, 1780**

Gates

swamp

de Kalb

Tarleton

swamp

Webster

Cornwallis

Rawdon

Saunders Creek

American retreat

British advance

American cavalry

British cavalry

0   .5 Mile

0   .5 Km

Virginia. His subordinates, who were familiar with the region, suggested a circuitous route to Camden through rich farming country, where anti-British sentiment was high and the troops would easily find sustenance. Unwilling to march an extra 50 miles, Gates ignored the advice and plotted a direct route through a barren, pro-British area that was permeated with sandy plains, swamps, and dense forests. Although he promised issues of rum and rations en route, none were forthcoming, and the soldiers were forced to subsist mainly on peaches, green apples, and green corn as they marched in the heat and humidity of a Carolina summer. As reinforcements slowly joined Gates's army, its strength in numbers grew, but the men were sick and debilitated. In Charleston, word reached Cornwallis of the rebel advance and he set off for Camden, ordering additional troops into the area so that ultimately about 2,200 men were at his command. Gates, on the other hand, was ignorant as to the size of his army. He believed he had over twice the number of available troops than the slightly more than 3,000 men who were actually fit for duty. Still, he confidently proclaimed they were enough for the purpose.

Gates continued to undermine his own operations. Planning a night march so as to surprise the enemy, he again ignored the advice of his officers by placing dragoons at the front of the line, despite protests that the enemy would be able to hear the horses' hooves from a great distance. Presumably trying to fortify the sick and hungry

army for the battle ahead, rations of beef, cornmeal, and molasses were procured and given to the men prior to breaking camp. The meal had severe gastrointestinal consequences, however, and throughout the march, soldiers continually broke ranks in order to relieve themselves, which only weakened them further. Around 2:30 A.M., British cavalry ran into Gates's dragoons, and after a flurry of gunfire and saber fighting in the dark, the American cavalry retreated to its line of infantry, both armies halting further action until daylight.

With the knowledge that Cornwallis was personally commanding the British forces and that the two armies were fairly even in size, Gates would have been wise to retreat to a stronger defensive position. As an ex-British officer, Gates must have known that, even with fewer men, the superior training and experience of the British gave them the advantage over the raw militia units that composed much of his army. Vacillating as to his course of action, Gates asked his officers for their opinions. None suggested a withdrawal, but one emphatically stated that it was too late to do anything but fight. Gates agreed and ordered them to their various commands straddling the Charlotte road. Stands of pine trees on either side of the route offered cover for sniper fire, and swamps on both sides of the trees protected against flanking movements. Gates positioned himself and his staff at the remote distance of some 600 yards to the rear of the American line. Following European military convention, which Gates would have known, the British placed their strongest unit on the right of their line. Gates, also a traditionalist, deployed his troops in similar fashion, which meant his inexperienced militia units would be on the left, facing the best of the enemy forces.

The British began their advance in the early morning hours, and American artillery opened fire as they approached. British artillery responded, and as their troops were moving from columns into line of battle, one of the American officers reported to Gates that he could attack them before they completed their deployment. Gates gave him the order to do so, which was apparently the last command he gave at Camden. Receiving their instructions, the militia on the left of the rebel line clumsily advanced. Many of these men had never been in battle and had little or no training with the bayonets they had been issued. Cornwallis noticed their hesitation and ordered a bayonet charge. Seeing the steady advance of the British regulars with their deadly steel implements and hearing their blood-curdling shouts, the raw troops ran for their lives. When over 2,000 of these men came storming through the reserve units behind the main line of battle, Gates, mounted on an excellent horse and believing the cause was lost, left the field in full gallop. He maintained the frantic pace until he reached the safety of Charlotte, 60 miles away. Meanwhile, the experienced troops at the left of the American line, though badly outnumbered, managed to push the enemy back with repeated bayonet charges. When the British dragoons finally joined the fray, the rebels gave up the fight and escaped into the woods and swamps, ending the battle. Total British casualties in killed, wounded, and missing comprised about 15 percent of the number engaged. Estimates of American losses reached as high as one-third of Gates's army, a devastating blow following the losses at Charleston. Gates, who claimed he went to Charlotte to rally the survivors of the battle, was exonerated for his conduct, but he never held command again.

Further reading: Robert Leckie, *George Washington's War: The Saga of the American Revolution* (New York: HarperCollins, 1992); Henry Lumpkin, *From Savannah to Yorktown: The American Revolution in the South* (Columbia: University of South Carolina Press, 1981); Page Smith, *A New Age Now Begins: A People's History of the American Revolution*, vol. 2 (New York: Penguin Books, 1989).

— Rita M. Broyles

camp followers

Civilian men and women who accompanied armies in the 18th century, camp followers provided various skills and services to the military establishment. The military and civilian components of the community that gathered around the army recognized their need for one another and that their mutual survival was vital for success. During the REVOLUTIONARY WAR (1775–83), the CONTINENTAL ARMY patterned much of its camp follower employment and organization after the long-established model of its enemy, the British. The army regulated the living and working arrangements, and under the articles governing them, camp followers could not be asked to perform military duty but were bound in every other way to maintain the peace and order of the command structure. Although a common assumption has been that camp followers were predominantly female prostitutes, the number of such women was actually quite small. Female camp followers were generally family members of the officers and soldiers, who were either refugees needing the protection of the army or women simply wanting to be near their loved ones and to tend to their needs. Countless wives and daughters worked as laundresses, cooks, seamstresses, and nurses during the war. However, the majority of nonmilitary personnel attached to the army were men. Many were sutlers, the name given to merchants and traders who were licensed to sell goods to the troops. A variety of employees, such as laborers, artificers, wagoners, cooks, and launderers, provided much-needed services to the army and freed soldiers

from these noncombatant duties. Some of the staff members in the quartermaster and commissary departments also were civilians working under contract. And AFRICAN-AMERICAN camp followers of both sexes, slave and free, performed domestic and labor-intensive tasks.

For those with a choice to do so, motives for following the army were undoubtedly as varied as the people themselves: contracts or financial arrangements with the military, devotion to family members, the need for protection, belief in the political cause, or the hope of personal freedom. For the parts they played, camp followers received various forms of rationing or compensation, but most also experienced equal portions of deprivation and suffering during the war. Sutlers and contract laborers did not get rich from their bargains with the military, and they frequently lost provisions and tools. African-American slaves did not necessarily obtain freedom by their service to either the British or American armies. Women and children often lost their husbands and fathers in battle. And everyone was susceptible to the diseases that spread through the camps. Though camp followers provided vital services to the army establishment and thus figured largely in the success of military ventures, when peace came and the troops disbanded, the civilian support services faded into oblivion, their contribution to the war efforts generally overlooked.

Further reading: Holly A. Mayer, *Belonging to the Army: Camp Followers and Community during the American Revolution* (Columbia: University of South Carolina Press, 1996).

— Rita M. Broyles

Canada

Sixteenth-century French explorers derived the name Canada from a Huron-Iroquois word *kanata*, meaning a village or settlement. In the 17th century the name became synonymous with New France, which eventually included not only the St. Lawrence River colony but also Acadia on the Atlantic coast. Throughout the colony's existence the fur trade provided a solid economic basis. Skillful and energetic French fur traders, or *voyageurs*, used their good relations with the Algonquin and Huron Indians to penetrate far into the interior of the continent. Political authority resided with a royal governor who exercised military and diplomatic power, an intendant who was responsible for internal affairs, and an appointed council. This highly centralized and authoritarian colonial government combined with a semifeudal landholding system was partly responsible for a much slower rate of growth than that of the English colonies to the south. By the mid-18th century, New France had a population of only 70,000 compared with over 1 million in the British colonies.

The French and their Indian allies relentlessly expanded the fur trade to the west, engaging in competition with the English and their Iroquois allies for land and strategic advantage. In 1754 fighting erupted in the Ohio River Valley, signaling the beginning of the French and Indian War (1754–63). This North American contest was the last of a series of colonial wars that began in 1689 and were part of a worldwide Anglo-French conflict. While the British colonists had a substantial advantage in numbers, the early victories went to the French, who had better-trained colonial troops, superior leadership, and more dependable NATIVE AMERICAN allies. Eventually the introduction of more troops and more competent leaders allowed the British to gain the upper hand. In 1758 the French fortress of Louisbourg in Nova Scotia fell to the British. The next year at the pivotal Battle of the Plains of Abraham, the British general James Wolfe defeated the French under the marquis de Montcalm and occupied Quebec. Finally in 1760, British forces captured Montreal. Under the terms of the Treaty of Paris (1763), the French gave up their possessions east of the Mississippi to the British.

This victory relieved the American colonists of the constant threat of attacks by the French and their Indian allies and lessened their dependence on British troops for protection. The British gained control of the Canadian fur trade and thousands of new subjects with an alien language, culture, and RELIGION. The Quebec colony was first governed under a royal proclamation (1763)—often referred to as the PROCLAMATION OF 1763—that provided for a governor and a legislative assembly. However, being CATHOLICS, the French colonists, or *habitants*, were not permitted to vote or sit in the assembly. In addition to creating the colony of Quebec, the proclamation excluded the inhabitants of the Atlantic Coast colonies from all the territory between the Appalachians and the Mississippi River. This move greatly angered the American colonists who wanted access to the western lands for land speculation and also resented British protection of the Indians.

After 1763 the population of Quebec remained overwhelmingly French, attracting only a few hundred English and Scottish traders who took control of the fur trade. The British military rulers were sympathetic with the *habitants*, however, they failed to adequately understand the dynamics of French Canadian society and chose to ally themselves with the French colonial elite of *seigneurs* (landlords) and churchmen. In 1774, at the urging of Governor GUY CARLETON, the colony was reorganized under the Quebec Act. This radical document allowed Catholics to hold office and provided for a governor and council, but no assembly. There were also protections for the French language, the Catholic religion, and French civil law. Despite some admirable features, the Quebec Act upset the delicate balance of colonial politics. The new regime alienated the *habitants* by granting new powers to the Catholic Church and the *seigneurs*. The residents of the other British American colonies viewed the Quebec Act with undisguised hostility. The British had resurrected a much feared enemy that American colonists thought had been vanquished a decade earlier.

In 1775 the CONTINENTAL CONGRESS, having failed to enlist the support of the French Canadians in their dispute with the British, decided to invade Canada. The invasion force led by Richard Montgomery and BENEDICT ARNOLD captured Montreal and laid siege to Quebec. However, poor training and lack of organization—combined with a harsh winter and the death of Montgomery—doomed the invasion. After an unsuccessful siege of Quebec City, the Americans retreated. The failed invasion of Canada guaranteed a British presence on the continent, and Quebec became a staging ground for the British military during the REVOLUTIONARY WAR (1775–83).

At the end of the Revolutionary War in 1783, about 100,000 LOYALISTS, many having fought with the British, left the United States. Half of that number went to Quebec and Nova Scotia. Although they were in many respects a diverse group, they shared a belief that their liberties were more secure within the British Empire than in an independent American nation. While the refugees were profoundly American, many coming from families that had been in the colonies for several generations, they had strong negative feelings about the new United States. The number of refugees was large in relation to the relatively small population of "old settlers" in Quebec and Nova Scotia, and they were destined to exert a powerful influence on the development of the British colonies.

The Loyalist IMMIGRATION had its greatest initial impact in Nova Scotia where 32,000 refugees, including several thousand AFRICAN AMERICANS who had fled to the British, joined a population of New England Yankees, Acadian French, and Maliseet and Micmac Indians. A new Loyalist colony, New Brunswick, was carved out of Nova Scotia in 1784 to accommodate half of the original group. In Quebec the problem of absorbing the Loyalists was more complicated. The initial influx of Loyalists amounted to only a few thousand, but following the war that number was swollen by "late Loyalists." The refugees occupying the unsettled lands north of Lake Ontario found it difficult to live under the Quebec Act. As Protestants they objected to the influence of the Roman Catholic Church. Being British they expected the traditional "rights of Englishmen," including the right to own land and, for some, representative government.

This put the British in a difficult position, as they could not easily renege on the concessions granted to the French by the Quebec Act. A solution was found in the Constitution Act (1791), which created two new colonies out of

Quebec. In Lower Canada (present-day Quebec), the new act retained protections for the French language, law, and religion while adding a legislative assembly. The British hoped that in such a system the French population would be gradually assimilated. Upper Canada (present-day Ontario) was given a conventional British-style colonial government that attempted as far as was practical to apply the principles of the British Constitution. Similar governments developed in Nova Scotia and New Brunswick. In each case British policy was aimed at avoiding a repetition of the AMERICAN REVOLUTION.

During the FRENCH REVOLUTION and Napoleonic Wars (1793–1815), British North America, like the United States, was at the mercy of international events beyond its control. The British colonies first suffered and then profited from the wartime ECONOMY. The Americans, on the other hand, were incensed when the British navy freely interfered with their shipping under the pretext of the war with France. The ongoing rivalry in the fur trade further added to existing international tensions. The Treaty of Paris (1783) and JAY'S TREATY (1794) should have effectively removed Canadian fur trappers and traders from United States territory. However, the Canadians justified an ongoing presence in the United States backcountry on the basis that the Americans had not paid reparations for Loyalist properties seized during the Revolutionary War.

Americans in the new western states blamed the Canadians for keeping the Indians stirred up and supplying them with arms. Western politicians known as War Hawks felt that conquering Canada would eliminate the Indian problem and give American land speculators access to huge amounts of new land in the British colonies. In 1812 the United States declared war, claiming British violation of its neutral shipping rights. In Canada, British colonists viewed the war as little more than an excuse for an American invasion.

The military conflict was inconclusive, and in the absence of a winner, both sides claimed victory. The Canadians had driven back an American invasion, and the Battle of Queenston Heights (October 13, 1812) became part of Canada's founding tradition. The Americans were equally pleased that they had frustrated British invasion attempts, and the Battle of New Orleans (January 8, 1815) provided a sense of national unity and pride for Americans. By the Treaty of Ghent (1814), both sides agreed to return to prewar conditions. The treaty served to reemphasize the continuing breach between the British colonies and the United States and thus initiated a clarification of the Canada–United States boundary that would continue until the 1840s. After 1814 relations between Britain, its North American colonies, and the United States remained strained for a time. However, starting in the 1820s, efforts to improve economic and political cooperation marked the beginning of a strong and stable Anglo-American relationship.

Further reading: W. J. Eccles, *France in America* (New York: Harper & Row, 1972); Desmond Morton, *A Short History of Canada* (Toronto: McClelland & Stewart, 1995); Francis Parkman, *France and England in North America*, 9 vols. (Boston: Little, Brown, 1885–92).

— Robert Lively

Carey, Mathew (1760–1839)

An Irish immigrant, Mathew Carey became one of Philadelphia's leading publishers in the 1790s and was a noted proponent of protective TARIFFS in the early 19th century. Born and raised in Dublin, Ireland, Carey did not receive much schooling as a child, even though his parents were relatively well-off. However, he read extensively and decided to become a printer and bookseller as a child. His father disapproved of this choice of a profession, but Carey persisted and apprenticed as a printer. As a young man, Carey—a Roman CATHOLIC—became interested in defending his RELIGION in Ireland, and he published an anonymous pamphlet on the issue in 1779. When a reward was offered for the identity of the author—the pamphlet was condemned in Parliament—Carey's family sent him to Paris. In the French capital he met the MARQUIS DE LAFAYETTE and BENJAMIN FRANKLIN. He even worked in a printing office set up by Franklin. After a year in exile, Carey returned to Ireland. He worked printing a newspaper until 1783, when his father underwrote the publication of his own newspaper, the *Volunteer's Journal*. This paper trumpeted the cause of Irish nationalism and created a great stir. After some articles led to a demonstration in which the young Carey took an active part, the British arrested him. When he was released after a short period but facing further legal action, Carey decided to head for America. Disguised as a woman, he departed Great Britain on September 7, 1784.

When he arrived in Philadelphia, he did not have much money. However, he quickly obtained the patronage of Lafayette. In January 1785 he was able to begin printing another newspaper, the *Pennsylvania Herald*. Newspapers in this era generally were strongly political, and Carey quickly aligned himself with those who wanted a weaker central government. He also published the debates in the Pennsylvania state assembly, a new practice. By October 1786 he seems to have abandoned the newspaper and began publishing the *Columbian Magazine*. He left this project to begin the *American Magazine* in 1787. During the 1790s Carey's printing business grew. He also authored an important book that described the conditions of the yellow fever epidemic of 1793 and played a vital role in dealing with the health crisis created by that epidemic. An avid DEMOCRATIC-REPUBLICAN (Jeffersonian), he became embroiled in several political controversies, most notably with the FEDERALIST PARTY spokesman and Englishman, William Cobbett. During the 1790s Carey did business worth more than $300,000 and kept as many as 150 men working in his print shop. In 1802 he was elected a director of the Bank of Pennsylvania, and in 1810 he was one of the few Democratic-Republicans to advocate rechartering the BANK OF THE UNITED STATES (FIRST). After the War of 1812 (1812–15) he became a strong advocate of the American System and in particular served as one of the most noted spokesmen for protective tariffs to encourage the development of manufacturing. Throughout his career he retained an interest in the Irish cause, forming a Hibernian Society in the 1790s and defending Irish Catholics in print.

See also DISEASE AND EPIDEMICS; JOURNALISM.

Further reading: Earl L. Bradsher, *Mathew Carey, Editor, Author, and Publisher: A Study in American Literary Development* (New York: Columbia University Press, 1912).

Carleton, Guy, first baron of Dorchester
(1724–1808)

An able administrator and brave soldier, Guy Carleton defended Quebec in the face of an American invasion in 1775 and 1776 and served as governor of CANADA. Born in 1724 to a middle-class Protestant family in Ireland, Carleton entered the army at a young age and quickly advanced through the ranks by his courage in battle and by making good political connections. In 1758 and 1759 Carleton served under General James Wolfe in the siege of French-held Quebec and was wounded in battle. He also took part in two other campaigns during the French and Indian War (1754–63): at Belle Isle en Mer in the Bay of Biscay, and in the conquest of Havana in 1762. In both campaigns he served with distinction and was wounded. For his service he was made a permanent colonel in the British army. After the war he was appointed lieutenant governor of the new British province of Quebec. Since the governor had been recalled, in essence he became the chief administrator of Quebec in 1766. He was also made a brigadier general and in 1768 became governor outright. Carleton consolidated power in his own hands in Quebec and sought to incorporate the French-speaking inhabitants into the British Empire. He supported the Quebec Act (1774) that tolerated the CATHOLIC religion, recognized French civil law in the province, and confirmed the land system that had been established under French rule. As the crisis with the North American colonies intensified in 1774–75, Carleton hoped that these policies would ally the French-speaking population to the British government. It may not have done so, but at least it convinced many Canadians to remain neutral.

When hostilities broke out in April 1775, Carleton had only about 800 regulars to defend Canada. Efforts to raise a militia among the French Canadians failed. Montreal quickly fell in November 1775 to a force under General Richard Montgomery, who then marched his small army of 300 Americans to join BENEDICT ARNOLD before Quebec. Carleton beat back their combined assault on December 31, 1775: Montgomery was killed, Arnold wounded, and almost 500 Americans captured. Having sustained great losses, the Americans settled in for a siege. Carleton drove off the remainder of the American army in the spring of 1776. He pursued the retreating Americans, defeating them again in the Battle of Trois Rivières (June 8, 1776). Carleton hesitated at Lake Champlain in his pursuit, waiting for the dismantling of a fleet on the St. Lawrence and then rebuilding it on the lake. With these forces, which had been greatly reinforced with troops under General JOHN BURGOYNE, he gained control of Lake Champlain at the BATTLE OF VALCOUR ISLAND (October 11, 1776). He did not take FORT TICONDEROGA, however, at the southern end of the lake. Instead, he withdrew to Canada to await the spring for a renewed offensive.

Despite his victories, command of the army destined to invade New York—and ultimately to surrender at SARATOGA (October 17, 1777)—fell to Burgoyne. Carleton was knighted and promoted to lieutenant general for his defense of Canada. Up until this point Carleton had enjoyed strong political support in Great Britain. But in 1775 a political enemy, Lord Germain, had become colonial secretary. Germain forced Carleton to resign as governor of Canada (June 27, 1777), and he returned to England in the summer of 1778. Once in Great Britain he avoided any blame for the Saratoga disaster and was provided a government position in Ireland. He lived quietly until 1781, when he was called upon to resume a command in North America and, as commander in chief, handle the negotiations for the removal of British troops and LOYALISTS at the end of the REVOLUTIONARY WAR (1775–83). Once again his administrative talents came to the fore. Having succeeded in this difficult and awkward task, Carleton became governor of all of Canada in 1786. At the same time, he was ennobled as the Baron Dorchester. He remained governor of all or part of Canada until 1796, when he retired from public life.

See also QUEBEC, BATTLE OF.

Further reading: George Athan Billias, *George Washington's Opponents: British Generals and Admirals in the American Revolution* (New York: Morrow, 1969).

Catholics

Before the REVOLUTIONARY WAR (1775–83) the British colonies in North America were overwhelmingly Protestant. In 1780 there were only 56 Catholic churches in the United States—mostly in Maryland and Pennsylvania—compared with nearly 2,900 congregations representing various Protestant denominations. Prior to the war many Americans—steeped in British political and religious traditions—associated Catholicism with the tyranny, oppression, corruption, and savagery they ascribed to their French and NATIVE AMERICAN enemies. Anti-Catholic feeling was especially strong in Congregationalist-dominated New England, where the pope was ritually burned each year on November 5. During the imperial crisis many Americans, especially in New England, came to believe that GEORGE III and his ministers were engaged in a new "popish plot" to subvert their liberties. Some WHIGS claimed that a campaign to establish an Anglican bishopric in the colonies, combined with the Quebec Act, was evidence that the Crown was giving precedence to Catholics at the same time that it was curtailing the rights of Protestants. In consequence, there was an upsurge in anti-Catholic feeling in America on the eve of independence. Anti-Catholicism, while not a major cause of the Revolution, contributed to the worsening relationship between the Crown and colonies.

The War of Independence undermined anti-Catholicism in America. American Catholics supported the rebels in proportions comparable to their Protestant neighbors. Perhaps the most famous Catholic among the revolutionaries was Charles Carroll of Carrollton, Maryland. Hailing from one of the wealthiest families in America, Carroll was a fervent supporter of the Revolution and served in a variety of positions at the state and local level during and after the war. Carroll was the only Catholic to sign the DECLARATION OF INDEPENDENCE (July 4, 1776). After the war his brother, John Carroll, became the first American Catholic bishop. Of greater importance than the contributions of the small number of American Catholics, like the Carrolls, were those of the French. In 1778 the new United States found itself allied with the traditional Catholic enemy—France. The FRENCH ALLIANCE undermined old assumptions and undercut the colonial anti-Catholic tradition.

The recognition that Catholics contributed materially to independence, combined with the libertarian ideology of the Revolution, resulted in greater religious freedom for Catholics. In their constitutions, many of the states repealed or weakened the legal restrictions they placed on Catholics. Even Massachusetts, where anti-Catholicism was strongest before independence, guaranteed religious and political freedom to Catholics under its 1780 constitution. With the adoption of the BILL OF RIGHTS in 1791, freedom of religion was guaranteed at the national level.

During the early republic, tens of thousands of Catholics immigrated to the new United States. Most came from Ireland and other parts of the British Empire. Some of these were radicals who fled from political repression in Britain in the wake of the FRENCH REVOLUTION (1789–1815). The small number of Catholic radicals and the much larger number of nonpolitical Catholic immigrants, usually of humble origin, were attracted by economic opportunity and religious freedom in the United States. They established Catholic institutions—schools, churches, and voluntary societies—throughout the United States, but especially in cities and towns. Boston, New York, Philadelphia, Baltimore, and Charleston all had significant Catholic populations by 1800. Politically, the growing Catholic population tended to identify with the DEMOCRATIC-REPUBLICANS (Jeffersonians). During the war scare of 1798, the FEDERALISTS adopted the ALIEN AND SEDITION ACTS intended, in part, to stifle internal dissent and to limit the political rights of immigrants. Although not specifically anti-Catholic, the acts adversely affected Catholics, who had become an important immigrant group. The Alien and Sedition Acts were short-lived and did little to stem Catholic IMMIGRATION, which continued to grow until the outbreak of the War of 1812 (1812–15). The LOUISIANA PURCHASE (1803) led to a further expansion of the American Catholic population by adding tens of thousands of French, Spanish, Méti, and Native American Catholics to the new nation.

In 1776 Catholics were a tiny minority with limited rights found in small pockets around the rebellious colonies. By 1815 the United States had a large, diverse, and growing Catholic population that enjoyed full civil and political rights. Although the United States would remain predominantly Protestant throughout the 19th century and anti-Catholic feeling would continue to be an occasional feature of national life, Catholics were among those who gained significant political and RELIGIOUS LIBERTY as a result of the Revolution.

See also RELIGION.

Further reading: Francis D. Cogliano, *No King, No Popery: Anti-Catholicism in Revolutionary New England* (Westport, Conn.: Greenwood Press, 1996); John Tracy Ellis, *Catholicism in Colonial America* (Baltimore: Helicon, 1965); Martin Griffin, *Catholics in the American Revolution*, 3 vols. (Philadelphia: Loyola University Press, 1909–11); Charles Henry Metzger, *Catholicism and the American Revolution* (Chicago: Loyola University Press, 1962).

— Francis D. Cogliano

Charleston, siege of (surrendered May 12, 1780)

In the spring of 1780, British forces under Sir HENRY CLINTON laid siege to Charleston, South Carolina, one of

America's largest port cities, the capture of which would play a vital role in British plans to subjugate the South. Already controlling Savannah and eastern Georgia, Clinton envisioned moving northward and conquering the Carolinas and Virginia, gathering support from the presumably large LOYALIST populations in those areas. The British might then have a better chance of crushing the rebellion in the northern colonies, a goal that had thus far eluded them.

Charleston was a strategic target for it boasted a good harbor and lay at the confluence of two navigable rivers, the Ashley and the Cooper. But these attributes also made the peninsular city vulnerable to attack from the water on three sides and along the narrow strip of ground, called the Neck, that connected it to the mainland. Clinton, with troops and ships at his disposal, made none of the mistakes that had doomed the previous attempt to capture the city in 1776. Nevertheless, with the advantages of troop strength and position, the British commander moved surprisingly slowly in the deployment of his men. Having landed below Charleston on February 10, 1780, it was not until March 29 that Clinton had guns in place on the peninsula. The delay should have facilitated the evacuation of the city before all avenues of escape were closed, but instead the inhabitants worked at strengthening their untenable defenses. Adding to the American tragedy of the situation, General Benjamin Lincoln, who commanded the 5,000 Continentals, the American ships in the harbor, and the considerable supply of military stores in Charleston, was an indecisive man who vacillated between the conflicting advice of his officers to abandon the city and the entreaties of the citizens and local leaders to stay and fight. Lincoln remained undecided as to his course of action even as the British continued digging in along the Neck and when, on April 11, eight British frigates easily passed the guns at Fort Moultrie to take command of the harbor and cut off Charleston by sea. A few days later, British troops under Colonel BANASTRE TARLETON surprised Americans north of the city at Monck's Corner and severed Lincoln's line of communications. Reinforcements under Lord Francis Rawdon and LORD CHARLES CORNWALLIS arrived to stretch British control from the Edisto Inlet, west of the Ashley River, to the Ashley, from the Ashley to the Cooper River, and from the Cooper to the Atlantic Ocean.

On April 21, acknowledging that the situation was hopeless, Lincoln naively proposed terms of capitulation that included an unmolested withdrawal of his troops from the city with full honors to any destination they chose. Clinton refused. Minor skirmishes took place as the British continued their advance, until finally on May 8, with opponents within shouting distance of one another, Clinton demanded the surrender of the city. In a final act of frustration, the Americans instigated further hostilities that brought on a frightful bombardment of the town. The citizens then insisted that Lincoln surrender. On May 12, the CONTINENTAL ARMY marched out of Charleston and laid down their arms. The militia were allowed to return to their homes, considered to be paroled prisoners, as were the civilians. Clinton's masterful siege of Charleston cost the Americans a valuable port, but had Lincoln been an authoritative commander, they might not have also lost virtually their whole southern army.

Further reading: John Buchanan, *The Road to Guilford Courthouse: The American Revolution in the Carolinas* (New York: Wiley, 1997); Robert Leckie, *George Washington's War: The Saga of the American Revolution* (New York: HarperCollins, 1993); Henry Lumpkin, *From Savannah to Yorktown: The American Revolution in the South:* (Columbia: University of South Carolina Press, 1981).

— Rita M. Broyles

Chase, Samuel (1741–1811)

The controversial Samuel Chase was a signer of the DECLARATION OF INDEPENDENCE (July 4, 1776) and was tried for impeachment as a SUPREME COURT justice by the Senate. Born in Maryland, Chase trained as a lawyer and was admitted to the bar in 1761. He served in the Maryland assembly from 1764 to 1784, quickly establishing his credentials as an opponent to the royal governor and as a leader of the RESISTANCE MOVEMENT (1764–75) to imperial regulation. Oddly, for a man who would later declare that expanding SUFFRAGE would lead to mobocracy, Chase took an active role in the Maryland anti-STAMP ACT mobs, served on a variety of revolutionary committees, and was a leading radical as the REVOLUTIONARY WAR (1775–83) broke out. He attended both CONTINENTAL CONGRESSES, orchestrated Maryland's support for the Declaration of Independence, and rode 150 miles in two days to Philadelphia in time to vote for that document in 1776. In 1777 and 1778 he was an important member of Congress and supported GEORGE WASHINGTON as commander of the armies without reservation. Toward the end of 1778, however, he became embroiled in a controversy concerning his efforts to speculate in flour using insider knowledge he had gained as a government official. Accused of corruption, he was compelled to withdraw from public life. When he was again chosen as a delegate to Congress two years later, he was not as active as he had been. Like many of his generation, he sought new opportunities in the independent United States, only to find that his speculations and business enterprises ended in failure. He declared bankruptcy in 1789.

At the same time, he again entered politics, opposing the United States Constitution that had been written in 1787 and voting against it at Maryland's ratifying convention. He became a Maryland judge in 1788 and chief justice of the Maryland general court in 1791. Although he had been rabidly anti-English, sometime in the 1790s he became more conservative. As a result, his old friend George Washington nominated him to the Supreme Court in January 1796.

Quickly ratified by the Senate, Chase played a prominent role in the pre-Marshall Court, writing several significant opinions. These opinions helped to assert national treaties over state laws, defined *ex post facto* laws, articulated procedures for amendments to the Constitution, and clarified the relationship between federal and common laws. At times, he also behaved high-handedly. When he delivered a charge to a Baltimore grand jury that attacked the DEMOCRATIC-REPUBLICANS and the expansion of the right to vote in 1803, President THOMAS JEFFERSON encouraged supporters to impeach Chase. This effort was part of a general Jeffersonian assault on a judiciary dominated by the FEDERALIST PARTY. Had the Senate managed to remove Chase, many scholars believe that the Jeffersonians would have acted against Chief Justice JOHN MARSHALL next. However, the case against Chase, presented in the Senate in 1804, was not particularly strong. Although he had uttered intemperate remarks and behaved so badly in the trial of John Fries for his role in a tax rebellion that President JOHN ADAMS had pardoned the convicted Fries (who had been sentenced to death in Chase's court), none

Samuel Chase. Reproduction of painting by Charles Wilson Peale *(Library of Congress)*

of the eight counts levied against Chase could stand up to an able legal defense and careful scrutiny. In short, they did not amount to high crimes and misdemeanors. Chase remained on the court for the rest of his life, although ill health limited his attendance.

See also FRIES'S REBELLION.

Further reading: William H. Rehnquist, *Grand Inquests: The Historic Impeachments of Justice Samuel Chase and President Andrew Johnson* (New York: Morrow, 1992).

Chauncey, Isaac (1782–1840)

A cautious naval officer, Isaac Chauncey served in the wars against the BARBARY PIRATES (1801–15) and in the War of 1812 (1812–15). Chauncey went to sea as a young man, and by the age of 19 was given command of his first vessel. When the United States Navy expanded because of a threatened war with France (the QUASI WAR, 1798–1800), he was commissioned a lieutenant to serve on the frigate *President*, which was then being built in New York. He took one cruise on that vessel to the WEST INDIES before peace was reestablished. Chauncey remained in the navy even after the Jeffersonians reduced the size of the peacetime force. He fought against Tripoli in 1804–06. Distinguishing himself in that conflict, he was promoted to captain in 1806. While taking a leave of absence from the navy, Chauncey made a merchant cruise for John Jacob Astor to the Far East. Upon his return, he went on active duty and was given charge of the navy yard in New York.

At the beginning of the War of 1812 Chauncey was sent to the Great Lakes to build a navy. An excellent and experienced administrator, he did well at this task, centering himself in Sacketts Harbor on Lake Ontario. Although he had several opportunities during the war, he was too cautious to risk his fleet in battle with the British. The result of his inaction was a stalemate in the war on Lake Ontario, with neither side gaining an advantage. At the conclusion of the war, he was about to be replaced.

Chauncey served in 1815 and 1816 in the Mediterranean against Algiers as captain of one of the United States's largest ships. From 1816 to 1818 he commanded the Mediterranean fleet. Thereafter he served the United States Navy in administrative positions.

Further reading: William M. Fowler, Jr., *Jack Tars and Commodores: The American Navy, 1783–1815* (Boston: Houghton Mifflin, 1984).

Cherokee Nation (Tsalagi)

The Cherokee in the second half of the 18th century were the most powerful NATIVE AMERICAN nation in the southern colonies. They played a crucial role during the REVO-LUTIONARY WAR (1775–83) and in the Creek War (1813–14). The Tsalagi also adopted many technological and governmental practices from their American neighbors. They were the only Native Americans to create their own writing system.

After ejecting the Muskogee (CREEK) from what is now northern Georgia, the Cherokee Nation controlled the mountains west of the Carolinas and southern Virginia. During the French and Indian War (1754–63), the Cherokee stayed neutral, though a strong anti-British faction held some influence. A few warriors fought for the British, but tensions between the colonists and the Cherokee mounted during the conflict. These tensions burst into full-scale war in 1760 after a party of Cherokee returning from fighting the French were ambushed by Virginians. The war took a heavy toll on the Tsalagi. They ceded some land to the colonies after the hostilities ceased.

Another round of concessions took place immediately before the Revolutionary War. The Watonga Treaty (1774) and Overhill Cherokee Treaty (1775) sold eastern and central Kentucky to the Transylvania Land Company. DRAGGING CANOE led a faction opposed to the land sale. He and his followers slipped into the rugged terrain in the Chickamauga Valley and conducted a bloody guerrilla war for nearly two decades against the European Americans trying to settle in the region.

The Cherokee sided with the British soon after the Revolutionary War began. This merely provoked the states of North and South Carolina, Georgia, and Virginia to send large militia expeditions into Cherokee territory. With attacks coming from several directions, the Cherokee soon asked for peace, and the Treaties of DeWitt's Corner and Long Island (both signed in 1777) surrendered the last Cherokee lands in the Carolinas. The Chickamaugans under Dragging Canoe fought on.

When the war ended the Cherokee still faced more demands to sell their lands. The Treaty of Hopewell promised to keep settlers off the remaining Cherokee hunting grounds, but in a few short years the Cherokee had to fight once more to protect their property. In 1791 President GEORGE WASHINGTON promised that if the Tsalagi ceded their land in eastern Tennessee, the Americans would not ask for any more territory. The promise spurred the Cherokee to learn to read and write English. They were sure that if they could understand the documents and treaties without the help of American interpreters, they could ward off swindlers.

The Chickamaugans continued to resist the Americans and aided the Miami in their wars of the early 1790s. After the crushing defeat at the BATTLE OF FALLEN TIMBERS (August 20, 1794), the Chickamaugans answered the invitation of the governor of Louisiana to move west of the Mississippi to act as a buffer against the land-hungry Americans already sneaking into Spanish territory.

Promises did not keep the American army from demanding that they be allowed to build a road through Cherokee lands. The road was supposed to be used only for military purposes, but the Cherokee leaders correctly feared that the road would bring settlers and, with them, more demands for land sales.

Early in first decade of the 19th century, the United States government opened trading posts in Cherokee lands. The idea behind these trading posts was to interest the Cherokee people in farming and other modern practices. The technologies that the trading posts brought were readily adapted by the Cherokee. The Cherokee had already formed the "Light Horse" (1799) as a police force for the tribe. Soon farms, ranches, and frame houses dotted the countryside. Some Cherokee even used slaves to work the new plantations.

TECUMSEH tried to enlist the Cherokee in his anti-American confederation of tribes. His pleas fell on deaf ears. When the War of 1812 (1812–15) broke out, the Cherokee cast their lot with the United States. The tribe assisted General Jackson in the Creek, or "Red Stick," War (1813–14) and attacked their ancient foes, the Muskogee. More than 500 mounted Cherokee warriors fought at the Battle of Horseshoe Bend (1814). They also aided the Americans in tracking down the "Red Sticks" that escaped into Spanish FLORIDA.

The service the Cherokee provided the United States did not prevent Andrew Jackson from demanding Cherokee lands at the negotiations at Fort Jackson in 1814. Nor did their adoption of farming and American-style government help them. The ever-increasing swarms of settlers ate up land faster and faster. In 1817 the Cherokee gave in to Jackson's demands. In 1819 they surrendered all their lands in eastern Georgia. These concessions set the stage for the final removal of the Cherokee from their homes in the East.

Further reading: Thomas M. Hatley, *The Dividing Paths: Cherokees and South Carolinians through the Era of Revolution* (New York: Oxford University Press, 1995); William G. McLoughlin, *Cherokee Renaissance in the New Republic* (Princeton, N.J.: Princeton University Press, 1986); Wilma Mankiller and Michael Wallis, *Mankiller: A Chief and Her People* (New York: St. Martin's Press, 1993).

— George Milne

Chesapeake-Leopard affair (June 22, 1807)

On June 22, 1807, the HMS *Leopard* attacked the USS *Chesapeake* just outside the Chesapeake Bay, forcefully removing four men that the British claimed were deserters.

This confrontation led to a major diplomatic crisis and contributed to the growing animosity between the United States and Great Britain that finally broke into the War of 1812 (1812–15).

The British had some legitimate concerns in manning their navy during their long struggle with the FRENCH REVOLUTION and Napoleonic France (1793–1815). They relied on their naval supremacy to prevent an invasion of Great Britain and to check the expansionist aims of the French. But they needed hundreds of thousands of seamen to do so. At the same time, American shipping expanded rapidly as a result of being neutral while France and Great Britain were at war. Although many Americans went to sea in this era, American merchant owners also recruited British and other foreign seamen. The British claimed that during this period as many as 10,000 sailors deserted the poor pay, harsh conditions, and dangers of His Majesty's Navy to sail under the American flag.

Aware of these problems, the senior British officer on the North American station in 1807 ordered his captains to forcefully remove any deserters that they knew were aboard American warships. At the time, a squadron of ships was stationed in Chesapeake Bay, hoping to capture two French vessels that had sought safety in a neutral American port. Officers from this squadron visited American ports and actually met British deserters in the streets, discovering that they were now in the American navy. This knowledge compelled the British to act when the *Chesapeake* put to sea. Not to intercept the American frigate would have been a violation of a direct order. The *Leopard* was dispatched to search the *Chesapeake* as soon as it entered international waters. The American vessel was not prepared for battle and had a new, untrained crew aboard. The Americans did not clear for action, a standard naval practice whenever a foreign warship approached. The British captain demanded to be allowed to search the American frigate for deserters. Commodore James Barron refused. Detecting the intent of the British, he ordered his men to quietly clear for action, but it was too little too late. The British were at close range and opened fire. There was nothing but confusion aboard the American vessel. Many of the cannons could not even be readied for fire. After one shot to save face, Barron surrendered to the British, who found four deserters aboard the vessel, one of whom eventually was hanged for desertion.

A tremendous public outcry arose against this attack. War was threatened, but President THOMAS JEFFERSON instead instituted the EMBARGO OF 1807, with devastating effects for the American ECONOMY. Ironically, the British issued an apology for the attack. However, American diplomats insisted on tying a discussion of the incident to the larger issues of IMPRESSMENT and neutral TRADE, two areas on which the British were not prepared to make many concessions. The result was increased tension between the two nations that ultimately led to the War of 1812.

See also FOREIGN AFFAIRS.

Further reading: Spencer C. Tucker and Frank T. Reuter, *Injured Honor: The* Chesapeake-Leopard *Affair, June 22, 1807* (Annapolis, Md.: Naval Institute Press, 1996).

China trade

After 1784, American and Chinese merchants carried on a lucrative TRADE in products such as silk, tea, porcelain, silver, and ginseng. American trade with China began during the colonial era, as Americans traded for various products under the guise of the British East India Company. Independent American trade with China began in 1784 when the ship *Empress of China* embarked on a long journey from New York City to Canton. The ship returned to New York in 1785 loaded with teas, silks, and porcelain from which its investors made a healthy 30 percent profit. American trade with China took place through the exclusive organization called the Co-Hong, or Hong, merchants. The Co-Hong had a corporate monopoly granted by the Qing (Ch'ing) dynasty to conduct trading operations with all foreigners. The Hong merchants also coordinated and directed various trading factories in Canton. These factories served as warehouses, offices, treasuries, and residences for foreign traders in Canton, including Americans.

The neutrality of the United States with regard to the European wars from 1790 to 1807 allowed American ships free trading opportunity in China, without fear that merchant ships would be captured. By the 1790s, trade between China and the United States focused mainly on a few products: silver, silks, and tea. American merchants carried millions of dollars worth of silver bullion garnered in South America to China in exchange for tea and silks. In Canton, American merchants competed for the Co-Hong's trade with merchants from various western nations, including Great Britain, France, Denmark, Spain, Holland, Portugal, and Sweden.

By far the largest rival to American trade with China was the British East India Company. The company dominated trade with China and was less dependent on silver than other western traders. Instead, the East India Company relied more on its own trade proceeds to purchase Chinese teas and silks, thereby reducing its need to provide the Hong merchants with silver. This put the other traders, including the Americans, at a considerable disadvantage due to the expense of purchasing and transporting silver for trade in Canton. By 1820 the British dominated trade in Canton with a majority of import and export traffic.

Between 1821 and 1839, American trade with China suffered as British importation of opium into China eclipsed other products. The opium trade took place against the Chinese government's wishes, thus forcing wars between Great Britain and China between 1839 and 1842. After the war, the British broke the Co-Hong monopoly, establishing and effectively maintaining an exclusive trading relationship with China.

Further reading: Yu-Kwei Cheng, *Foreign Trade and Industrial Development of China* (Washington, D.C.: University Press of Washington, D.C., 1956); Weng Eang Chong, *The Hong Merchants of Canton: Chinese Merchants in Sino-Western Trade* (Surrey, England: Biddles Limited, 1997).

— James R. Karmel

Choctaw Nation

The Choctaw people once lived in what became the state of Mississippi until they were forced to move west into Indian Territory in the 1820s and 1830s. They were expert diplomats, surviving in a world of strong enemies by playing the French, British, and Spanish against each other. Once the expansion of the American republic cut the Choctaw off from outside help, they soon fell prey to the white demands for their lands.

Before the French and Indian War (1754–63), the Choctaw dealt primarily with the French traders along the Mississippi. When the war broke out, the British strangled the flow of French goods by controlling the shipping lanes to New Orleans, and the Choctaw eventually drifted into the British camp by the end of the war. They found that the Anglo-American merchants trekking over the mountains to the east paid handsomely for the deerskins that the Choctaw harvested in the forests. They maintained contact with the Spanish Empire through New Orleans, which the French king gave to Spain after the war.

When the REVOLUTIONARY WAR (1775–83) broke out, many Choctaw sided with Britain. However, as the war progressed, the Spanish entered the fighting against the British in the hopes that they could reclaim FLORIDA. Some of the Choctaw began to doubt whether the English could win and started to make friends with the Spanish and the Americans. The British surrendered Florida to Spain at the TREATY OF PARIS (1783), and the Choctaw managed to keep the Americans and the Spanish bidding for their support during the years just after the war.

Spanish Florida and Louisiana were very sparsely settled places. In contrast, the United States was bursting over the Appalachian Mountains. Soon, American settlers appeared in the lands to the north of the Choctaw Nation. At the turn of the 18th century, the United States built a military road through the tribal land that funneled in immigrants from the East. The American government also opened trading posts in the region to encourage the Choctaw to take up farming and ranching. Many Choctaw adapted to the new ways quickly, some even using slaves to raise cotton on their plantations. Most Choctaw were not that rich but took up farming while still hunting deer for hides to TRADE. They also maintained their diplomatic contacts with Spain to keep the Americans from becoming too influential over Choctaw policy.

The American trading posts also had a hidden agenda. The tribe fell into debt buying goods at the stores. In 1804 and 1805, the Choctaw signed away some of their land in the Mississippi Territory to satisfy those debts. This agreement cut down on hunting grounds, and small parties of Choctaw began to cross into Louisiana to find game west of the great river. During the War of 1812 (1812–15), many Choctaw fought for the United States during the Creek War. However, their loyalty did not keep the Americans from demanding more land. Even though the Choctaw instituted a regular government and farmed like white people, the American government wanted them to sell all their land and move west.

See also CREEK NATION; NATIVE AMERICANS AND THE REVOLUTION.

Further reading: James Taylor Carson, *Searching for the Bright Path: The Mississippi Choctaws from Prehistory to Removal* (Lincoln: University of Nebraska Press, 1999).

— George Milne

Church, Benjamin (1734?–1777)

Doctor Benjamin Church was a LOYALIST who passed secret information to the British during the AMERICAN REVOLUTION. A citizen of Massachusetts, Church became involved in the revolutionary politics of Boston, making his way deep into the councils of the patriot leaders. He served on the Boston COMMITTEE OF CORRESPONDENCE, and in 1774 was selected as a delegate to the Massachusetts provisional legislature. Although some patriots such as PAUL REVERE were suspicious, the leadership remained unaware of Church's leanings. Suspicions probably should have been raised in late April 1775 when Church, supposedly going to Boston to pick up medicine, was captured (he said) and taken before British general THOMAS GAGE. At this meeting Church gave Gage information about business being discussed by the Massachusetts provisional congress and almost a full month's notice of the American army's plans to fortify Bunker Hill.

Events overtook Church in September 1775. American general NATHANAEL GREENE intercepted a coded letter from Church. Church claimed it was a letter to his brother, but when it was deciphered it was clear that he was providing military intelligence to the British. In October 1775 a council of war found Church guilty of communicating with the enemy, and he was jailed at Cambridge, Massachusetts, and then sent to Norwich, Connecticut. Church later petitioned for a reprieve claiming ill health. Although it took several months, Church was paroled to Boston. His end is somewhat unclear, but it seems he left Boston in poor health in 1777 for the WEST INDIES.

Further reading: Allen French, *General Gage's Informers* (Ann Arbor: University of Michigan Press, 1932).

— J. Brett Adams

Cincinnati, Order of

In April 1783, as the REVOLUTIONARY WAR (1775–83) was winding down, a group of CONTINENTAL ARMY officers led by General HENRY KNOX established the Order of Cincinnati. Looking upon their experience in the war and recognizing the special bond they had developed as a result of their sacrifices, these men wanted to create an association that would help them sustain their ties. The order took its name from the Roman general Cincinnatus, who had left his plow to defend the Roman republic, declined a crown after his victories, and returned to his life of agrarian simplicity. While clinging to a pose of humility, the officers were ambitious and anticipated that their organization would exert political influence in the new American republic. They also planned on using the Order of Cincinnati to lobby for overdue back pay. To add both visibility and additional honor, Knox persuaded GEORGE WASHINGTON to head the order. The Cincinnati, however, made one mistake: They limited membership to officers and their first-born sons.

The public outcry was tremendous. As an exclusive military club and as an inherited privilege, the order of Cincinnati was "full of danger to the rights of man" and seemed a violation of the ideals of REPUBLICANISM. As Knox explained to Washington, the organization was accused of being "created by a foreign influence, in order to change our form of government." SAMUEL ADAMS proclaimed that the Cincinnati represented "as rapid a Stride towards hereditary Military Nobility as was ever made in so short a Time." The eagle and blue ribbon of the society, instead of being a political asset, became a political liability. One Massachusetts candidate promised to withdraw from the order in an effort to get elected. The Rhode Island legislature went so far as to disenfranchise anyone who was a member. Amid this outcry, Washington resigned his leadership role. The organization survived, relegated to being one of many interest groups in the democratic politics of the new United States.

Further reading: Minor Myers, *Liberty without Anarchy: A History of the Society of Cincinnati* (Charlottesville: University Press of Virginia, 1983).

cities and urban life

American cities underwent a dramatic expansion in the years between 1754 and 1820. At the beginning of the period there were perhaps a half-dozen locations with 5,000 or more people; by 1820, there were 35. There were also two cities, New York and Philadelphia, that grew from around 20,000 to over 100,000. Although most Americans still lived in rural settings, cities had become vital in politics, the ECONOMY, and society.

During the 1760s and 1770s much of the RESISTANCE MOVEMENT (1764–75) took place in cities. Boston was the most prominent hub of activity, leading the way in the agitation against the STAMP ACT (1765), customs regulations, and the TEA ACT (1773). Cities were so important in the opposition to imperial regulation in part because of the

Photograph depicting Philadelphia's Elfreth Alley, near Independence Hall, appearing much as it did in the eighteenth century *(Library of Congress)*

TRADE that was funneled through their warehouses. But the fact that large numbers of people congregated in cites also mattered. Along the wharves of every port were sailors and dockworkers with plenty of grievances against Great Britain and eager to join a crowd. Large numbers of ARTI-SANS also populated the cities. These men had become increasingly articulate and schooled in the ideology of REPUBLICANISM. Many merchants and LAWYERS also resided in cities, providing further leadership for the resistance movement. In short, it was in the cities that each level of society met in enough of a concentration to provide an explosive mix that led to the revolution.

During the REVOLUTIONARY WAR (1775–83), most American cities suffered. Boston, Newport, New York, Philadelphia, and Charleston were each occupied by the British army. These occupations led to upheaval. When the British arrived, populations fled, buildings were commandeered, and churches were turned into stables. LOYALISTS flocked to the cities for asylum. Then, when the British evacuated, the Loyalists either left with their protectors or remained behind to be harassed by the revolutionaries. More people moved in to replace the exiles and the cities began to rebuild. Of the five major colonial cities, only Newport failed to recover rapidly. (Newport's decline had more to do with the competition from upstart Providence than to the effects of the war.)

During the early national era, cities became the locus of vibrant politics. The same artisans that had been so important to the resistance movement and revolution now viewed themselves as the bulwarks of society and rightful heirs to republican citizenship. Initially the FEDERALIST PARTY could use ties of patronage and the promise of commercial prosperity to attract the city voter. By the mid-1790s, however, mechanics, as artisans called themselves, asserted an equality that seemed more in concert with the ideals of the DEMOCRATIC-REPUBLICAN PARTY. This shift in allegiance contributed to the victory of THOMAS JEFFERSON in the ELECTION OF 1800. Artisans believed that as producers and craftsmen—men who lived by the work they did—they had a special role within the republic. No longer was the ideal to be a gentleman who did not labor with his hands; now the strong arm holding a tool and proclaiming "With Hammer and Hand, All Arts Flourish and Stand" became a symbol of the republic.

Concentrated in the city, mechanics, along with merchants, helped keep commerce moving. If cities had been central to the colonial economy, they became even more crucial to the economy of the new republic. While rural areas produced an agricultural surplus that could be exported overseas, it was the dock facilities, artisanal production, and banking services that kept goods moving. When France and Great Britain went to war in 1793, creating greater economic opportunity for the United States, cities became even more important.

City life, however, was not easy. Because it was difficult and expensive to develop the land on the edge of cites, builders relied upon multifamily dwellings. Crowding became typical of these urban spaces, with high-cost housing and great disparities between rich and poor. Streets were unpaved and often filthy. The most efficient garbage collectors were the hogs that roamed the streets. There were no sewers; people used privies in their backyards. Drinking water was not easy to come by, since everyone depended on a handful of wells or water carted from the countryside. Sickness and DISEASE AND EPIDEMICS spread rapidly. During the Revolutionary War smallpox was the biggest fear. In the 1790s and early 1800s there were repeated outbreaks of yellow fever that struck several cities. The affluent headed for the safety of the country during such epidemics. Those that remained behind, usually the poor, died by the hundreds and even thousands. Although by 1800 many cities required building with brick, there were still wooden structures around that burned all too easily in a fire. It was not unusual, with the city depending only on volunteer fire companies, for entire blocks to burn down in one conflagration. Police departments did not exist either. The main deterrent to crime was the night watch and a constable or two, who often were more concerned with gaining a reward than crime prevention. Prostitutes plied their trade openly, and public drunkenness and raucous behavior violated the sensibilities of the more refined. Disorderly mobs could break out at any moment in a tavern brawl or over some supposed affront. In case of popular disorder or RIOTS, the mayor or other municipal officer would try to step into the breach and use his personal connection with some in the crowd—the cities were still small enough where the official might know some of the rioters—to avert too much violence.

If there was a nasty quality to urban life in this period, there were also many positive features as well. The same streets that could be so repulsive could also be the source of entertainment; urban dwellers seemed to relish the hustle and bustle of the city. On special occasions crowds numbering into the thousands gathered in celebration or to watch a parade march by. Booths and small shops sold food and other items. TAVERNS and THEATERS also added to the enjoyments of the city, providing a level of entertainment impossible to match in the countryside. Printing presses rolled out newspapers, books, and pamphlets, providing a vibrant intellectual life. Associational activity was also easier in the city, with a greater variety of groups to join. Although it might be difficult to sustain a larger sense of community, it was easier to develop more personal networks along job, ethnic, or religious lines. Free AFRICAN AMERICANS, for example, flocked to cites to interact with others of their own race. Like the African Americans, other groups created their own institutions, including schools and churches. Neighborhoods began to emerge that developed a particular character all their own.

Finally, although there was a great deal of POVERTY in cities, there was also economic opportunity. African Americans sought to gain personal independence by moving to cities. Not every job was open to them, but many became storekeepers, ran oyster bars, or cut hair. Large numbers of African-American men found work on the waterfront or signed on as sailors. European Americans, too, came to the city in the hope of new careers. A building boom meant jobs for many laborers and skilled artisans, and the expansion of overseas commerce provided further skilled employment as shipbuilders, sailmakers, blockmakers, and coopers. For those further up the economic scale, starting as a clerk could be the first step to becoming a merchant and owning one of the fancy multistory brick houses that dominated the most prominent streets. While women had less opportunity, the city offered a more independent existence than the countryside, since it was possible for a woman to find employment as a seamstress or in the service industry.

Cities in the revolutionary and early national period were vibrant and expanding. Despite war and upheaval, or perhaps because of war and upheaval, they remained the epicenter of much of American life.

See also IMMIGRATION; POPULAR CULTURE; POPULATION TRENDS.

Further reading: Carl Bridenbaugh, *Cities in Revolt: Urban Life in America, 1743–1776* (New York: Knopf, 1955); Paul A. Gilje, *The Road to Mobocracy: Popular Disorder in New York City, 1763–1834* (Chapel Hill: University of North Carolina Press, 1987); Gary B. Nash, *The Urban Crucible: Social Change, Political Consciousness, and the Origins of the American Revolution* (Cambridge, Mass.: Harvard University Press, 1979).

Clark, George Rogers (1752–1818)

George Rogers Clark was a general during the REVOLUTIONARY WAR (1775–83). Clark was born in Virginia in 1752, the son of second-generation Scottish immigrant planters. One of his younger brothers was WILLIAM CLARK, of LEWIS AND CLARK fame. At age 20 Clark journeyed to Pittsburgh, traveled by boat down the Ohio River, and claimed land near modern-day Wheeling, West Virginia. He had hardly begun his life as a farmer when the Indian-British conflict known as LORD DUNMORE's War broke out in 1774. Clark joined the Kentucky settlers in defending their homes against Indian raids.

When the Revolutionary War began, Clark was sent by a group of settlers who wanted independence to acquire gunpowder from the governor of Virginia, PATRICK HENRY. Clark spent many months transporting the gunpowder to the FRONTIER. In 1777 the Ohio tribes, primarily the Shawnee, Miami, and Wyandot, rejected the American claim to Kentucky and, with British backing, attacked the settlers in an effort to drive them away. Clark, now a major and in charge of defending the settlements, decided on a seemingly outrageous scheme of cutting the Indian supply lines by capturing two British forts. These two forts were at the towns of Kaskaskia, on the Mississippi River in present-day Illinois, and Vincennes, on the Wabash River on the present-day Indiana-Illinois border. The plan was outrageous because it would require a small force to travel over 400 miles through wilderness with few supplies. However, Clark argued to Governor Henry that the element of surprise would make up for the difficulties. Clark's plan was approved and he was promoted to lieutenant colonel.

In June 1778 he led 175 men down the Ohio River from Pittsburgh to the mouth of the Tennessee River. To travel by boat would allow their enemies to discover them easily. Therefore, Clark's army marched through the wilderness, reaching Kaskaskia, a 125-mile distance, in six days. They easily took the unsuspecting forces in the fort. Clark learned that Vincennes was undefended and sent Captain Leonard Helm to occupy the fort. The seizure of Fort Vincennes was short-lived, however, as Henry Hamilton, the famous "Hair Buyer," retook the fort for the British using Canadian militia and Indians. Clark discovered the loss of Vincennes and led an army of 170 men through the cold and wet of winter to the fort. Using stealth and information provided by captives, he surrounded the fort and recaptured it.

Clark's seizure of the two forts helped to neutralize the British forces in the West. His victories also allowed the United States to claim the Northwest after the war. Clark earned the nickname "conqueror of the Northwest" for his efforts. However, his life after the war was marked by failure. Clark had borrowed substantial amounts of money from traders to finance his war efforts. The records authorizing the Virginia government to repay him were destroyed during the war, and repayments authorized by the American government in the 1780s were never made. To evade his creditors, Clark signed his property over to his relatives and lived on a small tract of land, where he became a loner and an alcoholic. Clark had a stroke in 1812 that partially paralyzed him. In 1818 he died of a second stroke.

See also NATIVE AMERICANS AND THE REVOLUTION.

Further reading: George Macgregor Waller, *The American Revolution in the West* (Chicago: Nelson-Hall, 1976).

— Michael L. Cox

Clark, William (1770–1838)

An influential figure in the Revolutionary era and the early republic, William Clark helped to navigate and describe the American West with his partner MERIWETHER LEWIS during the LEWIS AND CLARK EXPEDITION (1804–06). He then became closely involved with the management of western lands and their inhabitants in the decades of western settlement that followed.

Born in Caroline Country, Virgina, William Clark was the ninth child of prominent planter John Clark and Ann (Rogers) Clark. He spent his childhood, as did others of his class in Virginia, learning how to survey land, manage slave labor, and explore the natural world. He received minimal formal education, learning more through experience and observation of practical matters. He also developed his skills in drawing and cartography. His direct and pragmatic mind-set served him well in his later years on the rough American FRONTIER.

In 1784 the Clarks moved to Kentucky at the encouragement of William's older brother, frontier REVOLUTIONARY WAR hero GEORGE ROGERS CLARK. After a long journey down the Ohio River, the Clarks landed in Louisville, where General Clark helped them reestablish their enterprises on a new estate they called Mulberry Hill. William spent the rest of his formative years there, eventually inheriting the plantation from his parents. His life in frontier Kentucky was not a stationary one; at possibly as early as 16, William Clark accompanied General Clark on campaigns against the Indians in the Wabash region north of the Ohio. In 1789 he joined Colonel John Hardin in his battles against the Indians near the White River. He participated in several other campaigns in defense of the settlements in Kentucky.

Throughout the early 1790s, Clark engaged in military actions with various companies. In March 1792 he was commissioned lieutenant of infantry. While serving with General ANTHONY WAYNE, Clark acted as a representative to the Chickasaw near Memphis, negotiating a trade in rifles and ammunition in exchange for allegiance against the Spanish. Clark met the new enlistee Meriwether Lewis at Wayne's successful BATTLE OF FALLEN TIMBERS in 1794. After undertaking another negotiation with the Spanish along the Mississippi, Clark resigned his commission in 1796 and returned to Louisville. He spent the next few years as a private citizen, travelling and trying to salvage the fortune of his brother George Rogers Clark, who was deeply in debt.

Meriwether Lewis wrote to Clark in 1803, inviting him to join him in a transcontinental expedition. The expedition was proposed by President THOMAS JEFFERSON in order to explore the recently acquired Louisiana Territory and discover a new, all-water route to the Pacific Ocean. As a man who had lived on and explored the American frontier for most of his life, Clark was drawn to the planned expedition and brought with him the practical experience and resourcefulness necessary for such a dangerous trip.

Lewis, Clark, and their recruits set off from St. Louis in May 1804. Their party included officers, regular soldiers, and William Clark's slave, York. They traveled up the Missouri River, staying the winter with the Mandan Indians in what is now North Dakota. In spring they continued up the Missouri, now with a knowledgeable northern tribeswoman, SACAGAWEA, as their guide. The impossibility of an all-water route became evident in the Rocky Mountains, but the party continued overland, eventually finding the Columbia River. By autumn the expedition had reached the mouth of the Columbia at the Pacific Ocean, where it spent the winter. The party hoped to return by ship, but had to begin retracing its steps over land when they spotted no ships in the Columbia region. During the return trip they discovered new routes through the mountains. Clark separated from Lewis to navigate part of the Yellowstone River, meeting up with the rest of the party at the river mouth. They finally arrived in St. Louis in September 1806. While on the journey, Clark took responsibility for many of the practical tasks necessary to survival. He also drew the maps, measured mileage with remarkable accuracy, and described the new western landscape through his diaries and drawings. Thanks to Lewis and Clark's diligent recordkeeping, accounts of the journey could be communicated to the expectant American public. After many delays, the descriptions of the expedition were published in 1814.

In 1807 Clark resigned from the army and became brigadier-general of the militia for the Louisiana Territory he had just explored. In 1808 he married a young woman from his native Virginia, Julia Hancock. Of their four children, two sons—Meriwether Lewis Clark and George Rogers Hancock Clark—survived to adulthood. The couple lived in St.Louis, where Clark became superintendent for Indian affairs in the Upper Louisiana (later called Missouri) Territory. His old friend Meriwether Lewis became the governor of the territory. In the first years after their triumphant return, both men were preoccupied with establishing order in the administration of the West and the western TRADE. Clark fared better financially than his friend Lewis and often acted as his de facto caretaker as Lewis's mental state became more volatile.

After Governor Lewis's death in 1809, Clark declined the president's offer to make him Lewis's successor. Clark was eventually appointed to the office in 1813. During the War of 1812, Clark's forces defended St. Louis from attacks by Great Britain's Indian allies. He met with less success when he led an expedition to Prairie du Chien on the upper Mississippi—his forces were attacked there and down river at Rock Island. After the war ended, William Clark, his associates in the Chouteau family (traders and Indian agents), and other prominent men in the region needed to appease the Indians by conciliatory treaties. As was the established custom, most of these "peace and friendship" treaties required land cessions by tribes in exchange for credit, money, or goods. Some treaties established fur trading agreements as well, and William Clark was actively involved in the fur trade as regulatory agent and a private investor. Such conflicts of interest were common among the leading figures in the developing West.

After the successful negotiation of these treaties, Clark's duties became increasingly focused on maintaining stable Indian-white relations. He established a rapport with various Indian leaders and tried to cultivate a trusting, respectful relationship with them. As superintendent of Indian affairs, he was involved in every agreement between the tribes of his region and the federal government. He also facilitated meetings between different parties in his home and accompanied Indian delegations to Washington. As treaties began to unravel in the 1820s and 1830s (most notably during the 1832 uprising of the Sauk and Fox known as the Black Hawk War), Clark wielded enormous influence with the conflicting parties, managing to quell rebellions while also maintaining a sympathetic reputation among the tribes. Although Clark was sensitive to Indian concerns, he remained an imperious Virginia master when confronted by problems among his slaves. He refused to free York, even after the slave proved a valiant companion on the dangerous expedition. Instead, Clark forced York to leave his wife and children in Louisville to accompany his master to his new home in St. Louis.

During his later years, William Clark remained Indian superintendent but relinquished some of his other offices. After Julia Hancock Clark died in 1820, he married Harriet Kennerly, and they had a son, Jefferson Kennerly Clark. The Clarks' home continued to be a meeting place for Indian and white leaders, and William Clark continued to advocate for the humane treatment of Native Americans (while at the same time supporting Indian removal from the southern states). He was called the "Red-Headed Chief" among his Indian friends. While Clark's actions as an explorer, administrator, and businessman compromised the future vitality of western Indian tribes, he continued to act for what he considered to be their best interests. He leaves an ambiguous legacy of conquest and conciliation, which was not unusual for Indian agents during the early 19th century. William Clark died in St. Louis at the home of his eldest son in 1838.

See also LOUISIANA PURCHASE.

Further reading: John Bakeless, *Lewis and Clark: Partners in Discovery* (New York: William Morrow, 1947); Reuben Gold Thwaites, ed., *Original Journals of the Lewis and Clark Expedition* (1904–5; reprint, New York: Arno Press, 1969).

— Eleanor H. McConnell

Clinton, DeWitt (1769–1828)

DeWitt Clinton held many offices—United States senator, mayor of New York City, governor of the state of New York—but his most significant achievement was building the Erie Canal. Scion of an important political family and trained as a LAWYER, by the time Clinton was 20 he wielded considerable political influence. Much of this power was a legacy of his uncle, GEORGE CLINTON. Like his uncle, DeWitt opposed the United States Constitution and allied himself with the DEMOCRATIC-REPUBLICANS (Jeffersonians) in the 1790s. When his uncle was not reelected governor in 1795, DeWitt remained politically active. In 1797 Clinton was elected to the state assembly, and in 1801 he was appointed to the crucial council of appointments, the agency that doled out most of the state jobs. Previously the council had accepted a governor's nominations without question, but Clinton engineered something of a coup by challenging this practice. With a Jeffersonian state assembly to support him, he virtually took over the patronage that had been in the control of the FEDERALIST governor. With this success behind him, he was quickly selected to fill a vacancy in the United States Senate in 1802. But in 1803 he resigned that national office to become mayor of New York City. From Clinton's perspective, this office, which he held for most of the time until 1815, was more prestigious, had a greater income, and kept him close to the politics of his home state.

He was an active mayor, overseeing charities, pushing school reform and supervising the daily workings and expansion of what was quickly becoming the nation's largest city. While mayor he also served as a state senator (1806–11) and as lieutenant governor (1811–13). But in 1812 he allowed himself to be nominated by the Federalists, who had previously been his political opponents, as their candidate for president. He lost that contest to JAMES MADISON and also lost some credibility with many of his followers. By 1815 he was compelled to abandon all of his political offices. He then turned his energies to a new project, the building of the Erie Canal.

Clinton had been appointed a canal commissioner in 1810, but only after 1815 did he really push the project. As the state began to survey the area between Albany and Buffalo for construction, Clinton again found himself popular. In 1817 he was elected governor of the state and became wholly identified with what some derisively called "Clinton's Ditch." The building of the canal was one of the greatest engineering feats of the era, but before it could be completed, Clinton ran into some more political problems.

After a new state constitution broadened the franchise, Clinton failed at reelection to the governorship in 1822, losing the contest to Martin Van Buren and his developing Democratic Party. However, these politicians overplayed their hand when, as an additional affront to Clinton, they removed him from his role as a canal commissioner. This insult elicited the sympathy of many New Yorkers, who elected Clinton as their governor again in 1824, thus allowing him to preside over the opening of "his" 362-mile canal in 1825. The building of the Erie Canal guaranteed the future growth of both the state and city of New York. Clinton died in 1828 while still governor.

Further reading: Evan Cornog, *The Birth of Empire: DeWitt Clinton and the American Experience, 1769–1828* (New York: Oxford University Press, 1998); Craig Hanyan, *DeWitt Clinton and the Rise of the People's Men* (Montreal: McGill-Queen's University Press, 1996); Craig Hanyan, *DeWitt Clinton: Years of Molding, 1769–1807* (New York: Garland, 1988).

Clinton, George (1739–1812)

Known as the father of New York State, George Clinton served as governor for seven terms and then as vice president of the United States for two terms. Clinton came from middling origins and grew up in Ulster County, New York. He served briefly on a privateer during the French and Indian War (1754–63) and then fought as a junior officer in a British expedition against Fort Frontenac on Lake Ontario. After the war he became a LAWYER and was elected to the provincial assembly in 1768.

Clinton was an ambitious social and political climber. He gained a reputation as a defender of liberty by speaking out on behalf of ALEXANDER MCDOUGALL in 1770 and strengthened his political position by marrying into a locally prominent family. During the intensification of the imperial crisis in 1774 and 1775, he emerged as an important spokesman for the resistance to Great Britain and was selected to be a member of the state's COMMITTEE OF CORRESPONDENCE. In December 1775 he was elected to the SECOND CONTINENTAL CONGRESS. He voted for independence in 1776 but did not sign the DECLARATION OF INDEPENDENCE (July 4, 1776), since he was busy with the defense of New York. (Having gained some military experience in the French and Indian War, he had been appointed a brigadier general in the state's militia.) In 1776 and 1777 he organized the defenses of the Hudson highlands and recruited men into the militia and CONTINENTAL ARMY. He inspired confidence in his men and within the state, and as a result Congress appointed him a brigadier general in the Continental army in 1777. Because of his popularity, and much to the displeasure of

George Clinton *(Library of Congress)*

the aristocratic leadership in New York, he was elected as governor in the same year.

Few men have confronted more desperate times than Clinton when he was inaugurated as governor of New York in July 1777. The British occupied New York City, Long Island, and the lower reaches of the Hudson River Valley. A powerful army under General JOHN BURGOYNE was working its way south from CANADA, and a force of British soldiers and Indians threatened the state from the Great Lakes. The GREEN MOUNTAIN BOYS of Vermont were declaring themselves an independent state, even though their territory technically belonged to New York, and much of the population under the control of the state government was neutral at best, if not outright loyal to King GEORGE III. In short, there was not much left of New York State to govern. In the summer of 1777, Clinton set out to prevent a British army from moving up the Hudson to join with Burgoyne's forces heading south from Canada. Clinton was outmanned and outgunned; the best he could do was slow the British down. He lost the forts guarding the Hudson highlands, and the British were able to burn Kingston. Despite these defeats, he delayed the invasion long enough to leave Burgoyne isolated at SARATOGA, where he was forced to surrender on October 17, 1777. With the failure of the British thrust from the Great Lakes at Fort Stanwix, and Burgoyne's surrender, the British were compelled to withdraw to New York City. The state of New York survived its most perilous moment.

As wartime governor, Clinton followed a policy of rigorous prosecution of LOYALISTS, confiscating their property to pay for the war and thus relieving the yeomanry of the state from an excessive tax burden. He also sought to regulate the ECONOMY and limit inflation. The popularity of these measures secured the state for the revolutionary cause while making Clinton very popular, leading to his repeated reelection as governor. During the 1780s these policies put the state on such a sound financial base that Clinton did not see the need for a stronger central government. He therefore opposed the Constitution of 1787, writing ANTI-FEDERALIST tracts and working to defeat ratification of the Constitution. Despite his control of patronage as a political weapon, his political star began to fade as the FEDERALIST PARTY rose to power in the 1790s. He declined a reelection bid in 1795, believing defeat likely. After the DEMOCRATIC-REPUBLICAN (Jeffersonian) victory in 1800, Clinton returned from retirement and was elected governor again in 1801. In 1804 the Democratic-Republicans selected Clinton as THOMAS JEFFERSON's running mate, replacing the tarnished AARON BURR. The now aged and somewhat feeble Clinton became vice president. He considered a presidential bid in 1808, but he ended up as JAMES MADISON's running mate instead. Although he did not like Madison, he served as vice president until his death in 1812.

Further reading: John P. Kaminski, *George Clinton: Yeoman of the New Republic* (Madison, Wis.: Madison House, 1993).

Clinton, Sir Henry (1730–1795)

Sir Henry Clinton fought for the British during the REVOLUTIONARY WAR (1775–83), serving as commander in chief of the British army in North America from 1778 to 1782. Although Clinton was born in England, he spent much of his youth in New York, where his father was the royal governor. When he returned to England in 1749, he used his aristocratic connections to join the army. During the Seven Year War (known in the United States as the French and Indian War [1754–63]), he served with gallantry and distinction in the German campaign. By the end of the war he was appointed a general, and in 1772 he was promoted to the rank of major general and elected to Parliament.

Clinton was one of the three generals (along with WILLIAM HOWE and JOHN BURGOYNE) sent to Boston in 1775 to advise General THOMAS GAGE after LEXINGTON AND CONCORD (April 19, 1775). Before the BATTLE OF BUNKER HILL (June 17, 1775), he recommended a flanking maneuver to get behind the American lines to cut off retreat and to minimize casualties. Gage ignored the advice and opted for a frontal assault, carrying the hill with tremendous losses. When Howe replaced Gage, Clinton became his second in command. Clinton advocated action to destroy the enemy's army, while Howe was more concerned with conquering territory. However, it was Clinton who drew up the plan at the BATTLE OF LONG ISLAND (August 27–30, 1776) that led to a resounding victory and almost entrapped GEORGE WASHINGTON's army. Howe ignored Clinton's advice for a similar enveloping maneuver in the subsequent campaign that drove Washington out of New York and across New Jersey. Clinton also opposed Howe's move to take Philadelphia in 1777, arguing that he should move up the Hudson River and join with Burgoyne, who was advancing south from CANADA. Left with a relatively small detachment as Howe embarked on his Philadelphia campaign, Clinton struck up the Hudson in the fall of 1777, recognizing the desperate situation that was developing for Burgoyne. He seized the forts guarding the Hudson highlands and captured and burned Kingston. On the day that Burgoyne surrendered SARATOGA (October 17, 1777), British ships were within 45 miles of Albany. With the loss of Burgoyne's army, Clinton had to withdraw to New York City. Howe resigned command of the British armies in North America in February 1778, and Clinton became commander in chief.

After Saratoga, the French entered the war, and much of the British focus centered on the WEST INDIES, leaving Clinton with limited resources. He had to abandon Philadelphia, which Howe had captured the previous year, and withdraw to New York City. On the way to New York, he fought an inconclusive BATTLE OF MONMOUTH (June 28, 1778) in New Jersey. He later launched an attack on Georgia and began to develop a strategy for the war in the South. In 1780 he achieved his greatest victory by capturing CHARLESTON (May 12, 1780) and 5,000 American troops.

Clinton demonstrated flashes of military brilliance, but he had significant flaws that affected the outcome of the Revolutionary War: He had difficulty getting along with others, including his superiors and those below him; he never had strong political connections in England; and although he had many suggestions while second in command, they were rarely followed because Howe disliked him. Indeed, Clinton was generally disliked by his officers and the men under his command. He also had trouble with LORD CHARLES CORNWALLIS, who was his subordinate. Clinton had encouraged a slow and careful campaign in the South that would build upon a LOYALIST base. Cornwallis abandoned this policy in 1781, cutting his army loose to eventually invade Virginia. That campaign ended in failure when Cornwallis surrendered at YORKTOWN (October 19, 1781). Clinton's greatest flaw may have been his propensity to become more cautious when he was completely in charge. He could have ordered Cornwallis to withdraw from Yorktown before the French fleet arrived, but he hesitated and did not take direct command of the situation. The result was that Clinton, not Cornwallis, was blamed for the defeat at Yorktown. Cornwallis had returned to England first and had better political connections. By the time Clinton returned to England in 1782, he found himself with almost no support. Although he retired from active duty, Clinton again came into favor in the 1790s and briefly served as governor of Gibraltar in 1794.

Further reading: George Athan Billias, ed., *George Washington's Opponents: British Generals and Admirals in the American Revolution* (New York: William Morrow, 1969).

Coercive Acts (1774)

After the BOSTON TEA PARTY (December 16, 1773), the British government under FREDERICK, LORD NORTH decided that the colonists needed to be forced to recognize parliamentary sovereignty. To compel American compliance with imperial regulation, Parliament passed a series of laws called the Coercive Acts, sometimes called the Intolerable Acts, in the spring of 1774. The first measure passed was the Boston Port Bill (March 31, 1774), which closed the port of Boston until its inhabitants had paid the British East India Company for the tea that had been destroyed. This regulation effectively ended most business in Boston and threatened the inhabitants with starvation for lack of work and the inability to import food by sea. It also elicited the sympathy of many Americans for the people of Boston. If the king could close down the port of Boston to compel submission, he could do the same for any other community that might oppose him.

Believing that "the democratic part of government" had gotten out of hand in the colonies, Lord North also passed the Massachusetts Government Act (May 20, 1774). This law altered the charter of Massachusetts, providing greater royal control and reducing popular participation. Previously, the Massachusetts General Court (the lower house of assembly) had appointed members of the council. Now they were to be appointed by the king. The royal governor was given the absolute power to appoint many of the colony's judges and most civil officials. The long arm of the Crown was to reach into every community, as the law provided that there could be no town meetings without royal permission. Juries also were to be chosen by a royal official, the sheriff, rather than the freeholders. The alteration of

the colony's charter concerned many Americans because it meant that no written charter was inviolate. Parliament could alter the makeup of a government at will. The provision limiting town meetings brought the conflict into the countryside as well. Many farmers, who had viewed the debate over the TEA ACT (1773) or the TOWNSHEND DUTIES (1767) as far from their daily world, now came to see how their lives would be changed by an inability to sustain local control in politics.

The two remaining Coercive Acts were also viewed as steps toward tyranny. The Administration of Justice Act (May 20, 1774) was passed by Parliament to solve a real problem—the inability of colonial courts to convict violators of imperial regulations. This law therefore allowed the Crown to move the location of a trial to a different colony or to England if officials believed that it was impossible to prosecute a person in his own community with a local jury. While appearing as a logical solution to an ongoing problem for the British government, it struck Americans as unfair and unjust to have the trial moved. Moreover, changing the trial location would cost the defendant much more money. The fourth measure was a Quartering Act (June 2, 1774) that would have the colonies pay for the support of troops assigned to enforce these laws.

A fifth law was lumped together with the four Coercive Acts as also being intolerable. The Quebec Act (June 22, 1774) was passed to deal with a complex situation in CANADA, which had been conquered by the British in the French and Indian War (1754–63). Most Canadians spoke French and were Roman CATHOLICS. The British sought to incorporate these people into their empire in as fair a manner as possible. Thus, the Quebec Act tolerated the Roman Catholic faith, accepted provisions of the French legal code, and allowed the land-tenure system that had been in place to continue. It also created a huge boundary for Canada, including all of the territory between the Mississippi River and the Appalachians. Many Americans found this law distressing because it seemed to favor the French in Canada at the expense of the English in the colonies. Most Americans at this time viewed Catholics as agents of the devil, and toleration of Catholics was therefore unacceptable. Similarly, the Americans had eagerly participated in the French and Indian War and had expected to be rewarded with western lands. The PROCLAMATION OF 1763 had been a temporary measure to prevent settlers from crossing the Appalachians. The Quebec Act made that measure permanent, which seemed an infringement of American rights. NATIVE AMERICANS living in the area, on the other hand, supported this provision because it protected their homelands from an American invasion.

In reaction to the Coercive Acts, Americans formed COMMITTEES OF CORRESPONDENCE up and down the coast to pass resolutions against these measures. The committees also organized relief efforts to aid Boston and joined in a nonimportation movement to compel the British to rescind the laws. The colonies went on to organize the FIRST CONTINENTAL CONGRESS (1774) to discuss further actions. MINUTEMEN in Massachusetts and elsewhere began to collect arms and drill. The stage was set for a direct conflict, which would come on April 19, 1775, at LEXINGTON AND CONCORD.

See also RESISTANCE MOVEMENT.

Further reading: Robert Middlekauff, *The Glorious Cause: The American Revolution, 1763–1789* (New York: Oxford University Press, 1982).

committees of correspondence

Similar to the SONS OF LIBERTY, committees of correspondence were developed between 1772 and 1775 to exchange information between colonies and communities and to organize resistance to British imperial measures. There were two types of committees of correspondence: intercolonial and local. The intercolonial committees were established by colonial assemblies. The local committees, however, were more important. As the conflict with Great Britain intensified after the passage of the COERCIVE ACTS (1774), the local committees took on expanded roles. When government began to break down in the wake of the BATTLES OF LEXINGTON AND CONCORD (April 19, 1975), the committee system became more elaborate and began to assume administrative duties. The committees of correspondence began to adopt new names (like committee of safety) and became a central driving force behind the Revolution.

Although tensions between the colonies and Great Britain were reduced after the repeal of the TOWNSHEND DUTIES (1767; repealed 1770), many colonial Americans believed that they needed to be on guard against other encroachments on their liberty. Upon receiving news of the GASPÉE affair (1772), the Virginia House of Burgesses decided to establish a committee of correspondence to maintain contact with other colonial assemblies. Within a year, every colony but Pennsylvania had established a similar committee.

The local committees—developed at different times and in different places—acted as direct representatives of the people. Boston and smaller Massachusetts towns took the lead in organizing these committees. When the British government moved to make judges' salaries independent of the legislature, SAMUEL ADAMS was outraged. He convinced the Boston town meeting to call for the legislature to meet, and when the governor refused to gratify this request, Sam Adams thought that it was time to create an organization to help guard the liberty of the people. He

asked for a committee of correspondence to be formed "to state the Rights of the Colonists . . . as Men, as Christians, and as Subjects; to communicate and publish the same to the several Towns in this Province and the World as the sense of this Town, with the Enfringements and Violations thereof that have been, or from time to time may be made." He also wanted the committee to request that each town freely communicate "their Sentiments on this Subject." While not every community responded, by April 1773 half of the towns and districts in Massachusetts had set up committees of correspondence.

Sam Adams could not have timed his organizational efforts better. In May 1773 Parliament passed the TEA ACT, and the committees of correspondence were abuzz with discussions of this new presumed attack on American liberty. The Boston committee of correspondence organized the protest that culminated in the BOSTON TEA PARTY (December 16, 1773) and then guided the reaction to the Coercive Acts (1774), calling for a nonimportation movement. Outside Boston, the New England committees of correspondence began to respond, while committees of correspondence also started to appear elsewhere. As colonial Americans came to understand the full implications of the Coercive Acts, support for Boston grew. Committees organized the local militia as New England prepared for armed conflict. By the time hostilities broke out, the long organizational experience that had begun with the Sons of Liberty in 1765 and accelerated with committees of correspondence in the 1770s prepared men from a wide spectrum of society to assume the new responsibilities of self-government. During the REVOLUTIONARY WAR (1775–83) this experience would give the committeemen an edge over their LOYALIST opponents in gaining control over the local community.

See also RESISTANCE MOVEMENT.

Further reading: Richard D. Brown, *Revolutionary Politics in Massachusetts: The Boston Committee of Correspondence and the Towns, 1772–1774* (Cambridge, Mass.: Harvard University Press, 1970); Edward Countryman, *A People in Revolution: The American Revolution and Political Society in New York, 1760–1790* (Baltimore: Johns Hopkins University Press, 1981).

Common Sense (1776)

In January 1776 THOMAS PAINE published *Common Sense*, a radical pamphlet that urged Americans to declare independence from Great Britain. This work had a tremendous impact, selling over 100,000 copies within the year, and convinced many of the need to break free from King GEORGE III. Although hostilities had begun in April 1775— and even with George III asserting that the colonies were in a state of open rebellion in August 1775— Americans were unable to take the imaginative leap and sever their British ties. Paine's pamphlet paved the way for the DECLARATION OF INDEPENDENCE of July 4, 1776.

The pamphlet used plain diction, allusions to the Bible, and logic from the Enlightenment to present its argument. The language often relied on simple and direct assertions. For example, in his introduction Paine declared that "the cause of America is in great measure the cause of mankind" and thereby claimed a larger meaning for the conflict. He struck a similar note with brilliant imagery by arguing that "the sun never shined on a cause of greater

worth." Paine continued this line of thought with the statement, "Tis not the affair of a city, a country, a province, or a kingdom, but of a continent," further proclaiming that all posterity had a stake in its outcome. With phrases like these, Paine swept away opposition and pressed the idea that right then and there, in the winter of 1776, was the time to strike for independence and create the United States.

Paine understood that the Bible was the one book that most Americans were familiar with in the 18th century, and he used biblical references with skill and determination. Paine did not just attack King George III; he attacked the very idea of monarchy. He cited the Bible as proof of this position: "Monarchy is ranked in the scriptures as one of the sins about the Jews." Paine then went on to cite chapter and verse about how the Jewish insistence on having a king led to the downfall of ancient Israel, quoting long sections of Samuel to highlight God's displeasure with the idea of having a king. He then concluded in his straightforward prose: "These portions of scripture are direct and positive. They admit no equivocal construction. That the Almighty hath entered here his protest against monarchical government is true, or the scripture is false."

If Paine used RELIGION, he relied on the ideas of the Enlightenment even more. The influence of the Enlightenment, which centered on a belief in the relationship between nature and reason, can be seen in the repeated references to "natural principles." Paine also simplified Locke by putting complex ideas about the origin of government in prose that almost everyone could understand: "Society is produced by our wants, and government by our wickedness." Thus humans were seen as social individuals who must rely on government for some protection. Paine wrote that "society in every state is a blessing, but government is but a necessary evil; in its worse state an intolerable one." In short, "government, like dress, is the badge of lost innocence." From this perspective, "the palaces of kings are built on the ruins of the bowers of paradise."

Combining his forthright language, references to the Bible, and ideas from the Enlightenment, Paine leveled a devastating attack on the English Constitution, the king of England, and even hereditary aristocracy. Up until the publication of this pamphlet, most colonial Americans revered the English Constitution, believed that the king was ultimately good, and clung to notions of hierarchy. Thus *Common Sense* marked a radical break from the past. Paine had little respect for the balance of powers that supposedly lay at the core of the English Constitution. He posited that if the king could not be trusted and had to have his power balanced, then what good was a king in the first place? Moreover, the king held the greatest weight in the balance, tipping the scale in his favor

COMMON SENSE;

ADDRESSED TO THE

INHABITANTS

O F

A M E R I C A,

On the following interesting

S U B J E C T S.

I. Of the Origin and Design of Government in general, with concise Remarks on the English Constitution.

II. Of Monarchy and Hereditary Succession.

III. Thoughts on the present State of American Affairs.

IV. Of the present Ability of America, with some miscellaneous Reflections.

Man knows no Master save creating HEAVEN,
Or those whom choice and common good ordain.
THOMSON.

PHILADELPHIA;

Printed, and Sold, by R. BELL, in Third-Street.

MDCCLXXVI.

Front page of Thomas Paine's *Common Sense* (Library of Congress) through the use of patronage and pensions. The English had great faith in their supposed balanced constitution, but this confidence "arises as much or more from national pride as reason." From Paine's perspective, "the fate of Charles the First," who was executed in 1649 by the English people for abusing power, "hath made kings more subtle—not more just." Ultimately, it was the constitution of the people and not the constitution of the government that was the source of liberty.

Paine derided the monarchy. He wrote: "There is something exceedingly ridiculous in the composition of a monarchy." Paine argued that the king lived so removed from the people that it was impossible for him to truly know those he governed, yet he was daily expected to make decisions as if he understood what the world was like for common people. The origins of the king of England also could not bear close scrutiny. The kings of England claimed their descent from William the Conqueror. Paine wrote that this lineage was not "a very honorable one," since William was nothing more than "a French bastard landing with an armed banditti" who established himself king "against the consent of the natives." Such a claim to the throne "is in plain terms a very paltry rascally original—It certainly hath no divinity in it."

He continued this logic by attacking all hereditary succession, including an aristocracy. He believed that it was possible for a man to rise and show distinction in this world, and that it was just and right for him to be honored. But the fact that one person could stand out does not guarantee that his children and his children's children would also share the same qualities. By using hereditary succession, then, a society guaranteed that at some point power would fall into the hands of an incompetent, an imbecile, or someone even worse.

Ultimately, Paine's pamphlet argued not only for independence but also for a national republic. He called for a national single-house legislature with a weak executive chosen by the Congress. He also expressed tremendous confidence in the new nation's ability to wage a successful war against Great Britain and to create a government that would protect the rights of every citizen, including freedom of RELIGION, and thus meet the true objective of government. His would be an almost invisible republic, since he believed "that the more simple any thing is, the less liable it is to be disordered."

As compelling as these ideas appeared at the time, many American leaders opposed them. Men like JOHN ADAMS, who also advocated independence, thought that Paines radicalism went too far. Regardless of Adams's opinion, Paine's pamphlet had a tremendous impact and altered the course of history.

See also REPUBLICANISM.

Further reading: Eric Foner, *Tom Paine and Revolutionary American* (New York: Oxford University Press, 1976).

commonwealthmen

During the 18th century a group of thinkers and writers developed a critique of the British government, then dominated by the WHIG political party. This group, which historians call the commonwealthmen, saw themselves as the real or true Whigs, advocates of the tradition of limited government inherited from the English civil wars of the 1640s and the Glorious Revolution of 1688–89. While the commonwealthmen were only a minority in Great Britain and never wielded any political power, their writings had a profound influence in North America and were the source of many of the ideas held dear by the leaders of the RESISTANCE MOVEMENT (1764–75) to imperial regulation. The ideology of REPUBLICANISM grew out of the commonwealthman tradition.

Although they traced their roots to 17th-century thinkers like James Harrington, John Locke, and even Thomas Hobbes, the commonwealthmen emerged as an identifiable group shortly after the overthrow of James II in 1688. They wanted to push reform even further than set forth in the agreement between Parliament and William and Mary. They warned against the consolidation of power in the hands of the ministry, argued for full religious toleration, and wanted to reform Parliament to make it a truly representative body. A leading figure of this movement was Robert Molesworth, whose *Account of Denmark* (1694) outlined how a free state could fall into absolutism, especially through the combination of religious and political tyranny.

One of the most influential works for Americans was *Cato's Letters* (1723), by John Trenchard and Thomas Gordon, which offered a critique of the government of Sir Robert Walpole, the Whig Party, and the Bank of England. Trenchard and Gordon highlighted the inverse relationship between the power of government and the liberty of the people. From this perspective, "Whatever is good for the People, is bad for the Governors; and whatever is good for the Governors is pernicious to the People." They expressed tremendous faith in the will of the people: "It is certain that the whole People . . . are the best Judges whether things go ill or well with the Publick." The humblest individual could be trusted to understand the basic facts concerning liberty, since "every Cobbler can judge as well as Statesmen, whether he can sit peaceably in his Stall; whether he is paid for his Work; whether the Market, where he buys his Victuals, will be provided; and whether a Dragoon or a Parish Officer comes to him for his Taxes. . ." Therefore, it is up to the people to protect their liberty and, through the constitution—which in England was unwritten—ensure the limits on power. "Power is like Fire; it warms, scorches, or destroys, according as it is watched, provoked, or increased."

Commonwealthmen continued to express their ideals throughout the 18th century. They believed in a balanced English constitution and held that all Englishmen were entitled to be ruled by laws of their own choosing. Ultimately, they even extended this principle to all of mankind. As a corollary to this ideal, they argued for freedom of thought in RELIGION and in politics. They wanted to spread the benefit of education to include the poor as well as the middle classes. While commonwealthmen seldom pushed for a radical overhaul of the social structure, their ideas questioned privilege and encouraged equality. In the mid-18th century they took up the cause of Ireland, and much of the English support for colonial rights in the 1760s and 1770s could trace itself to commonwealth ideas. This last point is hardly surprising, since many revolutionary leaders had read extensively in the true Whig tradition and incorporated commonwealth ideas into their rationale for resisting imperial regulation.

Further reading: Bernard Bailyn, *The Ideological Origins of the American Revolution* (Cambridge, Mass.: Harvard University Press, 1967); Caroline Robbins, *The Eighteenth-Century Commonwealthman: Studies in the Transmission, Development and Circumstance of English Liberal Thought from the Restoration of Charles II until the War with the Thirteen Colonies* (Cambridge, Mass.: Harvard University Press, 1959).

Connecticut Wits

Sometimes referred to as the Hartford Wits, the Connecticut Wits were a group of writers who as young men expressed great enthusiasm for REPUBLICANISM and the AMERICAN REVOLUTION in the 1770s and early 1780s. Feeling betrayed by the democratic and egalitarian currents of the age, they generally became conservative by the late 1780s and identified with the FEDERALIST PARTY in the 1790s and early 1800s. Most notable of this group were TIMOTHY DWIGHT, John Trumbull (cousin of the painter JOHN TRUMBULL), David Humphreys, NOAH WEBSTER, and Lemuel Hopkins. JOEL BARLOW is also often counted as a Connecticut Wit in his early years, but he never underwent the conservative conversion and instead retained a commitment to revolution and the ideals of equality. Most of the Wits were from Connecticut and had attended Yale.

Even before the REVOLUTIONARY WAR (1775–83), the Wits expected great things of their culture. John Trumbull in 1771 wrote that "America hath a fair prospect in a few centuries of ruling both in art and arms." Hoping to be in the vanguard of this movement, the Wits became disillu-

sioned, especially in the wake of SHAYS'S REBELLION (1786–87). Several of the Wits had a hand in a long poem, "The Anarchiad," first published in the *New Haven Gazette* in 1786 and 1787, criticizing the rebellion. They accused the farmers of seeking luxury and corrupting the republic. The poem declared:

> Here shall my best and brightest empire rise.
> Wild riot reign, and discord greet the skies.
> Awake my chosen sons, in folly brave.
> Stab independence! Dance o'er Freedom's grave.

However betrayed they may have felt by overreaching farmers and "each leather-apron'd dunce," the Wits still had hope for United States. In his "Greenfield Hill" (1801), Timothy Dwight extolled the virtues of America—especially rural Connecticut—"where Freedom walks erect, . . . And mild Simplicity o'er manners reigns." In this vision the farmer becomes a repository of virtue, and

> The harmony of life more sweetly blend;
> Hence labour brightens every rural scene;
> Hence cheerful plenty lives along the green.

See also LITERATURE.

Further reading: Edwin H. Cady, ed., *Literature of the Early Republic*, 2nd ed. (New York: Holt, Rinehart and Winston, 1969); Henry F. May, *The Enlightenment in America* (New York: Oxford University Press, 1976); Robert E. Shalhope, *The Roots of Democracy: American Thought and Culture, 1760–1800* (Boston: Twayne, 1990).

Constitution, USS (1797–present)

The *Constitution* was one of six frigates authorized by Congress in 1794 to become the core of the young American navy and to meet threats from the BARBARY PIRATES and possibly the British and the French. Designed by Joshua Humphreys, these vessels were super frigates, larger than most vessels of that class and just as fast. Each was built in a different part of the United States. The *Constitution* was built in Boston and launched on October 21, 1797, just in time for the American conflict with France in the QUASI WAR (1798–1800). Although the *Constitution* cruised the waters of the Caribbean, protecting American commerce from 1798 to 1801, it was not involved in any sea battles. The frigate was laid up in Boston in 1802 during President THOMAS JEFFERSON's initial efforts to cut back on naval expenditures. However, in 1803 Jefferson sent the *Constitution* to the Mediterranean to take part in the campaign against the Barbary pirates in Tripoli (1801–05). As a part of that effort, the *Constitution* and other American vessels bombarded Tripoli. The final peace treaty with Tripoli was signed on the deck of the *Constitution* in June 1805.

The *Constitution* earned its reputation during the War of 1812 (1812–15). Soon after the war began, the men who served on the frigate demonstrated their fortitude—and the sailing qualities of their ship—when a squadron of five British ships pursued the *Constitution* for three days, starting on July 17, 1812. With all vessels becalmed, the crew of the *Constitution* towed their vessel in rowboats and then kedged—repeatedly towing an anchor away from the vessel, dropping the anchor, and pulling the vessel to the location of the anchor—it to avoid their pursuers. When a wisp of wind finally appeared, the speedy *Constitution* managed to escape. Over the next six months, the *Constitution* engaged in two battles of almost equal opponents and emerged victorious. On August 19, 1812, the *Constitution* met and defeated the HMS *Guerrière* about 600 miles east of Boston. In this short and brutal fight, the superior qualities of the *Constitution* came to the fore. Its thick wood oak sides seemed to repel the shots from the British vessel, and the crew dubbed her "Old Ironsides." The *Guerrière* was pulverized into surrender, losing 79 men to the *Constitution*'s 12. The British vessel was so badly damaged that it had to be scuttled. On December 29, 1812, the *Constitution* fought the HMS *Java* off the coast of Brazil. The battle lasted for over two hours, and both ships suffered damage. But by the time the *Java* surrendered, she was a wreck and had lost her captain and about 150 men. The Americans sustained 34 casualties. The *Java,* too, had to be scuttled. For most of the rest of the war, the *Constitution* remained blockaded in Boston. However, in December 1814 she managed to slip out of port. On February 20, 1815, unaware of the Treaty of Ghent (December 24, 1814), the *Constitution* ran across two smaller British warships, HMS *Cyane* and HMS *Levant.* She fought and captured both but only managed to return to the United States with the *Cyane,* the *Levant* having been recaptured by a British squadron.

After the War of 1812 "Old Ironsides" served for several decades as an American warship. After 1855 she was converted to a training ship and was later used as a barracks. Today, the *Constitution* can be visited at the navy yard in Boston, still part of the United States Navy and a proud representative of American national heritage.

Further reading: William M. Fowler, Jr., *Jack Tars and Commodores: The American Navy, 1783–1815* (Boston: Houghton Mifflin, 1984).

Constitutional Convention (1787)

The Constitutional Convention created the United States Constitution. It convened in Philadelphia in May 1787 with the purpose of revising the ARTICLES OF CONFEDERATION. Ultimately, the delegates acted beyond the scope of their original charge and created a greatly different form of government.

The convention was first suggested when the ANNAPOLIS CONVENTION of 1786 was unable to make much progress and the delegates called for a larger convention to be attended by all the states. Acting on the suggestion of the Annapolis Convention, Congress agreed that a new convention was necessary to review the Articles and then report the needed modifications to Congress and the state legislatures. However, the convention soon became much more than a simple discussion of revisions. In May delegates representing 12 states began assembling in Philadelphia (Rhode Island was never involved in the convention). Eventually, a total of 55 delegates, who were appointed by their state legislatures, would participate in the convention. There were usually only around 30–40 delegates in attendance on any given day. Most of the delegates had served in the CONTINENTAL CONGRESS or the CONTINENTAL ARMY, and many were officeholders in their respective states. The average age of the delegates was 42, but there were also some elder statesmen, such as BENJAMIN FRANKLIN, to lend dignity to the proceedings. GEORGE WASHINGTON was the unanimous choice for president of the convention, and his prestige increased the chances that the country would accept its outcome. A few of the other prominent active members were GOUVERNEUR MORRIS of Pennsylvania, RUFUS KING and ELBRIDGE GERRY of Massachusetts, and ALEXANDER HAMILTON from New York. Hamilton, in particular, was intent on promoting a nationalist vision. There were also a number of important statesmen who were absent, including JOHN ADAMS, who was in England; THOMAS JEFFERSON, who was serving as minister to France; and PATRICK HENRY, who had declined to participate, as he was a strong proponent of the sovereignty of the states and was suspicious about the intent of the proceedings. However, although these two well-known Virginians did not attend, Virginia sent JAMES MADISON, who would eventually be known as the "Father of the Constitution." The meticulous notes Madison kept were one of his most important contributions, as they remain our main source for the daily proceedings of the convention.

Much of the work and compromise took place during informal gatherings, of which we have little record. The meetings were held in INDEPENDENCE HALL in complete secrecy, although this had been a point of spirited debate. Each state was given one vote. The delegates realized that they needed to settle the problem of local state control as opposed to a centralized national government. They believed that the powers of the national government should be clearly stated and that functions not specifically given to the national government would be left for the states.

They also generally recognized that in order to operate efficiently, the central government had to have powers, especially to coin money and to deal with FOREIGN AFFAIRS.

The first issue of debate was the Virginia Plan, introduced on May 29 by EDMUND RANDOLPH. The Virginia Plan was Madison's idea for a new national government. Madison had worked hard to prepare for the convention, studying political theory and natural law. Ultimately, the Virginia Plan would provide the foundation of the new constitution, and the national government it proposed would be powerful. It provided for a bicameral legislature, with the lower house elected by the people and the upper house elected by the lower house. There was also to be a national judiciary and a national executive (a president named by Congress), with a committee formed from these two groups that would have a veto on national legislation. Although the national government would guarantee a republican form of government for each state, it would also take power away from the states by having an independent source of revenue, control over printing money, and guaranteeing contracts. Many nationalists believed that the state legislatures had become centers for radical democracy and that the turbulent common folk, such as those who participated in SHAYS'S REBELLION (1786–87), needed to be controlled.

The committee-of-the-whole reported the Virginia Plan to the convention, but it made a few changes, giving the election of the upper house of Congress to the state legislatures. It also gave the executive alone veto power and allowed for ratification of the new Constitution by state conventions. However, there were still those who feared a strong central government and wanted to preserve the power of the states. These delegates devised an alternative plan called the Paterson or New Jersey Plan. Support for the two competing plans was divided among large and small states. The smaller states objected to the Virginia Plan's proportional representation based on population; they favored equal representation of the states. The Paterson Plan intended to keep the Articles of Confederation but would give Congress the powers to regulate commerce and to tax. There were also more extreme proposals, such as Alexander Hamilton's, which called for a president who would be elected for life. The delegates debated for three days and finally adopted the essential outlines of the Virginia Plan.

The concerns brought up by the smaller states would not disappear, and other issues added to the difficulty of the convention's tasks. There was often sharp disagreement and conflict during the next four months. How could they create a government that was strong enough to be effective but would also preserve liberty? On July 16, 1787, the so-called Great Compromise was adopted, which gave representation based on population in the lower house with the exclusive power to originate money bills. Representation in the upper house, or Senate, would be equal for each state. To satisfy the concerns of the southern delegates, the convention agreed to count three-fifths of the slave population for representation in the lower house. Another important provision was that laws and treaties of the national government would now be the supreme law of the land and take precedence over state laws. The new Constitution followed the form of previous colonial and state governments.

Only 41 of the 55 original delegates were still present when the document was finished on September 17, 1787, and three of these refused to sign. The Constitution was then sent to the states for ratification, under the provisions the convention had created. Special ratifying conventions, rather than the state legislatures, were called, and only nine states had to approve the document before it would take effect. Other states could then approve it and join the union when they were ready. While ANTI-FEDERALISTS objected to the Constitution because it appeared to give the national government too much power while limiting the participation of the people, the FEDERALISTS supported the document, arguing that it rested on the sovereignty of the people and represented a republican form of government.

See also REPUBLICANISM.

Further reading: Catherine Drinker Bowen, *Miracle at Philadelphia: The Story of the Constitutional Convention, May to September, 1787* (Boston: Little, Brown, 1966); Paul Finkelman, *Slavery and the Founders: Race and Liberty in the Age of Jefferson* (Armonk, N.Y.: M.E. Sharpe, 1996); Gordon S. Wood, *The Creation of the American Republic, 1776–1787* (Chapel Hill: University of North Carolina Press, 1969).

— Crystal Williams

constitutions, state

American revolutionary leaders in 1776 were excited about the opportunity to create a government from, in John Locke's phrase, a *tabula rasa* (clean slate) JOHN ADAMS wrote, "how few of the human race have ever enjoyed an opportunity of making an election of government . . . for themselves and for their children." John Jay agreed, declaring that Americans were "the first people whom heaven has favoured with an opportunity of deliberating upon, and choosing the forms of government under which they should live." The government that so occupied the revolutionary leaders was not the ARTICLES OF CONFEDERATION and certainly not the Constitution of the United States that would be written over a decade later. Instead, these men abandoned the CONTINENTAL CONGRESS in order to write

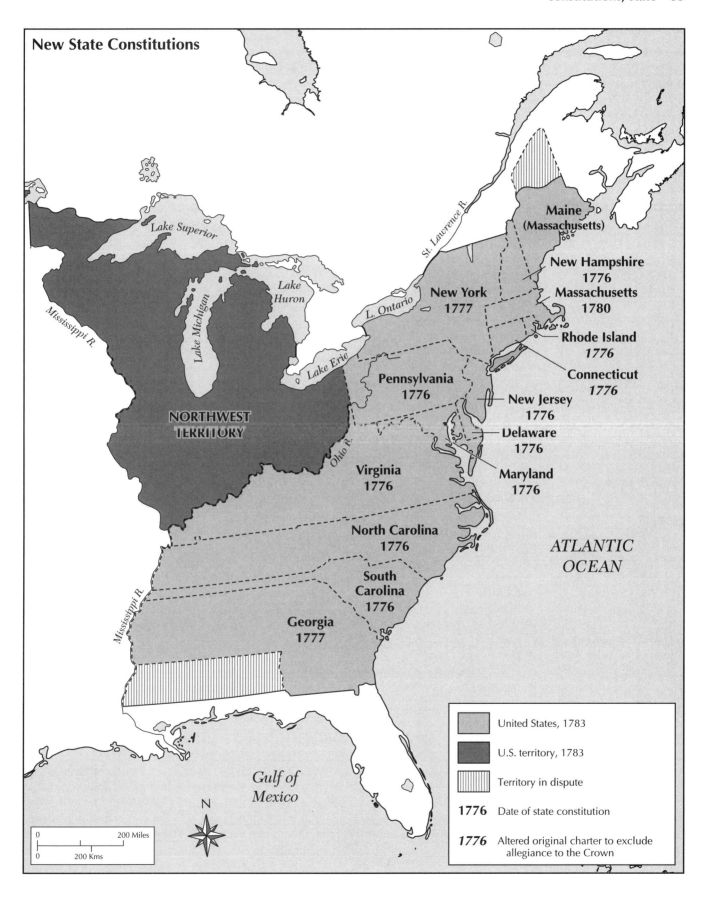

New State Constitutions

Lake Superior

Lake Michigan

Lake Huron

Mississippi R.

NORTHWEST TERRITORY

Ohio R.

Lake Erie

L. Ontario

St. Lawrence R.

Maine
(Massachusetts)

New York
1777

New Hampshire
1776

Massachusetts
1780

Rhode Island
1776

Connecticut
1776

Pennsylvania
1776

New Jersey
1776

Delaware
1776

Maryland
1776

Virginia
1776

North Carolina
1776

South
Carolina
1776

Georgia
1777

Mississippi R.

ATLANTIC
OCEAN

*Gulf of
Mexico*

N

	United States, 1783
	U.S. territory, 1783
	Territory in dispute
1776	Date of state constitution
1776	Altered original charter to exclude allegiance to the Crown

0   200 Miles

0   200 Kms

the original state constitutions. In the process, they experimented with a variety of forms of government in an effort to find the best balance and the safest means to guarantee a republic. While each state created its own government, we can divide the constitutions into two types: the extremely democratic frame of government, best represented by the constitution of the state of Pennsylvania, and the more conservative balanced constitution, such as that written in the State of Massachusetts.

Pennsylvanians wrote their state constitution at the height of revolutionary fervor in 1776. Believing that the king had sought to destroy the liberty of the people, Pennsylvania's radical revolutionaries created a government with a weakened executive. In fact, there was no single individual left to govern the state, only an executive council to carry out the directives of the popular assembly. Similarly, Pennsylvanians did not see any need for two houses of legislature. They were the only colony that had a single legislative body, since the idea of an upper house was still attached to the belief that, like the House of Lords, it represented the aristocracy. Such distinctions were of no use to the Pennsylvania radicals. The one-house legislature was always to have open-door sessions, allowing the people to see their representatives in action. All laws were to be published and placed in prominent locations for the people to read and discuss. There was a broad franchise including almost all adult male taxpayers, annual elections, and no law became permanent unless passed by two successive sessions. Judges were elected, and there was a guarantee of rotation of office. The constitution also created a Council of Censors that was to meet every seven years and review all legislation. For many more-conservative revolutionaries, this document created an unworkable form of government. The result was that Pennsylvanians abandoned their 1776 document in 1790 for a more conservative one.

The Massachusetts constitution of 1780 may well have been a model that the Pennsylvanians relied upon in 1790. Much of this document flowed from the pen of John Adams. It included a strong executive, who could make appointments and veto laws. The governor could be given so much power because, unlike the king, who had no direct connection to the people, the governor was a representative of the people and depended upon them for his election. The constitution also included two houses of legislature. There were high property qualifications to be a candidate for governor. Likewise, the property qualifications for the upper house, as a means of distinction, were higher than for the lower house. Massachusetts was also innovative in using a convention to write the constitution. Before 1780 states had relied upon their assemblies or revolutionary governing bodies to draw up their fundamental laws, but some critics began to argue that a legislature that could write a constitution could also change it at will. There

needed to be some extraordinary representation of the people that convened only to write fundamental law. Revisions would depend on a similar body that could be called into being under special circumstances. This special body was a constitutional convention.

Massachusetts, Virginia, and several other colonies all included a bill of rights as a guarantee of certain inalienable rights that each member of society retained regardless of the power of government. Having lived through a crisis that arose from a usurpation of rights, these states wanted to make sure that the liberty of the people would be protected from the power of government.

The writing of state constitutions entailed an important period of political experimentation that had as its legacy the creation of the United States Constitution at the Philadelphia Convention in 1787.

See also BILL OF RIGHTS; CONSTITUTIONAL CONVENTION; REPUBLICANISM.

Further reading: Gordon S. Wood, *The Creation of the American Republic, 1776–1787* (Chapel Hill: University of North Carolina Press, 1969).

Continental army

After the bloodshed at LEXINGTON AND CONCORD (April 19, 1775) and the formation of a New England army, the CONTINENTAL CONGRESS in Philadelphia began planning for a national force to assist with the deepening hostilities between England and her colonies. Because the New England defenders viewed their military struggle as one ultimately involving the protection of all the colonies against English aggression, they asked Congress to adopt the troops in Boston. This action would remove the impression that the conflict was merely a regional one and thus broaden the base for military support. Reports that Americans had captured FORT TICONDEROGA (May 10, 1775) in New York, which strengthened opinions that the British were planning to launch an attack from CANADA, and rumors that redcoats were moving toward New York City helped spur Congress to decisive action.

On June 14, 1775, Congress not only took financial responsibility for the existing New England troops and those requested to defend certain key positions in New York, but it adopted a Continental army as well. Creation of 10 companies of expert riflemen was authorized—though within a month this had swelled to 13—an enlistment form approved, and a committee organized to draw up regulations for governing the army. The riflemen were the first Continental troops raised, with six companies from Pennsylvania and two each from Maryland and Virginia. Each was allotted one captain, three lieutenants, four sergeants, four corporals, one drummer or horn player, and 68 privates. The term of enlistment was for one year. Delegates from the respective colonies turned over recruitment responsibilities to county committees, with commanders of the new units generally drawn from the local gentry.

On June 15, 1775, Congress unanimously named GEORGE WASHINGTON commander in chief of all the forces raised in America's defense. Thereafter, Congress authorized various staff positions to assist Washington with the administration of the army. Since some of the conflict with Great Britain centered on the presence of regular British forces in the colonies, Congress and Washington had to be careful in their use of the Continental troops so as not to undermine belief in the adequacy of the local militia or cre-

ate anxiety over an American standing army. To ease those fears, Congress carefully stressed the defensive nature of its actions, and the relatively small numbers of Continental troops to be raised and the short terms of enlistment were meant to bolster that position.

As the conflict widened and more companies were authorized, the army became a truly national institution. As militia units were increasingly called upon to reinforce the Continental troops, however, it became evident that they could not meet the British regulars on equal terms. Washington pressed Congress to lengthen enlistments so that he could retain experienced men, and in the autumn of 1776, Congress agreed to three-year terms and allowed

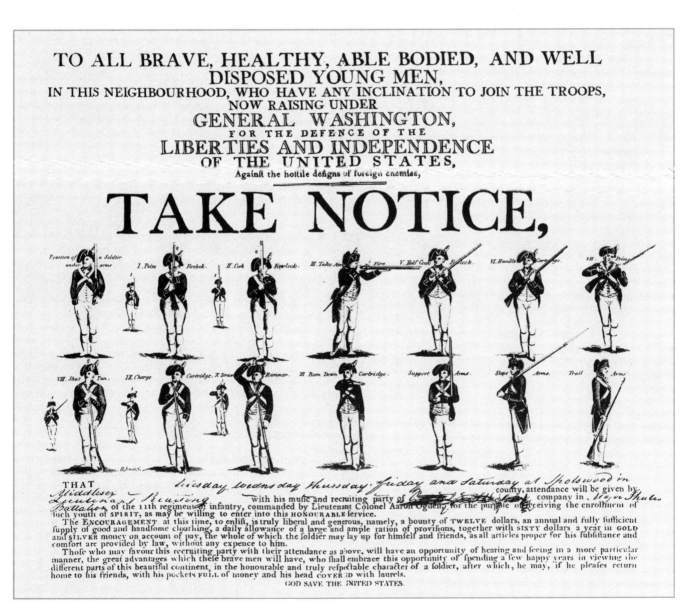

Recruiting poster for the Continental army *(Dover Publications)*

cash bonuses and postwar land grants as enticements. With longer enlistments and larger recruitment incentives, more men from the margins of society entered the Continental army. By the end of the war, the typical soldier was not an embattled farmer who owned property, because such men had too much to lose from long enlistments; instead, the typical soldier was a poor, often young man, who owned little or no property.

Military defeats were prevalent for the Continental army during 1777, often due to lack of resources and poor judgment within the officer corps. The arrival of Baron FREDERICK VON STEUBEN and his Prussian military expertise at the VALLEY FORGE encampment in the winter of 1777–78, however, brought discipline and inspiration to American forces. The drills and regulations von Steuben initiated gave uniformity to battlefield maneuvers, and their newfound precision instilled confidence in the men. The Continental army that marched out of winter quarters in June 1778 continued to have problems with pay and supplies, but it also had a revitalized spirit with which to engage the enemy. Washington's army persevered through all adversity until a decisive victory at YORKTOWN (October 19, 1781) signaled and end to the war. But the final peace in 1783 rekindled concerns over an American standing army. Not until June 1784 did Congress create a peacetime military establishment that was acceptable to all political factions, a small regular army led by Continental veterans and organized by von Steuben's regulations and drill manual.

Further reading: E. Wayne Carp, *To Starve the Army at Pleasure: Continental Army Administration and American Political Culture, 1775–1783* (Chapel Hill: University of North Carolina Press, 1984); Charles Royster, *The Revolutionary People at War: The Continental Army and the American Character, 1775–1783* (Chapel Hill: University of North Carolina Press, 1979); Robert K. Wright Jr., *The Continental Army* (Washington, D.C.: Center of Military History, U.S. Army, 1983).

— Rita M. Broyles

Continental army, mutinies of

There were four major mutinies in the CONTINENTAL ARMY during the REVOLUTIONARY WAR (1775–83). The men who joined these mutinies had serious grievances: They were poorly supplied and owed back pay. On December 25, 1779, two regiments in the Connecticut line assembled on the parade ground at MORRISTOWN, refused to obey their officers, and threatened more violent action. Officers called upon a veteran Pennsylvania brigade to arrest the ringleaders and force the rest of the men back to duty.

A year later, two other mutinies occurred. The men from the Pennsylvania line rebelled at Morristown on December 31, 1780. They had been unpaid for almost a year, and many of them were poorly clothed and fed. They also complained that their enlistments had run out and that new recruits were paid large bounties. Perhaps stimulated by additional rum to celebrate New Year's Day, they decided to take matters into their own hands. Officers who attempted to restrain them were roughly handled. The next day, under the command of a committee of sergeants, the Pennsylvania line marched with baggage and artillery toward Philadelphia. The mutineers got as far as Trenton before they were intercepted by loyal troops from New England. Authorities then negotiated with the Pennsylvanians, allowing those who claimed their three-year enlistment was up to go home and promising pay and supplies for the remainder. In the meantime the New Jersey line decided to revolt at Ringwood, New Jersey, on January 20. This time there was to be no compromising. General GEORGE WASHINGTON declared that "unless this dangerous spirit can be suppressed by force there is an end to all subordination in the Army, and indeed to the Army itself." New England soldiers were ordered to surround the New Jersey men, who were then mustered without their arms. Twelve men were selected as a firing squad and were compelled to shoot two of their leaders. This action quelled further mutiny.

The final mutiny took place in June 1783, just as the army was about to be demobilized. Some recruits from Lancaster, Pennsylvania, marched on Philadelphia. In the capital they were joined by other soldiers who wanted their pay. The disgruntled troops surrounded Congress and briefly held them hostage, but no serious harm was threatened and the representatives left the building unmolested. Before loyal soldiers could arrive, the mutinous crowd dispersed. Angered by this affront to its dignity, Congress left Philadelphia and reconvened at Princeton.

See also INDEPENDENCE HALL.

Further reading: E. Wayne Carp, *To Starve the Army at Pleasure: Continental Army Administration and American Political Culture, 1775–1783* (Chapel Hill: University of North Carolina Press, 1984); Lawrence Delbert Cress, *Citizens in Arms: The Army and Militia in American Society to the War of 1812* (Chapel Hill: University of North Carolina Press, 1982); Charles Royster, *The Revolutionary People at War: The Continental Army and the American Character, 1775–1783* (Chapel Hill: University of North Carolina Press, 1979).

Continental Congress, First (1774)

The First Continental Congress met in Philadelphia from September 5 to October 26, 1774. It passed three important resolutions: endorsing the SUFFOLK RESOLVES (1774), approving an economic boycott against Britain, and adopting a petition to the king detailing the colonies' rights and grievances. As an extralegal body, Congress depended upon obtaining and maintaining the support of colonial assemblies and the public. Thus delegates placed a premium on cooperation and compromise among the colonies, which were crucial for its success. Congress set the tone for future resistance to British rule and for the practice of politics in America.

Massachusetts called this meeting to formulate a response to the COERCIVE ACTS (1774) then being imposed upon the colony. Massachusetts's WHIG leaders sought advice and direction from the other colonies about how far they should go in resisting the Massachusetts Government Act, the Boston Port Act, and the new royal governor, THOMAS GAGE. Of the original 13 colonies, only Georgia did not send a delegation to Philadelphia.

Among the 56 delegates were men destined to lead the revolution and the new nation. Cousins JOHN ADAMS and SAMUEL ADAMS represented Massachusetts, and ROGER SHERMAN served for Connecticut. Virginia sent RICHARD HENRY LEE and GEORGE WASHINGTON. Future chief justice of the SUPREME COURT JOHN JAY represented New York, and JOHN DICKINSON and JOSEPH GALLOWAY of Pennsylvania attended. Not all delegates favored radical solutions. Men like Galloway searched for a moderate resolution to the crisis. Radical delegates did not dominate the proceedings, but this Congress succeeded because delegates were able forge a consensus that would help sustain unity among the colonies.

In its first public act on September 17, Congress unanimously endorsed the Suffolk Resolves. These resolutions declared the Coercive Acts unconstitutional and recommended economic sanctions against Great Britain as the best course of resistance. Thus Congress accepted resistance but strove to avoid direct confrontation with the British troops stationed in Massachusetts. It indicated its support for Massachusetts and issued a warning to Great Britain that other colonies supported Massachusetts's actions. In addition, Congress provided direction for Massachusetts's resistance. Yet, by only approving defensive measures and rejecting proposals for more forceful action, Congress cautioned Massachusetts that not every deed would meet with unanimous approval. For the time being, resistance would remain within guidelines proposed by the Suffolk Resolves. This first resolution established two important precedents: First, by accepting congressional direction, Massachusetts allowed Congress to assert similar authority over all colonies. Second, by seeking unanimity, delegates made consensus more important than radical resistance.

Congress's second accomplishment was to approve an economic boycott of Great Britain, Ireland, and the WEST INDIES. On September 22, Congress unanimously passed a resolution requesting the suspension of imports from

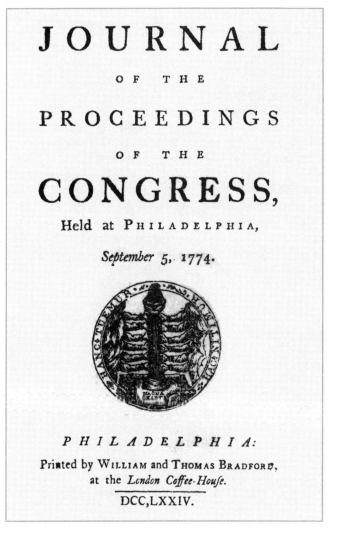

Title of a pamphlet summarizing the proceedings of the First Continental Congress *(Library of Congress)*

Great Britain until the sense of Congress was known. Just five days later, on September 27, delegates unanimously agreed to a resolution to stop importation of British and Irish goods after December 1. They further resolved to stop exports to Britain, Ireland, and the West Indies after September 10, 1775. Thus Congress endorsed the resumption of commercial resistance first tried during the STAMP ACT (1765) crisis. No one seriously questioned this path except Galloway. For the most part, the key issue was more a question of the scope of the boycott than whether to impose one at all. For example, Virginia delegates had been instructed to approve a boycott, but not one beginning before August 1775, and South Carolina wanted its staple crops—rice and indigo—exempted. Finally, on October 20, Congress formed the Continental ASSOCIATION to execute the "non-importation, non-consumption, and non-exportation agreement," Congress instructed that new local committees of safety be elected to oversee implementation and enforcement. It sanctioned extralegal committees and sought to direct and regulate their activities while allowing for local initiative and flexibility to fit each community's needs.

Third, Congress debated and approved a declaration of rights and grievances. During these debates, delegates considered the colonies' position within the British Empire and the proper interpretation of the unwritten British constitution. Galloway, who would become a LOYALIST, proposed a new imperial constitution. His plan of union would have created an intercolonial legislature responsible for "regulating and administering all the general police and affairs of the colonies" and during war to grant "aid to the crown." While the British Parliament would still have the power to enact laws for the colonies, all laws would have to be approved by both Parliament and the intercolonial assembly. Galloway's plan represented the most conciliatory proposal considered by Congress. Delegates effectively rejected it on September 28 on a procedural motion. New York delegates James Duane and John Jay proved more effective advocates of a moderate approach to the crisis than Galloway. Duane and Jay had the support of moderates from the middle colonies of New York, Pennsylvania, and Maryland.

Eight of the 10 resolutions considered for the declaration of rights passed unanimously, but not without debate. The debate focused on whether the colonies should base their grievances upon the law of nature or the British constitution. Delegates favored the latter over the former justification. The other main issue was how much authority and power colonies should concede to Parliament. The delegates rejected the resolution that defiantly asserted that colonial assemblies had the exclusive power of legislation in cases of taxation and internal policy, subject only to approval by the Crown. More conciliatory and ambiguous language replaced it. Congress agreed that colonial assemblies should assent to bona fide acts of Parliament concerning the regulation of external commerce for the general good of the British Empire. Taxation for the purpose of raising revenue was only acceptable if the colonial assemblies consented. The declaration of rights broke no new ground and was consistent with the constitutional arguments that had been made in the colonies for the past decade. In one conciliatory act, Congress decided against including complaints about parliamentary acts before 1763 among its grievances.

The First Continental Congress's actions further exacerbated rather than ameliorated relations between Great Britain and its colonies. It endorsed the autonomy of colonial legislatures and a very limited legislative role for Parliament over the colonies. It firmly accepted the proposition that conciliation had to be initiated by Britain.

Most importantly, Congress made future intercolonial cooperation and unified resistance possible.

Further reading: Merrill Jensen, *The Articles of Confederation; An Interpretation of the Social-Constitutional History of the American Revolution, 1774–1781* (Madison, Wis.: University of Wisconsin Press, 1948); Jack N. Rakove, *The Beginnings of National Politics: An Interpretative History of the Continental* Congress (New York: Knopf, 1979).

— Terri Halperin

Continental Congress, Second (Confederation Congress) (1775–1789)

The Second Continental Congress, or the Confederation Congress, convened May 10, 1775, and except for a few recesses met until the federal Constitution took effect in 1789. This body issued the DECLARATION OF INDEPENDENCE (1776), prosecuted the REVOLUTIONARY WAR (1775–83), and governed the new nation.

There was significant continuity between the First and Second Continental Congresses. Fifty of the 65 delegates who attended the initial session of the Second Continental Congress had served in the FIRST CONTINENTAL CONGRESS (1774). When the meeting was called, it seemed that this Congress would face many of the same issues as the First, but by the time delegates arrived in Philadelphia circumstances had changed significantly. Congress convened three weeks after the BATTLES OF LEXINGTON AND CONCORD (April 19, 1775) and only a little more than a month before BUNKER HILL (June 17, 1775).

While Congress continued to give advice and direction to the colonies, particularly Massachusetts, about the course of resistance, it began to transform itself from a purely deliberative body into one that assumed executive responsibilities as well. In mid-June, Congress created the CONTINENTAL ARMY and appointed GEORGE WASHINGTON as commanding general. Thus, it established the first national institution, an entity for which it would be responsible for supplying, financing, and regulating. To begin to fulfill those obligations, Congress issued its first bills of credit to finance the expanding war that same month.

Although many great men served in Congress, Congress was plagued by poor attendance even as early as December 1775. During the course of its existence, Virginia elected George Washington, PATRICK HENRY, Edmund Pendleton, Peyton Randolph, THOMAS JEFFERSON, and JAMES MADISON to the body. Massachusetts sent JOHN ADAMS and SAMUEL ADAMS, and JOHN HANCOCK and BENJAMIN FRANKLIN represented Pennsylvania. Concerns about political events at home, and their own livelihoods and families, however, made many delegates reluctant to spend months in Philadelphia or wherever Congress was meeting. Despite a rule adopted in November 1775 that no member could be absent without congressional permission, and several entreaties from Congress to the states to maintain their representation, absenteeism plagued the institution. The problem became particularly acute in the 1780s after the adoption of the ARTICLES OF CONFEDERATION. The Articles stipulated that two delegates be present for a state to be able to record its vote. Consequently, because the Articles also required nine states to agree on many issues, Congress often found it difficult to conduct business. Expertise, continuity, and stability were hard to achieve.

The exigencies of war created the necessary unity among the states and allowed delegates to delay addressing particularly prickly issues, be they substantive or organizational. Like the First Continental Congress, delegates voted by state and not individually. The president of Congress fulfilled many ceremonial and administrative duties, but he could not act without being directed to do so by Congress. Thus leadership was collective and variable rather than individual and institutionalized. Between 1774 and 1781, Congress experimented with several administrative arrangements to try to overcome the problems of a large workload and rampant absenteeism. At first, members relied on ad hoc committees, each created to tackle a crisis or issue as it was raised. Relatively soon thereafter, Congress decided permanent standing committees would better serve its purposes. Thus the Secret Committee imported munitions and procured supplies for the army. The Committee on Secret Correspondence conducted all diplomatic communications. The Marine Committee and Board of War oversaw naval operations and the conduct of the war, respectively. Two committees—on the treasury and accounts—managed finances. Committees would propose solutions that would be accepted or rejected by the whole Congress. Committees could not make decisions without such approval. Congress relied upon provincial officials, military personnel, or its own delegates to implement any resolutions adopted. Thus New Jersey delegates were charged with transporting gunpowder to Dobbs Ferry, New York, and JAMES WILSON of Pennsylvania was instructed to report on how much "Duck, Russian sheeting [etc.] . . . could be procured . . ." in Philadelphia. Many delegates felt overburdened by the workload and Congress's inefficiency.

This growing frustration culminated in December 1776 when ROBERT MORRIS of Pennsylvania complained that Congress should be relieved of the more mundane tasks and take advantage of outsiders' knowledge. The outcome was the creation of Executive Boards composed of delegates and nondelegates. Delegates would retain the ultimate control and authority, while the nondelegates could provide the necessary expertise. From the fall of 1777 through late 1779, Congress created four boards: Board of War, Board of Admiralty, Board of Treasury, and Committee of Foreign Affairs. Ultimately, Congress never fully trusted these quasi-independent organizations. Indeed, Congress could not resolve certain critical issues, particularly how much authority to delegate to the boards. The line between policymaking and simple execution of congressional directives was difficult to delineate, and Congress never found a comfortable position vis-a-vis the boards.

In late 1780 Congress abandoned the board system and began to establish civil executive departments with one administrator in command who was accountable and elected by Congress. Congress created four departments: war, marine affairs, treasury, and foreign affairs. Morris served as the superintendent of finance. Although these departments relieved delegates of the day-to-day operations, they did not significantly reduce their workload, as Congress insisted on retaining ultimate control.

Organizational issues were not the only ones that vexed this Congress during its 15-year existence. With victory assured at YORKTOWN (October 19, 1781) and the TREATY OF PARIS (1783), the underlying reason for unity among the states disappeared. Congress was ill-equipped to resolve some difficult issues, especially regarding repaying Revolutionary War debts, securing an independent source of revenue, regulating western lands, resolving disputes between states, and finding a permanent national capital. Despite debilitating problems, Congress did provide national leadership during the War of Independence and created the first national government. Perhaps its most singular achievement after the war was the passage of the NORTHWEST ORDINANCE in 1787.

The Confederation Congress participated in its own demise. Its delegates approved the CONSTITUTIONAL CONVENTION in Philadelphia in 1787 to revise the ARTICLES OF CONFEDERATION. Although Congress did not positively endorse the resulting Constitution, which abandoned the Articles, it did send the Constitution to the states for ratification. Congress continued to meet until the First Federal Congress convened in 1789.

Further reading: Calvin Jillson and Rick K. Wilson, *Congressional Dynamics: Structure, Coordination, and Choice in the First American Congress, 1774–1789* (Stanford, Calif.: Stanford University Press, 1994); Peter Onuf, *The Origins of the Federal Republic: Jurisdictional Controversies in the United States, 1775–1787* (Philadelphia: University of Pennsylvania Press, 1983); Jack N. Rakove, *The Beginnings of National Politics: An Interpretative History of the Continental Congress* (New York: Knopf, 1979).

— Terri Halperin

Continental navy

On October 13, 1775, the SECOND CONTINENTAL CONGRESS authorized a Continental navy. Previously, individual states had formed their own navies, scores of PRIVATEERS had been commissioned, and GEORGE WASHINGTON had even chartered a handful of vessels to attack the British off the coast of Boston. Now the national government stepped in and started to purchase some vessels. The Continental Congress also ordered the construction of 13 frigates. The Continental navy would experience a few spectacular successes but would often be mired in controversy and ultimately was no match for the British navy.

The first major naval action was typical of the experience of the Continental navy. A small fleet of ships was ordered to clear the Chesapeake of British and LOYALIST vessels. Esek Hopkins, the fleet's commodore, put to sea in February 1776. Instead of following orders, he launched a raid against Nassau in the Bahamas. Fortunately, he managed to capture the island and large quantities of supplies. He then sailed north, where his fleet was mauled by one British vessel of 20 guns off the coast of Rhode Island. Although the expedition to Nassau was a success, Hopkins had disobeyed his instructions and was embarrassed by the British warship. He was subsequently tried and acquitted at a court-martial.

Over the next two years there were several successful single-ship cruises. JOHN PAUL JONES cruised along the Nova Scotia coast in the fall of 1776, capturing seven prizes. In 1777 two captains, Lambert Wickes and Gustavus Conyngham, had solo cruises off the coast of Great Britain, wrecking havoc on British shipping and capturing scores of prizes. In the spring of 1778, Jones, now in Europe, took the *Ranger* into British waters, where he captured a British warship and four prizes while raiding the British coast at Whitehaven and Kirkcudbright. These three cruises led to near panic among British merchants and a dramatic increase in insurance rates.

Elsewhere, the news was not so good for the Continental navy. One vessel after another either had to be scuttled, burned, or was captured by the British. Most of the 13 frigates disappeared almost as quickly as they were launched. Often, the vessels were bottled up and destroyed by American forces in the face of invading British, as occurred with the frigates *Montgomery* and *Congress* in the Hudson River in October 1777 and the frigates *Effingham* and *Washington* in the Delaware River in 1778. During the siege of CHARLESTON (captured May 12, 1780) several other vessels were lost. One of the greatest naval disasters occurred in the spring of 1779 in the Penobscott expedition. After the British occupied Penobscot Bay in the District of Maine (then part of Massachusetts), the Americans sent a flotilla of three warships, 16 privateers, and 20 troop ships to drive the British out. Although initially the Americans had the advantage of numbers, they delayed their attack. By the time they were ready to move on August 13, 1779, British reinforcements had arrived. On seeing a British ship of the line, three frigates, and three sloops, the Americans scattered. Fourteen vessels were blown up or burned, including the American frigate *Warren,* and many other ships were captured by the British.

There were some successes to counterbalance these disasters. Jones's famous battle with the *Serapis* added to his reputation, although he failed to capture any of the merchantmen in the convoy that the *Serapis* was guarding. The *Alliance* fought a ferocious battle with a British warship in March 1783, pounding it to pieces while unaware that preliminary articles of peace had been agreed upon. By that time the Continental navy consisted of only two vessels. One of these, the *Hague,* was decommissioned in late 1783. The *Alliance* was sold as a merchantman in 1785, thus ending the Continental navy.

An American navy was revived in 1794, when the federal government began a building program to meet the threat of Algiers and the BARBARY PIRATES. Although some of the building program was scaled back after a treaty with Algiers in 1795, the navy was not entirely abandoned. Just as the United States entered the QUASI WAR (1798–1800) with France, several new super frigates were coming off the blocks. These vessels would become the centerpiece of the American navy in the conflict with France, the Barbary Wars of the early 1800s, and the War of 1812 (1812–15).

Further reading: Jack Coggins, *Ships and Seamen of the American Revolution: Vessels, Crews, Weapons, Gear, Naval Tactics, and Actions of the War for Independence* (Harrisburg, Pa.: Stackpole Books, 1969).

Conway Cabal

An ill-defined political and military intrigue that peaked and fizzled in the fall and winter of 1777–78, the Conway Cabal aimed at removing GEORGE WASHINGTON as commander in chief of the CONTINENTAL ARMY and replacing him with HORATIO GATES. The so-called conspiracy is named for the group's most tenacious and vocal member, Thomas Conway. The movement drew support from two sources: In Congress, detractors such as JOHN ADAMS and SAMUEL ADAMS, who were especially distrustful of a standing army, feared Washington might use his popularity with the people to become a military dictator. Within the army itself, a few of Washington's officers, among them Generals Conway and Gates, who had trained and served as professional soldiers in foreign armies, viewed their native-born commander as an incompetent amateur. And after the crucial victory at SARATOGA (October 17, 1777) under the command of Gates, the conspirators felt they had a suitable replacement.

Washington was soon aware of the maneuvering against him. In the afterglow of his victory at Saratoga, Gates became increasingly insubordinate, bypassing Washington and making his reports directly to Congress. Conway, a boastful self-enthusiast who lacked Washington's support for promotion, began badgering Congress for advancement and denigrating his commander's military leadership. Congress responded by aligning both Conway and Gates against Washington. Conway was promoted to inspector general, a position independent of the commander in chief and answerable to Gates as chairman of the Board of War. Infuriated, Washington treated Conway coldly but with the proper respect. Conway was nevertheless incensed, and his letters to Washington thereafter were insolent and duplicitous.

The crumbling of the cabal was already underway, however. Through indiscrete gossip and revelations from private correspondence, Washington had learned of a letter Conway had written to Gates disparaging the abilities of Washington and his aides. When he confronted Conway with the report, Conway tried to explain his meaning, but his condescending attitude only made matters worse. Gates, though merely the recipient of the damning communiqué, mired himself in the mess by foolishly accusing one of Washington's trusted aides of secretly copying the letter. His reputation was then further damaged when reports began filtering in from participants at Saratoga that BENEDICT ARNOLD, and not Gates, had been largely responsible for the victory. As exposure of the intrigue grew, most of the plotters shrank from sight, but Conway continued his attacks until a supporter of Washington shot Conway through the mouth in a duel. Only the thought of impending death prompted Conway to apologize for his disparaging remarks.

Further reading: Robert Leckie, *George Washington's War: The Saga of the American Revolution* (New York: HarperCollins, 1992); Page Smith, *A New Age Now Begins: A People's History of the American Revolution*, vol. 2. (New York: Penguin Books, 1989).

— Rita M. Broyles

Copley, John Singleton (1738–1815)
John Singleton Copley was one of America's most noted portrait artists, but he left the country of his birth in 1774, never to return. Copley was born in Boston and probably gained his artistic training from his stepfather Peter Pelham. By the 1760s he had become a well-known portrait painter in Boston and supported himself with an ample income from his painting. He married Susannah Farnham Clarke, whose father was a merchant, in 1769 and built a house on Beacon Hill (site of the present state capital building). In 1771 and 1772 he traveled to New York and Philadelphia, painting the portraits of many leading citizens there. Although he was not politically active, his family was strongly LOYALIST. Friends had long encouraged him to take a trip to Europe for artistic studies, and he left for England in 1774. The political climate in Boston helped to convince him to leave. To further his artist credentials he toured the continent in 1774 and 1775, visiting France and Italy. When he returned to England he found his wife and her family had left Boston as Loyalist refugees in 1775. He remained for the rest of his life in England. Although he was a successful painter, working on portraits and historical scenes, as he grew older he struggled to maintain his household. Copley painted portraits of members of the British royal family as well as many noted Americans, including JOHN ADAMS and John Quincy Adams when they stayed in England.

See also ART.

Further reading: Neil Harris, *The Artist in American Society: The Formative Years, 1790–1860* (New York: George Braziller, 1966); Kenneth Silverman, *A Cultural History of the American Revolution* (New York: Columbia University Press, 1976).

Cornplanter (Gyantwaka, John Abeel) (1732–1836)
A member of the Seneca tribe, Cornplanter sought to guide the IROQUOIS CONFEDERACY through the upheaval that accompanied the independence of the United States from Great Britain. He was born in the Genesee River Valley, according to some sources, to a Dutch father named John Abeel and a Seneca mother; his half brother was HANDSOME LAKE. The record of his early life remains unclear. Some documents place him on the French side during the French and Indian War (1754–63). He also was alleged to have taken part in the ambush of General Edward Braddock's column in 1755. During the REVOLUTIONARY WAR (1775–83), Cornplanter fought with the British, defending his homeland against the American invasion led by General JOHN SULLIVAN in 1779.

After the war he decided to work with the United States. The war devastated Iroquoia and split the confederation into pro-British and anti-British factions. The People of the Longhouse were also divided by an international border that ran between the settlement on the Grand River in CANADA and those living in New York State.

Cornplanter convinced the Iroquois to accept the terms of the second TREATY OF FORT STANWIX in 1784. This agreement gave the state of New York title to much of the old hunting grounds that were already filling up with

Cornplanter. Engraving from a painting by F. Bartoli *(Library of Congress)*

settlers from the coast. Several more treaties followed during the next decade and further whittled down the Iroquois lands. Cornplanter argued each time that to surrender to the territorial demands of the United States was the only way to save the lives of the people; the Americans were too strong and would destroy them if they resisted. GEORGE WASHINGTON sent Cornplanter on a peace mission to the tribes of the Ohio Territory in 1791. He failed to convince the NATIVE AMERICANS in the area to yield to American demands. However, he did manage to keep the Six Nations out of the Miami confederation that met with a disastrous defeat at the BATTLE OF FALLEN TIMBERS (August 20, 1794).

Cornplanter's unremitting accommodation of American demands cost him the respect of many of his own people. One of his most vocal opponents was RED JACKET, and the two men often debated the merits of the various treaties. Red Jacket almost always wanted to hold onto as much land as possible in defiance of the Americans; Cornplanter tried to make the best of a bad situation by getting the most desirable terms possible. In the early 1800s the rivalry came to climax when Red Jacket defended his positions in a debate at Buffalo Creek. Red Jacket won the debate and Cornplanter retired.

The old statesman lingered on. In 1802 he visited THOMAS JEFFERSON in the new capital in WASHINGTON,

D.C. He supported the Americans in the War of 1812 (1812–15), and he offered his services to the United States though he was 80 years old. His son led a band of warriors against the British in the Niagara region. Cornplanter died peacefully on a farm given to him by New York State in 1836.

Further reading: Anthony F. C. Wallace, *The Death and Rebirth of the Seneca* (New York: Knopf, 1969).

— George Milne

Cornwallis, Charles, Lord (1738–1805)

With all the advantages of wealth, education, and aristocratic birth, Charles, Lord Cornwallis expected only great military triumphs. While he did experience many successes, he is best known in the United States as the British general who surrendered at YORKTOWN (October 19, 1781), ending the last major military campaign of the REVOLUTIONARY WAR (1775–83). Cornwallis rose quickly in the British army because of his personal and political connections and his individual valor. Educated at Eton and instructed in military science by a Prussian officer, he also attended the Turin military academy. He was seventeen in 1756 when he obtained his first commission. He fought in several engagements in the German campaign of the Seven Year's War (known as the French and Indian War in the United States, 1754–63), was promoted to lieutenant colonel by 1761, and in 1766 became a colonel of his own regiment. His noble birth led to several offices within the king's household during the 1760s. In 1760 he was elected to the House of Commons, but he entered the House of Lords two years later when his father died and he inherited his title.

When the Revolutionary War broke out in 1775, Cornwallis was stationed in Ireland with his regiment. He volunteered for service in North America and was promoted to major general. His first exposure to battle in the war was not particularly noteworthy. He was sent to North Carolina to link up with General HENRY CLINTON, did little there, and took part in the misguided effort to capture Charleston in 1776. However, he also participated with distinction in the BATTLE OF LONG ISLAND (August 27–30, 1776) and in the following campaign that forced GEORGE WASHINGTON to flee across New Jersey. Cornwallis was about to return to England to visit his ill wife when Washington struck at TRENTON (December 26, 1776). Cornwallis took command of the advance troops but allowed Washington to slip away from Trenton, march around Cornwallis's flank, and attack Princeton (January 3, 1777). Cornwallis also took part in General WILLIAM HOWE's campaign against Philadelphia. It was Cornwallis who led the force that outflanked the CONTINENTAL ARMY at BRANDYWINE (September 11, 1777). Cornwallis also played an instrumental role in the

British victory at GERMANTOWN (October 4, 1777) and in driving American forces from the forts that controlled the Delaware River entrance to Philadelphia. The following year, Cornwallis became second in command behind Sir HENRY CLINTON and participated in the BATTLE OF MONMOUTH (June 28, 1778).

Clinton and Cornwallis had initially been friends, having known each and served together in the German campaign during the Seven Years War. But by 1778 their relationship had become estranged. Clinton was not the warmest of individuals and was never popular with officers and men. Cornwallis, on the other hand, was extremely well liked by officers and by the rank and file. Moreover, almost from the day Clinton replaced Howe, Cornwallis vied for an independent command and sought to be made commander in chief, a position his connections in England had promised him if and when Clinton stepped down.

This personal animosity and misunderstanding between the two generals increased in 1780 and contributed to the British disaster in 1781. Clinton and Cornwallis invaded the southern colonies in 1780, taking the city of CHARLESTON (May 12, 1780)—a victory that was largely due to Clinton's strategy. Clinton wanted to move slowly in South Carolina, expanding areas of control, supporting LOYALISTS, and consolidating the British position. But when he left for New York, placing Cornwallis in command of the southern campaign, the earl saw things differently. The Americans sent an army south to challenge British control. Cornwallis met this force under General HORATIO GATES at the BATTLE OF CAMDEN (August 15, 1780). In this battle, Britain's superior troops and Cornwallis's tactical abilities provided a smashing victory. Cornwallis became emboldened, believing that he had secured his base in South Carolina. However, he had been letting his men loot at will, often alienating the local population. This practice continued as he decided to head to North Carolina. He also seemed to ignore the depredations of several militia units that harassed Tories and threatened his line of communications. Nor did he fully support those Loyalists who took up arms to fight for the king. Disaster struck when a large Loyalist force was wiped out at KING'S MOUNTAIN (October 7, 1780) in the South Carolina backcountry. Cornwallis, faced with the appearance of another army of Continentals under General NATHANAEL GREENE, withdrew to South Carolina, dispatching Colonel BANASTRE TARLETON to deal with General DANIEL MORGAN's contingent of the rebel army. Unfortunately for Cornwallis, Morgan decisively beat Tarleton at the BATTLE OF COWPENS (January 17, 1781). Angered by this action and wishing to cripple the Americans the way he had at Camden, Cornwallis set off after Morgan with his whole army. Morgan proved elusive as the two forces shadowed each other through the North Carolina countryside. Cornwallis finally caught up to Greene and Morgan at GUILFORD COURTHOUSE (March 15, 1781), beating them in a battle that left the British with a costly victory. Cornwallis decided to reconnect with his supply lines and headed for the coast at Wilmington. Once there, he made another important strategic decision. Rather than returning to South Carolina and firm up his base, he headed for the Chesapeake, where other British forces had been active. Once in Virginia, the situation went from bad to worse. Although his force was greatly augmented to almost 8,500, he vacillated. Clinton wanted reinforcements to ward off a supposed threat to New York. Cornwallis started to send some men and then reversed himself. Asked to establish a base that would provide protection for a British fleet, he chose Yorktown, then changed his mind, then changed it again. Once at Yorktown, with the full summer heat affecting his men, he did not rigorously entrench his position. Finally, by the end of August he began to realize his desperate situation. By then it was too late. The French beat back a relief fleet in the Battle of the Capes on September 5, 1781. A huge French and American army surrounded Yorktown and lay siege to his positions. Outmanned, outgunned, and running out of supplies, Cornwallis agreed to surrender at Yorktown on October 19, 1781.

Oddly, Cornwallis was not really blamed for this defeat. His political connections were too strong. Instead, the blame fell to Clinton, who was commander in chief but had little influence on Cornwallis's southern campaign in 1780 and 1781. Cornwallis later had a brilliant career as governor general of India and lord lieutenant of Ireland.

Further reading: George Athan Billias, *George Washington's Opponents: British Generals and Admirals in the American Revolution* (New York: William Morrow, 1969); Franklin and Mary Wickwire, *Cornwallis: the American Adventure* (Boston: Houghton Mifflin, 1970).

corporations

Between 1789 and 1825, state legislatures chartered many new business corporations in banking, construction, insurance, and manufacturing. In the colonial period, the British government had granted corporate charters (detailed contracts between corporations and government institutions) to various organizations such as colleges, towns, and fire associations. These corporations enjoyed special and privileged licenses to govern or educate, for example. They were usually reserved for aristocrats or others with political connections, but they also served to maintain organizations devoted to public service. The British government granted only six corporate charters for business purposes during the entire colonial era. After independence, Americans re-defined the meaning of the corporation to focus on building the ECONOMY of the early republic. Thus, state governments granted over 300 corporate charters between 1789 and 1800, and 1800 business charters between 1800 and 1817. New York alone granted 220 charters to business corporations between 1800 and 1810. An important revolutionary ideological shift characterized the new approach to incorporation. Americans now looked at corporations as entities responsible to the democratic legislatures that granted them charters. Given this new public accountability, states permitted corporations designed to support the public interest. In the early republic, this public interest was tied to economic development. Therefore, state legislatures often looked favorably upon corporate proposals to build roads or bridges or to open new banks and insurance companies.

The new business corporations retained certain rights from the states that chartered them. These usually included powers to raise capital by various means, monopolistic control of a certain trade, and limited liability for stockholders. In addition, the new corporate charters became vehicles by which the states could regulate business enterprise. Consequently, states often restricted the new companies by defining boards of directors, qualifying limited liability, setting maximum interest rates in the case of banks, specifying dividend amounts, and setting prices in the case of utilities. The concept of limited liability sometimes became a flashpoint in debate over new charters, as public officials expressed reservations over allowing stockholders to be removed from debts incurred by the companies they owned. State legislatures sometimes connected new corporations to each other via investment mandates. For example, the corporate charters of many early republic banks in Pennsylvania required them to invest in specific internal-improvements companies.

Corporations gained an important measure of judicial support with a SUPREME COURT decision in 1819 in a ruling known as the Dartmouth College Case. Dartmouth had received a royal charter to operate independently in 1769. By 1819, the state of New Hampshire sought to bring it under the control of the state legislature. Supreme Court Chief Justice JOHN MARSHALL ruled that the state did not have the right to change the college's charter because it was protected under a constitutional stipulation that prevented states from impairing contractual obligations. In a controversial decision, Marshall ruled that corporations were contracts that included the right to property. The court ruled that these property rights were sacred and could never be subject to a state's authority. While the court struck a blow for corporate independence, state governments retained a high measure of control over corporations through standard clauses that allowed for modification of charters when necessary. These devices were known as reservation clauses. In the 1820s and 1830s, the number of business corporations continued to increase as Americans further expanded TRADE networks and business enterprise around the country.

Further reading: Morton J. Horwitz, *The Transformation of American Law, 1780–1860* (Cambridge, Mass.: Harvard University Press, 1977); George David Rappaport, *Stability and Change in Revolutionary Pennsylvania* (University Park: Pennsylvania State University Press, 1996); Gordon S. Wood, *The Radicalism of the American Revolution* (New York: Knopf, 1991).

— James R. Karmel

corporatism

In the 18th century, many people in colonial America and Great Britain believed that society consisted of a single giant interest. This ideal, which historians call corporatism, may not have fully reflected reality, but its proponents held that both society and politics were a single body, or corpus. Within this framework, there was no room for interest-group politics because anyone not working for the single interest was working against it. There was also no such thing as loyal opposition. Whether you were rich or poor, whatever your race or gender, all was subsumed to the ideal of the greater interest.

The cement that held this corporate, single-bodied society together was paternalism and deference. Paternalism was the belief that those who were on top of the social and political scale—the king, lords, governors, and gentry—would protect the single interest of society and take care of those below them as a father does for a child. Within the body of society, the elite were to be the head; the people were the body, the arms, and the legs. Common folk, therefore, would defer to the judgement of their betters, assuming that the elite knew best for everyone concerned.

This concept is crucial for understanding how people in the 18th century perceived the world. Faith in the king and a hierarchy was permeated with the ideal of corporatism. If an individual no longer believed that the king protected the welfare of the people, then the whole fabric of society, as it was then known, would unravel. On one level, the Americans who revolted from King GEORGE III began to lose their faith in corporatism. THOMAS PAINE attacked the whole notion of monarchy in COMMON SENSE and naturally included an assault on the concept of hierarchy as well. When THOMAS JEFFERSON wrote the DECLARATION OF INDEPENDENCE, which accused the king of no longer protecting the interest of the colonies, he began with an assertion of the antithesis of hierarchy by stating that "all men are created equal."

American Revolutionary leaders did not readily abandon the ideal of corporatism, despite the words in *Common Sense* and the Declaration of Independence. As American leaders struggled to create new government in the states and eventually to write the United States Constitution, they struggled with the ideal of corporatism. REPUBLICANISM as an ideology of the revolutionary era was dependent upon the ideal of corporatism. As republicanism gave way to the rise of a new democratic United States that emphasized equality, corporatism lost much of its hold on the minds of Americans, and it became possible to view the greater good as emerging out of competing political, economic, and social ideas.

Further reading: Gordon S. Wood, *The Radicalism of the American Revolution* (New York: Knopf, 1992).

Cowpens, Battle of (January 17, 1781)

Fought in northwestern South Carolina, the Battle of Cowpens was a significant victory for the CONTINENTAL ARMY under the command of General DANIEL MORGAN. The British were making substantial gains in the southern colonies, where they hoped to capture Virginia and force a colonial surrender. The Americans desperately needed a successful battle to turn the tide against the British and secure the southern militias' loyalty. Recently promoted by General GEORGE WASHINGTON, General NATHANAEL GREENE commanded the entire southern campaign. The British, brilliantly lead by CHARLES, LORD CORNWALLIS, covered most of South Carolina in December 1780. Attempting to flank the British, Greene divided his army. As a result, General Morgan led his men west toward the Cowpens.

In response to the American dispatch, Cornwallis ordered Colonel BANASTRE TARLETON to pursue Morgan. Tarleton was a tactician experienced in defeating forces larger than his own, and his ego often bolstered his military confidence. In this instance, Tarleton outnumbered the Americans. Morgan faced swollen rivers ahead and eager British regulars from behind. Instead of fording difficult waters, he decided to lead Tarleton to the Cowpens, forcing battle. The Cowpens was a large rolling pasture in the midst of forest and underbrush. General Morgan took full advantage of the terrain, placing his troops behind the soft embankments and out of Tarleton's sight. To further fortify his troops, Morgan deployed a line of marksmen at the entrance of the clearing. Tarleton confidently charged the American line ahead, and the commotion of early battle kept the colonel from detecting the bulk of the army, who remained hidden. On Morgan's command, the American detachment retreated, luring the British further into battle. Sensing victory, Tarleton brashly pressed Morgan's

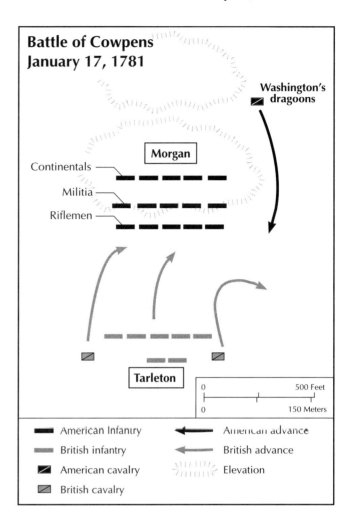

troops but quickly discovered the trap. The American forces, composed mostly of militia, soundly routed the British. Tarleton escaped capture, but he lost approximately 600 men. Morgan, on the other hand, suffered relatively small losses in an engagement that should have favored the British.

At the Battle of Cowpens the war's momentum turned in favor of the Americans, and the revolutionaries displayed their finest tactical performance. The victory at Cowpens also encouraged the colonial militiamen to continue in service, which boosted the manpower of the Continental army. Cowpens marked the beginning of the end for Cornwallis. Nine months after the rout in South Carolina, the British and Americans met again at YORKTOWN (October 19, 1781), where the British surrendered, ending the British campaign in North America.

Further reading: Lawrence E. Babits, *A Devil of a Whipping: The Battle of Cowpens* (Chapel Hill: University of North Carolina Press, 1998); Kenneth Roberts, *The Battle* *of Cowpens: The Great Morale-Builder* (Garden City, N.Y.: Doubleday, 1958).

— Lauren Held

Coxe, Tench (1755–1824)

Tench Coxe is best known as an advocate for a strong central government in the 1780s and 1790s and as a supporter for the development of American manufacturing. Coxe came from an affluent Philadelphia family, attended the College of Philadelphia (later the University of Pennsylvania), and was trained in the law. But he entered his father's countinghouse instead of practicing law, becoming a full partner in his father's business in 1776. During the early years of the REVOLUTIONARY WAR (1775–83), Coxe flirted with loyalty to the king. He was arrested for his support of King GEORGE III but was later paroled. This experience convinced him to side with the cause of independence. He seems to have repaired his fortunes by the end of the Revolutionary War. By the mid-1780s he had become a nationalist, advocating a more powerful central government. He attended the ANNAPOLIS CONVENTION in 1786 that issued the call for the CONSTITUTIONAL CONVENTION of 1787 in Philadelphia.

Coxe was a strong FEDERALIST at first, writing a pamphlet entitled *An Examination of the Constitution of the United States* (1788) supporting the Constitution. Once the new government was ratified and put into place, his talents were recognized by ALEXANDER HAMILTON and he was appointed assistant secretary of the treasury. In this position he had an important hand in guiding American fiscal policy and contributed significantly to Hamilton's "Report on the Subject of Manufactures" submitted to Congress on December 5, 1791. Coxe was involved in various efforts to start factories in the United States, including the Society for the Establishing of Useful Manufactures. Coxe also encouraged the development of cotton in the South. He believed that the safest way for the United States to become fiscally independent was to have a complete ECONOMY; he wanted cities and factories to develop so that they could produce more goods and provide larger markets.

Coxe had a strange political career. Not only had he switched sides during the Revolutionary War, he also seemed to switch parties in the 1790s. In 1792 he became commissioner of the revenue, holding that post until 1797, when a personality conflict with Secretary of the Treasury Oliver Wolcott led to his dismissal. Wolcott believed that Coxe was too sure of himself and had been insubordinate. Coxe then switched political parties, joining the DEMOCRATIC REPUBLICAN PARTY (Jeffersonian). During the ELECTION OF 1800 Coxe published a letter he had received from JOHN ADAMS in 1792 that politically embarrassed the president. In 1803 THOMAS JEFFERSON appointed Coxe as purveyor of public supplies, a position he held until 1812. Throughout his career, Coxe was involved in land speculation. In particular, he bought land in Pennsylvania with coal deposits, hoping that this investment would pay when manufacturing expanded. While he did not reap the rewards of this foresight personally his descendants profited from the investments.

Further reading: Jacob E. Cooke, *Tench Coxe and the Early Republic* (Chapel Hill: University of North Carolina Press, 1978).

Creek Nation (Muskogee)

The Creek (or Muskogee) Nation lived in what is today Georgia and Alabama. They survived by playing off the rivalries between Britain, France, and Spain until the end of the War of 1812 (1812–15), when they had to deal with the power of United States alone. The Muskogee Nation consisted of the Upper Creek and the Lower Creek. The Upper Creek lived further from the European settlers than the Lower Creek and therefore adopted fewer English ideas and practices.

In the years before the French and Indian War (1754–63), the Creek raided their neighbors to capture prisoners who were then sold at the slave markets in Charleston. During the war, the Creek stayed neutral for the most part, though many of the leaders favored the French. They felt little pressure from either the French or the English colonies until after 1763, when Georgia experienced an explosion of its nonnative population.

ALEXANDER MCGILLIVRAY, a Scot, moved into the Creek region and became an important figure in Creek politics before and during the REVOLUTIONARY WAR (1775–83). When the colonists rebelled against the English king, the Creek stayed neutral, although McGillivray led a pro-British faction that did some damage to the Continentals. John Stuart, a very capable agent for the Crown, also convinced some of the Creek to support the British cause.

After the Revolutionary War, the Creek started to drive away Americans who had illegally settled on Creek lands. The Spanish in FLORIDA helped the Muskogee in their efforts. However, once the United States established an effective central government, the State of Georgia could draw on the resources of the entire nation to fight the Creek. The federal government opened trading posts to encourage the Creek to adopt European-style farming and culture. These projects succeeded with the Lower Creek but not with the Upper Creek. A national council replaced the old system of clan government about 1800.

Many of the Creek objected to the federal road built through their lands. The United States government said it was to be used by the army to move troops, but the Creek feared that it would also bring settlers into the region. This fear proved to be correct. White settlers streamed into Georgia and the Mississippi Territory and demanded more land. Several times the Creek ceded parts of their hunting grounds. By the time the great Shawnee leader TECUMSEH visited the Muskogee in October 1811, many were ready to listen to him. Tecumseh called for a confederation of the native peoples to stand against the Americans, but the Lower Creek wanted to stay out of the coming war between Britain and the United States. Tecumseh gave those Creek who agreed with him bundles of sticks painted red. They were to use the sticks to count the days until they would launch their attacks on the white settlers. From this practice they got the name "Red Sticks."

In 1812 and 1813, war parties of Upper Creek raided isolated farms in southern Tennessee and northern Georgia. The people and politicians in Tennessee called for revenge and threatened to attack all of the Creek. In response, Creek leaders caught many of the raiders and executed them. Their actions staved off an invasion by the Tennessee militia, but it caused hard feelings between those who wanted to accommodate the Americans and those who wanted to make war on them. Some of the Red Sticks killed the Creek leaders responsible for the executions, and the Muskogee Nation soon spiraled into civil war.

The Red Sticks attacked American settlements throughout the region. At Fort Mims in 1813, they killed nearly all the defenders. This massacre stirred the Americans into action. The old Creek enemies, the CHEROKEE and the CHOCTAW, allied themselves with the Americans. Andrew Jackson led an army against the Red Sticks and finally cornered them at the Battle of Horseshoe Bend (March 27, 1814) and wiped them out. A few stragglers sought refuge in Spanish Florida only to be chased down by Jackson.

The Treaty of Fort Jackson (1814) forced cessions of land not only from the Upper Creek, but also from the Lower Creek who had fought for the United States. Andrew Jackson said this cession was to cut the Creek off from the Gulf of Mexico to prevent the Spanish or British from helping them in the future. Within a decade almost all the Muskogee lands had been seized, and the United States began to move all Creek west of the Mississippi.

Further reading: Michael Green, *The Politics of Indian Removal: Creek Government and Society in Crisis* (Lincoln: University of Nebraska Press, 1982).

— George Milne

Crèvecoeur, J. Hector St. John de
(Michael-Guillaume-Jean de Crèvecoeur) (1735–1813)

When J. Hector St. John de Crèvecoeur asked "What is an American?" in 1782, he could not have imagined how many times he would be quoted, cited, and misunderstood. Crèvecoeur had no intention of defining an American national character. Instead, Crèvecoeur was concerned with the special beneficial characteristics of *British* North America. While he painted a generally positive picture, Crèvecoeur included negative images when he described the horrors of slavery and the depredations of FRONTIER warfare. Whatever Crèvecoeur's intentions, scholars in the 20th century seized upon his question for their own purposes because it seemed to go to the heart of a national character pleasing to those with a European background, tracking it to a time when the United States was just beginning its independence. From this perspective, Crèvecoeur was reassuring: The American "is either an European, or the descendant of an European" who is a mixture of ethnic groups. More importantly "*He* is an American, who, leaving behind him all ancient prejudices and manners, receives new ones from the new mode of life he has embraced, the new government he obeys, and the new rank he holds." In short, "The American is a new man, who acts upon new principles; he must therefore entertain new ideas and form new opinions." For scholars and politicians who wanted to emphasize the European origins of America and claim an exceptional history without the relics of the past, Crèvecoeur and his book *Letters from an American Farmer* seemed tailor-made.

There was more to this Frenchman turned American than met the eye. Born to an impoverished aristocratic family in Normandy, France, Crèvecoeur was well-educated and became a junior officer in the French army in 1755. Stationed in New France during the French and Indian War (1754–63), he fought against the British and colonial Americans, taking part in the assault on Fort William Henry in 1757, and was wounded in the battle for Quebec on the Plains of Abraham (September 13, 1759). Shortly after the battle, he surrendered his commission and, with the money he was paid, set sail for New York, where he arrived in December 1759. During the next decade he traveled throughout the colonies, from Nova Scotia to Virginia, as a salesman and as a surveyor. He even joined one expedition to the West, visiting the Mississippi and the Great Lakes region. In 1765 he became a naturalized subject of King GEORGE III and a resident of New York. He settled down in 1769, marrying Mehetable Tippet, member of a prominent Westchester family in New York. Although in his writings he took on the persona of a farmer in Pennsylvania, the farm he now settled, called Pine Hill, was in Orange County, New York. He and his wife enjoyed seven years of peace, having three children and experiencing some prosperity.

The REVOLUTIONARY WAR (1775–83) shattered this life. While his *Letters From an American Farmer* sounds like a paean to the new American identity, Crèvecoeur was really describing an ideal world in colonial America under a beneficent King George. This position was only suggested at in the last chapter of *Letters,* where he described how war intruded on the peace of the American farmer. A second work, not discovered until 1923, revealed his LOYALIST sympathies more explicitly. Many editions of the *Letters* are now published with the addition of this second work, called *Sketches of Eighteenth-Century America.* In 1778, fearful of persecution as a Tory, concerned with the possibility of an Indian raid, and determined to protect his children's inheritance in France, Crèvecoeur left his farm and family to travel to British-occupied New York and seek passage to France. But in New York City the British arrested him under the suspicion that he was a rebel. Imprisonment brought illness and something of a mental breakdown. Friends managed to get him released, and after much travail he arrived in France in 1781. He did not return to New York until 1783, but this time he arrived as a diplomat—the French consul for that city. His appointment was in part due to the fame he had achieved by publishing the *Letters.* By then his wife had died and his children had been shipped to Boston. He remained in New York, reunited with his children, until 1790. During that time he was busy facilitating Franco-American commerce and was active in SCIENCE (mainly horticulture) and LITERATURE, gaining election to the AMERICAN PHILOSOPHICAL SOCIETY. He returned to France in 1790, retired from the diplomatic service, and lived in relative obscurity until his death in 1813.

More than anything, Crèvecoeur's written work was a product of the Enlightenment. He dedicated *Letters* to the Abbé Raynal, one of France's leading intellectuals. His main purpose was to argue that North America was a land where nature and reason existed side by side. Portraying himself as a humble farmer, Crèvecoeur asserted a moral superiority to the ancient relics of Europe. He proclaimed that "here [in North America] Nature opens her broad lap to receive the perpetual accession of newcomers" and that we "might contemplate the very beginnings and outlines of human society." From this perspective, the farmer was the happiest of men, "possessing freedom of action, freedom of thought" and lived in harmony with nature. This pleasant vision, which has attracted so much attention by scholars as representative of the new American, was also the vision that Crèvecoeur believed was wrecked by the revolution that created the new nation.

See also CORPORATISM; REPUBLICANISM.

Further reading: J. Hector St. John de Crèvecoeur, *Letters from an American Farmer and Sketches of Eighteenth-Century America,* ed. Albert E. Stone (New York: Penguin, 1981).

Cuffe, Paul (1759–1817)

A famed AFRICAN-AMERICAN ship captain and activist, Paul Cuffe was born free in colonial Massachusetts and died in New York. His father was a freed slave and his mother a Wampanoag Indian. Cuffe became perhaps best known as an advocate of voluntary black emigration to Africa. He undertook several voyages to Sierra Leone, the free black colony cofounded by African-descended slaves and British abolitionists. Cuffe also earned a distinction as one of the earliest black petitioners in revolutionary America. In 1780 Cuffe and six other men sent a memorial to the Massachusetts legislature complaining about being taxed without their consent. "We are not allowed the privilege of free men of the state," the petition, largely Cuffe's work, stated, "having no vote or influence on those that tax us." For the remainder of his life, Cuffe would be animated by this sense of injustice. Indeed, he became the leading black advocate of voluntary emigration from America during the early republic. Frustrated with white hypocrisy and expressing interest in uplifting Africa, Cuffe embraced plans by the 1790s to create a colony of free blacks in Sierra Leone.

Cuffe had a remarkable range of contacts in American, British, and African locales. He was a compatriot of black activists in the United States, including JAMES FORTEN of Philadelphia and Peter Williams of New York. In addition, he worked with white members of the Pennsylvania Abolition Society, gathering information on slave-trading activities in American ports and discussing voluntary emigration schemes to Africa. Cuffe also had strong connections with QUAKERS, a group known for its antislavery position, and he joined the Westport Monthly Meeting of Friends in 1808. He befriended British reformers such as Thomas Clarkson and William Wilberforce, working with them to establish the Sierra Leone settlement on the coast of West Africa.

Cuffe went to sea while in his teens, serving on a whaling vessel sailing for the Gulf of Mexico. He took other voyages up to the start of the REVOLUTIONARY WAR (1775–83). In 1776 British ships captured Cuffe and put him in prison for several months. After turning to farming for a few years and studying navigation, Cuffe began a career as a merchant seaman in the early 1780s. He constructed his own boat, as he put it, "from keel to gunwale," only to have it captured by pirates. A subsequent venture with a new craft brought Cuffe a big profit. By the mid-1780s, with the Revolutionary War over and Atlantic TRADE on firmer ground, Cuffe was successful enough to hire experienced seamen to aid his sea-travels. By the 1790s Cuffe had a 25-ton vessel called the *Sunfish* and then a 42-ton ship, the *Mary.* With 10 African-American crew members, Cuffe brought down several whales. By 1795 Cuffe christened an even bigger boat and set sail for Norfolk, Virginia, where he not only delivered cargo but viewed southern SLAVERY for the first time. On seeing a black captain, Cuffe observed that "the white inhabitants were struck with apprehension of the injurious effects on the minds of their slaves." He was violently confronted but escaped unharmed. Cuffe settled in Westport, New York, and continued to crisscross the Atlantic coast. He came to own several more ships of various sizes, not to mention land and houses.

Cuffe undertook several trips to Sierra Leone, the British colony of former slaves on the West African coast. In 1811 his all-black crew delivered cargo and surveyed the colony; he stayed for three months and vowed to return for an extended period of time, perhaps even to settle. Cuffe returned later in 1811–12 and then again in 1815. He died in 1817 on American shores just as debates over the American Colonization Society (ACS) prompted many black activists (including some friends and early advocates of Cuffe's back-to-Africa call) to organize against repatriation plans. The ACS, a white institution with many slaveholding members, had a different understanding of colonization. Where Cuffe wanted blacks to choose emigration freely and to use colonization as a way to bring demographic pressures on masters to liberate slaves, the ACS had many slaveholding advocates who merely wanted to rid America of free blacks. Cuffe hoped to persuade liberal elements of the ACS to put pressure on slaveholders. He even provided information to the ACS about Africa. James Forten, who initially saw potential in voluntary emigration (although he viewed the ACS warily), repudiated the plan by 1817. He joined other prominent blacks in stating that he would never voluntarily separate from the enslaved population. Although the ACS grew rapidly in the decade after Cuffe's death, the majority of the black population opposed colonization schemes, voluntary or otherwise. Still, generations of black reformers remembered Cuffe as both a legendary ship captain and entrepreneur, not to mention a fierce advocate of African uplift and redemption.

Further reading: Sidney Kaplan and Emma Nogrady Kaplan, *The Black Presence in the Era of the American Revolution,* rev. ed. (Amherst, Mass.: University of Massachusetts Press, 1982); Lamont D. Thomas, *Rise to Be a People: A Biography of Paul Cuffe* (Urbana: University of Illinois Press, 1986).

— Richard Newman

Currency Act (April 19, 1764)

Concerned with the issuance of paper money in the colonies, Parliament passed the Currency Act in 1764 to prevent the colonies from printing more money. Parliament had passed a similar measure in 1751 limited to only the New England colonies. The 1764 measure, however, was to include all of North America. The British passed the law because colonial currency had been highly inflationary. As a result, a note issued by a colony was not equal to a note of the same denomination in Great Britain. Colonists used their own notes to pay off debts to British merchants, thereby cheating their creditors of their full due. The simplest way to avoid this problem was to prevent the colonies from printing money.

From the colonists' point of view the law was unjust. Because colonial debt increased rapidly in the years around mid century, there was a constant drain of hard specie in the colonies. In other words, colonial Americans sent whatever gold and silver coin they had to Great Britain to pay their debts. The result was that it was difficult to make transactions of any kind since there was so little hard currency available. Notes printed by colonies, even inflationary notes, thus had an important use in the colonial ECONOMY. To further complicate the situation, the currency restriction was passed at about the same time as new parliamentary taxation—the SUGAR ACT (1764) and STAMP ACT (1765)—which increased the demand for more hard currency. While the Currency Act was not the focal point of the resistance to imperial measures that occurred in the 1760s and 1770s, it contributed to the overall sense of grievance that many colonial Americans developed at this time.

See also RESISTANCE MOVEMENT.

D

Deane, Silas (1737–1789)

An active revolutionary, Silas Deane was the first person sent by the CONTINENTAL CONGRESS to solicit support from the French during the REVOLUTIONARY WAR (1775–83). Born in Connecticut on December 24, 1737, and educated at Yale, Deane became a leading lawyer and merchant during the colonial period. Successful marriages also accelerated his career. During the 1760s and 1770s he became an active supporter of the RESISTANCE MOVEMENT (1764–75) and was chosen by Connecticut to serve in the FIRST and SECOND CONTINENTAL CONGRESSES. As a member of Congress he was largely responsible for supporting the attack on FORT TICONDEROGA in 1775. When he was not chosen for another term in Congress, his colleagues in Philadelphia decided to use his talents by sending him to France.

Deane's diplomatic efforts were important to the United States, but they were troubled by controversy. He arrived in Paris in July 1776 and encouraged the French to provide further assistance to the American cause. He was largely responsible for sending over the equipment and supplies that culminated in the successful campaign at SARATOGA in 1777. He worked closely with BENJAMIN FRANKLIN in convincing the French to form an alliance with the United States and to provide crucial supplies, although he may also have had some contacts with British agents. He subsequently became embroiled in a controversy over the finances of the war. Several members of Congress accused him of profiteering from his diplomatic mission. This controversy, triggered by the charges of ARTHUR LEE, who served in the diplomatic mission to France, seriously divided the Continental Congress when Deane returned to the United States.

Stripped of official duties, Deane returned to France in 1780 to pursue private business and resuscitate his reputation. He was not very successful in these efforts. In 1781 he began to despair over the outcome of the war. Unfortunately for Deane, he expressed his sentiments in several private letters that the British intercepted and published. As a result, many claimed that he was a traitor. He died in self-imposed exile on September 23, 1789.

Further reading: Coy Hilton James, *Silas Deane: Patriot or Traitor?* (East Lansing: Michigan State University Press, 1975).

Declaration of Independence (July 4, 1776)

The Declaration of Independence is the document by which the thirteen colonies proclaimed their independence from Great Britain. It was adopted in its final form on July 4, 1776. The goal of the document was to announce the independence of the colonies to the world and to list the reasons why the Revolution was legitimate. Although its statement that "all men are created equal" has received the most historical attention, the majority of the words in the document are devoted to a catalog of what the colonists saw as the transgressions of King GEORGE III.

The delegates of the FIRST CONTINENTAL CONGRESS in no way intended to declare independence from Great Britain. The delegates met simply to discuss forms of resistance to the British imperial regulation and the COERCIVE ACTS (1774). On October 14, 1774, the delegates passed a resolution called the Declaration of Rights and Grievances, which denied the right of Parliament to tax the colonies and presented the king with a list of grievances. Six days later they agreed to the Continental ASSOCIATION, setting up a timetable for banning all imports and exports to Great Britain. The Association also empowered local committees to take charge of the boycott on TRADE with the British. The members of the First Continental Congress were careful to maintain their loyalty to England, claiming they wanted to restore their relationship to what it had been. When the Congress adjourned, they agreed to meet again in May 1775.

By the time the SECOND CONTINENTAL CONGRESS convened, extralegal provincial assemblies were replacing learned that the king had hired German mercenaries to fight in America. It became increasingly clear that the British government was treating the colonies as a foreign body, and Congress increasingly acted like one. On April 6, 1776, Congress opened American ports to trade with other nations. Many Americans began to think that independence was inevitable. This rise in popular sentiment was partly due to the publication of COMMON SENSE in January 1776. By May 1776, eight colonies had decided that they would support independence. However, there were still some members of Congress who wished to continue to seek reconciliation with Britain. Although Congress voted to postpone discussion of the Lee resolution in early June, it also appointed a committee of five to draft a statement offering the arguments for independence.

The Declaration of Independence presented by the committee to the Continental Congress on July 1 was written almost entirely by THOMAS JEFFERSON. The Sage of Monticello worked on his draft from June 11 to June 28 in Philadelphia. BENJAMIN FRANKLIN and JOHN ADAMS offered some minor adjustments. Congress, meeting as a Committee of the Whole, made some more substantial changes to the wording. For example, Jefferson had wanted to blame the king for the SLAVE TRADE, but Congress thought better of addressing the issue of real SLAVERY. Regardless of the changes, the essential language and argument remained the same. The key to Jefferson's eloquence was his combination of lofty principles, pulling on the ideas of John Locke and the writings of the COMMONWEALTH-MEN, with an indictment of King George for usurping American liberty. The opening sections were especially compelling because they proclaimed that all men are created equal and asserted a social-contract theory of government. The list of grievances, while effective propaganda at the time, do not hold up to modern scrutiny as an accurate statements of events. Revolutionary Americans may have interpreted King George's actions as a concerted plan to destroy liberty, but there is little evidence to suggest that the various efforts at imperial regulation passed by Parliament and pursued by several different administrations in Great Britain reflected anything close to a conspiracy.

Americans celebrate July Fourth as the national holiday of American Independence, but the actual timing of events is more complex. On July 2 Congress voted—12 states to none—to declare independence (New York was allowed not to vote, since its delegation wanted to have approval of its state's convention). From the second to the fourth, Congress debated the wording of the document. When this process of revision was over, on the fourth, the Declaration of Independence became official. On the fifth of July Congress dispatched word of the Declaration to the states and the army. On the ninth, New York approved of the action. Finally, on August 2, 1776, most of the delegates

The Declaration of Independence was first read publicly in Philadelphia from the balcony of Independence Hall on July 8, 1776. According to John Adams, "The bell rang all day and almost all night," and the assembled crowd rejoiced. By the end of July, the document had been read and published throughout the colonies. *(Library of Congress)*

the legal legislative bodies and royal governors. The outbreak of actual fighting at LEXINGTON AND CONCORD (April 19, 1775) altered the mission of the Second Continental Congress. The Congress now had to operate as a governmental body in order to run a war.

Even though the war had begun, it was many months before the Congress issued the Declaration of Independence. On June 7, 1776, RICHARD HENRY LEE of Virginia read his resolution to the Congress which opened with: "Resolved: That these United Colonies are, and of right ought to be, free and independent States, that they are absolved from all allegiance to the British crown, and that all political connection between them and the State of Great Britain is, and ought to be, totally dissolved." Lee's sentiments echoed those of a growing number of Americans. In August 1775 the king had issued a proclamation declaring the colonies to be in rebellion. Congress also

Delegates to the Continental Congress approve the Declaration of Independence, held by Thomas Jefferson *(National Archives)*

signed the document that has become an American icon in the National Archives in WASHINGTON, D.C., including, and most conspicuously, the signature of the president of Congress, JOHN HANCOCK.

See also REVOLUTIONARY WAR; RESISTANCE MOVEMENT.

Further reading: Carl L. Becker, *The Declaration of Independence: A Study on the History of Ideas* (New York: Knopf, 1942); Garry Wills, *Inventing America: Jefferson's Declaration of Independence* (Garden City, N.Y.: Doubleday, 1978).

— Crystal Williams

Declaratory Act (1766)

When Parliament passed the repeal of the STAMP ACT (1765) in 1766, it was reacting as much to the petitions of merchants in Great Britain as it was to the opposition in the colonies. Based on those petitions, British officials stated that it was expedient at that particular moment to repeal the law. The British government still believed that it had the right to legislate for the colonies. In an effort to assert that authority, they passed the Declaratory Act, which claimed that Parliament had the right to bind the colonies "in all cases whatsoever." In other words, Parliament was saying that they would repeal the law now, but that they reserved the right to pass taxes and other legislation for the colonies in the future. Parliament agreed to this act in early March, and King GEORGE III assented to it on March 18, 1766. While clearly running counter to the beliefs of those colonists who had opposed the Stamp Act, most Americans did not worry too much about this face-saving measure. Amidst the jubilation and celebration, it appeared inconsequential compared with the fact that colonial Amer-

icans believed that they had compelled the British government to succumb to their will. This act would form the basis of later parliamentary taxes and would be cited by revolutionary leaders in the 1770s as an example of arbitrary and tyrannical government.

See also RESISTANCE MOVEMENT.

Further reading: Edmund S. Morgan and Helen M. Morgan, *The Stamp Act Crisis: Prologue to Revolution*, (Chapel Hill: University of North Carolina Press, 1953).

deism

Growing out of 17th century English intellectual traditions, and expanding in the 18th century with the spread of the Enlightenment, deism retained faith in the idea that God created the world but downplayed the roles of scripture and organized RELIGION. Deism also had an important impact on many leaders in the revolutionary generation.

The political and religious upheaval of the 17th century in England caused some individuals to question the identity between church and state. This questioning led to the beginnings of some toleration for different Protestant groups in England and colonial America. It also led to a general questioning of the role of organized religion. Some individuals held that God was a supreme being—a deity—who created the world. It was a person's duty to worship this deity, but everyone should do so in a personal manner by being moral and living a virtuous life. These ideas seemed to fit the new intellectual climate of the 18th century represented by the Enlightenment. The Enlightenment emphasized the relationship between nature and reason, holding that nature was organized according to scientific laws dictated by reason. Within this context, deism became a way to explain the origin of natural law. God created the mechanisms that dictated how nature operated. Humans could study nature and through reason discover how those mechanisms operated, but ultimately the splendor of nature and reason came from God. A few thinkers held that God was like a great clockmaker who created an elaborate machine—the world—wound it up, and allowed it to continue without his providential hand guiding every move. Prominent thinkers influenced by deism include John Locke in England and François-Marie Arouet (Voltaire) in France.

Several revolutionary leaders flirted with deism. BENJAMIN FRANKLIN wrote a deistic pamphlet as a youth, but he abandoned his commitment to its tenets and regularly attended religious services later in life. THOMAS JEFFERSON, too, was attracted to deism. In fact, his political opponents in the 1790s and early 1800s charged him with being godless based on earlier statements that clearly reflected the influence of deism. Even GEORGE WASHINGTON, although always pious and a churchgoer, expressed some support for deistic ideas. The most explicit statements of deism came from the pens of ETHAN ALLEN and THOMAS PAINE. Allen published a long manifesto, *Reason the Only Oracle of God* (1785). Placing reason over the Bible did not find a receptive audience in Vermont and contributed to the decline of Allen's political career. Thomas Paine wrote the most famous deistic tract while in Revolutionary France. His *Age of Reason* (1794–96) attacked all biblical revelation as falsehood. Paine, who had used the Bible to such good effect in *COMMON SENSE* (1776), now declared that the Bible was a forgery and packed with contradictions and immorality. He wrote, "It is a book of lies, wickedness, and blasphemy for what is more blasphemous than to ascribe the wickedness of man to the orders of the Almighty." Paine retained his faith in God as a deity; he merely rejected the Bible and organized religion. Although some readers in the United States, especially from the ARTISAN class, found his arguments convincing, the book was extremely unpopular and led to his being condemned by many as godless.

Further reading: Henry F. May, *The Enlightenment in America* (New York: Oxford University Press, 1976).

Democratic-Republican Party

During the 1790s, opposition to the program of ALEXANDER HAMILTON to create a stronger central government gradually coalesced into a political party. Initially, this party took its name from the DEMOCRATIC-REPUBLICAN SOCIETIES of 1794. Later, party members were often simply referred to as Republicans. History textbooks use a variety of labels for the party, including Democratic-Republican, Republican-Democratic, Republican, Democratic, Jeffersonian, Jeffersonian-Republican, and Jeffersonian-Democratic. Whatever the name, the party should not be confused with either the Democratic or Republican Parties that emerged later in American history. Centered on the ideas of JAMES MADISON and THOMAS JEFFERSON, the Democratic-Republicans supported limited government, extension of democratic rights to the "people" (white adult males), and strict construction of the Constitution.

The party began in Congress under the leadership of Madison. As secretary of state, Jefferson encouraged and worked with Madison, but it was Madison who coordinated a caucus in opposition to Hamilton's program. If there were some alliances among legislators in 1791 and 1792, local organization did not emerge until 1793 and 1794. In fact, it was more the FRENCH REVOLUTION (1789–1815) and France's war with Great Britain in 1793—rather than economic policy—that mobilized popular sentiment. Enthusiasm for republican France spilled onto the streets and

became a means of party identity. By 1796 party development remained only partial. The Democratic-Republican caucus in Congress nominated Jefferson for president; individual states had formed groups of alliances that called themselves Democratic-Republican; newspapers had clear party allegiances; and there were local organizations—but a national party structure hardly existed. The FEDERALIST PARTY helped party development along by pushing its policies too hard over the next four years. Increased taxation, expansion of the army and navy, the QUASI WAR (1798–1800), and the ALIEN AND SEDITION ACTS (1798) all demonstrated to many Americans the evils of a strong government run amok. By the ELECTION OF 1800 the Democratic-Republican Party had taken form, even if many of its leaders thought that the party was only a temporary expedient to save the republic.

After 1800 the Democratic-Republicans dominated the national scene, but they did not control every state and region. New England, in particular, remained a bastion of the Federalists. As a political party, the Democratic-Republicans were often divided into factions that vied with one another. In New York, for example, the Burrites (supporters of AARON BURR) contended with the Clintonians (adherents of GEORGE CLINTON and his nephew DEWITT CLINTON) and others for control of the state. Allegiances centering on a family or individual appeared in other states as well. By the end of the War of 1812 (1812–15), and in the wake of the Hartford Convention, the Federalists had lost almost all support. The United States became a single-party democracy. The unity of the Era of Good Feelings lasted only a few years, as different factions vied with each other nationally, eventually giving birth to a new party system in the 1820s and 1830s. By that time, although politicians still claimed a Jeffersonian legacy, the Democratic-Republican Party had also ceased to exist.

See also POLITICAL PARTIES.

Further reading: Richard J. Buel Jr., *Securing the Revolution: Ideology in American Politics, 1789–1815* (Ithaca, N.Y.: Cornell University Press, 1972); Richard Hofstadter, *The Idea of a Party System: The Rise of Legitimate Opposition in the United States, 1780–1840* (Berkeley: University of California Press, 1972).

Democratic-Republican societies

Founded during the first half of the 1790s, Democratic-Republican societies were the first grassroots organizations to oppose President GEORGE WASHINGTON. The societies broadened political participation by attracting men from the lower and middle classes to political action, thus precipitating debate about the legitimacy of such organized opposition to the government.

In May 1793 a group of Philadelphians founded the first and most prominent Democratic-Republican club. By the end of 1794 there were 42 known clubs. Societies were located in urban centers and the backcountry, and membership ranged from a handful to several hundred, with men of all ranks joining the societies. While most societies' leaders were prominent men in the community, many societies were led by less prosperous and more humble men. Thus, the Democratic-Republican societies attracted men of diverse status and, as a result, helped to broaden the scope of political participation in the early republic.

Originally founded as debating societies whose purpose was discussion and dissemination of information, the clubs soon became overtly political. Their immediate models were the SONS OF LIBERTY and COMMITTEES OF CORRESPONDENCE. Indeed, several members had also been active in these organizations. In addition, Democratic-Republican societies found a degree of inspiration from the FRENCH REVOLUTION (1789–1815) and the Jacobin clubs of France. Members of the Democratic-Republican societies saw the French Revolution as a continuation of the AMERICAN REVOLUTION, believing it their duty, and that of the American government, to support their brother republicans across the Atlantic. Nevertheless, the societies cannot be characterized as tools of the French. Although EDMOND GENET did suggest including "democratic" in the name for the Philadelphia society, he did not have undue influence over it or any other society.

In addition to being concerned about American policy toward France and Great Britain, the Democratic-Republican societies were troubled by the consolidating impact of Treasury Secretary ALEXANDER HAMILTON's financial schemes—assumption, national bank, and excise tax. Members believed that the Washington administration had betrayed the American Revolution and that, to combat such a betrayal, citizens needed to examine the conduct of all government officers, including Washington. Only a vigilant and virtuous citizenry could save America's republican experiment, and the societies hoped to fulfill this purpose.

By 1796 almost all of the societies had disappeared. There are several reasons their decline was almost as fast as their ascent. First, as the French Revolution deteriorated into the Reign of Terror and the war between Great Britain and France intensified, more Americans feared rather than celebrated the events in Europe. Hence, Democratic-Republicans societies lost support. Second, and more important, in November 1794 Washington denounced the societies for what he believed was their role in the WHISKEY REBELLION (1794). Despite efforts by individual societies outside of western Pennsylvania to condemn the rebels, the societies could not recover from Washington's public condemnation and challenge to their legitimacy. Significantly, Washington's comments precipitated a debate within the House of Representatives about whether to officially agree with him. Although DEMOCRATIC-REPUBLICAN PARTY leaders JAMES MADISON and THOMAS JEFFERSON never condoned the societies, they were not ready to denounce them either. The Democratic-Republican societies were one step in the growing acceptance of the legitimacy of a vocal opposition to the sitting administration.

Further reading: Eugene Perry Link, *Democratic-Republican Societies, 1790–1800* (New York: Columbia University Press, 1942).

— Terri Halperin

Dickinson, John (1732–1808)

A conservative revolutionary leader, John Dickinson was born November 8, 1732, in Maryland. He lived most of his life in Delaware and Pennsylvania, serving in the colonial legislatures of both colonies. He studied law in London but practiced in Philadelphia. Dickinson opposed both the SUGAR ACT (1764) and the STAMP ACT (1765), writing a pamphlet that advocated enlisting the support of British merchants to aid the colonies. In recognition of his vocal opposition, Pennsylvania sent him to the STAMP ACT CONGRESS in 1765. He objected to the use of force during the RESISTANCE MOVEMENT (1764–75).

Sometimes called the "penman of the revolution," he gained great fame for writing a series of essays that were later published as a pamphlet entitled *Letters from a Farmer in Pennsylvania to the Inhabitants of the British Colonies* (1768) in opposition to the TOWNSHEND DUTIES (1767). Although Dickinson was not really from Pennsylvania nor a farmer, his "letters" demonstrated a broad command of English history and the legal principles underpinning Anglo-American notions of liberty to express a fear of corruption and a necessity to resist arbitrary law. He still fell short of calling for force, although he implied that it might someday become necessary. He remained active in politics in the early 1770s in Pennsylvania but lost some influence in 1774, when he hesitated to support the radical measures that followed the COERCIVE ACTS (1774). He believed that New Englanders had acted rashly in the BOSTON TEA PARTY (December 16, 1773) and was afraid of taking any step that might prevent reconciliation.

Dickinson became a member of the FIRST CONTINENTAL CONGRESS in late 1774 and led the movement to petition the king for a peaceful resolution to the crisis. Also a member of the SECOND CONTINENTAL CONGRESS, he continued to seek reconciliation with the king while simultaneously joining in the preparations for war. He pursued the same policies in 1776, even voting against the DECLARA-TION OF INDEPENDENCE (July 4, 1776). During the war, however, he briefly served in the military fighting the British, was elected to Congress from Delaware in 1779, and became the chief executive officer in Delaware in 1781 and, later, in Pennsylvania. After founding Dickinson College in 1783, he advocated the creation of a stronger national government in the late 1780s, served as president of the ANNAPOLIS CONVENTION, and was a delegate for Delaware at the CONSTITUTIONAL CONVENTION, where he took an active role in its debates to draw up a new Constitution and wrote several essays, signed "Fabius," strongly supporting its adoption. Thereafter he retired from public life and died on February 14, 1808.

Further reading: Milton Embick Flower, *John Dickinson: Conservative Revolutionary* (Charlottesville: Va.: University of Virginia Press, 1983).

disease and epidemics

Americans in the revolutionary and early national period were frequently exposed to disease and suffered from several epidemics. As a result, their lives were shorter and often marred by physical debilitation and personal trial. Many of the diseases remain unnamed and resulted from poor sanitation, unhealthy drinking water, and unidentified microbes. The two most common diseases were malaria and tuberculosis, but the two most devastating diseases were smallpox and yellow fever.

Malaria, often called "intermittent fever," was endemic in much of the South wherever the *Anopheles* mosquito could breed year round. Creating recurrent bouts of fever, chills, weakness, and the shakes in its victims, malaria did not necessarily kill, but it left an individual susceptible to other illnesses. Most people with malaria struggled with the disease, attempting to maintain their work routine as best as possible. When there was no fever, they might function normally enough. If their hand started shaking or they had an "ague fit," they had to persevere and move on. Because many African Americans had a hereditary sickle cell trait in their blood, they were less susceptible to malaria.

Tuberculosis, known at the time as "consumption," was transferred by close contact when a sick person coughed or sneezed. The disease was prevalent in cities with compact housing and crowded workplaces. Consumption acted slowly, destroying its victim's lungs over the course of years. Although consumption became romanticized in the 19th century as a disease that struck young women, making them pallidly beautiful even as it stole their lives, the reality was more harsh. Tuberculosis had a devastating impact on poor families, removing its breadwinners from gainful employment, while one person after another caught the disease and slowly died.

If malaria and tuberculosis were persistent and worked their harm over time, smallpox and yellow fever were episodic and virulent. Smallpox was on the decline in the 18th century because of the practice of variolation—inoculation by purposefully exposing the blood of an individual to infected matter—which produced a milder form of the disease followed by a much lower mortality rate than if the person had caught the disease naturally. There was some popular opposition to this method, since it favored the affluent over the poor. Someone with extra money could afford both the medical expense and the time away from work to effect the treatment. Moreover, common folk feared that a person who was inoculated became a carrier of the disease to the rest of the community. By the end of the REVOLUTIONARY WAR (1775–83), with many men in the CONTINENTAL ARMY inoculated, objections decreased. In 1796 English physician Edward Jenner found a safer vaccination based on cowpox. Within a decade, this form of inoculation had become widespread in the United States, leading to a further decline in smallpox.

Yellow fever, which had appeared only occasionally in the colonial period, replaced smallpox as the disease most dreaded in the early national era. Like malaria, yellow fever was transmitted by a mosquito, but it was not endemic. Instead, the disease had to travel from hotter climates, usually the WEST INDIES. In the 1790s yellow fever appeared in American port cities with dramatic results. In 1793, the worst year for the epidemic, Philadelphia lost 10 percent of its population. The onset of the disease was sudden: A person would feel ill, run a fever, vomit black material, and turn a telltale jaundice yellow. Mortality was high. Within days, sometimes hours, the victim was dead. No one connected the disease with a mosquito, but everyone knew that it struck only in the summer and lasted until the first frost. Each June and July Americans began to watch for reports of yellow fever. At the first sign of trouble, masses of people exited the city. The poor, who often lived close to the waterfront, were left to suffer. Not every year brought yellow fever—the worst years for New York City were 1795, 1798, 1799, 1803, and 1819—but the experience became seared into popular memory. For decades after the outbreak of 1793, the people of Philadelphia would remember the call "bring out your dead" and the procession of coffins in the street.

See also MEDICINE.

Further reading: Elizabeth A. Fenn, *Pox Americana: The Great Smallpox Epidemic of 1775–82* (New York: Hill & Wang, 2001); Jack Larkin, *The Reshaping of Everyday Life, 1790–1840* (New York: Harper & Row, 1988); J. H. Powell, *Bring Out Your Dead: The Great Plague of Yellow Fever* *in Philadelphia in 1793* (Philadelphia: University of Pennsylvania Press, 1949).

Dorchester Heights, Battle of (March 4–5, 1776)

The Dorchester Heights were a series of hills lying to the south of Boston from which one could command the harbor. After the British forced the revolutionary army from BUNKER HILL (June 17, 1775) to the north of Boston, neither side fortified Dorchester Heights. When General GEORGE WASHINGTON took command of the armed forces surrounding Boston in early 1776, he and his officers determined that the best way to force the British to evacuate Boston was to capture these hills and establish batteries on them. Two problems confronted the Americans: First, they needed artillery. This difficulty was overcome by bringing an artillery train across the snow and ice from the recently captured FORT TICONDEROGA in New York. Second, they needed to occupy the heights in one night to prevent British interference. Since the ground was frozen, the troops could not dig regular earthworks. Instead, the troops prepared to build fortifications with logs and other materials and bring them to the top of the hills in one night. This maneuver was carried out the night of March 4–5, 1776. When the British awoke that morning they discovered that their position in Boston was untenable. They either had to attack the entrenched Americans, with possible results similar to the Pyrrhic victory at Bunker Hill, or evacuate. General WILLIAM HOWE had determined to evacuate Boston already. While he first contemplated an attack, he quickly gave up on the idea and merely accelerated his schedule for departure. On March 17, 1776, the last British ship left Boston Harbor, providing an important victory for Washington and the CONTINENTAL ARMY.

See also REVOLUTIONARY WAR.

Dragging Canoe (Cui Canacina, Cheucunsene, Tsiyu-Gunsini, Tsungunsini, Kunmesse) (1751?–1792)

Dragging Canoe led a NATIVE AMERICAN resistance movement during and after the REVOLUTIONARY WAR (1775–83) in the rugged region in what is now the Georgia-Tennessee border. He was born into the CHEROKEE NATION while it was still a powerful force in the southern colonies. Little is known about his early life.

A group of investors called the Transylvania Company bought a large tract in Kentucky from the Cherokee in 1774. This act infuriated the young Dragging Canoe, who told DANIEL BOONE that although the company had purchased the land, the white settlers would find that their new lands would be "a dark and bloody ground." Dragging Canoe refused to recognize the sale and vowed to kill any white person who tried to move into the region. When the Revolutionary War began, he immediately sided with Great Britain and declined American offers to negotiate with the Virginia representatives at Fort Patrick Henry.

Dragging Canoe led raids on settlements in Kentucky during the early part of the war, gathering a large band of nearly 600 men to attack the Americans living along the Watauga River. A militia detachment foiled the assault, and Dragging Canoe received a leg wound. He realized that his men could do better if they broke into small war parties rather than trying to fight in the white man's style, so he ordered raids all along the central and southern FRONTIER.

Sensing that he needed to establish a secure base, Dragging Canoe moved to the Chickamauga River Valley. Many warriors from different nations flocked to his cause. By 1778 as many as 1,000 Shawnee, Cherokee, CREEK and Miami men fought under his leadership. He was the single most powerful Native American at that time.

The CONTINENTAL ARMY sent a force under the command of Colonel Isaac Shelby to put an end to the raids. Dragging Canoe merely shifted his people to Chattanooga and parried the blow. The raids continued in their intensity.

The end of the Revolutionary War did not mean peace for Dragging Canoe, since he still considered the Americans to be invaders. He sent his men to attack the settlers flooding into Kentucky and Tennessee through the Cumberland Valley. His influence grew during these years and reached its peak in 1790. He attracted the allegiance of many warriors who would later become famous. TECUMSEH allegedly fought alongside the Chickamaugans in this time period.

Dragging Canoe died undefeated. The Americans eventually curbed some of his raids but never managed to stop them. After his death, the Chickamaugans joined forces with the Miami in Ohio. There they suffered defeat at the BATTLE OF FALLEN TIMBERS (August 20, 1794). In the years after the battle, Chickamaugans moved into Spanish Louisiana and joined up with their relatives, the Western Cherokee in what is modern Arkansas.

Further reading: Thomas M. Hatley, *The Dividing Paths: Cherokees and South Carolinians though the Era of Revolution* (New York: Oxford University Press, 1995).

— George Milne

Duane, William (1760–1835)

William Duane edited the stridently Jeffersonian *Aurora* newspaper in Philadelphia. He was born in upstate New York but moved to the British Isles at a young age. Trained as a printer, he went to India in 1787 to establish the *Indian World* in Calcutta. Although the paper was successful, his attacks on the East India Company led to his deportation.

He worked in London for a newspaper while seeking restitution of his seized property in India. Unsuccessful in this effort, he left for Philadelphia, where he began to work for BENJAMIN FRANKLIN BACHE and the *Aurora*. The yellow fever epidemic of 1798 killed Bache and Duane's wife, and Duane took over the editorship of the *Aurora*. In 1800 he married Margaret Bache, widow of Benjamin Franklin Bache and owner of the newspaper.

As editor, Duane made the *Aurora* the most important DEMOCRATIC-REPUBLICAN (Jeffersonian) paper in the country, attacking the JOHN ADAMS administration, the QUASI WAR (1798–1800) with France, and the ALIEN AND SEDITION ACTS (1798). As a result, Duane found himself hounded by mobs of FEDERALIST soldiers in the streets of Philadelphia and prosecuted by the courts. Neither legal nor illegal actions, however, were able to silence his biting pen. He was a major supporter of THOMAS JEFFERSON in the ELECTION OF 1800, and the Democratic-Republican triumph of that year seemed to guarantee his future. But the removal of the nation's capital to WASHINGTON, D.C., left his paper at a disadvantage, and promised patronage was not immediately forthcoming. Duane remained active in local Pennsylvania politics and eventually obtained a variety of government posts to supplement his income. He retired from the editorship of the *Aurora* in 1822 and traveled to South America. Upon his return he obtained another government office, which he retained until his death on November 24, 1835.

See also JOURNALISM.

Further reading: Kim Tousley Phillips, *William Duane: Radical Journalist in the Age of Jefferson* (New York: Garland, 1989).

Dulany, Daniel (1722–1797)

Born into a prominent Maryland family on June 28, 1722, Daniel Dulany gained enduring fame for a pamphlet he wrote against the STAMP ACT (1765). He was educated and trained as a lawyer in England. During the colonial period Dulany served in both Maryland's lower house and its council. He also held several important offices. In opposition to the Stamp Act he wrote a pamphlet entitled *Considerations on the Propriety of Imposing Taxes in the British Colonies, for the Purpose of Raising a Revenue, by an Act of Parliament* (1765). This essay attacked the notion that colonial Americans were virtually represented in Parliament. British politicians had argued that although colonial Americans were not directly represented in Parliament and elected no one to that body, members of Parliament virtually represented all subjects in the British Empire because Parliament had the general welfare of everyone in the empire at heart. Dulany denied this claim and asserted

that Americans could not effectively be represented in Parliament and that taxation without representation was a violation of English common law. If Dulany appeared one of the foremost colonial spokesmen in the 1760s, he faded in visibility in the 1770s. Dulany opposed the radical moves of resistance leaders in 1773 and 1774 and became a LOYALIST after independence. Most of his extensive property holdings were confiscated during the war, and he died in relative obscurity in Baltimore on March 17, 1797.

See also CORPORATISM; RESISTANCE MOVEMENT.

Further reading: Edmund S. Morgan and Helen M. Morgan, *The Stamp Act Crisis: Prologue to Revolution* (Chapel Hill: University of North Carolina Press, 1953).

Dunlap, William (1766–1839)

William Dunlap was born in Perth Amboy, New Jersey, on February 19, 1766, and moved to New York as a young boy because of his father's LOYALIST sympathies. Dunlap trained as an artist in New York and London, but he never became as skilled as some of his contemporaries. Having developed a taste for the THEATER in London, he was one of the driving forces behind establishing an American theater in New York in the 1790s and early 1800s. He also wrote almost 30 plays and translated about the same number from French and German. Throughout his career he struggled to earn a living. While involved in stage management, he usually operated at a loss. In particularly hard times he returned to painting portraits and miniatures. He also wrote several histories and other books. While never much of a personal success, he knew many of the leading intellectuals of his age and carried much of the burden of the early New York stage. He died in New York on September 28, 1839.

Further reading: Joseph J. Ellis, *After the Revolution: Profiles of Early American Culture* (New York: Norton, 1979).

Dunmore, John Murray, earl of (Lord Dunmore) (1732–1809)

At one time a popular Virginia governor, John Murray, Lord Dunmore became infamous among revolutionaries for offering freedom to AFRICAN AMERICAN slaves who joined in opposing colonial rebellion. Dunmore was born in Scotland in 1732 to a noble family. Inheriting his father's estates in 1756, he became a member of Parliament in 1761. In 1770 he was appointed royal governor of New York, where his lavish entertainments made him popular with the colony's elite. Within a year he was given a better position as the governor of Virginia. Here, too, he quickly gained popularity and even named a newborn daughter Virginia

(1772). Interested in the colony's welfare, he ordered the construction of Fort Dunmore at the forks of the Ohio River (modern-day Pittsburgh). He also engaged in a war against NATIVE AMERICANS in 1774, defeating the Shawnee in what is now Ohio.

Despite these successes, however, he was beginning to have problems with those who supported the RESISTANCE MOVEMENT (1764–75). He had dissolved the Virginia House of Burgesses in 1773 because of their efforts to set up a COMMITTEE OF CORRESPONDENCE. He did so again in 1774 when the burgesses declared a day of fasting and mourning after news of the Boston Port Bill arrived. He precipitated a crisis in 1776 when he seized gunpowder in Williamsburg belonging to the colony. While he was forced to back down, he ultimately fled to a British warship for protection. He then began to organize a LOYALIST force to support him against the rebels. As a part of this effort, he declared martial law and fought several small engagements with revolutionary forces.

On November 7, 1775, he made a controversial move that had a profound impact on the AMERICAN REVOLUTION when he issued what became known as Dunmore's Proclamation, which offered freedom for all slaves and indentured servants who rallied to the king's cause. Many white Americans now felt compelled to join the rebellion to protect their social system and SLAVERY. Many African Americans sought to escape from their masters and gain freedom by fighting for the king. Ultimately, hundreds of African Americans joined Dunmore, and thousands, in the spirit of the proclamation, escaped to the British lines during the rest of the REVOLUTIONARY WAR (1775–83). Although unintended by Lord Dunmore, his proclamation helped bring the issue of liberty for slaves to the fore during these years and contributed to the debate over emancipating slaves that became part of the American Revolution.

Dunmore's proclamation did not bring him victory. After being defeated at the Battle of Great Bridge (December 9, 1775), he again fled to British ships. Dunmore bombarded Norfolk on January 1, 1776, but could not gain a permanent foothold in Virginia. He left the Chesapeake in July 1776, later serving in Parliament and as governor of the Bahamas (1786–96). He died on March 5, 1809, in Ramsgate, England.

See also ANTISLAVERY AND ABOLITION.

Further reading: John E. Selby, *The Revolution in Virginia, 1775–1783* (Williamsburg, Va.: Colonial Williamsburg Foundation, 1988).

Dwight, Timothy (1752–1817)

Timothy Dwight was one of the leading intellectuals of his era, known as a conservative leader and as an important FEDERALIST. He was born on May 14, 1752, to a prominent New England family. His grandfather was Jonathan Edwards, New England's leading theologian and revivalist in the 18th century. Precocious as a child, he graduated Yale in 1769. Two years later he returned to Yale and served as a tutor. An intensive personal schedule of study ruined his eyes. Although he originally wanted to be a lawyer, he decided to become a minister instead. In October 1777 he became a chaplain in the CONTINENTAL ARMY, but the death of his father compelled him to resign that position in 1779 to settle his family's affairs. In 1783 he became pastor of a Congregational Church at Greenfield Hill, Connecticut, where he also established a school that helped spread his fame as a preacher, author, and educator. He emerged as a prominent conservative spokesman opposing democracy and the DEMOCRATIC-REPUBLICAN PARTY (Jeffersonian) of the 1790s. He thought that writers like François-Marie Arouet (Voltaire) advocated infidelity and believed that the FRENCH REVOLUTION (1789–1815) was a tragedy of global proportions.

In 1795 Dwight became president of Yale, where he remained for the next 21 years, educating New England's elite in his conservative ways. His enemies called him "Pope Dwight," while his followers looked upon him as a saint. A member of the famed CONNECTICUT WITS, he wrote extensively. Although his poetry was greeted positively at the time, it is difficult to read from a modern perspective. His most-lasting work is a four-volume book on his travels, entitled *Travels in New England and New York* (1821–22), which includes wonderful descriptions and insightful commentary on the areas covered. He died of cancer on January 11, 1817.

Further reading: John R. Fitzmier, *New England's Moral Legislator: Timothy Dwight, 1752–1817* (Bloomington: Indiana University Press, 1998).

E

Earle, Ralph (1751–1801)

Ralph Earle was one of the leading portrait artists of the revolutionary generation. He was born into an established New England family in Shrewsbury, Massachusetts, on May 11, 1751, but he was not to be a farmer. By 1774 he had moved to New Haven, Connecticut, and was painting portraits. At this time many affluent New Englanders were interested in having their portraits painted. However, the artist had to live something of an itinerant lifestyle, moving about the countryside seeking new customers. Earle reportedly visited LEXINGTON AND CONCORD in 1775 and made four paintings that became the basis of Amos Doolittle's famous engravings of the battles there. Although married in 1774, he does not seem to have spent much time with his wife. Either to desert her or maybe because of LOYALIST sympathies, he was in England by 1779. Here he obtained some success, studying in the studio of BENJAMIN WEST, becoming a member of the Royal Academy, and painting a number of important people, including the king. He also married for a second time. He had children with both of his wives. He deserted his second wife sometime in the 1780s and returned to the United States. Once again he became an itinerant portrait painter, traveling through New York and New England. Despite his skill and reputation—ALEXANDER HAMILTON was one of his patrons—he struggled because of habits of intemperance. At one point he was imprisoned for debt in New York City. He died on August 16, 1801.

See also ART.

Further reading: Neil Harris, *The Artist in American Society: The Formative Years, 1790–1860* (New York: Simon & Schuster, 1966).

economy

The rhythms of the American economy between 1754 and 1820 were dictated by war and revolution. During the French and Indian War (1754–63) prices remained high as long as the British campaigned in North America. Dangers lurked on the high seas as French privateers and warships threatened Anglo-American TRADE, but profits could also be made if the French cruisers could be avoided. After the conquest of CANADA and the end of the war, two economic problems loomed, and both played a role in the RESISTANCE MOVEMENT (1764–75) to imperial regulation. First, and more short-term, there was a postwar recession. Without armies and navies eating up excess production, prices collapsed and jobs became scarce. Unemployment in the port towns led to general discontent and provided the manpower for the mobs that opposed the STAMP ACT (1765) and TOWNSHEND DUTIES (1767). The second problem was more long-term. Colonial America produced raw materials, often in the form of staple crops, and imported finished and manufactured products. The result was a trade deficit that drained the colonies of specie and increased the overall level of debt. The specie shortage made exchange of money for goods more difficult. Efforts to remedy this difficulty were stifled by the CURRENCY ACT (1764), which prohibited the colonies from printing more money. The debt was a product of colonial affluence. The more the top echelon in colonial society was worth, the more they borrowed to purchase luxuries from their merchant connections in Great Britain. By the mid-1760s, the debt had climbed to 5 million pounds per year. Americans resented imperial taxation in part because they saw their trade deficit and their debt as a form of taxation already.

Trade and the economy did not rebound in the 1760s, especially with colonists proclaiming nonimportation as a part of the resistance movement. While the situation improved in the early 1770s, the flare-up of the conflict after the BOSTON TEA PARTY (December 16, 1773) and the outbreak of war hurt the economy further. The cost of the REVOLUTIONARY WAR (1775–83) to the economy was staggering. Per capita net worth actually went down between 1774 and 1805. The decline may have been even more dramatic

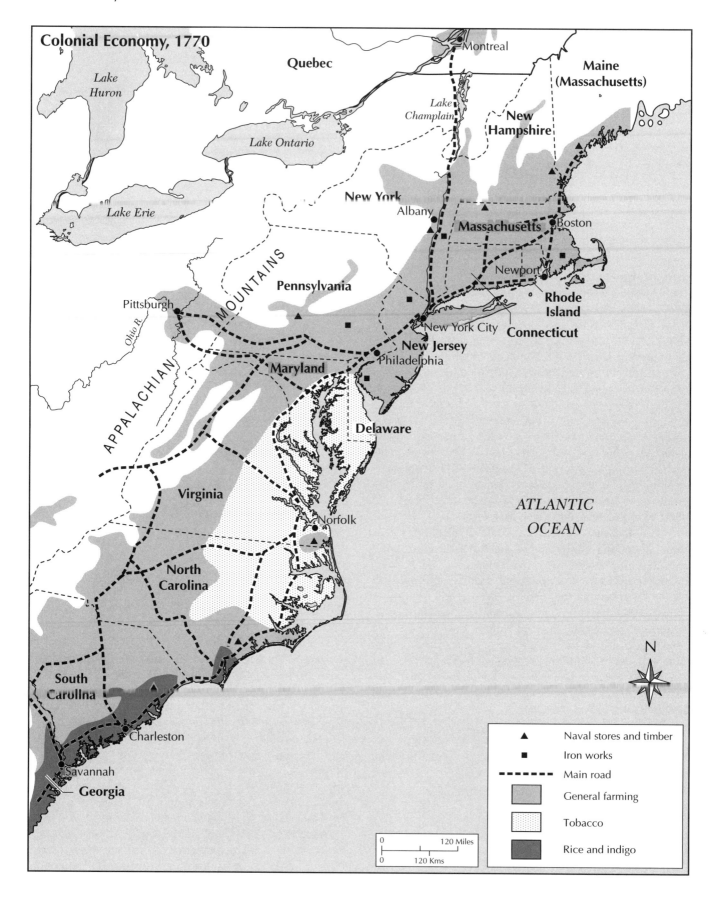

Colonial Economy, 1770

Quebec

Maine (Massachusetts)

Lake Huron

Lake Ontario

Lake Erie

New Hampshire

Lake Champlain

New York

Albany

Montreal

Massachusetts

Boston

Newport

Rhode Island

Connecticut

New York City

New Jersey

Philadelphia

Pennsylvania

Pittsburgh

Ohio R.

APPALACHIAN MOUNTAINS

Maryland

Delaware

Virginia

Norfolk

North Carolina

South Carolina

Charleston

Savannah

Georgia

ATLANTIC OCEAN

N

▲ Naval stores and timber

■ Iron works

▪▪▪ Main road

General farming

Tobacco

Rice and indigo

0   120 Miles

0   120 Kms

during the war and its immediate aftermath. Trade all but disappeared. Millions of dollars worth of property was destroyed as both sides pillaged each other. Armies devouring food may have driven up prices, but it was difficult to take advantage of the situation, since many now struggled simply to buy enough to eat. Depreciation of the Continental currency worsened the situation. In six months, from January to July 1777, Continental currency depreciated by 300 percent. With the cost of the war escalating, Congress printed more money. By 1781 the currency had depreciated 1,000 times and was not worth the paper it was printed on.

The immediate postwar period did not bring much relief. The United States was no longer bound by British imperial restrictions, but in a world of mercantilist monarchies, it was difficult to find many trading partners. The economy also suffered from a postwar recession. Some Americans became desperate. Farmers in western Massachusetts, unable to pay their taxes or their debts, closed courts and participated in SHAYS'S REBELLION (1786–87). By the time the CONSTITUTIONAL CONVENTION met in the summer of 1787, the economy was beginning to recover. The new Constitution may not have made an immediate difference, but it did provide a framework for national economic policy. Secretary of the Treasury ALEXANDER HAMILTON sought to strengthen the federal government and encourage economic development in the early 1790s.

What really turned the American economy around was the war that broke out between France and Great Britain in 1793. Suddenly markets that had been closed were opened. Not only could American farmers sell their own products, but merchants could also make great profits in the reexport trade. This economy, however, remained vulnerable. War threatened several times, and seizures of American ships occurred intermittently. These difficulties culminated in THOMAS JEFFERSON's attempt to use trade as a policy of diplomacy. The EMBARGO OF 1807 began a tailspin in the economy that hardly stopped until the end of the War of 1812 (1812–15). There was a slight upside to this economic decline. Textile manufacturing had begun in the 1790s after SAMUEL SLATER opened his mill in Pawtucket, Rhode Island. With imports stopped, industrial production increased. However, as soon as the war was over, the British dumped manufactured products into the American market, driving prices down. This development led to a call for TARIFFS to protect American industrialization. The economy recovered quickly after 1815. The Panic of 1819, however, led to a deep recession that lasted until the early 1820s. This last development marked a departure from the previous pattern. No longer held captive to war and revolution, the American economy entered a cycle of boom and bust based on expansion across a continent.

See also FOREIGN AFFAIRS; NATIONAL DEBT.

Further reading: Alice Hanson Jones, *Wealth of a Nation to Be: The American Colonies on the Eve of the Revolution* (New York: Columbia University Press, 1980); John J. McCusker and Russell R. Menard, *The Economy of British America, 1607–1789* (Chapel Hill: University of North Carolina Press, 1985); Douglass C. North, *The Economic Growth of the United States, 1790–1860* (Englewood Cliffs, N.J.: Prentice Hall, 1961).

education

Education throughout the period between 1750 and 1820 was most notable for its diversity. There was no common schooling system, much less any common experience shared by all children of a certain age. Children and adults were educated in multiple places and their experiences differed by region, gender, and class. This is not to say that no significant changes occurred during the period; after the REVOLUTIONARY WAR (1775–83), educators directly linked education to citizenship and founded new institutions to serve civic needs.

In colonial America, the home was the primary site for education. Boys and girls learned not only the skills attached to running a home or farm but also received their basic moral and literacy education from parents. The Bible and some religious tracts published for children were the primary texts people read. Indeed, the Bible was the only book many families owned. In New England, literacy had a larger significance, since Calvinists believed that each person should read the Bible individually. For boys, and especially for girls, literacy rates in New England were significantly higher than anywhere else in the British world.

Colonial homes often included people not directly related to the immediate family. In urban areas, ARTISANS and master craftsmen, such as blacksmiths and coopers, hired apprentices at young ages. These boys were usually hired out by parents who wanted to provide their children with productive skills. The apprentice lived with the master, who was responsible for general instruction as well as the teaching of a trade. In colonial America, where craftsmen were in demand, the skills of artisans should not be discounted. Master craftsmen were important educators.

Outside the home, churches were the primary formal educational institutions in colonial America. Ministers were called "public teachers" and were responsible for the moral instruction of their community. Most New England and southern states had an established church, and attendance and support of the church by members was mandatory. In the middle colonies, religious diversity prevented a single establishment. Nonetheless, most residents gained moral instruction from their particular church. Although not all colonists were members of the established churches, especially in the western regions of the South, most agreed that the minister had a central role to play in educating the public.

Formal academic training was available to a few. Each colony had only one, if any, college. Colleges trained ministers and prepared some children for careers as political leaders. While serving many of the children of elite parents, colleges also recruited children from middle-class backgrounds who showed particular promise. Apart from ministerial training, a college education was rare, and few students completed a full course of study. However, many

THE

AMERICAN

SPELLING BOOK;

CONTAINING,

THE RUDIMENTS

OF THE

ENGLISH LANGUAGE,

FOR THE

USE OF SCHOOLS

IN THE

UNITED STATES.

By NOAH WEBSTER, Esq.

JOHNSON'S SECOND REVISED IMPRESSION.

PHILADELPHIA:

PUBLISHED BY JACOB JOHNSON & CO.
NO. 147, MARKET-STREET.

1804.

Commonly known as the "blue-backed speller," *The American Spelling Book,* written by Noah Webster, was first published in 1783. *(Library of Congress)*

students used college as a stepping stone to a legal apprenticeship. There were no law schools in this period; college graduates served under the tutelage of established LAWYERS. Similar to the relationship between craftsmen and apprentices, lawyers provided their students with the appropriate legal education needed to practice law.

The AMERICAN REVOLUTION altered the ways in which Americans thought about education. Most importantly, revolutionary leaders believed that access to education for all citizens was necessary for the preservation of liberty. THOMAS JEFFERSON explained that since the people are the "only safe depositories" of power in a republic, "their minds must be improved to a certain degree." For Jefferson, improvement meant providing a state-supported common schooling system. In Virginia, he proposed a comprehensive school system consisting of different levels and culminating in a university for the best students. Although his plan was rejected, several states did pass mandatory schooling laws. The United States Congress approved Jefferson's draft of the NORTHWEST ORDINANCE (1787), which required every town in the northwest territory to set aside some land for schools. Although the state-supported common-school system really came into being after 1820, many private academies were established to serve both boys and girls. These academies proliferated throughout the nation, and while they often provided a superficial education, they did increase access to schooling.

Education was not limited to formal schooling. American leaders understood that Americans needed to learn less about Latin and more about what was called "practical knowledge." The rejection of formal knowledge was an act of patriotism. European aristocrats might have the time to learn arcane material, but hardworking Americans needed knowledge that they could use. Moreover, idleness was seen as the breeding ground for vice. Agricultural and mechanical societies were established so that ordinary Americans could spend their leisure time not in vice but in learning about their fields. Leaders hoped to provide interesting lectures about SCIENCE that related to the work of artisans and farmers. Such institutions were meant to increase the knowledge of the population as a whole while promoting values associated with republican liberty.

Female education was supported by most American leaders, and during the postrevolutionary period many female academies were established. Concerned about the values of the next generation, Americans thought that women, as mothers, played a vital role in shaping the character of their children. JOHN ADAMS explained that "it is by the female world, that the greatest and best characters among men are formed." As Adams suggested, female education was still centered around the needs of men. Only men could be citizens in the new republic. At the same time, the belief that women acted as moral teachers enabled women to gain not only greater access to education but also to fulfill an important public role.

The role of the minister as public teacher was also changed by the Revolution. In New England, ministers initially received heightened importance after independence. Indeed, Connecticut maintained an established church until 1818, while Massachusetts held on until 1833. Concerned about the character of citizens, New Englanders believed that the church would continue to be the central educational institution. In the words of the Massachusetts Constitutional Convention of 1780: "The Honor and Happiness of a People depend upon Morality," and "the Public Worship of GOD had a tendency to inculcate the Principles thereof, as well as to preserve a People from forsaking Civilization, and falling into a state of Savage barbarity." In their view, civilization itself depended on the ministry.

Not all Americans agreed that the established church was necessary, or even desirable, in an independent America. Thomas Jefferson believed that ministers were hucksters of superstition who would corrupt the morals of Virginia's citizens. In part, this hostility grew out of the different context in Virginia. In New England, the established church represented the majority of the population, whereas in the southern states the Anglican church represented the British Crown. Jefferson also inherited a hostility to priests that was a prominent aspect of the French Enlightenment Jefferson's opinions aside, many ordinary Americans rejected the established church not because they were hostile to RELIGION but because they found it in new places. New denominations such as the METHODISTS and BAPTISTS argued that no minister should interpose between oneself and the Bible. Using the revolution's egalitarian values against the established church, ministers without any formal training, such as the Methodist preacher Lorenzo Dow, gained many converts among ordinary Americans. While not educated in the formal sense, these ministers played important educational roles in the religious lives of many Americans in the early national period.

University education also changed dramatically during the early 19th century. Thomas Jefferson did not support the connection between higher education and religious training. After failing to gain state control over the Anglican William and Mary College, Jefferson decided to found a new secular college. In 1819 the University of Virginia was chartered by the legislature. To many Virginians, the lack of religious instruction at the university was scandalous, but Jefferson fought hard for this achievement. In reality, Jefferson's university did not represent the larger trend in American higher education. Instead of secularizing education, most states chose to allow denominations to found their own academies and colleges. The origins of this trend can be seen in the decades before 1820, when states chartered such institutions as the orthodox Congregational

Williams College in Massachusetts and Presbyterian colleges such as Transylvania in western Virginia and Dickinson in Pennsylvania. In addition, most colonial colleges were neither public nor private. Each college was an independent corporation, although its activities remained under the supervision of the colonial government. After independence, college trustees and state legislatures clashed in state after state over the question of who should control colleges. The question was settled in the 1819 United States SUPREME COURT case of *Dartmouth College v. Woodward,* in which the court ruled that Dartmouth was a private institution, independent of state oversight. This ruling cleared the space for the spread and growth of private denominational colleges.

Despite the spread of academies and colleges, much education took place outside schools in informal voluntary gatherings of men called "mutual improvement societies." These societies took seriously the need for civic education in a republic and gathered to hear lectures or give orations of their own work. Unlike the agricultural and mechanical societies, however, mutual improvement societies were subtly radical. By coming together in informal groups outside of the established institutions of school and church, members of these societies took control over their own education.

Education in the period 1754–1820 was quite different than today. Most education was informal and took place in myriad institutions and locations. Moreover, what it meant to be "educated" depended on one's place in society. Education was not seen as a stage of life one passed through and finished by a certain age. Moral and religious instruction were seen as requiring a lifelong attendance at church. The Revolution led to the establishment of new institutions and focused American attention on the relationship between education and citizenship.

See also WOMEN'S RIGHTS AND STATUS.

Further reading: Richard D. Brown, *Knowledge Is Power: The Diffusion of Information in Early America, 1700–1865* (New York: Oxford University Press, 1989); Richard D. Brown, *Strength of a People: The Idea of an Informed Citizenry in America, 1650–1870* (Chapel Hill: University of North Carolina Press, 1996); Lawrence Cremin, *American Education: The Colonial Experience, 1607–1783* (New York: Harper & Row, 1970); Lawrence Cremin, *American Education: The National Experience, 1783–1876* (New York: Harper & Row, 1980); Jürgen Herbst, *From Crisis to Crisis: American College Government, 1636–1819* (Cambridge, Mass.: Harvard University Press, 1982); Linda K. Kerber, *Women of the Republic: Intellect and Ideology in Revolutionary America* (Chapel Hill: University of North Carolina Press, 1980); Joseph F. Kett, *The Pursuit of Knowledge under Difficulties: From*

Self-Improvement to Adult Education in America, 1750–1990 (Stanford, Calif.: Stanford University Press, 1994).

— Johann Neem

election of 1800

In the election of 1800, Vice President THOMAS JEFFERSON defeated the incumbent President JOHN ADAMS. It was a campaign and election of many firsts for the new nation, with POLITICAL PARTIES dominating a presidential contest for the first time. The House of Representatives decided its first presidential election when the DEMOCRATIC-REPUBLICAN PARTY candidates tied, and it marked the first time in American history that power was peacefully transferred from one party to another.

Democratic-Republicans united behind Jefferson as their candidate, believing that a victory would rescue the principles of the AMERICAN REVOLUTION from the FEDERALIST PARTY. In particular, they believed that JAY's TREATY (1794), the ALIEN AND SEDITION ACTS (1798), and the QUASI WAR (1798–1800) with France proved that the Federalists wished to subvert the rights that had been secured by the Revolution.

Much greater division existed within the Federalist Party, particularly with regard to policy toward France. When Adams decided to send a new peace mission to France in early 1800, ALEXANDER HAMILTON and many high Federalists, who had never been enthusiastic supporters of Adams, decided to actively work against his election by promoting CHARLES COTESWORTH PINCKNEY of South Carolina. Pinckney thus became the de facto Federalist vice presidential candidate. The campaign was also noteworthy for the personal attacks against Jefferson and Adams. Jefferson's opponents charged him with atheism, while Adams was attacked for being a monarchist.

Under the Constitution, states determined how and when they chose their representatives to the electoral college. In 10 states—New Hampshire, Vermont, Massachusetts, Connecticut, New York, New Jersey, Pennsylvania, Delaware, South Carolina, and Georgia—the state legislature chose electors. Thus legislative elections were of particular importance in these states. Voters in Rhode Island and Virginia chose electors on a general ticket. In Maryland, North Carolina, and Kentucky, voters selected the electors by district, while Tennessee employed a combination of the district and legislative methods. The presidential election took place from May until December 1800.

Federalists felt confident that they would win New England (with the possible exception of Rhode Island) and Delaware. They also believed that they had a chance in South Carolina. Democratic-Republicans would safely capture Virginia, Kentucky, Tennessee, and Georgia. They needed to hold onto the South and win some votes in the mid-Atlantic states for victory. Because of the sectional nature of the parties, the outcome of the election primarily hinged upon the results in the mid-Atlantic states, particularly New York and Pennsylvania.

New York held its legislative elections in May 1800. AARON BURR masterfully assured a Democratic-Republican victory by capturing New York City's seats and thus the legislature for the party. He outmaneuvered his longtime rival Hamilton and earned a place on the ticket with Jefferson. Because of New York's national importance, Hamilton entreated Governor JOHN JAY to call the old Federalist-controlled legislature into session to alter the election law to ensure Federalist success. Jay rebuffed Hamilton because he believed it would embarrass the party to so transparently manipulate the election. With New York almost certainly in the Democratic-Republican column, Adams decided to dismiss Secretary of State TIMOTHY PICKERING and Secretary of the Treasury James McHenry, who were Hamilton Loyalists, and replace them with men more likely to help his cause in the South and hold an allegiance to him.

With New York decided, Pennsylvania assumed even greater importance. For months, however, Pennsylvania's participation was in jeopardy because the Democratic-Republican–controlled lower house and the Federalist-controlled senate could not agree on the method for casting the state's electoral votes. Finally, on November 29, the legislature agreed to split its vote by electing eight Democratic-Republican electors and seven Federalists.

By December 16, the nation knew the results of the election. Jefferson and Burr each captured 73 votes, Adams received 65 votes, Pinckney won 64 votes, and Jay had one. The three-fifths clause contributed to the Democratic-Republican triumph in the federal House and Senate because the party dominated the South. However, its victory in the electoral college was not overwhelming. Because Jefferson and Burr tied, the results created a new crisis for the nation.

At the time, the Constitution made no provisions for a separate vote for president and vice president. Electoral College members cast two votes for president. The candidate with the most votes became president and the second-place finisher became vice president. Unlike the Federalists—who threw away one vote to ensure there would be no tie between their candidates—Democratic-Republicans cast all their votes for both Jefferson and Burr because they feared a close election might give the vice presidency to Adams and they worried about offending Burr. Thus the old Federalist-controlled House of Representatives, voting by state, would decide the election between Jefferson and Burr.

Nine states were needed to win. Eight states were firmly for Jefferson; Federalists controlled six state delegations; and two states were divided. Burr would be crucial to any resolution. He never definitively denounced his interest in the presidency. Some Federalists saw the deadlock as an opportunity to keep control of the presidency and deny Jefferson his victory, and hence they courted Burr. The House began balloting on February 11, 1801, and agreed to remain in session until the election was decided. The House was working against the deadline of March 4, when the Constitution required the next president be inaugurated. No one knew what would happen if there were no president by that date. On the first 35 ballots, the results remained the same: eight states for Jefferson, six for Burr, and two divided. Rumors ran rampant of violence and the taking up of arms. The governors of Virginia and Pennsylvania prepared their states' militias for conflict if the Federalists took over the national government.

Finally, on February 17, the crisis was resolved. On the 36th ballot, 10 states voted for Jefferson, four for Burr, and two states did not vote. (Federalists from Vermont and Maryland absented themselves so that their states could move to Jefferson's column). The lone representative from Delaware, James Bayard, who had previously voted for Burr, submitted a blank ballot. South Carolina did the same. There are several reasons Federalists decided to break the deadlock. Hamilton, who detested Burr more than he feared Jefferson, prevailed upon his Federalist compatriots to end their flirtation with Burr. Bayard was convinced that he had received Jefferson's assurances regarding certain policies, appointments, and the removal of Federalists from federal offices, although Jefferson denied agreeing to these accommodations. Most importantly, representatives did not want to risk civil war and disunion in 1800.

On March 4, 1801, in a relatively smooth transition, Democratic-Republicans took control of the federal government for the first time. In his inaugural address, Jefferson pledged to restore the principles of 1776. A peaceful revolution had occurred. In 1804, the Twelfth Amendment requiring separate ballots for president and vice president was ratified.

Further reading: Stanley Elkins and Eric McKitrick, *The Age of Federalism* (New York: Oxford University Press, 1993); James Roger Sharp, *American Politics in the Early Republic: The New Nation in Crisis* (New Haven, Conn.: Yale University Press, 1993); Bernard Weisberger, *America Afire: Jefferson, Adams, and the Revolutionary Election of 1800* (New York: William Morrow, 2000).

— Terri Halperin

embargo of 1807

The Embargo Act, passed by Congress on December 22, 1807, was a declaration to Great Britain and France that the United States expected free and uninhibited access to the seas. President THOMAS JEFFERSON believed that a prohibition on TRADE with England and France would lead the European powers to acknowledge American maritime rights.

During the FRENCH REVOLUTION and Napoleonic Wars (1789–1815), the United States enjoyed an increase in trade as a "neutral carrier" on the high seas. NAPOLEON BONAPARTE, at war with Great Britain, attempted to blockade the British Isles by prohibiting any country from trading with England. Great Britain suspected American ships of supplying France. England claimed it had the right to search or capture any ships connected with France. England also insisted that it had the right to search American ships for British deserters and, if discovered, return those sailors to service in the Royal Navy. The British even searched an American warship in the *CHESAPEAKE-LEOPARD* affair (June 22, 1807). This incident could have led to war with Great Britain, but Jefferson sought economic redress instead, withholding trade and much-needed raw materials.

The Embargo Act, expanded twice the following year, was sweeping. It prohibited American ships from sailing to foreign lands and closed the border to imports. The embargo had little immediate effect on Great Britain, but in the United States it devastated American commerce. Even with the extralegal trade created by smuggling, the New England seafaring ECONOMY was hit especially hard. In New England, however, manufacturing expanded to compensate for some of the loss. Other regions, the South

A cartoon supporting the Embargo Act in which the cartoonist depicts the embargo as a turtle preventing a smuggler from selling a keg of New England rum to the British. The word "ograbme" is "embargo" spelled backwards. *(New York Public Library)*

in particular, were more dependent on trade and thus suffered greater economic losses.

The Embargo Act cost Jefferson much political capital, and the negative economic effects of the embargo divided his party internally. JOSIAH QUINCY, TIMOTHY PICKERING, and JOHN RANDOLPH denounced Jefferson in Congress. FEDERALIST PARTY members seized the opportunity to gain political mileage: a common image in Federalist cartoons showed American trading vessels being threatened by a sea monster or turtle named "Ograbme"—embargo spelled backward.

In the final days of Jefferson's term, the embargo was repealed. Congress replaced it with the NON-INTERCOURSE ACT of 1809, which eased trading restrictions with belligerent powers.

See also FOREIGN AFFAIRS; ORDERS IN COUNCIL.

Further reading: Louis Martin Sears, *Jefferson and the Embargo* (Durham, N.C.: Duke University Press, 1927).

— Jay R. Dew

Equiano, Olaudah (Gustavus Vassa) (1745–1797)

Probably born in West Africa, Olaudah Equiano became one of the leading ANTISLAVERY voices of the Atlantic world before his death. His memoir, entitled *The Interesting Narrative of the Life of Olaudah Equiano, or Gustavus Vassa, the African, Written by Himself,* is generally regarded as one of the canonical slave narratives. First published in 1789 and reprinted several times thereafter both in the United States and England, "the interesting narrative" was the most thorough and engaging document of the emerging genre of former slaves' written experiences. It remains a standard text, alongside later slave narratives by Frederick Douglass, Harriet Jacobs, and others.

Among other themes, Equiano focused early attention on the horrors of the overseas SLAVE TRADE, or the "Middle Passage," as it became known—the forced migration of Africans to the Americas. Historians now place the number of Africans who endured the Middle Passage at 12–15 million. Although some European and American statesmen, activists, and scholars began critiquing the slave trade during the era of revolutions (1770s through the 1790s), they often did so from philosophical or religious perspectives. While Equiano meditated on such themes too, he also provided firsthand testimony about the slave trade. In one of the most famous and often-cited passages, he wrote of the Middle Passage: "the stench of the hold [of the ship] while we were on the [African] coast was so intolerably loathsome, that it was dangerous to remain there for any time . . . the closeness of the place, and the heat of the climate, added to the number in the ship, which was so crowded that each had scarcely room to turn himself, almost suffo-

Opening pages of *The Interesting Narrative of the Life of Olaudah Equiano, or Gustavus Vassa, the African (Hulton/Archive)*

cated us . . . this wretched situation was again aggravated by the galling of the chains . . . the shrieks of the women, and groans of the dying, rendered the whole a scene of horror almost inconceivable." Equiano's book gained immediate notice after first being published in England: The London *Monthly Review* stated that "his publication appears very seasonable, at a time when Negro slavery is the subject of public investigation; it seems calculated to increase the odium that has been excited" against British planters operating in the Caribbean. The book would also become popular in Ireland, where it sold several thousand copies in the early 1790s, and in the United States, where white as well as black abolitionists used it to attack the slave trade.

Equiano's narrative traced his life from freedom to SLAVERY and back to freedom. Both he and his sister (who claimed Ibo ethnicity) were kidnapped and separated while still quite young (he was roughly 11–13 years old). Equiano was then transported to a slave pen on the western coast of Africa and sent to Barbados. He ended up on a Virginia plantation, then was sold again to an English owner who brought him to Britain and renamed him Gustavus Vassa. Sold again and brought to the Americas, Equiano worked on merchant ships and eventually bought his own freedom.

At his death in 1797, he was survived by a wife and two children in England.

Equiano was not just a writer but an early transatlantic antislavery activist. Not only did he publish his famous narrative but he presented petitions against the slave trade and gave public lectures about his experiences in bondage. Equiano's work was credited with helping stir popular as well as political sentiment against the slave trade, which England prohibited in 1807 and the United States banned in 1808. But as a writer of African descent, Equiano's narrative is also viewed as a means of establishing a proud racial identity through print. As Henry Louis Gates has argued, Equiano, like other black authors of the post–Revolutionary era, wrote to challenge stereotypes of African-descended people as savage and unlettered—and thus fit for enslavement. Equiano countered such pernicious views in a manner that remains powerful 200 years later.

See also AFRICAN AMERICANS.

Further reading: Robert J. Allison, ed., *"The Interesting Narrative of the Life of Olaudah Equiano, or Gustavus Vassa, the African, Written by Himself"* (Boston: Bedford Books, 1995); Henry Louis Gates, *The Signifyin' Monkey: A Theory of African American Literary Criticism* (New York: Oxford University Press, 1988).

— Richard Newman

Essex decision (1805)

The British Admiralty Court decision in the case of the American merchant ship *Essex* in 1805 altered official British policy toward American neutral shipping, aggravated diplomatic relations between Great Britain and the United States, and set the two nations on a collision course that ultimately led to the outbreak of the War of 1812 (1812–15). With France and Great Britain at war for most of the time from 1793 to 1815, there was a tremendous opportunity for the United States merchants to reap profits as long as both belligerents respected neutral rights. Initially, the British wanted to follow the Rule of 1756, which stated that any TRADE prohibited before wartime would remain prohibited after a declaration of war. In other words, if France had prohibited American ships from carrying goods from French colonies to France before the outbreak of war, then France could not allow such trade to occur after war broke out. Americans sidestepped this rule by shipping goods to the United States, unloading them, paying a small duty, and then reshipping the goods to France. Although such actions flouted British control of the seas—and allowed France to obtain goods from its colonies that would have been intercepted by the British had they been in French vessels—the British courts had allowed this trade to continue as indicated in the *Polly* decision of 1800.

With such favorable circumstances, American reexport trade rose from $40 million in 1800 to $60 million in 1805.

The *Essex* decision made it more difficult for Americans to evade British regulations. The court case involved the reshipment of wine between Spain (at the time an ally of France) and Cuba (a Spanish colony). The British court said that the reshipment of the wine in the United States was meant to deceive the British and did not represent a legitimate mercantile exchange. Since Spain had prohibited other nations from carrying goods to its colonies before it went to war with Great Britain, the trade was illegal and the ship was liable to seizure. Within the next few months, scores of American merchantmen were seized by the British navy. However, American merchants soon managed to make the reshipment of goods appear more legitimate, and the total amount of the reexport trade did not decline greatly.

Perhaps more important than the exact nature of the ruling was its symbolic significance. The courts put the burden of proof of neutral trade on the merchant owner instead of the captain of the British warship that seized a vessel. American merchants, in other words, were considered guilty of violating British regulations until they proved themselves innocent, rather than considered innocent until proven guilty. Such an approach showed little or no respect for the American flag. The British government had acted in what Americans thought was an arbitrary way, without warning or diplomatic discussion. When James Monroe, the American ambassador to Great Britain, attempted to discuss this ruling with the British government, he was told that it was nothing extraordinary and therefore not an appropriate topic for a special diplomatic meeting. The affront to American pride could hardly have been more direct. From the *Essex* decision until the outbreak of the War of 1812, the United States had an increasingly difficult time gaining the respect of both France and Great Britain and continuing its profits as a neutral trader amid a world at war.

See also FOREIGN AFFAIRS.

Further reading: Bradford Perkins, *Prologue to War, 1805–1812: England and the United States* (Berkeley: University of California Press, 1968).

Estaing, Charles-Henri Theodat, comte d' (Jean-Baptiste-Charles-Henri-Hector Theodat) (1729–1794)

When the French joined the REVOLUTIONARY WAR (1775–83) in 1778, Americans had high hopes that the conflict would soon be over. Much of the fulfillment of those hopes was placed on the shoulders of the Comte Charles Henri Theodat d'Estaing. This French aristocrat had fought in the French and Indian War (1754–63) with some distinction and was given command of the French forces to be sent to North America in aid of the American cause. Unfortunately, d'Estaing, while avoiding a total disaster, never succeeded in fulfilling American expectations.

The French fleet sailed from Toulon on April 13, 1778, but reached North American waters too late to trap the British fleet in the Chesapeake. Little came of a plan to attack the British in New York. Instead, d'Estaing decided to join up with American forces and capture the British army at Newport, RHODE ISLAND. This campaign never gained much momentum. The American forces under General JOHN SULLIVAN took too long to concentrate on Newport, delaying their attack. D'Estaing managed to bombard Newport and fought an indecisive action with a smaller British fleet from New York. Then nature interceded. A hurricane swept into both fleets, scattering the ships and severely damaging them. D'Estaing decided that he needed to take his fleet to Boston for a refitting. Without French support, the Americans were compelled to withdraw from their siege. In Boston, d'Estaing repaired his fleet and patched up some hard feelings, building a sense of camaraderie between the French and American forces. Then he headed for the WEST INDIES, where he conquered several British possessions, including St. Vincent and Grenada.

Late in 1779 d'Estaing, determined to aid the American forces fighting in the South, launched an attack on Savannah. Again, things did not work out for the French admiral. The British managed to reinforce the garrison despite the French blockade. Then in an all-out assault on October 9, 1779, the combined Franco-American armies failed to take the British fortification. D'Estaing was wounded twice in the battle and subsequently returned to France. This failure allowed General HENRY CLINTON to capture CHARLESTON (May 12, 1780) and extend the war for two more years. It was left to another French admiral, FRANCOIS-JOSEPH-PAUL, COMTE DE GRASSE, to defeat the British at the Battle of the Capes (September 5, 1781) and for a French general, JEAN-BAPTISTE-DONATIEN DE VIMEUR, COMTE DE ROCHAMBEAU, to join GEORGE WASHINGTON in the victory at YORKTOWN (October 19, 1781). D'Estaing was honored upon his return to France. When the FRENCH REVOLUTION (1789–1815) broke out, he tried to play to both sides and ended his life on the guillotine in 1794.

Eutaw Springs, Battle of (September 8, 1781)

One of the last and bloodiest major battles of the REVOLUTIONARY WAR (1775–83), the clash between the British and American armies at Eutaw Springs helped to determine the outcome of the war in the South. After CHARLES, LORD CORNWALLIS fought General NATHANAEL GREENE's Continentals at GUILFORD COURTHOUSE (March 15, 1781), the British general marched to Wilmington on the coast and then headed for Virginia. Greene, unaware of Cornwallis's intention, in the meantime decided to retake the rest of South Carolina. In the spring and summer of 1781 almost every British outpost fell to the American forces. Greene received a serious rebuff, however, at the Battle of Hobkirk's Hill (April 25, 1781) outside of Camden. The British commander, Lord Francis Rawdon, also successfully relieved a besieged garrison at Ninety-Six in May. However, the situation remained difficult for the British, as LOYALIST support within the state had evaporated. Rawdon, worn out by years in the field, headed for England, leaving Lieutenant Colonel Alexander Stewart in charge. By September, Stewart was encamped along the Santee River, about 30 miles northwest of Charleston. Without much local support, he had no idea about the location of Greene's army. Greene, on the other hand, knew exactly where to find his opponent.

Greene brought his army undetected to within a few miles of the British by the morning of September 8. Each side had about 2,200 men. Greene began to advance on the British position and might have caught Stewart entirely by surprise had the British not sent out a scavenging party of 80 men to collect yams for the troops. Greene's army met this small British force and quickly overwhelmed it, but the noise of the encounter brought a troop of cavalry that was also quickly dispatched. However, this encounter alerted the British army. Greene had deployed his force in what was now his usual fashion, with the militia in the front and the Continentals in the rear. The plan was that once the militia provided an initial volley or two, they would fall back and the British would rush ahead, expecting victory. Instead, they would meet well-trained Continentals. The plan almost worked. The militia fell back, and the British advanced in disorder. The Continentals broke the British advance and, joined by the militia, pursued the retreating enemy. But the cavalry, waiting on the wings, was unable to dislodge a British regiment in some thick underbrush. Their withering fire took its toll. Moreover, once the Americans reached the British encampment they began looting it, many drinking rum and creating disorder in the American ranks. Just behind the camp the British had drawn up a defensive position behind some walls at Burwell's plantation. From this protection they broke the American advance and compelled them to retreat. A complete disaster was avoided when a battalion of Maryland Continentals maintained order and delayed the counterattack. The Americans managed to withdraw with just enough order to prevent too hot of a pursuit.

The British held the field, but the battle cost both armies dearly. Greene lost one-fourth of his army as missing, killed, or wounded. The British fared worse. They had fewer dead but lost more than a quarter of their forces, many either missing or captured by the enemy. Soon after the battle, Stewart withdrew to Charleston, surrendering all of the South Carolina countryside. The British held the city until they evacuated it after the preliminary peace agreement that ended the war.

Further reading: Don Higginbotham, *The War of American Independence: Military Attitudes, Policies, and Practice, 1763–1789* (New York: Macmillan, 1971); Robert Middlekauf, *The Glorious Cause: The American Revolution, 1783–1789* (New York: Oxford University Press, 1982).

F

fairs, agricultural

In 1810 retired merchant and gentleman farmer Elkanah Watson organized the first agricultural fair in Berkshire County, Massachusetts. This grew to become a major American tradition—the agricultural fair. Watson had led an eclectic life, making and losing fortunes in a variety of enterprises before accumulating enough wealth to establish himself as a gentleman farmer in the first decade of the 19th century. He became a proponent of new agricultural techniques, importing special breeds of hogs, sheep, and cattle. Gaining support from the Berkshire Agricultural Society, which he spearheaded, Watson created a special "cattle show" in 1810. The idea was to demonstrate the scientific nature of American AGRICULTURE and to embody the pastoral ideal. From the beginning, the fair included more than a display of cattle; it also exhibited of wide range of farm produce and items manufactured domestically. Watson's fair relied upon an elaborate ritual to "seize the farmer's heart" as well as his mind. The idea quickly spread. Within a few decades there were hundreds of county fairs each year across the country, offering prizes and premiums; the county fair had become a highlight of the American agrarian culture.

See also RURAL LIFE.

Further reading: Catherine E. Kelly, "The Consummation of Rural Prosperity and Happiness: New England Agricultural Fairs and the Construction of Class and Gender, 1810–1860," *American Quarterly* 49 (1997): 574–602.

Fallen Timbers, Battle of (August 20, 1794)

Fallen Timbers was the final major battle in the Northwest Indian War of the early 1790s. Following the REVOLUTIONARY WAR (1775–83), the United States attempted to acquire new lands north of the Ohio River. Treaties were signed with some of the NATIVE AMERICANS in the area. However, many Indians did not see the treaties as valid because they were not signed by recognized leaders. As settlers began to cross the river into present-day Ohio, there were skirmishes between the Americans and the Indians. In response, the United States sent two armed expeditions, in 1790 and again in 1791. Indians of several tribes united under the leadership of Little Turtle and BLUE JACKET to soundly defeat both of these armies, led by General Josiah Harmar and Governor ARTHUR ST. CLAIR. These disasters crippled the United States Army and led President GEORGE WASHINGTON to appoint General "Mad" ANTHONY WAYNE to rebuild and train an army to defeat the Indians. Meanwhile, the Indians, who enjoyed a position of dominance, refused to make peace with the Americans and demanded that all of the treaties that surrendered land north of the Ohio River be abolished. They would make peace only if the Ohio River was restored as the boundary between Indians and Americans. Throughout 1793 and 1794, General Wayne trained his army and marched it into Ohio, destroying many villages and crops along the way.

The campaign culminated in the Battle of Fallen Timbers, in far northwestern Ohio, on August 20, 1794. Fallen Timbers was so-named because a recent thunderstorm had knocked down large numbers of trees. Wayne's army numbered about 3,000 men. The Indian forces numbered around 1,300, with a small number of Canadian militia volunteers also in their ranks. Many Indians were absent from the battlefield, however, because they had sought shelter from the storm at their village several miles away. Those who remained had ritually fasted in preparation for the battle. Unfortunately for them, the battle came a day later than anticipated, leaving the Indian warriors famished. Perhaps as few as 400 actually participated in the battle. Although the Indians provided stiff resistance to the American attack early in the battle, Wayne's army forced them to retreat. The Indians fled to nearby Fort Miami, a British post, where they had been assured in the past that the fort would offer them safe haven in times of trouble. In this instance, the British would not allow the Indians to enter, wishing to avoid conflict between themselves and the Americans. The Indians thus had to retreat farther from the field and lost additional warriors.

Although the casualties in the battle were nearly equal for the Americans and Indians, the victory clearly went to Wayne's army. The American army had displayed its new-found power, and the Indians now realized that the Americans would not be easily defeated. Due to the Fort Miami incident, the Indians also lost confidence in the British, who they had hoped would join them as allies. As a result, less than a year later the Indian confederacy signed the TREATY OF GREENVILLE (1795).

Further reading: Wiley Sword, *President Washington's Indian War: The Struggle for the Old Northwest* (Norman: University of Oklahoma Press, 1985).

— Michael L. Cox

Farewell Address of George Washington (1796)

In September 1796 President GEORGE WASHINGTON sent his farewell address to a Philadelphia newspaper. The address circulated around the nation and served two purposes: It let the public know that Washington would not run for reelection and offered the country some final advice. Washington began by announcing he would not seek reelection. At the end of the first paragraph he stated he had decided "to decline being considered among the number of those out of whom a choice is to be made." By so doing, Washington set a precedent that the American president would serve no more than eight years, a precedent that would be followed for over a century.

Washington advised his countrymen that the continued union of the states was their greatest hope for sustained independence, but he warned them that to maintain such a union would take vigilance and sacrifice. The dangers that Washington believed could most easily lead to trouble for the young republic were sectionalism, party politics, and foreign influence. Washington plainly stated that all sections—north, south, and west—were connected to each other politically, economically, and culturally, and that only by strengthening those bonds could the new nation survive. In order to form such a bond, citizens would have to recognize their responsibility to the national government. "The very idea of the power and right of the people to establish government presupposes the duty of every individual to obey the established government."

Another very real danger in Washington's view was the emergence of party politics or "factions" of competing visions of how the government should work. Washington was very clear in his warning that partisan differences, especially those based on geography, could weaken the republic. "I have already intimated to you the danger of parties in the State, with particular reference to the founding of them on geographical discriminations." Washington recognized that there were some who believed that parties "in free countries are useful checks upon the administration of government, and serve to keep alive the spirit of liberty." He admitted there was some truth to this, but that in a popularly elected government the danger of party politics was greater than the possible benefits. "But in those of the popular character, in governments purely elective, it is not to be encouraged."

In perhaps the most famous advice given in the address, Washington warned his fellow citizens to avoid becoming involved with foreign nations. He implored the American people to take advantage of their geographical isolation and to remain out of the affairs of Europe. The interests of the European powers, he argued, were not the interests of America. "Hence, therefore, it must be unwise in us to implicate ourselves by artificial ties in the ordinary vicissitudes of her politics or the ordinary combinations and collisions of her friendships or enmities." His advice to the country was: "The great rule of conduct for us in regard to foreign nations is, in extending our commercial relations to have with them as little political connection as possible. So far as we have already formed engagements let them be fulfilled with perfect good faith. Here let us stop."

See also FOREIGN AFFAIRS; POLITICAL PARTIES.

— J. Brett Adams

Federalist Papers (1787–1788)

The *Federalist*, more commonly known as the *Federalist Papers*, is a series of 85 newspaper essays on the United States Constitution written by ALEXANDER HAMILTON, JAMES MADISON, and JOHN JAY. Written to the citizens of New York under the pseudonym "Publius," a reference to the great defender of the ancient Roman Republic Publius Valerius Publicola, the *Federalist Papers* were originally published in two New York City newspapers: the *New York Packet* and the *Independent Journal*. The first essay appeared on October 27, 1787, and the series continued until April 2, 1788. Later that year, the collection of essays appeared as a bound book, edited by Hamilton and published by J. and A. McLean. A second edition, with Madison as editor, was published in 1818.

The purpose of the essays was to urge the people of New York to ratify the new Constitution, which had been drafted by the CONSTITUTIONAL CONVENTION and adopted on September 17, 1787. The Convention was held over the summer of 1787 in Philadelphia, with the purpose of planning for a more effective national government than the one provided for by the ARTICLES OF CONFEDERATION, which had been written in 1776. Initially the idea was to hold a convention with the responsibility of revising the Articles of Confederation, yet the delegates soon decided to not simply amend the Articles. Instead, they sought to create a new form of government altogether.

In order to establish the Constitution, the approval of at least nine of the 13 state ratifying conventions was required. Because of its thriving commerce and central location, New York's acceptance of the proposed document was deemed essential to the viability and success of a new government. The *Federalist* essays were reprinted in other newspapers across New York State and in several cities in other states, likely influencing the ratifying conventions in those places as well.

Alexander Hamilton, a member of the Constitutional Convention who strongly supported the proposed government, was the originator of the work. In an effort to win over public opinion in favor of the document, Hamilton decided to write a series of essays that would both defend the Constitution and explain its provisions. To complete the project, he enlisted the support of two prominent collaborators: Madison, a fellow Constitutional Convention delegate and brilliant scholar of political history, and Jay, the secretary of foreign affairs under the Articles of Confederation. Although the authorship of some of the essays was a subject of intense debate for well over a century, modern research suggests that of the 85 essays, Hamilton wrote 51, Madison wrote 29, and Jay wrote five. Collectively, the authors were experienced scholars on a variety of subjects, and their contributions tended to reflect their individual areas of expertise. Hamilton concentrated on military and financial affairs, while Madison addressed the historical experiences of confederacies, and Jay focused on foreign policy.

For the most part, the authors wrote independently, consulting each other infrequently due largely to time constraints imposed by newspaper deadlines. This loose collaboration was possible because, despite some minor differences, the authors generally agreed on the fundamental principles concerning the nature of the new government. They believed in the need for a strong central authority to correct what they saw as the political weakness inherent in the Articles of Confederation, and they thought that a vertical division of power of between the central and state governments would provide the best balance. They maintained that the separation of the legislative, executive, and judicial functions of government provided a further safeguard and would prevent any single branch from dominating the others.

Furthermore, Madison and Hamilton agreed about the fundamental question of human nature that underpinned all political systems. Like the English philosopher Thomas Hobbes, they believed that humans were inherently wicked beings who lacked self-control; therefore, the purpose of government was to curb the wild passions of people. This defect in human nature provided a constant state of struggle in which individuals sought their own selfish desires rather than the common good. This human propensity constituted the foundation of faction, which Madison and Hamilton believed should be incorporated into the function of good government. They thought that a strong republican government would recognize the existence of factions and force them to compete against one another to prevent tyranny by the majority. These ideas, as expressed in Madison's essay No. 10, constitute one of the most famous defenses of republican government.

Other notable essays include No. 51, in which Madison discussed the nature of human existence, quipping "if men were angels, government would not be necessary." Hamilton, anticipating objections to the expanded powers of the executive and judiciary under the Constitution, wrote two other influential series, Nos. 67–77 and 78–83.

The authors of the *Federalist* were confident that the new Constitution would provide the best foundation for a durable republic, but their view was not shared by all. Opposition organized against the Constitution, mainly because the document did not contain a BILL OF RIGHTS explicitly outlining powers reserved to both individuals and the states. Many opponents feared that the strong central government established by the Constitution would eventually usurp state sovereignty. Even those who agreed that a stronger central authority was necessary objected to particular details of the Constitution. Despite some public protest, such as editorials by anonymous writers like "Cato" and "Brutus," the opposition, formally known as ANTI-FEDERALISTS, never organized their campaign against the document and were thus overshadowed by the logical presentation in the *Federalist* papers.

In the end, the authors of the *Federalist Papers* achieved their goal: The Constitution won eventual ratification in all 13 states. Since that time, the *Federalist Papers* has become an important document in American history, evolving into a definitive treatise on American government and providing modern scholars and leaders alike with insight into the political minds of the founding era.

See also REPUBLICANISM.

Further reading: Alan Brinkley, *New Federalist Papers: Essays in Defense of the Constitution* (New York: Norton, 1997); Albert Furtwangler, *The Authority of Publius: A Reading of the* Federalist Papers (Ithaca, N.Y.: Cornell University Press, 1984); George Mace, *Locke, Hobbes, and the Federalist Papers: An Essay on the Genesis of the American Political Heritage* (Carbondale: Southern Illinois University Press, 1974).

— Amy Pharr

Federalist Party

The Federalist Party of the 1790s and early 1800s supported a platform that valued order and stability over freedom and personal liberty, a powerful national government, and diplomatic and commercial ties with Great Britain. The Federalist Party and the FEDERALISTS of 1787–88 should not be confused. The Federalists who advocated the ratification of the new Constitution in 1787 did not necessarily become members of the Federalist Party. Some men who had supported the Constitution, notably JAMES MADISON, became members of the DEMOCRATIC-REPUBLICAN PARTY, while others who opposed the Constitution became Federalists. The parties of the 1790s formed around the issues that faced the nation created by the Constitution; both sides accepted the new frame of government. The Federalist Party drew its strength from a curious mix ranging from wealthy merchants and large landowners to conservative farmers, who came mostly from the commercial cities and from slowly developing rural areas. Federalists were strongest in New England.

The Federalist Party developed during President GEORGE WASHINGTON's administration. Although Washington believed that parties, or factions, as they were often referred to in that period, were a negative force to be avoided, he is usually labeled a Federalist because of his policies and ideals. Under the leadership of Secretary of the Treasury ALEXANDER HAMILTON, the administration proposed several measures that became the core of the Federalist Party platform. Hamilton wanted to strengthen the national government by fully funding the NATIONAL DEBT, assuming the state debts, and creating the BANK OF THE UNITED STATES. The underlying theory of this plan was that such economic actions would provide the wealthy with a vested interest in seeing the United States succeed. Opposition to these measures formed around Secretary of State THOMAS JEFFERSON and Congressman James Madison. They believed that Hamilton's plan would give the federal government too much power. The supporters of Hamilton became the Federalists; the supporters of Jefferson and Madison became the Democratic-Republicans. The differences of opinion between the two groups solidified in the controversy over JAY'S TREATY (1794). The terms of this treaty angered many Americans, who saw it as too conciliatory to the British. Despite this opposition, the combination of Hamilton's fiscal program and expanding international markets created economic prosperity. The Federalists had also managed to get the new United States government operating efficiently and without major incident.

Politics in the late 1790s became more heated. The Federalists overplayed their cards during the QUASI WAR (1798–1800) crisis. War fever swept the nation, as many Americans wanted to fight the French for their depredations on American commerce and for the XYZ AFFAIR (1797–98). In an effort to stifle their political opponents, the Federalists passed the ALIEN AND SEDITION ACTS (1798), measures that sought to control criticism of the government and limit the impact of immigrants on politics. Although the navy was dispatched to attack French warships and preparations were made for war, President JOHN ADAMS decided to try to negotiate with the French. By 1800 an agreement was reached that avoided declared war. This statesmanlike action helped Adams lose the ELECTION OF 1800. Members of his own Federalist Party turned on him, while Democratic-Republicans attacked the unpopular Alien and Sedition Acts. Immediately before he left office, Adams created many new positions in the federal judiciary and filled them with Federalist appointees. These so-called midnight appointments caused great controversy and eventually led to the groundbreaking SUPREME COURT case *MARBURY V. MADISON*.

After the election of 1800, the Federalists fought a losing battle for national prominence. Previously, Federalist leaders had clung to older notions of politics and elections, believing that only the well-educated and relatively wealthy knew what was best for society. With Jefferson's victory, the party began to adopt more democratic campaign tactics to compete with the Democratic-Republicans. Yet the Federalists still became less important nationally and increasingly developed into a sectionally based minority. The party was revived temporarily because of the unpopularity of Jefferson's EMBARGO OF 1807, which devastated the national ECONOMY. Federalists hoped to gain similar political capital by opposing the War of 1812 (1812–15). But antiwar sentiment was much more regionally based. Many New Englanders believed that their interests were being pushed aside in favor of those of the South and West, and they were unhappy with the break in commerce brought by the war. Several government leaders in Massachusetts called for a convention to address these issues. Delegates from five New England states attended the Hartford Convention of 1814, where there was some talk of secession. Ironically, the Federalists became spokesmen for STATE'S RIGHTS when they declared at the convention that the states could deny the legitimacy of government acts that they believed were unconstitutional. However, these drastic steps allowed the Democratic-Republicans to attack the Federalists as treasonous, and the party looked foolish, as the convention occurred almost simultaneously with the end of the war. The Federalist Party never recovered. The party continued to run candidates for election, and while they had some local success, they never again were a strong national presence.

Although the failure of the Federalist Party was primarily due to its inability to recognize the growing importance of popular democracy, it left an important legacy. The Federalist Party may have lost, but its principles were preserved in the groundbreaking Supreme Court decisions of Chief Justice JOHN MARSHALL. The Federalists were also instrumental in setting up and operating the American government in the 1790s. It was thus the Federalists who successfully established national institutions, guided the economy, and shaped the judicial system in the most formative years of the United States.

See also POLITICAL PARTIES; REPUBLICANISM.

Further reading: James M. Banner Jr., *To the Hartford Convention: The Federalists and the Origins of Party Politics in Massachusetts, 1789–1815* (New York: Knopf, 1970); Stanley Elkins and Eric McKitrick, *The Age of Federalism: The Early American Republic, 1788–1800* (New York: Oxford University Press, 1993); David Hackett Fischer, *The Revolution of American Conservatism; The Federalist Party in the Era of Jeffersonian Democracy* (New York: Harper & Row, 1965).

— Crystal Williams

Federalists

Federalists were those who supported the Constitution and advocated its ratification, often in response to the strong opposition of the ANTI-FEDERALISTS. The Federalists who supported the Constitution should not be confused with the FEDERALIST PARTY, which formed later and did not necessarily include the same people. The opinions of the Federalists were most clearly expounded in the *FEDERALIST PAPERS*, which were published with the express purpose of convincing people to support the ratification of the Constitution. They were originally printed for the campaign in New York but were soon reprinted in other states. The primary authors of the *Federalist Papers* were JAMES MADISON, ALEXANDER HAMILTON, and JOHN JAY, who published the work anonymously under the pseudonym Publius.

The arguments of the Federalists were usually framed in defense of anti-Federalist attacks that government should be simple and power should be in the hands of the people. After the REVOLUTIONARY WAR (1775–83), many Americans were afraid of giving too much power to the national government for fear that it would become tyrannical. However, other Americans wanted to see the national government gain power at the expense of the state governments, especially in light of the weakness of the ARTICLES OF CONFEDERATION. Both the Federalists and the anti-Federalists wanted the new republic to succeed. Both also claimed to want to protect liberty. However, their two visions of how this would best be accomplished were completely at odds with each other. The Federalists argued that power was not a threat to liberty, but in fact would help to protect it.

The authors of the *Federalist Papers* also responded to the concern that having one large republic would include too many people with different needs and pursuits. The Feder-

alists believed that different interest groups, or factions, would have a positive effect. According to this theory, no one group could become an overwhelming majority and impose their will upon everyone else. To the Federalists, a larger political system was a much more reliable guarantee of liberty than the dependence on virtue and the idea that all citizens would give up their own interests for the public good. Under the Constitution, everyone would be forced to compromise, and in that manner the public good could be achieved. According to the Federalists, America was the perfect setting for a republic, because it was only in a large area that the public good could be protected. Small republics would be destroyed by the growth of interest groups. Federalists also explained that the states would not be wiped out by the formation of a strong national government. In fact, power would be divided between the states and the nation, providing yet another guarantee of liberty. Federalists were interested in the role of commerce and felt that the ownership of property and other economic interests would give people a stake in the continuation of the republic.

Federalists were split on how democratic the government should be, but they tended to believe that some limitation was necessary. Based on republican ideals of deference, many Federalists believed this limitation would occur naturally, as an aristocracy of talent would rise to power. Men of virtue, intelligence, and wisdom would be selected as leaders. In many ways, the views of the Federalists were much less democratic than those of the anti-Federalists. The Constitution they created was also less democratic than the government under the Articles of Confederation. The Federalists realized that the state assemblies would not be eager to ratify the Constitution and thereby give up a great deal of power, so the Federalists at the CONSTITUTIONAL CONVENTION (1787) provided for special ratifying conventions to be elected in each state. Ratification by such conventions would also give the Constitution greater legitimacy by grounding it directly in the people. They also knew it would be difficult to get all 13 states to agree, so they stated that only nine states had to ratify the Constitution for it to take effect. Other states could then join the union whenever they chose. Federalists won the debate with the ratification of the Constitution by nine states by the summer of 1788, and they eagerly set to work creating the nation they had envisioned. Federalist arguments have often been criticized as mere after-the-fact rationales for promoting their own economic interests, but their ideals have endured and, in many ways, form the basis of modern American politics.

Further reading: Forrest McDonald, *Novus Ordo Seclorum: The Intellectual Origins of the Constitution* (Lawrence: University of Kansas Press, 1985); Gordon S. Wood, *The Creation of the American Republic, 1776–1787* (Chapel Hill: University of North Carolina Press, 1969).

— Crystal Williams

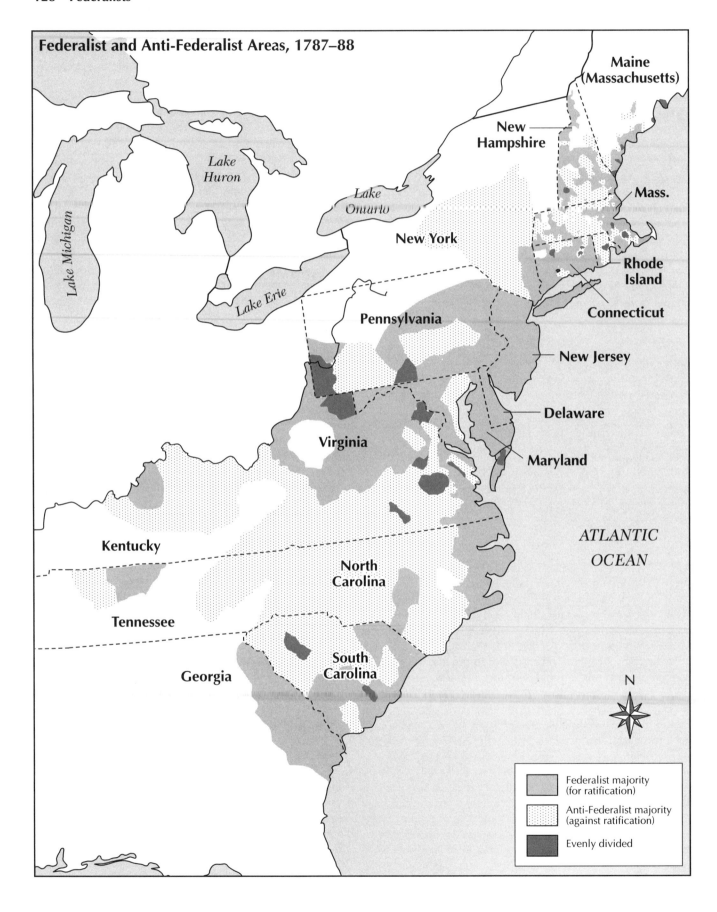

Federalist and Anti-Federalist Areas, 1787–88

Legend:
- Federalist majority (for ratification)
- Anti-Federalist majority (against ratification)
- Evenly divided

Florida

Between 1754 and 1820, Florida changed hands three times: The Treaty of Paris of 1763 transferred the territory from Spain to Great Britain; the TREATY OF PARIS of 1783 returned it to the Spanish; and in 1819 John Quincy Adams negotiated its acquisition by the United States. Throughout this period, Florida remained a sparsely settled borderland, often serving as a haven for illegal TRADE, escaped slaves, and NATIVE AMERICANS raiding across the border.

Until 1763, Spain's hold on Florida remained weak and centered on St. Augustine. The Spanish encouraged slaves from the British North American colonies to escape to Florida, assuring them freedom and using them to help protect the province. At the time, Florida had an ambiguous northern boundary and stretched only as far west as Pensacola. With the British victory in the French and Indian War (1754–63), Florida became part of the British Empire, since Spain had allied with France. The British encouraged settlement and organized the territory into two separate colonies: East Florida, which consisted of the swampy peninsula and the land directly south of Georgia, and West Florida, which had the Mississippi River as its western boundary and included as much as one-third of the present states of Alabama and Mississippi. As British settlers arrived in the two colonies, they sought to establish the slave ECONOMY that predominated in nearby Georgia and South Carolina.

The outbreak of the REVOLUTIONARY WAR (1775–83) left the two Florida colonies in an awkward position. While some of the colonists favored the opposition to British imperial regulation, many remained loyal to King GEORGE III, recognizing their vulnerability on the FRONTIER. Florida thus became a base for LOYALISTS and Native Americans during the war. When the war ended, however, the British returned the area to Spain, which had belatedly thrown its lot in with France and the United States. At this point, Florida again returned to its borderland status as a haven for escaped slaves and Native Americans. Its British and Spanish population were minimal.

Almost from its inception, the United States coveted Florida. The northern boundary remained in dispute, and the negotiators of the LOUISIANA PURCHASE (1803) were supposed to buy Florida and New Orleans, not the vast track of land west of the Mississippi. In fact, Robert R. Livingston claimed that most of West Florida was included in the Louisiana Purchase. The agreement with the French had merely stated that the territory that had been ceded from Spain to France was now given to the United States. The Spanish did not agree to this interpretation, nor did the United States push the interpretation immediately. But having Spanish control over Florida created problems for the United States, with British traders infiltrating the region and hostile Native Americans using Florida for a base of operations. In 1810 a group of American settlers in West Florida declared their independence from Spain and sought to become part of the United States. By 1811 American troops were stationed outside Mobile in West Florida, and President JAMES MADISON declared the Perdido River the boundary between Spanish and American territory. When Louisiana entered the union as a state in 1812, it included a good chunk of West Florida on the east bank of the Mississippi. During the War of 1812 (1812–15) Americans extended their efforts in Florida, including the seizure of Amelia Island by a band of Georgians and a failed attack on St. Augustine. The fact that the United States was at war with Great Britain—and not its ally Spain—seems not to have bothered the invaders.

In the years after the Treaty of Ghent (1814) the United States became even more aggressive in its bid for Florida. When escaped slaves established a fort and a haven for other runaways, an American expedition struck across the border, blew up the fort, and killed 270 AFRICAN-AMERICAN men, women, and children. In 1818 Seminole raids had become serious enough to draw the attention of General Andrew Jackson, commander for the southern district of the United States Army. Jackson crossed the border, defeated any Indians who opposed him, and arrested two British traders, John Ambrister and Alexander Arbuthnot. Convinced that both men had encouraged the Indians and supplied them with arms, Jackson saw to it that Ambrister and Arbuthnot were executed after conviction in an ad hoc court of law. Then, believing that President James Monroe wanted him to drive the Spanish out of Florida, Jackson occupied Pensacola and sent the Spanish governor and his officials to Cuba. These actions created an uproar in Monroe's cabinet and an international crisis. Eventually, the controversy subsided. John Quincy Adams convinced the Spanish to sell Florida for $5 million and, in an effort to concede something to the Spanish, set a western boundary to the Louisiana Territory in the Adams-Onís Treaty of 1819. While the purchase of Florida opened up more area for the expansion of SLAVERY, the Seminoles in central Florida were not easily subdued and would fight the United States government for decades to come.

See also FOREIGN AFFAIRS.

Further reading: Thomas D. Clark and John D. W. Guice, *Frontiers in Conflict: The Old Southwest, 1795–1830* (Albuquerque: University of New Mexico Press, 1989); Robert L. Gold, *Borderland Empires in Transition: The Triple-Nation Transfer of Florida* (Carbondale: Southern Illinois University Press, 1969); William Earl Weeks, *John Quincy Adams and American Global Empire* (Lexington: University Press of Kentucky, 1992).

foreign affairs

Between 1754 and 1820, Americans struggled with three major foreign policy problems: First, and most persistent, was defining their relationship with Great Britain and France as those two nations vied for world dominance. Second, Americans were confronted with a declining Spanish power on its southern and, for a while, western boundary. And third, once the United States became independent, it suffered periodic depredations from the BARBARY PIRATES on its Atlantic and Mediterranean shipping. By 1820, each of these problems had been all but solved. Great Britain and France no longer opposed one another, Spain had ceded FLORIDA and was losing its grip on its other colonies, and the Barbary pirates had at last been defeated. With these issues out of the way, an independent United States turned its back on Europe and focused on expansion in the North American continent.

In 1754 colonial Americans knew where they stood: They were Anglo-Britons locked in a death struggle to drive the French from the continent and subdue NATIVE AMERICANS. There can be no doubt about the enthusiasm colonial Americans had for the French and Indian War (1754–63) and the loyalty they felt to the British Crown. Victory on the Plains of Abraham above Quebec meant peace and security in a world that had been threatened repeatedly by the French and Indians. But if every colonial American was a British patriot, that did not mean that every colonial American followed British imperial regulations. Many merchants had earned a fortune trading with the French and others in the WEST INDIES, even during the war. This smuggling meant jobs for sailors and dockside workers. It also provided markets for goods produced by farmers. Efforts to change this illegal way of life were bound to bring opposition. However, Americans, even during the RESISTANCE MOVEMENT (1764–75), were not ready to jump into the arms of the French. The imperial debate was a debate within, not against, the British Empire.

The guns fired at LEXINGTON AND CONCORD (April 19, 1775) changed the situation. Once war broke out, the revolutionaries needed outside support. Inspired by the ideals of REPUBLICANISM, the CONTINENTAL CONGRESS drew up a model treaty it hoped all nations would sign onto; it offered free and open TRADE with the United States. In a world of power politics, no one took the treaty seriously. France, still resentful of its defeat, was willing to aid the rebellion, but it wanted concessions. The two treaties of 1778 provided most-favored-nation trading status to France and promised a defensive alliance. The Spanish and the Dutch joined in the war before the conflict was over. With this foreign assistance, the rebellion eventually succeeded.

In the years after the TREATY OF PARIS (1783) the United States did not get much respect. The diplomatic corps consisted mainly of THOMAS JEFFERSON in Paris and JOHN ADAMS in London. Limits were put on American trade; Barbary pirates threatened in the Mediterranean; the British occupied FRONTIER outposts; and Spain contested the southern boundary and navigation on the Mississippi River. Ratification of the Constitution did not materially change the situation. Only when war broke out in 1793 between France, inspired by its own revolution, and Great Britain did significant changes occur.

Once again Americans were confronted with a war between France and Great Britain. France wanted the United States to honor its 1778 treaty obligations and sent Citizen EDMOND GENET to convince Americans to fight for liberty. The administration of GEORGE WASHINGTON hesitated and then issued a NEUTRALITY PROCLAMATION (1793), declaring that the nation would not come to the aid of either power. Because of British seizures of American ships and the IMPRESSMENT of American sailors, Washington sent JOHN JAY to Great Britain. JAY'S TREATY (1794) left several issues unsettled, but it granted trading rights to the British. Distraught over this position, the French began to seize American ships, precipitating a crisis. When French agents insisted on a bribe before negotiations could begin in the XYZ AFFAIR (1797–98), the United States entered the QUASI WAR (1798–1800), an undeclared war in which Americans fought several naval engagements against the French. After NAPOLEON BONAPARTE seized power in France, peace was restored. The French agreed that their alliance with the United States was void and stopped capturing American merchantmen. The United States did not press for reparations and agreed to treat French trade on equal terms with British trade.

No sooner had Napoleon signed onto the agreement ending the Quasi War than he secretly had Spain cede the Louisiana Territory to France. Spain recognized its weakness and had already granted the United States free navigation of the Mississippi River, access to New Orleans, and a favorable Florida boundary in the TREATY OF SAN LORENZO (1795). Now it was surrendering a huge chunk of North America to Napoleon, who hoped to launch a Franco-American empire. Those dreams ended when a French expedition failed to secure the rebellious province of Saint-Domingue (HAITI). In an effort to raise money for his armies, Napoleon offered the Americans the opportunity to buy all of Louisiana. The Americans had sought to obtain New Orleans but capitalized upon the opportunity to double the size of the United States in the LOUISIANA PURCHASE (1803).

The war in Europe continued to create problems for America. The British insisted on stopping American ships and impressing seamen. In the *CHESAPEAKE-LEOPARD* affair (June 22, 1807), they even fired upon and searched an American naval frigate. Compounding the problem of impressment was the issue of neutral rights. American merchants profited greatly as a neutral carrier to both belligerents. The British and French sought to stifle each other's economy by putting limits on such trade. In the ORDERS IN COUNCIL the British demanded that all neutral ships stop in Great Britain before trading with the continent to ensure that there was no contraband or war materials on board. Napoleon issued the Berlin and Milan Decrees, which asserted that any vessel that stopped in Great Britain before entering French-controlled Europe would be liable to seizure. Caught between a rock and a hard place, President Thomas Jefferson opted to use trade as a diplomatic weapon. His DEMOCRATIC-REPUBLICAN-controlled Congress passed the EMBARGO OF 1807, which prohibited all exports, a measure that devastated the American ECONOMY. President JAMES MADISON therefore offered adjustments to this measure, first in the NON-INTERCOURSE ACT (1809), which promised not to trade with either power until they allowed neutral trade, then with MACON'S BILL NO.2 (1810), which allowed trade but promised to resume non-intercourse with one power if the other lifted its constraints against American merchant ships. When Napoleon suggested that he would do so, the United States reinstated non-intercourse with Great Britain. This precipitated a crisis that led to the outbreak of the War of 1812 (1812–15).

Although the Treaty of Ghent (1814) settled none of the outstanding issues between the United States and Great Britain, it marked the end of the biggest foreign policy problem for the United States during its first 50 years. Impressment and neutral rights became moot issues once Napoleon was defeated. The United States and Great Britain henceforth would settle their affairs amicably.

The other two foreign policy issues also moved toward settlement. Spain, ever weaker and facing rebellions in its American colonies, allowed itself to be bullied out of Florida in return for some compensation and a defined boundary between Texas and Louisiana. After the Adams-Onís Treaty (1819), Spain would not present a serious diplomatic challenge until the end of the 19th century. The Barbary pirates had been a nuisance and embarrassment for the United States since the 1780s. Wars with Algiers and Tripoli had been settled in part by agreeing to pay tribute. With an enlarged American fleet in 1815, Stephen Decatur forced the Barbary states to submit to treaties without any payment. In part through luck and in part through stint of arms, the United States emerged from this period in a position of relative strength, ready to tell the rest of the world that it would mind its own business if the world kept at arms length—a policy articulated by Secretary of War John Quincy Adams in the Monroe Doctrine (1821).

See also FRENCH ALLIANCE; FRENCH REVOLUTION.

Further reading: Reginald Horsman, *The Causes of the War of 1812* (Philadelphia: University of Pennsylvania Press, 1962); Paul A. Varg, *Foreign Policies of the Founding Fathers* (East Lansing: Michigan State University Press, 1963).

Forten, James (1767–1842)

James Forten was born to a free AFRICAN-AMERICAN family in Philadelphia and learned his father's sailmaking trade. While still in his teens, he served on a privateer during the REVOLUTIONARY WAR (1775–83) and, after his ship was captured, refused British offers of education in exchange for his service. After the war, Forten worked at, and then acquired, the sailmaking business of Robert Bridges. Forten then began to gather a fortune that made him one of the wealthiest people in Philadelphia, not to mention a leading member of the nation's so-called black elite. Yet no matter how far he progressed economically, Forten faced the obstacle of race. No matter how much he pledge to the American nation, often it refused to embrace him. In 1799, for example, an anti–slave-trading petition he and other black Philadelphians signed was rejected by Congress, 84–1. "We the People does not mean them," one southern congressman told Forten and the other petitioners. Forten wrote the lone supporter of the petition, a Massachusetts representative, and thanked him for joining the cause of justice. Throughout his life, Forten participated in other petition campaigns and struggles for racial equality, including opposition to segregated schooling in Pennsylvania and to the Quaker State's disfranchisement of black voters in 1838.

Forten was a model black activist for later figures such as Frederick Douglass. In 1849 Douglass told a New York City audience, "My heart swells with pride" at the mention of Forten's name. Like Douglass, Forten used American political beliefs in constitutional equality to condemn American racialist ideologies. One of Forten's most important pieces of writing was an 1813 pamphlet critiquing a Pennsylvania bill that sought to restrict African-American migration to Pennsylvania (and even threatened to reenslave those African Americans who migrated to the state and did not register their name with a local official). Forten's essay, entitled "Series of Letters by a Man of Colour," cited the DECLARATION OF INDEPENDENCE (July 4, 1776), Pennsylvania's 1780 gradual abolition act, and the state's 1790 constitution (which did not distinguish between so-called black and white rights) as evidence that American society rested firmly on beliefs of equality for all. "Let not the spirit of the father behold the son robbed of that liberty which he died to establish," Forten wrote, "but let the motto of our legislators be 'The law knows no distinction.'" The law was not passed. Forten's pamphlet gained prominence among black activists in other parts of America. In 1827, *Freedom's Journal,* the first independent African-American newspaper based in New York City, republished the essay so that younger generations of activists might learn the trade of written protest.

Although initially interested in voluntary emigration schemes to Africa, Forten came to oppose the American Colonization Society, which he believed an enemy of free African Americans. After its formation in 1816, Forten organized anticolonization protests in Philadelphia over the next decade and helped transform young white abolitionists' views on the subject. His most famous protégé was William Lloyd Garrison, the fiery Massachusetts editor of *The Liberator*. Garrison was initially a gradual abolitionist and a quasi colonizationist. Sometime in 1829 or 1830 he met Forten, who showed him African-American anticolonization pamphlets. Garrison used these and other documents to publish his first big work, *Thoughts on African Colonization* (1832). Forten remained an ally of new abolitionists coming on the American scene in the 1830s, speaking at interracial gatherings and providing African Americans with subscriptions to journals such as *The Liberator*. When he died in 1842, Forten was eulogized as a founding father of African-American protest in America. His motto remained, "America, with thy faults I love thee still."

See also ANTISLAVERY AND ABOLITION.

Further reading: Gary B. Nash, *Forging Freedom: The Formation of Philadelphia's Black Community, 1745–1840* (Cambridge, Mass.: Harvard University Press, 1988); Richard Newman, Patrick Rael, and Philip Lapsansky, eds., *Pamphlets of Protest: An Anthology of Early African American Protest Writing* (New York: Routledge, 2001); Julie Winch, *A Gentleman of Color: A Life of James Forten* (New York: Oxford University Press, 2002).

— Richard Newman

Fort Stanwix, Treaty of (1768)

The Treaty of Fort Stanwix between the British and Six Nations, or IROQUOIS CONFEDERACY, in 1768 opened much of the land south of the Ohio River to white settlement. The treaty was created as a response to further colonial demands for NATIVE AMERICAN lands west of the Appalachian Mountains. According to the PROCLAMATION OF 1763, white settlement had been forbidden beyond the Appalachians. Many people, called squatters, ignored the law and settled in small cabins in present-day Kentucky and Tennessee. The British government and the Virginia colonial legislature sought to obtain the lands through treaty and to regulate settlement in the West. Pennsylvania wanted more land on its western FRONTIER. Speculators also hoped for a new boundary, which would open land for sale.

In 1768 the British superintendent of Indian affairs, Sir William Johnson, organized a treaty council with the Iroquois at Fort Stanwix, now Rome, New York. The Iroquois's claims to the lands south of the Ohio River were not particularly valid. The Iroquois had once been the "conquerors and protectors" of the Ohio Indians. Therefore, they claimed to speak for the Ohio tribes, who actually lived and hunted in Kentucky, including the Delaware, Shawnee, and Ohio Seneca (sometimes called Mingo). These tribes did not recognize Iroquois land rights in Kentucky, but the British decided to use the Iroquois to acquire the land and did not let the Ohio Indians speak for themselves. They were allowed only to observe the treaty council. The British also chose to ignore the claims to lands north of the Tennessee River made by the CHEROKEE, who regarded the area as their hunting grounds.

The conference began on October 24, 1768, and ended on November 5 with the signing of the Treaty of Fort Stanwix. In this treaty, the Iroquois received financial compensation for selling a massive stretch of lands. The new boundary ran from Fort Stanwix southward to the Delaware River. The line then followed the Western Branch Susquehanna River to the Allegheny River in modern Pennsylvania. The largest tract of land acquired by the British extended from Pittsburgh down the length of the Ohio River to the mouth of the Tennessee River. The Iroquois justified their role in selling the land by stating that they had always considered their territory to extend to the Tennessee River. Their claims were unrealistic, to say the least, but the British accepted them as valid because the Six Nations were willing to sell, while the tribes who actually lived in the region would be less willing to sell. The Iroquois received all of the compensation for the lands, which was almost £10,000 worth of money and goods. The Ohio Indians were not satisfied with the treaty. Many would later say that the treaty was invalid because they had not consented to its stipulations. The Treaty of Fort Stanwix established a boundary between Indian and white settlement, but it did not ease tensions between settlers and Indians. Both groups crossed the boundaries to hunt and settle, creating conflict between colonists and Indians. The British government was unable to enforce the boundary, which led to skirmishing and eventually to war in 1774.

A second Treaty of Fort Stanwix was signed in 1784 between the newly independent United States and the Six Nations. It reaffirmed the stipulations of the 1768 treaty.

Further reading: Jack M. Sosin, *The Revolutionary Frontier, 1763–1783* (New York: Holt, Rinehart & Winston, 1967).

— Michael L. Cox

Fort Ticonderoga

During the French and Indian War (1754–63), Fort Ticonderoga, located near the southern end of Lake Champlain, was thought to be one of the most crucial outposts between CANADA and the British North American colonies. But with the British victory, and with both Canada and the colonies under the British flag, the fort became less important. At the outbreak of the REVOLUTIONARY WAR (1775–83), it was a backwater post with a small garrison. However, after LEXINGTON AND CONCORD (April 19, 1775), several revolutionary leaders recognized its strategic value. Encouraged by Connecticut backers, ETHAN ALLEN led 200 of his followers, called the GREEN MOUNTAIN BOYS, to capture the fort. The same idea had occurred to BENEDICT ARNOLD, who left his own Connecticut regiment to participate in the attack. Arnold and Allen argued over who should be in command. Nevertheless, both men set out with the Green Mountain Boys and surprised the garrison on the morning of May 10, 1775.

This capture was important. The guns from the fort would be brought to Boston the following winter and would be a part of the armament placed on DORCHESTER HEIGHTS to compel a British withdrawal. Fort Ticonderoga would also be the starting point of an American invasion of Canada in the late summer of 1775. The garrison served as the centerpiece in the defense against British invasions of New York in 1776 and 1777. The British under General JOHN BURGOYNE recaptured the fort on July 6, 1777.

Fort Washington, capture of (November 17, 1776)

The British victory at the BATTLE OF LONG ISLAND (August 27–30, 1776) made New York City at the tip of Manhattan Island indefensible. As GEORGE WASHINGTON began to withdraw his troops, General WILLIAM HOWE landed a powerful force at Kip's Bay on the East River, well above the city, on September 13, 1776. Although the British smashed any resistance to their landing, the units of the CONTINENTAL ARMY still in New York City slipped by them along the Hudson River, abandoning artillery and equipment to the British. The Americans, however, were able to hold the high ground called the Harlem Heights and beat back a British attack. Howe did not press a direct assault at this time, seeking instead to outmaneuver Washington. Howe put 4,000 men ashore on the mainland on October 12, first at Throg's Neck, and then at Pelham on October 18. To meet this threat Washington moved most of his men to WHITE PLAINS, where they fought an indecisive battle with the British on October 28.

Washington had left about 3,000 men at Harlem Heights, calling the entrenchments there Fort Washington. The Americans hoped that this position, which towered 230 feet over the Hudson River, combined with Fort Lee on the Palisades in New Jersey, could prevent the British navy from sailing up the Hudson. This was a mistake. Not only could the British pass the obstructions in the river and

the forts, but Fort Washington could easily be cut off and surrounded. On November 16, the British launched a coordinated assault from three directions, overwhelmed the outer defenses, and captured the fort. Although the British lost almost 300 soldiers, 2,858 Americans were captured, 54 killed, and 100 wounded. Precious stores, artillery, and ammunition were also taken. To compound the disaster, the British scaled the Palisades six miles above Fort Lee on November 20. They quickly took this outpost, although the main American force stationed there managed to escape. Washington, who by this time was in New Jersey, was forced to retreat with CHARLES, LORD CORNWALLIS close behind him. Washington had to fall back across New Jersey during the next month, one step ahead of the British. By late December, the British had control of most of New Jersey. Washington was across the Delaware River in Pennsylvania, planning his counterattack that would lead to the BATTLES OF TRENTON and PRINCETON (December 26, 1776, and January 3, 1777, respectively).

Further reading: Robert Middlekauf, *The Glorious Cause: The American Revolution, 1783–1789* (New York: Oxford University Press, 1982).

Franklin, Benjamin (1706–1790)

Benjamin Franklin, the first "real" American who rose from rags not only to riches but to greatness as a publisher, scientist, and statesman, was born in Boston, Massachusetts. At the age of 16 he fled from his brother James, to whom he had been apprenticed as a printer, to Philadelphia, the only other city in the colonies with a printing press. By the time he was 30, Franklin was publishing the *Pennsylvania Gazette*, handling all of the colony's official printing business, and issuing *Poor Richard's Almanac* each year. This annual compilation of information, advice, and stories achieved popularity throughout the American colonies. Franklin's business was so successful that he retired from it at age 42.

Franklin quickly became an important citizen of Philadelphia. He organized the Junto, a self-education study group for middle-class young men, like himself, who were not able to attend college; the colonies' first lending library, which survives today as the Library Company of Philadelphia; and the city's first (Union) Fire Company. He proposed a society for promoting useful knowledge, which became the AMERICAN PHILOSOPHICAL SOCIETY that still flourishes today, and he was among the founders of the College of Philadelphia that became the University of Pennsylvania. Franklin was the first great organizer of the VOLUNTARY ASSOCIATIONS Americans have frequently founded to accomplish civic projects outside government channels. At the same time, he was inventing the Franklin stove and bifocal eyeglasses. His electrical experiments, including the dangerous flying of a kite with keys attached, led to the invention of the lightning rod and membership in Britain's Royal Philosophical Society.

Franklin emerged as an intercolonial statesman when he represented Pennsylvania at the unsuccessful Albany Congress of 1754. His plan for a colonial union—consisting of an American parliament and British governor-general with responsibility for intercolonial defense—was accepted by the delegates but was turned down by both the British Parliament and the colonial assemblies. Franklin proved crucial in organizing supplies and volunteer troops for General Edward Braddock's unsuccessful expedition to Fort Duquesne the next year during the French and Indian War (1754–63). He became the leader of the QUAKER faction in the Pennsylvania Assembly, to which he was elected in 1751. That body sent him to England in 1757 to present the case against the Penn family, which governed Pennsylvania but refused to pay taxes for the common defense.

Franklin spent the years 1757–62 and 1764–75 in England. Opponents pointed to the appointment of his son WILLIAM FRANKLIN as governor of New Jersey and his nomination in 1765 of John Hughes to be Philadelphia's stamp master to suggest he might have become a tool of

Benjamin Franklin. Portrait by Charles Willson Peale *(Library of Congress)*

British administrators who were trying to curtail American liberty. Franklin was unprepared for the outrage the STAMP ACT (1765) provoked: Crowds in 40-odd communities throughout the colonies compelled stamp masters to resign. In Philadelphia, only a hastily organized defense by Franklin's wife Deborah—who, though almost unknown to history, managed his household during his long absences—prevented his own house from being attacked.

Thereafter Franklin was less willing to compromise with the British. The most famous American in Europe, he became the agent for several colonies and presented their case as Parliament passed laws such as the TOWNSHEND DUTIES (1767), TEA ACT (1773), and COERCIVE ACTS (1774), restricted westward settlement, clamped down on illegal TRADE, and sent troops to Boston. In his 1766 examination before the House of Commons concerning the Stamp Act disturbances, he warned the British that the colonists paid heavy taxes of their own and had supported the mutual cause as well during the French and Indian War. Colonial Americans, Franklin asserted, were proud to be British, and only infringements of the rights they perceived as theirs (whether correctly so did not matter) would change their minds. Were military forces sent to America, he predicted, "they will not find a rebellion; they may indeed make one."

Franklin's British career ended in scandal. In 1773 he had conveyed copies of letters addressed to the British ministry by Massachusetts royal officials, including Governor THOMAS HUTCHINSON, to the Massachusetts Assembly. Although specifying they were only to be viewed privately so patriot leaders could know of plots to alter their government, Franklin could hardly have been surprised when the letters were published. British solicitor general Alexander Wedderburn made the most of this incident, denouncing Franklin as a thief before the Privy Council. In January 1775, having been dismissed as the colonies' postmaster, he left for America. His parting gift to the British was a letter of recommendation for a dismissed excise collector, THOMAS PAINE, who would soon move to Philadelphia and write *COMMON SENSE*, the pamphlet that persuaded many colonists to favor independence.

Franklin himself, upon his return from Europe, was one of the five-man committee chosen by the CONTINENTAL CONGRESS to frame the DECLARATION OF INDEPENDENCE (July 4, 1776), although he only added a few minor corrections to THOMAS JEFFERSON's draft. The same year, he was one of the peace commissioners chosen by Congress to meet with the British general Sir WILLIAM HOWE on Staten Island, and he joined his fellow delegates in refusing any offer save independence. Meanwhile, Franklin emerged as first President of the Commonwealth of Pennsylvania. Unlike most members of the old Quaker and Proprietary factions who became LOYALISTS, he became head of the "radicals" who took over the government of the new state of Pennsylvania. The government disfranchised Quakers and Tories, handed over local rule to militia committees, and gave power at the state level to the prorevolutionary counties and Philadelphia workers from whose ranks Franklin had sprung.

Franklin did not remain long in Pennsylvania. In 1777, Congress sent him to France to negotiate the alliance that would be signed the following year. Franklin was an instant hero in France: He wore a fur cap to symbolize the "natural man" praised by the philosopher then in vogue, Jean-Jacques Rousseau, and charmed the court and the ladies, although legends of his sexual conquests are greatly exaggerated. Franklin's popularity enabled him to negotiate not only treaties but to deal with the animosity among the American diplomats. JOHN ADAMS, for instance, resented Franklin's popularity and thought him too pro-French and lacking in care. (Franklin's private secretary was a British spy.) Nevertheless, it was Franklin who decided to accept the advantageous peace offered by Britain—putting the boundary of the new nation at the Mississippi River— rather than obey Congress's instructions that he approve of no treaty unacceptable to France. And then Franklin's friendship with the French foreign minister, CHARLES GRAVIER, COMTE DE VERGENNES, proved crucial in getting the French to accept a treaty obnoxious to their Spanish allies, who claimed a good deal of that territory.

Returning to America early in 1785, Franklin abandoned the Pennsylvania state's-rights radicals. Like most people who had represented the United States as a nation in the army, Congress, or diplomatic service, he became convinced that only a strong national government could save 13 disunited states from disaster. Elected to the CONSTITUTIONAL CONVENTION, the aged statesman slept a good deal during a stifling Philadelphia summer while his speeches were read by JAMES WILSON. Nevertheless, his final statement—which urged his countrymen to accept the proposed document as the best possible despite reservations they, like he himself, might have—was circulated throughout the states and had some role in achieving ratification.

Ill and in pain from gallstones, Franklin spent the final years of his life in Philadelphia, teaching the printing business to his grandson BENJAMIN FRANKLIN BACHE. But he never totally retired. Although he had owned five slaves at different times in his life, he became president of the Pennsylvania Anti-Slavery Society. In his last published writing in 1790 he impersonated an African Muslim who held American sailors captive and parroted the arguments proslavery advocates used to justify SLAVERY (civilize slaves and teach them the true RELIGION). During his last years he frequently sat in his front yard with a model of a bridge designed by Thomas Paine and tried to persuade his countrymen to support its construction over the Schuylkill River to further economic development.

Even after his death, Franklin continued to be a public benefactor: His will left a substantial amount of money for the EDUCATION of youth, much of which became the endowment of the Franklin Institute. Americans best remember "printer Ben" as the most down-to-earth of the founding fathers, who appeared in Philadelphia with a loaf of bread under each arm, as he described in his *Autobiography,* a literary classic. But beneath this friendly surface lurked as capable and clever a diplomat and statesman as ever lived. Without Franklin's European negotiations, his role in declaring independence, and his presence at the Constitutional Convention, the United States would have emerged differently—how and to what extent we will never know.

See also FOREIGN AFFAIRS; FRENCH ALLIANCE.

Further reading: Benjamin Franklin, *Writings* (New York: Library of America, 1987); J. A. Leo Lemay, ed., *Reappraising Benjamin Franklin* (Newark: University of Delaware Press, 1993); Esmond Wright, *Franklin of Philadelphia* (Cambridge, Mass.: Harvard University Press, 1986).

— William Pencak

Franklin, state of

The short-lived state of Franklin in what is now eastern Tennessee demonstrated the confused nature of politics on the western slopes of the Appalachians in the late 18th century. Men and women from the backwoods of the Carolinas, Virginia, and Pennsylvania came to the region in the tumultuous years following the REVOLUTIONARY WAR (1775–83). To the south a confederation of NATIVE AMERICAN tribes from the Chickamarga River Valley, led by DRAGGING CANOE, fought their advance. These so-called Chickamargans—CREEK, Shawnee, CHEROKEE, and Miami—also came to the Tennessee Valley to start new lives.

North Carolina had ceded the lands to the federal government, but when the state did not receive payments for its war debt, it reclaimed the territory. Despite this claim, in August 1784, delegates from the far western counties of North Carolina met in Jonesborough to organize the state of Franklin. In March 1785, John Sevier accepted the governorship of the infant state. The loyalty of many of the settlers to Franklin rested on the fact that they had settled illegally on land that North Carolina had set aside for the Indians. The Franklinites launched several raids against the Cherokee. The situation remained complicated, with Sevier representing land speculators from the East who sought to eventually maneuver the region back into North

Carolina. Sevier was even elected to the North Carolina Senate in 1789. Conflict over land claims also led to some fighting between individuals holding deeds under the state of Franklin and those who had North Carolina deeds. By 1790 the state of Franklin had ceased to function. North Carolina established control over the area until it became part of the new state of Tennessee in 1796. Sevier served as Tennessee's first governor.

Further reading: Wilma Dykeman, *Tennessee: A Bicentennial History* (New York: Norton, 1975).

— George Milne

Franklin, William (1731–1813)

A LOYALIST and last governor of colonial New Jersey, William Franklin was the son of BENJAMIN FRANKLIN and an unknown mother. Benjamin and Deborah Read, Franklin's common-law wife, always treated him like a legitimate child. Although privately tutored and put to work in Franklin's print shop, he longed to leave home. When his father prevented him from sailing on a privateer during King George's War, he enlisted in the Royal American Regiment. Although only 16 years of age, by 1747, he had served with distinction on the New York FRONTIER and was a commissioned captain of a company of grenadiers. That year he assisted his father in raising Pennsylvania's volunteer militia. In 1748 he accompanied Conrad Weiser to the Ohio Valley to negotiate with Indians, and in the early 1750s was sufficiently involved in his father's electrical experiments that when Benjamin received his honorary doctorate from Oxford in 1762, William obtained a master's degree.

A political supporter of his father, William served as his clerk when he left for England in 1757 in an effort to remove Pennsylvania's proprietary Penn family and replace them with a royal governor. William's behavior in England was as impressive as it had been in Pennsylvania. He became governor of New Jersey in 1762 and at first was extremely successful. He urged the improvement of roads and bridges, supported the colony's college, and punished whites who invaded NATIVE AMERICAN rights. However, when Britain passed the STAMP ACT (1765), Franklin felt it his duty to uphold the law. His father, now an agent for several colonies in England, denounced him as "a thorough government man." When the REVOLUTIONARY WAR (1775–83) broke out, William and New Jersey's Loyalist assembly were overthrown by the Provincial Congress. "An enemy to the liberties of this country," William was imprisoned in Connecticut for two years until he was exchanged on November 1, 1778. His wife had died in the meantime, and his health suffered greatly after 250 days served in solitary confinement.

Franklin immediately went to New York upon his release, where he organized the Board of Associated Loyalists, of whom he served as the first president. The Board cared for thousands of refugees while planning military ventures in cooperation with the British army. The guerrilla tactics Franklin urged were responsible for much of the vicious, small-scale warfare in southern New York and northern New Jersey that accompanied the last years of war.

Leaving America in August 1782, William received a generous pension and compensation for his losses from the British government. In 1785 he briefly met his father in England as the latter was returning from France to America, but he received as an inheritance only some worthless land in Nova Scotia to which the elder man retained title. Benjamin sarcastically noted in his will that since William remained loyal to England, English land was all he deserved. William helped other Loyalists receive reimbursement for sufferings, married Mary D'Evelyn, and lived in London until his death in 1813.

Further reading: Sheila L. Skemp, *William Franklin: Son of a Patriot, Servant of a King* (New York: Oxford University Press, 1990).

— William Pencak

freemasonry

In an era in which Americans increasingly joined clubs and associations, the Freemasons became one of the most important fraternal organizations in the country. Although it claimed ancient origins, freemasonry expanded beyond its guildlike roots in 1717 when a group of four lodges, including craftsmen and noncraftsmen, met in London to create a grand lodge. The Masonic Order's original purpose remains unclear, reflecting both the Enlightenment's concern for reason and older notions of the occult. A benevolent group and fraternal brotherhood, the Freemasons quickly became identified with 18th-century notions of gentility. While still clinging to a mythology connected to the craft of working with stone, the Masons provided a way for gentlemen to earn distinction. As such, the organization spread to Europe and the colonies. Philadelphia's St. John's Lodge, probably the first in the colonies, began meeting sometime around 1730. The colonial lodges that sprang up in community after community in the 1730s and 1740s were exclusive and were a means for the local elite to become more English.

Even before the REVOLUTIONARY WAR (1775–83), however, the Freemasons began to change into something else—a broader-based organization that included not only those who stood at the top of society, but also those who strove to join them. In America, that second group grew ever larger in the revolutionary and early national periods. A debate over ritual was the entering wedge for this expansion, as Masons divided into the Ancients and the Moderns. It was the Ancient lodges, claiming a superiority in the antiquity of their ritual, that were newer and had a more open membership. The Ancients allowed ARTISANS in the cities and elites in the backcountry to join, and by sheer force of numbers gained precedence in the fraternity. The Revolutionary War created something of a crisis for the Masons, since its membership was divided between LOYALISTS and WHIGS. Officers in the CONTINENTAL ARMY, however, organized their own lodges. By the end of the war, masonry became identified with the ideology of REPUBLICANISM. Masons, in part by the example of the officers' sacrifices during the war, claimed to be willing to put aside their own interests for the interests of the general public.

The early national period was the heyday of masonry. Lodges appeared in every part of the country, and the membership created elaborate rituals. Masons were more than a fraternal organization and engaged in benevolent activities and charities. But it became increasingly apparent to men on the make that one path to success lay through the Masonic lodge. As an organization that asserted the ideals of mutuality and brotherhood, it was only natural for Freemasons to seek business relationships with each other. Similarly, while the Masons did not support one political cause or another, many elected officials were Masons and gained support because of their affiliation. By the 1820s, the secret nature of the organization, and the apparent political and economic connections of its membership, led to growing suspicion. When William Morgan disappeared after threatening to reveal some of the Masonic secrets in 1826, an anti-Masonic movement erupted on the scene that almost destroyed the Masonic Order.

See also VOLUNTARY ASSOCIATIONS.

Further reading: Steven C. Bullock, *Revolutionary Brotherhood: Freemasonry and the Transformation of the American Social Order* (Chapel Hill: University of North Carolina Press, 1996).

French alliance

Without the support of France, the REVOLUTIONARY WAR (1775–83) would have been difficult, if not impossible, to win for the United States. The French provided aid in the form of munitions and equipment before a formal treaty of alliance (February 6, 1778). After that agreement, the French supplied troops and a navy that played a crucial role in the conflict, especially in the YORKTOWN campaign that led to the surrender of CHARLES, LORD CORNWALLIS (October 19, 1781).

Almost as soon as hostilities broke out at LEXINGTON AND CONCORD (April 19, 1775), some Americans began to look toward France for help. The French, for their part, had long seen the British crisis in the colonies as an opportunity, hoping that it might lead to armed conflict and the chance to weaken its traditional enemy, Great Britain. But there were several factors impeding the relationship. Americans had fought for most of a century against the French when they had controlled CANADA. Such animosities did not easily disappear. Moreover, the vast majority of colonial Americans were anti-CATHOLIC and viewed the French as agents of the Pope. Finally, even after the first guns were fired, many Americans hoped for reconciliation with King GEORGE III. The French also hesitated. They, too, remembered that their wars against Great Britain had included the colonies. They feared moving too quickly and forcing the Americans and Britons back together. The lack of a clear goal in the rebellion in 1775 and early 1776 was also cause for concern. The objectives of the CONTINENTAL CONGRESS became clarified after the DECLARATION OF INDEPENDENCE (July 4, 1776), but the war went badly that summer, with one defeat after another for GEORGE WASHINGTON and his CONTINENTAL ARMY.

Despite these problems, the French provided 1 million livres for munitions for the colonies as early as May 2, 1776. Negotiations for a more formal relationship began in earnest after the arrival in France of BENJAMIN FRANKLIN in December 1776. But not even his widespread fame as an American genius and simple philosopher could overcome all of the difficulties. News of the American victory at SARATOGA (October 17, 1777) dramatically altered the situation. France became fearful that the loss of an entire army would convince the British to reconcile with the Americans. By December 17, 1777, the French foreign minister, the COMTE DE VERGENNES, had agreed to recognize the United States and sign a formal alliance.

There were two treaties between the United States and France. First was a commercial treaty that opened up American and French ports to TRADE and gave France most-favored-nation trading status. Second was the alliance. Although the alliance was contingent on a declaration of war between France and Great Britain, all parties recognized that the agreements made such a war inevitable. Once that war occurred, the French promised to fight until American independence was guaranteed. They also renounced all territorial claims in the contended areas of North America. Both sides agreed to make peace only with the consent of the other.

Not only did this treaty have a tremendous impact on the course of the Revolutionary War, but it also affected the politics of the new nation. During the FRENCH REVOLUTION (1789–1815), many on both sides of the Atlantic believed that the United States should join the French in their struggles against the powers of reaction. When Great Britain went to war against France in 1793, Citizen EDMOND GENET came to the United States to convince the Washington administration to help the French. His failure, and the granting of most-favored-nation trading status to Great Britain in JAY'S TREATY (1794), led to a crisis with France and the QUASI WAR (1798–1800).

See also FOREIGN AFFAIRS.

Further reading: Samuel Flagg Bemis, *The Diplomacy of the American Revolution* (Bloomington: University of Indiana Press, 1957); Ronald Hoffman and Peter J. Albert, eds., *Diplomacy and the Revolution: The Franco-American Alliance of 1778* (Charlottesville: University Press of Virginia, 1981).

French Revolution (1789–1815)

The French Revolution stands as one of the most significant events of world history and had a major impact on the United States. Driven to the verge of bankruptcy, in part by aiding the Americans during the REVOLUTIONARY WAR (1775–89), King Louis XVI called the Estates General to meet in the spring of 1789. This group was unsatisfied with simply discussing the financial needs of the monarchy and instead called for a host of reforms, including reorganizing itself as a national assembly, demanding control over taxation, and writing a constitution. Efforts by the king to oppose these measures led to a popular revolt and the storming of the Bastille (July 14, 1789), a Parisian prison that had come to symbolize the absolute power of the king. The National Assembly abolished feudal privileges (August 4, 1789) and issued the Declaration of the Rights of Man (August 26, 1789). This document asserted as "natural rights" the right to liberty, property, and security, as well as the freedom of the press, opinion, and RELIGION. The document also proclaimed that sovereignty lay with the nation and not with the king.

The French Revolution began in the spirit of the Enlightenment and was in part inspired by the example of the AMERICAN REVOLUTION. Because so many of the ideas pushed by the French Revolution seem to coincide with the REPUBLICANISM shared by most Americans, few people in the United States at first opposed it. The fact that the MARQUIS DE LAFAYETTE emerged as one of the leaders of the early phase of the French Revolution brought even more support. But even from its earliest phases, the violence of the rioting that accompanied the revolt concerned some Americans. Over the next few years, as the French Revolution became more violent and as the forces of reaction in Europe began to send armies against the revolutionaries, opposition to the French increased. By 1793 radicals had assumed power in France, executing the king

on January 21, 1793, and establishing the Reign of Terror (September 1793–July 1794) that executed approximately 40,000 royalists and opponents to the Jacobin regime. In large part as a result of the radical turn of the French Revolution, in February 1793 Great Britain declared war against the French Republic, creating a diplomatic crisis for the United States.

France called upon the United States to come to the aid of its sister republic, reminding Americans of the FRENCH ALLIANCE that had been so instrumental in winning the Revolutionary War. France sent Citizen EDMOND GENET as ambassador to the United States in 1793. Genet sought to recruit men for French war vessels and wanted President GEORGE WASHINGTON to commit to supporting the French. If Genet's entreaties fell on deaf ears in the Washington administration, many Americans seemed to support him. The French Revolution contributed to the division of the Americans into two POLITICAL PARTIES: FEDERALIST PARTY, who supported ALEXANDER HAMILTON's program for a stronger central government and who opposed the French Revolution; and the DEMOCRATIC-REPUBLICANS PARTY, who supported THOMAS JEFFERSON and had continued enthusiasm for the French.

The radical Jacobins did not remain in power in France for long. In July 1794 Maximilian Robespierre was overthrown, and a conservative reaction took place. As the French moved away from the extreme implications of their revolution, power fell into the hands of a group of directors (1795–99) who restored order and prosperity to France while conducting wars against Britain and several European powers. Eventually NAPOLEON BONAPARTE emerged as the first consul (1799) and the emperor of the French (1804). Napoleon continued to rule France, conquering much of Europe, until he was forced into exile in 1814. Napoleon had a brief return to power in the spring of 1815, but he was defeated by a coalition army at Waterloo (June 18, 1815).

Although the excitement for the republican aspects of the French Revolution declined in the United States as the Thermidorian reaction (conservatives in France retreating from excesses of democracy) took over, and then as Napoleon took control, the ongoing power struggle in Europe continued to exert influence on the United States. Americans remained divided in their sympathies. Perhaps more important was the series of diplomatic crises faced by the United States because of the war between Britain and France. As long as America could remain neutral, great profits could be made by shipping goods to both belligerents. The problem was maintaining neutrality in the face of TRADE restrictions and IMPRESSMENT of American sailors by the British. Indeed, the United States almost went to war with Great Britain in 1794 because of the seizure of American merchant ships, until JAY'S TREATY

(1794) settled some outstanding issues. But that treaty, which favored the British over the French, helped to bring on the QUASI WAR (1798–1800) with France. After 1807 neutral American trade became more difficult to sustain as both Britain and France sought to limit access to each other's ports. Ultimately, this problem helped to bring on the War of 1812 (1812–15). Although the United States fought this war while Britain was engaged in a death struggle with France, the United States never came to a formal alliance with Napoleon. By the close of 1814, and with the exile of Napoleon, Britain was willing to agree to the Treaty of Ghent to end the American war, since the issues of neutral trade and impressment were no longer significant in an era of peace.

The legacy of the French Revolution on the United States and the world transcended war and diplomacy. During the 1790s a set of ideas, first brought into focus in the American Revolution, set the stage for the transformation of the world. Americans had fought for liberty; the French added equality and fraternity to the vocabulary of revolution.

See also FOREIGN AFFAIRS.

Further reading: E. J. Hobsbawm, *The Age of Revolution, 1789–1848* (New York: New American Library, 1962); George Lefebvre, *The French Revolution* (London: Routledge, 1964); R. R. Palmer, *The Age of Democratic Revolution*, 2 vols. (1959. Reprint. Princeton, N.J.: Princeton University Press, 1964).

Freneau, Philip (1752–1832)

One of the most significant poets in American history, Philip Freneau was born to a prosperous family in New York. Freneau was educated by tutors as a young man and entered the sophomore class at the College of New Jersey (now Princeton) at age 15; there he began to prepare for a life in the clergy and immediately started writing. With the collaboration of one of his classmates, HUGH HENRY BRACKENRIDGE, Freneau wrote his first published poem in college. Brackenridge read their "The Rising Glory of America" during their 1771 graduation ceremonies, and the poem was issued as pamphlet the next year in Philadelphia.

Freneau was tied to family duties after graduating college, which kept him from immediate further publication. Unable to make a living as a clergyman, he taught school for a short while and continued to write poetry on his own time. The coming of the REVOLUTIONARY WAR (1775–83) inspired Freneau to publish "American Liberty" in July 1775. Within a few months he published more than eight pamphlet satires aimed at Great Britain. Freneau's pamphlets were widely reprinted and were most popular among moderate WHIGS. Poetry, however, did not earn him much money.

He soon acquired a job as a secretary for a planter who lived on the Island of Santa Cruz in the WEST INDIES. Freneau lived there for three years, where he continued to write some of his most significant poems, including "Santa Cruz," "The Jamaica Funeral," and "The House of Night." He returned home in 1778 after being captured and released by the British. In New Jersey, he joined the militia and continued to publish his poetry.

Freneau loved the sea and took many voyages during his life. When he set out in the spring of 1780 to return to the West Indies, he was captured by a British man-of-war and sent to the prison ship *Scorpion* in New York Harbor. Freneau suffered brutal treatment and starvation as a prisoner and was soon sent to the hospital ship *Hunter* before he was able to return home to New Jersey. Based on this experience, he wrote a poem entitled "The British Prison Ship." After his imprisonment, Freneau worked in the Philadelphia Post Office for three years and continued to write poetry, most of which was published in Francis Bailey's *Freeman's Journal*. Freneau's extensive publications earned him the title "Poet of the Revolution."

For the next several years Freneau took to the sea again as an officer on merchant ships. He settled down in 1789 when he married Eleanor Forman and immediately became involved in newspaper work as editor of the New York *Daily Advertiser*. THOMAS JEFFERSON offered him a government job in 1791, so he moved to Philadelphia. Although a federal employee, he also edited the partisan *National Gazette*. Freneau was a passionate DEMOCRATIC-REPUBLICAN and published many wild political remarks in this paper—so much so that he often had to write anonymously.

When the *National Gazette* dissolved in 1793 and Jefferson retired, Freneau had to resign his government position. He tried his hand at a number of rural newspapers for the next few years but quickly retired from JOURNALISM, spending the rest of his life alternating between the sea and his farm in New Jersey. He also continued to write poetry. Freneau died in 1832 when he lost his way home during a raging blizzard.

Further reading: M. W. Bowden, *Philip Freneau* (Boston: Twayne, 1976); Harry Hayden Clark, *Poems of Freneau* (New York: Hafner Publishing, 1960).

— Meghan A. Earl

Fries's Rebellion (1798–1799)

In 1798 German-American inhabitants of eastern Pennsylvania rose in protest to a direct tax on land, houses, and slaves. As a result of the Anglo-American JAY'S TREATY

(1794), diplomatic relations between the United States and France had been strained. When the undeclared QUASI WAR (1798–1800) broke out between the United States and France, President JOHN ADAMS asked Congress to raise money to fund and strengthen the army and navy. At about the same time, the federal government also passed the ALIEN AND SEDITION ACTS (1798) to protect national security by making it more difficult for immigrants to become citizens and prohibiting public speech against the government.

Open rebellion to the tax started in July 1798 in the Pennsylvania counties of Northhampton, Montgomery, Berks, and Bucks. The new law placed a tax on houses that was assessed by the number and size of windows in the dwelling. The federal government believed that this type of graduated tax assessment would not be as burdensome on the poor, requiring the rich to carry the bulk of the tax. Many German-American citizens did not view the tax in this manner. Rather, they remembered a series of transgressions from the 1791 excise tax, which in their view only benefitted wealthy land speculators. Additionally, they believed that the unequal collection of taxes put the largest burden on average citizens rather than wealthy speculators who owned uncultivated lands. Additionally, many southeastern Pennsylvanians believed that it was no coincidence that the federal government had passed the Alien and Sedition laws to stop protest against the new tax.

When attempts were made to collect the new tax in eastern Pennsylvania, tempers began to flare. First, angry citizens dumped boiling water on collectors who were trying to measure windows. Throughout the fall of 1798 and into the winter and spring of 1799, enraged citizens continued to protest the tax, harassing collectors and seizing their records. After several incidents of federal collectors being attacked and their records destroyed, the Federal District Court had 23 men arrested and jailed in the Sun Tavern at Bethlehem. On March 12, 1799, a Bucks County auctioneer and former militia captain named John Fries rode into Bethlehem with a group of men and freed the protest leaders, thus giving his name to what came to be known as "Fries's Rebellion."

After hearing of the jailbreak, President Adams gave the insurgents six days to stand down, and he also called out the militia. The Pennsylvania militia, in cooperation with federal authorities, managed to put down the uprising. On April 4 troops sent from Philadelphia marched into the southeastern countryside, arresting many citizens simply based on rumor and little hard evidence; there was no sign of open rebellion by the local inhabitants. Fries himself was apprehended while trying to escape into a swamp when the barking of his own dog gave him away to the authorities. Approximately 60 prisoners were taken back to Philadelphia.

John Fries was especially singled out for prosecution on the charge of treason, quickly tried, found guilty, and sentenced to death. Fries's LAWYERS argued that the actions committed by the defendant, while they could be construed as sedition or riot, were certainly not treason worthy of the death penalty. Under strict instructions from the judges, the jury returned a verdict of guilty. However, Fries was granted a second trial because one of the jurors had broken the confidentiality rule. Nevertheless, Fries was again found guilty and sentenced to hang.

President Adams, who had followed the trials closely, became uneasy over the decisions of the courts and therefore pardoned Fries and two others of treason, as well as several others of lesser crimes. Adams's action caused a firestorm among the Federalists, many of whom felt that the president should allow justice to run its course. Moreover, Fries's Rebellion marked the end to Federalist political domination in Pennsylvania. Many Pennsylvania Germans now viewed the FEDERALIST PARTY as the party of elites and the wealthy, unconcerned with the rights and liberties of the common citizen. In fact, in the 1799 election, Pennsylvanians elected Thomas McKean, the state's first DEMOCRATIC-REPUBLICAN (Jeffersonian) governor, and in 1800 Pennsylvania played a large role in electing THOMAS JEFFERSON as president.

See also ELECTION OF 1800; LAND RIOTS; RIOTS.

Further reading: Paul Douglass Newman, "Fries Rebellion and American Political Culture, 1798–1800," *Pennsylvania Magazine of History and Biography* 119 (1995): 37–73.

— Jeffrey A. Davis

frontier

Americans have customarily defined the frontier as the limit of European-American agricultural settlement. This definition ignores the fact that many NATIVE AMERICANS farmed and lived in towns. More recently, historians have viewed frontiers less as a boundary and more as a zone of communication between cultures—between European Americans and Native Americans as well as between Anglo-Americans and colonists from other European powers. In particular, scholars have emphasized the role of the individuals who lived along and traveled through the frontier as cultural intermediaries. Whatever definition one uses, the period between 1754 and 1820 witnessed a pushing back of the frontier from east of the Appalachians to just beyond the Mississippi River.

Traditional ideas of the frontier were in large part molded by the Enlightenment thought of the revolutionary generation, whose REPUBLICAN beliefs held that all societies could be placed on a spectrum from primitive to advanced. A primitive society was one that depended on hunting and gathering. Many Americans falsely assumed that Native Americans were at this level of development. As a society moved toward civilization, it became more dependent upon AGRICULTURE. As new layers of complexity were added to society, commerce became more important, cities developed, and industrial production expanded. The revolutionary generation, however, believed that there were cycles in history: The more advanced stages of civilization were symptoms of decay, leading to the destruction of the society and the beginning of the cycle all over again. From this perspective, the expansion of the frontier was crucial. New areas of settlement promised to sustain America as an agricultural nation and postpone the end of European-American society.

Concerns with the frontier played a role in the origins of the AMERICAN REVOLUTION. After victory in the French and Indian War (1754–63), colonial Americans hoped that new lands west of the Appalachians would be open to settlement. However, in an effort to protect its Native American subjects and to reduce military expenditures, the British government issued the PROCLAMATION OF 1763, prohibiting settlement west of the Appalachians. The Quebec Act of 1774 granted this territory to CANADA and also sought to limit colonial American settlement in the west. This barrier to frontier expansion became an important colonial grievance. At the end of the REVOLUTIONARY WAR (1775–83), the TREATY OF PARIS (1783) provided a generous boundary for the United States, stretching to the Mississippi River. During the 1770s, DANIEL BOONE and a few other European Americans had begun to cross the mountains. Following the war, thousands of Americans streamed across the Appalachians to settle the new frontier. Efforts of the United States government to guide and limit the settlement to below the Ohio River proved fruitless, leading to a series of wars with Native Americans that culminated in the BATTLE OF TIPPECANOE (November 7, 1811) and Andrew Jackson's campaign against the CREEK NATION in the War of 1812 (1812–15).

Popular images of the frontier reflect only some of the reality. Men did wear coonskin caps, and the first dwellings erected were often lean-tos or crude log cabins. But as soon as anyone on the frontier could afford to, they bought clothing in stores and improved their houses. Perhaps equally important in the mythology was the idea that every frontiersman wanted his own piece of land to farm and raise a family in some agrarian paradise. Few on the frontier had such limited ambitions. Those who settled south of the Ohio often hoped someday to own a plantation with slaves; those further north may have simply wanted to produce a cash crop for the market. Speculation was rampant on the frontier. Those with the grandest dreams sought to engross thousands of acres.

More humble men merely wanted to improve the land to sell it for a higher price. Within such an aggressively capitalistic atmosphere, more fortunes were lost than won. The frontier, in other words, was less rough and tumble and more boom and bust.

Further reading: Andrew R. L. Cayton and Fredrika J. Teute, eds., *Contact Points: American Frontiers from the Mohawk Valley to the Mississippi, 1750–1830* (Chapel Hill: University of North Carolina Press, 1998); Drew R. McCoy, *The Elusive Republic: Political Economy in Jeffersonian America* (Chapel Hill: University of North Carolina Press, 1980); Alan Taylor, *William Cooper's Town: Power and Persuasion on the Frontier of the Early American Republic* (New York: Knopf, 1995).

Fulton, Robert (1765–1815)

Robert Fulton was an early American inventor who designed canals, submarines, mines, and the first steamboat to travel on American waterways. Fulton was born in 1765 to a SCOTCH-IRISH family in southeastern Pennsylvania. He grew up in the town of Lancaster in a family of modest wealth. As a young man, Fulton became a portrait painter for a number of wealthy Pennsylvania families in the 1780s. In 1787 he traveled to England to advance his artistic career and did not return to the United States for 20 years. In England, Fulton shifted the direction of his career from portrait painting to canal engineering. With the financial backing of a few landholders and industrialists, he developed sophisticated plans for canals. His designs employed various mechanical devices, such as wheels, inclined planes, and aqueducts, all of which Fulton illustrated well using his artistic talents. In 1796 he published a book on canal design and sent letters to President GEORGE WASHINGTON and Pennsylvania's Governor Thomas Mifflin advocating canal projects in the United States. Although none of these projects came to fruition, a canal system later constructed in Pennsylvania followed Fulton's basic design.

In 1797 Fulton traveled to France, where he quickly established connections to the French government. By the end of 1797 he had refocused his energies on naval warfare and proposed a plan for a cigar-shaped submarine that could be used to plant bombs in the water to destroy enemy ships. Between 1797 and 1801 Fulton developed a submarine called the *Nautilus* and experimented with it along the French coast of the English Channel and the Seine River. Though the *Nautilus* proved successful, Fulton declined to present it formally to French leader NAPOLEON BONAPARTE and dismantled it before French naval engineers could investigate and copy the design. Fulton steadfastly considered himself a private entrepreneur with control of his creations independent of the will of the

French regime under Napoleon. Between 1800 and 1802, Fulton also developed plans for submerged bombs—he called them "torpedoes"—that would either be released by submarines or anchored on the seafloor. He also drew plans for a steamboat that he presented to Napoleon, although these plans were not developed at that time. In 1804 English agents lured Fulton to England to work for the Royal Navy. In two years of service, Fulton designed and launched two torpedo attacks on French ships—and successfully tested a larger mine—before deciding to return to the United States.

In the United States, the newly famous Fulton resumed his work on torpedoes for the United States Navy. He also returned to his steamboat project in partnership with New Yorker ROBERT R. LIVINGSTON. With Livingston's financial support, Fulton completed his steamboat, which he and Livingston officially named the *North River Steam Boat,* commonly known as the *Clermont.* It caused a national sensation with a trip up the Hudson River in 1807. By 1809 Livingston and Fulton had created another steamboat and established a commercial steamboat line with an exclusive right to operate on New York waters.

During the War of 1812 (1812–15), Fulton contracted with Captain Stephen Decatur and the American navy to create the first-ever steam warship, which unfortunately was not completed until mid-1815. He continued testing mines and more sophisticated torpedo boats, and many were employed in various naval engagements. During the war, Fulton also became embroiled in legal action, successfully defending his company's patent and monopoly rights to operate steamboats in New York. Fulton died unexpectedly in February 1815. His steamboat interest was sold off to competitor Aaron Ogden, who later lost the New York monopoly in the 1824 SUPREME COURT case *Ogden v. Gibbons.*

See also SCIENCE.

Further reading: Cynthia Owen Philip, *Robert Fulton: A Biography* (New York: Franklin Watts, 1985).

— James R. Karmel

Robert Fulton. Wood engraving *(Library of Congress)*

fur trade

The fur trade helped to fuel the competition for an empire in North America. Colonists along the Atlantic coast had hoped to profit from victory in the French and Indian War (1754–63) by increasing their share of the fur trade. But with CANADA in the hands of the British, most furs were traded through the St. Lawrence River Valley after 1763. Even after the REVOLUTIONARY WAR (1776–83), the British retained posts north of the Ohio River on American territory in part to control the fur trade. By the time the British evacuated those posts after JAY'S TREATY (1794), much of the region had been depleted of furs. The trade shifted westward across the Mississippi River.

Americans began to compete for western furs from two directions. First, merchant ships in the Pacific sailed to the Columbia River to obtain furs to trade in China. The LEWIS AND CLARK'S EXPEDITION in 1804–06 furthered the American claim to the region of the Pacific Northwest and encouraged the fur trade. John Jacob Astor pursued this trade, organizing the American Fur Trading Company in 1808 and the Pacific Fur Company in 1810. He established his trading fort at Astoria at the mouth of the Columbia River in 1811. Astor, however, wisely sold Astoria to the British at the outbreak of the War of 1812 (1812–15). The Hudson Bay Company, the main British agent in the North American trade after 1800, soon controlled the Columbia River Basin.

Second, Americans began to move up the Missouri River and into the Rocky Mountains after the LOUISIANA

PURCHASE (1803) and the Lewis and Clark expedition. Based in St. Louis, these fur traders tapped into a huge territory with plenty of beaver. They also explored much of the GREAT PLAINS and Rocky Mountains in their pursuit of furs.

Further reading: David J. Wishart, *The Fur Trade of the American West, 1807–1840: A Geographical Synthesis* (Lincoln: University of Nebraska Press, 1979).

G

Gabriel's Rebellion (1800)

Born a slave in 1776 in Henrico County, Virginia, Gabriel took the name of the Biblical prophet. After he planned a slave rebellion in 1800, Gabriel's name became synonymous with the ultimate act of black resistance to enslavement. Although he left no written record of his plan, Gabriel's Rebellion has been widely chronicled. For African-American novelist Arna Bontemps (1902–73), Gabriel was a deeply introspective man who sought to conquer SLAVERY's psychological as well as physical oppression. Most recently, historian Douglas Egerton has placed Gabriel's Rebellion in a broader context of early national political life.

Gabriel was the slave of Thomas Prosser, a member of the Virginia gentry and a tobacco farmer who owned one of the largest plantations in Henrico County. Yet, of the Prosser plantation's over 50 slaves, Gabriel stood out: He was literate in a time and place when most African Americans were not (and when teaching blacks to read and write was forbidden); he was an ARTISAN, learning the smithing trade of his father on the Prosser plantation; and Gabriel's talent allowed his master to hire him out during the 1790s to other masters in need of labor. Thus Gabriel traveled away from plantation life, often going to the urban environment of Richmond. There he encountered free blacks, some white ANTISLAVERY advocates, and working-class whites, all of whom lashed out at the deferential codes of Virginia politics and society. By the late 1790s, democratic movements emerged to challenge the Virginia gentry. These social and political currents established a foundation for Gabriel to begin planning a slave rebellion. In addition, Gabriel's travels and experience of being hired out further convinced him of slavery's oppression: No matter whom he worked for, Gabriel's wages went back to his master. By the fall of 1799, Gabriel had in fact moved toward open rebellion against slavery.

Gabriel planned to marshal forces in late August 1800, capture guns and ammunition from local depots, march to the capital of Richmond (capturing political leaders such as the governor), and demand both an end to slavery and equal treatment. When the rebellion was betrayed and Gabriel was captured, he refused to speak. But if the details of his plan remain sketchy, its larger import remains clear: Gabriel hoped to rout bondage and revolutionize Virginia society. Indeed, he demanded that "QUAKERS, METHODISTS, and French people"—generally known as antislavery advocates—be spared. He also hoped that laboring white people who opposed the aristocratic sentiments of Virginia's ruling elite would join him. Unlike South Carolina's Denmark Vesey, a slave rebel who planned to flee the United States, and Virginia's Nat Turner, who sought to wreak as much havoc on the white population as possible in revenge for slavery's brutality, Gabriel sought to radically alter both American race and class relations.

The plot was betrayed by an enslaved person on a nearby plantation and put down before Gabriel's troops could march. A torrential rainstorm had delayed Gabriel in any event. For much of the fall of 1800, white Virginians remained alarmed that other rebellions might occur. Governor James Monroe, who would eventually succeed JAMES MADISON as president of the United States, called out special militia forces to put down any possible revolt. As reports of Gabriel's plot rippled throughout the United States, and even through Europe, Virginia authorities began prosecuting the accused. Although fewer than 100 enslaved people were ever formally deemed part of Gabriel's ranks, trial testimony by some of the rebellion's other leaders put the number at 150 to 500 strong, perhaps more. Over two dozen black conspirators were eventually executed, including Gabriel. For the next decade, at least, Virginia masters tightened control over slavery and moved further away from Revolutionary era antislavery sentiments.

Further reading: Arna Wendell Bontemps, *Black Thunder* (Boston: Beacon, 1968); Douglas Egerton, *Gabriel's*

145

Rebellion: The Virginia Conspiracies of 1800 and 1802 (Chapel Hill: University of North Carolina Press, 1993); James Sidbury, *Plowshares into Swords: Race, Rebellion, and Identity in Gabriel's Virginia, 1730–1810* (New York: Cambridge University Press, 1997).

— Richard Newman

Gage, Thomas (1719?–1787)

The younger son of an aristocratic family, Thomas Gage pursued a military career that brought him to the colonies and placed him as commander in chief of the British army in North America at the outbreak of the REVOLUTIONARY WAR (1775–83). A capable administrator with a likable personality, he was not a good combat officer. His influence in guiding British imperial policy, and his military missteps, helped shape the crisis that led to American independence.

His military career followed a typical and unexceptional path for a member of the British aristocracy before the French and Indian War (1754–63). He saw service in the low countries against France and fought against the Jacobite invasion in Scotland in 1745. Gage rose through the ranks by purchasing vacant positions, and by age 30 he was a lieutenant colonel. His regiment was sent to North America when hostilities with the French and Indians broke out in 1754. During that conflict he served in several campaigns with mixed results. He was in command of the vanguard of General Edward Braddock's army as it approached Fort Duquesne and was ambushed by the French and Indians. While he did not get blamed for this disaster, he also did not rise to the occasion. He showed some bravery but managed to leave the field and escape the disaster with his life. In 1757 he took part in the failed attempt to capture Louisbourg on Cape Breton. In 1758 he was promoted to colonel and developed the concept of using light infantry companies to replace colonial rangers to reconnoiter and protect the flanks of regiments of regulars. He also participated in another botched campaign, this time before FORT TICONDEROGA. Shortly thereafter, he married Margaret Kemble, daughter of a wealthy New Jersey family. In 1759 he obtained an independent command and was made a brigadier general with orders to take charge of the siege of Fort Niagara. After the fall of that French outpost he was to attack La Galette at the head of the St. Lawrence to help relieve pressure on British armies advancing up the St. Lawrence and invading from New York along Lake Champlain. Gage failed at La Galette and saw himself relegated to supervising the rear guard of the invasion of CANADA in 1760.

Gage might have fallen into obscurity at that point, except fate had other plans. Serving as military governor of Canada after 1760, Gage suddenly found himself commander in chief in North America after Sir Jeffrey Amherst was recalled because he had miscalculated the Indian threat in 1763. It fell to Gage to supervise the suppression of PONTIAC'S REBELLION (1763). Once his subordinates crushed the uprising, Gage remained in the colonies in command of the permanent British army stationed there. Although the imperial crisis and the RESISTANCE MOVEMENT (1764–75) sorely tested his patience, Gage's strengths were as an administrator. Throughout the 1760s and early 1770s he was a model of caution. Left to his own devices, he might have pursued a more aggressive policy to put down the street disorder and resistance to imperial measures. But he hesitated to do anything without firm direction from England, and such direction was not forthcoming. He sought to limit further settlement of colonists west of the Appalachians and encouraged the stationing of troops in Boston after the customs RIOTS of 1768. But he also oversaw the withdrawal of British troops from the same city after the BOSTON MASSACRE (March 5, 1770). Even as late as 1774, this middle course kept him relatively popular with both his superiors in England and colonial Americans. After his appointment as governor of Massachusetts to enforce the COERCIVE ACTS (1774), he had the hopes of King GEORGE III and many Americans riding on his shoulders. JOSEPH WARREN believed Gage "a man of honest, upright principles" who might some how find "a just and honourable settlement." Unfortunately for the British Empire, Gage's shoulders were not broad enough for this burden.

As the situation deteriorated in the fall and winter of 1774, Gage became convinced that dramatic and forceful action was called for to regain control of the colonies. A provincial congress beyond his control or influence replaced the official colonial assembly in Massachusetts. The SUFFOLK RESOLVES (1774) were put into effect, all but nullifying the Coercive Acts outside of Boston. Gage and the British troops felt isolated in Boston, surrounded by a hostile countryside where MINUTEMEN trained and prepared for war. Gage's reputation in England also declined that winter, as the British government rejected his recommendations to repeal the Coercive Acts as unenforceable, withdraw from Boston, and set up a naval blockade to shut off all TRADE with colonies and compel submission. The British government, however, agreed that some action should take place to demonstrate its authority. On April 14, 1775, Gage received orders to use force to suppress what he had previously described as an open rebellion. These orders led to the ill-fated expedition to LEXINGTON AND CONCORD (April 19, 1775). Gage had planned a quick surprise strike to the countryside to arrest leaders and seize supplies, but he did not catch the colonists by surprise. No leaders were captured and only a few supplies were destroyed. The column of British regulars, however, suffered dramatic loses. Gage soon found himself besieged by thousands of minutemen and all but superseded by the arrival of three new British generals: WILLIAM HOWE; CHARLES, LORD CORNWALLIS; and JOHN BURGOYNE. All hopes that the conflict might subside disappeared on June 17, 1775, after the Americans occupied BUNKER HILL. With Gage's blessing, the British launched a frontal assault on the entrenched positions. After three advances, they drove the Americans off. But as on April 19, they suffered catastrophic loses. Gage was soon recalled, and Howe replaced him in command. Gage then retired to the relative obscurity that had eluded him earlier in his career.

Further reading: George Athan Billias, ed., *George Washington's Opponents: British Generals and Admirals in the American Revolution* (New York: William Morrow, 1969); David Hackett Fischer, *Paul Revere's Ride* (New York: Oxford University Press, 1994).

Gallatin, Albert (1761–1849)

Albert Gallatin was a Swiss immigrant to British North America who eventually became a congressman from Pennsylvania, secretary of the treasury under Presidents THOMAS JEFFERSON and JAMES MADISON, and an American diplomat in Europe. Born in 1761 in Geneva, Switzerland, Gallatin grew up in a Genevan mercantile family and eventually saved enough money to embark for North America in 1780. His ship landed in Boston and he joined a FRONTIER expedition to Maine. This adventure was short-lived, and he traveled back to Boston, where he became a tutor in French at Harvard College in 1782.

Gallatin soon moved to western Pennsylvania, and by 1784 he had become involved in land speculation in the western country. He and a partner purchased large tracts in the Ohio River Valley in western Virginia and Pennsylvania. In 1785 Gallatin began work on a frontier farm and manor that he named Friendship Hill on the Monongahela River in Fayette County, Pennsylvania. In 1788 he entered local politics and was elected to represent Fayette County at the state ratifying convention in Harrisburg for the United States Constitution, where he advocated a BILL OF RIGHTS. In 1789 he was an influential participant in the Pennsylvania state constitutional convention, again advocating guaranteed civil liberties. In the early 1790s Gallatin established his political reputation as a legislator representing Fayette County in the Pennsylvania General Assembly. There he often voted with factions loosely aligned with the DEMOCRATIC-REPUBLICANS in national politics. In 1793 he played an important role in the establishment of the Bank of Pennsylvania.

Gallatin gained a national profile in 1794 when he acted as an intermediary between western Pennsylvanians involved in the WHISKEY REBELLION (1794) and federal troops led by President GEORGE WASHINGTON. As a Jeffersonian in Congress between 1795 and 1800, Gallatin was often in the middle of the partisan battles of the era. He openly protested the ALIEN AND SEDITION ACTS (1798) on the House floor and encouraged moderation with regard to France in the wake of the XYZ AFFAIR (1797–98). Simultaneously, Gallatin launched a glassworks and a gun factory in the frontier town of New Geneva, Pennsylvania.

Gallatin's national influence increased with his appointment as secretary of the treasury in 1801. In that position, he symbolized moderate Democratic-Republican practicality on financial issues and therefore became a lightning rod for political criticism throughout his years as secretary (1801–14). Under Jefferson, his most important role was as advocate for the BANK OF THE UNITED STATES. Gallatin and Jefferson disagreed over the legitimacy and necessity of the bank, and Gallatin worked hard to overcome the president's reluctance to accept the bank's status as national repository and lender. Gallatin's understanding of the bank was akin to ALEXANDER HAMILTON's original position on the bank. Like Hamilton, he believed that the government could maintain some debt and that the bank had clear constitutional legitimacy. In 1804 Jefferson actually signed legislation authorizing new branches of the bank in New Orleans and WASHINGTON, D.C., on Gallatin's recommendation. Gallatin also disagreed with Jefferson over the president's controversial EMBARGO OF 1807. In 1808, Gallatin presented a comprehensive plan for Internal Improvements that Jefferson rejected on the grounds that the federal government did not have the authority to fund transportation projects.

Gallatin stayed in the cabinet under Madison and soon became embroiled in controversy over rechartering the Bank of the United States in 1810 and 1811. Gallatin steadfastly defended the bank against Democratic-Republican critics and sought to maintain its existence in the face of impending war with Britain. In doing so, he became a symbol of lost principles to many antibank Jeffersonians. Despite Gallatin's best efforts and Madison's support, Congress voted to kill the bank by a tie-breaking vote cast in the Senate by Vice President GEORGE CLINTON. This action contributed to financial distress during the War of 1812 (1812–15). In 1814 Gallatin served on the American delegation negotiating the Treaty of Ghent. Later, he served the nation as minister to France and then minister to Britain. In the 1830s he wrote and published a number of influential essays on banking, financial policy, and TARIFFS. He died peacefully at home in 1849, just a few months after the passing of his wife Hannah.

See also BANKS.

Further reading: Ray Walters Jr., *Albert Gallatin: Jeffersonian Financier and Diplomat* (New York: Macmillan, 1952).

— James R. Karmel

Galloway, Joseph (1731–1803)

Joseph Galloway was a Philadelphia LAWYER who remained loyal to the British Crown during the REVOLUTIONARY WAR (1775–83). Galloway came from a prominent Delaware family. His father had achieved great wealth through land investments and a successful family mercantile business. Although he had no formal schooling, Galloway received a first-rate education from private tutors and a private attorney. He moved to Philadelphia in 1747, where he was admitted to the bar and began practicing law. Galloway was an excellent lawyer and between his flourishing practice and inherited wealth, he quickly became a force in Philadelphia politics. He became friends with WILLIAM FRANKLIN, son of BENJAMIN FRANKLIN, and Galloway and the elder Franklin became partners in Pennsylvania politics. With Franklin's help, Galloway was elected to the state assembly for the first time in 1756. He and Franklin both lost their seats in the assembly in 1764, when they supported a plan that would have made Pennsylvania a royal, instead of a proprietary, colony. He was reelected to the assembly in 1765 and served there until 1775.

Galloway rejected the idea of American independence but supported a new relationship between Great Britain and her North American colonies. He advocated an American congress that could speak for the colonies as a whole and a reform of British mercantile regulations. After the STAMP ACT (1765) protests, however, Galloway found himself increasingly at odds with the radical faction gaining popularity in Philadelphia. Galloway remained influential, though, and was selected to be one of Pennsylvania's delegates to the FIRST CONTINENTAL CONGRESS in 1774, where he proposed a plan that would address the colonies' grievances and keep the bonds between America and England intact. His "A plan of proposed Union between Great Britain and the Colonies" called for a president-general for the colonies appointed by the king and a legislature that would represent all the colonies. The Congress rejected the plan.

Galloway consistently opposed independence and left Philadelphia for the protection of General Sir WILLIAM HOWE's British army, returning to serve as a civil administrator for the Crown during the British occupation of Philadelphia in 1777–78. Galloway continued to hope that America and the British Empire could be reunited, and after the DECLARATION OF INDEPENDENCE (July 4, 1776), he formulated several plans of union that he thought could be used when the American rebels were defeated. When the British evacuated Philadelphia in the summer of 1778, Galloway went to British-occupied New York. He left New York City for England in December 1781.

Galloway was reviled by the Americans, who viewed him as a traitor who supplied information to General Howe's army. The new American government seized his estates, and Galloway never received compensation. In 1793 he applied for readmission to the state of Pennsylvania. His request was rejected. He died in 1803 in Watford, England.

Further reading: John E. Ferling, *The Loyalist Mind: Joseph Galloway and the American Revolution* (University Park: Pennsylvania State University Press, 1977); Benjamin H. Newcomb, *Franklin and Galloway: A Political Partnership* (New Haven, Conn.: Yale University Press, 1972).

— J. Brett Adams

Gaspee affair (June 9, 1772)

A crowd of Rhode Islanders, which probably included merchant John Brown, boarded a grounded British naval schooner in Narragansett Bay, forced the crew ashore, and burned the vessel. The *Gaspee* affair contributed to the sense of mistrust and anger between the colonies and Great Britain.

After the repeal of the TOWNSHEND DUTIES (1767, repealed 1770), except for the duty on tea, relations between the colonies and Great Britain improved and TRADE grew rapidly. While most merchants were involved in legal trade, some also continued to trade illegally. Rhode Island was a hotbed of illicit trade. Several confrontations occurred between smugglers and customs officials in the 1770s. To protect customs officials and to seize smugglers, the Royal Navy stationed a schooner, the HMS *Gaspee*, in Narragansett Bay in March 1772. The officer in charge of the vessel, Lieutenant Dudington, rigorously pursued smugglers and captured several vessels. In retaliation, the local sheriff threatened to arrest him for false seizure. The British admiral and the Rhode Island governor exchange threats, further inflaming the situation.

While in pursuit of a suspected smuggler, Dudington ran the *Gaspee* aground. Rhode Islanders boarded the vessel, overwhelmed the crew, examined the ship's papers, and then set fire to this threat to their livelihood. To make matters worse, Dudington had been wounded during the engagement and was arrested a few days later by the sheriff. After the British admiral paid a stiff fine and obtained Dudington's release, the British government launched a full-scale investigation into the affair. Although the British could not identify any of the rioters, the investigating commission had been empowered to send those accused of the crime to England for trial. This provision violated the traditional right of an Englishman to a trial by a jury of his peers, and Americans throughout the colonies became concerned about this threat to their liberty. Largely in response to the *Gaspee* affair, the Virginia House of Burgesses organized its COMMITTEE OF CORRESPONDENCE.

Gates, Horatio (1727–1806)

Horatio Gates was an English-born American general in the REVOLUTIONARY WAR (1775–83). Born to a lower-class family at Maldon in Essex, Gates entered the British army at an early age with a lieutenant's commission and served his first tour of duty in Nova Scotia from 1749–50. After receiving a captaincy, he was seriously wounded in July 1755 while a member of General Edward Braddock's unsuccessful attack on the French at Fort Duquesne during the French and Indian War (1754–63). He later served several posts in New York before obtaining a promising position under General Robert Monckton. After participating with Monckton in the expedition that defeated French resistance on the island of Martinique, Gates was granted a major's commission in 1762. His promotion turned out to be a disappointment, however, and he subsequently returned to England. There, as a major on half pay, a lack of further military advancement coupled with social prejudice led Gates to retire from the army and move to Virginia with his family, where he established himself as a planter and lived a life of substantial middle-class comfort.

Although Gates did not initially become involved in the political affairs of Virginia, he did accept a position as lieutenant colonel in the local militia. Sympathetic to colonial complaints against the British, Gates joined the American cause when the Revolutionary War began. He was commissioned a brigadier general and was given the position of adjunct general in the CONTINENTAL ARMY at Cambridge, Massachusetts, on June 17, 1775.

In May 1776 Gates was promoted to major general by the CONTINENTAL CONGRESS at the behest of his prominent friends and was then appointed to command the American army in CANADA. When he arrived in Albany to assume the new post, however, he learned that the Canadian army had retreated to Crown Point, which was under the jurisdiction of General PHILIP SCHUYLER, commander of the northern department. Gates was forced to subordinate himself to Schuyler, who appointed him to command FORT TICONDEROGA. In the summer of 1777, General JOHN BURGOYNE made an advance on Ticonderoga, upon which Gates was able to supersede Schuyler to command the defeated northern troops. Gates's fame was firmly established at SARATOGA (October 17, 1777) when the major general won two battles and forced the surrender of Burgoyne. Although Gates was not solely responsible for the success of the Saratoga campaign, the victory marked a turning point in the war, for which Gates reaped the glory and was named president of the board of war.

In June 1780 Congress appointed Gates as commander of the southern army in the Carolinas without consulting General GEORGE WASHINGTON, who wanted NATHANAEL GREENE to take the post. The Carolina campaign was poorly organized, and a lack of supplies coupled with untrained troops led to a terrible defeat at CAMDEN, South Carolina (August 16, 1780). After this battle, Gates was forced to relinquish his command to Greene. Congress ordered an official investigation of Gates's conduct in the affair, but it was never completed. Gates returned to active service in August 1782, but he never fully recovered his reputation. He retired to Virginia the following year.

In September 1790 Gates sold his plantation in Virginia, sold his slaves, and moved to Rose Hill Farm, an estate in Manhattan, New York. There he renewed an interest in politics, even serving one term in the New York legislature as a DEMOCRATIC-REPUBLICAN in 1800. Gates was a controversial figure in the Revolutionary War and died at home on April 10, 1806.

Further reading: Max M. Mintz, *The Generals of Saratoga: John Burgoyne and Horatio Gates* (New Haven, Conn.: Yale University Press, 1990); Paul David Nelson, *General Horatio Gates, A Biography* (Baton Rouge: Louisiana State University Press, 1976).

— Amy Pharr

Genet, Edmond Charles ("Citizen Genet") (1763–1834)

Edmond Charles Genet, "Citizen Genet," served as the French minister to the United States in 1793. During his short tenure as minister, Genet managed to antagonize President GEORGE WASHINGTON and members of his cabinet, including Secretary of State THOMAS JEFFERSON, who sympathized with the FRENCH REVOLUTION (1789–1815). Thus Genet added to a crisis in Franco-American relations as American leaders were trying to maintain neutrality in the war between Great Britain and France.

Genet was born at Versailles on January 8, 1763. A prodigy, Genet learned to read English, Swedish, Italian, and Latin by the time he was 12 years old. Previous to his American mission, he served as secretary of legation and chargé d'affaires to Russia. A full convert to the revolutionary cause, Genet was appointed minister to the United States in late 1792 and set sail for America in February 1793.

The Girondin government instructed Genet to negotiate a new treaty with the United States that would expand upon the Treaty of 1778. Genet was to use debt payments received from Americans to fund his mission and purchase supplies for French forces in the region. In essence, the French government wanted Genet to use the United States as a base for French operations. In addition, Genet was instructed to undertake "all measures which comported with his position" to foment rebellion in Spanish Louisiana and FLORIDA and British CANADA.

Genet arrived in Charleston, South Carolina, on April 8, 1793. Upon his arrival, he issued letters of marque for four French privateers and established procedures for condemning the British prizes they captured. Genet then traveled by land to Philadelphia. At almost every stop, local residents feted Genet and the French Revolution, causing him to believe that Americans fully supported his cause. Simultaneously, President Washington's cabinet was debating how the United States should treat the French Revolution, the new French minister, and the expanding war between France and Great Britain. Genet became an issue in this increasingly partisan dispute between Secretary of the Treasury ALEXANDER HAMILTON and Jefferson.

Genet took his frustrations with American neutrality directly to the people, thereby jettisoning traditional diplomatic practices. The *Little Sarah* affair typified Genet's disregard for American neutrality: In June and July 1793, Genet oversaw the conversion of the British ship *Little Sarah* into the privateer *La Petite Democrate* (the *Little Democrat)* in the Philadelphia harbor. Upon learning of Genet's activities, Jefferson demanded the ship remain in port. However, Genet ordered the ship to sea and consequently alienated his one ally within Washington's administration. Washington was deeply offended by Genet's actions. In August 1793 the United States requested Genet's recall.

Because the government had changed in France, Genet could not return to France without endangering his life. In 1794, at the age of 31, Genet married a daughter of Governor GEORGE CLINTON of New York and settled into the life of a gentleman farmer in upstate New York.

Further reading: Henry Ammon, *The Genet Mission* (New York: Norton, 1973).

— Terri Halperin

George III (1738–1820)

In the DECLARATION OF INDEPENDENCE (July 4, 1776), the CONTINENTAL CONGRESS asserted, "The history of the present king of Great Britain is a history of repeated injuries and usurpations all having in direct object the establishment of an absolute tyranny over these states." There followed a long indictment of more than 20 crimes committed by George III against the rights and liberties of his American subjects. After a decade of attacking parliamentary authority, American radicals turned their attention

King George III. Painting *(Library of Congress)*

to their monarch. This action was necessary for propaganda and ideological reasons. If Americans were to sever their ties with Britain, then they had to declare their independence from the king as well as his government and empire. The Declaration did much to cast an image of George III as tyrant in the minds of Americans during and after the REVOLUTIONARY WAR (1775–83). This view, while good politics, was based on a poor understanding of history. The monarch from whom Americans declared independence in 1776 was not a tyrant. Although the titular head of the British state, he was not primarily responsible for the policies, adopted in his name, that provoked rebellion in America. In many respects he was a sympathetic and tragic figure whose long reign witnessed the collapse of the first British empire and the birth of the second.

George III had the second longest reign in British history. Born on June 4, 1738, he was the son of Frederick, Prince of Wales, and Princess Augusta of Saxe-Coburg. He was not a prodigy and experienced educational difficulties as a child. He did not learn to read properly until he was

11 years old. A year later his father died and George became Prince of Wales, heir to his grandfather King George II. In 1760 George assumed the throne upon the death of his grandfather. He was the third Hanoverian king of Great Britain and the first who spoke English as his native language. As a new king, George III oversaw the final stages of the British triumph in the French and Indian War (1754–63), which ended with the Peace of Paris in 1763. When George III acceded to the throne, he was heavily influenced by JOHN STUART, EARL OF BUTE, who had been his tutor (and was reputed to be his widowed mother's lover). Bute helped to arrange the marriage of George to Princess Charlotte of Mecklenburg-Strelitz in 1761. This marriage proved to be a happy and durable one, lasting for more than 50 years and producing nine sons and six daughters. George III was a successful family man, devoted to his wife and children.

If George III's private life gave him stability and happiness, the same could not be said of his monarchical responsibilities. During the 1760s, a succession of short-lived governments grappled with imperial administration and the fiscal and political problems that came with a global empire. George III had hoped to recover for the monarchy some of the powers that had been assumed by Parliament since the Glorious Revolution, but he enjoyed little success in this area. He ruled in the style of his Hanoverian predecessors, through the extensive use of patronage to establish a group of supporters in Parliament known as the "king's friends." The early part of George III's reign was dominated by the problem of governing Britain's American colonies. The king favored the policies of his ministers and supported the efforts to tax and, later, to subdue the rebellious colonies by force. He was not, however, the author of these policies. It is often said that the loss of America cost George III his sanity, as he periodically displayed evidence of dementia. While the strains and stresses of governance took their toll on George III, modern research suggests that the king suffered from porphyria, a hereditary nervous disorder. The king suffered prolonged bouts of the illness in 1788–89 and again in 1801. He was permanently incapacitated by the disease in 1810 and his eldest son—later George IV—acted as Prince Regent during the last decade of George III's reign.

Apart from his illness, the second half of George III's reign was dominated not by events in America but by those in Europe, particularly the FRENCH REVOLUTION (1789–1815). Between 1793 and 1815 Britain led the successful movement to contain and defeat the French and NAPOLEON BONAPARTE. This effort included the inconclusive War of 1812 (1812–15) with the United States over maritime TRADE and western expansion. Simultaneously, Britain enlarged its colonial holdings in the WEST INDIES and south Asia. Despite the loss of the American colonies, when George III died in 1820 there had been a great expansion of empire and trade under his reign. At home the British population doubled in size, agricultural production increased, the INDUSTRIAL REVOLUTION had begun, and Enlightenment ideas found wide currency in Britain. Although George III cannot be credited with these developments, he did encourage them. He took a keen interest in SCIENCE and AGRICULTURE—his subjects nicknamed him "Farmer George"—and created and generously supported the Royal Academy of Arts. George III could be obstinate, and he did not always rule with wisdom or foresight. However, he was not, despite the claims of the Declaration of Independence, a tyrant. Rather, he was a good man of limited abilities and considerable health problems who sought with mixed results to grapple with massive responsibilities.

Further reading: John Brooke, *King George III* (New York: McGraw Hill, 1972).

— Francis D. Cogliano

Germantown, Battle of (October 4, 1777)

After defeat at the BATTLE OF BRANDYWINE (September 11, 1777) and the British occupation of Philadelphia (September 26, 1777), General GEORGE WASHINGTON sought to redeem the CONTINENTAL ARMY and force General Sir WILLIAM HOWE to retreat by launching a surprise attack at Germantown. Howe, for his part, may have been too confident because he did not entrench his position and spread his troops out in Pennsylvania and New Jersey near Philadelphia. Washington, however, developed an overly complicated plan: He ordered four separate columns to march on the British position at night for a coordinated assault in the morning. With the best troops, such a maneuver would have been difficult. With poorly trained Continentals and militia, it was courting disaster. The first Americans stumbled into British sentries about 4:00 A.M., easily pushing them back. But it was unusually foggy that morning and confusion began to reign on both sides. The American columns did not attack together. One American division even fired into another, and the militia never came up into position. At a crucial moment in the battle, the disciplined British shored up their line and gained reinforcements. Confronted with this defense, running out of ammunition, and confused by the smoke and fog, some American soldiers began to withdraw. The panic spread, and soon the whole American force was in retreat. Washington was convinced that had they persisted just a little longer, his men would have been victorious. The battle lasted under three hours. Each side had put about 8,000 men in the field: Howe lost about 500 men, the Americans had more than 1,000 killed, wounded, and captured.

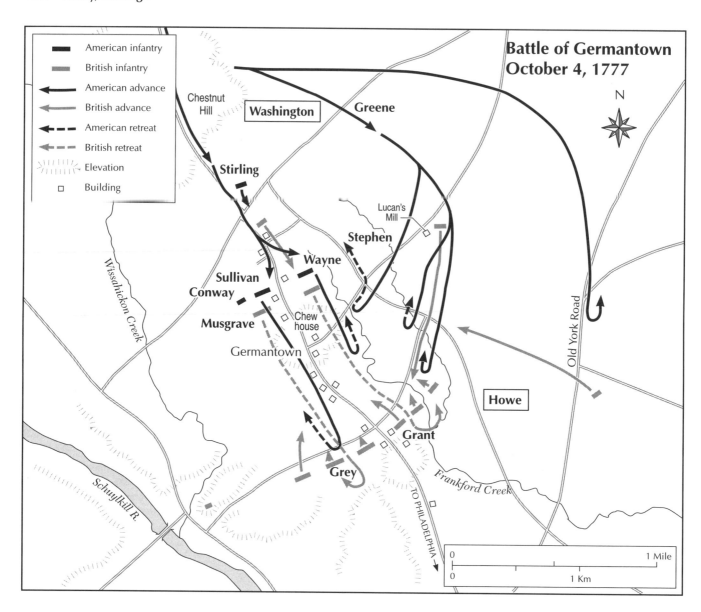

Battle of Germantown
October 4, 1777

Gerry, Elbridge (1745–1814)

One of the revolutionary era's most dedicated politicians, Elbridge Gerry was born in Marblehead, Massachusetts, in 1745. Gerry was the third of 12 children, son of a wealthy, respectable, and politically active father. In 1758 Gerry entered Harvard College and graduated in 1762. Upon graduation, Gerry joined his father's business, exporting dried fish to British colonies in the Caribbean.

Gerry's political career began after the BOSTON MASSACRE (March 5, 1770). Marblehead residents elected Gerry as town inspector to enforce an ongoing boycott of British imports protesting imperial regulation. In 1772 Marblehead elected Gerry to the colonial legislature, where SAMUEL ADAMS befriended him. Gerry used the

imperial crisis and the REVOLUTIONARY WAR (1775–83) to bolster his political and economic fortunes. He supplied military material to Massachusetts after the British closed Boston Harbor (1774), and he served in the CONTINENTAL CONGRESS between 1776 and 1780.

During the CONSTITUTIONAL CONVENTION in 1787, Gerry's REPUBLICANISM led him to oppose the effort to create a powerful central government because he believed it would threaten people's liberties and undermine state independence. Gerry signed the document despite his opposition. After the Constitutional Convention, he attempted to avoid partisan politics. In 1798 President JOHN ADAMS sent Gerry, JOHN MARSHALL, and CHARLES PINCKNEY to France to negotiate an end to the diplomatic impasse with France and repair relations that had deteriorated since JAY'S TREATY (1794). The French believed that the Americans had abandoned the alliance of 1777 and now favored Great Britain. American officials were angry about French meddling in American politics and seizures of American shipping. The resulting negotiations led to the infamous XYZ AFFAIR: Before Gerry and his cohorts could meet the French minister of foreign relations CHARLES MAURICE TALLEYRAND-PERIGORD, lower dignitaries demanded a bribe. When news of this diplomatic affront reached the United States, Adams insisted that the delegation return to the United States. However, Gerry defied Adams's order, believing that he could defuse the crisis and avoid war. In 1798 Adams recalled Gerry to face FEDERALIST PARTY scorn.

After the XYZ affair, Gerry again became active in partisan politics, aligning with the DEMOCRATIC-REPUBLICAN PARTY because of its devotion to small government. Suffering four consecutive defeats, Gerry was finally elected governor of Massachusetts in 1810. During his second term he supported Democratic-Republican redistricting measures, and Federalist opponents coined the term "gerrymander" to describe the practice of drawing voting district boundaries to favor one party. Gerry was elected JAMES MADISON's vice president in 1812 and died on November 23, 1814.

Further reading: George Athan Billias, *Elbridge Gerry: Founding Father and Republican Statesman* (New York: McGraw Hill, 1976); William Stinchcombe, *The XYZ Affair* (Westport, Conn.: Greenwood Press, 1980).

— William J. Bauer, Jr.

Girard, Stephen (1750–1831)

Stephen Girard was a prominent American of French descent who became a wealthy merchant, banker, investor, and philanthropist in Philadelphia during the early republic. Born in 1750, Girard arrived in New York from France in 1774 as the son of a successful ship captain and merchant. He quickly established himself in the mercantile field in New York and spent the next few years sailing between New York and the WEST INDIES. During the REVOLUTIONARY WAR (1775–83) he relocated to Philadelphia, where he built a very successful trading business and became one of the wealthiest persons in the United States by 1810. Girard faced financial complications between 1807 and 1812 due to the EMBARGO OF 1807 and escalating tension between the United States and Great Britain. However, he successfully liquidated most of his physical holdings in European ports and turned to domestic banking. In 1812 he opened the Girard Bank in the building that had housed the late BANK OF THE UNITED STATES with $1.2 million of his own capital. The Girard Bank operated between 1812 and 1832 as a privately owned bank, without a state charter. Nevertheless, the bank achieved financial parity with the other major Philadelphia BANKS by 1816.

Girard played a pivotal role in financing the War of 1812 (1812–15). Along with merchants David Parish and John Jacob Astor, he invested approximately $10 million in government stock to fund the war effort in 1813. He also used his political influence and financial holdings to support the successful effort to establish a Second Bank of the United States in 1816. Girard distinguished himself in service to the people of Philadelphia by personally volunteering and funding yellow fever relief efforts in the 1790s. In his will, he left substantial funds for the operation of a home for orphaned boys in Philadelphia, which would become known as Girard College. Girard died in 1831 with no immediate family and left most of his $7.5-million estate to the city of Philadelphia.

Further reading: Donald R. Adams Jr., *Finance and Enterprise in Early America: A Study of Stephen Girard's Bank, 1812–1831* (Philadelphia: University of Pennsylvania Press, 1978); Belden L. Daniels, *Pennsylvania: Birthplace of Banking* (Harrisburg, Pa.: Pennsylvania Bankers Association, 1976).

— James R. Karmel

Golden Hill, Battle of (January 18, 1770)

A series of confrontations between New York civilians and British soldiers culminated in a riot in 1770, popularly known as the Battle of Golden Hill, in which the two groups fought each other in the street. There were no fatalities, but several on both sides were injured. This disturbance demonstrated how local issues, like competition over jobs, could be given a larger ideological meaning within the context of the imperial crisis.

To commemorate the repeal of the STAMP ACT (1765, repealed 1766), the New York SONS OF LIBERTY organized a celebration of the birthday of King GEORGE III in June 1766, centered on a flagstaff erected on the city's common and parade ground. Within days of this holiday, the New York assembly refused to comply with the QUARTERING ACT (1765), and suddenly the flagstaff became a symbol of colonial opposition to the presence of British troops. Recognizing the significance of this symbol, British soldiers cut the pole down on the night of August 10, 1766. New Yorkers were outraged by this attack on their "Tree of Liberty" and put up a new pole shortly thereafter. Further confrontations followed through August and September, but the pole remained in place. On March 18, 1767, New Yorkers held their celebration of the anniversary of the Stamp Act repeal around their LIBERTY POLE. The following night British soldiers chopped it down. Several more confrontations ensued, but a new pole remained in place until January 1770.

That winter there were several major controversies swirling through the colony of New York. Opposition to the TOWNSHEND DUTIES (1767) had finally gained momentum, and a nonimportation movement had begun to succeed. New Yorkers were also agitated over the treatment of ALEXANDER MCDOUGALL, who had been imprisoned for his outspoken opposition to the New York assembly's compliance with the Quartering Act. Finally, in the middle of winter and with a sluggish ECONOMY, many workers found it difficult to obtain employment. Making matters worse was the fact that off-duty British soldiers competed for jobs, laboring for as little as half the pay of a civilian. On January 16, 1770, New York WHIGS issued broadsides complaining of the presence of the British army and suggesting that merchants and other employers should show "care and benevolence" to their neighbors and not hire any redcoats. Angered by the broadside, British soldiers destroyed the liberty pole that night. The next day the soldiers printed their own handbill. Two New Yorkers seized two soldiers distributing the broadside, intending to turn them over to the authorities. A group of soldiers came to rescue their comrades, and the confrontation quickly escalated into a riot. Scores of soldiers and civilians fought until officers and local officials parted the two sides. The next day, New Yorkers patrolled the waterfront, beating any soldiers they found working at jobs that should have gone to civilians.

See also BOSTON MASSACRE; RESISTANCE MOVEMENT; RIOTS.

Further reading: Paul A. Gilje, *The Road to Mobocracy: Popular Disorder in New York City, 1763–1834* (Chapel Hill: University of North Carolina Press, 1987).

Grasse, François-Joseph-Paul, comte de
(1722–1788)

The son of a nobleman, de Grasse played a vital role in helping win the BATTLE OF YORKTOWN (October 19, 1781) and securing an American military triumph in the REVOLUTIONARY WAR (1775–83). He entered the Garde de la Marine at age 11 to pursue a life in the French navy. He became a page to the grand master of Malta at age 12, saw action against corsairs in the Mediterranean, and in 1747 was captured by the English during the Battle of Cape Finisterre. Upon his release he resumed his stellar naval career, and by 1781 he was a rear admiral and commander in chief of French naval forces in the WEST INDIES. Contemporaries considered him the finest French admiral of the age, and he was widely admired for his good looks, commanding bearing, and coolness under fire.

Ordered by King Louis XVI to attack British forces in the Caribbean and then assist French and American armies in North America during the Revolutionary War, de Grasse sailed for the West Indies in the spring of 1781. He defeated a British force commanded by Admiral Samuel Hood, captured St. Eustatius and St. Kitts, and in August entered Chesapeake Bay with 28 ships and 3,000 French soldiers. He arrived in time to block the seaward escape of a British army commanded by CHARLES, LORD CORNWALLIS from Virginia. Combined French and American armies under GEORGE WASHINGTON and the COMTE DE ROCHAMBEAU had surrounded Cornwallis at Yorktown. On September 5, 1781, de Grasse blocked a British naval attempt to relieve Cornwallis by defeating Admiral Thomas Graves in the Battle of the Chesapeake Capes. Graves cautiously decided to retreat to New York for repairs and reinforcements before returning to save Cornwallis, but the delay proved fatal to British interests in North America. Without hope of rescue because of the presence of de Grasse's fleet, Cornwallis was forced to surrender his besieged army at Yorktown on October 19th. The American victory proved decisive in convincing leaders in Great Britain that prolonging the war was pointless. They soon began negotiations to end the war, leading to the TREATY OF PARIS (1783).

By then de Grasse had been decisively defeated and captured by British Admiral George Rodney in the famous Battle of the Saintes off Dominica (April 12, 1782), and the Royal Navy reigned supreme as the unquestioned master of the world's oceans. De Grasse died six years later, a disappointed man.

Further reading: Barbara Tuchman, *The First Salute: A View of the American Revolution* (New York: Knopf, 1988).
— Lance Janda

Great Plains

The Great Plains, sometimes referred to as the Great American Desert, was teeming with life in the century after 1750. Before 1750, only limited numbers of NATIVE AMERICANS had ventured onto its vast open spaces. But the introduction of the horse in the late 17th century from New Mexico allowed many Indians to alter their culture and pursue the huge herds of buffalo that wandered the region. Comanche trekked from the Great Basin area in eastern Utah, and the Sioux moved from the east and the prairies of Minnesota. This transformation took decades to develop. By the second half of the 18th century, these tribes had created the elaborate Plains Indian culture that was largely dependent on the horse for mobility and the buffalo for almost everything else.

There were several key characteristics of this culture: First, tribes became decentralized, since there was less need for cooperation in a nomadic lifestyle; AGRICULTURE had required greater group organization for labor and for protection. Second, the gender division of labor changed.

Women had previously been the primary food producers by gathering food or growing crops (or both). Now their labor focused on the dressing of meats and the tanning of hides. With this shift also came some diminution of the status of women within the tribe. Finally, the Plains Indians developed extensive TRADE networks that reached from New Mexico and the Rio Grande to Hudson's Bay in CANADA, and from beyond the Rockies to the European Americans on the Atlantic.

There were also important shifts in the balance of power in this period. The Comanche drove the Apache into the deserts of the Southwest. Further north, the sedentary tribes of the Mandan and Hidasta, visited by LEWIS AND CLARK, had been vital as trading centers around 1800, but they soon lost ground, devastated by DISEASE AND EPIDEMICS. Because of the dispersed nature of the mobile Plains Indians, they suffered less from disease at this time. Europeans also laid claim to the Great Plains. French fur traders traveled throughout the area in the late 18th century. Spain held title to most of the Plains after 1763 but did not colonize it beyond southern Texas and the Mississippi outposts established by the French. Shortly after the LOUISIANA PURCHASE (1803) by the United States, American explorers like Lewis and Clark and Zebulon Pike crossed the Great Plains, and American fur trading penetrated into the Rockies. European-American settlement of the Great Plains would have to wait until later in the 19th century.

See also FRONTIER.

Further reading: Gary Clayton Anderson, *The Indian Southwest, 1580–1830: Ethnogenesis and Reinvention* (Norman: University of Oklahoma Press, 1999); Andrew C. Isenberg, *The Devastation of the Bison: An Environmental History, 1750–1920* (Cambridge, U.K.: Cambridge University Press, 2000).

Greene, Nathanael (1742–1786)

One of General GEORGE WASHINGTON's ablest lieutenants, Nathanael Greene, served in the army from the siege of Boston until after the British surrender at YORKTOWN (October 19, 1781). He fought in several battles and took over command of the southern campaign at a critical juncture after the defeat of HORATIO GATES at the BATTLE OF CAMDEN (August 16, 1780).

There was little in Greene's background to suggest that he would become an important military figure. He was born in Warwick, Rhode Island, to QUAKER parents. He was brought up in some comfort and became an anchor smith and ironmonger. By the time of the REVOLUTIONARY WAR (1775–83), he had left the Society of Friends and was eager to fight against the British. Somehow the Rhode Island Assembly recognized his greatest assets—tremendous organizational skills and the ability to instill confidence and lead men—and appointed him in May 1775 as the general in command of the Rhode Island Army of Observation with orders to join the siege of Boston. Once the Rhode Island troops arrived in the Boston area, Greene's talents quickly came to the fore as he helped to organize supplies for the army and eased intercolonial tensions. On June 22 he was appointed a brigadier general in the CONTINENTAL ARMY, and after the British evacuated Boston in the spring of 1776, he was put in charge of the army of occupation for the city.

During the next few years, Greene participated in every major campaign led by General Washington. In April 1775 Greene brought his Rhode Island regiments to New York City and helped to prepare the defenses against a British attack. He was promoted to major general on June 22, 1776. Although he was ill and did not fight in the BATTLE OF LONG ISLAND (August 27–30, 1776), he recovered in time to take command of the Continental forces in New Jersey in the fall of 1776. His attack in October on Staten Island had to be called back after General WILLIAM HOWE threatened Washington at the BATTLE OF WHITE PLAINS (October 28, 1776), and he had to oversee the retreat from Fort Lee after the disastrous loss of FORT WASHINGTON (November 17, 1776) on Harlem Heights. He retained Washington's confidence in the face of defeat and had command of one of the columns at the BATTLE OF TRENTON (December 26, 1776), cutting off the retreat of many HESSIANS and forcing their surrender. He was important in setting up the winter camp at MORRISTOWN and in skirmishing with the British in New Jersey in the spring of 1777. During the BATTLE OF BRANDYWINE (September 11, 1777), his stout defense in the center and careful retreat helped save the Continental army from destruction. In the attack at GERMANTOWN (October 4, 1777), which depended upon coordinated assaults at dawn and in the fog, Greene failed to bring his division into play early enough to have an impact on the battle. Greene was also unable to hold onto the Delaware River forts in November after the main Continental forces retreated to VALLEY FORGE (1777–78) and the British occupied Philadelphia.

Recognizing the difficulties of the military situation, Washington did not blame Greene for these reverses. When the CONTINENTAL CONGRESS wanted to appoint a new quartermaster general for the army, Washington immediately suggested Greene. As quartermaster from February 25, 1778, to July 15, 1780, Greene once again demonstrated his talents for organization in supplying the army. He also continued as a field commander, participating in the BATTLE OF MONMOUTH (June 28, 1778) and an abortive attack on Newport that led to the BATTLE OF RHODE ISLAND (August 29, 1778). Although often adept at smoothing relations between different men, politics ultimately compelled Greene to resign as quartermaster. His greatest service to the cause of independence was yet to come.

In the summer of 1780 CHARLES, LORD CORNWALLIS's invasion of the southern colonies had almost ended the rebellion in that region. The capture of CHARLESTON (May 12, 1780) followed by the Battle of Camden all but eliminated the presence of the Continental army in South Carolina. At this crucial moment, Washington needed to send someone to the South he could depend on. He chose the Rhode Island ironmonger, Nathanael Greene. As soon as he received his appointment on October 14, 1780, Greene began planning and organizing. Oddly, without ever winning a major victory himself, Greene managed to drive the British back to a small area around Charleston and so frustrated Cornwallis that he abandoned the Carolinas and marched north to Virginia and his eventual surrender at Yorktown.

Greene's first order of business was to make sure that his army would be adequately supplied. As he reformed the Continental army in North Carolina, he made the unorthodox move of splitting his forces. Cornwallis obliged him by splitting his own army, sending BANASTRE TARLETON after DANIEL MORGAN in the South Carolina backcountry. Morgan so severely trounced Tarleton at the BATTLE OF COWPENS (January 17, 1781) that Cornwallis abandoned his baggage and set off after Greene in an effort to corner him and regain the initiative. But Greene was wily and kept one step ahead of the pursuing British. When Cornwallis at last gave up the chase in northern North Carolina, Greene advanced. Cornwallis's troops were still superior to the Continentals and defeated them at the BATTLE OF GUILFORD COURTHOUSE (March 15, 1781). But this victory was so costly that Cornwallis marched to Wilmington on the coast and then headed to his ill-fated invasion of Virginia. Greene did not follow him. Instead, he marched into South Carolina and captured several British outposts. Greene was still no match for concentrated British forces. The British, for example, beat back his attack at EUTAW SPRINGS (September 8, 1781), but he continued to apply pressure until the British withdrew all their forces except those that held Charleston. As Greene explained: "We rise, get beat, rise, and fight again."

At the end of the war, Greene faced financial difficulties. Although he was granted land by South Carolina and Georgia and made profits as a supplier when he was quartermaster, he also used his own credit and resources to sustain the army. The war also took a physical toll on him as well. In the last few years of his life, he divided his time between property he owned in Rhode Island and in Georgia.

Further reading: Theodore Thayer, *Nathanael Greene: Strategist of the American Revolution* (New York: Twayne, 1960).

Green Mountain Boys

The Green Mountain Boys of Vermont began as land rioters, organized themselves as a WHIG militia in the opening days of the REVOLUTIONARY WAR (1775–83), and became a regular regiment in the CONTINENTAL ARMY. Starting in 1770 and headed by ETHAN ALLEN and several of his relatives, New England settlers formed the Green Mountain Boys. Their aim was to protect their land titles based on New Hampshire grants from landlords whose deeds rested on New York's claim to territory north of Massachusetts and between the Hudson and Connecticut Rivers. Ultimately, the British government sustained the New York right to these lands. But that right became a dead letter in the face of the Green Mountain Boys and their riotous tactics. Calling themselves a militia, the Green Mountain Boys harassed New York sheriffs attempting to evict settlers with New Hampshire deeds, tore down fences, and even destroyed houses built by settlers from New York. Such actions made Allen and his followers outlaws in New York.

The Revolutionary War offered a new opportunity to the Green Mountain Boys. By siding with the Whigs, they hoped to legitimize their claim and gain recognition. Allen led a group of his followers in a surprise attack on the British, capturing FORT TICONDEROGA (May 10, 1775). Seth Warner and Allen convinced the CONTINENTAL CONGRESS to incorporate the Green Mountain Boys into the Continental army in June 1775, and the new regiment elected Warner its colonel. The regiment participated in the invasion of CANADA that winter. After that disaster left the regiment devastated, other Vermont regiments were recruited and given the Green Mountain label. These units fought against the invasion that led to the British surrender at SARATOGA (October 17, 1777) and in subsequent campaigns along the northern border. This commitment to independence may have strengthened the case of the Green Mountain Boys for secure title of their lands, but it was not until 1791 that Vermont became a separate state.

See also LAND RIOTS.

Further reading: Michael A. Bellesiles, *Revolutionary Outlaws: Ethan Allen and the Struggle for Independence on the Early American Frontier* (Charlottesville: University Press of Virginia, 1993); Robert E. Shalhope, *Bennington and the Green Mountain Boys: The Emergence of Liberal Democracy in Vermont, 1760–1850* (Baltimore: Johns Hopkins University Press, 1996).

Greenville, Treaty of (1795)

The Treaty of Greenville in 1795 marked the end of a long series of battles between the American army and the Miami confederacy led by Little Turtle. By the terms of the treaty, the NATIVE AMERICANS deeded away most of what is now southern Ohio in return for the promise that the United States government would keep settlers from trespassing further on tribal lands. The Americans paid for the lands with trade goods that were distributed over the course of many years.

In the early 1790s, the Miami confederation kept a strong hold over the lands west of Pennsylvania. Any Europeans that tried to settle in the region north of the Ohio River took their life in their hands. President GEORGE WASHINGTON sent several expeditions into the region to establish the authority of the United States. Little Turtle and his warriors defeated a force of militiamen and regular troops commanded by General Josiah Harmar. In 1791 the Miami crushed another army under General ARTHUR ST. CLAIR. Washington then sent one of his best commanders, ANTHONY WAYNE, to conquer the territory. Wayne planned carefully, but on August 20, 1794, his men ran into an ambush around FALLEN TIMBERS. This time the Americans did not run away, and they regrouped and defeated the Miami. They chased the Native American warriors back to the British-held Fort Miami, where the Indians sought refuge. The English did not fire on the Americans nor open the gates to their old Indian allies. The campaign against the Confederation of Great Lakes Native Americans was over.

General Wayne wanted to demonstrate to the various Indian tribes that the United States was now in charge of the region. He prepared for a large conference to show that the Americans could be as generous and as powerful as the former British and French rulers of the Ohio. The members of various tribes gathered the next summer around Greenville to attend the meeting.

General Wayne wanted to conclude the parley quickly, since the volunteers that made up his army had left to go home. The Indians surrendered southern Ohio and southeastern Indiana in exchange for $20,000 worth of goods and another $9,500 the next year. The United States in turn promised to keep settlers and hunters off of the land beyond the boundaries marked out in the Treaty of Greenville. On August 3, 1795, leaders of the Wyandot, Delaware, Shawnee, Potawatamie, Kickapoo, Wea, and Miami signed the document.

The treaty put an end to British hopes for an Indian state that would act as a buffer between the land-hungry Americans and CANADA. England soon withdrew its troops from American territory. For the Native Americans the treaty was only a breathing spell; American swarmed into Indian lands almost as soon as the ink dried.

Further reading: Andrew R. L. Cayton, "'Noble Actors' on 'the Theatre of Honour': Power and Civility in the Treaty of Greenville," in *Contact Points: American Frontiers from the Mohawk Valley to the Mississippi,* *1750–1830,* eds. Cayton Teute and Frederika J. Teute (Chapel Hill: University of North Carolina Press, 1998); Richard White, *The Middle Ground: Indians, Empires, and Republics in the Great Lakes Region, 1650–1815* (New York: Cambridge University Press, 1991).

— George Milne

Grenville, George (1712–1770)

George Grenville was chief minister in the British government in the period 1763–65 and is remembered for passing tax reform in the British Empire that angered the American colonists. A well-known and successful politician, he had held a number of important positions before becoming the king's chief minister in 1763. Oxford educated, he began his public career as a member of Parliament in 1741. He rose in the political ranks quickly: In 1744 he became Lord of the Admiralty; in 1747 he was appointed a lord of the treasury; in 1754 he assumed the dual responsibility of treasurer of the navy and privy councillor; in 1761 he was given a leadership role in the House of Commons; in May 1762 he was appointed secretary of state; and in 1763 he gained the top position in the British government. He inherited a government that was £145 million in debt from fighting the French and Indian War (1754–63). A master of finance, he proposed a plan to put the empire back on a sound financial footing and to ease the tax burden of the British subjects.

To accomplish this, he encouraged the British government to pass a number of financial reforms known as the Grenville Acts. The acts angered the American colonists, inciting them to begin the RESISTANCE MOVEMENT (1764–75) to British imperial policy. Although his primary goal was to make the colonists pay for part of the protection provided to them by British troops, many Americans viewed Grenville's actions as unacceptable impositions on both their wallets and their freedoms. Under the Grenville government, the British parliament passed the CURRENCY ACT (1764), the SUGAR ACT (1764), and the STAMP ACT (1765). While all three of the acts irritated the colonists, it was the Stamp Act that provoked widespread resistance. The Stamp Act levied taxes on every newspaper, pamphlet, almanac, legal document, pair of dice, and all other legal and commercial papers in the colonies. RIOTS and other forms of violent protest were widespread, and the tax prompted an intercolonial meeting attended by delegates from nine colonies known as the STAMP ACT CONGRESS.

The failure of the Grenville Acts, and the surprising American reaction to them, cut short Grenville's ministership. He was replaced by Charles Watson-Wentworth, Lord Rockingham, in 1765. Grenville continued to defend his policies and, as a member of Parliament, he voted against the repeal of the Stamp Act in 1766.

Further reading: Allen S. Johnson, *A Prologue to Revolution: The Political Career of George Grenville* (Lanham, Md.: University Press of America, 1997).

— J. Brett Adams

Guilford Courthouse, Battle of (March 15, 1781)

The Battle of Guilford Courthouse on March 15, 1781, was an American defeat, but the heavy price of victory in North Carolina drew CHARLES, LORD CORNWALLIS into Virginia and ultimately to his surrender at YORKTOWN (October 19, 1781). After the BATTLE OF COWPENS (January 17, 1781), the Americans withdrew into North Carolina. Hoping to catch and crush General DANIEL MORGAN, recapture prisoners, and dispel the impression of British vulnerability, Cornwallis followed, destroying all his excess baggage and supplies to increase the army's mobility and speed. Upon learning of the victory at Cowpens, General NATHANAEL GREENE, in turn, maneuvered his forces to reunite with Morgan.

When the two armies finally reached Guilford Courthouse, the Americans had approximately 4,400 men to the 2,200 British. Despite superior numbers, the rebels lacked the experience and training of their enemy. Militia units, many that had never been in combat, formed the bulk of Greene's army. Generally considered to be highly unreliable on the battlefield, the militia men were unused to formal drills and military discipline, and they carried a mixture of rifles, muskets, and fowling pieces, none of which were equipped with bayonets for close-order fighting. Though better equipped and trained, the soldiers in the CONTINENTAL ARMY at Greene's disposal were of uneven quality, their ranks continually depleted of veterans as terms of enlistment ended. Yet, the terrain at Guilford Courthouse favored the Americans. The woods, shrubs, and underbrush provided cover for rebel attackers and made it difficult for the British to march in their conventional long, tightly formed files. With these factors in mind, Greene deployed his men in three rows, the first two composed of North Carolina and Virginia militia and the third of Continentals.

The redcoats began their approach early in the morning. Greene's first line of militia performed better than expected, but they quickly fell back. As anticipated, the terrain hindered the British advance on the second column, and they took heavy losses. Exhausted, the redcoats engaged the third line, where, quite unexpectedly, a veteran Continental unit bolted and opened a serious breech in their position. Greene was forced to order a retreat. The British carried the day but lost a staggering 27 percent of their engaged forces as compared with only 6 percent for

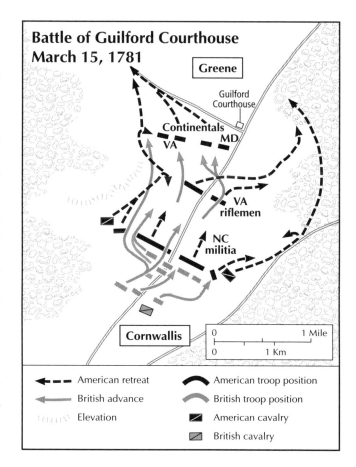

Battle of Guilford Courthouse March 15, 1781

the Americans. An English Parliamentarian later remarked, in fact, that "another such victory would ruin the British Army."

In the aftermath, Cornwallis considered his options. Having generated little LOYALIST support in North Carolina, in desperate need of supplies and rest, and viewing Virginia as the key to victory in the South, he elected to move his tattered army north. This allowed Greene to return unopposed to South Carolina. With the surrender at Yorktown in October, however, and Greene's reclamation of the South, England soon resolved to end the war and relinquish her rebellious colonies.

See also REVOLUTIONARY WAR.

Further reading: Thomas F. Baker, *Another Such Victory: The Story of the American Defeat at Guilford Courthouse That Helped Win the War for Independence* (New York: Eastern Acorn Press, 1981); Robert Leckie, *George Washington's War: The Saga of the American Revolution* (New York: HarperCollins, 1993).

— Rita M. Broyles

H

Haiti

In 1791 revolution broke out in the French colony of Saint-Dominigue, later called Haiti. The Haitian Revolution would send ripples not just through Europe but through North America as well. One of the wealthiest European outposts in the New World, the Caribbean island's western third became home of some of the largest and most brutal slave plantations anywhere. Slave laborers cultivated sugar and coffee, and they endured horrible death rates, requiring constant infusions of slaves from Africa. On the eve of the Haitian Revolution, roughly 450,000 black slaves lived in the colony along with fewer than 40,000 whites. Another group of Haitians—roughly 30,000 so-called mulattos—came from black/white parentage. Although the mulattos might own land and accrue wealth (and while many were free), mixed-race Haitians had no political rights. In 1791 this tense racial situation exploded.

The FRENCH REVOLUTION (1789–1815) prompted the mulatto class to seek political recognition. In May 1791 the French Assembly granted freeborn mulattos equality, much to the consternation of middle-class whites, who lashed out (often violently) against them. By the summer, slave uprisings began occurring in various parts of Haiti. By 1793 a full-scale revolution against French colonial rule was under way. Haitian rebels coalesced around the dynamic figure of Toussaint Louverture. A former slave, Toussaint gathered a force of several thousand and issued a proclamation in 1793 declaring all slaves free. At first an ally of Spanish forces fighting the French, Toussaint and his army soon backed French Republican forces seemingly sympathetic to their revolution. War continued throughout the 1790s, often pitting slave rebels against free blacks. By 1801 Toussaint claimed control of the entire island. Haiti eventually became the first independent black republic in the Western Hemisphere.

The significance of the Haitian rebellion transcended time and place. American masters of the 1790s nervously watched events in the Caribbean, dreading the possibility of the slave rebellion spreading to their own plantations. Such fears intensified when Haitian masters sought refuge in various American states, bringing their slaves (and their slaves' knowledge of the revolution) with them. Some northern states, such as Pennsylvania, refused to allow Haitian masters to maintain their slave property (Pennsylvania had already passed a gradual emancipation act). On the other hand, South Carolina admitted many masters and their slaves. As president in the early 1800s, THOMAS JEFFERSON refused diplomatic recognition of Haiti, a policy that continued until Abraham Lincoln's presidency.

Among enslaved peoples, the memory and example of Haiti remained strong. Black seamen brought news of the rebellion to various ports, from New England down to the Carolinas. South Carolina eventually passed a law requiring black seamen to be locked up while in the state's ports. The Haitian Revolution would also inspire free-black activism: In 1797 Boston's PRINCE HALL encouraged his brethren to unify and recall Haitian rebels to fight American racial prejudice. Decades after it had occurred, other black activists would similarly invoke the memory of Haiti. At a convention of AFRICAN-AMERICAN activists in Buffalo in 1843, Henry Highland Garnet likened Toussaint Louverture to Moses, for his "tremendous movement shook the whole empire of slavery!"

See also ANTISLAVERY AND ABOLITION; SLAVERY.

Further reading: C. L. R. James, *Black Jacobins: Toussaint L'Ouverture and the San Domingo Revolution* (New York: Random House, 1963); Lester Langley, *The Americas in the Age of Revolution, 1750–1850* (New Haven, Conn.: Yale University Press, 1996).

— Richard Newman

Hale, Nathan (1755–1776)

Most famous for his patriotic last words before being put to death by the British on September 22, 1776, Nathan Hale became a symbol of the American struggle for independence. Born in Coventry, Connecticut, on June 6, 1755, he was one of 12 children of the wealthy and influential Edward and Elizabeth Strong Hale. After a sickly childhood, Hale grew into an intelligent and athletic young man. His parents encouraged him to pursue his education, and the young Hale became an avid reader. While his father hoped he would become a minister, he chose instead to pursue a life as a teacher after graduating from Yale at age 18. He taught in East Haddam, Connecticut, in 1773 and 1774 and then in New London, Connecticut, in 1774 and 1775.

After a brief tenure as a schoolmaster, Hale joined the fledgling CONTINENTAL ARMY and received a commission as a first lieutenant in 1775. Shortly after participating in the siege of Boston, he was promoted to captain. His exemplary performance in the ill-fated BATTLE OF LONG ISLAND (August 27–30, 1776) earned Hale further recognition, and he served as captain of the prestigious "Congress's Own," a company of the Connecticut rangers among 120 handpicked men under the command of Lieutenant Colonel Thomas Knowlton. Hale then distinguished himself by volunteering for a risky assignment to spy on the British general WILLIAM HOWE, a mission which no one else in his regiment would accept.

The 21-year-old Hale quickly assumed his undercover assignment. He lacked any formal training in intelligence gathering and was given very little guidance in his mission. Left to his own ingenuity, Hale posed as a Dutch schoolmaster in search of a job. He traveled from Harlem Heights to Long Island and successfully gathered a good deal of information about British operations, which he kept hidden in his shoes. While in the process of returning to Harlem Heights, Hale was captured by the British.

Interestingly, the details of his capture remain murky. Some believed he had been betrayed by his cousin, Samuel Hail, a LOYALIST who served as General Howe's deputy commissioner of prisoners. Others claimed that he mistakenly boarded a British ship that he believed to be an American vessel sent to pick him up, or that British soldiers captured him at Cedars Tavern, just north of New York City. Regardless of how he came to be captured, his detailed notes and sketches regarding British military positions that were hidden in his shoes led his captors to condemn him as a spy.

On September 21, 1776, General Howe sentenced Nathan Hale to die without a trial. The following day the British hanged Hale, but not before reportedly uttering his famous last words: "I only regret that I have but one life to lose for my country." Hale's statement earned him the legacy of a martyr in the cause of independence.

Further reading: Henry Phelps Johnston, *Nathan Hale, 1776 Biography and Memorials* (New Haven, Conn.: Yale University Press, 1914).

— Sarah Eppler Janda

Hall, Prince (1750?–1807)

Although the precise date of his birth remains unknown, Prince Hall lived in Massachusetts for most of his life and became one of the most celebrated AFRICAN-AMERICAN figures of the post–Revolutionary era. A former slave to a leather merchant, Hall was freed in 1770. He soon formed the African Masonic Lodge, which grew out of meetings Hall and roughly a dozen other blacks began holding in 1775. The Lodge received formal status in 1787—and then, ironically, from British Masons. Hall was also a longtime black activist. In the late 1770s he petitioned the Massachusetts Legislature to end SLAVERY. A decade later, he memorialized the same body to fund voluntary African-American emigration to Africa. At the end of the 1790s, Hall asked Boston officials to start a school for black youth. When these officials delayed such action, Hall used his own home for the school.

Hall remains equally famous for authoring two protest pamphlets during the 1790s, both entitled *A Charge*. The first of the essays was published in 1792, and it focused on the significance of religious piety and racial uplift for black Masons. Hall distributed copies of it, one of the earliest African-American pamphlets, from his Lodge. His second publication dated from 1797. This work addressed more directly racial oppression and the need for African-American unity. Although Massachusetts had declared slavery unconstitutional in the early 1780s, the state's racial situation remained tense for decades. In 1788 the legislature even approved a law stating that black émigrés could not remain in Massachusetts, forcing them to leave or face incarceration. Hall confronted racial mobs angered by his independence and activism. In his 1797 essay, Hall told African Americans that God was firmly on the side of the oppressed and that masonry offered not only brotherhood but protection to African Americans. In addition, Hall's second pamphlet made reference to the Haitian Revolution, which began in the early 1790s as a slave revolution and ended in 1801 with the declaration of the first independent black republic in the Western Hemisphere. At a time when even white abolitionists referred to the event cautiously, Hall encouraged American blacks to think of HAITI in positive terms. The reverence with which African-American communities held Hall may be gauged by one simple fact: After his death in 1807, the African Grand Lodge of Masons referred to itself as the Prince Hall Masons.

See also ANTISLAVERY AND ABOLITION; FREEMASONS.

Further reading: Sidney Kaplan and Emma Nogrady Kaplan, *The Black Presence in the Era of the American Revolution* (Amherst: University of Massachusetts Press, 1985); Richard Newman, Patrick Rael, and Philip Lapsansky, eds., *Pamphlets of Protest: An Anthology of Early*

African American Protest Writing, 1790–1860 (New York: Routledge, 2001).

— Richard Newman

Hamilton, Alexander (1757–1804)

Born in the British WEST INDIES on January 11, 1757, Alexander Hamilton was a close friend of GEORGE WASHINGTON, a leading founding father, and the first secretary of the treasury. His mother was a planter's daughter of French-Huguenot descent, and his father was an itinerant Scottish merchant. However, his mother had been previously married, and as a result her union with Hamilton's father was not legally recognized, rendering Hamilton illegitimate. At a young age, Hamilton learned to speak fluent French as his mother and a Presbyterian minister provided him with a basic EDUCATION. In 1768 his mother died, and Hamilton became an apprentice to a local mercantile establishment, whose owner perceived his intelligence and organized a fund for a proper education. In 1772 Hamilton left the West Indies for the American colonies. He arrived in New York with letters of introduction and attended grammar school at Barber's Academy in Elizabethtown, New Jersey. He excelled in his studies, and upon graduation he enrolled at King's College in New York City, which is presently Columbia University.

However, the REVOLUTIONARY WAR (1775–83) interrupted his studies. A fervent patriot, Hamilton made his first public speech denouncing the British on July 6, 1774. He also authored and distributed fiery pamphlets responding to those who decried the FIRST CONTINENTAL CONGRESS. While still in school, Hamilton joined a volunteer militia, drilling every morning before classes. When the war came to New York City (summer of 1776), Hamilton was commissioned as a captain of an artillery company. He participated in the BATTLE OF LONG ISLAND (August 27–30, 1776) and BATTLE OF WHITE PLAINS (October 28, 1776), quickly earning the attention of General NATHANAEL GREENE. At the Battle of Princeton (January 3, 1777) (see TRENTON AND PRINCETON, BATTLES OF), Hamilton fired upon Nassau Hall when the British refused to surrender, earning himself an introduction to General George Washington. Impressed with Hamilton, Washington promoted him to lieutenant colonel. Later, Hamilton joined the general's staff as aide-de-camp and became Washington's close confidant. However, Hamilton yearned for military glory, and upon a slight reprimand from General Washington, he left his staff position for a command in the field. On the night of October 14, 1781, he led American troops in an attack at YORKTOWN (surrendered October 19, 1781), earning high praise. Toward the end of the war, Hamilton married Elizabeth Schuyler, the daughter of a wealthy and politically powerful New York family. His new family connections set the stage for the next phase of his career: politics.

He opened an office on Wall Street, founded the Bank of New York, and was elected to the Congress within two years of his military discharge. His political skills were honed during this time; in his letters he described the weaknesses of the confederation and asserted the necessity for a strong central government, ideas that he would spend the rest of his public life defending. He was a key participant at the ANNAPOLIS CONVENTION in 1786, where he personally drafted the call to summon the CONSTITUTIONAL CONVENTION in Philadelphia. Hamilton's presence in Philadelphia at the Constitutional Convention in the summer of 1787 was relatively limited due to professional commitments. However, he sat on the Committee of Style and was the only New York delegate to sign the final document. Upon return from Philadelphia, Hamilton put all his energy into securing the Constitution's ratification in New York. He waged an ardent campaign, coauthoring the *FEDERALIST PAPERS* with JOHN JAY and JAMES MADISON. His work remains an enduring commentary on constitutional law and the principles of American government. Hamilton

Alexander Hamilton. Engraving *(Library of Congress)*

succeeded in his campaign; the Constitution narrowly won ratification on July 26, 1788.

Once the federal government was securely established, Hamilton accepted President Washington's invitation to head the new Department of the Treasury. In this position, Hamilton's views supporting strong, centralized government could be acted upon. He likened himself to being the chief minister of England, which made him appear elitist. He immediately attacked the nation's disorganized financial system. In a four-point program, Hamilton built the foundation of American finance and established the nation's credit abroad. He proposed the establishment of a national bank, full funding of the national debt, assumption of state debts, and government support of industry as means by which the United States would take its place in the world. The BANK OF THE UNITED STATES was a unique hybrid of public and private institutions, lending considerable support for government finance and international TRADE. Hamilton argued that a funded NATIONAL DEBT would secure public loyalty to the new government by directly connecting wealthy interest with federal stability. To further consolidate the government, he insisted upon the assumption of state debts, a point that settled the location of the national capital through a compromise with THOMAS JEFFERSON. Finally, Hamilton argued that the United States must become more like Great Britain, both in industry and finance. To achieve such a goal, the government must take the lead in investment. Hamilton had an impressive sphere of influence; both the president and SUPREME COURT listened to his advice.

However, Hamilton was grossly unpopular with others who were equally significant. Jefferson and Madison in particular despised his viewpoint, and with Jefferson in Washington's cabinet as secretary of state and Madison in Congress, they could not avoid confrontation. Madison and Jefferson disagreed vehemently with Hamilton's entrepreneurial programs, affinity for the British, elite attitude toward the general public, and opposition to the FRENCH REVOLUTION (1789–1815). This division ultimately spawned the first two-party political system; Hamilton led the FEDERALIST PARTY, and Jefferson and Madison headed the DEMOCRATIC-REPUBLICANS. Hamilton prevailed with President Washington, but personal and financial needs forced Hamilton from the Treasury in 1795. He returned to his law practice in New York but continued to advise the president through correspondence. In fact, Hamilton helped Washington write the presidential FAREWELL ADDRESS in 1796. Hamilton continued to develop the Federalist Party from New York, opposing a fellow Federalist, JOHN ADAMS. In this stage of his career, Hamilton mastered the art of intrigue as he sought to block Adams's election to the presidency in 1796. Hamilton refused to capitulate after Adams's election, manipulating the cabinet members as best he could. The tension between the two men became public in 1800 when a letter of Hamilton's fell into the hands of AARON BURR, one of Hamilton's larger enemies. The letter disclosed private cabinet information and a bitter attack on Adams.

Hamilton now shifted his focus to Burr's demise and to thwart his pursuit of the presidency in the ELECTION OF 1800. Burr was tied with Jefferson in the electoral college vote, and the election had to be settled by Congress. Rather than allow Burr victory, Hamilton ultimately sided with his old enemy, Jefferson. He persuaded the House to vote in favor of Jefferson to break a deadlock, despite Jefferson's intentions to reverse Hamiltonian policy. Later, in 1804, Burr sought the New York governorship, and Hamilton opposed him again, publicly denouncing Burr's character. Burr responded by challenging Hamilton to a duel. The two met at Weehawken, New Jersey, on July 11, 1804. Hamilton did not intend to fire, but he wrote before the meeting that the duel was inseparable from his future in politics. Aaron Burr mortally wounded Hamilton, whose pistol fired involuntarily as he was shot. Hamilton died the next day at the age of 49. His death was lamented nationally, and Burr was forced to flee. Hamilton was buried in Trinity Churchyard in New York City.

Further reading: Jacob Cooke, *Alexander Hamilton* (New York: Scribners, 1982); Joseph Ellis, *Founding Brothers* (New York: Knopf, 2000); Broadus Mitchell, *Alexander Hamilton: A Concise Biography* (New York: Oxford University Press, 1976).

— Lauren Held

Hancock, John (1737–1793)

John Hancock was a merchant and politician who became an influential leader during the AMERICAN REVOLUTION. Born to a poor clergyman in Braintree, Massachusetts, on January 23, 1737, Hancock was orphaned at an early age and was subsequently adopted by his uncle Thomas Hancock, one of the wealthiest merchants in Boston. With his uncle's support, Hancock attended the Boston Latin School and later Harvard College, where he graduated at age 17 ranked near the top of his class. After graduation, he joined his uncle's firm as an apprentice clerk, a job at which he proved skilled. In 1760 he was sent to London on business for his uncle, where he watched the coronation of GEORGE III and developed a taste for high-style living that would later mark his life in Boston. Upon his uncle's death in 1764, the 27-year-old John Hancock was the principal heir, inheriting the mercantile business as well as what was reputed to be one of the greatest fortunes in all America.

After his uncle's death, Hancock proved to be an adequate businessman, but a growing interest in politics was beginning to consume his attention. Due to a post-French and Indian War (1754–63) economic decline, TRADE had slumped in the colonies, causing several Boston firms to collapse, and Hancock was feeling the effects of the economic situation in his own increasingly sluggish business. By the mid-1760s, Hancock had become deeply involved in colonial politics and was an ally of SAMUEL ADAMS and other prominent leaders in the RESISTANCE MOVEMENT (1764–75). After the imposition of the STAMP ACT in 1765, Hancock, an ardent opponent of the measure because of its negative impact on trade, was elected to the STAMP ACT CONGRESS. Soon after the act's repeal he found himself popular enough to obtain a seat in the Massachusetts legislature.

While Hancock's role in the opposition to the Stamp Act brought him notice and acclaim, he remained a relatively undistinguished member of the increasingly radical resistance faction until the *Liberty* affair of 1768 propelled him into the spotlight. In June of that year, customs officials impounded the *Liberty,* a small sloop owned by Hancock, charging that the ship was running contraband goods in defiance of provisions of the SUGAR ACT (1764). The seizure of the *Liberty* prompted a Boston mob to riot (June 10, 1768), burning a customs boat and forcing customs officials to flee the city. When the condemned *Liberty* was later purchased for use by customs officials, rioters burned it in protest.

Hancock's dramatic efforts in court during the *Liberty* affair won him wide support among radical Bostonians, and he emerged as a symbol for the cause. Riding on his enhanced prestige, Hancock delved further into politics and was elected to the Massachusetts General Court in 1769. He took a vocal role in the wake of the BOSTON MASSACRE (March 5, 1770) when, as a leader of the Boston committee, he demanded the removal of British troops from the city. He also supported the BOSTON TEA PARTY (December 16, 1773), although he did not personally attend. From 1774 to 1775 he served as president of the Massachusetts provincial congress. Because of his inflammatory rhetoric and association with Samuel Adams, Hancock caught the attention of British general THOMAS GAGE, who ordered him arrested. With word of the impending arrest, PAUL REVERE made his famous ride just before the opening battles of the REVOLUTIONARY WAR (1775–83) at LEXINGTON AND CONCORD (April 19, 1775).

Hancock was elected to, and soon became president of, the SECOND CONTINENTAL CONGRESS in May 1775. By virtue of his presidency, he was the first to sign the DECLARATION OF INDEPENDENCE (July 4, 1776), thus forever linking his name to the word "signature." Despite his political success, Hancock harbored military ambitions and was deeply disappointed when GEORGE WASHINGTON was named commander in chief of the Continental forces by

John Hancock. Engraving *(Library of Congress)*

the Congress. Hancock eventually received a military appointment as the first major general of the Massachusetts state militia, but his tenure in the military was unexceptional.

After relinquishing his presidency in 1777 and resigning from Congress three years later, Hancock returned to Boston and focused his attention on Massachusetts affairs. He was elected to be the state's first governor in 1780, a position that he held for nine terms from 1780 to 1785 and from 1789 until his death in 1793. During this time he also served as a member of the Massachusetts constitutional convention, helping to frame the state constitution. Despite initial misgivings about the United States Constitution, he also presided over the state ratifying convention in 1788, where his support for the document was pivotal to its eventual acceptance.

John Hancock was an ambitious and sometimes arrogant man who loved public glory, yet he believed deeply in the revolutionary cause and sacrificed a great deal, including much of his personal fortune, to support it. He died on October 8, 1793, at his home in Quincy, Massachusetts.

Further reading: William M. Fowler, *The Baron of Beacon Hill: A Biography of John Hancock* (Boston: Houghton Mifflin, 1979).

— Amy Pharr

Handsome Lake (Skaniadariio, Ganeodiyo) (1735?–1815)

A member of the Seneca tribe of the IROQUOIS Nation, Handsome Lake created a religious movement that blended NATIVE AMERICAN and European-American culture. Prior to his three visions in 1799 and 1800, Handsome Lake had lived like many other Seneca Indians. He had fought against the CHEROKEE in the 1760s and had sided with the British during the REVOLUTIONARY WAR (1775–83). He also drank alcohol to excess and had been demoralized by defeat. He was, however, a member of a prominent family; his half brother was CORNPLANTER; and he had some leadership positions before 1799. Life was changing dramatically for the Iroquois in the 1790s, and as a people they had to either adjust or face increased difficulties. QUAKERS became active on the New York reservations—all the land that was left to the Iroquois in the state had been limited to a handful of reservations—teaching religion, European-style AGRICULTURE, and handicrafts. At the same time, there were ripples of religious revitalization among some Iroquois.

Experiencing three visions over the space of seven months, Handsome Lake incorporated all of these developments into his own apocalyptic view of the world, creating a revitalized RELIGION. He proclaimed that if the Iroquois did not change their ways, they would be visited by even worse disasters than military defeat. He advocated TEMPERANCE and the adoption of European-style agriculture. He melded Christianity with the Iroquois creation myth. At times he could become excessively proscriptive, and his accusations of witchcraft led to executions that threatened to divide the Iroquois by blood feuds. But his message had a staying power, since it allowed Indians to retain their native identity while still making the adjustments necessary to survive in a changing world.

Further reading: Anthony F. C. Wallace, *The Death and Rebirth of the Seneca* (New York: Knopf, 1969).

Hawaii

The arrival of Captain James Cook on January 18, 1778, began a great transformation in Hawaii. The Polynesians who lived in the island group had migrated to Hawaii in two waves: first from the Marquesas sometime between A.D. 500 and 750, then from Tahiti about A.D. 1100. Before Cook, contact with Europeans had been intermittent. After Cook, who was killed on Maui (February 14, 1779), contact became more frequent. The consequences were staggering. Beginning in 1782, a local leader named Kamehameha I embarked on a conquest of all the islands and the creation of a Hawaiian kingdom. Using English gunners and European weaponry, he managed to unite the islands by 1810, thus dramatically altering the social and political systems. European contact also brought the spread of DISEASE AND EPIDEMICS. Between 1778 and 1823 Hawaii's native population declined from about 400,000 to 142,050.

Americans from the United States began to visit Hawaii as they explored different TRADE opportunities in the 1790s and early 1800s. New England missionaries arrived in March 1820, and missionary influence rose steadily thereafter. Simultaneously, American whalers started to frequent the islands for resupply and even recruited natives to work on their ships. Hawaiians thus continued to be besieged by European-American culture, ranging from evangelists, who wanted to mold their behavior to Christian standards, to whalers and sailors who sought to sexually and economically exploit the natives.

Further reading: Gavan Daws, *Shoal of Time: History of the Hawaiian Islands* (New York: Macmillan, 1968); Ralph Kuykendall, *The Hawaiian Kingdom: Volume I, 1778–1854, Foundation and Transformation* (Honolulu: University of Hawaii Press, 1938); Gananath Obeyesekere, *The Apotheoses of Captain Cook: European Mythmaking in the Pacific* (Princeton, N.J.: Princeton University Press, 1992).

Hemings, Sally (1773–1835)

From the early republic, when a journalist first suggested that THOMAS JEFFERSON and his slave Sally Hemings had been lovers, through the late 1990s, when DNA evidence implicated Jefferson as the father of one of Hemings's children, Sally Hemings has been the subject of publicity, innuendo, and gossip. Biographer Fawn Brody's 1974 book on Jefferson highlighted the relationship, scandalizing Jefferson in the process. AFRICAN-AMERICAN novelist Barbara Chase-Riboud also authored a best-selling story of the two, entitled simply *Sally Hemings,* with Hemings herself as the protagonist. Filmmakers Merchant and Ivory featured the affair prominently in their hit movie of the mid-1990s, *Jefferson in Paris.* Yet until DNA evidence pointed more definitively to Jefferson's involvement with Hemings, much of the focus on the relationship was relegated to the realm of speculation. In light of the scientific findings, however, contemporary scholars have begun reexaminations of Thomas Jefferson's racial beliefs and have taken a fresh look at the young enslaved woman, Sally Hemings.

Sally Hemings was born in 1773, the daughter of a Virginia plantation owner named John Wayles and one of his enslaved women, Elizabeth Hemings, herself the product of interracial parentage. John Wayles was also Jefferson's father-in-law, and after his death, Jefferson assumed control of the Hemings family, which included six children. As a young teenager, Sally Hemings traveled to Paris with one of Jefferson's daughters to serve Jefferson, who was then minister to France. According to the most recent and perhaps the most illuminating treatment of the subject, Annette Gordon-Reed's book *Thomas Jefferson and Sally Hemings: An American Controversy* (1997), "the story begins in Paris because it was there, some have alleged, that Thomas Jefferson and Sally Hemings began a relationship that lasted for 38 years." Although rumors of the affair followed the two back to the United States during the 1790s, it was not until Jefferson's first term as president (1801–04) that journalist James Callender alleged in print that Jefferson had fathered one of Hemings's children. Callender was none too friendly to Jefferson or Jeffersonian principles. Thus, for well over a century, Jefferson confidants and then scholars denied the story's plausibility, calling it merely malicious gossip. On the other hand, Sally Hemings's descendants long claimed kinship to Jefferson. Madison Hemings, one of Sally Hemings's children (Gordon-Reed states that she had "either six or seven children"), told a journalist in 1873 that he was indeed the son of Jefferson and Hemings.

As Gordon-Reed tells the story, not until "Dr. Eugene Foster, a retired professor of pathology, working with scientists at the universities of Oxford, Leicester, and Leiden, devised a [DNA] test" was there solid evidence of Jefferson's paternity of Hemings's children. Because the test only identified someone in Jefferson's bloodline as the father, a few doubters remain. But documentary evidence—the fact that Jefferson was often the only one of his lineage around Hemings at Monticello nine months before some of her children were born—also suggests that Jefferson was romantically involved with Hemings. In addition, of his over 200 slaves, Jefferson manumitted only a small fraction after his death—but he did free Sally Hemings's two remaining children (Madison and Eston), not to mention Sally Hemings herself. Sally Hemings died in 1835 in Virginia.

In one sense, the Jefferson-Hemings affair has vindicated African-American oral testimony. Long dismissed simply as implausible, now scholars must at least reexamine the Hemings family's claims to the Jefferson line. In another sense, the affair raises questions about Jefferson's racial beliefs: how deep did his feelings of black infe-riority go if he loved, in some way, Sally Hemings? Finally, and perhaps most interestingly, Sally Hemings has been treated less as an object and more as a person. Her life illuminates the narrow choices available to enslaved African Americans in postrevolutionary Virginia, but it also reveals how she shaped her own personal history, from the relationship she had with Jefferson to her children's eventual freedom. Gordon-Reed sums up the matter: "Some commentators have deemed the possibility that Sally Hemings could have loved Thomas Jefferson and that he could have loved her as fanciful . . . [But] we're talking about human beings."

See also SLAVERY.

Further reading: Fawn Brodie, *Thomas Jefferson: An Intimate History* (New York: Norton, 1974); Annette Gordon-Reed, *Thomas Jefferson and Sally Hemings: An American Controversy* (Charlottesville: University of Virginia Press, 1997).

— Richard Newman

Henry, Patrick (1736–1799)

A major figure of the revolutionary era, Patrick Henry is most famous for his passionate rhetoric in defense of liberty. He was also an early opponent of the United States Constitution. Born to a substantial Hanover County, Virginia, family, Henry's father John was a surveyor and county court justice. Young Patrick received only the most basic education, supplemented by some tutoring from his father. In 1754 he married Sarah Shelton and began the first of several unsuccessful ventures in business and farming. Eventually he decided on a career in the law, and in 1760 he was admitted to the Virginia Bar. As it turned out, this was a wise choice of career. Although his knowledge of the law was not great, Henry soon displayed outstanding abilities as a courtroom orator. That gift would eventually lead him to a profitable legal career and success in colonial politics.

Like his contemporary, SAMUEL ADAMS of Massachusetts, Henry was a man of strong passions but narrow vision. His views reflected the local interests of backcountry planters and yeoman farmers, and he used his skill as a speaker to sway juries and legislators alike. Henry's rhetoric was rooted in the English radical WHIG tradition, and his opposition to the Constitution was characteristic of libertarian and state's-rights tendencies among the ANTI-FEDERALISTS. However, despite his obvious talents, his contemporary THOMAS JEFFERSON credited him with little intellectual depth. While his memorable phrases helped to crystallize public opinion in opposition to British imperial measures, his unwillingness to compromise encouraged confrontation and made negotiation difficult.

An important role in the Parsons Cause of 1763 firmly established Henry's reputation. This dispute resulted from a royal veto of a Virginia law that had effectively lowered the salaries of Anglican clergymen. Anglican churches in Virginia had traditionally paid clergy salaries in tobacco. The Virginia law permitted payment in tobacco certificates at the reduced rate of two pence a pound rather than the market rate for tobacco of six pence a pound. Henry's fiery courtroom defense of the Virginia law, based on the radical doctrine of natural rights, won him the case and a name for himself. Two years later in the Virginia House of Burgesses, Henry further bolstered his reputation by putting forward a series of resolutions opposing the STAMP ACT (1765). It was on this occasion that the Speaker of the House accused him of treason. Although it makes a wonderful story, it appears unlikely that he ever said, "if this be treason, then make the most of it."

From 1765 to 1774 Patrick Henry was a leading opponent of British colonial policies. He was one of a small group of men who organized the first Virginia COMMITTEE OF CORRESPONDENCE. Elected to the CONTINENTAL CONGRESS in both 1774 and 1775, he spoke often and eloquently in support of colonial rights. At the second Virginia Convention of 1775, he argued that the colonial militia should be readied for what he saw as an inevitable war. It was at the end of his speech on that occasion that he spoke the words, "I know not what course others may take, but as for me, give me liberty or give me death."

During the war years Henry was very active politically. He helped to draft the Virginia constitution in 1776, served as governor for three one-year terms from 1776 to 1778, and provided able support for General GEORGE WASHINGTON. After the war he retired with his second wife Dorothea to his country estate in Hanover County but remained active in politics. He served in the House of Burgesses from 1780 to 1784 and again from 1786 to 1790. From 1784 to 1786 he served another term as governor of Virginia.

In 1787 Henry refused to attend the CONSTITUTIONAL CONVENTION in Philadelphia, saying he "smelled a rat." He became an active opponent of the new Constitution and a leading anti-Federalist, fearing that the excessive central ization of power would do irreparable damage to both state and individual rights. The addition of the BILL OF RIGHTS, for which he was partly responsible, satisfied Henry's major objections.

In the years following 1790 Henry refused several high-ranking offices in the new national government and did not enter politics again until 1799, when he was reelected to the Virginia House of Burgesses. He died at his home in Red Hill, Virginia, before he could take his seat.

See also RESISTANCE MOVEMENT.

Further reading: Richard R. Beeman, *Patrick Henry: A Biography* (New York: McGraw Hill, 1974); Robert D. Meade, *Patrick Henry*, 2 vols. (Philadelphia: Lippincott, 1957–69).

— Robert Lively

Hessians

The name *Hessians* was used to collectively describe the German soldiers Great Britain hired to help fight the REVOLUTIONARY WAR (1775–83), most coming from the principality of Hesse-Cassel. In response to the eruption of violence at LEXINGTON AND CONCORD (April 19, 1775) and the growing spirit of independence, the British Parliament voted an army of 55,000 men to be raised to suppress the rebellion. Men were needed quickly, but the British army was already below strength, and recruiting and training would take time. Moreover, English subjects were not eager to take up arms against their American brethren, nor could the government count on filling the ranks through traditional methods, such as press gangs and judicial sentencing. Parliament chose instead to hire foreign troops to augment the British regulars. Many European princes were in the soldier trade, entering into treaties in which they supplied auxiliaries in exchange for financial subsidies to benefit the princedom. This was a different arrangement than that of individual mercenaries, who received certain sums of money or special conditions for their services and who were also among the forces sent to America.

Though some ministers argued that the Germans might desert once in America, Parliament granted generous sums of money in hopes of acquiring troops quickly to crush the colonial rebellion in one campaign and return the hirelings to Europe at relatively little expense. More than half of the mercenaries came from Hesse-Cassel, with princes from Hesse-Hanau, Brunswick, Waldeck, Anspach-Bayreuth, and Anhalt-Zerbst also hiring soldiers to Britain. Among the units assembled for service in America were grenadier battalions, a field hospital, three artillery companies, field regiments, garrison battalions, and two Jäger companies. The men in these units had various skills and degrees of experience. The field regiments were made up of professional servicemen enrolled for 24 years, adept at keeping troops supplied in the field. Garrison battalions were similar to American militia or modern army reserve units. These men, mostly farmers, assembled four weeks a year between sowing and harvest times in order to drill, and they served as a local police force to quell disturbances. In times of war, they were used for home defense and performed garrison duties. The Jägers were skilled marksmen, recruited from foresters and huntsmen, who were capable of acting independently as light troops.

The situation of the German mercenaries remained awkward throughout the war. On the one hand, anti-British propaganda promoted a fear and loathing among the Americans for hired killers; on the other hand, Congress urged the Hessians to desert. Relations between the British and Hessians were also strained. British officers were condescending to the Germans, excluding their officers from councils, giving their troops unpleasant posts to occupy, and sending them on missions without proper support. Indeed, Hessian officers were not of the same caliber as those in the British army, many being considerably older than their English counterparts and showing no particular genius for independent command. A second weakness was that their close Prussian order inhibited their attacking a more mobile enemy.

The Hessians served throughout the war with mixed results. They performed well in the BATTLE OF LONG ISLAND (August 27–30, 1776) and with gallantry at WHITE PLAINS (October 28, 1776) and FORT WASHINGTON (November 17, 1776), but they suffered devastating defeats at TRENTON (December 26, 1776) and Redbank (October 22, 1777). Most of the war, however, was spent in dull garrison duty, interspersed periodically with marching and periods of intense activity, and fighting off boredom and monotony. Approximately 18,970 Hessians were actually mustered into British service between 1776 and 1782, with only 292 returning home during the war. Hessian casualties were approximately 535 killed and 1,309 wounded, but from all causes, the Hessian dead amounted to a staggering 4,983. Approximately 10,492 returned to Europe between 1783 and 1784, while roughly 3,014 chose to remain in America. About 190 went to CANADA and settled in Nova Scotia.

Further reading: Rodney Atwood, *The Hessians: Mercenaries from Hessen-Kassel in the American Revolution* (Cambridge, U.K.: Cambridge University Press, 1980); Edward J. Lowell, *The Hessians and the Other German Auxiliaries of Great Britain in the Revolutionary War* (Williamstown, Mass.: Corner House, 1975).

— Rita M. Broyles

Holland Land Company

The Holland Land Company consisted of a consortium of Dutch investors who formed a company in 1792 that purchased, sold, and developed 3.3 million acres of land in western New York obtained from revolutionary merchant and financier ROBERT MORRIS. Following the advice of surveyor and consultant Joseph Ellicott, the company decided to sell off part of its purchase in 1800 to agricultural settlers lured from the mid-Atlantic states. As the sale evolved between 1800 and 1810, a few patterns emerged. First, the company tried to discern good settlers—who would actively clear, improve, and cultivate the land—and bad settlers who would simply strip the land of its valuable resources. Second, the company directed extensive road construction to connect settlements to market points to the north, south, and east. Under Ellicott's direction, the company paid settlers and other contractors to build roads that created an extensive commercial network throughout the region. Many of the new roads relied on old Indian trails and pathways. The company further directed settlement by establishing towns throughout the purchase. The land purchases picked up momentum between 1804 and 1812. By 1812, the company had sold over half of the surveyed lots at prices adjusted frequently according to market conditions and the quality of the land. The region was well-marked in a neat grid replete with central villages such as Buffalo, Batavia, and Attica. The region was characterized by cooperative efforts by settlers and company agents to develop neat, agricultural villages for market expansion, cultural achievement, and profit.

Further reading: Charles E. Brooks, *Frontier Settlement and Market Revolution: The Holland Land Purchase* (Ithaca, N.Y.: Cornell University Press, 1996); William Wyckoff, *The Developer's Frontier: The Making of the Western New York Landscape* (New Haven, Conn.: Yale University Press, 1988).

— James R. Karmel

Howe, Richard, Lord (1726–1799)

One of Great Britain's most illustrious naval heroes, Richard, Lord Howe served as commander in chief of the British navy during the REVOLUTIONARY WAR (1775–83), from the summer of 1776 to the summer of 1778. These were two crucial years during which Howe's efforts at reconciliation may have cost Great Britain the war. Howe had distinguished himself repeatedly in the Seven Years' War (known in the colonies as the French and Indian War, 1754–63) and was highly respected in both the colonies and England. In 1775 he saw the conflict with the North American colonies as a national tragedy and wanted nothing more than to have the opportunity to bring the two sides together. He was finally given the chance in 1776 when he managed to get appointed as both commander in chief in North America and a peace commissioner. In July 1776 he joined his brother, Sir WILLIAM HOWE, in New York. Sir William had command of the British land forces and was also a peace commissioner.

Because he saw himself as much of a peacemaker as anything else, Admiral Howe did not prosecute the war as vigorously as he might have. He did not press to trap the CONTINENTAL ARMY in the BATTLE OF LONG ISLAND

(August, 27–30, 1776), and contrary to the orders he had received, he did not use the navy to punish rebellious Americans. Despite overwhelming strength at sea, he did not order a tight blockade, nor did he launch punitive raids on coastal towns. He even allowed American fishermen to pursue their trade unmolested. The appeal for peace seemed to have some effect in New Jersey in November and December of 1776, but Washington's strike across the Delaware and the BATTLES OF TRENTON AND PRINCETON (December 26, 1776, and January 3, 1777, respectively) revived the revolutionary cause.

Although Howe recognized that force would have to be used in the 1777 campaign, he did not pursue a vigorous course in that year either. He agreed to tie much of his fleet to his brother's army in its long transport from New York to the Chesapeake on its way to Philadelphia. Once Sir William captured Philadelphia, the Howe brothers struggled to clear away American outposts on the Delaware River. With General JOHN BURGOYNE's surrender at SARATOGA (October 17, 1777), both brothers offered their resignations.

While William's replacement, Sir HENRY CLINTON, was on the scene and could take charge of the army in the spring, Richard had to wait until someone could be sent from England. In the meantime, he had to face a large French fleet under the comte D'ESTAING. The French fleet joined General JOHN SULLIVAN in his attack on the British outpost in Newport. Howe sailed to Rhode Island Sound and began to maneuver for position with the French on August 10, 1778. Before the two fleets could fully engage, a hurricane struck, dispersing both forces. Although Howe did not defeat the French, D'Estaing's fleet was in such bad shape from the storm that it sailed for Boston to refit. This withdrawal compelled Sullivan to abandon his attack on Newport in the BATTLE OF RHODE ISLAND (August 29, 1778).

Despite Howe's failure in the American campaign, he later served with distinction in the command of an expedition to relieve Gibraltar in 1782 and in the opening phases of the wars with France that began in 1793. Popular among the common seamen, who nicknamed him "Black Dick," Howe was the government's chief negotiator during the mutinies at Spithead and the Nore in 1797, when British sailors demanded a redress of grievances and improved treatment.

Further reading: Ira D. Gruber, *The Howe Brothers and the American Revolution* (Chapel Hill: University of North Carolina Press, 1972).

Howe, Sir William (1729–1814)

Many scholars believe that Sir William Howe could have won the REVOLUTIONARY WAR (1775–83). As British com-

mander in chief from the fall of 1775 to the spring of 1778, he squandered repeated opportunities to annihilate General GEORGE WASHINGTON and the CONTINENTAL ARMY. Whether this evaluation is correct or not, Howe played a central role in the drama that led to American independence.

Like many officers in the British army of the 18th century, Howe came from an aristocratic background, pursued a military career as a younger son, and—through personal connections, purchase, and some ability—worked his way up to a position of command. Howe served in the Flanders campaign of 1747–48 as a junior officer and fought in the French and Indian War (1754–63) in North America. He commanded a regiment at the siege of Louisbourg in 1758 and led the vanguard of light infantry that scaled the Heights of Abraham in the attack on Quebec in 1759. By 1760 he commanded a brigade during the advance on Montreal. Later he participated in the British capture of Havana in 1762. In short, he was a respected and experienced field commander when the Revolutionary War broke out. Along with CHARLES, LORD CORNWALLIS and JOHN BURGOYNE, the British government sent him to Boston in the spring of 1775 to take charge of the conflict. Howe was to replace General THOMAS GAGE as commander in chief when he was finally recalled.

During the war Howe achieved some brilliant successes that, if the advantage gained had been pushed, might have meant complete victory for the British. At the BATTLE OF LONG ISLAND (August 27–30, 1776), Howe outmaneuvered the Continental army, compelling it to retreat to Manhattan. A final attack before the American withdrawal from Long Island might have led to the capture of half the Continental army. Similarly, had Howe moved quickly against New York City, cutting Washington off from the mainland, another smashing victory would have been his. Advantage gained at the BATTLE OF WHITE PLAINS (October 28, 1776) was lost when Howe did not renew the attack. He again did not push his troops hard enough in pursuit of Washington as he retreated across New Jersey after the fall of Fort Lee on November 20, 1776. And while his army outflanked Washington at the BATTLE OF BRANDYWINE (September 11, 1777), he again delayed and failed to totally defeat his enemy. Howe also allowed opportunities to attack slip through his fingers through inaction. He failed to occupy the heights around Boston in the winter of 1775–76 and to harass the newly formed and barely organized Continental army. He did not attack Washington in his winter quarters at MORRISTOWN (1776–77) or, a year later, at VALLEY FORGE (1777–78). Finally, and perhaps most notably, he failed to understand the larger strategic goals of the war. While General Burgoyne advanced south from CANADA, he attacked Philadelphia. Moreover, rather than moving through New Jersey, he took his army on a long sea voyage to the head of Chesapeake Bay to approach the rebel capital from the south. This maneuver put him out of contact with his other forces and prevented any possibility of linking up with Burgoyne, who surrendered at SARATOGA (October 17, 1777). Thus, despite capturing Philadelphia, the British ended 1777 recognizing that the war had taken a turn for the worse.

Three main reasons are given for Howe's failure to achieve the victory that could have been his. First, some scholars believe that Howe was not up to the task of commanding armies. A younger regimental commander, he had flashes of brilliance. They argue that as an older commanding officer, Howe turned lethargic and overly cautious, in large part because he was more interested in seeking pleasure than seeking the enemy. This evaluation is unfair and overlooks his many successes in the Revolutionary War. Second, other scholars argue that Howe did not have the heart to destroy the American forces. As a member of Parliament, he had opposed harsh measures to compel the colonies to submit to the imperial regulations. As a general, Howe, along with his brother, Admiral RICHARD HOWE, had been given commissions to negotiate a settlement. These scholars hold that Howe, believing that most Americans were loyal subjects of King GEORGE III, simply wanted to defeat the Americans enough to give them a reason to come to the bargaining table. While there may be some truth to this position, ultimately the fault may lie more with Howe's military training. The third explanation of Howe's military failures is that professional 18th-century armies were expensive to train and maintain. Howe may not have pushed his advantages for fear of disaster and losses that would be impossible to replace. His first experience in battle in the Revolutionary War was as commander of the assault on BUNKER HILL (June 17, 1775), where he saw column after column of redcoats smashed and over 1,000 casualties. Although the British won the battle, many victories like Bunker Hill would have meant losing the war. Instead, Howe planned carefully and moved cautiously, trying not to lose the British army in a final frontal assault. By not taking risks, however, he guaranteed ultimate failure.

Many in England criticized him when he returned in 1778, but Howe did not lose complete favor with the king. He kept his rank and was appointed to military and civilian domestic posts that brought honor and monetary rewards. He retired from the army in 1803 and died 11 years later.

Further reading: George Athan Billias, ed., *George Washington's Opponents: British Generals and Admirals in the American Revolution* (New York: William Morrow, 1969); Ira D. Gruber, *The Howe Brothers and the American Revolution* (Chapel Hill: University of North Carolina Press, 1972).

humanitarianism

At the heart of modern humanitarianism is the assumption that human beings can be reformed through the charitable efforts of individuals and institutions. This idea developed in the decades after the REVOLUTIONARY WAR (1775–83). In the colonial period, while there were examples of charitable giving (John Harvard's bequest in 1638 to Massachusetts's new college being the most notable), "charity" was a pragmatic response to local needs. Towns and parishes were responsible for their own poor, and most charitable donations came from friends and families. Other than POVERTY, the greatest local problem was crime. In a world that believed in original sin, criminal behavior was expected, although churches and courts sought to prevent it as much as possible. Criminals were punished but not reformed. Few colonial charitable efforts were voluntary. Colonial laws followed England in obliging localities to care for their own needy. Local political elites considered charitable work an extension of their position as "fathers" of the community; it was an obligation not taken voluntarily but out of necessity and expectation. Localities responded to individual problems concerning individual people as they arose.

Dating back beyond John Calvin, Christians had been taught to love their neighbors. Before the Revolutionary War, however, most people simply accepted that social problems would not be solved. During the religious revivals of the Second Great Awakening, Americans started to think seriously about their obligations to each other. They sought to eradicate poverty, crime, and vice. To do so, humanitarians in the early republic organized VOLUNTARY ASSOCIATIONS as never before. Charitable, moral, bible, and TEMPERANCE societies spread from urban areas into the small towns of the West. Moreover, evangelicals were not simply the elite; now ordinary Americans had a role to play in fighting social problems.

While most voluntary associations between 1780 and 1810 remained locally oriented, Americans learned that these associations were effective ways to pool human energy and money in the battle against social problems. By the 1810s, religious leaders hoped to increase the scope of humanitarian activity from the local to the state and national levels. Bible societies, for example, were originally founded in towns to distribute Bibles to a community's needy. After the founding of the American Bible Society in 1816, most bible societies became members of the national organization, which collected and distributed resources throughout the country. Local voluntary efforts were now placed in the context of national problems and national solutions. Humanitarians, unlike colonial "fathers," did not respond to local and individual problems. Instead, they organized to combat specific structural problems through national institutions. In doing so, they redefined the meaning of humanitarian work. The new humanitarian organizations assumed that particular social problems, such as intemperance, poverty, or immorality, were longstanding and could best be addressed through constant vigilance and not on a case-by-case basis.

Humanitarianism was not limited to men; women were important agents in the organization of charitable institutions. In fact, early republicans believed that women were more virtuous than men and thus more likely to feel sympathy for those who suffered. Women took advantage of the opportunity provided by charitable work to become active agents in public life, lobbying on behalf of various charitable causes. They used their supposed moral superiority as assets in the fight against criminal or antisocial behavior and, later, against SLAVERY.

Humanitarian organizations did not take hold throughout the nation. In the South, humanitarianism lagged behind the other states. In Virginia, especially, many leaders followed THOMAS JEFFERSON's unease with charitable trusts. Trusts, Jefferson believed, represented the dead hand of the past; they were legal entities that could hold land and wealth indefinitely, taking them away from the use of the present generation. When Virginia repealed its English laws in 1792, it eliminated legal support for charities. Thus, when Virginian Silas Hart donated money to the Philadelphia Baptist Association upon his death in 1795, Virginia's courts refused to acknowledge the bequest. In the 1819 case of *Philadelphia Baptist Association v. Hart's Executors,* the United States SUPREME COURT agreed with Virginia. In the absence of laws upholding charitable gifts, individuals could not leave money to voluntary associations. For humanitarian institutions to develop, they needed both the animating ideas of evangelical Christianity and a legal system that encouraged and protected their efforts.

See also EDUCATION; RELIGION; REPUBLICANISM; WOMEN'S RIGHTS AND STATUS.

Further reading: Lori Ginzberg, *Women and the Work of Benevolence: Morality, Politics, and Class in the Nineteenth-Century United States* (New Haven, Conn.: Yale University Press, 1990); David J. Rothman, *The Discovery of the Asylum: Social Order and Disorder in the New Republic* (Boston: Little, Brown, 1971); Conrad Edick Wright, *The Transformation of Charity in the Postrevolutionary New England* (Boston: Northeastern University Press, 1992).

— Johann Neem

Husband, Herman (1724–1795)

Inspired in part by millennial ideas, Herman Husband supported several radical reforms from the 1760s to the 1790s. Born into a planter family in Maryland, Husband's life was transformed by listening to a sermon of evangelist George Whitefield in 1739. Husband began a spiritual odyssey that eventually took him into the Society of Friends in 1743. In 1765 the QUAKERS disowned Husband because he objected to the sect's strict control of conscience. Husband moved to North Carolina in the 1760s, purchasing thousands of acres in the backcountry. However, he soon became involved with the NORTH CAROLINA REGULATION movement, objecting to the corrupt nature of the colony's legal system. Although he did not take an active part in armed resistance, he became a spokesman for the Regulators. After the BATTLE OF ALAMANCE (May 16, 1771), Governor William Tryon put a price on Husband's head and confiscated his property. To escape prosecution, Husband fled the colony and found sanctuary in the mountains of Pennsylvania.

This experience did not alter Husband's radicalism. He supported the movement for independence from Great Britain, serving in a minor government position in Pennsylvania during the REVOLUTIONARY WAR (1775–83). Still inspired by RELIGION, he became convinced that the world was on the precipice of the millennium. He did not think that the revolution went far enough in creating democratic government, and he opposed the ratification of the Constitution. During the 1790s, he was against the financial program of ALEXANDER HAMILTON and supported the FRENCH REVOLUTION (1789–1815). When the WHISKEY REBELLION broke out in 1794, his neighbors selected him to represent them. Because of this activist role, he was arrested when the United States Army marched into western Pennsylvania and brought back to Philadelphia for trial. He was never indicted, but he spent the winter in jail and died shortly after his release in 1795.

Hutchinson, Thomas (1711–1780)

Statesman and historian, Thomas Hutchinson was the last civilian royal governor of Massachusetts (1770–74) before the REVOLUTIONARY WAR (1775–83). As a young man, he won election to the assembly in 1736 and rose to become speaker by 1747. By 1749 his administrative abilities had made him known to friend and foe alike as the "prime minister" for Governor William Shirley. That year, he persuaded the legislature to use British reimbursement for Massachusetts's capture of Louisbourg during King George's War to fund a stable currency based on silver. Immediately before the French and Indian War (1754–63) broke out, he and BENJAMIN FRANKLIN were the two leading delegates at the Albany Congress (1754), where their proposal for a colonial union—wherein an American parliament and British governor-general would handle matters of defense—was approved by the delegates but rejected by colonial assemblies and the British Parliament.

Hutchinson's appointment as chief justice of Massachusetts in 1760 by new governor FRANCIS BERNARD (at the time Hutchinson was also serving as lieutenant-governor) brought cries of plural office-holding and charges that he favored imperial tyranny, chiefly from a rival faction headed by James Otis Sr. and his son JAMES OTIS JR. The younger Otis won election to the assembly from Boston and soon became head of the opposition. Once on the bench, Hutchinson played into their hands in 1761 by supporting customs officials who acquired general search warrants, or WRITS OF ASSISTANCE, which enabled them to seize merchants' illegal cargoes. When Parliament proposed the STAMP ACT (1765), Hutchinson's refusal to oppose it in public—although he wrote a powerful tract incorporating most of his opponents' arguments that he circulated privately to influential Englishmen—provoked rumors that the law was his personal idea. When he did not deny this to a mob that menaced his house on August 26, 1765, Hutchinson had to flee for his life as his splendid mansion was destroyed.

Hutchinson cemented his position as a supporter of British authority by refusing to open Massachusetts's courts when the required stamps were not distributed and by supporting the unpopular customs commissioners sent to Boston in 1767. Yet he was not the tyrant his opponents claimed: When troops came to Boston in 1768, he refused to authorize their use to crush the opposition, as he thought this would end the rule of law and the balance between British rule and colonial rights he was desperately trying to restore. Hutchinson also ordered the troops out of Boston following the BOSTON MASSACRE (March 5, 1770) rather than risk the potential all-out confrontation that might have followed what was essentially a minor brawl. However, when ships bearing tea from the East Indian Company anchored in Boston Harbor in 1773, Hutchinson played the key role in ensuring they were not, as in every other colony except Georgia, persuaded to return to England by the populace. Hutchinson had British warships to command, and he ordered the cargoes brought to port under their guns. Planning to unload the tea (which he was sure the people would buy due to its low price), Hutchinson reckoned without considering the possibility of patriots boarding the ship in the middle of the night of December 16 and dumping the tea in the harbor—which they did during the BOSTON TEA PARTY.

When Britain responded with the COERCIVE ACTS (1774) that altered Massachusetts's government, Hutchin-

son realized his usefulness was at an end. Replaced by General THOMAS GAGE, he went to England in an effort to reconcile the two sides. However, just as the patriots blamed him for supporting British power in an effort to become a virtual dictator, the British condemned his failure to use the troops and his underestimation of the protestors' strength. As his powerful writings, "A Dialogue Between a European and an American Englishman" and his three-volume history of Massachusetts (still the single most important source for the colony's history), show, he was neither weak nor arbitrary. Instead, he hoped to restore the balance between British authority and colonial rights that he was sure was responsible for the liberty and order that 18th-century Massachusetts enjoyed. A sincere lover of Ameri-

Thomas Hutchinson. Engraving *(Library of Congress)*

can liberty as he understood it, Hutchinson is now generally appreciated by scholars for his keen insights into how the stubborn behavior of both contending parties led to a revolution neither desired.

See also LOYALISTS; REPUBLICANISM; RESISTANCE MOVEMENT.

Further reading: Bernard Bailyn, *The Ordeal of Thomas Hutchinson* (Cambridge, Mass.: Harvard University Press, 1974); William Pencak, *America's Burke: The Mind of Thomas Hutchinson* (Lanham, Md.: University Press of America, 1982).

— William Pencak

I

immigration

Although not as extensive as it would be later in American history, immigration was important to revolutionary and early national America. Perhaps as many as 300,000 immigrants arrived in what became the United States from 1754 to 1820. Before independence, many European immigrants came to North America as indentured servants. After 1776, bound white LABOR seemed to contradict the ideals of REPUBLICANISM, and the number of bound servants as immigrants declined. Ethnically, in the years before and immediately after the REVOLUTIONARY WAR (1775–83), many immigrants were SCOTCH-IRISH, although large numbers of Scotch, English, and Germans also arrived. In the 1790s and early 1800s the same groups continued to immigrate to the United States, but there were also increased numbers of CATHOLIC Irish and refugees from the FRENCH REVOLUTION (1789–1815).

Whether driven from their home countries by hard times and oppression, or attracted by America as the land of opportunity, immigrants could achieve the same status as native-born denizens through the process of naturalization. Parliament's Plantation Act of 1740 allowed all non-Catholic aliens to become English citizens if they paid a small fee, resided in a colony for seven years, received the sacraments at a Protestant church, swore allegiance to the king, and declared that they were Christians. Special provisions were added for JEWS and QUAKERS. Concerned with the loss of population to the colonies, Great Britain shifted its policy in 1773 by ordering governors to disallow any laws within the colonies for naturalization. When the revolutionaries declared their independence, they included a statement that King GEORGE III had obstructed the "naturalization of foreigners" and discouraged immigration. After 1776, naturalization fell into the hands of state legislatures, which passed a variety of laws, usually encouraging early citizenship. In some cases, however, states created new categories, granting immigrants only partial citizenship rights. The entire process became more uniform when the Naturalization Act of 1790, passed by the First Congress, established a two-year waiting period before an immigrant could apply for citizenship. In 1795, under pressure from the FEDERALIST PARTY, the period of residence was extended to five years. At the height of anti-French feeling from the XYZ AFFAIR, the Federalists in 1798 managed to increase the waiting period to 14 years. In 1802, when THOMAS JEFFERSON was president, the DEMOCRATIC-REPUBLICAN PARTY reduced the waiting period again to five years.

As suggested in the various shifts in naturalization law, immigration was a political issue from the very beginning of the United States. Not only did the DECLARATION OF INDEPENDENCE (July 4, 1776) blame the king for limiting immigrants, but subsequent state laws were written in part to punish immigrants who might have been LOYALIST. During the 1790s, the nature of the immigrant changed. Many were political exiles from Ireland or France. These individuals were often Catholic, and hence often seen as agents of the pope, and they also frequently espoused republican principles. In 1797 Federalist politician HARRISON GRAY OTIS declared that he did "not wish to invite hordes of wild Irishmen, nor the turbulent and disorderly of all parts of the world, to come here with a view to disturb our tranquility, after having succeeded in the overthrow of their own Governments." Within this context the Federalists sought to make it more difficult for an immigrant to become a citizen.

Immigrants faced other difficulties. While some immigrants achieved success, like ALBERT GALLATIN and SAMUEL SLATER, others struggled to get by. They often clung to their own ethnic groups, both in cities and in the countryside. Prejudice emerged, especially against the rising numbers of Catholics. Nativist crowds, for example, might parade with a "stuffed paddy" to mock the Irish or harass a Catholic Christmas celebration, as they did in New York City in 1806. In short, although the mass immigration awaited future decades, there were by 1820 important precedents for later developments.

See also ALIEN AND SEDITION ACTS; RIOTS.

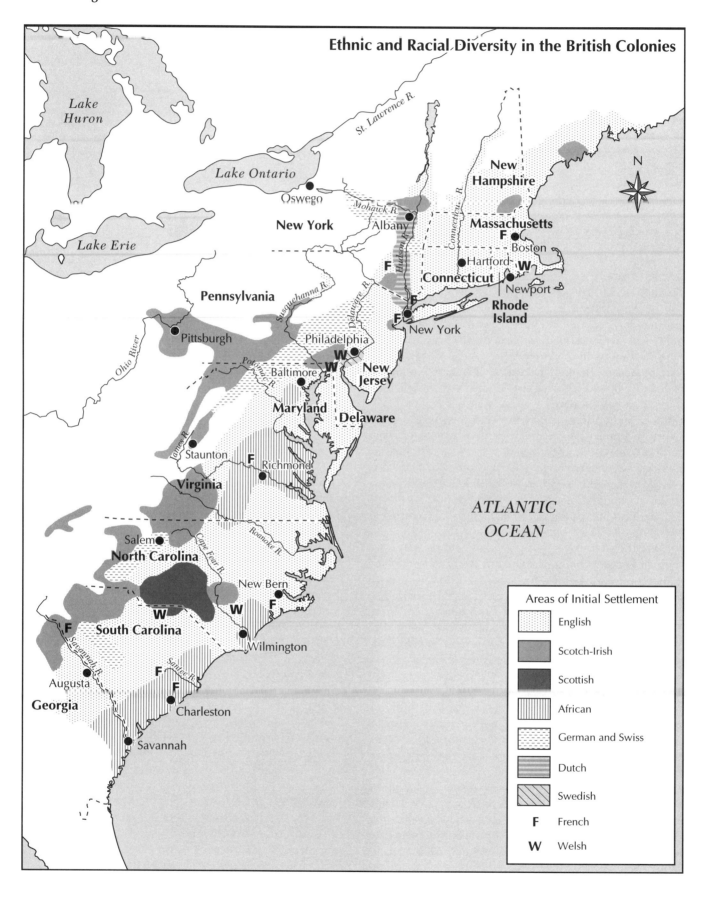

Ethnic and Racial Diversity in the British Colonies

Further reading: Marilyn C. Baseler, *"Asylum for Mankind:" America, 1607–1800* (Ithaca, N.Y.: Cornell University Press 1998); Maldwyn Allen Jones, *American Immigration*, 2nd ed. (Chicago: University of Chicago Press, 1992).

impeachment

The concept of impeachment evolved during the 18th and early 19th centuries from a means of protecting colonists from corrupt British officials and executive officers into a partisan tool for FEDERALIST and DEMOCRATIC-REPUBLICAN PARTIES. Ultimately, the latter use proved to be untenable, and impeachment became an important part of the Constitution's system of checks and balances.

In America, impeachment was modeled upon the English process. The House of Commons impeaches and the House of Lords conducts the trial and issues judgment. This process crossed the Atlantic relatively unchanged. From the 1750s through the 1770s, in cases against British officials, colonists challenged British authority. Significantly, colonial assemblies asserted their supremacy as representatives of the people over other branches of government.

Most states included impeachment provisions in their constitutions. Unlike the British system, STATE CONSTITUTIONS placed restrictions on impeachment. Only officeholders could be impeached for offenses committed while in office, and their punishment was limited to removal from office and being prohibited from occupying any public offices in the future. In the states, lower houses of the legislature could impeach officials for corruption, bribery, and misuse of power.

During the CONSTITUTIONAL CONVENTION in 1787, impeachment engendered significant debate. No one seriously questioned the power of the House of Representatives to impeach a civil officer, but the Senate's role provoked controversy. Eventually, most delegates felt comfortable giving the Senate authority to conduct trials. The two-thirds majority requirement for a conviction helped to ensure that the Senate would engage in due deliberation.

Through three impeachment trials from 1797 to 1805, Congress narrowed the definition of an impeachable party and offenses. In the end, participants found that impeachment was not an effective partisan tool but, rather, was useful in stemming corruption and malfeasance in office. In the first case, the House impeached Senator WILLIAM BLOUNT of Tennessee for allegedly conspiring with Britain to foment rebellion in the Louisiana Territory. Blount resigned his office and returned to Tennessee before the Senate could try him. Eventually, the Senate dismissed the charges against Blount without definitively declaring whether senators were indeed impeachable. However, the House never again impeached a senator.

The second and third impeachment trials involved federal judges and tested the principle of using impeachment as a partisan tool. In 1804 the House impeached Judge John Pickering of New Hampshire for incompetence. It was general knowledge that Pickering was insane and often presided over court while intoxicated. The Senate convicted Pickering and removed him from office. The most important case was that of SUPREME COURT Associate Justice SAMUEL CHASE. In 1805 the Democratic-Republican House indicted Chase for making partisan comments from the bench. This Federalist Justice proved to be a formidable opponent. Even Democratic-Republican senators were uncomfortable convicting a man for his opinions. The Senate acquitted Chase, bringing to a close the era of partisan impeachments.

Through these early impeachment trials, the Senate established rules and proceedings that would direct future trials. It established itself as a deliberative body determined to conduct trials in a fair manner guided by judicial principles. Impeachment proved to have limited use as a party tool and became, instead, an infrequently used method for removing corrupt officials.

See also POLITICAL PARTIES.

Further reading: Michael J. Gerhardt, *The Federal Impeachment Process: A Constitutional and Historical Analysis*, 2nd ed. (Chicago: University of Chicago Press, 2000); Peter C. Hoffer, and N. E. H. Hull, *Impeachment in America, 1635–1805* (New Haven, Conn.: Yale University Press, 1984); Buckner F. Melton Jr., *The First Impeachment: The Constitution's Framers and the Case of Senator William Blount* (Macon, Ga.: Mercer University Press, 1998).

— Terri Halperin

impressment

The British practice of forcing American sailors to enter the British navy was a major grievance between the United States and Great Britain and became a leading cause of the War of 1812 (1812–15). Throughout the 18th and into the 19th century, the British navy used this form of recruitment in British ports and on the high seas. During the colonial period, the British navy occasionally resorted to impressment in American seaports or the nearby coast. American sailors greatly resented the press gang—the naval patrol that searched the waterfront for seamen—and several times rioted to prevent impressment. It should be pointed out that there were also anti-press-gang RIOTS in Great Britain as well. During the REVOLUTIONARY WAR (1775–83) men captured from American merchant vessels were often forced to serve in the British navy, and even sailors from American PRIVATEERS and warships, instead of being imprisoned, sometimes were recruited into His Majesty's service. After independence, the press gang could no longer haunt the American waterfront, and since the demand for seamen in the British navy declined, impressment of Americans on the high seas, or even in British ports, was not an issue until Great Britain went to war with France in 1793.

In the war against the French, the British relied heavily upon their navy. The number of seamen in the navy rose from 36,000 in 1792 to approximately 120,000 by 1805. At that point, the British needed to recruit an additional 10,000 men a year just to keep their ships manned. This manpower requirement created a crisis for the British. They took as many men from the British merchant marine as they could while still keeping goods and services flowing. The British therefore offered incentives to foreign nationals to join the navy, and men from almost every nation could be found on British warships. Many Americans, unable or unwilling to find a berth aboard a private vessel, joined the British navy. But the navy still needed men.

From the British perspective, the expanding American merchant marine was an appropriate place to find seamen. As the American merchant fleet grew, so did its need for men. By 1807 over 65,000 men worked on American ships. While the sons of New England and elsewhere in the United States provided much of this workforce, seamen flocked to the American merchant marine from other countries in search of high wages. American vessels often paid $12–14 a month for an able-bodied seaman who would make half of that in the British navy. Many men born in Great Britain signed aboard American vessels; some of whom were deserters from the British navy.

Recognizing that the king's subjects were on American ships, officers in the British navy believed they had a right to search those vessels, even on the high seas. To help distinguish between American sailors and foreigners on board, the United States offered an official document, called a protection, that indicated that a sailor had been born in America. But protections quickly became an easily forged commodity, and for a few dollars, any foreign seaman could purchase a protection that looked authentic. To make matters more complicated, the British did not recognize the process of a British subject becoming a naturalized citizen of the United States. The result was that the British navy searched countless American ships, taking the men it needed. In this process from 1793 to 1812, at least 10,000 Americans were swept onto the gundecks of British warships, along with thousands of men born in Britain and other countries. As one British officer told some American sailors in the WEST INDIES, "Men I will not look at your protections—my ship is in distress, and I will have men to carry me to England."

American diplomats repeatedly decried the practice to little avail, reflecting the lack of respect the United States suffered on the international scene. At the end of the War of 1812, the Treaty of Ghent (1814) made no mention of impressment, but since the French had been defeated, the demand for seamen in the British navy declined, and the issue became moot.

See also CHESAPEAKE-LEOPARD AFFAIR; FOREIGN AFFAIRS.

Further reading: Bradford Perkins, *Prologue to War, 1805–1812: England and the United States* (Berkeley: University of California Press, 1968); James Fulton Zimmerman, *Impressment of American Seamen* (1925. Reprint, Port Washington, N.Y.: Kennikat Press, 1966).

Independence Hall

Originally constructed between 1732 and 1756, the Georgian-style brick building now known as Independence Hall was the State House of colonial Pennsylvania. In 1775 the SECOND CONTINENTAL CONGRESS used it as a meeting place. GEORGE WASHINGTON accepted command of the CONTINENTAL ARMY and Congress agreed to the DECLARATION OF INDEPENDENCE (July 4, 1776) within its walls. The building remained the seat of the national government during much of the REVOLUTIONARY WAR (1775–83). Congress abandoned Philadelphia briefly in the winter of 1776–77 and again when the British captured the city of Philadelphia on September 26, 1777. After the British evacuation in June 1778, Congress continued to meet in Philadelphia until June 1783, when mutinous troops surrounded the building seeking back pay. Considering this action an insult, Congress decided to reconvene in Princeton, New Jersey.

Independence Hall, a name that did not come into common usage until much later, continued to function as the Pennsylvania State House until the state capital moved in 1799. The building, however, had been used in the summer of 1787 when the CONSTITUTIONAL CONVENTION met in Philadelphia. After 1799 the building was abandoned for several years until CHARLES WILLSON PEALE was allowed to use it for his museum. Only after the visit of the MARQUIS DE LAFAYETTE in 1824 and the resurrection of all things having to do with the Revolutionary War did Americans begin to consider the structure a national shrine. The trademark tower was redesigned and rebuilt after 1828, and for most of the rest of the 19th century the building was used for exhibitions and civic receptions. In 1943 Independence Hall became part of the National Park system. Today it is one of the most-visited historical sites in the nation, with its interior restored to its 18th-century appearance.

industrial revolution

The American ECONOMY grew increasingly mechanized and oriented around mass production during the years of the early republic. New industries emerged and old industries changed the nature of their operations to meet the needs of an increasingly market-oriented society. By 1825 Americans had utilized innovative technologies in areas such as textiles and cotton production, despite a predominant agricultural lifestyle in most areas. Slowly, Americans pursued comprehensive industrialization similar to the British model.

The mechanization and industrialization of the American economy began with using English inventions in the late 18th century and some political encouragement from protective TARIFFS in 1792. Crucial to American and English industrialization was a device invented by Englishman James Hargreave called the spinning jenny, which increased textile production by allowing workers to spin many different cotton threads at once. Spinning jennies were run by water and then steam power until they were massive in size and producing vast quantities of cloth in new mills or production centers. An English immigrant named SAMUEL SLATER established the first American textile mill in 1790. Later, these operations utilized power looms that connected many different spinning jennies or spindles. These larger machines were first perfected by Francis Cabot Lowell in 1813 and were operating throughout the United States by 1820. Between 1814 and 1823, Lowell and other Massachusetts capitalists built textile mills on the rivers of eastern Massachusetts. The new textile mills received funding through a combination of private investors and local BANKS. By 1825 Americans were purchasing much more manufactured clothing than before, rather than spinning at home. In 1807 approximately 15–20 textile mills were operational and using around 8,000 spindles. By 1831 around 1.25 million spindles operated in textile mills located primarily in New England and producing cotton cloth. The textile industry also changed due to the increasing use of the "putting out" system, in which merchants hired out individuals (often women and children) to produce clothing. In return, the merchants would pay workers for each piece of clothing received. By 1825 the textile industry had pioneered the American factory system, in which mass numbers of identical goods were produced through a large operation involving many specialized workers. Mechanization in the early republic also increased the production of woolen items, glass, lead, wool carpets, sugar and molasses, salt, and anthracite iron.

The use of interchangeable parts and assembly lines was fundamental to early American industrialization. Interchangeable machine parts and assembly-line production allowed for the standardization of the small parts of engines and other machines in order to end up with the same products consistently. Rifle manufacturer ELI WHITNEY is associated with this development. The factory system gradually replaced individual craftsmanship as the chief method of manufacturing.

In order to run a factory, a reliable source of power was needed. American industrialists used wood extensively in contrast to Great Britain, where coal was used as fuel in early industrial processes. By the 1820s, woodworking carpenters, hatmakers, and shoemakers were using machines such as the Woodworth planer and Blanchard lathe as timesaving devices. Although early factories relied on water, steam engines—invented in 1775 by Englishman James Watt—ultimately became the main source of power in factories. Steam was also used extensively by early Americans who built and operated boats to travel the nation's rivers. By 1825 boats powered by steam engines, or steamboats, were a regular feature of American transportation and had expanded TRADE and transport throughout the nation. In the 1820s, steam-engine factories opened everywhere to meet the demand for engines to equip steamboats. The booming steamboat industry of the 1820s is a good example of early-American industrialization. Independent ARTISANS were contracted to produce smaller parts of boats that were then constructed in factories. By 1830 the cities of Pittsburgh and Cincinnati produced 100 and 150 steamboats per year, respectively.

Several factors beyond mechanization contributed to industrial development. Turnpikes, canals, and eventually railroads all facilitated industrialization by creating new pathways to transport resources and market products. International political dynamics also shaped early American industrialization. Domestic manufacturing rose and fell in the early republic as a consequence of relations with the European powers. As overseas trade declined at the outbreak of the REVOLUTIONARY WAR (1775–83) through the 1780s, domestic manufacturing increased. This production dropped from around 1790 to 1807 as international commerce expanded substantially. The EMBARGO OF 1807 and the War of 1812 (1812–15) encouraged domestic manufacturing generally through the multiplication of local commercial operations such as sawmills, ironworks, paper mills, breweries, and tanneries. From 1816 to 1825, successful protectionist legislation at the national level spurred domestic manufacturing while simultaneously reflecting and sparking a strong popular desire in northeast, northwest, and mid-Atlantic states to become economically independent from European manufactured goods.

Early industrial progress also had a substantial impact on the lives of average Americans. From the consumer's point of view, industrialization meant a greater variety and cheaper assortment of goods. This aspect of the industrial revolution meant that even relatively poor people had access to nicer textiles, home furnishings, and everyday items such as dishes, pots, and pans. While daily life for many Americans may have become better, conditions for workers could often be harsher and meant a complete change of lifestyle. For example, the booming New England textile industry had a large impact on the lives of thousands of young people who worked in the mills. Most of the mill workers were girls and young women, aged 8–24, from the small farms around the region, while others were members of entire families recruited into mill work. They lived and worked in a very regimented culture that structured their waking hours from approximately 5 A.M. to 6 P.M., six days a week. Often, church attendance was mandatory, as was participation in basic courses and social events. They earned money while theoretically learning obedience and domestic skills suitable for marriage. The mill workers were specialized by task, with young children often used to maintain machinery because their size allowed them to reach into small areas and fix or replace parts. Historians disagree over the primary economic motivations for the mill workers. Some emphasize the ability of the workers to make and use significant amounts of money for personal goals, such as clothes, education, and marriage dowries. Other historians suggest that most or all the workers' earnings went home to cash-strapped families to pay mortgages or for a brother's education.

Industrialization also had an impact on the environment. In part, the early industrial revolution was responsible for the fast growth of American cities in the first half of the 19th century. In the 1820s, the growth of manufacturing enterprises contributed significantly to an increase in the urban populations. For example, the city of Philadelphia drew people from its hinterlands to live and work amidst various industrial shops. By 1820 two-thirds of Philadelphia's population was involved in manufacturing and its related commercial operations, like transport. Beginning around 1825, coal-mining operations began to operate without much regard to environmental change or best practices for efficiency and the safety of miners. These early shortcomings would haunt the mining industry later in the 19th century. The industrial revolution was in a very early stage of development in the United States through 1825. Despite the changes taking place between 1790 and 1825, the American industrial revolution did not take off until the middle and late 19th century in terms of production and comprehensive popular participation. Yet, the industrial revolution of the early republic did set some important precedents for later and more extensive development.

See also CITIES AND URBAN LIFE.

Further reading: Stuart Bruchey, *Enterprise: The Dynamic Economy of a Free People* (Cambridge, Mass.: Harvard University Press, 1993); Louis C. Hunter, *A History of Industrial Power in the United States, 1780–1930* (Charlottesville: University of Virginia Press, 1979–85); Charles Sellers, *The Market Revolution: Jacksonian America, 1815–1846* (New York: Oxford University Press, 1991).

— James R. Karmel

Ingersoll, Jared (1722–1781)

Jared Ingersoll was a moderate LOYALIST who believed the American colonists should accept British policies in good faith. Ingersoll was born in Connecticut and attended school at Yale College. He graduated with a bachelor's degree in 1742 and remained in New Haven for a year reading law. He then set about making a name for himself by establishing a successful law practice in New Haven.

In 1751 Ingersoll became the king's attorney for New Haven, and in 1758 Connecticut appointed him as their representative to London. Here he met several influential individuals, such as BENJAMIN FRANKLIN. On his second trip to London in 1764, the English government persuaded him to support the STAMP ACT (1765). Initially he was skeptical and opposed the measure, but, after being convinced the act was justified, he agreed to be a stamp collector for Connecticut. He returned home amidst a public outcry. He stood his ground and refused to surrender his position as stamp agent unless specifically told to do so by the Connecticut Assembly. A mob met him on the way to the assembly and forced him to resign. Ingersoll then read his resignation before the assembly and retired from political life.

After retiring, Ingersoll focused on his law practice. He gained respect as a good LAWYER and in 1771 the British government appointed him as a judge to the new vice admiralty court in Philadelphia. His Loyalist sympathies forced him to flee Philadelphia in 1777. He returned to his beloved New Haven, Connecticut, where he died in 1781.

Further reading: Lawrence Henry Gipson, *Jared Ingersoll, a Study of American Loyalism in Relation to British Colonial Government* (New Haven, Conn.: Yale University Press, 1920).

— Brant Day

Iroquois Confederacy (Iroquois League)

The Iroquois were a powerful alliance of NATIVE AMERICAN nations that played an important role in American history from the early 1600s until the end of the War of 1812 (1812–15). They lived in what is now New York State and CANADA. The confederacy originally consisted of the Onondaga, Seneca, Mohawk, Oneida, and Cayuga Nations, all of which shared similar languages and cultures. The various tribes formed the confederacy sometime before the

Europeans arrived. (Historians are not sure of the exact date; many think that it was some time in the 1400s or 1500s.) In the 1720s the Tuscarora came north from the Carolinas to join the confederacy as the sixth nation. Each tribe agreed to submit internal disputes to the chiefs of the Iroquois tribes at the Great Council Fire (in the town of Onondaga) and to never fight each other. Iroquois women held a great deal of influence over decisions made at these meetings because they chose the chiefs. They could also stop their men from going to war. Their unity made the Iroquois the strongest and most influential people for two centuries in eastern North America after the arrival of the English and the French.

Once the French lost Canada (1763), the Iroquois faced the British and their colonists alone. The American colonists took more and more land from all of the native peoples. When the British issued the Proclamation of 1763, making it illegal for the colonists to settle west of the Appalachian Mountains, the Americans simply ignored the order and streamed west, often killing any Native American who stood in the way. In 1768 the British negotiated the TREATY OF FORT STANWIX with the Iroquois. The Iroquois agreed to cede southern New York, parts of Pennsylvania, and all of Kentucky. In exchange the Iroquois expected the settlers to stop trespassing and respect the new border. Britain lacked the power over the colonists to keep the bargain. Before long, the British had even more serious problems with the Americans. GEORGE WASHINGTON asked the Iroquois to remain neutral in the REVOLUTIONARY WAR (1775–83). Most Iroquois, however, sided with their old friends, the British. The Americans seemed too eager to take even more land, and the British had promised to keep them away. However, some Iroquois, especially the Oneida, fought for the Americans and often faced fellow Iroquois in battle. The American War for Independence became a civil war for the Iroquois.

War parties raided American farms and settlements on the FRONTIER from New York to Virginia. Washington ordered General JOHN SULLIVAN to put an end to those raids. In 1779 Sullivan led a large army through Iroquois country, burning villages and crops. Most of the time the villagers escaped into the woods before the soldiers came. However, the Iroquois never recovered from the blow.

The TREATY OF PARIS (1783) ceded all the Iroquois land to the new United States. The Americans showed little interest in respecting the old agreements with the Iroquois, and settlers rushed in. The British government gave the Iroquois land in Canada as a new home. Many Iroquois moved there under the leadership of the Mohawk JOSEPH BRANT. However, the border between the United States and Canada separated those who stayed and those who took up life under British rule.

During the War of 1812, the Iroquois found themselves divided once more. Some fought on the British side and some with the Americans. The British wanted peace with the Americans after the war because they wanted to protect Canada, so they could not help the Iroquois left in the United States. The American government showed little thanks to the Iroquois that fought as allies during the war with Britain, forcing them into small reservations in New York or moving them to Indian Territory in what is now Oklahoma.

Further reading: James Thomas Flexner, *Mohawk Baronet, a Biography of Sir William Johnson* (Syracuse, N.Y.: Syracuse University Press, 1979); Daniel K. Richter, *The Ordeal of the Longhouse, the Peoples of the Iroquois League in the Era of European Colonization,* (Chapel Hill: University of North Carolina Press, 1992); Ian K. Steele, *Warpaths: Invasions of North America* (New York: Oxford University Press, 1994).

— George Milne

J

Jay, John (1745–1829)

Diplomat and first chief justice of the SUPREME COURT, John Jay negotiated JAY'S TREATY (1794), resolving important grievances between the United States and Britain. Descended from French Huguenot immigrants, Jay's Protestant family was wealthy and politically powerful. Jay was born in New York and educated at King's College (later Columbia University), from which he graduated in 1764. After several years of further study, he was admitted to the bar in 1768 and began his legal career. Politically conservative, Jay opposed independence until settlement with Britain was impossible; indeed, the Jays were among only a handful of New York patrician families who sided with the WHIGS. In 1774 Jay was named as a delegate to the FIRST CONTINENTAL CONGRESS. His conservatism continued in the Congress, and Jay fought against a radical move toward war with Britain. However, as resolutions against Parliament passed, Jay acceded to the will of the majority and drafted the Congress's *Address to the People of Great Britain,* in which he censured Parliament for its taxation of the colonists without their consent. Notwithstanding his compromise, Jay was opposed to an outright declaration of independence until hostilities with Britain began. Jay then joined completely with the independence movement.

He accepted an invitation to help draft the New York Constitution and, upon its ratification, was elected chief justice of the state supreme court. A provision of the constitution permitted the chief justice to serve also as a delegate to the SECOND CONTINENTAL CONGRESS, and Jay was sent to Philadelphia. Almost immediately upon his arrival in 1778, the delegates elected Jay to the presidency of Congress. In 1779 the Congress appointed Jay as minister to Spain, and at the same time selected him to serve with JOHN ADAMS and BENJAMIN FRANKLIN on an American peace commission seeking terms from Britain. Jay's stay in Spain was unfortunate and he did not secure Spanish cooperation with the American revolutionaries. Jay was incensed at Spain—and at France for failing to help him

with the Spanish—so that by the time Jay joined Franklin, he urged him to ignore instructions from the Congress advising them to rely on France; instead, Jay counseled Franklin to seek the best possible terms without reliance on France. Jay, Franklin, and Adams secured a favorable treaty, one that recognized American independence and enlarged the new nation's borders to the Mississippi River. In 1783 the United States, Britain, France, and Spain signed the TREATY OF PARIS. Upon his return to the United States in 1784, Jay was elected secretary of FOREIGN AFFAIRS under the ARTICLES OF CONFEDERATION.

Chief Justice John Jay *(Library of Congress)*

181

Though Jay was not a member of the CONSTITUTIONAL CONVENTION, he supported ratification of the federal Constitution and wrote at least five *FEDERALIST PAPERS* in favor of the new system. After ratification of the new Constitution, President GEORGE WASHINGTON appointed Jay chief justice of the Supreme Court. As chief justice, Jay continued to support a strong federal government. In 1793 Jay delivered the majority opinion for an important case, *Chisholm v. Georgia,* that upheld the right of an individual to sue a state in federal court. An outcry ensued about this blow to state sovereignty, and in 1798 the states ratified the Eleventh Amendment, which denied such federal judicial power.

In 1794 President George Washington appointed Jay as special envoy to Britain in order to resolve a conflict stemming from the Royal Navy's capture of American ships and merchantmen. The treaty Jay negotiated resolved many unsettled questions in Anglo-American relations. Under the terms of Jay's Treaty, Britain agreed to remove its troops from the American western territories, to pay reparations to American merchants, and to permit American TRADE in the WEST INDIES, though under restrictive conditions. Many Americans were dissatisfied with the treaty because it did not recognize American neutral rights to trade with nations at war with Britain. Furthermore, Jay's Treaty committed the American government to repay outstanding British prerevolutionary debts, an issue still being discussed at home. Jay was accused of betraying American interests, and a huge political storm ensued. The public debate over Jay's Treaty contributed to the political rivalry between the FEDERALIST and the DEMOCRATIC-REPUBLICAN PARTIES.

In 1795 Jay was elected governor of New York and served two terms; as governor he signed an act calling for the gradual abolition of SLAVERY in the state. He declined, in 1800, to be reappointed as chief justice of the Supreme Court because he regarded the federal judiciary as too weak, though JOHN MARSHALL saw the court differently. Jay retired to Bedford, New York, where he lived a private life until his death in 1829. His contributions tend to be overshadowed by the reputations of his more widely esteemed contemporaries, but Jay was nevertheless instrumental to the creation of the American republic.

Further reading: Richard B. Morris, *John Jay: The Making of a Revolutionary: Unpublished Papers, 1745–1780* (New York: Harper & Row, 1975); Richard B. Morris, *John Jay: The Winning of the Peace: Unpublished Papers, 1780–1784* (New York: Harper & Row, 1980); Richard B. Morris, *Witnesses at the Creation: Hamilton, Madison, Jay and the Constitution* (New York: Harper & Row, 1985).

— Robyn Davis McMillin

Jay-Gardoqui treaty negotiations (1785–1786)

Beginning in the summer of 1785, and lasting for a year, JOHN JAY, secretary of foreign affairs for the United States, and Don Diego Gardoqui, representing Spain, strove to forge an agreement on TRADE and navigation of the Mississippi. Congress had intended to send Jay to Spain for the negotiations, but before Jay left, Gardoqui arrived in the United States. The negotiations therefore took place in New York, which was then the seat of the American government.

Throughout the discussions, Gardoqui was adamant that Spain would not allow free navigation of the Mississippi. At the time, Spain's hold on its Louisiana and FLORIDA possessions was not strong, and Americans were just beginning to settle on the western side of the Appalachians. Gardoqui was willing to open up Spanish ports for trade. In 1786 Jay proposed to Congress that the United States accept the restrictions on navigation on the Mississippi for 25 to 30 years in exchange for the immediate benefit of the trade agreement. Seven states voted to do so, but under the ARTICLES OF CONFEDERATION, nine states were needed to make the treaty official. Without congressional approval and with the opposition of powerhouse Virginia, the negotiations ended in failure. However, the results left all parties upset. Spain refused both trade and navigation of the Mississippi, allowing room for future conflict. Those Americans willing to go along with the treaty were distraught that the majority had not been able to pass it, while those who opposed the treaty deeply resented the fact that several eastern states had been willing to sell out on westward expansion to gain profits from Spanish trade for themselves. It would be another decade before Spain and the United States settled their differences in the TREATY OF SAN LORENZO (1795).

See also FOREIGN AFFAIRS.

Jay's Treaty (1794)

Negotiated by American jurist JOHN JAY and British Foreign Secretary William Grenville, Jay's Treaty attempted to settle problems that had plagued the United States and Britain since the REVOLUTIONARY WAR (1775–83). It was also an attempt by Great Britain to ensure American neutrality during the FRENCH REVOLUTION (1789–1815), which threatened to destabilize Europe. Jay's Treaty was signed on November 19, 1794.

The treaty addressed several issues that were either unresolved by or grew out of the TREATY OF PARIS (1783). The main points of disagreement were the continued British presence in FRONTIER forts, collection of prewar debts, violation of property rights of returning LOYALISTS, and unsettled boundary disputes. Other differences included the treatment of American ships in British colonies as well as Britain's influence over several NATIVE AMERICAN tribes along the western frontier.

Chief Justice John Jay was dispatched to England to resolve these outstanding problems. Britain's main concern was that the United States remain neutral in the growing crisis of the French Revolution. Jay and Grenville fashioned a compromise. Jay's Treaty included limited access of United States merchant ships in British ports, effective most-favored-nation trading status for British imports, and the final evacuation of British troops from frontier forts. Commissions of American citizens and British subjects would be formed to settle the questions of debt and boundary locations.

The treaty was not popular in the United States. Many claimed it was overly favorable to Great Britain. THOMAS JEFFERSON's supporters in the House of Representatives attempted to subvert the treaty by blocking funding. DEMOCRATIC-REPUBLICANS also turned on John Jay as a result of his role in the agreement. Jay's Treaty survived the Senate ratification process by a slim margin, and even then it passed only because of pressure from President GEORGE WASHINGTON.

The treaty had mixed results on American diplomacy and politics. It helped to preserve peace with Great Britain. However, it antagonized the French and contributed to the animosity that broke out into the QUASI WAR (1798–1800). The bitter and contentious debate over the treaty also furthered political divisions between the emerging FEDERALIST and Democratic-Republican Parties.

Further reading: Samuel Flagg Bemis, *Jay's Treaty: A Study in Commerce and Diplomacy* (New York: Macmillan, 1924); Jerald A. Combs, *The Jay Treaty: Political Battleground of the Founding Fathers* (Berkeley: University of California Press, 1970).

— Jay R. Dew

Jefferson, Thomas (1743–1826)

Thomas Jefferson, the author of the DECLARATION OF INDEPENDENCE (July 4, 1776), was born near present-day Charlottesville, Virginia, at Shadwell on April 13, 1743 (old style, April 2, 1743; Britain did not adopt the Gregorian calendar until 1752). Jane Randolph, Jefferson's mother, was a member of the prominent Randolph family of Virginia. His father, Peter Jefferson, was a self-taught surveyor who died on August 17, 1757, bequeathing his land and slaves to his son Thomas Jefferson. However, Jefferson declared that his father's most valuable legacy was his provision for his children's EDUCATION.

After his father's death, Thomas Jefferson studied under the tutelage of a Virginia clergyman, the Reverend James Maury. In 1760 he moved to Williamsburg, the capital of colonial Virginia, to attend the College of William

Thomas Jefferson. Painting by Thomas Sully *(National Archives)*

and Mary. After completing his studies there in 1762, he read law under George Wythe, a prominent jurist and classical scholar, and entered the bar in 1767. Two years later, he began political life as a member of Virginia's House of Burgesses. Although not yet a conspicuous politician, Jefferson began to put his thoughts on paper. In 1774 he authored "A Summary View of the Rights of British America," a resolution protesting British imperial policy. Considered too radical for approval, the "Summary View" nevertheless earned Jefferson notoriety after it was published and circulated throughout the colonies.

A year later, when Jefferson arrived in Philadelphia as one of Virginia's delegates to the SECOND CONTINENTAL CONGRESS, JOHN ADAMS noted that he enjoyed "a reputation for LITERATURE, SCIENCE, and a happy talent for composition." Jefferson served on a number of important committees, including the one charged with the preparation of a declaration of independence. Jefferson drafted the document, which the committee altered slightly and then presented to Congress. There the document was further edited; one change was the removal of Jefferson's assertion holding the king responsible for the existence of SLAVERY on the North American continent. On July 4, 1776, Congress approved the Declaration of Independence.

Three months later, Jefferson returned to work and family in Virginia. In Williamsburg he contributed to the drafting of his state's new constitution; among other things he advocated complete separation of church and state. His "Statute for Religious Freedom" was so bitterly disputed that it was not enacted until a decade later.

Jefferson married Martha Wayles Skelton on January 1, 1772. The couple had their first child, a daughter Martha, in the autumn of 1772. By 1777 they had four children, but only two had survived. Few of their children would survive the perilous months of infancy.

In 1779 Jefferson was elected wartime governor of Virginia (1779–81). After the fall of CHARLESTON (May 12, 1780) and the ensuing defeat of General HORATIO GATES by CHARLES, LORD CORNWALLIS at CAMDEN (August 15, 1780), Virginia stood vulnerable to British invasion. Despite Jefferson's attempts to reinforce defenses, British troops commanded by BENEDICT ARNOLD easily took Richmond. By the spring of the following year, general wartime destruction under British occupation had heightened, and the capital was moved from Richmond to Charlottesville. British mounted infantry led by Colonel BANASTRE TARLETON attacked Charlottesville but failed to capture Jefferson and members of the assembly. The British success led members of the assembly to make a formal inquiry into possible misconduct by Jefferson. Although cleared of any wrongdoing during Arnold's invasion, Jefferson was deeply wounded by the episode and pledged to his friends that he would never again enter public life.

Jefferson and his family remained at his Poplar Forest plantation until August 1781. While there, Jefferson undertook to complete a request for information on the state of Virginia forwarded to him by a good friend. The answers to the marquis de Barbé-Marbois's circulated list of inquiries eventually became Jefferson's Notes on the State of Virginia, one of the most important scientific works of the 18th century. In the manuscript, Jefferson articulated a position on such issues as slavery, education, RELIGION, and government. Jefferson was the second largest slave owner in Albemarle County and owned at any one time some 200 people. His ruminations in the Notes on the State of Virginia were controversial and contradictory. Jefferson advocated freeing slaves at some point in the future, but he considered African Americans inferior. He also asserted that slaves could not be freed and then incorporated into the state due to "deep rooted prejudices entertained by the whites; [and] ten thousand recollections, by the blacks, of the injuries they have sustained. . . " and therefore argued for colonization. However, Jefferson never followed up on his beliefs; he freed only a handful of favored slaves, retained possession of the rest, and never sent any slave back to Africa.

Within the household of the Monticello plantation, Jefferson's family had grown. Martha had given birth to two more daughters, although only one of them survived more than a year. Tragically, Martha never recovered after the birth of their daughter Lucy in May 1782, dying two months later on September 6, 1782. Jefferson never remarried.

Although he had been named as one of the negotiators for the treaty of peace to be worked out with Great Britain, he was unable to travel to France in 1782. Instead he entered Congress in the fall of 1783. As a member of Congress, Jefferson proposed a plan of government for the Western Territory. The Ordinance of 1784 was "significant historically," as Jefferson scholar Dumas Malone writes, "because it embodied the principle that new states would be formed from the western region and admitted to the Union on an equal basis with the original commonwealths." Never put into effect, the Ordinance of 1784 served as the basis for the NORTHWEST ORDINANCE of 1787. That same year Jefferson wrote his Notes on Coinage, proposing the American system of money.

In May 1784 Congress elected Jefferson minister plenipotentiary. Within a week he had his instructions from Congress and soon thereafter sailed to France with his eldest daughter Martha. Jefferson had left his daughters Mary and Lucy with his sister-in-law in Virginia, but after the death of his youngest daughter Lucy, Mary, with SALLY HEMINGS, a slave, sailed to join her father in Paris. In the spring of 1785, when BENJAMIN FRANKLIN returned to Philadelphia, Congress appointed Jefferson to the Court of Versailles as his successor. On May 17, Jefferson presented his credentials to Louis XVI and became the American minister to France. He remained in France until the fall of 1789 and thus witnessed the birth of the FRENCH REVOLUTION (1789–1815).

After Jefferson's return to the United States he received notification (December 12, 1789) of his appointment to GEORGE WASHINGTON's cabinet as secretary of state. Hesitant to accept, Jefferson nevertheless responded that he would join the administration. Once in the cabinet, Jefferson began to advocate policies in opposition to the ideas of ALEXANDER HAMILTON, the secretary of the treasury. Washington often asked the opinions of both the secretaries of state and treasury, but he seemed to favor his close personal friend, Hamilton. His advice often rejected, Jefferson became frustrated. He resented Alexander Hamilton's pro-British stance, as well as his influence over the president. By January 1792, Jefferson had decided to retire from Washington's cabinet, but his friend JAMES MADISON persuaded him to remain in the post. Jefferson continued as secretary of state until he resigned at the close of 1793.

Jefferson described his plantation home at Monticello as his "essay in ARCHITECTURE." Chiefly influenced by the works of Andrea Palladio (1508–80), an Italian architect, Jefferson's home was designed in the neoclassical style. Jefferson also designed the Capitol in Richmond; the University of Virginia, in Charlottesville; and his plantation house at Poplar Forest in the Palladian manner. Originally planned as a two story, eight-room dwelling, the first house at Monticello was never completed. After he retired from Washington's administration he began to remodel the home extensively. Enslaved and hired workmen carefully demolished the house in an effort to salvage the bricks, while construction supplies were primarily made on the plantation. Owing to Jefferson's continued absence from home, construction was often delayed; in fact Jefferson's 21-room plantation house was completed in 1809, 40 years after construction began.

Jefferson was drawn back into politics in the presidential contest of 1796, advocating small government and anti-British policies. He lost the presidential election, but since the Constitution originally provided that the person who earned the second largest number of electoral votes became vice president, in 1796 Jefferson assumed this office. John Adams, once a close personal friend, had received 71 electoral votes and Jefferson 68. Although vice president, Jefferson opposed many of Adams's Federalist policies, viewing them as tending toward monarchy. After the federal government passed the ALIEN AND SEDITION ACTS in 1798, Jefferson drafted the Kentucky Resolutions (November 13, 1798), arguing for nullification of the acts. He justified his position by claiming the laws represented an unconstitutional use of power by the FEDERALIST PARTY. The Kentucky Resolutions were adopted just prior to the opening salvo of what Jefferson later termed the revolution of 1800, the presidential ELECTION OF 1800.

Jefferson had predicted prior to the election of 1800 that "our campaign will be as hot as that of Europe, but happily we deal in ink only; they in blood." He said the nation's newspapers were "teeming with every falsehood they can invent for defamation." Jefferson supporters labeled John Adams a monarchist; Adams supporters called Jefferson an atheist; each side declared their opponents enemies of the Constitution. Scandalmonger James T. Callender was one of the writers who took up his pen against the Federalists. After he was arrested and successfully tried for sedition, Callender assumed that since he served as a political martyr, he would be rewarded for his political service with an appointment. Once Jefferson became president, Callender became angered when a reward did not materialize. Consequently, he switched allegiances and turned against Jefferson, publishing rumors that Jefferson had fathered children by his slave, Sally Hemings. The debate over these charges continues even today. A DNA study conducted in 1998 produced evidence suggesting that Jefferson did father at least one of the children of Sally

Hemings, the same slave who had accompanied his daughter Mary to Paris.

When the electoral votes were cast on December 3, 1800, Adams was defeated, but Jefferson did not win the presidency. Instead, he tied with AARON BURR, his DEMOCRATIC-REPUBLICAN running mate. The Twelfth Amendment to the Constitution, ratified in 1804, would change the process for electing the president and vice president by directing the electoral college vote separately for each; in 1800, however, Jefferson's place at the top of the Democratic-Republican ticket counted for little. The election was finally decided in the House of Representatives, where the Federalists worked to block Jefferson's election by throwing their support behind Burr. The House convened in WASHINGTON, D.C., on February 9, 1801, but after several days of balloting there was still no decision. Finally, on the 36th ballot, Jefferson attained a majority and the presidency.

On March 4, 1801, Thomas Jefferson was inaugurated as the third president of the United States. He attempted to ease party faction in his inaugural address by declaring, "We are all republicans, we are all federalists;" however, party strife did not end. As John Adams left office, he packed the courts with Federalist judges, a move that was coined the "midnight appointments." In 1801 three judges—including William Marbury—demanded confirmation of their appointments, but Jefferson considered those appointments void. Chief Justice JOHN MARSHALL ordered the appointments to be ratified but was ignored. The ensuing court case, *MARBURY V. MADISON* (1803), and Marshall's ruling established the precedent of judicial review.

Jefferson also pursued policies to reverse the Federalist effort to strengthen the central government at the expense of the states. He reduced the size of the army and navy and shrank the already small federal bureaucracy. Jefferson advocated a policy that held that the best government was one that limited its interference in the daily lives of the people.

Presiding over not only the nation but also the national scientific organization, the AMERICAN PHILOSOPHICAL SOCIETY, Jefferson was a lifelong student of science. Interested in the scientific world of the West, Jefferson sponsored various North American expeditions, including the "voyage of discovery" led by Captains MERIWETHER LEWIS and WILLIAM CLARK. On January 18, 1803, Jefferson sent a secret message to Congress explaining the planned expedition to the western territories. Charged, among other things, to find the Northwest Passage to the Pacific Ocean, to establish contact with the various NATIVE AMERICAN tribes of the territory, and to make detailed scientific observations of animal and plant life, the Corps of Discovery—cocaptained by LEWIS AND

CLARK—departed on the journey on July 4, 1803. On the same day, the government announce the purchase of the Louisiana Territory.

The greatest achievement of Jefferson's first term was the LOUISIANA PURCHASE, which doubled the nation's size, adding 828,000 square miles of land and moving the western boundary to the Rocky Mountains. However, this triumphant purchase came with a cost: It breached the limits of the Constitution, and Jefferson feared that it might establish a dangerous precedent. In remedy, Jefferson drafted a retroactive Constitutional amendment, but the document found no support in Congress.

In 1804 Jefferson was overwhelmingly reelected president. His first term had been marked with domestic success. Unconscious of the toll it was to take on his second term, Jefferson in his second inaugural address made little mention of international affairs. However, the nation was soon engulfed in international power politics. British IMPRESSMENT of sailors often resulted in desertion, which produced a policy of searching other vessels for those who had absconded from service. On June 22, 1807, the British HMS *Leopard* fired upon the USS *Chesapeake* when the American vessel refused to allow the British to search for deserters (CHESAPEAKE-LEOPARD affair). Three sailors were killed in an action that violated American territorial waters and sovereignty. After the incident, war fever spread through the United States. President Jefferson worried about jeopardizing American concord by becoming entangled in the European contest between France and Britain. The recognized choices were conceding to a foreign power, war, or "peaceable coercion" by establishing a commercial embargo. In December 1807 the Embargo Act became law. The once-lucrative shipping industry fell prey to "Jefferson, worms, and embargo," as one broadside read. Commerce, with the exception of blockade-runners, came to a standstill and economic depression set in. Unwavering in his belief that Europe would yield to the economic power of the United States, Jefferson clung to the embargo, but the nation saw the policy as a failure. As his presidency came to an end, Congress repealed the EMBARGO OF 1807. The economic experiment had failed and, as a consequence, the United States would have to fight the War of 1812 (1812–15).

Jefferson returned to his beloved Monticello in 1809, where he was surrounded by his daughter Martha's family, the enslaved plantation community, and a constant stream of visitors. In retirement he campaigned for public education and rejoiced when the state chartered the University of Virginia in 1819. Jefferson, the father of the University of Virginia, was its architect, chose the faculty, and selected the curriculum and corresponding books for its library. The "Sage of Monticello" saw the University of Virginia open its doors to scholars a year before his death.

He also reconciled in 1812 with his one-time friend and political opponent John Adams, sharing with Adams a correspondence that stands as a testament to the brilliance and political statesmanship of both men. On July 4, 1826, the 50th anniversary of American Independence, John Adams died in Quincy, Massachusetts. His last words were in regard to his friend and fellow revolutionary Thomas Jefferson. He said, "Thomas Jefferson still survives," unaware that Jefferson had died earlier that day. Jefferson's last words were, "Is it the fourth?"

Jefferson's legacy today is marked by contradiction, most strikingly as the author of the words, "We hold these truths to be self-evident: That all men are created equal" while simultaneously owning slaves. However, Jefferson did attempt to secure his legacy. He wrote the epitaph on his grave marker, which reads: "Here was buried Thomas Jefferson Author of the Declaration of American Independence, of the Virginia Statute for Religious Freedom, and Father of the University of Virginia."

See also FOREIGN AFFAIRS; JUDICIARY ACT OF 1801; RELIGIOUS LIBERTY; REPUBLICANISM; VIRGINIA AND KENTUCKY RESOLUTIONS.

Further reading: Noble E. Cunningham Jr., *In Pursuit of Reason: The Life of Thomas Jefferson* (Baton Rouge: Louisiana State University Press, 1987); Dumas Malone, *Jefferson and His Time,* 6 vols. (Boston: Little, Brown, 1948–81); Peter S. Onuf, *Jefferson's Empire: The Language of American Nationhood.* (Charlottesville: University of Virginia Press, 2000); Merrill Peterson, *Thomas Jefferson and the New Nation.* (New York: Oxford University Press, 1970).

— Christine Coalwell

Jersey, HMS

The *Jersey* was an infamous British prison ship. In the wake of their capture of New York in 1776, the British found themselves with thousands of rebel prisoners. The British army and navy struggled to cope with the captives, and prisoners were interned in all large public and private buildings, including churches and warehouses. When these were filled to capacity, the transport ships that had carried WILLIAM HOWE's soldiers to America were used to hold prisoners, most of whom were privateersmen and naval prisoners captured by the Royal Navy.

The most notorious of the British prison hulks in New York harbor was HMS *Jersey,* in Wallabut Bay, Brooklyn. The *Jersey* was built as a 64-gun ship of the line in 1736. In 1776 the vessel was used as a transport to convey hired HESSIAN troops to America for the campaigns in and around New York. After the British invasion of LONG ISLAND and subsequent capture of New York City, the *Jer-*

sey was used as a storage vessel and then as a hospital ship. During the winter of 1779–80, after prisoners set fire to two other prison ships, the *Jersey* was converted to accommodate captives. It was gutted and dismasted, its rudder was unhung, and its guns were removed. The *Jersey's* portholes were bolted shut and a series of holes—20 inches wide at 10-foot intervals and blocked by iron bars—were cut into the sides of the ship to afford its unfortunate residents with light and air. Between 1780 and 1783 thousands of American, French, and Spanish sailors were held aboard the *Jersey.* At any one time between 400 and 1200 captives were confined to the ship. They were allowed to walk the ship's deck by day and confined below at night.

Between 1776 and 1783, more than 18,000 rebel prisoners were held aboard more than 20 prison ships in New York harbor. Of these, approximately 8,500 captives (nearly 47 percent) died in British custody. Most died from the combined effects of neglect, disease, malnutrition, overcrowding, and exposure to the elements. During the REVOLUTIONARY WAR (1775–83), the treatment of rebel prisoners aboard the *Jersey* and the other prison ships was a subject of controversy. GEORGE WASHINGTON and the CONTINENTAL CONGRESS wrote to the British authorities in New York to protest the maltreatment of captured seamen. The British brushed aside the criticisms. During the decades after the conflict, a number of memoirs were published by former prisoners who emphasized the ill treatment they had received from their captors. Many of these memoirs were written by *Jersey* survivors, and they guaranteed the ship's reputation as the worst of the New York prison hulks.

After the British evacuated New York in 1783, the *Jersey* was abandoned and slowly rotted and disappeared below the surface of Wallabut Bay early in the 19th century. During the 19th century there were repeated unsuccessful attempts to erect a monument to commemorate the victims of the *Jersey* and the other prison ships.

Further reading: Francis D. Cogliano, *American Maritime Prisoners in the Revolutionary War: The Captivity of William Russell* (Annapolis, Md.: Naval Institute Press, 2001).

— Francis D. Cogliano

Jews

Although the Constitution of the United States does not specifically mention Jews, its RELIGIOUS LIBERTY provisions in essence granted Jews the honor of citizenship. The United States was thus the first non-Jewish country, ancient or modern, that included Jews as political equals. Official tolerance of RELIGION is one of the most enduring victories of the AMERICAN REVOLUTION.

At the time of the REVOLUTIONARY WAR (1775–83), approximately 2,500 Jews lived in the English colonies, or about 1 percent of the general population. Most Jews in the revolutionary era lived in urban areas and worked as ARTISANS and merchants. Leading Jewish merchants of the period included Barnard and Michael Gratz of Philadelphia, the Lopez family of Newport, and Isaac DaCosta of Charleston. Several port cities became centers of Jewish life, including New York, Newport, Charleston, Savannah, Philadelphia, and New Haven. Like QUAKER and Huguenot merchants, Jews enjoyed special cultural relationships with coreligionists who still lived in western Europe and with those who had moved to the Caribbean. These connections greatly assisted transatlantic trade. Moreover, ritual necessities such as prayer books and special silverware were produced and distributed throughout the colonies, providing links between communities. Mercantile ties were further solidified through kinship relations. Internationally arranged marriages also were a common means of bringing merchant houses together.

Jewish communities tended to follow a simple pattern of religious development: The communities usually employed a ritual slaughterer, which allowed them to enjoy kosher meat. A religious leader, known as a hazan, would then be brought into the community, as the Jews of New York did in 1757 when they hired one from London to lead services and to teach Hebrew, English, and Spanish to their children. Private homes served as the sites of prayer meetings until the community developed a synagogue complex, which typically included a place of worship, a ritual bath, and a schoolhouse. The Touro Synagogue in Newport still stands as one of the earliest examples of colonial Jewish architecture.

Jews were active in the RESISTANCE MOVEMENT (1764–75) and participated on both sides of the Revolutionary War. Jewish merchants during the STAMP ACT Crisis of 1765 signed the nonimportation agreement promising to stop English imports. Later, New York's Jewish merchants protested the levy on tea. Once the war broke out, the Jewish community, like the larger American community, was divided. Some men, like the affluent David Franks, became LOYALISTS, while others strove to remain neutral. A few shifted sides during the conflict. Many supported independence. In 1775 Mordecai Sheftall of Savannah ordered English captains to leave port without unloading their cargoes. Throughout the country, Jews volunteered for military service in state militias and in the CONTINENTAL ARMY. Between 25 and 35 Jews participated in the Battle of Beaufort in 1779 and in the defense of Charleston in 1780.

Perhaps the most famous Jewish WHIG during the war was Haym Salomon, who has sometimes mistakenly been called the "financier of the Revolution." Salomon began the war in obscurity, probably serving as a sutler with the

American forces on the Canadian border in 1776. Upon his return to New York City, which by then was occupied by the British, he was arrested. Somehow he obtained his release and began working as a supplier to HESSIAN troops, opened up a shop, and made a small fortune. However, he also worked as an agent for the Americans, inducing Hessians to desert and assisting escaping American and French prisoners. When he was betrayed in August 1778, he left the city and moved to Philadelphia. By 1781, Salomon had reestablished his fortune and begun working with ROBERT MORRIS to arrange financing for the United States. Salomon became a bill broker, selling notes and raising cash to supply the army in the last years of the war. While he did not exactly finance the revolution, he facilitated the financial arrangements made by Morris.

When the war was over, the Jewish community in America enjoyed a status that was distinctively different from that of their European counterparts. In Europe, Jews belonged to a legal category separate from all other natives, comprising an official and distinct social and political body in which participation was mandated both by the Jewish community and by the host European government. In the United States, however, association with the Jewish community was completely voluntary. The Constitution of the United States prohibited a religious test for government office (Article VI), and the First Amendment prohibited Congress from establishing any religion, thus permitting Jews to participate as equal citizens on the federal level. President GEORGE WASHINGTON captured the significance of the change in Jewish legal and political status when he wrote warmheartedly to the congregation of the Newport Synagogue that "the government of the United States, which gives to bigotry no sanction, to persecution no assistance requires only that they who live under its protection should demean themselves as good citizens, in giving it on all occasions their effectual support."

State governments moved more slowly concerning religious liberty. While some states like Virginia quickly disestablished religion, others clung to some state support for specific denominations into the 19th century and limited the right of citizenship to Protestants. Pennsylvania, home to a large Jewish community, did not grant the privileges and immunities of citizenship to Jews until 1790. By 1820, most STATE CONSTITUTIONS eliminated religious qualifications that had kept Jews from participating in public affairs and government office, though Rhode Island, New Hampshire, and North Carolina maintained these religious requirements until later in the 19th century.

Further reading: Eli Faber, "A Time for Planting: The First Migration, 1654–1820" in Henry Fiengold, ed. *The Jewish People in America,* 5 vols. (Baltimore: Johns Hopkins University Press, 1992); Jacob Rader Marcus, *United States Jewry, 1776–1985,* vol. 1 (Detroit: Wayne State University Press, 1989); Samuel Rezneck, *Unrecognized Patriots: The Jews in the American Revolution* (Westport, Conn.: Greenwood Press, 1975).

— Michael Alexander

Johnson, Sir John (1742–1830)

Sir John Johnson was a royal Indian agent and an important landlord in the Mohawk River Valley, as was his father, Sir William Johnson, before him. During the REVOLUTIONARY WAR (1775–83), he remained loyal to the Crown and raised a regiment of his tenants and supporters to fight for the British. After the war he became an important LOYALIST leader in CANADA.

John Johnson was the eldest son and heir of Sir William Johnson and was the product of Sir William's liaison with a Dutch woman named Catherine Weisenberg. By the beginning of the Revolutionary War, John Johnson was an important man in his own right, having been knighted in 1765 for his military service during PONTIAC'S REBELLION (1763). When Sir William Johnson died in 1774, John Johnson inherited his father's huge estates with thousands of Scottish and SCOTCH-IRISH tenants, many of whom had been British soldiers. He also inherited his father's influence among the Indians. By the time of the Revolutionary War, Johnson was the most powerful man in the Mohawk Valley.

American colonists began to choose sides as the Revolutionary War broke out. Those who supported King GEORGE III were often forced to flee or to join Loyalist regiments. This fact, along with the personal devotion of his tenants and supporters, allowed Sir John to recruit more than 1,000 men to his two battalions of the King's Royal Regiment, the "Royal Greens." It was Johnson's intention to organize the settlers and Indians of the Mohawk Valley to fight the revolutionaries. However, in 1776, superior American forces under General PHILIP SCHUYLER forced Sir John to flee to Canada with his men.

During the early years of the war Johnson and other Loyalist leaders were often able to return from Canada to check on their homes, spy, and sometimes carry out raids. However, they were never able to stay long for fear of capture. Johnson served with the British colonel Barry St. Leger in his attack from Lake Ontario in the summer of 1777 and participated in the Battle of Oriskany (August 6, 1777). Following that campaign, he and several other Loyalist leaders, including his brother-in-law Guy Johnson, participated in an often-vicious border war. From Canada, the "Royal Greens" periodically staged raids against revolutionary forces in the Mohawk Valley and adjoining areas. However, while the raids were an annoyance, they were never able to inflict any substantial damage. Johnson and his regiment spent the later years of the war on garrison duty in Montreal.

Both during and following the Revolutionary War, tens of thousands of Loyalists fled across the border into Canada. With the end of hostilities, the British called on Sir John Johnson and other leaders to administer the resettlement of Loyalists along the upper St. Lawrence River. However, the British refused to recreate in Canada the large semifeudal estates that had existed in New York. This policy prevented powerful Loyalist leaders from reestablishing their dominant positions after the war. In the new Canadian settlements, the king was the only landlord, and all Loyalists received grants of land. Nevertheless, despite his loss of property and power, Johnson remained influential among the Loyalist settlers. He lived in Montreal until the end of the war and eventually became superintendent of Indian Affairs.

— Robert Lively

Jones, Absalom (1746–1818)

Born a slave in British colonial America, Absalom Jones became one of the leading free-black activists of the early American republic. Before his death in 1818, Jones helped found the Free African Society in Philadelphia (a mutual aid society dedicated to racial uplift through education and insurance), the first independent black church, and, with RICHARD ALLEN, coauthored the first copyrighted black pamphlet. Jones was born into SLAVERY in Delaware. He learned to read at an early age and acquired both a Bible and a speller before he was 16 years old. In the early 1760s, Jones went to Philadelphia with his master and worked in a dry-goods store. After a colaborer helped him learn to write, Jones obtained permission from his master to attend a QUAKER-run school. Jones married in the 1770s and saved enough money to buy his wife out of bondage (thus allowing any children of theirs to be free as well). Jones remained in Philadelphia during the REVOLUTIONARY WAR (1775–83), finally purchasing his own freedom in 1784. Over the next three decades, Jones solidified his reputation as one of Philadelphia's preeminent AFRICAN-AMERICAN leaders.

In the newly independent American nation, Jones was in the vanguard of black activists who tried to use the ideals of the Revolution to attack racial subjugation. Pennsylvania had adopted the world's first gradual abolition law in 1780, declaring that bondage would slowly but surely be ended in the Quaker State over the next few decades. Between the 1780s and early 1800s, Philadelphia's African-American population swelled. Leaders such as Jones, Allen, and JAMES FORTEN created autonomous African-American institutions (in particular, African-American churches) to aid black Pennsylvanians' transition from slavery to freedom. Jones and Allen eventually broke over denominational affiliations, although they remained friends. Allen

gravitated toward METHODISM, while Jones founded St. Thomas's African Episcopal Church in 1794. In 1804 Jones became the first black priest ordained by the Episcopalian Church.

Jones and Philadelphia's other black leaders attempted to keep ANTISLAVERY momentum going both in Pennsylvania and nationally. Allen, Jones, and Forten aided blacks falsely accused of being fugitive slaves, putting them in contact with white abolitionist LAWYERS. Jones and Allen also led an anti-slave-trading petition drive in 1799 aimed at the federal Congress, meeting then in Philadelphia. The petition attempted to ban slave imports immediately and gently urged Congress to consider a gradual abolition act for the nation. By a vote of 84 to 1, the petition was rejected.

Jones combated racial injustice by wielding his pen. When Philadelphia was ravaged by a yellow fever epidemic in 1793, and European Americans accused African Americans of ransacking the stricken, Jones helped Richard Allen compose a rebuttal to the unjust charges. Entitled "A Narrative of the Proceedings of the Black People During the Late Awful Calamity in Philadelphia," the pamphlet pointed out that African Americans aided white Philadelphians even though they too suffered tremendous casualties. In addition, Jones and Allen attacked the root of the antiblack charges: slavery and racial injustice. If white Americans would free slaves and give them equal opportunities to succeed, they asserted, then Africans Americans would become valuable citizens. Jones published his own pamphlet in 1808, "A Thanksgiving Sermon," which celebrated the recent Congressional ban on the SLAVE TRADE. In his last years, Jones joined Allen and Forten in opposing the American Colonization Society (formed in 1817), which sought to export free blacks from American shores.

Further reading: Gary B. Nash, *Forging Freedom: The Formation of Philadelphia's Black Community, 1745–1840* (Cambridge, Mass.: Harvard University Press, 1988); Richard Newman, Patrick Rael, and Philip Lapsanky, eds., *Pamphlets of Protest: An Anthology of Early African American Protest Writing* (New York: Routledge, 2001); Julie Winch, *Philadelphia's Black Elite: Activism, Accommodation, and the Struggle for Autonomy, 1787–1848* (Philadelphia: Temple University Press, 1993).

— Richard Newman

Jones, John Paul (1747–1792)

John Paul was born near Kirkcubright in southwest Scotland, a region bordering the Solway Firth and the Irish Sea. Most local men were compelled to choose between the farm and the sea in seeking their livelihoods. Paul opted for the latter. At age 12 he went to sea as a ship's boy aboard a merchant ship sailing between Britain, the WEST INDIES, and Virginia. Over the next decade he gained wide experience and proved to be a capable mariner. By the age of 21 he was captaining merchant vessels plying the route between the West Indies and Britain. Paul, like most of his peers, could be ruthless in dealing with his subordinates. In 1769 he ordered a ship's carpenter whipped. When the sailor died as a result of the whipping, Paul was charged with murder and subsequently cleared of wrongdoing. In 1773 his crew mutinied in the West Indies, and Paul killed one of the mutineers. Fearing that he would not beat another murder charge, he fled to British North America and added the surname "Jones" to his name.

As an experienced mariner and man of action, John Paul Jones arrived in the colonies at a fortuitous time. Based on his experience and connections with rebel officials, which were a legacy of his prewar career as the master of merchant vessels, Jones obtained a commission as a lieutenant aboard the *Alfred,* one of the ships in the fledgling CONTINENTAL NAVY. Jones proved himself to be a capable officer and was given command of the sloop *Providence* in 1776. In 1777 Jones was given command of the ship *Ranger* with orders to wreak havoc on commerce in British waters. His most notable achievement as commander of the *Ranger* was a patrol in the Irish Sea in April 1778, during which Jones returned to the scenes of his boyhood, attacking Whitehaven on the English side of the Solway Firth and leading a quixotic raid in Kirkcubrightshire in a failed effort to capture the earl of Selkirk, whom he hoped to exchange for American prisoners. Nonetheless, the *Ranger's* cruise was a success—Jones captured seven British prizes and many prisoners. He had, moreover, spread fear around coastal Britain and earned himself a notorious reputation.

In 1779 Jones led a small Franco-American squadron on another cruise in British waters. He commanded the *Bonhomme Richard,* a converted French merchant vessel named in honor of BENJAMIN FRANKLIN's "Poor Richard." The squadron met with some success. On September 23 the *Bonhomme Richard* engaged in a bloody night battle with HMS *Serapis* off Flamborough Head in Yorkshire. The two ships fought a close action and were badly damaged. When the captain of the *Serapis* asked whether Jones was willing to surrender the sinking *Bonhomme Richard,* Jones replied, "I have not yet begun to fight." Eventually the captain of the *Serapis* was forced to strike his colors. Jones and his crew took possession of the British vessel as the *Bonhomme Richard* sank. Jones had won the most famous American naval victory of the war.

Jones was driven by a desire for fame and recognition, and he found these briefly after his victory over the *Serapis.* After the war Jones unsuccessfully sought to become the first admiral in the United States Navy. Frustrated, he served in the navy of Catherine the Great in Russia's war with Turkey in 1788–89. Jones died in Paris in 1792. At the time of his death, Jones was trying to revive his reputation—he had sunk into relative obscurity—and obtain a commission in the French navy.

While American privateers captured thousands of British prizes at sea during the War of Independence, the Continental navy made only a minor contribution to the final victory. Despite Jones's individual heroics, the American navy could never seriously challenge the might of the Royal Navy during the war. Rather, it was the advent of the French navy in the struggle in 1778 that helped to shift the balance of the war at sea. Posterity has been kinder to Jones than his contemporaries were. With the growth of American naval power during the 19th and 20th centuries, Jones has come to be viewed as the father of the American navy. The culmination of this transformation occurred in 1905, when Jones's remains were exhumed in France for burial in the United States. In death Jones has received the fame and approbation that he enjoyed only briefly in life.

Further reading: Samuel Eliot Morison, *John Paul Jones: A Sailor's Biography* (Boston: Little, Brown, 1959).

— Francis D. Cogliano

journalism

Newspapers became a major agent of change in American society by the mid-18th century. With the rise of egalitarianism, increased literacy, rapidly evolving postal and transportation systems, and a booming population, printed matter became widely accessible. The revolutionary era was one of the most politically and journalistically dynamic periods in American history. During this period the American press played an important role in determining the direction of the emerging political system.

Newspaper publishing expanded rapidly after 1750. The press, originally born to serve religious fervor and society's elite, became a powerful political instrument that served all individuals. Circulation might have been limited during this era, but total readership accounted for much more than the numbers show. For example, large groups of people often shared one newspaper. TAVERN and coffeehouse owners subscribed to newspapers for their customers to read. Ministers would even read the latest news to their congregations. As the revolutionary period wore on, Americans increasingly turned to newspapers for news.

Papers during this period usually were one large sheet folded once to create four pages. Type size was very small, and no large headlines or fancy graphics were used. The first and last sheets of a newspaper usually consisted of advertising, while the middle two sheets included news and LITERATURE. Local news was less common in 18th-century newspapers but became more prominent in the early 1800s.

Throughout the revolutionary and early republican periods, printed dissent was never fully accepted. The John Peter Zenger trial of 1733 is popularly known for establishing the jury's right to decide whether or not a publication is defamatory or seditious, as well as the admissibility of evidence about the truth of an alleged libel. But this interpretation is misleading. Publishing any kind of official document or legislative debate was still dangerous for printers during this period, because neither of these precedents was established in American law until 50 years after the Zenger trial. While newspapers still played a prominent role in affecting public opinion, printers remained on guard. But despite their vulnerable position, many colonial newspaper editors gave voice to the opposition to imperial regulations after 1765.

When the British imposed the STAMP ACT of 1765—requiring all legal documents, official papers, books, and newspapers to be printed on specially taxed, stamped paper—printers denounced the action and refused to print on the stamped paper. By the time Parliament repealed the unenforceable Stamp Act in 1766, many colonial newspapers openly opposed British authority, and their continuing opposition helped lead the country into revolution.

Colonial American newspaper publishers faced trying times during the REVOLUTIONARY WAR (1775–83). Publishing was disrupted by military operations, and there was a shortage of printing materials. Paper prices rose sharply during the war, mostly because of the need for rags in making paper. News coverage was limited. Major events sometimes appeared as no more than one paragraph, and English newspapers, which were a prime source for information, were scarce. Thus, most news was delayed. But although many newspapers stopped publishing during the war, nearly as many were started, and readership continued to grow. Editors were also threatened by politics and the events of the war. Whether for or against independence, each paper served only one political point of view. Rebel publications denounced all loyalty to Great Britain, and Tory newspapers declared opposition to the king as treason. Both the printers' and the newspapers' safety hung in the balance as troops moved from town to town.

After the TREATY OF PARIS of 1783, newspapers remained highly political. LOYALIST publications closed, and other newspapers supported a variety of political issues, depending on local circumstances. The Constitution of 1787 created a national debate in the press. Newspapers throughout the country printed the first proposal of the Constitution. Attacking each other more vehemently than ever, newspapers published articles either for or against the ratification of the United States Constitution. Among the most popular in favor of ratification was the

series known as the FEDERALIST PAPERS, written by ALEXANDER HAMILTON, JAMES MADISON, and JOHN JAY. All but 12 newspapers favored ratification. Thus, editorial support was very strong, and opponents—claiming their views were not fairly heard in the press—received one reply: that all views were printed, and the reason such a small number of opposing articles had been published was that few were submitted.

During the 1790s the two new POLITICAL PARTIES—the FEDERALIST and DEMOCRATIC-REPUBLICAN—used newspapers extensively. The "partisan press" was technically born in 1789 when John Fenno published the *Gazette of the United States*. Fenno's newspaper was the first founded solely as an organ of one political faction. Alexander Hamilton and other leading Federalists financially supported the *Gazette*. Democratic-Republican political leaders also

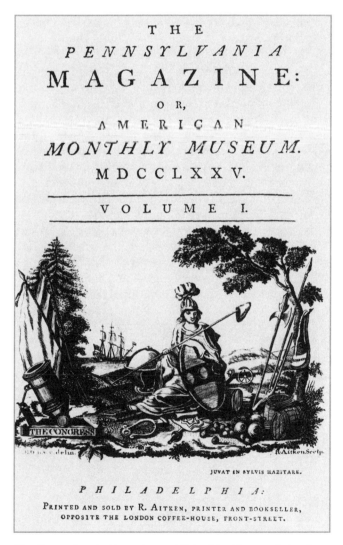

The Pennsylvania Magazine, published by Thomas Paine in 1775 and 1776 *(Library of Congress)*

helped establish a number of newspapers. One of the most prominent Democratic-Republican newspapers during this period—and one of the biggest threats to Federalists—was BENJAMIN FRANKLIN BACHE's *Aurora*. Because of Bache's inside knowledge of politics, many Democratic-Republican leaders looked to his paper for guidance. He was threatened verbally and physically, first by a Federalist mob, and when that failed, by the Federalist-controlled government. Both parties feared for the future of their new nation, and one of the most prominent acts of oppression during this period was the Sedition Act, imposed by the Federalists in 1798. This law, forbidding the printing of "false" and "malicious" material, gave authorities power over the Democratic-Republican press. Federalist courts prosecuted over a dozen editors under the Sedition Act. But when THOMAS JEFFERSON was elected president in 1800, the Democratic-Republican Party and its sympathetic press started to gain the upper hand.

Politicians and editors still viewed the press as a major political instrument into the 1800s. Both Democratic-Republican and Federalist editors continued their attempts to silence the opposition, and thus newspaper content remained highly political, filled with opinion and argument. The split continued into the War of 1812 (1812–15), with Democratic-Republicans and Federalists disagreeing about the necessity of the war. Newspaper attacks were plentiful, and several Federalist papers fell victim to the Democratic-Republican mob. The Federalist Party disappeared after the War of 1812, but newspaper expansion continued.

Newspapers were able to reach out farther than ever during this era. They set the public agenda during the RESISTANCE MOVEMENT and the Revolutionary War, and they continued to shape public opinion throughout the ratification process and the party-press period—newspaper expansion paralleled political expansion. Ultimately, it was the revolutionary era that first introduced the power of the press to the American public.

See also ALIEN AND SEDITION ACTS.

Further reading: Bernard B. Bailyn and John B. Hench, eds., *The Press and the American Revolution* (Worcester, Mass.: American Antiquarian Society, 1980), Richard D. Brown, *Knowledge Is Power: The Diffusion of Information in Early America, 1700–1865* (New York: Oxford University Press, 1989).

— Meghan A. Earl

Judiciary Act of 1789

Article III, Section 1 of the United States Constitution vested the federal judicial power in the SUPREME COURT and "in such inferior courts as the Congress may, from time to time, ordain and establish." The Judiciary Act of 1789 was the first attempt by Congress to establish inferior federal courts. President GEORGE WASHINGTON signed the act on September 24, 1789. The principal architects of the act were Senators Oliver Ellsworth of Connecticut, William Paterson of New Jersey, and Caleb Strong of Massachusetts. All three were LAWYERS. Ellsworth and Paterson would later serve on the Supreme Court, Ellsworth as the second chief justice. The act established a judicial structure very different from what we have today. The act provided for United States district courts, each presided over by a district judge, and for circuit courts, which, unlike circuit courts today, heard appeals from the district courts and acted as trial courts. The most important sorts of cases heard by the circuit courts as trial courts were cases between persons who resided in different states where the amount in controversy was greater than $500.

This sort of jurisdiction is called "diversity" jurisdiction: the parties are citizens of diverse states. Perhaps surprisingly, the courts were not at this time given what we call "federal question" jurisdiction: the jurisdiction to hear claims involving federal law, regardless of the home states of the parties. Under the 1789 act, the circuit courts were composed of three judges: the same district judge whose decision was being challenged and the two Supreme Court justices who had been assigned to the circuit. There were initially three circuits: Eastern, Middle, and Southern. Riding the Southern Circuit was especially onerous for the justices, and the elimination of the circuit system was one of the most popular features of the JUDICIARY ACT OF 1801. The 1801 act, however, was repealed the following year, and the practice resumed. Circuit riding did have its positive side. The appearance of the Supreme Court justices was a major event for most communities, an opportunity to socialize with an important federal official. JOHN MARSHALL, when on circuit duty in Raleigh, North Carolina, regularly played quoits with members of the community. Conversely, circuit riding enabled the justices to keep in touch with the country.

The Judiciary Act of 1789 also empowered the Supreme Court to hear appeals from state courts in certain cases involving federal law. Section 25 of the act, which granted this authority, was extremely controversial. States were resistant to the idea that the federal Supreme Court could reverse the judgments of the highest state courts. Nevertheless, the section stood.

Section 13 of the Judiciary Act of 1789, among other things, empowered the Supreme Court to issue writs of mandamus (court orders that state "we command") against public officers. This provision was held unconstitutional in *MARBURY V. MADISON* (1803).

The Judiciary Act of 1789 governed the federal judicial structure during virtually the whole of the early republican period. Its peculiarities both reflected and helped shape the legal culture of the early republic.

Further reading: Maeva Marcus, *The Origins of the Federal Judiciary: Essays on the Federal Judiciary Act of 1789* (New York: Oxford University Press, 1992); Wilfred Ritz, *Rewriting the History of the Judiciary Act of 1789: Exposing Myths, Challenging Premises and Using New Evidence* (Norman: University of Oklahoma Press, 1990).

— Lindsay Robertson

Judiciary Act of 1801

Perceived deficiencies in the federal judicial structure established by the JUDICIARY ACT OF 1789—particularly deficiencies relating to the circuit court—led the JOHN ADAMS administration to overhaul the system by means of a new judiciary act that became law on February 13, 1801. The chief innovation of the Judiciary Act of 1801 was the abolition of circuit court duty for the justices of the SUPREME COURT and the creation of six new, independent circuit courts presided over by 16 newly appointed circuit court judges. Other new positions created by the act included United States marshals, clerks, and attorneys.

The Act became the subject of political controversy almost immediately. THOMAS JEFFERSON and the DEMOCRATIC-REPUBLICAN PARTY had won the presidency and control of the House of Representatives in the ELECTION OF 1800, and President Adams moved to fill the new judicial offices with members of the outgoing FEDERALIST PARTY before turning over the reins of power. Adams also took the opportunity presented by the resignation of Chief Justice Oliver Ellsworth to appoint his secretary of state, JOHN MARSHALL, to the position of chief justice of the Supreme Court. "[T]hey have retired into the judiciary as a stronghold," Jefferson bitterly observed. "There the remains of federalism are to be preserved and fed from the treasury, and from that battery all the works of republicanism are to be beaten down and erased." The judges appointed under the Act were known as the "midnight judges," an allusion to their having been appointed in the closing hours of the outgoing administration.

The new Congress immediately set about orchestrating the repeal of the 1801 Judiciary Act. However, repeal was constitutionally tricky. Article III of the Constitution provided that federal judges would hold their offices "during good behaviour." This meant that the only way to oust a federal judge was by impeachment. The repeal debate centered on the question of whether Congress could get around this safeguard by abolishing the court over which the judge presided. If it could, then why couldn't Congress abolish the courts of all politically unpopular judges and reestablish the same courts with new judges? On the other hand, if it couldn't, then would any reform of the judicial system have to await the death or retirement of all affected federal judges? In the end, Congress decided that repeal was constitutional and in 1802 voted the 1801 act out of existence. The Supreme Court was soon slated to reconvene, however, and a majority feared that the Marshall Court would claim the power of judicial review (the power to examine legislation for constitutionality) and hold otherwise, precipitating a constitutional crisis. Accordingly, they passed companion legislation abolishing the August term of the Supreme Court, effectively postponing Supreme Court consideration of the constitutionality question until February 1803, by which time things had cooled down a bit. The Judiciary Act of 1801 thus passed into history.

— Lindsay Robertson

K

Kalb, Johann, baron de (1721–1780)

Baron de Kalb was a German-born officer in the French infantry who served with the CONTINENTAL ARMY in the REVOLUTIONARY WAR (1775–83). De Kalb began his military career in 1743 as a lieutenant in the French army and served with distinction in France's European wars. In 1769 the French government sent him to the British North American colonies to observe the relationship between the colonies and Great Britain. He sent back detailed reports, but when the British intercepted his communications, French officials ordered him home. De Kalb returned to the American colonies in 1777 after receiving a promise from SILAS DEANE that he would be given a command in the Continental army. He did not receive his own command, but de Kalb served admirably for the American cause, spending the harsh winter of 1777–78 in VALLEY FORGE with General GEORGE WASHINGTON and participating as second in command under the MARQUIS DE LAFAYETTE in an aborted raid on CANADA in 1780. De Kalb moved south in the spring of 1780, taking an active role in the southern campaign under the command of General HORATIO GATES. On August 16, 1780, the Americans fought against the British army commanded by CHARLES, LORD CORNWALLIS at CAMDEN, South Carolina. Although de Kalb had advised against the attack, he led his men into battle, where he was mortally wounded.

Further reading: A. E. Zucker, *General de Kalb: Lafayette's Mentor* (Chapel Hill: University of North Carolina Press, 1966).

—J. Brett Adams

King, Rufus (1755–1827)

Rufus King was an American political leader. Throughout his life he served as a state legislator, a member of Congress under the ARTICLES OF CONFEDERATION, a delegate to the CONSTITUTIONAL CONVENTION, a United States senator, a minister to England, and a presidential and vice presidential candidate. He was a member of the FEDERALIST PARTY, an ardent Anglophile, and a successful lawyer. King was at the center of many of the key issues of his day and an outspoken opponent of SLAVERY.

Born in Scarboro, Massachusetts (present-day Maine), King left home at the age of 12 to attend the Dummer Academy in South Byfield, Massachusetts, and later went to Harvard College, where he graduated in 1777. After Harvard he moved to Newburyport, Massachusetts, to read for the law. He received his license to practice law in 1780 and began practicing in Newburyport. King was a smart, articulate man and a good public speaker. He first joined the Massachusetts state legislature in 1783 and was reelected three times. From 1784 to 1786 he served in the Congress, where he introduced a resolution banning slavery in the Northwest Territory.

His personal life changed during this time, when he married Mary Alsop of New York in 1786. They moved to New York, but before he left Massachusetts he served as a delegate to the Constitutional Convention in Philadelphia in 1787. King went to the convention convinced that the Articles of Confederation could be saved, but he was converted to an ardent supporter of the new Constitution. After settling in New York, he served in the state legislature and in 1789 was chosen as one of New York's senators. King aligned himself with the Federalist Party and supported the economic goals of Treasury Secretary ALEXANDER HAMILTON. In 1791 he was appointed director of the FIRST BANK OF THE UNITED STATES. A year later he became minister to England, a post he held from 1796 to 1803. It was not the easiest time to be a diplomat. The FRENCH REVOLUTION (1789–1815) had led to war in Europe, and both France and Great Britain were interfering with American merchant vessels. Opinion in the United States was particularly negative toward the British because of their use of IMPRESSMENT, the forcible conscription of American sailors into the British navy. King could not stop impressment, but he provided a calming presence that helped ease tensions between the two nations.

Returning to the United States in 1803, King ran unsuccessfully for vice president on the Federalist ticket in 1804 and 1808. During the War of 1812 (1812–15) he was again elected to the Senate. In 1816 he ran for president against James Monroe and lost. In 1820 his longstanding opposition to slavery was again on display, when he argued against the Missouri Compromise. He believed that the issue of slavery had to be settled by compensated emancipation and colonization. In 1825 he once again served as minister to England at the request of President John Quincy Adams, but he soon fell ill and had to return home. Rufus King died in 1827, less than a year after his return.

See also FOREIGN AFFAIRS.

Further reading: Robert Ernst, *Rufus King: American Federalist* (Chapel Hill: University of North Carolina Press, 1968).

— J. Brett Adams

King's Mountain, Battle of (October 7, 1780)

The crushing defeat of LOYALIST forces at King's Mountain, South Carolina, was a turning point in the REVOLUTIONARY WAR (1775–83) in the South and a sobering reminder that the conflict with Britain was also a brutal civil war. With the capture of Savannah (December 29, 1778) and CHARLESTON (May 12, 1780) and the overwhelming victory at CAMDEN (August 16, 1780), the British commander CHARLES, LORD CORNWALLIS reasoned that the subjugation of North Carolina would secure the pacification of South Carolina and Georgia and, further, would lead to the invasion and conquest of Virginia. If that hotbed of revolution could be crushed, the rebellion might finally end. In preparation for the campaign, Cornwallis dispatched Major Patrick Ferguson into the northwestern region of South Carolina, where he was to recruit and train Loyalist soldiers, intimidate rebel sympathizers, and cover the left flank of the main army.

Having defeated a contingent of North Carolina militia, who took refuge over the western mountains, Ferguson issued a message that if these men did not cease their opposition to British arms, he would cross the mountains, hang the rebel leaders, and ravage the area with fire and sword. Failing altogether to browbeat the enemy into submission, Ferguson's words only served to bring together WHIG militia units and civilians determined to track him down and attack first. Two deserters from the American army warned Ferguson of the enemy pursuit, and though only 35 miles from the safety of the main British army, he chose to make a stand at King's Mountain.

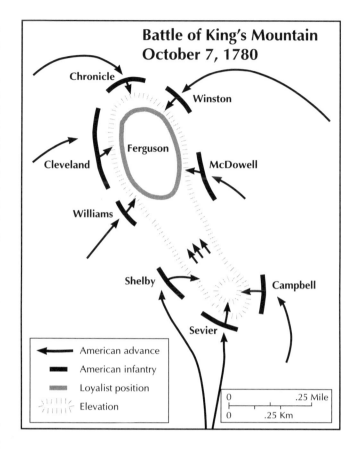

**Battle of King's Mountain
October 7, 1780**

American advance
American infantry
Loyalist position
Elevation

0 .25 Mile
0 .25 Km

The site was a curious choice for a seasoned veteran to have made. The Loyalists took a position on the widest portion of a bare, tapered ridge ranging from 60 to 120 yards wide, offering no readily available source of water, and whose summit was about 60 feet above the surrounding countryside. The slopes leading up to the ridge, however, were heavily wooded and provided excellent camouflage for an approaching enemy. Though time permitted and timber was readily available, Ferguson failed to reinforce his position with barricades. An elevated position also put Ferguson's men at a disadvantage, since firing downhill meant that they would often overshoot their attackers, while the rebels firing uphill could easily hit the Loyalists at long range and from under cover of the trees.

Of the combatants at King's Mountain, only Ferguson, a Scot, was not an American. Under his command were roughly 800 North and South Carolina Loyalist militia and 100 provincial infantry. Opposing them were approximately 940 men from the backcountry farms and villages of the Carolinas, Virginia, and Georgia, as well as hardened pioneers living in settlements west of the Appalachians in what is now Tennessee. Unlike Ferguson's troops, the Americans had no formal training or discipline, no uniforms, and no supply train. They wore hunting shirts with buckskin leggings and moccasins, and each man carried his own food, bedding, and spare ammunition. Experience fighting Indians on the FRONTIER had taught them savage, no-quarter warfare. The most significant difference between the two armies was the weaponry. Most of the Loyalists carried smooth-bore muskets that had an effective range of about 90 yards, while the "back watermen" and "mongrels," as Ferguson disparagingly called his adversaries, were armed with rifles. Though not fitted with bayonets or sturdy enough for use as a club in hand-to-hand fighting (as were muskets), these weapons had a killing range of 300 yards.

Ferguson's arrogant belief in the superiority of his men over undisciplined frontiersmen and militia—along with his apparent overestimation in the strength of his position—spelled his ruination. The American force divided into two columns, surrounded the ridge on both sides, and launched attacks from all directions. The Loyalists countered with bayonet charges down the hill, which was a difficult task on the wooded slopes. The Americans simply fell back, reloaded, and renewed their assault. As the Loyalists retreated back up the hill to the barren summit, they were easy targets for the enemy riflemen. As the encirclement of the ridge tightened, some Loyalists tried to surrender, but Ferguson twice cut down their white flags. Finally, in a desperate attempt to break through the enemy line, Ferguson led a mounted charge that resulted in his death and that of every man who followed him. When his second in command tried to capitulate, some of the attackers shouted, "TARLETON's quarter," and kept killing Loyalists even after the white flags were raised, in retribution for the massacre by British dragoons of Virginians who had surrendered at the Waxhaws. The Loyalists suffered 119 killed, 123 wounded, and 664 captured. Rebel losses were extremely light, with only 28 killed and 62 wounded.

The victory boosted flagging morale among the revolutionary forces, who had suffered a string of military defeats, and paved the way for the resurgence of the American army in the South. For the British, the defeat of the king's forces by rebel militia and civilians thoroughly intimidated would-be sympathizers of the Crown in the Carolinas and forced Cornwallis to delay the invasion of North Carolina.

Further reading: Henry Lumpkin, *From Savannah to Yorktown: The American Revolution in the South* (Columbia: University of South Carolina Press, 1981); Hank Messick, *King's Mountain: The Epic of the Blue Ridge "Mountain Men" in the American Revolution* (Boston: Little, Brown, 1976).

— Rita M. Broyles

Knox, Henry (1750–1806)

Henry Knox was one of GEORGE WASHINGTON's most competent officers in the REVOLUTIONARY WAR (1775–83). Knox quickly moved through the ranks to become major general. Knox's father, a ship master, died impoverished, and thus 12-year-old Henry became the sole provider for a family of eight working in the Boston bookstore of Wharton and Cornhill. He opened his own bookstore on his 21st birthday. Although most of his bookstore customers consisted of British officers and their wives, he strongly identified himself with the American colonies rather than Great Britain. Far from being bookish, Henry Knox was interested in the military and joined the Boston militia company. At the BOSTON MASSACRE (March 5, 1770) he tried to restrain a British officer from firing on the mob. Despite a hunting accident where he lost two fingers of his left hand, he joined the Boston Grenadier Corps in 1772 as second in command under Captain Joseph Pierce. While serving in the regiment he studied military science, specializing in artillery warfare and logistics. In 1774 he married Lucy Flucker, the daughter of the royal secretary of Massachusetts.

At the outbreak of the Revolutionary War, he left Boston with his family and volunteered for service in the newly formed CONTINENTAL ARMY. Knox advised that fortifications be constructed around Boston, including Bunker Hill, thus attracting the attention of JOHN ADAMS and George Washington. Consequently, the CONTINENTAL CONGRESS appointed him colonel of his own artillery regiment in 1775. His heavy artillery participated in the siege of Boston until the British evacuated the city. Afterward, he was stationed at the Battery in New York City but had to retreat when SIR WILLIAM HOWE seized the city in the summer of 1776. Knox again saw action in the BATTLES OF TRENTON AND PRINCETON (December 26, 1776, and January 3, 1777, respectively) and the BATTLE OF BRANDYWINE (September 11, 1777), and spent the winter camp in VALLEY FORGE (1777–78) with Washington.

Knox was made major general in 1782 and became the chairman of a committee of officers to draft a petition to Congress that demanded payment of their salaries and future pensions for the soldiers. When Congress denied these demands, a mutinous spirit spread among the officers, but Knox made great efforts to calm down the unruly soldiers. Congress reconsidered the proposal and granted it in 1783. Learning from this experience, and to foster loyalty in the officer corps, Knox founded the ORDER OF CINCINNATI in 1783. After the British evacuated New York City (November 24, 1783), he triumphantly led his troops into the city and took his final leave from the army.

Congress elected Knox secretary of war in 1785. Washington appointed Knox to the same position after the formation of the United States government in 1789. Knox helped to establish the United States Navy in 1794. In the same year he retired from public office.

Further reading: Noah Callahan, *Henry Knox: General Washington's General* (New York: Rinehart, 1958).

— Dirk Voss

Kościuszko, Tadeusz (1746–1817)

Champion of independence on two continents, Tadeusz (sometimes Thaddeus) Kościuszko was born in Poland. Briefly educated by an uncle and at the Jesuit College at Brest, he soon began an extensive study of military science. After graduating from the Royal Military School in Warsaw in 1765, Kościuszko went on to the École Militaire in Paris. He immersed himself in the study of artillery and military engineering. He returned to Poland in 1774 and found the Polish army to be a shadow of its former self. A failed courtship to the daughter of a nobleman added to Kościuszko's discontent.

The REVOLUTIONARY WAR (1775–83) provided the restless Kościuszko with an opportunity to use his military skills. The rhetoric of REPUBLICANISM also fit nicely with the liberal philosophy he had been exposed to while in France. With borrowed money, Kościuszko traveled to America, where in October 1776 he received a commission as colonel of engineers in the CONTINENTAL ARMY. Kościuszko's counsel was not followed at FORT TICONDEROGA, which the British recaptured on July 6, 1777. However, during the campaign that led to the British surrender at SARATOGA (October 17, 1777) Kościuszko oversaw the fortifications and battlefield placement, contributing significantly to the American victory. Kościuszko continued to direct the successful construction of fortifications, most notably at West Point, New York, and CHARLESTON, South Carolina. After the war, Kościuszko was granted American citizenship, land, and the rank of brigadier general.

He returned to Poland in 1784 to lead a peasant army in the quest for Polish independence. Despite significant victories, the army was defeated and Kościuszko was forced into exile. Before his death in October 1817, in a final demonstration of liberty, he freed the serfs on his Polish estate. Kościuszko's will instructed that his Ohio property be sold and the proceeds directed toward the founding of a school for AFRICAN AMERICANS in Newark, New Jersey.

Further reading: Miecislaus Haiman, *Kościuszko in the American Revolution* (Boston: Gregg Press, 1972).

— Jay R. Dew

L

labor and labor movements

During the revolutionary and early national periods there were two basic categories of labor: unfree and free. Unfree labor was performed by a person who was bound by deed or contract to work for an individual for a set period of years or for life. In free labor, a worker might or might not have had a contract, but he felt free to leave employment at any time. The ideals and experiences of revolution challenged unfree labor and put a premium on free labor. However, even within free labor, there were changes in the ECONOMY that altered the conditions of employment and led to the first stirring of an American labor movement.

In the mid-18th century there were several different types of unfree labor. First and most important was SLAVERY. By 1750 AFRICAN-AMERICAN slavery was a well-established fact in North America. Slaves comprised about one-fifth of the population. Although most slaves worked in AGRICULTURE and lived in colonies south of Pennsylvania, slaves could be found in every colony and appeared in almost all aspects of the economy. As a labor system, slavery had several distinguishing characteristics. First it was perpetual; a slave served for life. Second, slave status was handed down from generation to generation through the mother. Third, it was uncompensated. The master either inherited or purchased the slave, but he did not pay him or her a wage. Finally, slavery depended upon coercion. Without payment, ultimately violence, or the threat of violence, had to be used to get the individual to work. The ideals of the AMERICAN REVOLUTION and the disruption caused by the REVOLUTIONARY WAR (1775–83) threatened to end slavery. Northern states gradually abolished the institution during the early national period. Most southern states flirted with this idea but did not pursue it. Starting in the 1790s, the southern economy became even more tied to slavery. By 1820 most slaves in the North had been freed, while the South had started to identify itself with its peculiar institution.

Another form of bound labor involved European immigrants. Indentured servants signed contracts to work for a set number of years to compensate for their passage to North America. This form of labor had predominated in the earliest years of settlement in the Chesapeake. While slaves replaced many indentured servants in the tobacco fields of the late 17th century, this form of labor continued to exist. During the 18th century, in addition to the traditional indentured servant, Great Britain shipped thousands of convicted criminals to the colonies. In lieu of punishment in England, these individuals were bound to service for several years. The 18th century also saw another form of contract labor emerge—the redemptioners. Unlike an indentured servant, who signed his indenture contract in Europe, a redemptioner promised to pay for passage once he or she arrived in the colonies. Unable to redeem the price of passage, the individual signed a contract in America to work to discharge the debt. This form of bound labor was prevalent among Germans.

These three forms of bound labor—indentured servitude, convict, and redemptioner—were interrupted by the

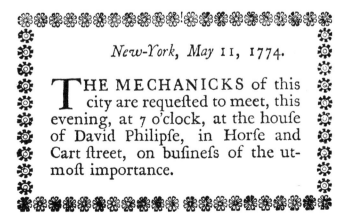

New-York, May 11, 1774.

THE MECHANICKS of this city are requeſted to meet, this evening, at 7 o'clock, at the houſe of David Philipſe, in Horſe and Cart ſtreet, on buſineſs of the utmoſt importance.

A handbill announcing a meeting of New York's "mechanicks" *(Library of Congress)*

199

Revolutionary War and virtually disappeared during the early national period. Indentured servitude and redemptioning seemed to violate the REPUBLICANISM of the Revolution. One New York newspaper reported in 1784 that "the traffick of white people . . . is contrary to . . . the idea of liberty this country has so happily established." But pragmatic circumstances also had an effect. Great Britain passed legislation against indentures in the 1790s, and the wars in Europe triggered by the FRENCH REVOLUTION (1789–1815) all but stopped the redemptioner trade. The British had halted the export of convicts to the colonies in 1776 but reinstated it after the TREATY OF PARIS (1783). By the late 1780s, however, they stopped sending criminals to North America and shipped them to Australia instead.

Another form of bound labor, apprenticeship, was for youths. In exchange for an education in a trade, a young person, usually in the teens, would agree to work without payment for seven years or until reaching the age of 21. The employer usually agreed to provide room and board and the rudiments of EDUCATION. Most apprentices were male, although some young women also signed apprentice papers. Apprentices could also sign indentures for farming or seamanship, as well as for a skilled craft. Throughout the 18th century it was difficult to keep apprentices on the job. BENJAMIN FRANKLIN ran away from his apprenticeship as much because he argued with his master (his brother) as because he sought opportunity elsewhere. By the early national period the institution was being challenged further. Employers, seeking to minimize costs, began to hire apprentices instead of skilled workers, pay them by the day, and abdicate their other responsibilities for the youth. Apprentices, in other words, were becoming a form of free labor.

A final form of bound labor, one that remained unchallenged in the period, was family labor. Technically, although no contract was ever signed, sons and daughters were bound to their parents until they were 21 years of age. The family farm depended on such labor. Parents often hired out their children to others beyond the immediate family, either through apprenticeship or through informal agreements. Rural households frequently included an adolescent who was not directly related to the family.

Most adult white Americans worked as free labor, with no binding contract. Farm labor might depend on some form of exchange of work between two individuals, although cash payments became more common in the 19th century. Similarly, laborers and tradesmen often signed on for the season or month in the 18th century. By 1800 they more frequently hired themselves by the day or sometimes by the week. It was not even unusual to see someone listed as laboring only a part of a day in an account ledger. Maritime workers, however, continued to sign contracts for a voyage.

There was no national labor movement during this period, although some workers began to organize and occasionally there were strikes. Skilled workers were the most likely to organize. During the early republic there was a growing distance between master and journeyman among ARTISANS. Masters began to expand production and become more entrepreneur than craftsman. To push profits, masters not only hired more apprentices without fully training them, they also lowered the journeyman's wage and sought other ways to cut costs. Journeymen, like shoemakers and tailors, organized their own associations to negotiate wages and working conditions. When they could not agree with their employers, they might "turn out"—go on strike. Philadelphia shoemakers, for example, went on strike in the fall of 1805 to gain control of the workshop. They met with a hostile reception, and in a famous court case they were convicted of forming a conspiracy to restrain trade. Protests that the masters had colluded to lower wages fell on deaf ears.

The labor movement struggled before 1820. Worker "turn outs" were sporadic. When they occurred at all, they most likely took place in early spring, when there was the greatest demand for labor, or in the fall, before employment became scarce. But beyond a few local journeymen's associations, there was no larger labor organization. Laborers would have to wait until the late 1820s before a national workingman's movement would develop.

See also ABOLITION AND ANTISLAVERY; IMMIGRATION.

Further reading: Marilyn C. Baseler, *"Asylum for Mankind:" America, 1607–1800* (Ithaca, N.Y.: Cornell University Press, 1998); Paul A. Gilje, *The Road to Mobocracy: Popular Disorder in New York City, 1763–1834* (Chapel Hill: University of North Carolina Press, 1987); Paul A. Gilje and Howard B. Rock, eds. *Keepers of the Revolution: New Yorkers at Work in the Early Republic* (Ithaca, N.Y.: Cornell University Press, 1992); Ronald Schultz, *The Republic of Labor: Philadelphia Artisans and the Politics of Class, 1720–1830* (New York: Oxford University Press, 1993).

Lafayette, Marie-Joseph-Paul-Yves-Roche-Gilbert du Motier, marquis de (1757–1834)

The marquis de Lafayette served as a major general in the REVOLUTIONARY WAR (1775–83) and as a commander of the French army in the early stages of the FRENCH REVOLUTION (1789–1815). Lafayette was born in Chavaniac, France, and by the time he was 12, Lafayette's parents and grandfather had died, leaving him a very wealthy orphan. At 14 he joined the royal army, and at 16 he married a relative of King Louis XVI. Lafayette first heard of the AMERICAN REVOLUTION at a dinner party in August 1775. Sympathetic to the cause and seeking adventure, Lafayette made plans without the king's permission to sail with several other French officers to North America. They arrived in Charleston on June 13, 1777, and traveled directly to Philadelphia, where Lafayette volunteered his service, without pay, to the CONTINENTAL CONGRESS. Due to his noble rank, Congress commissioned Lafayette, at 19 and with little military experience, a major general.

Lafayette became a member of General GEORGE WASHINGTON's staff, and the two men began a lifelong friendship. Lafayette was wounded in the leg at the BATTLE OF BRANDYWINE (September 11, 1777). In early 1778 General HORATIO GATES obtained Congressional support for an invasion of CANADA, and Congress chose Lafayette as the expedition's commander. Lafayette headed to Albany, New York, in February to begin preparation, but he found only a small band of poorly clothed and equipped soldiers whom Congress had not paid in months. Lafayette sent word to both Congress and Washington that such forces could not attack a well-defended Canada without sustaining massive loses. Congress canceled the expedition, and Lafayette returned to Washington's staff at VALLEY FORGE (1777–78). In June 1778 Lafayette and other junior officers suggested to Washington that the CONTINENTAL ARMY should attack the rear of the British army in New Jersey to see if a more general battle was possible. Washington agreed and offered the command to Major General CHARLES LEE, who at first rejected the offer, believing the plan to be futile. Washington then gave the command to Lafayette. When Lafayette began his advance in late June 1778, Lee changed his mind about the appointment and urged Lafayette to resign the command, since Lee was the more experienced officer. Lafayette agreed, and in the subsequent BATTLE OF MONMOUTH (June 28, 1778), Lee retreated three times. After this battle, Washington sent Lafayette to Rhode Island to help the forces fighting the entrenched British at Newport. Lafayette made it to Newport in time to participate in the BATTLE OF RHODE ISLAND (August 29, 1778) and to direct the retreat of 1,000 men and their supplies that had become trapped by a quickly advancing British attack.

With the end of the 1778 campaigns, Congress granted Lafayette's request for a furlough so he could return to France. Lafayette spent most of his furlough attempting to secure more aid from his government. His efforts paid off, and in early July 1780 Washington received 12 battalions of French troops, along with the return of Lafayette. In the spring of 1781, Washington dispatched Lafayette to Virginia to join FREDERICK VON STEUBEN in his push to stop the British invasion of the South. By early fall, Lafayette and von Steuben's forces had pursued General CHARLES, LORD CORNWALLIS's troops into YORKTOWN. The British surrendered on October 19, 1781. With the main fighting at an end, Congress granted Lafayette's wishes to return to France.

During the early 1780s, Lafayette returned to American once for a tour initiated by Washington, and he assisted THOMAS JEFFERSON who served as American minister to France in the 1780s. Back on his family estate, Lafayette supported the rights of Protestants in France and joined with the Third Estate to form the National Assembly in the summer of 1789. In August the assembly named him commander of the National Guard, and Lafayette saved Louis XVI and Marie Antoinette from a Paris mob in October. When France declared war on Austria in 1792, Lafayette commanded the French army until Jacobins took control of Paris politics and replaced him. Lafayette then fled to Belgium to avoid the Reign of Terror, but Austrians captured Lafayette and held him prisoner until 1797, when NAPOLEON BONAPARTE's forces freed him. When Lafayette returned to France in 1800, he found his property confiscated. Lafayette spent most of the rest of his life restoring his estate, La Grange, which became a pilgrimage site for revolutionary thinkers. Lafayette continued to support revolutionary causes, playing a leading role in France's Revolution of 1830 and corresponding with revolutionary agents in Italy. He returned to the United States in 1824, touring the country as a living revolutionary hero. He died in Paris on May 20, 1834.

See also FRENCH ALLIANCE.

Further reading: Olivier Bernier, *Lafayette: Hero of Two Worlds* (New York: E. P. Dutton, 1983).

— Heather Clemmer

land riots

Between the mid-1750s and the early 1800s, a series of land riots erupted in the northern colonies/states from New York to New Hampshire and Maine. FRONTIER settlers, tenant farmers, and proprietary landlords disputed land claims, which led to these uprisings. Lands in frontier Maine, the Hudson Valley of New York, and the disputed area between New York and New Hampshire (which eventually became Vermont), all saw organized efforts by settlers and tenants to challenge land claims and protect their property.

The way in which the land was divided in the Hudson Valley made that system unique as compared with other regions in the colonies. Manors and patents divided the land in such a way as to resemble a medieval tenant system that did not allow for eventual ownership by the occupants. Moreover, by the 1750s, there were serious questions as to whether many of these tracts of land had been obtained legally or through fraud. Indian claims to the same land—as well as the disputed boundary between New England lands and New York lands—also added confusion and tension to the situation in the region. The reluctance of some of the more prominent families, such as the Livingstons and Van Rensselaers, to sell their lands to the tenants (or at least modify some of the harsh terms of the leases) caused two major uprisings by tenant farmers, one in 1755 and the other in 1766. Both of these disturbances were caused by the sudden eviction of tenants by the landlords. In each case, rioters would attack the property of the landlord, destroying crops, tearing down buildings, or in some cases, displacing new tenants and replacing them with the original occupants. Landlords acted swiftly to put down these riots, usually calling out the militia or local law enforcement. In the case of the 1766 riots, British troops were utilized. The tenant riots in the Hudson Valley were put down as quickly as they started, and the end result solidified the standing of the landlords.

Both New York and New Hampshire claimed the territory that would eventually become Vermont until 1764, when the Crown ruled in favor of New York claims. Before the ruling, however, both colonies had granted some of the same lands to settlers. The unrest that shook the region after 1764 stemmed from New Hampshire grantees who feared that submitting to New York authority would cost them their land or, at the least, increase their payments for rents and taxes. Many of the insurgents came from the Green Mountains in Vermont; hence, the insurgents became known as the GREEN MOUNTAIN BOYS, who were led by ETHAN ALLEN. This movement was much more organized than the Hudson Valley riots. In fact, in 1772 and 1773, the resistance became far more organized, and New Hampshire grantees formed committees, organized militia units, held courts, and tried and punished those whom they considered to be enemies of the movement. Sometimes, authorities who tried to enforce New York laws found themselves jailed and even lashed by members of the Green Mountain Boys. Most of the violence, however, was acted out on property rather than persons, in the form of crops and buildings being destroyed. By 1775–76, New York was in the throes of the Revolutionary cause, and the Green Mountain movement managed to establish the independent state of Vermont.

In Maine the process of settlement was similar to that of New York and Vermont. Before, during, and immediately after the REVOLUTIONARY WAR (1775–83), Maine saw a huge influx of settlers from southern New England who were looking for land to farm. These settlers improved the land, established towns, and developed an evangelical style of worship that ran counter to the established Congregational church. Resistance began in the 1760s and died down during the war, and then sprang up again in the 1780s and 1790s when proprietors tried to reestablish their land claims and instill a social and religious order that fit with their idea of democratic society. The insurgents in Maine called themselves Liberty Men, after the SONS OF LIBERTY from the RESISTANCE MOVEMENT (1764–75) to British imperial regulation. The proprietors called them White Indians, on account of their dress during attacks on the proprietors' property and agents. Resistance on the Maine frontier did not have a single climactic event or moment. Rather, the threat of resistance would simmer when a proprietor pressed his land claims or tried to have land boundaries surveyed and redefined. When this occurred, settlers turned their attention to committee meetings, petitions, militia patrols, and physical threats to land agents or potential traitors within the Liberty Men. This pattern of resistance in Maine lasted well into the 1810s, finally subsiding around 1820.

All of the land riots that occurred from the 1750s to the 1820s shared certain characteristics. In most cases, the violence was against property or agents of the great proprietors rather than against the proprietor himself. Also, the resistance often took the form of extralegal meetings and alternative government organization (although the tenant riots in the Hudson Valley were an exception), which typically mirrored the revolutionary direct-action organizations. Lastly, the land riots represented a continuation of the struggle to clarify the meaning of the AMERICAN REVOLUTION regarding property, central power of government, and the legitimacy of extralegal crowd action that lasted well into the early republic.

See also RIOTS.

Further reading: Edward Countryman, "'Out of the Bounds of the Law:' Northern Land Rioters in the Eighteenth Century," in *The American Revolution: Explorations in the History of American Radicalism*, ed. Alfred F. Young (DeKalb: Northern Illinois University Press, 1974); Alan Taylor, *Liberty Men and Great Proprietors: The Revolutionary Settlement on the Maine Frontier, 1760–1820* (Chapel Hill: University of North Carolina Press, 1990).

— Jeffrey A. Davis

Laurens, Henry (1724–1792)

Merchant, planter, and statesman, Henry Laurens was born in Charleston, South Carolina, in 1724. His education was not classical but met the requirements of a colonial-merchant society. By the 1760s he had emerged as a leading merchant in Charleston. His firm primarily managed the ventures of investors and exporters of rice, indigo, slaves, and indentured servants. Laurens grew increasingly uncomfortable with the SLAVE TRADE, and by 1763 he ended his direct involvement with it. In 1776, corresponding with a son who served as an aid to GEORGE WASHINGTON, Laurens wrote, "I abhor SLAVERY." Such comments would be resurrected by abolitionists later, even though

Laurens did not free his own slaves. In the 1790s, well after the inspired letter to his son, Laurens continued to hold around 300 slaves.

Laurens turned away from the merchant life to focus on planting. He eventually controlled three plantations in South Carolina and two in Georgia, as well as significant land holdings in the South Carolina backcountry. Laurens's involvement in public affairs increased as well. He served in a variety of local and church offices, including the colonial assembly.

The RESISTANCE MOVEMENT (1764–75), which Laurens generally supported, affected Laurens personally. During the STAMP ACT (1765) crisis, his home was invaded by radicals searching for stamped paper. During the uproar over the TOWNSHEND DUTIES (1767), however, British customs officers seized two of Laurens's ships. Laurens wrote pamphlets criticizing the royal officials, including *A Representation of Facts* (1767). In 1775 Laurens was elected to the first provincial congress of South Carolina and later the president of the Council of Safety. In June 1777 he was chosen to be a delegate to the CONTINENTAL CONGRESS. In November he became president of the Congress, succeeding JOHN HANCOCK. Laurens held that office for over a year, presiding over the fits and starts of the early revolutionary government. His relationship with Congress grew strained at times, and Laurens frequently allowed himself to be drawn into factional disputes. He eventually resigned the presidency because of a growing lack of support and confidence.

Laurens was appointed envoy to the Dutch to negotiate a commerce treaty in 1780. He was captured en route, however, by the British navy off the coast of Newfoundland. As the British boarded the *Mercury,* Laurens attempted to scuttle his papers, which were retrieved and used against him in charges of treason. Held prisoner in the Tower of London from October 1780 to December 1781, Laurens was eventually released in a prisoner exchange for CHARLES, LORD CORNWALLIS, who had surrendered to the Americans at YORKTOWN (October, 19, 1781).

The imprisonment took its toll on Laurens's health, and he began to withdraw from public life. Notable exceptions included his contribution to the TREATY OF PARIS (1783) negotiated by JOHN ADAMS, BENJAMIN FRANKLIN, and JOHN JAY in 1782. Laurens was appointed to the CONSTITUTIONAL CONVENTION but chose not to serve. He spent the final years of his life attending to his estates and repairing the damage caused by the war. His will directed that his body be cremated, an unusual practice at that time. He died on December 8, 1792.

Further reading: David Duncan Wallace, *The Life of Henry Laurens* (New York: Knickerbocker Press, 1915).

— Jay R. Dew

lawyers

Law was the profession of most of the leading political figures of the early republican United States. Indeed, the "nation of laws" was almost a "nation of lawyers." More than one-third of the members of the First Congress were members of the bar, as were four of the first five presidents of the United States (JOHN ADAMS, THOMAS JEFFERSON, JAMES MADISON, and James Monroe).

The large number of lawyers in the early republic, which increased dramatically during the Jacksonian era, resulted in part from the relative ease with which one could enter the profession. The College of William and Mary, at Thomas Jefferson's prompting, established the nation's first dedicated law professorship in 1779, and the first law school in the United States was founded in 1784 (in Litchfield, Connecticut, by Litchfield lawyer Tapping Reeve). But institutional learning was not the means by which most attorneys learned their trade. Instead, most "read" law in the offices of practicing lawyers, copying documents, serving process, and drafting simple forms. The quality of the instruction these aspiring lawyers received depended on the knowledge and attentiveness of the sponsor. Moreover, apprentices were subject to abuse: Jefferson complained that he had "ever seen that the services expected in return [for instruction] have been more than the instructions have been worth." Nevertheless, by the Jacksonian era, reading law was almost universal. Some aspiring lawyers might supplement time in a practicing attorney's office with formal institutional instruction. JOHN MARSHALL, for example, spent six weeks studying law at the College of William and Mary, much of which he appears to have devoted to pining for his soon-to-be wife, Mary Ambler. Most, however, did not. Apprentices supplemented their office work with outside reading. The standard texts were English. Sir WILLIAM BLACKSTONE's *Commentaries on the Laws of England* was the most popular. Other popular English legal treatises included works by Sir Edward Coke and Henry Bracton.

The completion of an apprenticeship, or an academic program, did not guarantee one the right to practice law. The practice of law was rather tightly regulated under the British Empire, and after the REVOLUTIONARY WAR (1775–83), licensing restrictions continued. Admission to practice before the courts of a particular state was a matter of state law and requirements varied widely, even among courts within a particular state. In 1783, for example, the supreme court of New York required that practitioners have three years apprenticeship experience, be of good moral character, and pass an examination. In 1797 the court increased the required years of apprenticeship to seven, but allowed that four of these might be satisfied by years devoted to the study of the classics. Most courts also required applicants for admission to demonstrate they were of good moral character and loyal to the state.

Once admitted to practice, lawyers had to prove themselves in order to win clients. Interestingly, in addition to its many other profound effects, the AMERICAN REVOLUTION had an enormous impact on the style of legal advocacy. Most cases today are won by lawyers who understand precedent—past instances in which the courts have considered the questions they are arguing—and are able to persuade that court that the same or a different rule ought now to apply. In other words, success at the practice of law depends on one's ability to outresearch one's opponent. Before independence, lawyers succeeded by mastering the precedential decisions handed down by English courts. In the courts of the new states, however, references by lawyers to decisions of English judges were not always well received. Lawyers consequently turned more to creative analogy, common sense, and references to the classics in arguing cases. This tendency is evident in the SUPREME COURT opinions of John Marshall, who issued his most important pronouncements, including *MARBURY V. MADISON*, with barely a nod to precedent. The move away from reliance on precedent further democratized the legal profession in that young lawyers with limited library access but common sense could still win cases.

Despite their contributions to the cause of independence, lawyers were not the most popular class in the United States. This lack of popularity resulted in part from the perception that lawyers were part of a conspiracy to manipulate the common law. The common law, which evolved in England and which applied in all of the new states, was judge-made law. When parties appeared before a court with a dispute, the court would look not to acts of the legislature but, rather, to precedent and the court's own sense of fairness in deciding the case. A complicated vocabulary developed to explain the court's reasoning, as did an elaborate system of writs and motions that had to be filed to initiate a lawsuit and keep it going. Legal education consisted in large part of learning the vocabulary and procedures. Complexity was increased by the fact that much of the terminology was in Latin or Legal French. Law was thus largely inaccessible to nonlawyers, and this seemed to many flatly antidemocratic. In the revolution's immediate aftermath, a movement was started to abandon the common law in favor of the civil-law system embraced by most European countries. In civil-law countries, the law is all written down, and nonlawyers as easily as lawyers can look it up in a civil code. Opposition from the bar—the members of which had devoted long years to mastering the complexities of the common law—and from many who saw advantages to the common law system (in particular, that life was too complicated to cover all situations in a written code) defeated the move to abandon it. The United States would remain a common-law country, its dispute-resolution mechanisms largely inaccessible to nonlawyers.

Further reading: Robert F. Boden, *The Colonial Bar and the American Revolution* (Chicago: Callaghan, 1976); Anton-Hermann Chroust, *The Rise of the Legal Profession,* vols. 1–2 (Norman: University of Oklahoma Press, 1965); Gerald W. Gawalt, *The Promise of Power: The Emergence of the Legal Profession in Massachusetts, 1760–1840* (Westport, Conn.: Greenwood Press, 1979); A. G. Roeber, *Faithful Magistrates and Republican Lawyers: Creators of Virginia Legal Culture, 1680–1810* (Chapel Hill: University of North Carolina Press, 1981).

— Lindsay Robertson

Lee, Ann (Mother Ann) (1736–1784)

Ann Lee, also known as Mother Ann, brought the Shaker religious sect to America from Britain in 1774. She was born in Manchester, England, on February 29, 1736. Although she came to be known as Ann Lee, her family name was most likely Lees. In her early 20s, Lee joined the Shaking QUAKERS, or SHAKERS, religious group in 1758, which had been founded in Manchester only 11 years before. The sect derived its name from the shaking and dancing its members exhibited while engaged in worship. Shakers believed in both the imminence of the second coming of Christ as well as in the public confession of sin.

Although she married Abraham Standerin on January 5, 1762, Lee became increasingly disillusioned with the idea of marriage. She promoted celibacy because she felt that sexual relations between men and women negatively influenced their spiritual work. Inspired by a vision, Lee persuaded her husband, brother, and others to travel to America and settle in an area called Niskayuna (later called Watervliet), near Albany, New York. Among the Shakers, Mother Ann came to be considered the second appearance of Christ, the female embodiment of God's dual nature.

During the REVOLUTIONARY WAR (1775–83), Lee and her fellow Shakers drew much criticism for their pacifist beliefs and for their refusal to sign oaths of allegiance. Revolutionaries accused the Shakers of being pro-British sympathizers; in fact, Lee was briefly imprisoned in 1780 for high treason. She toured New England from 1781 to 1783, preaching her beliefs to the Shaker faithful. Returning home, Mother Ann Lee died in 1784.

See also RELIGION.

Further reading: Stephen J. Stein, *The Shaker Experience in America: A History of the United Society of Believers* (New Haven, Conn.: Yale University Press, 1992).

— Linda English

Lee, Arthur (1740–1792)

Arthur Lee was a voice for colonial grievances in the years leading up to the REVOLUTIONARY WAR (1775–83) and a diplomat who attempted to secure European support for the United States during the war. At age 11 Lee's parents died and his eldest brother sent him to England to attend Eton College and then Edinburgh University for training in MEDICINE. Lee returned to Virginia in 1766 with the intention of starting a medical practice, but his interest in imperial issues led Lee back to England in 1768. As tensions between the government in London and the colonists in North America grew, Lee began writing petitions to Parliament and articles for London papers detailing colonial grievances. He also corresponded with colonists, especially his brother RICHARD HENRY LEE and the Boston radical SAMUEL ADAMS, concerning the state of English politics, and providing analysis of the colonial situation from the view in London. For his efforts in support of the colonies, Massachusetts in 1770 made him a substitute agent for the colony in London (BENJAMIN FRANKLIN was Massachusetts's primary agent at the time). He also became a spokesman for the FIRST CONTINENTAL CONGRESS in December 1774, presenting the Congress's petition to Parliament.

When Franklin returned to America in March 1775, Lee became the London agent for the Massachusetts House of Representatives and the Assembly of New Jersey. When fighting broke out in 1775, Lee became an informant for the SECOND CONTINENTAL CONGRESS's Committee of Secret Correspondence. In 1776 Lee found himself again working with Benjamin Franklin; this time the two men were emissaries to the French court, along with SILAS DEANE. Deane, Franklin, and Lee worked to convince France to assist the Americans in their fight. While these negotiations continued, Congress sent Lee to Spain in February 1777 to elicit support for American independence. While Lee did not receive open recognition, Charles III agreed to send secret funds and supplies to America. In May 1777 Lee set off for Berlin to attempt a similar agreement with Frederick the Great, but this trip proved fruitless and Lee returned to France. As negotiations with the French intensified after the American victory at SARATOGA (October 17, 1777), tension mounted between Silas Deane and Lee. Lee warned Congress that Deane was only in Europe seeking a private fortune and not the common good. As a result, Congress recalled Deane a month after the treaty with France was signed in February 1778. After returning to North America, Deane began a crusade to have Lee recalled. Deane claimed Lee had leaked information to the British about the treaty with France before it had been finalized. Congress responded by recalling Lee in September 1779. The recall was not the end of Lee's political career. He was also appointed one of four commissioners to form a peace treaty with the IROQUOIS in 1784, leading to the cession of 30 million acres to the new American government. He served in Congress from 1782 to 1785 and on the Board of Treasury until its elimination by the Constitution in 1789. Lee then returned to Virginia to practice law and died December 12, 1792, at his estate in Middlesex County.

See also FRENCH ALLIANCE; FOREIGN AFFAIRS.

Further reading: Louis W. Potts, *Arthur Lee, a Virtuous Revolutionary* (Baton Rouge: Louisiana State University Press, 1981).

— Heather Clemmer

Lee, Charles (1732–1782)

Charles Lee was a controversial military figure whose loyalty to the American cause became suspect because of his actions at the BATTLE OF MONMOUTH (June 28, 1778), which led to his court-martial and dismissal from the army. Lee was born in Cheshire, England, and began his military career when he was 18. He fought in the French and Indian War (1754–63) and was promoted to the rank of major in 1760. In 1762 Lee joined Brigadier General JOHN BURGOYNE in Portugal and was made a colonel by the Portuguese government. When Lee returned to England, the English army retired him from active service. With no prospect of military advancement, Lee decided to seek employment in the Polish army, where he courted the favor of King Stanislaus Poniatowski. After learning of his mother's death in 1766, Lee returned to England with a letter from King Poniatowski recommending that GEORGE III find Lee an army appointment. George III refused, adding to Lee's growing resentment of what he saw as monarchical tyranny and leading Lee to return to the Polish army, where Poniatowski made him a major general.

Due to illness, Lee returned to England in 1770, but his restless nature and political sentiments brought him to the American colonies in August 1773. Lee resumed a friendship with GEORGE WASHINGTON, whom he had served with under General Edward Braddock. He also wrote a number of anonymous essays for colonial papers and corresponded with THOMAS JEFFERSON and SAMUEL ADAMS, emphasizing the need for bold action to protect the rights of British subjects. In 1776 the CONTINENTAL CONGRESS, desperately in need of experienced officers, commissioned Lee as a major general, making him the third-highest-ranking officer in the CONTINENTAL ARMY.

After the British evacuated Boston, Washington sent Lee to New York City to gauge the Continental army's ability to hold the city. After surveying the city, Lee created a plan that called for extensive fortification. As Washington's troops made their way to New York, Congress ordered Lee to take charge of the southern military department, especially the organization of defenses for Charleston Harbor. On June 28, 1776, Lee's troops repulsed an attack by British ships on Sullivan's Island, leading the British to set sail for northern harbors in July. Upon Washington's insistence, Lee was recalled to New York, where he repeatedly disregarded Washington's commands to cross the Hudson and join Washington's army in New Jersey. When Lee finally did cross the river in December 1776, the British captured him at a boardinghouse. While a prisoner, Lee offered Admiral LORD RICHARD HOWE and General Sir WILLIAM HOWE his services as a mediator between Great Britain and America. He promised the two men that, upon his release, he would use his influence with American leaders to bring about peace negotiations.

Released in April 1778, Lee did attempt to push for peace before Congress, arousing some suspicion regarding his loyalty to the American cause. Despite the suspicion, Lee returned to duty and Washington placed him in charge of the advance corps in what would be the Battle of Monmouth. During the battle, Lee ordered his forces to withdraw to more secure locations three times. When Washington arrived on the scene, he chastised Lee verbally for retreating and ordered the troops to stand their ground. The British abandoned the field, but Lee felt he had been right in ordering the retreats and demanded a court-martial to clear his name and show Washington's error. Lee's plan backfired; he was court-martialed and suspended from command for one year, a ruling Congress supported when Lee appealed it. Lacking vindication for his action, Lee sent Congress an insulting letter in January 1780, which led Congress to dismiss him from the Continental army. Lee died in Philadelphia two years later.

Further reading: John Richard Alden, *General Charles Lee: Traitor or Patriot?* (Baton Rouge: Louisiana State University Press, 1951).

— Heather Clemmer

Lee, Henry (Light Horse Harry) (1756–1818)

Henry Lee, known as "Light Horse Harry," served as a cavalry officer in the REVOLUTIONARY WAR (1775–83), supported the ratification of the United States Constitution, became a FEDERALIST politician, and was a friend of GEORGE WASHINGTON. He served as governor of Virginia and as a congressman from that state. Lee is also remembered for his famous description of George Washington as "first in war, first in peace, and first in the hearts of his countrymen." Lee was from a prominent Virginia family, attended the College of New Jersey (present-day Princeton University), and was on his way to England when the war broke out and changed his plans. He entered the CONTI-

NENTAL ARMY in June 1776 as a captain in the cavalry. He began his military career in the northern theater and saw combat in the 1777 Philadelphia campaign. By 1778 he had under his command three troops of cavalry and three companies of infantry known as Lee's Legion. In 1779 his troops, in a daring raid, captured the fort at Paulus Hook, New Jersey. He was sent south with General NATHANAEL GREENE, where he and his troops won distinction in several battles, including the one at YORKTOWN (October 19, 1781).

Lee left the army on a leave of absence in 1782 and never returned, having been honorably discharged during his absence. Lee adjusted to civilian life by getting married and entering politics. He married his cousin Matilda Lee, a Virginia heiress. He entered political life as a Federalist and supporter of George Washington, whom he greatly admired, serving in both the state legislature and the CONTINENTAL CONGRESS. After his wife Matilda died in 1790, he served as governor of Virginia from 1792 to 1795. During that time he remarried, this time to Anne Hill Carter, daughter of another prominent Virginia family. After briefly reentering the military for service in the WHISKEY REBELLION in 1794, Lee returned to Virginia, where he was elected to Congress in 1799 and served until 1801.

But, as successful as he was in war and politics, success in business eluded him. Lee speculated in western land and lost large sums of money. By the time he left Congress, he had moved from his late wife's Stratford estate to Alexandria, where he was living on his second wife's money. It was during this period that his and Anne's famous son Robert E. Lee was born (1807). By this time Lee was living well beyond his means, and he spent time in 1808–09 in jail for failure to repay his debts. In 1812 Lee was injured by a mob in Baltimore while trying to help a friend defend his printing press. He never recovered his health and the next year left for the WEST INDIES to recuperate (though some said he left to flee debts). His health did not improve, and Lee returned to the United States when it became clear he was dying. On the return trip he was put ashore in Georgia, where General Greene's daughter took him in and cared for him until his death.

Further reading: Charles Royster, *Light-Horse Harry Lee and the Legacy of the American Revolution* (New York: Knopf, 1981).

— J. Brett Adams

Lee, Richard Henry (1732–1794)

Richard Henry Lee was one of the first politicians who boldly demanded independence for the American colonies. Lee was born into a wealthy planter family in Westmoreland County, Virginia. After an education in England, he entered the Virginia House of Burgesses in 1758 and proposed in his first speech the restriction of the importation of slaves. In opposition to the STAMP ACT (1765), Lee joined a committee to write protest notes to the king and the Parliament, and he led a "mob of gentlemen," forcing a stamp distributor to give up his commission. In 1766 Lee organized a boycott of British imports in Virginia. The TOWNSHEND DUTIES (1767) provoked Lee to advocate intercolonial contacts to counteract British policies.

After the death of his wife in 1768, Lee concentrated on the business of growing and shipping tobacco to England. In 1773 THOMAS JEFFERSON and PATRICK HENRY joined Lee in advocating colonial cooperation to resist British imperial regulation. In May 1774 the three politicians "cooked up," as Jefferson wrote, a protest resolution against the closing of the port of Boston and convinced the Virginia House of Burgesses to call for a general congress in Philadelphia. In the CONTINENTAL CONGRESS and in the Virginia legislature, Lee resisted British conciliatory offers and boldly advocated national independence, foreign alliance, and a confederation. Increasingly radicalized, Lee supported Patrick Henry's proposal to arm the Virginia militia and urged the appointment of GEORGE WASHINGTON as commander in chief. Lee wrote in an address to the people of Great Britain that "these united colonies are, and of right ought to be, free and independent states, that they are absolved from all allegiance to the British crown; and that all political connection between them and the state of Great Britain is, and ought to be, totally dissolved." Lee might have drafted the Declaration of Independence, but an illness in his family caused his absence from Congress at that time. Lee signed the finished document and prepared to form a new government in Virginia.

In the following years he narrowly escaped capture by British troops and remained an important figure in national politics. When internal strife over the western lands divided the states and prevented the establishment of a confederation, Lee used his influence to convince the Virginia legislature to give up all claims to western territories. Increasingly ill since 1779, Lee continued to serve in the Virginia House of Delegates (1780–84) and even returned to Congress in 1784. In Congress he stubbornly resisted any plans to replace the ARTICLES OF CONFEDERATION with a new constitution. Lee feared a strong central government, arguing that one should never "grant to Rulers an atom of power that is not most clearly and indispensably necessary for the safety and well being of Society." Richard Henry Lee resigned from Congress in bad health in 1792 and died two years later.

Further reading: James C. Ballagh, *The Letters of Richard Henry Lee* (New York: Macmillan & Company, 1911); O. P. Chitwood, *Richard Henry Lee: Statesman of the Revolution* (Morgantown: West Virginia University Press, 1967).

— Dirk Voss

L'Enfant, Pierre-Charles (1754–1825)

Pierre-Charles L'Enfant planned the original layout of public buildings, parks, and streets of WASHINGTON, D.C., the capital of the United States of America. L'Enfant, born in Paris in 1754, was educated as an architect and engineer. While serving in the French army in 1777, the king granted him and eight other soldiers the permission to serve in the American forces to fight Great Britain. He joined the CONTINENTAL ARMY as a volunteer captain in the corps of engineers in Philadelphia. In the 1779 failed attack on Savannah, he was left for dead but recovered and returned to his unit. During the siege of CHARLESTON (captured by the British May 12, 1780), the British army took L'Enfant as prisoner but exchanged him for a HESSIAN officer in 1782. A year later GEORGE WASHINGTON recommended his promotion to a major of engineers.

After the war he became a leading member of the ORDER OF CINCINNATI, designed its insignia, and founded the society's French branch. Washington sent him on a mission to France, but L'Enfant had already made up his mind to remain in the United States. In 1784 he wrote a memo to Congress recommending a permanent peacetime corps of engineers. A year later he moved to New York City, where he supervised the construction of several impressive buildings and remodeled the old City Hall, since the city fathers expected New York City to become the capital of the new country. When Congress decided against New York City, President Washington commissioned L'Enfant to plan, design, and erect the streets and public buildings of the new capital in the District of Columbia. L'Enfant selected the site of the Capitol, laid out the street pattern radiating from the Capitol and the White House, designed the parks, and arranged the buildings on the Mall. Although L'Enfant had great freedom to plan the city, disagreements between L'Enfant and the congressional commission arose concerning how the construction should be conducted. When L'Enfant refused to loan his plans to the commission, Congress pressured the reluctant Washington to dismiss him.

President Washington proposed 500 guineas and a city lot for him, but the embittered L'Enfant refused and charged Congress with a bill of $95,500 for his services. Ten years later he settled for $1,394.20. ALEXANDER HAMILTON attempted to give him a job developing an industrial city in New Jersey, but financial backing failed to materialize. He became the engineer of a fort near Philadelphia, and after the burning of Washington in 1814, he worked designing better fortifications for Fort Washington. He was, however, charged with extravagance and was removed from office.

L'Enfant spent the rest of his life in POVERTY at the home of a benefactor in Maryland.

Further reading: H. Paul Caemmerer, *The Life of Pierre Charles L'Enfant, Planner of the City Beautiful, the City of Washington* (Washington, D.C.: National Republic Co., 1950).

— Dirk Voss

Lewis, Meriwether (1774–1809)

One of the most important explorers of the early republic, Meriwether Lewis helped to navigate and describe the newly acquired Louisiana Territory with his partner WILLIAM CLARK during the LEWIS AND CLARK EXPEDITION (1804–06). Lewis's journals from the expedition are some of the most significant accounts of the early American expansion to the West. After returning from the expedition, Lewis became closely involved with the administration of western land, serving as governor of the Louisiana Territory.

Meriwether Lewis was born in Albemarle County, Virginia, in 1774, the oldest child of William Lewis, a CONTINENTAL ARMY officer, and Lucy (Meriwether) Lewis. His father died when Meriwether was five years old, leaving a substantial estate. Soon after, Lucy Meriwether Lewis married John Marks. The extended Marks-Lewis family moved to FRONTIER Georgia when Lewis was 10 years old. Marks established plantations in what is now Oglethorpe County, Georgia, where the young Lewis spent his time hunting, exploring, and reading. At 13, Lewis returned to Virginia to begin his formal education under the tutelage of Reverend Matthew Maury. Maury instructed him in Latin, as well as science and mathematics. For the next five years he studied under private tutors and intended to continue his education at the College of William and Mary. However, the death of his stepfather obliged Lewis, then 18 and the oldest son, to return to his Virginia plantation and manage the family estate. As head of the family, he supervised the education of his younger brother, Reuben, and his half brother and half sister, John and Mary Marks.

Lewis's career as a soldier began in 1794, when he enlisted in the Virginia militia and journeyed to western Pennsylvania to help quell the WHISKEY REBELLION. He then participated in General ANTHONY WAYNE's successful campaigns against the Indians in the Northwest Territory, serving under his future partner William Clark at the pivotal BATTLE OF FALLEN TIMBERS (1794). The following year, Lewis enlisted in the regular army, commissioned as an ensign in the Second Legion. He was with Wayne during the making of the TREATY OF GREENVILLE, which ended the wars in the Northwest. In 1796 Ensign Lewis was transferred to the First Infantry. He spent the next four years in the army moving around to different stations, developing his reputation as an honest and diligent soldier. In 1799 he was commissioned lieutenant, and by 1801 he was a captain and paymaster in the First Infantry.

In early 1801 Meriwether Lewis received a letter from his Virginia neighbor and friend, President-elect THOMAS JEFFERSON. Jefferson asked the promising young officer to become his private secretary—an offer Lewis immediately accepted. Jefferson chose Lewis not only because of his ability to manage private household matters but also because of the officer's practical understanding of the western frontier. After the LOUISIANA PURCHASE was finalized in 1803, Jefferson saw an opportunity to implement a project he had been promoting for several years: a transcontinental expedition. Lewis began to prepare for the proposed expedition soon after he became Jefferson's secretary. He gathered information about possible routes to the Pacific, acquired essential equipment, and went to the University of Pennsylvania for additional scientific training. Congress officially sanctioned the expedition in 1803, with Lewis as commander. Lewis then asked his army comrade William Clark to be coleader of the expedition. Lewis was the true leader of the voyage, but the two men divided administrative and navigational tasks according to their particular strengths. Clark took responsibility for many of the practical elements of the journey, while Lewis performed the intellectual work, recording scientific information about western flora and fauna and personal observations about the NATIVE AMERICANS they encountered. Lewis's thoughtful, introspective journal entries demonstrate the seriousness with which he undertook this mission of exploration.

Lewis, Clark, and their recruits departed from St. Louis in May 1804. The party traveled up the Missouri River, staying over the winter with the Mandan Indians in what is now North Dakota. In the spring, they continued along the Missouri with the help of the Shoshone guide SACAGAWEA. Reaching the Rocky Mountains, Lewis and Clark realized that an all-water route to the Pacific would not materialize. The party continued overland to the Columbia River, and thus to the Pacific Ocean. They spent the winter of 1805–06 at the mouth of the Columbia and then began the arduous overland journey back to St. Louis. Now two years later, Americans had given up the party for lost. The nation rejoiced when Lewis and Clark returned to St. Louis in September 1806, their mission successfully completed.

Jefferson appointed Lewis governor to Louisiana Territory in 1807. His record during his short tenure as governor was mixed. By codifying laws and organizing a state militia, he established the institutions necessary for effective territorial administration. He helped William Clark, now superintendent of Indian affairs, in negotiations with local tribes over land cessions. In other respects, however, the experienced soldier was ill-suited for administrative work. He frequently disagreed with his staff and became increasingly alienated from many of the settlers. He hardly ever communicated with his superiors in Washington and failed to inform the federal administration of his policies concerning Indians. Federal and local officials accused him of mismanagement when the government refused to honor some of the bills he issued. These accusations troubled him greatly, and his governorship seemed to be in jeopardy.

In September of 1809 Lewis left St. Louis for Washington, hoping to clear his political reputation. He also planned to look into publishing his journals from the expedition. During the journey, while staying at a tavern on the Natchez Trace in southwest Tennessee, Meriwether Lewis died. The circumstances surrounding his sudden death remain mysterious. Scholars continue to debate whether he was murdered or committed suicide. Accounts of his troubled mental state and introverted nature have led many to believe that it was the latter. Whatever the truth may be, Jefferson, Clark, and many other Americans mourned the premature loss of this courageous explorer.

Further reading: John Bakeless, *Lewis and Clark: Partners in Discovery* (New York: William Morrow, 1947); Richard H. Dillon, *Meriwether Lewis: A Biography* (New York: Coward-McCann, 1965).

Eleanor H. McConnell

Lewis and Clark Expedition

MERIWETHER LEWIS (1774–1809) and WILLIAM CLARK (1770–1838) trekked across the American continent from 1803 to 1806 to reach the Pacific Ocean in one of the greatest exploratory expeditions of all time. Much of their success was due to the diplomatic and linguistic skills of one of their guides, a 16-year-old Shoshone woman named SACAGAWEA. When the party of soldiers, scouts, and traders returned to St. Louis, they brought with them one of the first pictures of the continent west of the Mississippi. The United States would base its future claims to what is now Idaho, Oregon, and Washington State on their journeys to the mouth of the Columbia River. They also put an end to the last hope for a "Northwest Passage," an easy water route from the Atlantic to the Pacific Oceans.

THOMAS JEFFERSON proposed to send explorers to the lands west of the Mississippi almost as soon as he became president in 1801. Spain claimed the vast territory from that river to the Pacific Ocean and south to Mexico. Only the NATIVE AMERICANS who lived in the plains, deserts, and mountains actually knew the terrain. A few traders from Spain, CANADA, and the United States ventured into the region. The Spanish did not want Americans trespassing in their country, especially since many settlers had already

Captain Clark and his men shooting bears *(Hulton/Archives)*

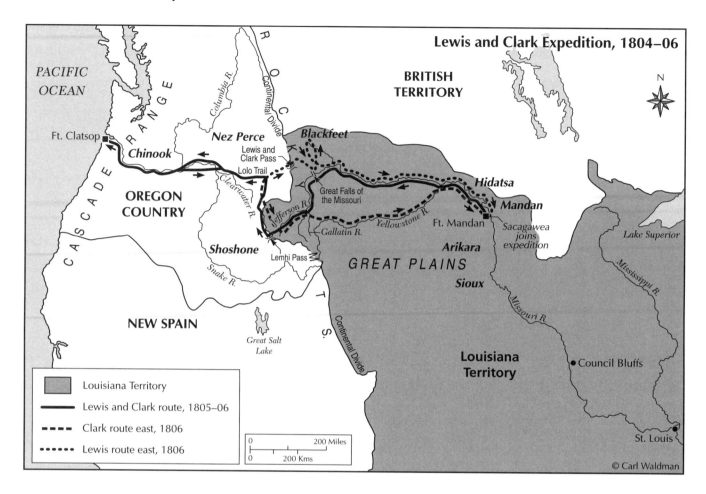

illegally slipped across the border from Kentucky and Tennessee to set up farms in what is now Missouri.

When Jefferson sent a delegation to offer to negotiate the sale of New Orleans from NAPOLEON BONAPARTE (Spain secretly returned Louisiana to France in 1800), they were surprised when the French offered to sell them all of Louisiana. At that time, Louisiana encompassed all the lands drained by the Mississippi and Missouri Rivers. No Europeans knew where these rivers began or how much land they drained. President Jefferson asked Meriwether Lewis to lead a party to find the sources of those rivers and a way to the Pacific. Lewis chose to bring Captain William Clark as a joint commander of the group. The expedition included over two dozen soldiers as well as guides and translators.

Calling themselves "the Corps of Discovery," the party left the Ohio Valley in 1803 and wintered on the lower Missouri River just above its junction with the Mississippi. The next spring they set off up the Missouri in a large boat along with several canoes and smaller boats. The soldiers and other men used poles to push the boats upriver, sometimes with the assistance of sails to catch the wind.

In September 1804 the Lewis and Clark Expedition encountered the mighty Sioux near where the Missouri and the Cheyenne Rivers meet. The Sioux thought that the party was stingy with the amount of gifts the white men gave to them. Serious trouble was averted when Lewis ordered the men on to the boats and set off quickly up the river.

Since they labored against the current, they made slow progress. It took them all summer and fall to reach the Mandan villages in what is now central North Dakota. The Mandan conducted a thriving trade with the tribes of the interior. There Lewis and Clark questioned the Hidatsa who came to barter at the villages. Timing would be critical for the next year's journey. The expedition had to reach the source of the river in the Rocky Mountains, then find the Shoshone in order to trade with them for horses to carry them through the passes before the first snows. Sacagawea spoke Shoshone (she had been captured as a girl by the Hidatsa and traded to a fur trapper named Toussaint Charbonneau) and would prove essential in these efforts.

In the late summer of 1805, Lewis and Clark reached the headwaters of the Missouri and desperately looked for the Shoshone. When the party finally found them, the

Shoshone appeared less than enthusiastic about the presence of strangers until Sacagawea recognized one of the warriors, her brother whom she had not seen since childhood. The party traded for horses and headed west.

After great difficulty the group reached the last ridge of the Missouri drainage system in early September 1805. When they saw more mountains reaching as far west as the eye could see, they knew that there was no easy water route across the continent—the dream of a Northwest Passage ended forever. Along the way, in the Bitterroot Mountains, they met and traded with the Nez Perce. These Native Americans had never seen a European before. A Nez Perce named Twisted Hair guided the party across the difficult terrain. By mid-autumn, the expedition had reached the uppermost courses of the Columbia River. They bought canoes and traveled down some of the most dangerous rapids in North America. On November 2, 1805, they passed the last rapid and reached the tidewaters of the Columbia River. They made good progress downstream, reaching the Pacific Ocean on November 6.

Spending the winter near the mouth of the Columbia River, Lewis and Clark started their return voyage in the early spring of 1806. After a treacherous passage over the Rockies they paddled back down the Missouri. Several times, Lewis and Clark split up and led the groups in different directions to find alternative routes. In late September 1806 they ended their 28-month journey with a triumphant entry into St. Louis. By early November, news of Lewis and Clark's success reached WASHINGTON, D.C.

Lewis and Clark brought back a rich record of their trip in the journals that they kept. The journals represented more than just an account of their journey, containing descriptions of plants, animals, and fish that had never been seen by European Americans before. The books told about the numerous Native American peoples and the rich lands the party saw along the way. A few years later settlers streamed into the lower reaches of the Missouri Valley into a land that had been a mystery to white people before the Corps of Discovery set forth on its journey.

See also LOUISIANA PURCHASE.

Further reading: Stephen Ambrose, *Undaunted Courage: Meriwether Lewis, Thomas Jefferson, and the Opening of the American West* (New York: Simon & Schuster, 1996).

— George Milne

Lexington and Concord, Battles of (April 19, 1775)

On April 14, 1775, General THOMAS GAGE received the orders that he had been waiting for. Responding to Gage's reports that the colony of Massachusetts was in a virtual state of rebellion, Lord William Dartmouth, the British secretary of the colonies, wrote that if the colonists had decided to revolt, then "Force should be repelled by Force." Believing that the Massachusetts militia could not effectively face British regulars, Dartmouth urged a military action to arrest opposition leaders and nip the rebellion in the bud. If there was bloodshed, Dartmouth maintained, "it will surely be better that the Conflict should be brought on, upon such ground, than in a riper state of Rebellion." Armed with this authority, Gage launched the expedition to Lexington and Concord that led to bloodshed and began the REVOLUTIONARY WAR (1775–83).

Gage had been preparing for the expedition for some time. He had served as commander in chief of the British army for over a decade and had witnessed much of the disorder that had accompanied the RESISTANCE MOVEMENT (1764–75) that had confronted efforts at imperial regulation. In 1774 King GEORGE III appointed him as governor of Massachusetts to enforce the COERCIVE ACTS (1774) and to compel Massachusetts to submit to British authority. His task in Massachusetts was formidable. When he refused to call the colony's assembly, fearing it would jump to the forefront of resistance, colonial leaders simply met as a provincial congress external to his authority. Worse, COMMITTEES OF CORRESPONDENCE appeared in community after community to coordinate resistance and nullify the effects of the Coercive Acts throughout the colony. A nonimportation movement stopped trade with Great Britain. Militia formed bands of MINUTEMEN, smuggled arms into the colony, and prepared for conflict. The commander in chief and royal governor of Massachusetts had no authority beyond the range of British warships and the presence of

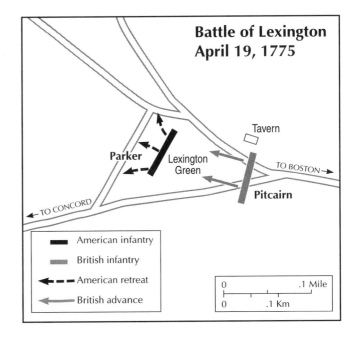

Battle of Lexington
April 19, 1775

British troops; his control was limited to Boston and its harbor. A well-planned raid into the countryside on September 2, 1774, successfully seized a large supply of powder from the colonists, but it also brought a surprise to the British general. Tens of thousands of colonists had begun to march on Boston in response to the raid. The mission was so swift that there was little that the colonists could do but harass loyal supporters of the king. A message had been delivered, however. Future British raids were either canceled or were not successfully carried out.

Gage reported the situation to England, sending the letters that eventually brought the orders of April 14. He also declared that he would need 20,000 troops—he only had 3,000 in Boston—to subdue the colony. Dartmouth and the king thought that request was preposterous. Isolated in Boston and determined to assert royal control, Gage planned another, larger raid into the hinterland. He had spies identify the targets: SAMUEL ADAMS and JOHN HANCOCK were said to be in Lexington, and there were military supplies stockpiled in Concord. He would send 800 hand-picked grenadiers and light infantry under the command of an experienced officer, Lieutenant Colonel Francis Smith. When the April 14 letter arrived, it was the signal that he had support for action from Britain.

Secrecy was hard to come by in Massachusetts in April 1775. Men loyal to the king provided details of every movement of provincial leaders and messengers like PAUL REVERE. Deserters and supporters of the opposition to imperial regulation reported on the British. Although the expedition was supposed to be secret, the colonists knew it was coming. When the 800 regulars began their thrust into the countryside, a signal went up in the Old North Church, indicating that the approach was to be by sea, across the Back Bay, and along the Concord Road through Lexington. Paul Revere, William Dawes, and others set out to spread the alarm. Anticipating this action, the British had mounted patrols of officers and sergeants along the roads to intercept the messengers. Paul Revere was almost intercepted by the British officers on his way to Lexington, but he arrived safely and provided his warning: "The regulars are coming out!" (He did not say that "the British are coming", colonists considered themselves Englishmen at the time.) After he left Lexington, he was captured by a British patrol, held for awhile, and then released without his horse. The patrol, aware of the alarm, wanted to head east to the safety of the British lines.

By the time the column of regulars reached Lexington Green, the local minutemen had collected and prepared to meet them. It was an uneven contest. As columns of light infantry filed onto the Green and formed a battle line, Captain John Parker quickly realized the folly of some 70 minutemen facing a larger force of professional soldiers. As the British officers demanded the colonists lay down their arms, Parker told his men to disperse. The Lexington men began to withdraw but held on to their weapons. A shot rang out. No one knows who fired, but the regulars didn't wait for orders. Eager for action, they leveled two volleys at the colonists before Major Pitcairn, who had command of the advance column, managed to stop them. A few minutemen fired back and then fled. Within a minute or two a war had begun, with eight colonists killed and 10 wounded. One regular was slightly injured. Hancock and Adams had escaped, however, and the British column pushed on to Concord.

Without much opposition, the British occupied the town of Concord and burned some military stores, but they did not find nearly as much equipment and powder as they had expected. In anticipation of the raid, Concord had been emptied of most of its stores. The fire, however, accidentally spread to some buildings. The British and the townsmen on hand worked to put out the flames, but from a distance, it looked like the British were burning the town. Light infantry companies had been sent to secure the North and South Bridges beyond the town, and four companies had been sent past North Bridge to Colonel James Barret's farm, which had been the location of a stash of equipment earlier that month. But like the material that had been in Concord, most of it had been moved. Meanwhile, Colonel Barret was with a large militia force on a hill overlooking the North Bridge. Seeing the smoke from their town and convinced that the British had set the fire, Barret ordered his men to advance. Confusion reigned in the British companies at the bridge. Unprepared for the advance and in some disorder, a regular fired a shot, followed by some others, and then a disorganized volley. The regulars generally missed their mark and most shots went over the heads of the militia. Upon closing within 50 yards, the colonials opened fire, wounding four of the eight officers at the bridge in their first volley and adding to the confusion among the British. After a short hesitation, the regulars broke and ran back toward Concord. The militia remained on the hill, however, and even allowed the advance column from Barret's farm to march past them and across the bridge. With his troops gathered together in Concord, Colonel Smith hesitated before withdrawing. Then, at about noon, he began the long march back to Boston.

It was during that march that the real disaster for the British occurred. Thousands of minutemen from the surrounding towns had been collecting since the alarm had spread. In a series of running actions, they attacked the column mercilessly. Even with the use of flankers to protect the column, the casualties began to mount. The Americans did not just fight from behind rock walls and bushes. On several occasions they sought to form ranks and fight the regulars. When the British responded and fired into the

Americans as they attacked, they also inflicted punishing casualties. Smith's men might have been wiped out if Gage had not sent out a relief column of 2,000 men under Lord Hugh Percy. This force met up with the retreating British just east of Lexington. With the added reinforcement and some artillery, Smith's troops were saved. The fighting continued, with the Americans avoiding direct confrontations and continuing to inflict casualties on the British until the regulars reached the protection of Boston. The British lost 273 men killed, wounded, or missing; the Americans lost 95. Perhaps more importantly, colonists throughout North America now realized that they were confronted with a war, and their cousins on the other side of the ocean became convinced that only greater force could suppress the rebellion.

Further reading: David Hackett Fischer, *Paul Revere's Ride* (New York: Oxford University Press, 1994); Robert A. Gross, *The Minutemen and Their World* (New York: Hill and Wang, 1976).

liberty tree/pole

Scholars are not sure where the idea for a liberty tree and pole first came from. Liberty trees may have been connected in some colonial minds to the freedom of the forests of North America, and several colonies had special trees identified with their history, such as Connecticut's "Hartford Charter Oak," Maryland's "Annapolis Tulip Poplar," and Pennsylvania's "Treaty Elm." There may also be some connection to the English maypole, a traditional fertility symbol and the focal point of community festivities in the spring. Whatever the lineage, the use of a liberty tree first appeared in Boston during the STAMP ACT (1765) controversy. On August 14, 1765, anti-Stamp Act demonstrators hung effigies of ANDREW OLIVER (the colonial stamp distributor) and the EARL OF BUTE (an unpopular adviser of King GEORGE III) from a tree and made it the centerpiece of their protest. Soon Bostonians were calling the tree the Liberty Tree. The SONS OF LIBERTY hung a plaque commemorating August 14th around the tree. On November 1, 1765, the day the Stamp Act was to go into effect, a crowd

John McRae's engraving shows Americans in 1776 reacting to news of independence by hoisting a liberty pole festooned with flags while another group cuts down a tavern sign emblazoned with a figure of George III. *(Library of Congress)*

celebrated by hanging effigies of GEORGE GRENVILLE and John Huske, who was popularly believed to be an initiator of the Stamp Tax. On December 17, 1765, the Sons of Liberty compelled Oliver to repeat his resignation as the colonial stamp distributor in front of the Liberty Tree.

New Yorkers took the next step by changing the tree into a pole. To celebrate the repeal of the Stamp Act and the birthday of George III, New Yorkers raised a flagpole on their commons in June 1766. But with the New York assembly refusing to comply with the QUARTERING ACT (1765), the flagstaff soon became a symbol of resistance to imperial regulation. Since it stood on the parade ground, it was a constant irritant to the British soldiers stationed in the city. After soldiers tore down the pole, New Yorkers, resentful of this attack on their "Tree of Liberty," erected a new pole. This liberty pole became a rallying point for anti-imperial demonstrators and was torn down by soldiers, and put up again by New Yorkers, several times. On January 18, 1770, soldiers and citizens skirmished in a street fight over the liberty pole in what popularly became known as the BATTLE OF GOLDEN HILL. Other communities began to erect their own liberty poles, and by the time of the REVOLUTIONARY WAR (1775–83), liberty poles could be found in almost every colony.

After the war, liberty poles occasionally appeared, but they were revived as an important political symbol in the 1790s. The French began using liberty poles during the FRENCH REVOLUTION (1789–1815). In part because of the French example but also harking back to their use in the 1760s and 1770s, DEMOCRATIC-REPUBLICANS began using poles in their celebrations. Liberty poles also appeared during the WHISKEY REBELLION (1794) and FRIES'S REBELLION (1798). Supporters of THOMAS JEFFERSON rallied around liberty poles, called sedition poles by the FEDERALIST PARTY, to register opposition to the ALIEN AND SEDITION ACTS (1798). After 1800, although liberty poles symbolized the Jeffersonian triumph, they lost some significance. During the 1820s supporters of Andrew Jackson raised hickory poles, while the followers of Henry Clay had the ash pole. The Republican Party of the 1850s occasionally used liberty poles.

See also RESISTANCE MOVEMENT; RIOTS.

Further reading: Arthur M. Schlesinger, "Liberty Tree: A Genealogy," *New England Quarterly* 25 (1952): 435–458.

literature

The modern reader often struggles with American literature from the revolutionary and early national periods. It is not that the language was so different. The words and sentences are easy enough to comprehend. But the purpose of the writer reflected a different world and culture—a world in revolution and a culture moving from the reason of the Enlightenment to the emotion of Romanticism.

In the 18th century the political treatise was considered an art form. During the RESISTANCE MOVEMENT (1764–75) countless pamphlets were published exploring the imperial relationship. Reflecting the Enlightenment, authors usually used a pseudonym, like JOHN DICKINSON's "Pennsylvania Farmer"; packed their tracts with references to antiquity; and constructed arguments following logic and careful reasoning based on law and history. Most of these essays were written for a limited audience of educated gentlemen. THOMAS PAINE broke this mold, although he too was influenced by the Enlightenment, in his *COMMON SENSE* (1776) and *Crisis* (1776–77). Paine sought to broaden the appeal by simplifying the language and relying more heavily on the Bible than any other source. Political writing continued to reach a wider audience after the REVOLUTIONARY WAR (1775–83). While not quite in Paine's same straightforward style, much of the debate over the United States Constitution in 1787–88 appeared as essays in newspapers, notably the *FEDERALIST PAPERS* by "Publius." During the 1790s and early 1800s political rhetoric became even more heated, so much so that the FEDERALIST PARTY sought to stifle its opposition through the ALIEN AND SEDITION ACTS (1798).

Another important form of literature in the period was the description of nature or travel account. These publications were often seen as a direct contribution to enlightened discourse. THOMAS JEFFERSON wrote his *Notes on the State of Virginia* (1787) to demonstrate that the natural world in North America was superior to Europe. He was thus entering an ongoing debate among the philosophers of his generation concerning the relationship between nature and society. Similarly, HECTOR ST. JOHN DE CRÈVECOEUR published his *Letters from an American Farmer* (1782) to extol the virtues of the agrarian life in North America and contrast it to the ancient relics of civilization found in the Old World. Both books are difficult to understand without placing them in the context of the Enlightenment.

Although Crèvecoeur was critical of the Revolutionary War (he cut out his most severe comments for publication, and they were not found and published until the 20th century), many American writers seized upon the contest for American independence as a moment of glory and an opportunity to create a new age in literature. PHILLIS WHEATLEY wrote largely on religious themes but also penned several patriotic poems, including an ode to GEORGE WASHINGTON. PHILIP FRENEAU was inspired by the Revolutionary War, writing about the conflict and emphasizing the sacrifices of common men. The CONNECTICUT WITS were at first thrilled by the possibilities of America and sought to compose a literature that a new republic could be proud of. In the years after the war, several authors, including JOHN MARSHALL and MERCY OTIS WARREN, wrote history and biography to celebrate the new nation. While not explicitly patriotic, the portrayal of the self-made man in BENJAMIN FRANKLIN's *Autobiography* (1791) seemed to give definition to what it meant to be American. Parson MASON WEEMS's fabricated, or mostly fabricated, popular life story of Washington equally contributed to the image of the American.

In the years after the war, however, two new trends began to emerge. First, the debate over the direction of the nation divided authors. Some writers remained committed to the ideals of revolution; others began to feel ambiguous about the nature of the republic. Philip Freneau continued to be enthusiastic about the rights of man. During the party battles of the 1790s Thomas Jefferson hired him at the state department and had him edit a partisan newspaper. In 1795 Freneau wrote: "Let us with France agree, And bid the world be free." Upon the death of Thomas Paine in 1809, Freneau proclaimed that it is easy to replace "Princes and kings," but

> In vain the democratic host
> His *equal* would attain:
> For years to come they will not boast
> A second Thomas Paine.

The Connecticut Wits saw things differently and were dismayed to find that the revolution led to unexpected changes. They decried SHAYS'S REBELLION (1786–87) and anything that sounded of democratic rhetoric. Supporting the stronger central government of the Federalist Party, they believed equality led to mob rule and the rise of men unfit for office. John Trumbull (cousin of JOHN TRUMBULL the painter), using a metaphor to describe the "tatter'd legislator," wrote:

> For in this ferment of the stream,
> The dregs have work'd up to the brim,
> And by the rule of topsy-turvy,
> The scum standing foaming on the surface.

DEMOCRATIC-REPUBLICANS, however, could express the same apprehensions. HUGH HENRY BRACKENRIDGE's novel, *Modern Chivalry* (1792–1815), traces the exploits of a natural aristocrat, Captain John Farrago, and his Irish immigrant sidekick, Teague O'Regan, across the American democratic landscape. While Farrago is the voice of enlightened reason, O'Regan is provided with repeated opportunities for personal advancement, from scientist to congressman, despite his ignorance and unsuitability for any position beyond Farrago's servant.

The second trend developed in conjunction with the first Confidence in the role of reason waned, and nature became volatile, unpredictable, and mysterious. This shift did not occur all at once. A Democratic-Republican poet like Freneau might as easily praise "the uniformity and perfection of nature," as ask, "What friendship can in tempests be, what comforts on this raging sea?" in which "skill and science both must fall; And ruin is the lot of all." Similarly, Federalist FISHER AMES might wish to cling to a world dominated by natural aristocrats, comparing a "mobocracy"—the inevitable end of democracy—to a "West-India hurricane" that "instantly strews the fruitful earth with promiscuous ruins, and turns the sky yellow with pestilence." This mixture of rationality and irrationality can also be seen in the work of novelist CHARLES BROCKDEN BROWN, who used the appearance of the supernatural to advance his plots while ultimately offering a logical explanation for the seemingly illogical. By the 1810s and 1820s, authors like James Fenimore Cooper and Washington Irving had begun writing, and the stage had been set for the development of a truly great American literature firmly rooted in sentiment and emotion.

Further reading: Edwin H. Cady, ed., *Literature of the Early Republic*, 2nd ed. New York: Holt, Rinehart and Winston, 1969); Cathy N. Davidson, *Revolution and the Word: The Rise of the Novel in America* (New York: Oxford University Press, 1986); Emory Elliot, *Revolutionary Writers: Literature and Authority in the New Republic, 1725–1810* (New York: Oxford University Press, 1986); Henry F. May, *The Enlightenment in America* (New York: Oxford University Press, 1976); Robert E. Shalhope, *The Roots of Democracy: American Thought and Culture, 1760–1800* (Boston: Twayne, 1990).

Little Belt incident (May 16, 1811)

The American frigate USS *President* fought a battle with the British sloop of war HMS *Little Belt* on the evening of May 16, 1811, an event that increased the animosity and distrust of both Americans and British before the War of 1812 (1812–15). At the time several British warships had stopped American merchantmen just outside of American ports to impress seamen. This behavior outraged American public opinion. When the *President* set sail from the Chesapeake Bay in May, many believed that Commodore John Rogers had orders to stop this violation of American rights. Rogers had no such orders. But when he spotted the *Little Belt*, he initially thought it might be the HMS *Guerriere*, which had just pressed a native of Maine named John Diggio. Rogers decided to see if he could get the man returned to the United States. The *Little Belt* also closed with the American, thinking that it was either another British ship or perhaps a French frigate. When the captain of the *Little Belt*, Arthur Bingham, recognized the vessel as an American, he resumed his original course. The Americans, however, decided to chase the British vessel, still hoping it was the *Guerriere*. The American frigate soon closed the gap with the British, at which point Bingham hoisted his colors and cleared for action (standard procedure whenever a warship came near to another country's warship). Neither ship would respond to the hail of the other, since to identify oneself first was the duty of the inferior to the superior. At this point a gun went off. Both captains later claimed that the other had fired first. Regardless of who began the firing, the *President* had twice the armament of the *Little Belt* and it was an uneven contest. After 45 minutes the *Little Belt* was in shambles, with 13 men killed and 19 wounded. The *President* had only one boy slightly wounded. When the battle ended, Bingham finally responded to the American hail. Rogers then offered assistance, which was refused. The *Little Belt* made some repairs and sailed on to Halifax, Nova Scotia.

This victory was greeted in the United States with much popular acclaim. Many Americans saw it as striking a blow at last to defend national honor in the face of repeated IMPRESSMENT and as a redemption for the *CHESAPEAKE-LEOPARD* AFFAIR (June 21, 1807). The action agitated the British public, who decried the attack as unprovoked and between mismatched foes. The *Little Belt* affair therefore contributed to the hostility between the two countries that would break out in the War of 1812.

See also FOREIGN AFFAIRS.

Further reading: William M. Fowler Jr., *Jack Tars and Commodores: The American Navy, 1783–1815* (Boston: Houghton Mifflin, 1984); Bradford Perkins, *Prologue to War, 1805–1812: England and the United States* (Berkeley: University of California Press, 1968).

Livingston, Robert R. (1746–1813)

A member of one of New York's leading families, Robert R. Livingston played an important role in the AMERICAN REVOLUTION. He also became a supporter of the Constitution of the United States and a prominent member of the DEMOCRATIC REPUBLICAN PARTY. As a diplomat he served as minister to France during the crucial negotiations for the LOUISIANA PURCHASE (1803).

Livingston was educated at King's College (later Columbia University) and trained as a LAWYER. An ardent WHIG, he supported the revolutionary cause both as a member of the CONTINENTAL CONGRESS and in his home state. Although he served as one of the committee of five that drafted the DECLARATION OF INDEPENDENCE (July 4, 1776), through an odd set of coincidences he neither voted for the document (New York was excused from voting on the issue until its convention gave a go-ahead) nor

signed it (urgent demands concerning the war forced him to return to New York while the document was being signed). However, during his terms in the Continental Congress (1775–76, 1779–81, 1784–85), he was usually one of the most active and influential members. Livingston became the first secretary of the department of FOREIGN AFFAIRS established by Congress in 1781. In this position, Livingston shaped not only American diplomacy but also helped order the Confederation government. He retained this position until May 1783. When not working in the Continental Congress, Livingston was active on committees overseeing the conduct of the REVOLUTIONARY WAR (1775–83) in New York and serving as chancellor—the state's highest judicial office—to which he was appointed in 1777. Livingston also was influential in writing New York's first STATE CONSTITUTION. He was an important member of the state's ratifying convention in 1788, helping to assure the acceptance of the Constitution of the United States.

During the 1790s he led his family into the ranks of opposition to the FEDERALIST PARTY program of ALEXANDER HAMILTON. Although he failed in his election bid for governor in 1795, he remained influential in the Democratic-Republican Party. THOMAS JEFFERSON appointed him minister to France in 1801. The choice was fortunate. Livingston worked hard to gain the respect of the French government and was a good negotiator. When the opportunity came to purchase all of the Louisiana Territory, Livingston, along with James Monroe, managed to close the deal. Although Livingston at first believed that West FLORIDA was not part of the purchase, he quickly changed his mind and provided the arguments that became the basis of the United States policy toward this contested area. Livingston resigned as minister in 1804 and returned to the United States.

While in France, Livingston had encouraged ROBERT FULTON in his experiments with a steamboat. Once back in the United States, he continued to work with Fulton, both technically and financially, in the development of steam navigation. Fulton's *Clermont* derived its common name from Livingston's Hudson River family home. Livingston used his political connections to get exclusive navigational rights to the steamboat, a contract that became highly contested in the courts.

Further reading: George Dangerfield, *Chancellor Robert R. Livingston of New York, 1746–1813* (New York: Harcourt Brace, 1960).

Livingston, William (1723–1790)

William Livingston was an active revolutionary, served as New Jersey's first governor, and attended the CONSTITU-

TIONAL CONVENTION. Livingston went to Yale and was trained as a LAWYER. An early proponent of WHIG ideas in New York politics, he led the attack on the effort to establish King's College (later Columbia University) with a royal charter and as an Anglican institution. Although he lost this battle, his essays in the *Independent Reflector* in the 1750s not only warned against the dominance of the Anglican Church, but used the writings of the COMMONWEALTHMEN to decry any usurpation of liberty. He and his family came to control the provincial assembly in 1758 after defeating the DeLancey faction at the polls. During the STAMP ACT (1765) crisis and the resistance to the TOWNSHEND DUTIES (1767), Livingston played an important and restraining role: He encouraged resistance while seeking to curb the excesses of the mob. The DeLanceys regained control of the legislature in 1769. Livingston retired to his estate in Elizabethtown, New Jersey, in 1772, calling his home "Liberty Hall."

Livingston was soon sucked into the vortex of revolutionary politics, serving on the local COMMITTEE OF CORRESPONDENCE and becoming a delegate to both the FIRST and SECOND CONTINENTAL CONGRESSES. He left Congress shortly before the DECLARATION OF INDEPENDENCE (July 4, 1776) to take command of the New Jersey militia. As soon as New Jersey created its own constitution organizing a state government, he was elected as governor, an office he held for 14 years. After the war, Livingston did not seek retribution against LOYALISTS and opposed unrestricted paper money. He also hoped for the gradual abolition of SLAVERY. Livingston became a supporter of a stronger national government, and at the Constitutional Convention he was important in forging a compromise between the large and small states over representation. In short, Livingston was a typical advocate of REPUBLICANISM of his generation and social standing: He wanted to see the Revolution, but he worked to ensure that it would follow a moderate course.

See also RESISTANCE MOVEMENT.

Further reading: Dorothy Rita Dillon, *The New York Triumvirate: A Study of the Legal And Political Careers of William Livingston, John Morin Scott, William Smith, Jr.* (New York: Columbia University Press, 1949).

Long Island, Battle of (August 27–30, 1776)

The Battle of Long Island was an early defeat for the CONTINENTAL ARMY in the REVOLUTIONARY WAR (1775–83). The battle was the first major conflict in the state of New York, initiated as part of a British strategy to seize control of the central colony. A capture of all of New York would have allowed the British control of the Hudson River, an important water route to CANADA, as well as enabled them to isolate New England from the rest of the colonies.

After the British evacuation from Boston in March 1776, the British general SIR WILLIAM HOWE decided to move his troops to New York, where a British fleet commanded by his brother LORD RICHARD HOWE controlled the surrounding waters. Before arriving in New York, however, General Howe decided to strengthen his forces by sailing to Halifax, Nova Scotia, where he was able to recruit thousands of new troops to join his army. Howe finally arrived in the New York harbor on June 30 and immediately set up camp on Staten Island. For the next seven weeks, daily shipments of British troops arrived by boat, and Howe's forces swelled to well over 30,000.

Anticipating that New York City would be the site of the next conflict, General GEORGE WASHINGTON, commander of the Continental army, followed Howe's move to New York. He sent word to colonial forces in New York warning them of Howe's advance, and the colonials immediately began efforts to fortify their city and to organize their own forces. General NATHANAEL GREENE planned a defense strategy for the Continentals, and General ISRAEL PUTNAM organized the incoming regiments. With Washington's arrival, the Americans had amassed some 25,000 Continental soldiers, the largest force ever commanded by the general, and they began lining the New York Harbor with the heavy cannons and mortars used in the fighting in Boston.

Washington, understanding that holding Brooklyn was essential to maintaining control of New York, stationed a force of about 19,000 men on the Long Island side of the East River to defend his left flank. There they quickly erected fortifications on Brooklyn Heights and created a defensive position behind a ridge running eastward from Gowanus Bay at the western end of Long Island. Washington's eastern flank at Jamaica Pass, however, was left undefended. At dawn on August 22, General Howe led a British force of 32,000 from Staten Island to Gravesend Bay, Long Island, to launch an assault on Washington's isolated flank. After four days' reconnaissance, Howe attacked on August 27, eventually surrounding the colonial forces through the unprotected Jamaica Pass. The Continental Army fought bravely, but they were outnumbered and simply no match for the better-trained British forces. Approximately 1,400 American and 400 British soldiers were wounded, captured, or killed during the battle, and the Continentals fell back to Brooklyn Heights.

Realizing the futility of his position on Long Island, Washington took advantage of Howe's decision to lay siege rather than storm Brooklyn Heights, and he evacuated the Continental troops. During a storm on the night of August 29–30, Washington orchestrated an escape, moving the entire Continental force along with equipment and supplies across the East River into New York City. Thus, according to both territory acquired and casualties, the battle was a British victory. This battle also opened the way for the British to capture New York City and much of the lower Hudson River Valley.

Further reading: Henry Phelps Johnston, *The Campaign of 1776 around New York and Brooklyn . . .* (Brooklyn: Long Island Historical Society, 1878); Robert Middlekauff, *The Glorious Cause: The American Revolution, 1763–1789* (New York: Oxford University Press, 1982).

— Amy Pharr

Louisiana Purchase (1803)

The Louisiana Purchase nearly doubled America's territory overnight, moving the border to the Rocky Mountains. This enormous addition of land brought new sources of wealth in the form of timber, game, and minerals as well as millions of acres of potential farmland. Louisiana, Nebraska, Missouri, Iowa, and parts of North and South Dakota, Kansas, Oklahoma, Minnesota, Montana, Wyoming, and Colorado were formed out of the purchase. The purchase also brought additional populations that did not share a common British heritage. NATIVE AMERICANS and descendants of French and Spanish colonists lived in the new territory.

Before 1763, Louisiana had been claimed by France. With defeat in the French and Indian War (1754–63), France ceded the territory to Spain. The TREATY OF PARIS (1783) granted the area east of the Mississippi and north of FLORIDA to the United States and guaranteed the United States free navigation of the Mississippi. Unfortunately for the Americans, the last few hundred miles of the river lay completely in Spanish territory. If farmers in the new states west of the Appalachian Mountains wanted to send their crops to markets using the Mississippi, they had to ship them through the Spanish port of New Orleans. The governor of Spanish Louisiana allowed some Americans to settle around St. Louis if they promised to help keep others out of the territory. The Americans also had the "right of deposit"—the privilege to ship goods through New Orleans with Spanish permission. Many Americans resented the control Spain had over their commerce.

In 1800 the Spanish secretly gave Louisiana back to France, though Spain continued to guard it for its new owners. NAPOLEON BONAPARTE hoped to use Louisiana as a foothold in North America to start a new empire in the Western Hemisphere. When the revolutionaries in HAITI defeated French troops sent to retake the island colony of Saint-Dominigue, his hopes faded. Without the failure in Haiti, Napoleon may never have considered selling the

territory. Late in 1802, the Spanish colonial government suspended the "right of deposit" for Americans goods. President THOMAS JEFFERSON sent James Monroe and ROBERT R. LIVINGSTON to negotiate a sale of the Isle d'Orleans, the land on the east bank of the Mississippi that ran from the American border to the mouth of the river and secure navigation along the entire course of the river. After the initial rejection of the offer to buy the Isle d'Orleans, the negotiators were shocked when the French officials offered to sell them the entire Louisiana Territory. In April 1803, the talks yielded a deal. Napoleon knew that he could never hold on to Louisiana; the Americans would overrun it eventually. If he sold it to the United States, he would strengthen a potential rival that could trouble England for years to come. The United States was to pay $15 million for nearly 830,000 square miles of land. This agreement not only solved the problems of shipping on the Mississippi, it placed the United States in control of what would prove to be one of the richest regions of the world.

President Jefferson had doubts about the constitutional legitimacy of the purchase. Recognizing the opportunity to gain a huge addition to the country, he put aside such questions. He hoped to trade land in the West for the remnants of Native American lands in the rapidly growing states of the Old Northwest and Southwest. He also believed that the lands in the West would guarantee the agrarian nature of the American nation for centuries.

The Louisiana Purchase faced opposition from the FEDERALIST PARTY. Some of Jefferson's political enemies thought that he had overreached his authority. Like Jefferson, they believed the Constitution made no provision for this kind of sale, and they were unwilling to put aside this issue. Many of these eastern-based politicians feared that those who settled the new territory would lose their loyalty to the United States and might declare themselves independent or ally with a foreign power. Although much of the purchased territory remained unsettled by European Americans for decades, the opening of the Mississippi encouraged further settlement west of the Appalachians. Americans rapidly flooded west to stake out farms and build cities. No longer would the United States be hemmed into the lands along the Atlantic; the nation was on its way to becoming a continental power.

See also LEWIS AND CLARK EXPEDITION.

Further reading: Alexander DeConde, *The Affair of Louisiana* (New York: Scribner's, 1976); D. W. Meinig, *The Shaping of America: A Geographical Perspective on 500 Years of History,* vol. 2, *Continental America, 1800–1867* (New Haven, Conn.: Yale University Press, 1993).

— George Milne

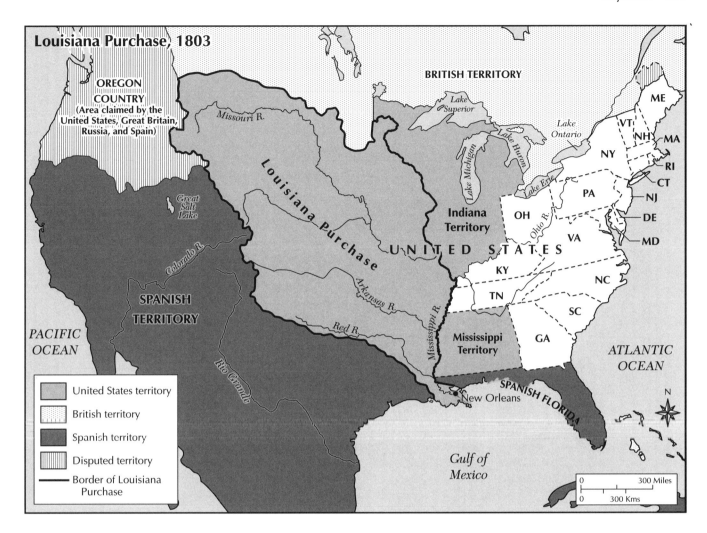

Loyalists

Called *Tories* by their political opponents, Loyalist Americans refused to support independence and remained faithful to the British Crown during the REVOLUTIONARY WAR (1775–83). There were Loyalists in every colony. New York, Pennsylvania, and South Carolina had the largest number while New England had relatively few. However, accurately estimating the total number of Loyalists in the population is difficult. JOHN ADAMS thought that one-third of the colonial population opposed independence, one-third supported independence, and one-third were neutral or did not care. More recent estimates suggest that a smaller number, perhaps 20 percent of the population, were Loyalists. Approximately 100,000 left the United States after the war. This amounted to between 3 and 4 percent of the population of the United States. Some of these people emigrated to Britain, several thousand went to the WEST INDIES, and as many as 50,000 traveled north to CANADA and Nova Scotia. Complicating these estimates are the thousands of "late Loyalists" who crossed the border into Canada in the years immediately after the war and those that eventually returned to the United States when anti-Loyalist feelings subsided.

The traditional stereotype pictured the Loyalists as officeholders or Anglican clergymen with ties to the British government. It was commonly assumed that they shared an innate conservatism sharply in contrast to the political radicalism of the revolutionaries. There were certainly some who fit that stereotype, but the Loyalists were in many respects a diverse group. Aside from a small elite, they were largely common people. Many were farmers and ARTISANS of modest means. Among those who left the United States there was a substantial representation of minorities, including AFRICAN AMERICANS from the South and Dutch, Huguenots, and QUAKERS from the middle colonies. A large number of Loyalists were members of the Church of England, although there were at least an equal number representing other denominations, including evangelicals from

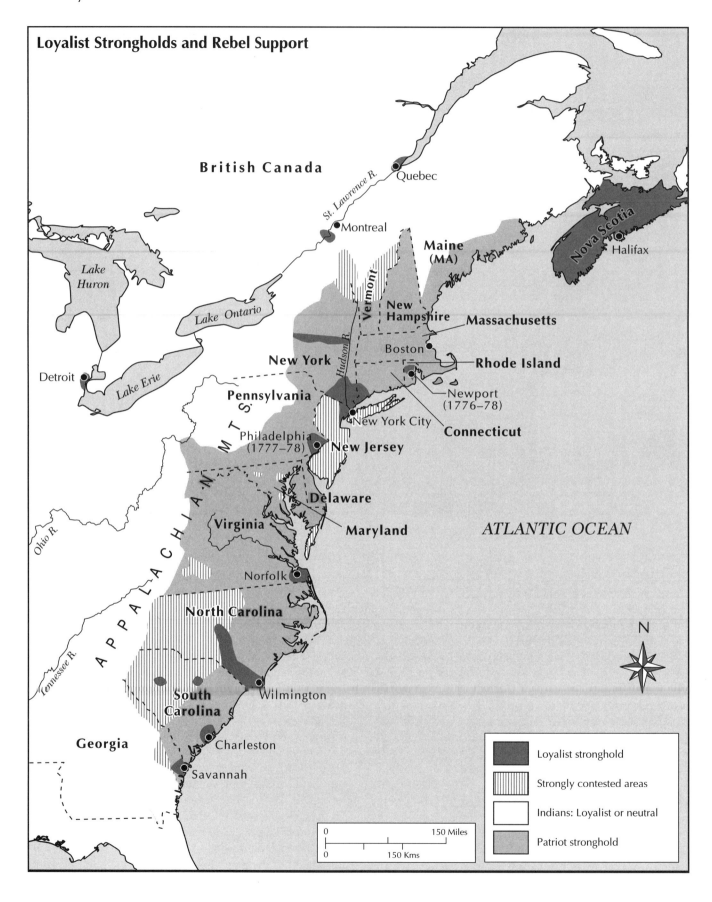

Loyalist Strongholds and Rebel Support

groups such as the METHODISTS and BAPTISTS. Many of the Loyalists came from families that had been in North America for several generations. Of the group that went to Nova Scotia, over 90 percent were born in North America, and many left relatives in the United States.

The Revolutionary War was a civil war as well as a struggle for independence. Conflicting loyalties often divided communities, congregations, and families. The decision to remain loyal to the Crown was often a difficult one and the reasons for it were complex. Like most political decisions, the choice was usually a function of personal principles and self-interest. It was, above all, a decision based on local conditions. In areas where political conflicts resulted in one side depending on the Crown, loyalism was common. The political enemies of the people who became revolutionaries were the people who supported the British forces. Tenants in the Hudson River Valley sought British support in their quarrels with their landlords. Backcountry farmers in South Carolina sided with the British against WHIG planters and merchants in Charleston.

Loyalism presupposed no particular political creed. Studies of Loyalist political thought indicate that a variety of political opinions were common among Loyalists both during the revolution and in exile. Loyalists and revolutionaries were often united in their opposition to British policies. But the Loyalists rejected the solution of independence, feeling strongly that their rights would be most secure within the British Empire. Many Loyalists actively argued their cause by speaking out and writing articles. While they did not rise as a group to support Britain, a substantial number eventually volunteered to fight alongside the British in Loyalist regiments or in guerrilla groups. Some performed other duties for the occupation forces. However, the majority of Loyalists simply attempted to survive and hold on to their homes. Most Loyalists remained in the United States after the war and quietly assimilated into the general population.

Of those who left the United States, some did so on the basis of a conscious decision, while others had no choice. Both the CONTINENTAL CONGRESS and the state assemblies approved repressive measures against the Loyalists. In most areas Loyalist property was confiscated, and Loyalists often were subject to violence by their neighbors. Some were tortured and killed. They were usually barred from political activity. During the war, large numbers of Loyalists lived under the protection of British forces in New York and Charleston. In 1783 when the war ended, they had little choice but to leave with the retreating British.

Of the 50,000 Loyalists who went to what is today Canada, 32,000 went to Nova Scotia. The remainder went to Quebec, most of those to the unsettled lands north of Lake Ontario. In the TREATY OF PARIS (1783), the Americans agreed in principle to compensate the Loyalists for lost and confiscated property. That agreement was never honored. The British provided some compensation for wartime losses, but fewer than 10 percent of the refugees owned enough property before the war to justify filing a claim with the Loyalist Claims Commission. All Loyalists were eligible for land grants, but in most cases they were a poor substitute for what they had lost. In contrast with civilian refugees, Loyalist troops, or *provincials*, had the added incentive of staying with trusted leaders and units. In many cases they also enjoyed the benefit of retirement on half-pay.

For the Loyalists, being on the losing side of the war was a bitter experience, particularly for those who went into exile. Many had lost much of what they owned and were forced to start over in mid-life and in difficult circumstances. However, most of the refugees persisted and eventually exerted a powerful influence on the colonies that received them. The modern nation of Canada may be considered as much a product of the Revolutionary War as was the United States. Two of the four colonies that united to form the Dominion of Canada in 1867, New Brunswick and Canada West (present-day Ontario), were created specifically for the Loyalists. In the other two, Nova Scotia and Canada East (present-day Quebec), the Loyalists exerted a substantial influence. While often overlooked or vilified in American history, the Loyalist tradition came to play an important role in the development of Canadian political culture.

Further reading: Bernard Bailyn, *The Ordeal of Thomas Hutchinson* (Cambridge, Mass.: Harvard University Press, 1974); Wallace Brown, *The Good Americans: The Loyalists in the American Revolution* (New York: William Morrow, 1969); Wallace Brown, *The Kings Friends: The Composition and Motives of the American Loyalist Claimants* (Providence, R.I.: Brown University Press, 1965); William H. Nelson, *The American Tory* (New York: Beacon Press, 1961); Paul H. Smith, *Loyalists and Redcoats: A Study in British Revolutionary Policy* (Chapel Hill: University of North Carolina Press, 1964).

— Robert Lively

Loyal Nine

In the summer and fall of 1765 a group of men from the middle ranks of Boston society called themselves the Loyal Nine and organized the initial street resistance to the STAMP ACT (1765). The group may have been a social club before the Stamp Act crisis. By the beginning of 1766 the Loyal Nine began to use the name adopted by similar groups in other communities—the SONS OF LIBERTY. The Loyal Nine strove to keep their activities a secret. They printed handbills calling for crowd action against stamp agent ANDREW OLIVER and built the effigies used by the mob. They developed a close relationship with mob captain EBENEZER MACINTOSH, who had previously been known for his role in Pope Day celebrations. They also organized other demonstrations and elicited a second public resignation of Oliver as stamp distributor in December 1765.

Because JOHN ADAMS visited one of their meetings in January 1766, we have a list of names of the probable members. Adams's diary included the following names: John Avery, a distiller or merchant; John Smith, a brazier; John Smith, a printer; Joseph Field, a ship captain; Benjamin Edes, a printer; Stephen Cleverly, a brazier; Henry Bass, a merchant; George Trott, a jeweler; and Thomas Crafts, a painter. Some scholars believe that Field, like Adams, was just visiting the meeting and that Henry Wells was the ninth member. There is also strong evidence indicating that SAMUEL ADAMS was closely connected to the Loyal Nine. Whatever the exact membership of this organization, they played the central role in the Stamp Act resistance in Boston.

See also RESISTANCE MOVEMENT.

Further reading: Pauline Maier, *From Resistance to Revolution: Colonial Radicals and the Development of American Opposition to Britain, 1765–1776* (New York: Knopf, 1972); Edmund S. Morgan and Helen M. Morgan, *The Stamp Act Crisis: Prologue to a Revolution* (Chapel Hill: University of North, Carolina Press, 1953).

Lyon, Matthew (1750–1822)

Matthew Lyon rose from humble beginnings to become a leading DEMOCRATIC-REPUBLICAN politician. He was born in Ireland and emigrated to the American colonies at age 15. After acquiring enough money to purchase land, Lyon settled in Cornwall, Connecticut, in 1772. Marrying Mary Hosford (niece of ETHAN ALLEN) one year later, he moved again in 1774 after purchasing land in the Hampshire Grants (Vermont) from the Allen Brothers.

Lyon quickly became involved in the local militia (the GREEN MOUNTAIN BOYS) where he was promoted to colonel, and was prominently known in the border country of Lake Champlain. He played an important role in the capture of FORT TICONDEROGA on May 10, 1775. When the DECLARATION OF INDEPENDENCE was signed on July 4, 1776, Lyon immediately joined the CONTINENTAL ARMY. Serving as a second lieutenant during the REVOLUTIONARY WAR (1775–83), Lyon fought near the Canadian border. He was dishonorably discharged from the army after his troops got into some disciplinary trouble, but he was soon reinstated, serving with distinction during General ARTHUR ST. CLAIR's retreat before General JOHN BURGOYNE's invasion in the summer of 1777. Lyon resigned from the army after Burgoyne's surrender at SARATOGA (October 17, 1777), heading back to the Green Mountains region, where he became involved in politics and the business world.

Although Vermont still technically was a part of New York, settlers in the Green Mountains wrote their own state constitution in 1777. (The United States admitted Vermont as a state in 1791.) In this breakaway state government Lyon served as deputy secretary to the governor and as a representative in the legislature. After his first wife died in 1782, he married Beulah (Chittenden) Galusha, and one year later he moved to Fairhaven, where he became a leading businessman. There, Lyon owned 400 acres of land rich in iron, timber, and water power, and he successfully used these resources. Lyon established his own printing press and newspaper (the *Farmer's Library*) in 1793, with which he openly advocated direct representation, sympathized with the FRENCH REVOLUTION (1789–1815), and opposed the views of ALEXANDER HAMILTON. With cloth paper not meeting his publishing needs, he invented a new process of making paper out of basswood.

Lyon was known for boasting of the role his press played in the formation of the Democratic-Republican Party. He began running for federal office, winning his first seat in Congress in 1796. Because of his background and party affiliation, Lyon received contempt from his fellow congressmen and was the object of suspicion and many cruel jokes. The FEDERALIST PARTY press was unrelenting in their personal attacks on Lyon; his Irish birth was ridiculed, as was his former status as an indentured servant. The most popular instance of this occurred in 1798, when, after Roger Griswold insulted his military record, Lyon spat in his face. Griswold then assaulted him with a cane, whereupon Lyon grabbed a pair of fire tongs and a fencing match ensued on the floor of the House of Representatives.

After this incident, the Federalists watched Lyon with a sharp eye, waiting for the first sign of seditious libel worthy of prosecution. They got their wish when Lyon published a letter in the *Vermont Journal* that same year. He served as his own attorney during the trial and was sentenced to four months in jail and a $1,000 fine. Lyon continually published throughout his imprisonment and was reelected to federal office before his release date. While Federalists tried to bar him from his political seat, Democratic-Republicans defended his innocence.

In 1801 Lyon resettled to Kentucky, where he founded the city of Eddyville. There his life mirrored that of the successful businessman he had been in Vermont. He remained politically active as well, until, due mostly to his opposition to the policies leading to the War of 1812 (1812–15), he was defeated for election in the 12th Congress. Lyon's business suffered during the war, but his friendship with President James Monroe brought him a political appointment in 1820. Lyon moved to Spadra Bluff, Arkansas, where he managed the trading activities of the CHEROKEE NATION until his death two years later.

See also ALIEN AND SEDITION ACTS; JOURNALISM.

Further reading: Aleine Austin, *Matthew Lyon, "New Man" of the Democratic Revolution, 1749–1822* (University Park, Penn.: Pennsylvania State University Press, 1981).

— Meghan A. Earl

M

MacIntosh, Ebenezer (1737–1816)

Ebenezer MacIntosh was a shoemaker who achieved brief fame and notoriety for the role he played in Boston's RIOTS against the STAMP ACT in 1765. MacIntosh was born to an impoverished family and apprenticed as a shoemaker. He had few career prospects. Shoemakers in Boston were generally poor, and in the years prior to the REVOLUTIONARY WAR (1775–83) their fortunes were declining.

In the 1760s MacIntosh emerged as a popular leader among the poor in Boston's South End. He was a prominent and leading participant in the town's celebrations of Pope Day (November 5). Pope Day was an American celebration of the British folk holiday Guy Fawkes Day (held to remember the discovery of the CATHOLIC Fawkes's "gunpowder plot" to destroy Parliament). In Britain, Guy Fawkes Day was commemorated with bonfires and burning of effigies of Fawkes. In colonial America, especially the seaports of New England, the celebrations were popular, with particular emphasis given to the anti-Catholic aspects of the day. Boston held two processions—one in the town's North End and one in the South End—that entailed large crowds traveling door-to-door with an effigy of the pope soliciting donations of money or liquor. In the evening the two processions met and fought a battle. The winners were able to burn the popes in a massive bonfire. Wealthy Bostonians saw Pope Day as unsettling because poorer Bostonians engaged in rowdy and unruly behavior.

During the early 1760s, Boston's Pope Day celebrations had become increasingly violent. On November 5, 1764, prior to the procession, a young boy fell under the carriage carrying the South End pope and was killed. In response, the sheriff and militia were called out to destroy the North and South End popes and to cancel to celebration. The officials destroyed the North End pope but a South End crowd, under the leadership of MacIntosh, defended their effigy. The North Enders rebuilt their pope

and a raucous, violent celebration was held. For his part as "captain" of the South End procession, MacIntosh was arrested and subsequently acquitted in a trial in February 1765.

Soon after MacIntosh's acquittal in Boston, Parliament adopted the Stamp Act. In Boston, opposition to the Act was coordinated by a group of ARTISANS and lesser merchants known as the LOYAL NINE. In August 1765 the Loyal Nine mediated the unification of the North and South End mobs prior to the disturbances that led to the resignation of ANDREW OLIVER, a Boston merchant suspected as the likely Stamp Act collector in Massachusetts. MacIntosh led a crowd of over 3,000 in demonstrations on August 14, which included destroying an effigy of Oliver as well as the merchant's office and home. The next day Oliver resigned as stamp distributor (a post to which he had not yet been appointed). Bostonians had rendered the Stamp Act a dead letter. The solution proved infectious, and soon similar demonstrations—followed by resignations—were held throughout the colonies. MacIntosh also helped to lead the mob that attacked and gutted THOMAS HUTCHINSON's house on August 26.

Although Ebenezer MacIntosh was a popular leader in 1765, many of the men who tried to guide the RESISTANCE MOVEMENT (1764–75) may have been uncomfortable with him because of his social standing. He reappeared in the streets on Pope Day in 1765, wearing a blue and gold uniform trimmed with lace, bearing a rattan cane and a speaking trumpet, in mockery of men like Andrew Oliver whom he had humbled. MacIntosh, however, soon returned to obscurity. There is no record of his participation in any of the crowds protesting imperial regulations in the late 1760s and 1770s. In fact, he ran upon economic hard times and languished for a while in debtor's jail. Many years later he claimed to have led the BOSTON TEA PARTY (December 16, 1773), but there is no evidence to back this assertion. In 1774 Macintosh left Boston to settle in Haverhill, New

Hampshire. He spent most of the rest of his days there in poverty, dying in 1816 in the local poor farm.

Further reading: George P. Anderson, "Ebenezer Mackintosh: Stamp Act Rioter and Patriot," *Publications of the Colonial Society of Massachusetts* 26 (1924–26): 15–64; Gary B. Nash, *The Urban Crucible: Social Change, Political Consciousness, and the Origins of the American Revolution* (Cambridge, Mass.: Harvard University Press, 1979).

— Francis D. Cogliano

Macon, Nathaniel (1758–1837)

A veteran of the REVOLUTIONARY WAR (1775–83) and 37 years as a member of Congress, Nathaniel Macon was born near Warrenton, North Carolina, in 1758. He emerged from the Revolution as one of the leading figures in his home state and became a vigorous supporter of STATE'S RIGHTS and a committed ANTI-FEDERALIST. Macon fought against ratification of the Constitution because he believed it concentrated too much power in the hands of the central government. However, he became an influential political figure in the new republic upon his election to the House of Representatives in 1791.

Macon served as Speaker of the House between 1801 and 1807 and remained a DEMOCRATIC-REPUBLICAN despite his brief association with a political faction known as the "Quids," who supported James Monroe over JAMES MADISON as the man they wanted to succeed THOMAS JEFFERSON as president. He successfully ran for a seat in the Senate following the War of 1812 (1812–15) and served as a senator from 1815 to 1828. During his last two years in office he also served as president pro tempore of the Senate, thus retiring as the fourth-most-powerful elected official in the United States.

In both houses of Congress, Macon vigorously opposed FEDERALIST PARTY policies, from the ALIEN AND SEDITION ACTS (1798) to protective TARIFFS, and strongly attacked the reestablishment of the BANK OF THE UNITED STATES. He was a champion of personal liberty and limited government throughout his life, and ironically he opposed a bill that bears his name and represents his most enduring legacy in the popular mind. MACON'S BILL NO. 2, which Congress passed in 1810, reopened American TRADE with Britain and France, which the EMBARGO OF 1807 had banned three years earlier. Like its predecessors, however, the bill failed to stop the drift toward war between the United States and Great Britain in 1812. Macon died in 1837.

Further reading: William E. Dodd, *The Life of Nathaniel Macon* (Raleigh, N.C.: Edwards and Broughton 1903).

— Lance Janda

Macon's Bill No. 2 (1810)

Passed by Congress in 1810, Macon's Bill No. 2 was one of many American actions designed to force Britain and France to recognize the rights of neutral countries on the high seas in time of war. It grew out of the NON-IMPORTATION ACT of 1806, which forbade American merchants from importing specific British goods, and the EMBARGO OF 1807, which prohibited all international TRADE to and from American ports. President THOMAS JEFFERSON approved these measures under the mistaken impression that the United States had sufficient economic leverage to persuade Britain and France to stop interfering with American trade in the midst of wars between those two countries, but the acts succeeded only in ruining many United States merchants.

Congress ended the effort to break Britain and France economically when it passed Macon's Bill No. 2, which took its name from NATHANIEL MACON, a member of the House of Representatives from North Carolina who, ironically, opposed it. The bill reopened American trade with both Britain and France despite their continued interference with American trade. It provided, however, that if one country stopped its interference, the United States would trade with that country to the exclusion of the other. Like previous efforts to influence French and British policy, this bill also failed. When France indicated it was going to repeal its restrictions on American trade, the United States, following Macon's Bill No. 2, stopped trade with Britain. This action helped to precipitate the War of 1812 (1812–15).

See also FOREIGN AFFAIRS.

— Lance Janda

Madison, Dolley Payne Todd (1768–1849)

Dolley Madison, the wife of JAMES MADISON and fashionable Washington hostess, was born on May 20, 1768, in Piedmont, North Carolina. Dolley Payne was one of eight children of QUAKER parents Mary Coles and John Payne. Three years after Dolley's birth the family moved to her mother's family estate, Cole Hill Plantation in Hanover County, Virginia. After the conclusion of the REVOLUTIONARY WAR (1775–83), Dolley's father, in accordance with those members of the Quaker faith advocating emancipation, freed his slaves and moved the family to Philadelphia, where Dolley married her first husband, John Todd, in January 1790.

John Todd, a successful lawyer in Philadelphia, and Dolley Payne Todd shared only a few years of happiness, highlighted by the births of two sons, John Payne Todd, born in 1790, and William Temple Todd, born in 1792. In 1793 a yellow fever epidemic struck the city of Philadelphia, killing over 5,000 people. For Dolley Todd the toll of the plague proved acute. Her husband, in-laws, and son William died within one week's time. Although the Payne family no longer resided in Philadelphia, Dolley decided to stay in the city with her surviving son, John Payne Todd (called Payne), where she was surrounded by friends. In the spring of 1794, Congressman James Madison asked his friend AARON BURR to introduce him to the vivacious widow, and by September of the same year Dolley married the representative from Virginia.

The Madisons resided in Philadelphia, living within the domestic circle occupied by visits from her siblings and her son Payne; the couple remained childless. With the election of FEDERALIST JOHN ADAMS to the presidency in 1796, James Madison retired from politics, and he and Dolley moved to the Madison family plantation, Montpelier, in Orange County, Virginia. The retirement proved brief. In 1801, President THOMAS JEFFERSON appointed James Madison as secretary of state, and the Madisons moved to the nation's new capital, WASHINGTON, D.C. Jefferson was their good friend, and their first residence in the city was in the president's house. During this time, Dolley Madison acted as the unofficial "first lady" for Jefferson, who was himself a widower, initiating a public role she held for over 16 years, through Jefferson's two terms (1801–09) and her husband's presidency (1809–17).

Upon the election of James Madison to the presidency, the Madisons moved back into the president's house, and aided by architect Benjamin Henry Latrobe, Dolley undertook to decorate the home. The result was a social space that was the talk of the town. Mrs. Madison's "drawing room," especially on Wednesday night, became the place to be in Washington. Dolley accentuated her image as a hostess through clothing; her grand and colorful costumes, highly influenced by French fashion, commanded attention. Admirers called her "Queen Dolly" and her "crown" of choice was the fashionable turban. During the War of 1812 (1812–15), the British invaded Washington, D.C., in 1814, burning the public buildings of the capital, including the president's house. It was due to Dolley's efforts that the portrait of GEORGE WASHINGTON, an American icon, was saved. When the couple returned to the capital, Dolley resumed her role as first lady. In 1817, with the election of James Monroe as president, James Madison permanently retired from politics. The couple left Washington, and although Dolley missed the society she found in Washington, visitors flocked to their plantation in Virginia.

See also DISEASE AND EPIDEMICS.

Further reading: Catherine Allgor, *Parlor Politics: In Which the Ladies of Washington Help Guild a City and a Government* (Charlottesville: University of Virginia Press, 2000), 48–146; Lewis L Gould,. ed., *American First Ladies: Their Lives and Their Legacy* (New York: Garland, 1996), 45–68.

— Christine Coalwell

Madison, James (1751–1836)

Born into a prominent Virginia family and a leading founding father, James Madison was a member of the CONTINENTAL CONGRESS, an architect of the Constitution, a close ally of THOMAS JEFFERSON in the formation of the DEMOCRATIC-REPUBLICAN PARTY, a secretary of state, and president during the War of 1812 (1812–15).

In 1762 Madison began his education under the tutelage of the Presbyterian minister Donald Robertson of King and Queen County, Virginia. After five years with Robertson he returned to his family home at Montpelier, where he studied for the next two years with the Reverend Thomas Martin. In 1769 Madison attended the College of New Jersey (present-day Princeton University), where he studied under the Reverend JOHN WITHERSPOON, a prominent classical scholar and staunch WHIG. Madison graduated in the fall of 1771 but remained in Princeton to read law under Witherspoon's direction.

By the spring of 1772, Madison later remembered, he was "under very early and strong impressions in favor of liberty both civil and religious." In the years prior to the REVOLUTIONARY WAR (1775–83), when provincial committees of safety formed to prepare for war with Great Britain, Madison and his father joined the local Orange County organization. In 1774, when members of the BAPTIST community were imprisoned in the neighboring county of Culpepper, Madison denounced the suppression of their freedom.

Two years later, Orange County elected Madison to the Virginia convention in Williamsburg. There Madison supported Virginia's formal declaration of independence. Soon thereafter, Madison became a member of the committee to prepare a Declaration of Rights and a plan of government. In committee, Madison suggested the disestablishment of the state church, and although this proved too progressive, the legislature did adopt Madison's amendment entitling "all men" the right to "free exercise of religion." In October 1776 he first met Thomas Jefferson who, having recently returned from the SECOND CONTINENTAL CONGRESS, was anxious to contribute to the formation of Virginia's new government. They served together on several committees, including the committee on religion; the "great collaboration" of Madison and Jefferson, however, was yet to begin.

Madison, who did not win reelection as a legislative delegate, soon returned to Williamsburg as a member of Virginia's executive council and served under Governors PATRICK HENRY and Jefferson. In 1779 he became a delegate to the Continental Congress, and in March 1780 he left Virginia for Philadelphia. When Madison arrived, the nation still awaited unanimous state ratification of the ARTICLES OF CONFEDERATION. At this time Madison helped to persuade large states to cede their western lands, thus opening the way for smaller states like Maryland to ratify the Articles. The western territories, Maryland argued, were the common property of the confederation and the federal government should control the proceeds of public sale of the land.

Another major difficulty for the Continental Congress was financing the war. Since Congress did not possess the power to impose taxes, it remained dependent on the states. In 1781 Congress established federal departments of finance, war, and FOREIGN AFFAIRS. ROBERT MORRIS headed finance and undertook to set up an efficient method of supplying the troops, while several members of Congress, including Madison, sought additional French aid to rescue the southern states from British occupation. At the close of Madison's first year in Congress, he began to recognize the value of a more energetic government. After victory in the Revolutionary War, Madison began to believe that with independence won on the battlefield, Americans must now work to secure it.

Madison turned his attention to the problem of national finance. Working to help Congress in the transition to a peacetime government, he lobbied for an amendment to the Articles of Confederation authorizing a 5 percent duty on imports that would generate the revenue necessary to operate government and repay accumulated wartime debts. Many congressmen, however, opposed a more central authority and the amendment failed to pass. Madison left Congress in November 1783 after serving four years, longer than any other representative. Already an authority on federal affairs, he now studied the problems of ancient confederacies.

Madison returned to represent Orange County in the Virginia House of Delegates in April 1784. In June he persuaded the legislature to appoint a commission to negotiate Virginia's right to navigate the Potomac River. After the commission successfully completed its task, Representative JOHN TAYLOR OF CAROLINE suggested, with the urging of Madison, that delegates from the various states convene to consider a uniform system of commercial regulations. In January 1786 Virginia sent out a national request for delegates to meet in Annapolis, Maryland, in September. Although only five states sent representatives, the ANNAPOLIS CONVENTION recommended that another meeting occur in Philadelphia in order "to render the Constitution of the federal government adequate to the exigencies of the Union."

In the meantime, Madison pursued RELIGIOUS LIBERTY in Virginia, shepherding through the state legislature Jefferson's "Act for Establishing Religious Freedom," which secured, as the preamble states, "that our civil rights have no dependence on our religious opinions." Jefferson cheered "the first legislature who had the courage to declare, that the reason of man may be trusted with the formation of his own opinions." The Virginia Statute of Religious Freedom would be a precursor of the First Amendment to the United States Constitution.

Late in 1786 Madison was elected to the Confederation Congress, and in February 1787 he took his seat as a representative in New York, the temporary capital of the confederacy. Within months, Madison left New York for Pennsylvania to attend the CONSTITUTIONAL CONVENTION. In Philadelphia, the delegates decided not to revise or amend the Articles of Confederation but, rather, to draft a new Constitution, voting on May 30 that "a national Government ought to be established." Madison declared, "We are laying the foundation of a great empire." Although the deliberations were kept secret, Madison kept notes, and his account of the convention's transactions, published posthumously, provides the only full record of the proceedings.

For four months the delegates deliberated on the nature of a sound republic. Madison recognized that the new central government must possess the power necessary to operate efficiently. EDMUND RANDOLPH proposed Madison's "Virginia Plan," which recommended an entirely new form of government with an executive, judiciary, and a bicameral legislature. The Virginia Plan backed proportional representation in the bicameral legislature—a plan that representatives from the larger states supported; smaller states, however, backed New Jersey's plan for equal representation. ROGER SHERMAN's "Connecticut Compromise" finally decided the issue: States would have representation based on population in the House of Representatives, while in the Senate they would be represented equally. Yet, who would be represented? Madison said that it would be "wrong to admit . . . the idea that there could be property in men," but northerners wanted slaves to be counted as taxable property, and southerners wished to count them when determining representation in the House. The "Great Compromise" was the settlement reached: Slaves would count as three-fifths of a person. Madison referred to SLAVERY as a "blot" or a "stain" and worried that this compromise might later jeopardize the Constitution. On September 17, 1787, the final document was signed. The framers of the Constitution in Article VII imparted the power of ratification to the individual state conventions. Considering state conventions a more direct representation of the will of the people, Madison called this procedure "the highest source of authority."

Madison, a fervent advocate of the Constitution, believed that the success or failure of the Constitution "would decide for ever the fate of republican government." A complex and innovative document, it did not excite unqualified approval. Supporters of the Constitution called themselves FEDERALISTS, and opponents were ANTI-FEDERALISTS. Before returning to Virginia, Madison worked with ALEXANDER HAMILTON and JOHN JAY to produce 77 essays, written under the pseudonym "Publius," to explain and defend the new system against the anti-Federalists' charges. Along with the publication of the FEDERALIST

PAPERS, Madison led the campaign for ratification against anti-Federalist Patrick Henry, who supported the widespread call to postpone ratification until another convention could be held to add a declaration of rights.

Running against James Monroe and promising that, if elected, he would work to add a BILL OF RIGHTS to the Constitution, Madison won a seat in the House of Representatives. He wanted the first Congress to provide "additional guards in favour of liberty" and was the leader of the reform movement. "I should be unwilling to see a door opened for a re-consideration of the whole structure of the government," Madison wrote, "[b]ut I do wish to see a door opened to consider, so far as to incorporate those provisions for the security of rights." On June 8, 1789, Madison proposed that the Congress adopt a Bill of Rights. Altogether a dozen amendments would be proposed, 10 of which were ratified.

While framing the Constitution, Madison worked in harmony with GEORGE WASHINGTON and Hamilton. Political discord, however, arose under the new federal government. When Secretary of the Treasury Hamilton advanced a series of controversial proposals in 1791 to strengthen the federal government, Madison led the resistance. For Washington and Hamilton, their former collaborator's opposition was a shocking blow both personally and politically. Siding with Secretary of State Jefferson, Madison viewed Hamilton's plan as a threat to liberty—one that went beyond the limits authorized in the Constitution. By rallying opposition against Hamilton, Madison and Jefferson—the acknowledged leaders of the movement—began to organize a factional alliance that they described as Democratic-Republican.

Jefferson resigned from Washington's administration in 1793, leaving Madison as the leader of the loosely organized group. Partisan strife heated up during the presidential election of 1796, which resulted in the election of JOHN ADAMS of the FEDERALIST PARTY to the president; Jefferson was elected vice president. In 1797, after Congress adjourned, Madison, having declined reelection to another term in the House of Representatives, left Philadelphia for Montpelier.

Madison did not return to Montpelier alone. In the 1780s, Madison had fallen in love with Catherine "Kitty" Floyd. Although she initially accepted his proposal, she broke off the engagement within months. In 1794 Madison was more fortunate. He had his friend AARON BURR introduce him to Dolley Payne Todd, a beautiful and vivacious widow. The couple married that September, and DOLLEY MADISON went on to earn enduring fame as a Washington hostess for both Jefferson and Madison.

Madison's retirement from politics proved brief. In opposition to Adams's ALIEN AND SEDITION ACTS (1798), Madison drafted the Virginia Resolutions. (Jefferson wrote similar resolves for Kentucky's legislature.) The VIRGINIA AND KENTUCKY RESOLUTIONS questioned the federal government's right to exercise powers not delegated to it by the Constitution and helped to establish the STATE'S RIGHTS theory of government.

Jefferson was elected president in 1800 and named Madison his secretary of state. The Madisons moved to the nation's new capital, WASHINGTON, D.C., where they would live for the next 16 years. For the duration of Jefferson's presidency (1801–09), Madison served as secretary of state and the president's most trusted advisor. In the election of 1808, Madison won 122 of 173 possible electoral votes, and on Saturday, March 4, 1809, he was inaugurated as the fourth president of the United States.

At Madison's inaugural ball, departing President Jefferson was asked why he seemed so happy and Madison so serious and sad. He replied that "I have the burthen off my shoulders, while he has now got it on his." Madison inherited a crisis: France and Britain were seizing United States merchant vessels, and the British were using IMPRESSMENT to force American men into naval service.

James Madison *(Library of Congress)*

Efforts to use TRADE to force Great Britain to respect the United States failed. Impotent to protect American ships and men, and with the War Hawks in Congress pressing for a fight, Madison asked Congress to declare war against Great Britain on June 1, 1812.

After the declaration of war, Madison easily won reelection. For two and one-half years the United States fought the War of 1812, and oftentimes it seemed uncertain that the young nation would endure. American forces were, with few exceptions, badly led, underfinanced, and poorly trained. In the summer of 1814, Madison watched as one of his officers, commanding twice the number of troops as the opponent, fled almost without firing a shot. The British then marched into Washington, where they burned a number of buildings, including the executive mansion. When Madison returned to Washington, however, he received news of the British defeat at the Battle of Baltimore (September 12–14, 1814). On Christmas Eve 1814, the war ended in stalemate with the signing of the Treaty of Ghent.

In 1817, after Monroe assumed the presidency, Madison retired to Montpelier. Together with Jefferson and Monroe, he worked to establish the University of Virginia (1819) and served as its second rector (1826–36) after Jefferson's death. "Having outlived so many of my contemporaries," he said, "I ought not to forget that I may be thought to have outlived my self." The last of the "founders" died at the age of 85 on June 28, 1836, and he was buried in the family cemetery at Montpelier. Dolley Madison inherited his papers, most particularly his notes from the Constitutional Convention, which she published as Madison directed. While she received most of the proceeds, Madison had earmarked some of the funds for various causes, particularly EDUCATION. He also bequeathed $2,000 to the American Colonization Society. Although a lifetime slave owner, Madison held an unyielding commitment to abolishing slavery in the United States. Nevertheless, he made no provision in his will for his nearly 100 slaves. On August 12, 1844, Dolley Madison sold the Montpelier estate, including its enslaved workforce, to Henry Moncure.

In 1834, two years before his death, Madison wrote "Advice to My Country," not to be read "till I am no more." He wrote that "the advice nearest to my heart and deepest in my convictions is that the Union of the States be cherished and perpetuated." He professed an "inexhaustible faith that a well-founded commonwealth might be immortal." Today James Madison is remembered as the "father of the Constitution."

See also POLITICAL PARTIES; REPUBLICANISM.

Further reading: Ralph Louis Ketcham, *James Madison: A Biography* (New York: Macmillan, 1971); Drew R. McCoy, *The Last of the Fathers: James Madison and the Republican Legacy* (Cambridge, U.K.: Cambridge University Press, 1989).

—Christine Coalwell

Marbury v. Madison (1803)

Marbury v. Madison is the most important decision issued by the early republican SUPREME COURT. It established that the Supreme Court of the United States can exercise the power of judicial review—the power to declare governmental acts unconstitutional. The decision represented one volley in the ongoing war between the DEMOCRATIC-REPUBLICAN president and Congress and the FEDERALIST judiciary over who would control the future development of the nation.

On the heels of the JUDICIARY ACT OF 1801, by which President JOHN ADAMS acquired the power to appoint 16 new federal judges, Adams signed legislation creating a new court for WASHINGTON, D.C. This act became law on February 27, 1801, four days before Adams left office, and empowered Adams to appoint three more federal judges and numerous marshals, clerks, attorneys, and justices of the peace. Adams and his secretary of state, JOHN MARSHALL, signed commissions naming Federalists to these positions, but not all the commissions were delivered to the intended officeholders before Jefferson's swearing-in. Among those who did not receive his commission was William Marbury, who had been named a justice of the peace for the District of Columbia. When Jefferson took office, his secretary of state, JAMES MADISON, refused to deliver Marbury's commission, and Marbury filed suit in the Supreme Court of the United States, asking the court to issue a writ of mandamus (a court order that stated "we command") ordering Madison to turn over his commission.

Marbury's case was unusual. In filing the action directly with the Supreme Court, he relied on that court's having what the Constitution calls "original" jurisdiction—the jurisdiction to preside over the trial of a case—as opposed to "appellate jurisdiction,"—the jurisdiction to preside over an appeal. The Constitution authorizes the Supreme Court to exercise original jurisdiction in only a few types of cases, including cases involving ambassadors, cases between states, and the like. Marbury, however, could point to Section 13 of the JUDICIARY ACT OF 1789, which authorized the Supreme Court to issue writs of mandamus in cases involving public officers.

The Supreme Court thus had three issues to resolve: Did it have jurisdiction to hear the case? Had Madison done anything wrong? and Was a mandamus order the appropriate remedy? In a move derided by contemporaries as political, Chief Justice Marshall (who might well have recused himself, as he had signed Marbury's commission) answered the last two questions first. Madison, he held, had wronged Marbury by failing to deliver his commission, and under the Judiciary Act of 1789 mandamus was an available and appropriate remedy. The administration of THOMAS JEFFERSON, in short, had got it wrong. Madison had failed in his public duties, and William Marbury had been injured. Pursuant to the Judiciary Act of 1789, the Supreme Court would be acting within it rights by ordering the secretary of state to deliver the commission. Had Marshall issued the writ, of course, it is not at all clear that Madison would have obeyed it. A constitutional crisis of the first order would have been precipitated. Could the judiciary tell the executive what to do? The answer of the Jeffersonians, who controlled both the presidency and the Congress, might well have been "no." In this case, what future did the Supreme Court have? Understanding this, John Marshall opted to lose the battle and win the war. The Supreme Court would not issue Marbury's writ of mandamus, but not because the facts did not warrant it or because the statute did not allow it. It would not order Madison to deliver Marbury's commission because, in granting the Supreme Court the authority to issue writs of mandamus against public officials in the Judiciary Act of 1789, Congress had passed an unconstitutional act. The Supreme Court, therefore, was without jurisdiction.

Marbury v. Madison was an astonishing opinion. It was the first case in which the Supreme Court of the United States exercised the power to declare acts of Congress unconstitutional. The Jeffersonians counterattacked by impeaching Justice SAMUEL CHASE and threatening to impeach the Supreme Court's entire Federalist component. So effective was this counterattack that the Marshall Court never again invalidated a federal statute. But the opinion was on the books, and generations would look to it as the defining moment in the Court's establishment as the guardian of the Constitution. In modern times, the power is exercised regularly, and for many it defines the central role of the Supreme Court.

Further reading: Robert Lowry Clinton, Marbury v. Madison: *The Origins and Legacy of Judicial Review* (Lawrence: University Press of Kansas, 1986); Donald Odell Dewey, *Marshall versus Jefferson: The Political Background of* Marbury vs. Madison (New York: Knopf, 1970); William E. Nelson, Marbury v. Madison *and Judicial Review* (Lawrence: University Press of Kansas, 2000).

— Lindsay Robertson

Marion, Francis ("the Swamp Fox") (1732–1795)

One of the REVOLUTIONARY WAR's most colorful and legendary leaders, Francis Marion was instrumental in organizing guerrilla warfare against the British enemy in the South. Born in South Carolina in 1732, the last of six children, Marion was a rather puny, sickly boy, who lived much of his youth in the port at Georgetown. Fascinated by the ships and sailor's tales, he went to sea at age 15. Though his maritime experience strengthened his health, he was lucky to survive a disastrous voyage into the Caribbean. Subsequently, he gave up the sea, returned to his parents' home, and settled into farming. Around the age of 25, near the end of the French and Indian War (1754–63), Marion began his army career with a local militia company. He first came under fire against the CHEROKEE, who were threatening South Carolina's border settlements. Holding the rank of lieutenant, Marion led his men into the woods, taking cover from tree to tree, as they battled the Indians. This irregular military service would serve him well in the future. The Cherokee eventually sued for peace, and Marion, having earned respect as a courageous veteran and leader, returned to his farm.

The years that followed witnessed a deterioration in the relations between Great Britain and her North American colonies. Of Huguenot descent, Marion knew of the hardships that had driven his grandparents from France to the Carolinas in search of religious and political freedom. His background made him sympathetic to the cause of separation from England, and Marion's district elected him as their representative to South Carolina's first provincial congress, which met in Charleston in January 1775. When news came of the bloodshed at LEXINGTON AND CONCORD (April 19, 1775), the provincial congress agreed to raise three regiments from South Carolina. Because of his distinguished service against the Cherokee, Francis Marion was appointed one of the captains of the Second Regiment, and by 1778 was its commandant with the rank of lieutenant colonel. He served in the defense of CHARLESTON until it fell to the British on May 12, 1780. The Second Regiment was captured, but Marion escaped and joined the CONTINENTAL ARMY that was heading south into the Carolinas.

Despite his standing as a Continental officer, Marion soon took command of a homespun-clad militia force. The American forces were at a disadvantage against South Carolina's LOYALISTS and the invading British army, one of the most efficient fighting forces in the world. Marion knew his untrained and often temperamental band of volunteer farmers and shopkeepers could not compete in numbers or expertise in conventional battlefield warfare. Instead, Marion and his men utilized their intimate knowledge of the local geography and executed daring hit-and-run raids against the enemy to burn or destroy matériel and free rebel prisoners.

Marion's wily tactics and habit of hiding in the numerous bogs and morasses of South Carolina soon earned him the nickname of "the Swamp Fox." By December 1780, Marion's astute abilities as strategist, tactician, fighter, and disciplinarian merited his promotion to brigadier general. His gallant conduct at the Battles of Parker's Ferry and EUTAW SPRINGS (September 8, 1781) brought grateful thanks from the CONTINENTAL CONGRESS. As the British steadily lost control of South Carolina and civil government was reestablished, Marion's precinct elected him to the state senate. When the British finally evacuated Charleston in December 1782, the militia disbanded and the Swamp Fox was free to return home. His plantation was in ruins and he was destitute. In 1786, at age 54, Marion wed his first cousin, Mary Esther Videau. He ended his political career after serving as a delegate to the state's constitutional convention of 1790 and retired from militia service in 1794. He died without heirs at his Pond Bluff home on February 27, 1795.

Further reading: Robert D. Bass, *Swamp Fox: The Life and Campaigns of General Francis Marion* (Lexington, S.C.: Sandlapper Store, 1974); P. Horry and M. L. Weems, *The Life of General Francis Marion: A Celebrated Partisan Officer, in the Revolutionary War, against the British and Tories in South Carolina and Georgia* (1854; reprint, Winston-Salem, N.C.: Blair, 2000).

— Rita M. Broyles

marriage and family life

From 1756 to 1820 white families in the United States changed from units of economic pragmatism into smaller households focused on emotional bonds between husbands and wives and between mothers and children. AFRICAN-AMERICAN families constructed slave communities to help lessen the constant threat and reality of family separation, while NATIVE AMERICAN families continued to develop their matrilineal families and tribes.

During the mid-18th century the educated elite began adjusting their vision of marriage. In the 17th and early 18th centuries a woman's father arranged her marriage, preferably to a man who was both an economic provider and a patriarch intent upon transforming the woman into a "good wife" who was submissive, obedient, and quiet. Marriage was considered the "state writ small," where the husband was the king of his family and his wife's job was to be his "helpmeet." White women had some rights, notably the right to refuse to permit her husband to sell land that she brought into the marriage, the right to one-third of the husband's property upon his death, and the right to testify in court (although she could not sue). Essentially, however, a wife was the property of her husband.

Demographics reinforced this system of patriarchal marriage. Most women in New England and the middle colonies married in their early 20s. Men tended to marry in their mid-20s, so that husbands were often three to four years older than their wives. A colonial wife generally had five to seven children, so that from her marriage until menopause in her early 40s, she was usually pregnant or breastfeeding a baby. German, French-Canadian, and SCOTCH-IRISH women often worked in the family's farm fields. English women typically did not work in the fields unless absolutely necessary, but they were responsible for all work inside the house, such as preserving food, making candles, dairying, brewing beer, and sewing clothes, as well as caring for the livestock and the vegetable and herb gardens.

As the 18th century progressed, the notions of marriage began to change in response to the declining ability of fathers to bequeath sizeable farms to their children, the popularity of the new sentimental LITERATURE like *Pamela* (where heroines married poor men out of love and passion), and the rhetoric of liberty. Early American fathers typically divided their land upon their deaths to grant some land to each male child. Over time, fathers were no longer able to leave adequately sized farms to their children in long-settled areas. Sons started migrating to less populated areas in order to acquire land, and fathers began losing control over their sons. At the same time, young women who read the new sentimental literature began to expect more than an economic partnership out of marriage. They wanted to marry for love and found a way to force their parents to permit them to marry the men of their own choosing by entering into sexual relationships with the men they wanted to marry. Divorce applications, though rare in the 18th century, show applicants requesting a divorce because a partner had "alienated affections," meaning that men and women were coming to expect affection and love in marriage, not merely economic partnership.

The rhetoric that led to the AMERICAN REVOLUTION and the founding of the republic furthered the trend towards companionate marriage and gave women a larger role in the American family. The question for the new nation's leaders was how to instill citizens with virtue. They turned toward women. Literate women had long been responsible for early childhood EDUCATION, particularly for teaching children how to read. With the founding of the new republic, reading mothers became republican mothers, responsible for instilling virtue into each child. Despite these changes, restrictions remained. Once a woman became a wife she could no longer own property and had no legal control over any of her children; in case of divorce, children went with the father, and upon his death his family had the right to take the children.

White southern men and women followed the same trend toward companionate marriages, but while the status of white wives in New England and the middle colonies may be seen as improving, southern white women's position declined in some ways. In the 17th century the shortage of women in the South gave a white southern woman the ability to choose her husband, and she usually inherited all of his property upon his death. By 1750, as sex ratios evened, white women lost these powers, and white family life in the South became more like that of the middle colonies and New England.

The new emphasis on companionate marriage, wherein republican mothers instilled virtue in their children, encouraged a change in attitudes toward childhood in America that began with the QUAKERS. Portraiture of 17th-century Puritans shows how they thought of children: as small adults whose wills had to be broken. The Quakers, however, believed that each man and woman contained a small spark of light that led them toward God, so they thought that children should be nurtured in order to encourage this spark. As a result, Quakers developed child-centered families that focused on the development of the children. The desire among republican Americans to instill virtue into future citizens led them to adopt child-centered families.

Declining birth rates and improving mortality rates permitted parents to spend more time with each child and encouraged the trend toward child-centered families. A farm family in 1700 would have had six or seven children. In 1800 that number dropped to five or six overall, and in long-settled communities where years of dividing inheritance had decreased the size of farms, a family frequently had only four children.

White families also began to enjoy more material comforts. In the 17th century a family frequently shared a bed, might have only one chair and one bowl, and perhaps a spoon. The material culture of American families began to improve because of long-term inflation, the development of cheaper production methods, and the determination of increasing numbers of people to settle in the colonies permanently. Men began to exchange temporary wooden houses for larger, permanent brick homes that offered more privacy to family members. Eighteenth-century inventory and probate records show that families were purchasing more beds, chairs, clothing, forks, knives, and more varied food. The wealthier sort imported books, furniture, Madeira wines, sugar, and tea pots. Americans had begun their quest for comfort.

A white family in the early republic usually involved more members than only parents and children. A widowed grandmother, aunt, or sister might join a family until she died. Such situations were frequently painful for the "relic" (the common term for a widowed woman), since she gave up much of her independence. Frequently a middling-class family would have a servant or two to help with the washing, cooking, livestock, and farming. In addition, a family might have an apprentice, a young man living with them from age 13 or so to learn a trade like coopering, shoemaking, or harness-making from the family's father. Young

girls might live with the family to help with weaving, milking, food preservation, and sewing. Wealthy families hired academic tutors to live with them and train their children. Particularly in the South, where families lived far apart because of the large land requirements to grow tobacco, visiting family members and friends might stay for months.

Middling families might have an indentured servant or two, men and women who owed seven years service in exchange for their passage to America. Life could be wretched for these indentured servants, who were not allowed to marry during service, and in fact female indentured servants who became pregnant during service, sometimes because they were raped by their masters, owed extra time. Particularly in the South, many indentured servants would not survive their servitude. After the REVOLUTIONARY WAR (1775–83), indentured servitude became less common as increasing white IMMIGRATION and availability of slaves—both from the SLAVE TRADE and birth rates—made indentured servitude less necessary, and fewer families would have included an indentured servant.

Life was even more difficult for African-American slaves. It is hard to speak of the "family life" of slaves, who often showed great ingenuity in establishing family relationships only to have them broken by their owners. Slaves were forbidden by American law to marry, and so were denied the foundation of Anglo-American family life. Slaves' desires to marry were often so strong, however, that they devised their own custom of "jumping the broomstick" while holding hands in order to establish a marriage. Although this marriage was then recognized by slaves and African Americans, it often was not recognized, or not considered sacrosanct, by white owners. Married slaves went to great lengths to maintain their marriages when they had been separated by their owners, traveling secretly during the night to visit partners and children.

During the early years of SLAVERY, blacks often maintained their tribal identities by marrying slaves of similar tribal backgrounds and speaking tribal languages. Over time these identities disintegrated as enslaved men and women of different tribal backgrounds began to intermarry. Slaves started speaking English or a new Gullah dialect of English and African words. The end of the legal slave trade in 1808 reduced the importation of new slaves who could teach tribal ways to slaves who had forgotten them or had been born in the United States. Slaves managed to recreate aspects of African life nonetheless, singing African songs to African-style instruments and building the "I"-shaped structures typical of African regions.

Slave families could not always form the same child-focused families that white families were creating. Slave mothers carried their babies as they worked in the fields, and their children often began working themselves at the age of four. Some of these children were the spawn of white

Much of the interaction in a colonial family occurred around the fireplace. This hearth scene was photographed at the Joseph Gilpin House, near Chadd's Ford, Delaware County, Pennsylvania. *(Library of Congress)*

owners or their white sons and female black slaves, from either mutual sexual liaisons or rape. Regardless of the father's status, children of slave mothers were counted as slaves. There was no guarantee that slave children would remain with their mothers. Not only did plantation owners sell slaves to other planters, but they also bequeathed slaves to their white sons and daughters, who might move far away for marriage or more land.

To mitigate the constant threat and the reality of separation, slaves developed a sense of community that in some ways superseded that of individual families. An older man or woman who could no longer work in the fields would care for the plantation's children during the day while their parents were out. Such women were often called "aunts" even when they were no relation. Giving members of the community family relationship names helped to foster a sense of family.

Over the course of the early 19th century, slaves were able to build more stable families. The end of the legal importation of slaves increased the cost of purchasing a slave and made slave owners loathe to allow their slaves to purchase their freedom, so it became increasingly difficult for a slave to become free. At the same time, the increasing economic value of slaves made them ever more valuable to plantation owners, who in turn tried to safeguard their investments by looking after the health of the slaves. Plantation owners hired doctors to visit ill slaves, at a time when most whites could not afford a doctor, and provided small plots of land for slaves to grow vegetables for themselves. The increasing economic value of slaves also made plantation owners hesitate to separate slave families, since stable slave families were less likely to rebel.

Historians unfortunately know much less about slave family life than that of white families, in part because most slaves were illiterate and so left few records. Historians know something more about the family life of Native Americans, but many questions remain. One striking difference between Native American and white families is that Native Americans often were polygamous, meaning that a man had more than one wife and fathered children by several women. Early explorers and previous generations of historians have used this fact as a symbol of Native Americans' lack of "civilization." More current research has demonstrated that women often appreciated sharing the labor of child-raising with other wives, as well as sharing other household work.

In most Native American societies, men were in charge of hunting, while women were responsible for the hoe AGRICULTURE that provided the tribes' basic food supplies of corn, squash, and beans. Pounding the maize for corn meal alone was a tremendous task that was made less onerous by sharing the labor. Just as Native American tribes generally shared labor, so they shared land. Tribes held land in common rather than having each family buy a plot. The right to cultivate or hunt on a portion of land passed from mother to daughter, a matrilineal inheritance system, rather than the European-American method of transmitting rights from father to son. So, Native Americans identified with their mothers' clan and accorded women much higher status than they held in white families.

See also EDUCATION; REPUBLICANISM; WOMEN'S RIGHTS AND STATUS.

Further reading: Kathleen Brown, *Goodwives, Nasty Wenches, and Anxious Patriarchs: Gender, Race, and Power in Colonial Virginia* (Chapel Hill: University of North Carolina Press, 1996); Eugene D. Genovese, *Roll, Jordan, Roll: The World the Slaves Made* (New York: Random House, 1974); Linda K. Kerber, *Women of the Republic: Intellect and Ideology in Revolutionary America* (Chapel Hill: University of North Carolina Press, 1980); Peter Kolchin, *American Slavery, 1619–1877* (New York: Hill & Wang, 1993); Barry Levy, *Quakers and the American Family: British Settlement in the Delaware Valley* (New York: Oxford University Press, 1988); Daniel K. Richter, *Ordeal of the Longhouse: The Peoples of the Iroquois League in the Era of European Colonization* (Chapel Hill: University of North Carolina Press, 1992); Merril D. Smith, *Breaking the Bonds: Marital Discord in Pennsylvania, 1730–1830* (New York: New York University Press, 1991); Laurel Thatcher Ulrich, *A Midwife's Tale: The Life of Martha Ballard, Based on her Diary, 1785–1812* (New York: Knopf, 1991); Michael Zuckerman, *Peaceable Kingdoms: New England Towns in the Eighteenth Century* (New York: Knopf, 1970).

— Sarah Hand Meacham

Marshall, John (1755–1835)

John Marshall was the first great chief justice of the United States. Born near Germantown, Virginia, on September 24, 1755, he was raised on the Virginia FRONTIER. The oldest of 15 children, he was educated by his father, Thomas Marshall, a friend of GEORGE WASHINGTON. He fought in the REVOLUTIONARY WAR (1775–83) in the Third Virginia Continental Regiment, rising to the rank of captain. He was at VALLEY FORGE (winter 1777–78), where he helped keep up morale by starting impromptu snowball fights. While on a break in service, he studied law for six weeks at the College of William and Mary. This was Marshall's only formal instruction. He left the CONTINENTAL ARMY in 1781, and the following year was elected to the Virginia legislature. In 1783 he married Mary Ambler of Yorktown and began the practice of law in Richmond, Virginia.

His wartime experiences persuaded Marshall of the need for a strong central government, and he was a vocal supporter of the proposed Constitution when it was sent to the state ratifying convention. After Washington's election to the presidency, Marshall was recognized as the leader of the FEDERALIST PARTY in Virginia. In 1795 Washington offered him an appointment as attorney general of the United States, but he declined. In 1796 Marshall similarly declined an appointment as minister to France, but the following year, he agreed to accept President JOHN ADAMS's nomination as one of the commissioners sent to France to resolve the XYZ AFFAIR (1797–98). In 1798 Marshall was offered deceased justice James Wilson's place on the SUPREME COURT of the United States, but he declined, instead running successfully for a seat in Congress in 1799. As a member of the United States House of Representatives, Marshall quickly became prominent as a staunch defender of the Adams administration. In May 1800, without consulting him, Adams moved to reward Marshall's loyalty by appointing him secretary of war, but Marshall again declined. A few days later, however, Marshall accepted appointment as Adams's secretary of state, to succeed TIMOTHY PICKERING, who had just been fired. He would hold this position for less than a year.

Chief Justice Oliver Ellsworth resigned in January 1801, and after the position had been rejected by Adams's first nominee, JOHN JAY, who had served as the first Chief Justice, Adams offered the post to Marshall. Despite widespread opposition, particularly from DEMOCRATIC-REPUBLICANS, who thought that Ellsworth's resignation was strategically timed and that the appointment should be left to the incoming president, THOMAS JEFFERSON, Marshall accepted the nomination and was confirmed by the Senate. He took his seat on February 4, 1801.

The Supreme Court's position was precarious as Marshall took office. Before leaving office, President Adams had signed the JUDICIARY ACT OF 1801, creating many new federal judgeships. He then filled these positions in the waning days of his administration with Federalist Party Loyalists (the "midnight judges"). Among the first acts of the incoming Jefferson administration was the repeal of the Judiciary Act of 1801 and the dismissal of the new judges. Profound questions arose during the repeal debate, however, about the constitutionality of firing the judges, who were entitled under the Constitution to lifetime tenure. The Supreme Court was next scheduled to meet in August 1802. To put off a legal challenge, Congress abolished the August term, thus postponing any judicial hearing until February 1803.

Marshall heard one case in the August 1801 term, his first, and he took the opportunity to prepare the Supreme Court for war with the Democratic-Republicans. Previously, the Supreme Court's opinions had regularly appeared *seriatim*—each justice had written a separate opinion, offering different (and sometimes conflicting) rationales for decisions. In *Talbot v. Seeman*, the Supreme Court's one August 1801 case, Marshall issued one opinion for the entire court. The abolition of *seriatim* opinions and the reserving of important decisions for his hand alone were a major reform and greatly strengthened the Supreme Court's authority.

Chief Justice John Marshall *(Alonzo Chappell, Collection of the Supreme Court of the United States)*

The new authority of the Supreme Court was put to the test when it convened in February 1803. The first case on the docket was the effective challenge to the repeal of the Judiciary Act of 1801: MARBURY V. MADISON. President Adams had appointed William Marbury a justice of the peace for the District of Columbia under legislation establishing federal courts in the district passed at the same time as the 1801 Judiciary Act. John Marshall, as secretary of state, had signed Marbury's commission, but the Adams administration left office before delivering it to Marbury. When Jefferson took office, he and his secretary of state, JAMES MADISON, refused to follow through with Marbury's appointment. Marbury filed suit in the Supreme Court, asking for a writ of mandamus ordering Madison to deliver his commission. The political stakes in *Marbury v. Madison* were high. If the Supreme Court granted the writ, Madison might well refuse to abide by it, and a constitutional crisis would result. John Marshall was hardly sure of being on the winning side in such a crisis. The Democratic-Republicans had already taken control of the executive and legislative branches: Could the Supreme Court stand against them?

Marshall was not the sort to bow to the new administration, and he found an ingenious solution. First, he declared that Madison had indeed wronged Marbury by not delivering his commission. Next, he determined that a writ of mandamus was the appropriate remedy under the JUDICIARY ACT OF 1789. Finally, however, he held that the Supreme Court could not issue such a writ because the section of the 1789 Judiciary Act authorizing the Supreme Court to issue writs of mandamus against public officers was unconstitutional. In one fell swoop, Marshall had chastised the Jefferson administration, avoided a constitutional showdown, and claimed for the Supreme Court the power to determine the constitutionality of acts of Congress and invalidate them when it found them to be unconstitutional. *Marbury v. Madison* was a landmark in constitutional law.

The battle between the Supreme Court and the administration was not over. Marshall's colleague, Justice SAMUEL CHASE, had assailed the Jeffersonians in a series of grand jury charges, and on March 12, 1804, the House of Representatives voted to impeach him. Chase was not convicted, but Marshall was clearly intimidated. By 1807, however, he had recovered his composure, and when AARON BURR was tried before him for treason, he denied Jefferson the conviction he sought.

Hostility between the branches cooled somewhat after Jefferson left office. In 1811 JOSEPH STORY and Gabrial Duval were appointed to the Supreme Court, and the court's personnel would remain essentially the same for the next 18 years. The justices met for one term each year and regularly lived together in the same boarding house, an arrangement that afforded Marshall the perfect opportunity to assert his personality. A series of important constitutional decisions followed. In 1810 the Supreme Court decided *Fletcher v. Peck*, a challenge to Georgia's repeal of the YAZOO grants. Marshall found the repeal unconstitutional and invalidated it, the first time the Supreme Court had invalidated the act of a state legislature. Four years later, the Supreme Court decided *Martin v. Hunter's Lessee*, this time invalidating an act of the Virginia legislature. The single most important term of the Marshall court was the 1819 term, in which the Supreme Court decided the cases of *McCulloch v. Maryland, Sturges v. Crowninshield*, and *Trustees of Dartmouth College v. Woodward*. In *McCulloch*, the Supreme Court found constitutional a federal act creating the Bank of the United States and invalidated a tax Maryland had imposed on the bank, in the process interpreting broadly Congress's power to legislate. In *Sturges*, the Supreme Court invalidated New York's bankruptcy law. In *Dartmouth College*, the Supreme Court invalidated an act of the New Hampshire legislature repealing that college's charter. All three decisions were blows against STATE'S RIGHTS and fixed the Supreme Court as the guardian of national power.

The 1819 term precipitated a crisis similar to the crisis that threatened the Supreme Court in 1803. This time, the states were up in arms. Virginia and Kentucky, in particular, assailed the Supreme Court during the early 1820s, challenging its claimed power to interpret the Constitution and invalidate the acts of sovereign states. Ultimately, the Supreme Court was rescued by the federal executive, when, in 1832, the overly aggressive acts of South Carolina Nullifiers (who claimed the power to "nullify" within the boundaries of the state those of the Supreme Court's constitutional decisions with which they disagreed) prompted President Andrew Jackson to threaten to send in the troops. By this time, John Marshall was nearing the end of his life. The court over which he had presided began to slip from his control with a series of retirements during the Jackson years. He died in Philadelphia on July 6, 1835. In fitting tribute, during the public ceremonies marking his death, the Liberty Bell cracked.

Further reading: Albert J. Beveridge, *The Life of John Marshall,* 4 vols. (New York: Oxford University Press 1916–19); Jean Edward Smith, *John Marshall: Definer of a Nation* (New York: H. Holt & Co. 1996); G. Edward White, *The Marshall Court and Cultural Change, 1815–1835* (New York: Houghton Mifflin, 1991).

— Lindsay Robertson

Mason, George (1725–1792)

George Mason authored some of the most compelling political treatises of the revolutionary period. He wrote the Fairfax Resolves of July 18, 1774; Virginia's Declaration of Rights; and "Objections to the Federal Constitution." An ardent constitutionalist, advocate of the disestablishment of RELIGION, and enemy of SLAVERY, he was a strong supporter of the BILL OF RIGHTS.

Mason began a life of politics in 1754 when he served as the trustee for the town of Alexandria, Virginia, and on the local court of Fairfax County. He also gave his time to Truro Parish as a vestryman, overseeing its relief activities for the poor. In 1752 Mason assumed the role of treasurer in the OHIO COMPANY. In this capacity he authored *Extracts from the Virginia Charters, with Some Remarks upon Them* (1773), a study inspired by Great Britain's attempt to abrogate Virginia's claims to what later became the Northwest Territory.

As the events leading toward the REVOLUTIONARY WAR (1775–83) unfolded, George Mason assumed an increasingly central role in the process of founding the new nation. During the late 1750s, Mason had served in Virginia's House of Burgesses with GEORGE WASHINGTON. Although he had a low estimation of the political wrangling within the House and resigned from it, he agreed to serve at the July convention in 1775.

Mason authored stinging criticisms of the Crown's efforts to levy and collect taxes. In so doing, he provided constitutional rationales with far-reaching import. In June 1766 he penned an open letter in opposition to the STAMP ACT (1765), underscoring the colonists' resolve to be loyal, but not at the cost of their independence. His argument against the Boston Port Bill (1774) and other COERCIVE ACTS (1774)—entitled the Fairfax Resolves of July 18, 1774—was adopted as the constitutional position of Fairfax's county court, the Virginia convention, and the CONTINENTAL CONGRESS. In this bitter attack, Mason contended that through laws like the Boston Port Bill, the English government endeavored "to fix the shackles of slavery upon us."

Mason's crowning achievement was his authoring of the Declaration of Rights at Virginia's May convention in 1776. This document influenced the DECLARATION OF INDEPENDENCE (July 4, 1776), was readily adopted by several other colonies, and served as the foundation for the Bill of Rights. At the same convention, Mason wrote significant portions of Virginia's constitution. During the succeeding five years, he played a critical role on the state's Committee of Five, carefully attending to the revision of the state's laws.

After a brief retirement, Mason returned to public life during the late 1780s. Though absent from the ANNAPOLIS CONVENTION, he attended the CONSTITUTIONAL CONVENTION held in Philadelphia in 1787. He argued against the creation of too strong a federal government, implored his colleagues not to allow state militias to languish in favor of a standing army, and looked askance at the provision for presidential pardons. To defend against the accretion of too much power in the executive, Mason proposed a three-person executive that included one representative from the nation's three regions. Later in the Convention he advocated a six-person council of state, also regionally representative, that would serve as a constitutional council. Its primary responsibility would have been to make appointments and to serve as an advisory body. The Convention rejected these provisions. Consistent with his skepticism toward consolidated power, Mason also expressed concern over the vesting of legislative, executive, and judicial authority in the Senate.

Mason argued for a bill of rights, a position that became the cornerstone of ANT-FEDERALIST dissent. The failure to include a bill of rights pushed Mason reluctantly into the anti-Federalist camp. A propertied gentleman, he loathed the very state politics that anti-Federalists sought to defend—it was his distaste for this pettiness that had driven him into retirement not once, but twice. Nonetheless, his opposition to certain clauses in the Constitution and the absence of a bill of rights compelled him not to sign the founding document. Mason seconded EDMUND RANDOLPH's proposal to allow state conventions to propose amendments to the Constitution that would be further considered by a second national General Convention. In so doing, Mason opined, "This Constitution has been formed without the knowledge or idea of the people. A second Convention will know more of the sense of the people, and be able to provide a system more consonant with it." Through his "Objections to the Federal Constitution," Mason focused on the issue of popular sovereignty and urged the Virginia convention not to ratify. In this pamphlet, Mason called for a bill of rights and opposed the convention's compromise on slavery.

Further reading: H. H. Miller, *George Mason: Gentleman Revolutionary* (Chapel Hill: University of North Carolina Press, 1975); Jack N. Rakove, *Original Meanings: Politics and Ideas in the Making of the Constitution* (New York: Knopf, 1996).

— Daniel M. Cobb

Mayhew, Jonathan (1720–1766)

Jonathan Mayhew helped pave the way for American independence by using his influence in religious matters to preach against the British government. Mayhew was born at Martha's Vineyard, Massachusetts, to parents Experience and Remember Mayhew. The Mayhew family included a number of successful ministers and missionaries, and Jonathan's career was to be no different. He attended Harvard for four years, graduating in 1744. In

1747, after being ordained, he was invited to be the pastor of the West Church in Boston. He held this post until his death in 1766.

Mayhew was industrious, cheerful, intelligent, and a powerful speaker. In his theology, he moved away from the rigid Protestantism of the Puritans and instead preached a simpler faith. This Christianity was sensible and rational, based on the Holy Scriptures. By his unusual proclamations of faith and his mastery of speech, Mayhew soon gained a wide influence and popularity, both at home and in Britain. He received an honorary degree from the University of Aberdeen and exchanged letters with prominent British religious leaders.

While many found his ideas refreshing, others, especially the British, found them too extreme. On the 100th anniversary of the execution of the English king Charles I, Mayhew preached a sermon on the responsibilities of rulers. Mayhew felt that rulers had an obligation and duty to rule in the best interests of their subjects and do them no harm. In 1750 he published his influential *Discourse Concerning Unlimited Submission and Non-Resistance to the Higher Powers*. In this treatise, Mayhew argued that subjects had a duty to obey their rulers. However, if temporal rulers made laws that interfered with spiritual laws given in the Bible, then subjects were no longer obligated to serve their worldly leaders.

As his career progressed, Jonathan Mayhew grew more outspoken. He attacked the divine right of kings, vigorously opposed the introduction of Anglican bishops to the colonies, and gave a sermon against the STAMP ACT (1765). In fact, he opposed the act so passionately he was accused of provoking the Stamp Act RIOTS in Boston. He believed that if rulers became tyrannical, citizens had a right and an obligation to take the government into their own hands. In order to distance himself from the British government, he dedicated a sermon to the British politician WILLIAM PITT. Pitt was famous for his opposition to the British government's policies towards the colonies.

Mayhew proved to be a powerful influence. JOHN ADAMS believed Mayhew was one of the most important figures of the prewar era. From his pulpit, Mayhew wielded an enormous influence. Those American colonists that did not attend his Boston church could read the published versions of his sermons, which were even printed and distributed in England. Mayhew is famous for declaring, "For Brethren, ye have been called unto Liberty." He believed the British government had failed to properly govern the American colonies, but he did not live to see the American independence; he died in 1766 at the age of 46.

Further reading: Charles W. Akers, *Called unto Liberty: A Life of Jonathan Mayhew, 1720–1766* (Cambridge, Mass.: Harvard University Press, 1964); John Corrigan, *The*

Hidden Balance: Religion and the Social Theories of Charles Chauncy and Jonathan Mayhew (Cambridge, U.K: Cambridge University Press, 1987);. Mark Valeri, "The New Divinity and the American Revolution," *William and Mary Quarterly,* 46 (Oct. 1989): 741–769.

— Brant Day

McCrea, Jane (1752?–1777)

Jane McCrea was killed by NATIVE AMERICANS during General JOHN BURGOYNE's invasion of New York in 1777. This act of FRONTIER warfare became an important symbol of Indian brutality and female helplessness. Although McCrea was a real person, much that is known about her is mixed with legend. Born in New Jersey, she was a member of a family that supported the revolution. She reportedly fell in love with a man who was a LOYALIST with Burgoyne's army. They had planned to rendezvous and marry during the British invasion. Unfortunately, she was captured and killed by an Indian raiding party while waiting for her beloved at a friend's house. The story spread quickly at the time and helped to fuel American anger at the British before Burgoyne's surrender at SARATOGA (October 17, 1777). After the REVOLUTIONARY WAR (1775–83), the incident remained in American folklore and appeared in poetry and in art. John Vanderlyn's early-19th-century painting of the murder was an instant success and has been reproduced countless times. It has become the standard depiction of the horrors of frontier warfare in the late 18th century.

Scholars believe that the story, which has several different versions, has had such staying power for a variety of reasons. In part—ignoring the fact that both sides could fight the war with brutality—Americans could claim that the British were villains for using Native Americans in the war and decry Indians as savages. Some scholars have argued that the popularity of McCrea's story reflected dominant ideas about the status of women in the era of the early republic by indicating that all women needed male protection. Moreover, because McCrea had fallen in love with a Tory, her fate demonstrated that women did not have judgment enough to make decisions about politics. These messages were reassuring to men in a period in which civil identity was a male identity.

See also ART; WOMEN'S RIGHTS AND STATUS.

Further reading: Jay Fliegelman, *Prodigals and Pilgrims: The American Revolution against Patriarchal Authority* (Cambridge, Mass.: Cambridge University Press, 1982).

McDougall, Alexander (1732–1786)

Alexander McDougall mobilized public opinion against British rule and entered a successful military career during the REVOLUTIONARY WAR (1775–83). McDougall was born in Scotland and immigrated with his parents to New York in 1738. During the French and Indian War (1754–63), he commanded the privateers *Tyger* and *Barrington.* After the war he returned to New York and became a merchant.

In December 1769 McDougall published a pamphlet, signed "A Son of Liberty," criticizing the New York assembly for raising money to support the British troops quartered in the city. On the following day a mob rallied around a LIBERTY POLE in the "fields" (today City Hall Park) denouncing the assembly's decision. After McDougall's second pamphlet, local authorities offered a reward for the discovery of the writer. On the testimony of the printer, authorities arrested McDougall and held him without bail. Instead of breaking his will, McDougall's arrest made him a popular hero in New York City. Supporters visited him so often in prison that he had to schedule appointments. On the anniversary of the repeal of the STAMP ACT (1765), 300 New Yorkers toasted him at a celebratory dinner, and a delegation of New York's respectable citizens dined with him in jail. Because of the death of the main witness, he was never brought to trial and was released. The general assembly summoned him for questioning, and when McDougall refused to answer, the assembly confined him again until March 1771.

McDougall emerged from these travails as one of the most prominent radical leaders in New York. In 1774 he became a member of the New York Committee of Fifty-one. He presided over a demonstration in the "fields," where ALEXANDER HAMILTON made his first appearance as a public speaker on July 6, 1774. McDougall was also one of the Committee of One Hundred that organized a provisional government for New York on May 5, 1775. In the same year he was appointed colonel of the first New York regiment. In 1776 he was promoted to brigadier general in the CONTINENTAL ARMY and advanced to major general in 1777. He participated in the battles of WHITE PLAINS (October 28, 1776) and GERMANTOWN (October 4, 1777) and secured for the Americans the control of the upper Hudson River Valley. After BENEDICT ARNOLD committed treason, GEORGE WASHINGTON appointed McDougall as the commander of West Point.

In 1781 McDougall was offered the position of minister of marine to oversee the navy and maritime affairs, but he declined the offer. In 1782 General William Health charged him with insubordination. McDougall insisted that the West Point commandant was responsible only to the commander in chief and Congress, while Health demanded obedience as the superior officer. After a long trial, McDougall was acquitted of most of the charges but was convicted on insubordination.

This experience did not destroy McDougall's political career nor his ambitions. He headed the delegation sent by the officers of the army to negotiate questions of pay with the CONTINENTAL CONGRESS. McDougall twice represented New York in the Continental Congress (1781–82 and 1784–85), and served as state senator (1783–86). He was also the first president of the Bank of New York.

See also RESISTANCE MOVEMENT.

Further reading: Roger J. Champagne, *Alexander McDougall and the American Revolution in New York* (Schenectady, N.Y.: Union College Press, 1975).

— Dirk Voss

McGillivray, Alexander (1750–1793)

Alexander McGillivray led the CREEK NATION during the difficult times after the REVOLUTIONARY WAR (1775–83). Born of a Creek mother and a Scottish father, he introduced many European methods of AGRICULTURE, law, and government to the NATIVE AMERICANS of the Southeast.

McGillivray was born somewhere in Creek country in what is now the Georgia and Alabama border. He moved to his father's plantation outside Augusta and later spent two years at school in Charleston, South Carolina. He learned to read and write English, skills that proved to be very useful. When he came of age he maneuvered himself into a position of authority over the Creek. McGillivray owned a large plantation with a European-style house, slaves, and cattle.

In the 1780s and 1790s, the Creek found themselves caught between the growing United States and the Spanish in FLORIDA. McGillivray took advantage of this situation by playing off the two powers. He drew a salary from the Spanish as their representative while the Americans made him a brigadier general with a salary of $1,200 a year. In 1790 he traveled to New York City and signed a treaty ceding the Creek lands in Georgia to the federal government. Since most of the Creek leaders could not read, McGillivray was the only one of them fully aware of what the document meant. The Treaty of New York also made him a very wealthy man. Many Creek were very angry when they found out about the sale of their lands. To avoid being killed, McGillivray slipped across the border into Spanish Florida, where he died in Pensacola in 1793.

Further reading: John Walton Caughey, *Mcgillivray of the Creeks,* (Norman: University of Oklahoma Press, 1938); Michael D. Green, *The Politics of Indian Removal: Creek Government and Society in Crisis* (Lincoln: University of Nebraska Press, 1982); Claudio Saunt, *A New Order of Things: Property, Power, and the Transformation of the Creek Indians, 1733–1816* (Cambridge, U.K.: Cambridge University Press, 1999).

— George Milne

medicine

The practice and study of medicine in the second half of the 18th and early 19th centuries experienced some changes while still remaining firmly rooted in tradition. Although the number of doctors with formal medical schooling increased, most practitioners simply served an apprenticeship with a doctor or were self-taught. There were also few specialists; the majority of doctors were surgeon-apothecaries: individuals who mixed medicines, treated illness, and even on occasion performed operations. Female midwives delivered most babies and often were responsible for medical care when the expense of a doctor was either not called for or was too high. By 1820 midwives were being replaced by male doctors as the medical profession began to organize itself and medical training in a college and hospital became more frequent.

In the 18th century the predominant European-American theory of medicine found its roots in the ancient humoral thesis, which held that all illness was caused by an imbalance in the natural humors of the body. Doctors typically sought to purge the patient of whichever humor was in excess. Medicine was slow to move away from this theory because few doctors did medical research; doctors were too busy treating patients, and the general population had moral objections toward using human bodies for research.

By the second half of the 18th century there was some change. Medical men began to study anatomy, pathology, and physiology, even if they had to use stolen cadavers to do so. Doctors also began to change their approach to illness. They started to view DISEASES AND EPIDEMICS as different from each other, which, in turn, required different treatments. The most important step in this development was the establishment of hospitals and medical schools. The first hospital was built in Philadelphia in 1752, and the associated medical school opened at the College of Philadelphia in 1766. Prior to the opening of this school, Americans had to go to Europe for their formal medical education. Following the success in Philadelphia, New Yorkers started a medical department at King's College (now Columbia University) in 1768. The REVOLUTIONARY WAR (1775–83) put plans at other schools on hold, but by 1799 Harvard, Dartmouth, and Transylvania University had medical programs of their own.

There were also a few advances made in the areas of surgery during this time, mostly in the fields of obstetrics and gynecology. John Bard, in 1759, and John King, in 1818, successfully treated extrauterine pregnancies. Ephraim McDowell, in 1809, performed the first ovariotomy. There may have been other advances, but we have no record of them. Surgeons focused more on the practice of medicine and often did not seek publication of their procedures.

Public health issues also played an important role in American society. A community's ability to protect itself from contagious diseases was vital to its survival. Most cities had ordinances related to quarantining outbreaks of a contagious disease and the inspection of incoming vessels. However, the major outbreaks of yellow fever in the years after 1793 brought the need for public health standards to the forefront. The problem with yellow fever was that it did not behave in the same way as other contagious diseases. Communities had to revise their policies on quarantine and sanitation. First, however, they had to settle on the cause of these epidemics, an argument that would last through most of the 19th century.

Another disease that had a major impact on America during this era was smallpox. Before the invention of vaccines, doctors tried to prevent epidemics of contagious diseases such as smallpox using a treatment called inoculation, or variolation. This treatment involved the doctor collecting pus from an infected patient and injecting it into a healthy one. As a result, healthy patients contracted a milder case of smallpox from which they had a better chance of surviving. The survival rate increased from 20 percent to 95 percent. While this method of treatment appeared in the American colonies in the early 18th century, it became more prominent during the Revolutionary War. At the outset of the war smallpox epidemics were again on the rise, but with the spread of inoculation, including within the CONTINENTAL ARMY, the impact of the disease decreased.

During the Revolutionary War the CONTINENTAL CONGRESS set up a medical department for the Continental army. While it achieved some success, especially in dealing with hygiene and smallpox, it was plagued with problems. The first head of the army medical department was Dr. BENJAMIN CHURCH. He turned out to be a British spy and was dismissed from service. Dr. John Morgan, who had helped to establish Philadelphia's medical school, was appointed to replace Church in October 1775. But he became embroiled in controversy as he wrangled over policy and authority with his longtime rival, Dr. William Shippen, Jr. Shippen replaced Morgan in January 1777, only to be charged with war profiteering. Shippen resigned in 1781. Throughout the war these political problems only made the shortage of supplies and personnel more difficult.

The foremost doctor of this time was BENJAMIN RUSH, who gained fame as a revolutionary, reformer, and medical man. He served as a regional director in the army medical corps and sided with Morgan in the jurisdictional disputes. As a doctor, Rush was an important teacher at the medical school in Philadelphia and wrote extensively on medicine. Rush clung to the "heroic" theory of disease, and because of his support and influence it continued as the dominant approach to disease in the United States. The heroic theory was rooted in the humoral theory of disease. Rush believed that all diseases could be tied to one problem, vascular tension. The differing levels of tension in the small capillaries of the body resulted in the symptoms manifested by the patient. This meant that the only cure was bloodletting and purging. The "heroic" theory of disease was slowly replaced by new theories formulated by Rush's students in the 19th century. Ironically, it is the emphasis that Rush placed on observation while teaching his students that led them to discard his theory.

Rush also had a huge impact on the treatment of mental illness. The abandonment of supernatural causes for insanity shifted the condition from the realm of religion to the realm of medicine. If there were natural causes for mental illness, then there had to be natural cures. This development in the conception of psychological derangement began in Europe and had crossed the Atlantic by the mid-18th century. The Eastern Lunatic Hospital in Williamsburg was the first separate institution devoted to the insane. The founders of the Philadelphia Hospital hoped that they could treat and cure the insane, and by 1796 they had built a separate wing to house only those with mental illness. Other communities and states built asylums in the following decades. Europeans emphasized "moral treatment," which separated the individual from his family and provided a rigid schedule and disciplined habits. Following the leadership of Rush, Americans believed that a medical treatment should accompany this separation. Using his "heroic" theory of disease, Rush advocated bloodletting, daily purges, and other procedures that today sound like torture. He restrained patients by strapping them in a chair, then applying cold water and ice to the head and warm water to the feet.

Beyond the European-American population, NATIVE AMERICANS and AFRICAN AMERICANS developed their own medical practices with a more holistic approach. Neither group separated the spiritual from the physical world. While this left them open to criticism from European Americans, it also meant that they treated social and physical symptoms. Both groups also relied heavily upon plants and herbs. Native Americans had centuries to experiment with plants that might help in the context of the North American environment. African Americans were relative newcomers to the continent, but their experiences in Africa, where the environment had some similarities to the American South, helped them to seek out local cures. Distinctions between male and female medical practitioners, which increased in this period in European-American society, had little meaning for either African Americans or Native Americans.

See also SCIENCE.

Further reading: James Bordley and A. McGehee, *Two Centuries of American Medicine, 1776–1976,* (Philadelphia: Saunders, 1976); Lamar Riley Murphy, *Enter the Physician: The Transformation of Domestic Medicine, 1760–1860* (Tuscaloosa: University of Alabama Press, 1991); William D. Piersen, *Black Legacy: America's Hidden Heritage* (Amherst: University of Massachusetts Press, 1993); Oscar Reis, *Medicine and the American Revolution: How Diseases and Their Treatments Affected the Colonial Army* (Jefferson, N.C.: McFarland and Company, 1998); Richard Harrison Shyrock, *Medicine and Society in America, 1660–1860* (New York: New York University Press, 1960); Laurel Thatcher Ulrich, *A Midwife's Tale: The Life of Martha Ballard, Based on Her Diary* (New York: Knopf, 1990).

— Susan Jorgenson

Methodism

Methodism played an important role in increasing the religiosity of American society and was particularly influential among ordinary men and women, many of whom would become the core of the emerging middle class. Between 1770 and 1820, American Methodism grew from fewer than 1,000 members to over 250,000. By 1812, one out of every 36 Americans was Methodist.

Initially, Methodism had an egalitarian appeal, attracting Americans of European and African descent, and spread rapidly among the poor and the backcountry. Following the lead of John Wesley, the founder of Methodism in England, American Methodists began to support ANTISLAVERY in the 1770s. In 1780 the Methodist Church declared that SLAVERY "is contrary to the laws of God, man, and nature." Methodists encouraged state petitions to abolish slavery and in 1785 moved to have all members free their slaves. This antislavery position was difficult to maintain in the South, and after 1800 the church retreated from its radical position against slaveholding.

The Methodist Church also struggled with its own identity in the closing years of the 18th century. Methodism began in England and spread to North America before the REVOLUTIONARY WAR (1775–83). The war left the Methodists in an awkward position, since Wesley discouraged his preachers from taking political stands. It was not an easy time to remain neutral. Many of the itinerants spreading Methodism were from Great Britain, and therefore triggered the suspicions of the revolutionary committees. More than one Methodist preacher found himself a victim of an anti-Tory mob. FRANCIS ASBURY, the emerging Methodist leader, waited to the last possible moment before taking a loyalty oath to the state of Maryland in 1778, and he still had to flee to Delaware to escape possible prosecution. In 1784, with national independence assured, the Methodist conference in Baltimore created a church structure separate from British Methodism.

Methodism's success had much to do with its embrace of popular religious practices that were resisted by the older denominations. Two particular Methodist qualities proved appealing to many Americans: The first was their use of camp meetings—multiday religious extravaganzas in which enthusiastic preachers and participants built on each other's energies. Camp meetings provided many people with the sense that the divine was present and that they were in need of salvation. Methodists, however, also embraced the mystical and supernatural beliefs still held by many ordinary Americans. At camp meetings and elsewhere, American Methodists believed in the power of dreams, speaking in tongues, and even miracles. These ideas were denounced by the other denominations, providing Methodism with an advantage in the spiritual marketplace.

Methodism also benefitted from the cultural environment following the AMERICAN REVOLUTION. The Revolutionary War led to a breakdown in religious authority in many parts of the nation, most notably in the South, were the Anglican church was delegitimized. Moreover, the idea of RELIGIOUS LIBERTY created space for new denominations and preachers to challenge existing hierarchies. Finally, ordinary Americans, inspired by the democratic beliefs of the Revolution, desired to make their own choices about religious affiliation. Early Methodist ministers took advantage of these changes. Many ministers lacked a formal education and thus were better able to speak to and as an "ordinary person." Methodism grew not only in the South but in the West as well, where Methodists proved more successful than other denominations at bringing RELIGION to settlers.

Methodism was also influential among AFRICAN AMERICANS. Not only did its democratic theology include all individuals, but the Methodists' enthusiastic style proved compatible with that of African Americans' own spiritual traditions. Methodism, however, could not avoid the racism of American society. In the North, congregations were often divided by race, and in 1816 the African Methodist Episcopal Church (AME) was founded as a separate entity. The AME would become one of the most important religious institutions for black Americans. In the South, some congregations were integrated following the Revolutionary War, but they quickly became segregated as whites strengthened the racial slavery regime. In fact, slave owners worried that black churches would threaten the hierarchy and submission necessary for slavery to function, forcing many African Americans to worship in secrecy.

Despite its limitations, early American Methodism thrived among ordinary people and invigorated American

Christianity. By the second decade of the 19th century, however, many Methodists, now middle class, turned away from their denomination's earlier practices. Seeking respectability, middle-class Methodists hoped to limit the enthusiasm and exuberance that, in the post-revolutionary period, had proven so central to Methodist growth. Nonetheless, by the 1820s and 1830s, Methodism had already established itself as one of America's largest and most important denominations.

Further reading: Dee E. Andrews, *The Methodists and Revolutionary America: The Shaping of an Evangelical Culture* (Princeton, N.J.: Princeton University Press, 2000); Nathan Hatch, *Democratization of American Christianity* (New Haven, Conn.: Yale University Press, 1989); John H. Wigger, *Taking Heaven by Storm: Methodism and the Rise of Popular Christianity in America* (New York: Oxford University Press, 1998).

— Johann Neem

minutemen

In September 1774, WHIG leaders in Worcester County, Massachusetts, decided to reorganize their militia companies. They had two goals: First, they wanted to purge their ranks of LOYALISTS who might be untrustworthy in a potential confrontation with King GEORGE III. Second, they wanted to develop rapid-response light-infantry companies that could act quickly to a call of battle at a moment's notice. Composing 25 percent of each militia regiment, these hand picked men became known as minutemen. In the following months, encouraged by the provincial congress, other Massachusetts counties followed the same policy. By the time the British sent their large raiding party to LEXINGTON AND CONCORD (April 19, 1775), the minutemen had become a well-trained and effective fighting force. Indeed, it was the minutemen who responded to this raid. While unsuccessful on Lexington Green, the minutemen beat back British light-infantry units on Concord Bridge and inflicted heavy casualties on the British column on its retreat back to Boston. The Massachusetts minutemen were absorbed into the army that lay siege to Boston in 1775 and early 1776. Other states formed minutemen units during the REVOLUTIONARY WAR (1775–83) largely to protect their communities when the CONTINENTAL ARMY was busy fighting the British elsewhere.

Molly Pitcher (1753?–1832)

Perhaps the most famous female image to emerge from the REVOLUTIONARY WAR (1775–83) is that of "Molly Pitcher," the American camp follower who, at the BATTLE

Molly Pitcher at the Battle of Monmouth *(National Archives)*

OF MONMOUTH (June 28, 1778) in New Jersey, stepped forward to aid her wounded husband and his artillery unit. While the nickname "Molly Pitcher" has been generally applied to other women who participated in battlefield action, research most consistently identifies Mary Hays as the woman of Monmouth fame. Apparently a Pennsylvanian by birth, Mary was only one among hundreds of women who accompanied their menfolk during the war. William Hays, her husband, was with the Pennsylvania State Regiment of Artillery at the Battle of Monmouth. The weather was fiercely hot that day, and men were succumbing to the heat as much as to the British enemy's gunfire. Mary, or "Captain Molly," as one contemporary observer later called her, carried canteens of water to many of the stricken soldiers. Another eyewitness noted that while Mary was assisting her husband with the artillery piece, she had a portion of her petticoat shot away by an enemy cannonball. Yet another report claimed that when William became incapacitated, Mary took over the loading and firing of the gun, keeping it in service during the conflict. When the battle was over, however, she moved on with the American army and remained an obscure heroine until years later, when reports of her actions at Monmouth gained wider recognition.

During her marriage to William, Mary had one son, John. William died in 1787, and after a short widowhood, Mary wed John McCauly. A widow again by 1822, Pennsylvania records of that year showed that a "Molly McKolly," apparently Mary Hays McCauly, petitioned for financial aid as the widow of a Revolutionary War soldier and received a pension of $40 per year for the rest of her life. Approximately 79 years of age at the time of her death in 1832, Molly McCauly is buried at Carlisle, Pennsylvania, beneath a monument proclaiming her

"Renowned in History as Mollie Pitcher, the heroine of Monmouth."

See also CAMP FOLLOWERS.

Further reading: Samuel Stelle Smith, *A Molly Pitcher Chronology* (Monmouth Beach, N.J.: Philip Freneau Press, 1972); "The Search for Molly Pitcher," *DAR Magazine* (April 1975): 292–295.

— Rita M. Broyles

Monmouth, Battle of (June 28, 1778)

The first test of the newly trained and disciplined CONTINENTAL ARMY since VALLEY FORGE (1777–78), the Battle of Monmouth was also the last major battle fought on northern soil during the REVOLUTIONARY WAR (1775–83). With the change of commanders from WILLIAM HOWE to HENRY CLINTON, the British decided to abandon Philadelphia, move the army back to New York, and concentrate their efforts on conquering the South. Since the French navy in the Atlantic made it too risky to move everything by sea, only the heavy guns and baggage and approximately 3,000 LOYALIST refugees and their belongings were placed aboard transports at Philadelphia. The British army was to march across New Jersey. Encumbering the movement of the roughly 15,000 troops was an enormous column of carriages, carts, and wagons loaded with baggage, provisions, and equipment that stretched at times from eight to 10 miles in length. Knowing the vulnerability of his position, Clinton's objective was to reach New York, not to provoke a battle.

General GEORGE WASHINGTON, proceeding with caution, initially sent only a small detached force to watch Clinton's flank and determine his intentions. Once it was clear Clinton was not going to initiate an attack, however, Washington reinforced the detachments until almost one-third of his men were within striking distance of the enemy. Washington then made a critical mistake. He had wanted the MARQUIS DE LAFAYETTE to lead the vanguard, but he instead selected the more senior general, CHARLES LEE. Lee vocally opposed an attack on what he regarded as the vastly superior British army. In the comedy of errors, inde-

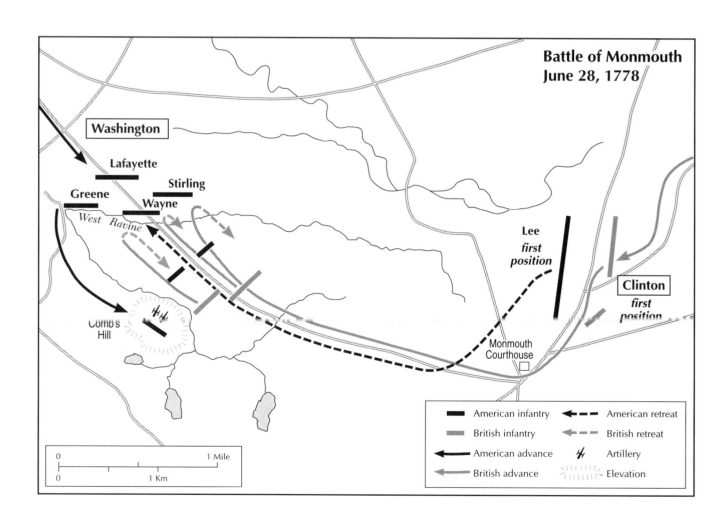

cision, and faulty communication that followed, Lee deferred to Lafayette, changed his mind and accepted command, then stepped aside once again. In camp near Freehold, Clinton learned that a large Continental force was approaching in battle formation and decided to move on to Monmouth Courthouse, having CHARLES, LORD CORNWALLIS to the north and Wilhem von Knyphausen and his HESSIANS to the east. Washington, informed of Clinton's destination, sent another 1,000 men to Lafayette with orders to attack the British rear guard at the first opportunity. When Lee realized that Lafayette had the chance to attack Clinton, he wrote him begging to be allowed to assume command. The Frenchman generously agreed to serve under Lee as the overall commander of the advance units if Washington sent Lee with more men. Inexplicably, Washington allowed Lee to resume command although Lee had no plans of his own, preferring, as he informed Lafayette on the eve of battle, to wait and see what circumstances warranted. Nor had he undertaken any reconnaissance of the surrounding terrain, which was dissected with brooks, ravines, roads, and woods. Clinton anticipated an attack and ordered Knyphausen to move before dawn toward the sea, with Cornwallis covering the rear of the column.

When he received word the enemy was on the march, Washington ordered Lee to attack, but it was almost midmorning before the indifferent leader got his troops underway. Orders were vague or contradictory and, consequently, the advance proceeded in a confused and halting manner. The Continental army finally came upon Cornwallis, who organized a series of attacks designed to give Clinton time to bring men back to their aid. The Americans, having repulsed a cavalry charge and an infantry detachment, were holding their own when suddenly, instead of pressing the attack, Lee ordered a general retreat. The command angered the men, but they retired in an orderly manner. Upon hearing of the retreat, Washington, who had been moving forward with the main army, immediately rode to intercept the soldiers, halted their withdrawal, and assigned them to defensive positions. When Lee appeared on the scene wondering why the retreat was not proceeding as ordered, he found an enraged Washington. Lee explained his decision by claiming that contradictory reports of the enemy's movements had caused confusion he could not control, and he reminded Washington of his opposition to the attack. Though Lee had no good answer when asked why he had assumed command if he had not intended to obey orders, Washington then put Lee in charge of the defensive positions while he personally took charge of forming the army in the rear. In the meantime, Clinton, sensing a chance to soundly beat the enemy, mounted a counterattack. Striking first at the American left, the British were met by dev-

astating musket and artillery fire. Bringing their own guns into position, a long artillery duel ensued in the searing temperatures of the day. Men on both sides collapsed from heat exhaustion, and it was during the battle at Monmouth that the legend of the water bearer, MOLLY PITCHER, was born. When the Americans held on the left, Cornwallis attacked the right, but was forced back. At the same time, Clinton launched a series of assaults against the center. Not until the fourth charge did the Americans withdraw, but the defensive position in the rear was too strong for Clinton to risk another charge. Washington wanted to strike back with fresh troops, but night fell and the attack was canceled.

When morning came, he discovered that Clinton had quietly put his men back on the road to New York during the night, making a renewed assault impossible. Washington's decision to allow Lee to command the advance units may have cost him the chance to inflict serious harm on the British. In the end, Monmouth was virtually a stalemate. Both armies remained on the field and counted almost equal numbers of casualties from the battle. Clinton got his troops to New York and Washington's men, though forced onto the defensive, fought well against the European professionals. Seeking to retrieve his damaged reputation after his conduct at Monmouth, Lee demanded and was given an immediate court-martial, which found him guilty of disobeying orders and suspended him from his command for a year. When he contested Congress's approval of the sentence, he bitterly denounced their action and was dismissed from the service altogether.

Further reading: Alfred Hoyt Bill, *New Jersey and the Revolutionary War* (New Brunswick, N.J.: Rutgers University Press, 1992); Robert Leckie, *George Washington's War: The Saga of the American Revolution* (New York: HarperCollins, 1993); Page Smith, *A New Age Now Begins: A People's History of the American Revolution.* vol. 2 (New York: McGraw Hill, 1989).

— Rita M. Broyles

Monroe-Pinkney Treaty (December 31, 1806)
President THOMAS JEFFERSON rejected the Monroe-Pinkney Treaty because it failed to address the unsolved problems of British IMPRESSMENT of American sailors and the restraint of American TRADE. Both issues would become major causes of the War of 1812 (1812–15).

With the resumption of war in 1803, Great Britain and France challenged American neutrality. Both European powers restricted neutral trade to deprive each other of the means to support the war. The British tried to curtail neutral commerce with French and Spanish colonies in America to cut off staples to NAPOLEON BONA-PARTE's armies. Under the pressure of Congress, President Thomas Jefferson sent two special envoys, James Monroe and William Pinkney, to Britain to negotiate a new treaty to replace the expiring JAY'S TREATY (1794). Great Britain made some minor concessions but would not address the issues of impressment of American citizens into the British navy and the indemnities for previous ship and cargo seizures. Monroe optimistically believed that Britain would give up the practice of impressment while asserting it in principle. The American delegation finally signed the treaty not knowing that American public mood had dramatically changed after the killing of an American sailor by a British warship.

Thus President Thomas Jefferson refused to submit the treaty to the Senate and pressed for further negotiations. The British foreign secretary, George Canning, felt deceived and rebuffed any proposed changes. James Monroe was also disappointed about this outcome after he had spent so much time and energy in these negotiations. The episode left Monroe estranged from Secretary of State JAMES MADISON because Monroe believed that Madison should have kept him informed about the political developments at home.

See also FOREIGN AFFAIRS.

Further reading: Harry Ammon, *James Monroe: The Quest for National Identity* (New York: McGraw Hill, 1971).

— Dirk Voss

Morgan, Daniel (1736–1802)

Leader of a Virginia rifle company raised during the REVOLUTIONARY WAR (1775–83), Daniel Morgan gave meritorious service in several of the war's most significant actions. Morgan's early life is obscure, but he lived in New Jersey until about the age of 17, when he moved to Virginia. He was a crude, illiterate, hardworking youth who loved fistfighting, card games, and strong drink. During the French and Indian War (1754–63), Morgan acquired his nickname of "The Old Wagoner" from driving supply wagons for the British army. In 1756, he struck a British officer and was sentenced to 500 lashes on the back. He later joked that the British miscounted and only 499 strokes had been delivered. Undeterred by the experience, he joined the British army the following year. Ambushed by Indians while on a mission, a bullet passed through the back of Morgan's neck and knocked out the teeth in his left jaw before exiting his cheek. He carried his service scars for life. Morgan's relationship with Abigail Bailey was more rewarding. Her influence brought positive changes in his personal and moral behavior. Together since 1759, the couple finally married in 1773 and had two daughters.

When the Revolutionary War erupted in 1775, Morgan accepted a captain's commission with a newly formed Virginia rifle company and joined General GEORGE WASHINGTON in Boston. By December, the riflemen were with BENEDICT ARNOLD in the failed assault on QUEBEC (December 31, 1775), where Morgan was captured and paroled eight months later. His exemplary performances at SARATOGA (British surrender October 17, 1777) received little acknowledgment, however, and Morgan resigned from the CONTINENTAL ARMY in 1779 when he was not promoted to brigadier general. But a strong desire to help his country prompted him to rejoin the service in the fall of 1780, and Congress awarded his long-awaited promotion. At the BATTLE OF COWPENS (January 17, 1781), General Morgan was the chief architect for the British defeat. He knew what he could expect from the Continental soldiers and lesser-trained militia under his command and, more importantly perhaps, understood how his opponent, BANASTRE TARLETON, would behave. Morgan employed his men accordingly, and his expertise carried the day, Tarleton losing all but a handful of men. Shortly after the victory, Morgan retired from military service due to chronic pain in his back. After the Revolutionary War, he briefly led a militia unit against protesters during the WHISKEY REBELLION (1794) and was elected to a single term in the Virginia House of Representatives. Morgan died in 1802.

Further reading: Don Higginbotham, *Daniel Morgan, Revolutionary Rifleman* (Chapel Hill: University of North Carolina Press, 1961); Robert Leckie, *George Washington's War: The Saga of the American Revolution* (New York: HarperCollins, 1993).

— Rita M. Broyles

Morris, Gouverneur (1752–1816)

Gouverneur Morris was an able statesman, a framer of the United States Constitution, and the principal designer of the United States decimal coinage system. Born on the family estate "Morrisania" (in the Bronx, New York) to a family of high status, Morris was the youngest of three sons. Choosing the law as his profession, he was educated at King's College (later Columbia University) and admitted to the bar in 1771, at age 19. As a member of the landed elite, Morris feared the social effects of popular uprising. He also succeeded, however, to a long family tradition of colonial self-rule and, after the BATTLES OF LEXINGTON AND CONCORD (April 19, 1775), lent his support to the revolutionaries.

In 1775 Morris was elected to New York's provincial congress and served on the committees that drafted the state's constitution in 1776. He was appointed a delegate to the CONTINENTAL CONGRESS of 1778, where he signed the ARTICLES OF CONFEDERATION. His opposition to New

York's land claims in Vermont cost him his seat, and in 1779 he was not reelected to another term in Congress. He moved to Philadelphia, became a citizen of Pennsylvania, and published in 1780 a series of essays on finance under the pen name of "An American." In consequence, Morris was appointed assistant to ROBERT MORRIS (no relation), the superintendent of finance (equivalent to the secretary of the treasury today). As assistant superintendent, Morris drafted the proposal to establish the BANK OF NORTH AMERICA and was responsible for the nation's change to decimal coinage.

Morris was appointed a delegate from Pennsylvania to the Philadelphia CONSTITUTIONAL CONVENTION. Always an articulate orator, Morris made more speeches than any other delegate, and his ideas contributed much to the final product. He helped reword the preamble to the Constitution, naming the "People of the United States" as supreme power, thereby strengthening the new national democratic principles and introducing an obstacle to state separatism. (The original wording enumerated each of the states.) Nevertheless, as a member of the landed elite, Morris held that property was the basis of civil society, and he wished for government to remain in the hands of the wealthy few. His major contribution as a framer of the Constitution was in the creation of the executive, though he initially proposed a president elected for life. It was Morris who put forward the idea of the electoral college system, as well as limitations on the power of the president by a two-thirds vote of the Senate.

President GEORGE WASHINGTON in 1792 named Morris minister plenipotentiary to France, where he witnessed the excesses of the FRENCH REVOLUTION (1789–1815). In retaliation for the rejection of EDMOND GENET, the French in 1794 requested that Morris be recalled. Returning to New York, he purchased the family manor from his older brother. In 1800 Morris was elected to the Senate, and he served three years. In 1809 Morris married Anne Cary Randolph, despite the rumors surrounding her past (including adultery and murder).

Though his arguments against universal franchise and popular government can obscure his contributions at the Constitutional Convention, Morris should be seen as the principal architect of the American presidency and a significant contributor to the Constitution.

Further reading: Max M. Mintz, *Gouverneur Morris and the American Revolution,* (Norman: University of Oklahoma Press, 1970).

— Robyn Davis McMillin

Morris, Robert (1734–1806)

Robert Morris was a prominent merchant and financier of the REVOLUTIONARY WAR (1775–83), most well-known for founding the BANK OF NORTH AMERICA. Morris was born in England in 1734 and immigrated to colonial Philadelphia when he was 13. He joined a mercantile firm as an apprentice and accumulated enough capital to become a partner by age 20. He soon built his firm into one of the most successful mercantile houses in British North America.

In 1775 he became a member of the CONTINENTAL CONGRESS and eventually opposed independence in 1776. Nevertheless, he continued to serve in the Congress and was appointed to manage the finances of the new nation in 1778. Despite his original opposition to independence, Morris's sharp financial expertise made him a strong choice to supervise American financial efforts to sustain the war effort. At the beginning of the Revolutionary War, no organized BANKS existed in the United States, and people like Morris who understood complicated financial operations were rare. As revolutionary financier and manager, he developed a system of paper notes known as Continental Certificates that the government and military used to pay debts. He established the Pennsylvania Bank to act as an exclusive capital source for the CONTINENTAL ARMY and the American government. He also sunk much of his own fortune into the effort to establish public credit, and he personally directed American ministers abroad to borrow funds from foreign governments and banks for the war effort. Morris remained superintendent of finance under the ARTICLES OF CONFEDERATION government until 1784.

Morris was also active in Pennsylvania politics during the Revolutionary War. In particular, he became part of the conservative faction in the state that opposed the democratic STATE CONSTITUTION. Radicals from the middling ranks advocated a program that would help the common man during the stressful war years. Morris spoke out against these policies. In 1779 he attacked price regulations to prevent profiteering in times of scarcity. Morris, as coauthor with Peletiah Webster, wrote: "Freedom of Trade, or unrestrained liberty of the subject to hold or dispose of his property as he wishes is absolutely necessary to the prosperity of every community, and to the happiness of all who compose it." This position was not popular, and Morris often found himself the target of plebeian wrath, charged with monopolistic practices and not fulfilling his obligations as a citizen.

On one level the radicals were right: Morris remained an entrepreneur even as he served in public office. He organized a group of Philadelphia merchants for the purposes of establishing the Bank of North America, which received a charter to operate from the Continental Congress in 1781 and opened for business in Philadelphia in January 1782 as the first commercial bank in the United States. Immediately, the new bank underwrote the financial position of the national government and also provided financial support to the state of Pennsylvania. In 1784 the bank received a charter from the Pennsylvania General Assembly. The state charter caused some significant problems for Morris, who had become a member of the assembly. In 1785 the legislature took up the charter issue, and a substantial number of assemblymen from central and western Pennsylvania expressed outrage over the bank because they considered it to be an exclusive monopoly, catering to wealthy Philadelphia merchants at the expense of middling farmers and ARTISANS. Morris became the target of sharp political rebuke as various assemblymen pointed out his dual interests in the assembly and in the bank, which they assumed to be a natural condition for corruption. They supported a state loan office to provide paper notes to farmers and others not typically accommodated by Morris's bank. The antibank forces succeeded by garnering enough votes to revoke the state charter after a long and substantive debate. However, the political tide in Pennsylvania changed again, and Morris's bank received a new charter from the state in 1787.

In the 1790s Morris became heavily involved in land speculation through a company called the North American Land Company. The venture failed miserably, and Morris ended up in debtor's prison in 1798, owing millions to his creditors. He left prison in 1801 and lived out the last few years of his life in a modest home in Philadelphia with his wife Mary White Morris. He died in 1806.

See also REPUBLICANISM.

Further reading: Belden L. Daniels, *Pennsylvania: Birthplace of Banking* (Harrisburg, Pa.: Pennsylvania Bankers Association, 1976); Clarence Ver Steeg, *Robert Morris, Revolutionary Financier* (New York: Octagon, 1972).

— James R. Karmel

Morristown, New Jersey, encampment of
(1779–1780)

Although the VALLEY FORGE encampment of 1777–78 has come to epitomize the suffering endured by soldiers in the REVOLUTIONARY WAR (1775–83), those quartered at Morristown during the winter of 1779–80 braved perhaps the most severe winter of the 18th century. One American officer claimed that soldiers who had experienced the Valley Forge winter "but have not tasted the cruelties of this one, know not what it is to suffer."

In a hilly, wooded area of northern New Jersey, Morristown was a small settlement containing iron and powder works strategically located about 25 miles from British-occupied New York. It provided a secure defensive position from which General GEORGE WASHINGTON could watch for signs of enemy troop movements. In fact, the CONTINENTAL ARMY had wintered there once before, in early 1777, after the triumphs of TRENTON (December 26, 1776) and PRINCETON (January 3, 1777). At that time, privations were acute and smallpox had ravaged the troops, but those ordeals paled in comparison to the hardships of the second Morristown encampment.

The weather was the greatest adversary at Morristown. There had been at least three storms in the last two weeks of November, and when Washington arrived on December 1, it was amid snow and hail. The army filtered into camp throughout the month. The men were to occupy the wooded area known as Jockey Hollow, about four miles from Morristown, and immediately began to fell trees for building shelters. Approximately 1,200 log huts eventually made up the encampment, and most of the soldiers were housed within a month. But during the building process, sleet, freezing temperatures, and numerous blizzards dumped more than six feet of snow on the area, burying men in their tents and erasing all traces of the roads. Area waterways froze to such a depth that heavy carriages could be driven across them. In early January, the quartermaster reported that half the men in camp were naked and two-thirds were starved. One soldier later noted a time when four days passed without anything to eat. When the storms abated, many men either deserted or plundered neighboring farms for provisions.

Supplies were a persistent problem. Hoping to stop the marauding bands and yet provide for the army's needs, Washington divided New Jersey into 11 districts and assigned a quota of grain and cattle for each. Local magistrates cooperated willingly with the apportionment of requisitions, and foodstuffs began arriving at Morristown as the roads became passable. The bounty lasted for only a short time, however, and by late February supplies were scarce once again. In addition, the depreciation of the Continental currency made purchasing provisions increasingly difficult. Without adequate negotiable funds, the army's supplies were only a few days ahead of consumption, which kept the men in constant need of food, clothes, medical supplies, and other necessities.

The bleak conditions lowered morale and caused behavior to deteriorate. Officers were court-martialed for unbecoming conduct, trading with the enemy, and unapproved absences. Enlisted men were guilty of neglecting their weapons, plundering, drinking, desertion, and rowdy conduct. Mindful of the severe deprivations the men faced, as well as the boredom, Washington judiciously tempered the punishments for infractions of discipline and encouraged recreational activities and declared holidays, including St. Patrick's Day.

Washington and his officers, of course, fared somewhat better during their stay at Morristown. Those encamped at Jockey Hollow had larger cabins than the enlisted men, who slept 12 to a hut. Washington, believing he must maintain a style befitting the importance of his office and that comfort was a prerogative of command, moved into the Ford mansion in Morristown. The general and his staff occupied most of the house, leaving two rooms for the widow Theodosia Ford and her four children. And the general had the pleasure of Mrs. Washington's company for the winter. Washington's administrative labors were enormous, and he handled much of the burden alone. He was overindulgent in granting furloughs to his officers, so there were too few remaining to assist him with the problems of supply, personnel, intelligence, and enlistment.

The limited military operations Washington undertook had disastrous results. In January he planned a raid on Staten Island, but the British learned of it in time to prepare. Consequently, hundreds of ill-clad Americans suffered frostbite from exposure, six were killed, 16 captured, and those returning had only a few prisoners and some meager provisions to show for their effort. Even worse, the ill-fated mission and the plundering done by some of the Americans along the way sparked retaliatory raids by the British, which inflamed tempers on both sides. Furthermore, Washington's fear that continuing shortages in food, clothing, and money might lead to mutiny were realized on May 25 with the rebellion of part of the Connecticut line. Though the uprising was quickly subdued, Washington was still struggling with these problems and the need for more men when British troop movements were detected in early June. By the end of the month, with the supplies that had been accumulated removed to safety and a small detachment left behind, the Continental army marched out of Morristown, ending a brutal encampment that had seen the ranks depleted by 86 deaths and 1,066 desertions.

Further reading: U.S. Department of the Interior, *Morristown: A History and Guide, Morristown National Historical Park, New Jersey* (Washington, D.C.: National Park Service, 1984); Page Smith, *A New Age Now Begins.* Vol. 2 of *A People's History of the American Revolution* (New York: McGraw Hill, 1989).

— Rita M. Broyles

Morse, Jedidiah (1761–1826)

Known as the "father of American geography," Jedidiah Morse published widely read studies of the American landscape. His *Geography Made Easy* (1784) and *The American Geography* (1789) each saw multiple printings, with the former achieving some 25 editions. Based on his own travels, the works of contemporaries, and correspondence with people across the country, Morse's work advanced the reading public's knowledge of the North American continent. These studies were followed by a children's book entitled *Elements of Geography* (1795), *The American Gazetteer* (1797), and *A Compendious History of New England* (1804).

Morse was born in Woodstock, Connecticut. The eighth child of Jedidiah and Sarah Morse, he honed his intellectual skills as a student at Yale College. It was here, however, that he resolved to commit his life to the ministry, a decision that prolonged his academic career. To support his studies, Morse taught and wrote a geography book for students. He also developed a staunch nationalist ideology and a vigorous devotion to orthodox Christianity.

In 1786 Morse, now an ordained and licensed Congregationalist minister, accepted a position at a church in Midway, Georgia, but he soon returned to the northeast to lead the First Congregational Church in Charlestown, Massachusetts. Morse married Elizabeth Ann Breeze in 1789, and together they enjoyed a 30-year tenure at this church. A tremendously popular preacher, Morse launched an unrelenting assault on the liberal Christian views espoused by UNITARIANS. From his perspective, enlightened thought—and particularly DEISM—presented a threat to orthodox belief. THOMAS PAINE's *Age of Reason* (1794) came under especially close scrutiny. "The existence of God is boldly denied [in such texts]," Morse observed. "Atheism and materialism are systematically professed. Reason and Nature are deified and adored. The Christian religion and its divine and blessed author are not only disbelieved, rejected and contemned, but even abhorred." In 1805 he carried forward his defense of orthodoxy with the publication of *True Reasons on which the Election of a Hollis Professor of Divinity in Harvard College was opposed at the Board of Overseers, 14 February 1805* (1805). This diatribe set out his rationale for denying the Hollis Professorship to Henry Ware, whose liberal theology Morse considered antithetical to the man for whom the chair was named. Morse carried his efforts against deism forward through the organization of the General Association of Massachusetts, the launching of *The Panoplist* (1805), the establishment of Andover Theological Seminary (1808), and the founding of the Park Street Church in Boston (1809).

Morse considered the propagation of the gospel across the country to be no less important than purging the church from within. He therefore committed much of his time to evangelical endeavors such as the American Board of Commissioners for Foreign Missions, on which he served as a board member from 1811 to 1818, the New England Tract Society (founded in 1814), and the American Bible Society (founded in 1816). Until his tenure at the First Congregational Church ended in 1819, he also played an active role as secretary for the Society for the Propagation of the Gospel. After his voluntary removal from the church, Morse returned to New Haven, Connecticut, and spent the last years of his life in relative quietude, studying, preaching, and involving himself in Indian affairs.

Further reading: Joseph W. Phillips, *Jedidiah Morse and New England Congregationalism* (New Brunswick, N.J.: Rutgers University Press, 1983).

— Daniel M. Cobb

Murray, Judith Sargent Stevens (1751–1820)

During the early republic, Judith Sargent Murray published numerous essays and commentaries on REPUBLI- CANISM, especially with regard to women's rights. Born in Gloucester, Massachusetts, in 1751, Sargent was the daughter of the wealthy shipping merchant, Captain Winthrop Sargent. Studying with her brother, she received an unusually comprehensive EDUCATION for a female during this time period. In 1769 Judith Sargent married sea captain John Stevens, also of Gloucester, Massachusetts. He was later killed at sea while sailing in the WEST INDIES.

The prevalence of revolutionary ideas in the 1770s inspired Judith Stevens to write essays on the role of women in the new republic. In 1784, under the pseudonym Constantia, she published her first essay "Desultory Thoughts upon the Utility of Encouraging a Degree of Self-Complacency, Especially in Female Bosoms," in the Boston magazine, *Gentleman and Lady's Town and Country Magazine.* She argued that women needed both a strong sense of themselves and a thorough education to resist rushing into marriage to merely better their social status. Through education, women could develop sound judgment and intellectual competence so that they might become better citizens and, more importantly, better mothers to the future leaders of the new nation.

In 1788 Judith Stevens married the Reverend John Murray, who had moved to Gloucester in 1774 to serve as minister for the Universalist church. Through Murray, Judith developed a devout interest in Universalism and its principles. She accompanied her new husband on his various preaching tours, often keeping written accounts of their experiences. In 1790 the *Massachusetts Magazine* featured the first of many poems submitted to the magazine by Murray; she later published poems in the *Boston Weekly Magazine* and *Boston Magazine.* She also began a column in the *Massachusetts Magazine* that ran from February 1792 to August 1794 under the title "The Gleaner." Murray's column offered insights on the political questions of the day, particularly those regarding women's rights. She argued that "The [female] sex should be taught to depend on their own efforts, for the procurement of an establishment in life." Murray stressed that women needed access to a good education to become model republican citizens. She fervently promoted the idea of republican motherhood.

In addition, Murray wrote two plays: *The Medium, or A Happy Tea Party* (1795) and *The Traveller Returned* (1796). Unfortunately, her plays met with little public success, critically or economically. In 1798 these plays and a number of her essays from her column were collected and published in three volumes under the title *The Gleaner.* As Reverend Murray's health declined, she gathered her husband's letters and papers together for the publication of his *Letters, and Sketches of Sermons* (three volumes, 1812–13), adding additional chapters to his autobiography after his death in 1815. Judith Sargent Murray established herself as one of the preeminent voices on women's rights and responsibilities in the early republic. Murray died at her daughter's home in Natchez, Mississippi, on July 6, 1820.

See also REPUBLICANISM; WOMEN'S RIGHTS AND STATUS.

Further reading: Linda K. Kerber, *Women of the Republic: Intellect and Ideology in Revolutionary America* (Chapel Hill: University of North Carolina Press, 1980); Sheila Skemp, *Judith Sargent Murray: A Brief Biography with Documents* (Boston: Bedford Books, 1998).

— Linda English

music

Music during the late 18th and early 19th centuries was an important part of American life. Religious services, usually focused on the Psalms, had long included music, but in the 1760s and 1770s a transformation occurred. Following English fashions, Americans increasingly introduced sacred music. This practice led to the importation of organs, the use of more hymns, and the development of singing schools in New England and elsewhere. Initially, Americans imported their music. But in 1770, WILLIAM BILLINGS published *The New-England Psalm Singer; or American Chorister. . . ,* a collection of music that was entirely American. Billings not only wrote the tunes, but he also included singing instructions to be used in schools. The book was immensely popular and had a dramatic impact on American music.

Music also had more secular uses. Within the gentry, or upper class, music lessons were part of the children's curriculum. The best homes often had numerous instruments for their occupants' use. Robert Carter's plantation in Virginia, for example, had a harpsichord, harmonica, forte-piano, guitar, violin, and flutes. Sheet music published in London, Paris, Vienna, and other European centers was available in book shops and specialty stores, and featured composers of the period such as Haydn, Mozart, Beethoven, Schubert, and others. With chores and lessons done for the day, an evening's entertainment often consisted of family members gathering together and playing music.

Those European Americans further down the social scale also enjoyed music. They might have had fewer instruments available, but that did not stop them from playing or singing music. Billings, for instance, came from an obscure background, apprenticed as a tanner as a youth, and worked as a tradesman most of his life. For such individuals, whether in the church, at home, or in a TAVERN, music was a major form of entertainment.

Equally as important as well-played music was mastering the art of dance. Carter's home also boasted a separate ballroom, and in Virginia, where farms and plantations were often far apart, a ball drew people from miles around for a chance to socialize and exchange news and information. The children learned the complicated steps for stately court dances, such as the minuet, as well as those for hornpipes and country dances, the cotillion, and the quadrille, a dance that became increasingly fashionable after the turn of the 19th century. Many of the leading European composers also wrote for the dance. Although they may not have had formal training, common folk also danced, ordinarily to popular country tunes of unknown origin.

The enjoyment of music and dance was not confined to the free white population or to the upper classes. On more than one occasion, the slaves at Carter's plantation met to play the fiddle or the banjo and to dance. Music often had a poignant meaning for enslaved AFRICAN AMERICANS. It was a means to express resentment over their condition and also a release from the harsh realities of their daily world. By the beginning of the 19th century, as more and more African Americans turned to Christianity, the so-called Negro spiritual developed to fulfill these functions while also serving as a means of teaching stories from the Bible. Free African Americans used music, especially at certain festivals such as Pinkster, a secular celebration of Pentecost. African Americans would gather and play banjos, fiddles, and drums, shake rattles made up of pebbles or shells in a basket, and sing. These venues gave them the opportunity to maintain elements of their African heritage and ritual while creating a distinct African-American culture.

In addition to its uses in religious services and for private enjoyment, music also had important public functions. During the RESISTANCE MOVEMENT (1763–75), music was a means to deride opponents and to garner collective support. Once the REVOLUTIONARY WAR (1775–83) broke out, the political role of music became even more important. "YANKEE DOODLE," which emerged before the war as a popular tune, became identified with the cause of independence. Other songs were more spontaneous and are lost to us today. Common sailors and soldiers composed stanza after stanza in camps and aboard ships trumpeting their cause and their heroes. Some of the music flowed

from the pens of men like Billings. The patriotic undertones in the *New-England Songster* became explicit in his more secular *The Singing Master's Assistant, or Key to Practical Music*, first published in 1778. In this work, which soldiers often carried with them, Billings joined the American cause with the Bible and portrayed the British in an "Infernal League" conspiring against "New England's God."

Music also had a military purpose. The British, Hessians, and French had the most elaborate bands for performances. While GEORGE WASHINGTON believed that "nothing is more agreeable, and ornamental than good music," the CONTINENTAL ARMY had only a few bands of musicians accompanying its regiments. In all of the armies that fought in the war, fifers and drummers were used primarily for signaling purposes. The sound emitted by an 18th-century drum could be heard for long distances over the din of battle. Certain beats were used to transmit orders on the battlefield, as well as for regulating routine when in camp.

After the war, music continued to serve an important function in civic occasions and celebrations, such as military training days, Election Day, and the Fourth of July. The local tavern was usually the focal point for public meetings and political rallies. Much of the music-making that occurred in these situation was informal, however, so little documentation of it remains. Popular songs found a spirited audience in tavern patrons and were sung alone or to the accompaniment of a dance fiddle or other instrument. Prominent tunes, reset to new words, easily lent themselves to the purpose of political criticism or satire. In the emerging party politics of the 1790s and early 1800s, the FEDERALIST and DEMOCRATIC-REPUBLICAN PARTIES had their own political tunes to taunt each other. The Democratic-Republicans sang French Revolutionary tunes, while the Federalists, influenced in part by Great Britain, developed songs such as "Hail Columbia." Similarly, when Francis Scott Key wrote his "Star Spangled Banner" in 1814, it quickly got put to the music of an English drinking song.

Although music was usually participatory, there were also public concerts in taverns, theaters, and other public spaces. Before the Revolutionary War, concerts were relatively infrequent and featured amateur musicians, usually prominent gentlemen. After the war, an increasing numbers of professional musicians came to the United States. Many had been trained in Germany and France, and offered their talents as performers, teachers, and instrument makers. Benefit concerts sometimes raised money for the needy, but were usually for the support of the musician who organized it. Subscription concerts were a series of performances, usually two per month for a total of 10 or 12, that were advertised in the newspapers, with tickets for individual concerts available for sale at various locations.

Most of the music presented featured the works of composers still living or only recently deceased. Franz Haydn was especially popular, but Mozart apparently was not very popular with American audiences during his lifetime.

See also POPULAR CULTURE; THEATER.

Further reading: Richard L. Bushman, *The Refinement of America: Persons, Houses, Cities* (New York: Knopf, 1992); Philip Vickers Fithian, *Journal and Letters, 1767–1774* (Freeport, N.Y.: Books for Libraries Press, 1969); James R. Heintze, ed., *American Musical Life in Context and Practice to 1865* (New York, Garland, 1994); John Fitzhugh Millar, *Country Dances of Colonial America* (Williamsburg: Thirteen Colonies Press, 1990); Jane C. Nylander, *Our Own Snug Fireside, 1760–1860* (New York: Knopf, 1993); Kenneth Silverman, *The Cultural History of the American Revolution: Painting, Music, Literature, and Theatre in the Colonies and the United States from the Treaty of Paris to the Inauguration of George Washington, 1763–1789* (New York: Columbia University Press, 1976).

— Rita M. Broyles

N

national debt

The American national debt was created during the REVOLUTIONARY WAR (1775–83). The extent of this debt remains unclear since it came from several different sources. Continental and state currencies were both a form of public debt, but when the Continental dollar became worthless, it wiped out most of this obligation. The individual states and the CONTINENTAL CONGRESS borrowed money to support the war effort. Some of this money was in loans from the American people and some of it was borrowed from foreign powers. Millions, too, were issued in military supply certificates and pay vouchers to soldiers. State governments assumed some of the national debt and began paying it during the 1780s. By the time the CONSTITUTIONAL CONVENTION met in the summer of 1787, the debt was estimated at about $80 million.

In the early 1790s, Secretary of the Treasury ALEXANDER HAMILTON sought to strengthen the federal government using the national debt. His financial program offered to take over the state debts. Hamilton believed that this assumption of state debts would leave the business interests of the country tied to the national government, since it would owe them money. People who had money would want to make sure that the federal government had the power to guarantee the integrity of government securities. Hamilton also wanted to provide full funding for the national debt. Because the Congress under the ARTICLES OF CONFEDERATION had not paid interest and looked like it would never be able to pay back the debt, the government notes had been sold at a discount. Now Hamilton wanted to reward the speculators who had bought the notes at a fraction of their original worth by offering to redeem the notes at face value. Hamilton had no intention of paying off the debt. He was willing to honor any note but preferred to make regular interest payments on the debt, ensuring continued support for the government. As a safe and profitable place for money, he believed, investors would eagerly hold on to these securities. To further demonstrate the worth of government notes, he was willing to accept them as payment for stock in the BANK OF THE UNITED STATES.

Hamilton's financial plan was supported by the FEDERALIST PARTY and opposed by the DEMOCRATIC-REPUBLICANS. THOMAS JEFFERSON and JAMES MADISON saw the entire scheme as an effort to corrupt the American people and create a too powerful government. During the course of the 1790s their opposition grew more adamant. When Jefferson won the ELECTION OF 1800 he worked to shrink the size of government and began to pay off the national debt. The Democratic-Republicans continued to make progress in this direction until the War of 1812 (1812–15), when government expenditures outstripped income. The debt increased to $127 million. However, in the years after the war, the federal government again sought to pay down the debt, erasing it completely during the administration of Andrew Jackson.

Further reading: E. James Ferguson, *The Power of the Purse: A History of American Public Finance, 1776–1790* (Chapel Hill: University of North Carolina Press, 1961); Stanley Elkins and Eric McKitrick, *The Age of Federalism: The Early American Republic, 1788–1800* (New York: Oxford University Press, 1993); Gerald Stourzh, *Alexander Hamilton and the Idea of Republican Government* (Stanford, Calif.: Stanford University Press, 1970).

Native Americans and the Revolution

The REVOLUTIONARY WAR (1775–83) had a profound and devastating effect upon the Native American peoples east of the Mississippi. When the war ended, they faced the power of a new nation that had little respect for their lands, their cultures, or their lives. Most Native Americans remained neutral at the request of both the British and the Americans when the war started. As the war continued, however, it became more difficult for them not to pick one

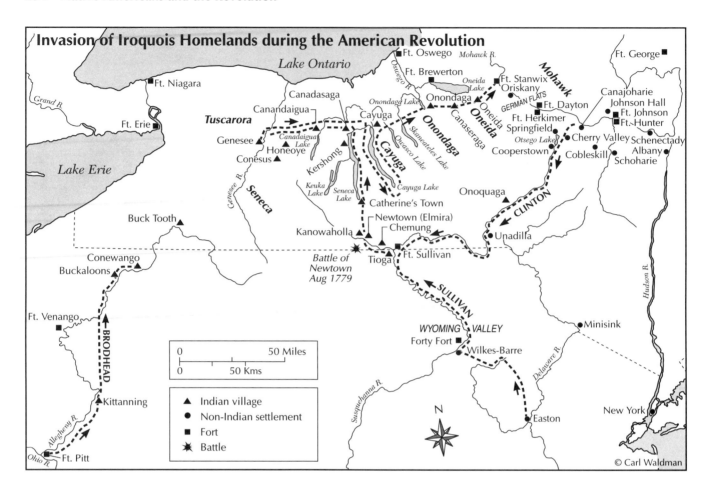

Invasion of Iroquois Homelands during the American Revolution

side or the other. Since the British promised to protect them from the land-hungry colonists and provided a steady supply of trade goods, most Native Americans came to support Great Britain. Members of many tribes also had relatives and strong relationships with the English living among them.

The stress of the Revolutionary War highlighted the fact that tribal leaders were losing control over their young men. Frequently, warriors from the same nations—sometimes from the same villages—faced each other in battle while fighting for one side or the other. Besides the lack of unity within tribal groups, many Native-American nations were bitter enemies, with some of these conflicts going back generations. The IROQUOIS in New York hated the CHEROKEE in the Southeast, while the Cherokee had a running feud with their neighbors, the CREEK. Both the British and the Americans took advantage of the rivalries and the internal divisions to get Native Americans to fight for them. The older leaders often wanted to stay neutral in the war, but the young warriors looked forward to proving themselves on the battlefield. The agents for both sides—British and American—exploited these desires for glory and gave the eager warriors a chance to

make a name for themselves and to settle old scores with their tribe's enemies. The Native American leaders had no real authority to stop the young men from fighting; their real power was in their ability to persuade their people. Consequently, when a white representative of one side appeared in a village, they might enlist a few men for their cause without getting the support of the entire tribe. This created hard feelings among the people of the different villages and between different tribes that might have been at peace with one another before the war. It also provided the various state legislatures with an excuse to attack Native Americans whose lands they coveted. When a few warriors of a certain tribe were seen fighting for the British, state militias quickly raided the tribe's otherwise peaceful villages and drove their inhabitants away. American settlers and traders were usually not long in moving in and claiming the vacated land.

Before the war, Great Britain spent much time and effort making and keeping friendships with Native-American peoples. In the North, William Johnson lived with the Mohawk and other Iroquois as the king's Indian agent. John Stuart played a similar role among the Cherokee and the Creek in the South. Johnson secured Iroquois help for

Britain during the French and Indian War (1754–63). Although Johnson died before the war started, his hard work and that of his replacement, his son Guy Johnson, kept most Iroquois loyal to the king. Stuart spent the rest of his life working with southern Native Americans to get them to fight for the English side. In contrast, the Americans had few effective representatives with the Native Americans. The American Reverend Kirkland was an exception to this. He kept the Oneida Nation of the Iroquois confederacy neutral during the war. In general, the British were able to draw upon the goodwill and diplomacy of its agents throughout the conflict.

When the shooting started, neither the British nor the Americans wanted to involve the Native Americans. The Americans did not want to face any more enemies than they already had; the British did not want to upset the delicate balance among the tribes. English merchants stood to lose the profitable fur and deer-hide TRADE with the Native Americans if the fighting diverted the young men from hunting. The Americans could also make it difficult to transport the goods from the backcountry if the tribes became caught up in the struggle. GEORGE WASHINGTON sent messages to many tribal councils asking them to stay out of the fighting.

By 1776 it was clear that the rebellion was serious and that neither side could safely ignore the potential military contributions of the native peoples. The British held a decisive advantage in raising support for their side because of their longstanding relationships. In contrast, the colonists had constantly trespassed on tribal lands before the war despite treaties and agreements. This conflict made it easier for the British to make allies with many tribes. Moreover, the Crown promised to keep the Americans out of the hunting grounds west of the Appalachian Mountains.

The Cherokee were one of the first nations to strike out at the Americans. During the spring and summer of 1776 they launched a series of raids against FRONTIER towns. The states reacted quickly. Georgia, South Carolina, North Carolina, and Virginia all mounted devastating militia invasions of the eastern Cherokee lands. The lack of coordination among the states actually worked against the Cherokee, with their enemies coming from many directions at once. The invaders burned villages and fields and killed or drove off horses and other livestock. By the end of the year the Cherokee chiefs asked for peace.

Not all of the Cherokee wanted to stop fighting the Americans. DRAGGING CANOE led a party of warriors into the mountains of northern Georgia and southern Tennessee. From his base along the Chickamauga River, he gathered over 1,000 fighting men. Dragging Canoe raided the backwoods settlements and farms in the South, and the CONTINENTAL ARMY was unable to stop him throughout the war.

In the North, the Iroquois (except the Oneida) fought for the king. Warriors from the Six Nations accompanied British forces in the invasion of New York in 1777. When the British suffered defeat at SARATOGA (October 17, 1777) and withdrew from the siege at Fort Stanwix (August 1777), the Iroquois broke off into small bands to raid the frontier from Vermont to Virginia. JOSEPH BRANT led a mixed force of LOYALISTS and Iroquois on some of the most devastating forays against the American settlements. These raids had the unintended consequence of forcing Americans who had previously been neutral to join the fight for independence.

The Americans struck back in the summer of 1779. George Washington sent a large army of militia and Continental soldiers under General JOHN SULLIVAN to destroy the Iroquois's ability to make war. The force brushed aside Iroquois resistance and marched into the heartland of the Six Nations. As in the invasion of Cherokee territory, the soldiers burned the villages and cornfields throughout the region. The troops made no distinction between the neutral Oneidas and the other five nations: All suffered from the wrath of the Continentals. Many of the Americans were amazed at the rich Iroquois farms complete with cattle and horses and the sturdy cabins with glass windows and wooden floors. The Iroquois lived more comfortably than many settlers. The memories of these homesteads stayed with the raiders, suggesting that this region might be the place for them to start new lives after the war. The invaders marched back home after laying waste to Iroquoia. The Six Nations would never recover from the blow.

Other Native Americans had spent their entire lives living among the colonists in the Atlantic colonies. When the war broke out, some fought for either side. The Mohegan preacher Samson Occom and his son-in-law, Joseph Johnson, had made plans to move their people out of Connecticut to a grant of land in Iroquoia. Johnson had acted as Washington's agent to the Iroquois in 1776, asking them to stay neutral. The fighting disrupted their plans until 1784, when they established the Brotherton Settlement in New York State.

The story was different in the West. While the Continentals had some successes under General GEORGE ROGERS CLARK, the vast distances and the difficulty of keeping an army supplied made it hard for the Americans to hold onto the fruits of their victories. Powerful tribes also made the region very unstable for the Americans. The British agents kept the Shawnee supplied with powder and lead. The nations south of the Great Lakes also made contact with Dragging Canoe's warriors in the Southeast. Together, these groups prevented the Americans from establishing dominance in the lands to the west of the Appalachians. In 1782 the Shawnee defeated an American force in the Ohio country.

The terms of the TREATY OF PARIS (1783) between the Americans and the British shocked most Native Americans: Their British allies had given away Native American lands. The new United States claimed everything from the Great Lakes to Spanish FLORIDA and from the Atlantic to the Mississippi River, an area containing vast tracts that few Americans had ever seen. The new borders also divided many nations like the Iroquois and the Creek. The American Revolution proved to be devastating to the native peoples, even those who fought alongside the Americans.

Further reading: Colin G. Calloway, *Crown and Calumet: British-Indian Relations, 1783–1815* (Norman: University of Oklahoma Press, 1987); Barbara Graymont, *The Iroquois in the American Revolution* (Syracuse, N.Y.: Syracuse University Press, 1972); Tom Hatley, *The Dividing Paths: Cherokees and South Carolinians through the Revolutionary Era* (New York: Oxford University Press, 1995); James H. Merrell, *The Indians' New World: Catawbas and Their Neighbors from European Contact through the Era of Removal* (Chapel Hill: University of North Carolina Press, 1989); Richard White, *The Middle Ground: Indians, Empires, and the Republics in the Great Lakes Region, 1650–1815* (Cambridge, U.K.: Cambridge University Press, 1991).

— George Milne

Neutrality Proclamation (April 22, 1793)

GEORGE WASHINGTON issued the Neutrality Proclamation on April 23, 1793, to solve a problem: What role should the United States play in the war between Great Britain and France that began on February 1, 1793? No one in the president's cabinet wanted to enter the war, even though the United States had signed a treaty with France in 1778. Secretary of State THOMAS JEFFERSON, however, was not eager to stake out a position, especially because he was suspicious of Great Britain and supported the principles of the FRENCH REVOLUTION (1789–1815). Secretary of the Treasury ALEXANDER HAMILTON, on the other hand, sought ways of distancing the administration from the FRENCH ALLIANCE and hoped to placate Great Britain.

The Neutrality Proclamation was drafted by Edmund Randolph and made three key points. First, it urged "a conduct friendly and impartial toward the belligerent powers." Second, it advised all American citizens to avoid acts that would be construed as helping one side or the other. And third, it declared that any American who committed such an act would not be protected by the United States government. Interestingly, the document never used the word "neutrality," although that was the intended effect.

The proclamation was generally popular in the United States, but it contributed to the developing partisan fervor. JAMES MADISON and Alexander Hamilton engaged in a newspaper debate over the policy of neutrality under the pen names "Pacificus" and "Helvidius." When Citizen EDMOND GENET, the new French ambassador, ignored the proclamation, the Washington administration demanded his recall.

The policy of neutrality has been held up as an example of Washington's statesmanship and as a precursor of his FAREWELL ADDRESS's advice to avoid "entangling alliances." It has also been used a precedent for calls for neutrality and isolationism throughout American history.

See also FOREIGN AFFAIRS.

Further reading: Stanley Elkins and Eric McKitrick, *The Age of Federalism: The Early American Republic, 1788–1800* (New York: Oxford University Press, 1993).

Newburgh conspiracy (1782–1783)

The Newburgh conspiracy occurred during the winter of 1782–83, when officers in the CONTINENTAL ARMY threatened to coerce the CONTINENTAL CONGRESS into providing pensions after the war. General GEORGE WASHINGTON defused this potential conflict between the military and civilian authority in the new republic by refusing to countenance any military interference in politics.

As the REVOLUTIONARY WAR (1775–83) wound to a close in 1782, many officers began to express their concerns that the Continental Congress would not keep its promise of lifetime pensions at half pay for officers. With no guaranteed revenue, Congress appeared unlikely to be able to provide even the back pay owed to the army. In the last week of December, a group of officers sent a petition to Congress asking for compensation, either in a lump-sum payment or a full pension for a set number of years. Nationalist leaders in Congress, like ROBERT MORRIS, seized the opportunity of this petition to work toward creating additional revenue for the federal government under the ARTICLES OF CONFEDERATION. The exact details of the nationalist manipulations remain unclear, but they apparently encouraged the most extreme military officers, led by HORATIO GATES, to threaten mutiny and a possible coup d'etat if their demands were not met.

The crisis came to a head in March 1783 at the military cantonment in Newburgh, New York, when army officers issued two addresses anonymously. These addresses argued that the officers should abandon "milk-and-water style" and moderation, and demand that Congress recognize their sacrifices and provide pensions. They urged that the officers act immediately before the army was disbanded and implicitly threatened military action. The addresses called for a meeting on March 11. At this point Washington stepped in to prevent the officers from plunging "themselves into a gulph of Civil horror." He agreed to a meeting on March 15—the extra days would allow tempers to cool—and suggested that Gates preside. As soon as the meeting began, Washington entered and requested to speak. Gates could not deny the commander in chief the floor. Washington agreed that the officers had a legitimate complaint and talked of all of their sacrifices, but he also exclaimed "My God! What can this writer [the author of the addresses] have in view, by recommending such measures? Can he be a friend of the army? Can he be a friend of the country? Rather is he not an insidious foe?" Opposition to Washington disintegrated and the conspiracy came to naught. Within days, news of the peace agreement arrived and the army began to disband.

There were several important ramifications of the Newburgh conspiracy. First, the nationalists in Congress managed to pass an impost, although it was never effectively collected. Second, Washington emerged from the controversy with an enhanced reputation. Third, and most significant, the army avoided interfering in politics. Other revolutions have ended with a military coup and dictatorship. The AMERICAN REVOLUTION eluded a similar fate, and in the United States the military would remain subordinate to civilian authority.

Further reading: Richard H. Kohn, *The Eagle and Sword: The Federalists and the Creation of the Military Establishment in America, 1783–1802* (New York: Free Press, 1975).

New Spain (Mexico), northern frontier of

The northern FRONTIER of New Spain (Mexico), the area of the current Southwest United States, was a backwater of the Spanish Empire from 1754 to 1820. Although Spain devoted limited resources to the region, it had two main goals for this frontier: to restrict the influence of other European powers and to subdue hostile NATIVE AMERICANS.

No European power posed a direct threat to Spain's tenuous hold on this part of its empire, but Spain continuously

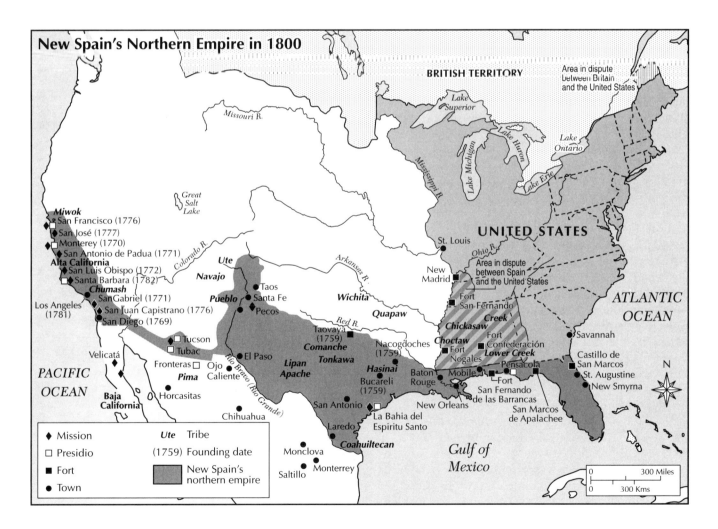

looked at its rivals with a wary eye. To forestall Russian advances and possible English interest, Spain colonized CALIFORNIA beginning in 1769. The acquisition of Louisiana in the treaty that ended the French and Indian War (1754–63) provided a territorial cushion for Spain's settlements in New Mexico and Texas. The English, however, now had outposts on the Mississippi River, and English traders soon began penetrating the GREAT PLAINS, competing with the Spanish. The defeat of Great Britain in the REVOLUTIONARY WAR (1775–83) minimized this threat. It also brought an aggressive and, as it turned out, expansive United States into the picture. By the time Spain retroceded Louisiana to NAPOLEON BONAPARTE, who in turn sold it to the United States during the LOUISIANA PURCHASE in 1803, the Spanish had their hands full in Europe and in the rest of their empire. The vague boundary between American Louisiana and the Spanish possessions in northern New Spain was clarified in 1819 by the Adams-Onís Treaty. Two years later, Spain withdrew entirely from North America, and Mexico gained its independence.

The Indian problem was dealt with by two separate orders that reoriented Spanish policy. The *Regulations of 1772* shifted Spanish-Indian relations from diplomacy to force. The Spanish government proposed the creation of a line of 15 presidios (forts) from the Gulf of California to the Gulf of Mexico, spaced at a distance of approximately 100 miles. These 15 outposts, roughly along the 30th parallel, or near the current United States–Mexico border, were to be manned by well-paid and heavily armed mounted soldiers. All settlements, except for a few around Santa Fe in New Mexico and San Antonio in Texas, were to be abandoned north of the line. Although this plan was more difficult to carry out than originally envisioned, it helped to provide frontier security. The second set of orders, the *Instructions of 1786,* created an aggressive Indian policy that sought to exterminate all Native Americans who opposed the Spanish, while making other Indians more dependent on the Spanish for trade. This policy was calculating and brutal. Captured Apache, including women and children, were shipped to Cuba to serve as slaves. Previously, captives had been sent to Mexico, where some would escape and return to the frontier. A pact was arranged with the Comanche. Before this time, the Spanish had been reluctant to trade firearms with the Indians. Now they did so willingly, with the idea that the Indians would become dependent on the Spanish for gunpowder and repairs. By the 1790s a relative peace settled over the border region, leading to increased Hispanic settlement and relative prosperity. After 1810, the Mexican independence movement disrupted this peace. Texas experienced the greatest disorder, as competing government and republican forces seized control of the province and pirates, such as Jean Laffite, infested the coast.

Throughout this period, Franciscan friars never abandoned their efforts to bring Christianity to the Indians. Despite decreased government support, the Franciscans maintained missions in New Mexico and Texas and established several in California. Although Christian Indians often suffered a high mortality, especially among seminomadic peoples that were compelled to settle near the missions, these institutions were important in spreading Hispanic culture in the region.

Further reading: Gary Clayton Anderson, *The Indian Southwest, 1580–1830: Ethnogenesis and Reinvention* (Norman: University of Oklahoma Press, 1999); David J. Weber, *The Spanish Frontier in North America* (New Haven, Conn.: Yale University Press, 1992).

Niles, Hezekiah (1777–1839)

Hezekiah Niles was born to QUAKER parents in Pennsylvania. Apprenticed at a young age to a printer named Benjamin Johnson, Niles quickly earned a reputation as one of the most efficient typesetters in America. Niles first published in Philadelphia in 1794, when he wrote several essays for local newspapers favoring TARIFF protection. He started a short-lived literary magazine in the early 1800s and soon moved to Baltimore, where he bought and became editor of the *Baltimore Evening Post.* He sold the *Post* five years later and almost immediately published the prospectus for his most memorable publication, *Niles' Weekly Register.*

The first issue of the *Niles' Weekly Register* was published on September 11, 1811. The paper was later renamed *Niles' National Register,* but it was often simply referred to as *Niles' Register.* The newspaper was read in every state and several foreign countries and attained over 10,000 subscriptions within its first seven years of publication. THOMAS JEFFERSON, JAMES MADISON, and Andrew Jackson were faithful readers, and Congress received 10 copies of the newspaper each week for its members. The *Register's* popularity sprang from its differences from other publications. During a time when linguistic eloquence and editorial bias abounded, the *Register* printed facts and statistics of national interest, endorsed no particular political candidates, published no advertisements, and refused all anonymous material.

Despite the newspaper's objectivity, Niles remained politically outspoken. He was a DEMOCRATIC-REPUBLICAN until about 1817, when he described himself as belonging to no party. Differing with Jackson's policies, Niles became a WHIG in 1829. He also openly declared for the abolition of SLAVERY and was an officer of Delaware's abolitionist society.

The *Register* lived on for 10 years after Niles's death in Wilmington, Delaware, in 1839.

See also ANTISLAVERY AND ABOLITION; JOURNALISM.

— Meghan A. Earl

Non-Importation Act (1806)

Concerned with the tightening British blockade of Napoleonic Europe, the United States passed the Non-Importation Act in the spring of 1806 in an effort to convince the British to ease its restrictions. With the DEMOCRATIC-REPUBLICANS dominating both houses of Congress and the presidency, the main debate over the measure came from within Jeffersonian ranks. One group of Democratic-Republicans wanted to put a comprehensive ban on most imports from Great Britain as a statement of American determination. Ultimately, this group was defeated by another set of Democratic-Republicans with close ties to the administration of THOMAS JEFFERSON. These men wanted only a partial ban. The measure that was passed would proscribe some metal goods, cloth made of hemp or flax, certain expensive woolens, glass, finished clothing, beer, ale, and a few other items. The largest imports from Great Britain were not included—cottons, cheap woolens, iron, and steel.

The hope was that this symbolic gesture would convince the British to negotiate an acceptable agreement on the role of the United States as a neutral trader in a time of war. To emphasize this fact, the law was not to take effect until November to give the British time to consider treating with the Americans. JOHN RANDOLPH, a Democratic-Republican who was against all commerce as a violation of the agrarian nature of the United States, proclaimed the law "a milk-and-water bill, a dose of chicken broth to be taken nine months hence." British politicians also scoffed at the bill, considering it mere bluff and bluster. They believed that Americans wanted to buy English goods and would as soon as forgo TRADE with Britain as they would go naked. From their perspective it was a "foolish and teasing measure." Randolph and the British were right. The law was ineffective and a sign of the weakness of the United States on the world stage. It eventually had some impact on Anglo-American trade after it was allowed to go into effect early in 1808, but only because it became an important addition to the restraints imposed by the EMBARGO OF 1807. The law remained in place into the War of 1812 (1812–15).

See also FOREIGN AFFAIRS.

Further reading: Bradford Perkins, *Prologue to War, 1805–1812: England and the United States* (Berkeley: University of California Press, 1968).

Non-Intercourse Act (1809)

By the beginning of 1809 the EMBARGO OF 1807 had failed. Instead of compelling Britain and France to end their restrictions on neutral TRADE, the measure had wrecked havoc on the American ECONOMY. With THOMAS JEFFERSON leaving the presidency and JAMES MADISON replacing him, it was time to find a new solution for the diplomatic and commercial problem of neutral trade while Europe was engulfed in war. Some politicians clamored for a declaration of war against either or both belligerents. Others sought more-peaceful solutions. Amid this drift there emerged the Non-Intercourse Act. This legislation repealed the embargo, closed both export and import trade with Britain and France, and prohibited warships of either power from visiting American ports. The law held out the possibility of resuming normal trade with either European power if it repealed its trade restrictions. In such a circumstance, the United States would maintain nonintercourse against the other power.

The law was a farce. As JOHN RANDOLPH eloquently explained: "We have trusted our most precious interests in this leaky vessel." Merchants could easily avoid its provisions once their ships put to sea. They could either ignore the law directly or sail to some neutral port to exchange goods with a British (more likely) or French ship. The law also favored Great Britain, since its navy could intercept neutral shipping more effectively than the French, and since it had ports in CANADA and the WEST INDIES that it could use for provisioning. Neither the British nor the French could take the measure seriously. In 1810 Congress recognized the futility of the Non-Intercourse Act and replaced it with MACON'S BILL NO. 2, which reopened trade with both the French and the British but promised to reinstate nonintercourse with one power if the other repealed its trade restrictions.

See also FOREIGN AFFAIRS.

Further reading: Bradford Perkins, *Prologue to War, 1805–1812: England and the United States* (Berkeley: University of California Press, 1968).

North, Frederick, Lord (Lord North of Kirtling) (1732–1792)

Lord North was British chief minister during the critical years from 1770 to 1782. The actions taken by his government intensified the crises that led to the REVOLUTIONARY WAR (1775–83), and his weak wartime leadership contributed to Britain's defeat.

North was the son of the first earl of Guilford and received an English aristocrat's education at Eton and Trinity College, Oxford. In 1754 at the age of 22 he began his political career as a member of Parliament for Banbury. He quickly obtained influential positions as a lord of the treasury and a member of the Privy Council. In 1765 he became Chancellor of the Exchequer, and with the defeat of the WHIG government in 1770 King GEORGE III made him chief minister of a new Tory government. The king preferred the Tories, who were strong supporters of the monarchy, and North was the only Tory capable of forming a stable government.

Lord North was a popular and competent politician who possessed the debating and negotiating skills necessary for survival in Parliament. However, as chief minister he was often forced to support policies with which he himself did not agree. He was also frequently under sharp attack from a capable opposition that included the likes of EDMUND BURKE and Charles James Fox. The outbreak of war served only to emphasize his shortcomings as a leader. He lacked the initiative to take strong action and the optimism needed to withstand the pressures of wartime politics.

North failed to understand the deep dissatisfaction of the American colonists and the degree to which American political ideals had come to differ from those of Great Britain. This lack of understanding became evident during the tea crisis. North misjudged the effect of the TEA ACT (1773), a measure meant to bail out the floundering East India Company. The law granted the company a monopoly in the colonial tea trade, and by lowering the price of tea, would subtly compel compliance with the remaining TOWNSHEND DUTY (1767). These actions were potentially damaging to colonial merchants. In protest, colonists dumped a valuable cargo of tea into Boston Harbor. North's government retaliated for this BOSTON TEA PARTY (December 16, 1773) by passing the COERCIVE ACTS (1774) that closed the port of Boston and intervened in the operation of the Massachusetts government. These actions increased tensions between Britain and the colonists and led to the outbreak of hostilities.

North also miscalculated the capacity of the colonists to wage war. Early American successes distressed him. What little enthusiasm he had for the war quickly evaporated after the surrender of General JOHN BURGOYNE at SARATOGA (October 17, 1777). However, he proved unable to resist King George III and unwilling to resign. The resulting period of weak and indecisive leadership eventually cost Britain the war.

In 1782, after the surrender at YORKTOWN (October 19, 1781), North resigned and left politics briefly, but he reappeared in a coalition government with his old enemies the Whigs. In 1786 he left politics for good due to failing eyesight. Following the death of his father in 1790 he became the second earl Guilford, only to die two years later. Despite what might have been considered in other times a successful political career, his name is today primarily associated with Britain's loss of the 13 colonies.

See also RESISTANCE MOVEMENT.

Further reading: Don Cook, *The Long Fuse: How England Lost the American Colonies, 1760–1785* (New York: Atlantic Monthly Press, 1995); Edmund S. Morgan, *The Birth of the Republic, 1763–89* (Chicago: University of Chicago Press, 1992); Peter D. G. Thomas, *Lord North* (New York: St. Martin's Press, 1976).

— Robert Lively

North Carolina Regulation (1766–1771)

The North Carolina Regulation was a social movement in the Piedmont region of the colony aimed at combating corruption among local officials, creating a more equitable economic system in the backcountry, and increasing the participation of farmers in the political system. Settlers had first moved to the North Carolina Piedmont, or backcountry as it was then known, beginning in the 1740s. Most came from the colonies to the north, with others coming directly from Europe or from eastern North Carolina. The majority of immigrants were dissenters from the Anglican established church. They were eager to follow their own religious principles and to obtain sufficient land to ensure family independence. Their hopes for autonomy in economic and religious matters were threatened by backcountry elites who used their control of the legal system, the land market, and credit to fleece the population. Farmers were particularly outraged by three key issues: the high costs associated with using the courts, which served as the only local government institution in the southern colonies; the sheriffs' embezzlement of people's hard-earned tax monies; and usury laws that favored creditors over debtors.

The movement began in 1766 when farmers in Orange County organized the Sandy Creek Association. The core of the organization consisted of a group of QUAKERS led by HERMAN HUSBAND, a deeply religious and prosperous farmer from Maryland who had first come to the Piedmont in the mid-1750s. Husband quickly became the main spokesman for the farmers' movement and its chief ideologue. His ideas about social justice and the duty of Christians to help bring it about were tremendously influential among Piedmont farmers. Within two years of its organization, the Sandy Creek Association ceased to exist, but the seeds for more widespread resistance had been sown; early in 1768, many of its members joined with other reform-minded farmers under the name of "Regulators," a term used in England for people appointed to reform government abuse.

Regulators organized throughout all Piedmont counties. They pursued legal and extralegal means to put a stop to the extortionate practices of local officials. They repeatedly petitioned the governor and the colonial assembly for relief, tried to set up meetings with local officials to talk things over, and brought suits against officials. When such legal measures had little effect, they resorted to extralegal action: They refused to pay taxes, repossessed property seized for public sale to satisfy debts and taxes, and disrupted court proceedings. In September 1768 Governor William Tryon and his militia confronted a large number of Regulators outside of Hillsborough, but violence was avoided. Two years later, a large group of Regulators disrupted the superior court in Hillsborough; roughed up a number of LAWYERS, merchants, and officials; and destroyed the house of Edmund Fanning, the most hated official in the area. The authorities retaliated forcefully.

Almost as soon as the colonial assembly opened later that fall, Herman Husband, who had been elected a legislator for Orange County in 1769, was accused of libel, expelled from the assembly, and jailed. Next, the assemblymen passed a sweeping riot act that, among other things, gave Governor Tryon the authority and funds he needed to raise the militia and march against the Regulators. On May 16, 1771, about 1,100 militiamen confronted upwards of 2,000 farmers in the BATTLE OF ALAMANCE about 20 miles west of Hillsborough. Two hours after the first shot was fired, 17–20 farmers lay dead, along with nine militiamen; more than 150 men on both sides were wounded. One Regulator was hanged on the spot without benefit of trial; six others were hanged in Hillsborough on June 19 after a hasty trial. At least 6,000 Regulators and sympathizers took the oath of allegiance as the victorious troops marched through backcountry settlements, burning farms and requisitioning foodstuffs. Some of the best-known Regulators, including Herman Husband, fled the province. By summer, the Regulation had been suppressed. Just five years later, the same men who had opposed the Regulators in the assembly and on the battlefield led North Carolina into the REVOLUTIONARY WAR (1775–83). Perhaps not surprisingly, many former Regulators were little interested in the imperial struggle. The economic, religious, and social independence they had fought for did not become a reality in the wake of the AMERICAN REVOLUTION. Yet their hopes for social justice in an agrarian setting would live on, finding expression in later social movements such as Populism.

See also LAND RIOTS; RIOTS; SOUTH CAROLINA REGULATION.

Further reading: Marjoeine Kars, *Breaking Loose Together: The Regulator Rebellion in Pre-Revolutionary North Carolina* (Chapel Hill: University of North Carolina Press, 2002); William S. Powell, James K. Huhta, and Thomas J. Farnham, eds., *The Regulators in North Car-*olina: A Documentary History, 1759–1776 (Raleigh, N.C.: State Dept. of Archives and History, 1971).

— Marjoeine Kars

Northwest Ordinances (1785 and 1787)

The Northwest Ordinances were acts passed under the ARTICLES OF CONFEDERATION government that provided the basic framework for government and settlement of the Northwest Territory, the present-day states of Ohio, Indiana, Illinois, Michigan, Wisconsin, and part of Minnesota. Following the REVOLUTIONARY WAR (1775–83), the states agreed to give up their individual claims to western lands to the national government. The national government needed a method to govern and sell the land, since the sale of land in the Northwest Territory would raise money for the government and allow it to pay off the debts accumulated by the states during the Revolutionary War. Congress attempted to construct a plan to govern the territory. THOMAS JEFFERSON suggested a division of the territory into over a dozen smaller entities, each with classical, or Roman, names. When a territory contained as many residents as did the smallest of the 13 original states, it could gain statehood. This proposal alarmed many of the people in the existing states, who feared that the western states would dominate the government. Congress eventually amended Jefferson's plan to create a temporary government and to establish universal rights for all men in the territory. Although never enforced, this plan, called the Ordinance of 1784, was endorsed by Congress and became the basis for the Ordinance of 1787. Before that act, however, Congress passed another law in 1785.

The Ordinance of 1785 simplified the process of the sale and distribution of land. The act called for the survey of rectangular townships. Each township would then be subdivided into 36 square-mile sections, each containing 640 acres. These sections were to be auctioned off for not less than one dollar per acre. Four sections in each township were reserved for future sale by Congress. Section 16 of each township was set aside for the establishment of educational institutions.

While the Ordinance of 1785 laid the groundwork for settlement of the Northwest Territory, it did not provide a governmental or legal system to oversee the territory and manage the land. Therefore, two years later Congress passed the Ordinance of 1787, which contained several new clauses. One of the most important features of the Ordinance of 1787 was the establishment of a system for a territory to become a state. Congress, which in effect owned the territory, would appoint a governor, a secretary to serve under the governor, and three judges. These people would govern the territory as agents of Congress and were subject to the authority of Congress. Once the terri-

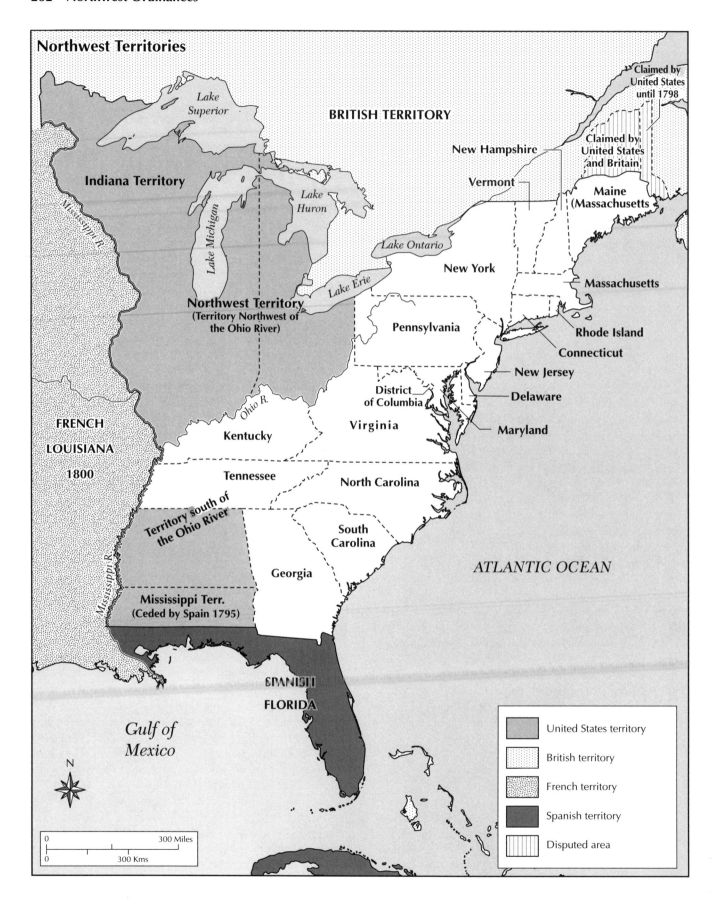

Northwest Territories

Lake Superior

BRITISH TERRITORY

Claimed by
United States
until 1798

Claimed by
United States
and Britain

Indiana Territory

Lake Michigan

Lake Huron

New Hampshire

Vermont

Maine
(Massachusetts)

Mississippi R.

Lake Ontario

Lake Erie

New York

Massachusetts

Northwest Territory
(Territory Northwest of
the Ohio River)

Pennsylvania

Rhode Island

Connecticut

New Jersey

Ohio R.

District
of Columbia

Delaware

FRENCH

Kentucky

Virginia

Maryland

LOUISIANA

1800

Tennessee

North Carolina

Territory south of
the Ohio River

South
Carolina

ATLANTIC OCEAN

Mississippi R.

Georgia

Mississippi Terr.
(Ceded by Spain 1795)

SPANISH

FLORIDA

Gulf of
Mexico

N

0   300 Miles

0   300 Kms

United States territory

British territory

French territory

Spanish territory

Disputed area

tory, or a section of the territory, contained 5,000 adult white males, the territory would elect a legislature and send a speaking, but not voting, delegate to Congress. Finally, once the total population rose above 60,000, the territory could send application to Congress and be admitted "on equal footing with the original states."

In addition to the organization of government, the Ordinance of 1787 contained six articles that created laws within the territory. Article I established freedom of worship and RELIGION in the territory. Article II contained the equivalent of a bill of rights for all individuals within the territory. Some of the most important features of Article II were the right to trial by jury, laws against cruel and unusual punishment, the right to reasonable bail and fines, and the legal sanctity of property and contracts. Article III stressed the importance of EDUCATION in the territory, which added emphasis to the establishment of schools in the Ordinance of 1785. Article III also provided for the fair treatment of NATIVE AMERICANS. It declared that "the utmost good faith shall always be observed to the Indians" and promised that their property would not be taken from them without their consent. Moreover, the article assured that "they [Indians] shall never be invaded or disturbed" unless the United States had just cause, and that "laws founded in justice and humanity" shall be made to protect the Indians. These provisions were often ignored. Article IV opened the waterways of the Northwest Territory to tax-free navigation. Article V divided the Northwest Territory into no less than three but no more than five separate states. This provision limited the potential Congressional power of the new western states, easing the fears of western domination felt by some people in the existing states. Finally, Article VI stated, "There shall be neither slavery nor involuntary servitude" in the territory except in the punishment of crimes. However, it also provided for the capture and return of fugitive slaves from "one of the original States." This act constituted the first federal-level legislation against SLAVERY. Article VI was very controversial, and despite numerous attempts to repeal Article VI, it remained in force.

When combined, the Ordinance of 1785 and the Ordinance of 1787 provided the framework for the governance of the Northwest Territory and established a method for the territory to be divided into states. However, these two pieces of legislation had an impact well beyond their intended purpose. The same basic rules used in the Northwest Territory were used in the establishment of nearly every western state. This may make the Ordinances of 1785 and 1787 the most important legislation passed by the Articles of Confederation government.

Further reading: Peter Onuf, *Statehood and Union: A History of the Northwest Ordinance* (Bloomington: Indiana University Press, 1987).

— Michael L. Cox

Ohio Company of Associates

The Ohio Company of Associates was an organization formed by land speculators in Massachusetts who hoped to capitalize on the settlement of Ohio by exchanging Continental certificates for a large tract of land in present-day southeastern Ohio and then selling the land to settlers. Composed of REVOLUTIONARY WAR (1775–83) officers and soldiers who obtained rights to lands northwest of the Ohio River, partially in repayment for military service, the Ohio Company of Associates was formed in 1786 by Rufus Putnam and Benjamin Tupper, generals in the CONTINENTAL ARMY. In 1787 the company received Congressional approval of their claim to 1,500,000 acres (1,781,760 acres when school and Congressional lands were added in). The Ohio Company established the first permanent American settlement in Ohio at Marietta in 1788.

— Michael L. Cox

Ohio Company of Virginia

One of the many land-speculation companies formed in Virginia prior to the REVOLUTIONARY WAR (1775–83), the Ohio Company was created in 1747 through a partnership between a London merchant named John Hanbury and a group of Virginia gentlemen led by Thomas Lee. The Ohio Company hoped to obtain land and TRADE rights in the area west of the Appalachian Mountains. The company would in turn sell the lands at a higher price to immigrants and turn a handsome profit. In 1748 the group petitioned the English government in an attempt to acquire a 500,000-acre grant. In 1749 the British government approved the grant, giving the Ohio Company 200,000 acres immediately. The one stipulated condition required the company to settle 200 families on their lands within seven years. The Ohio Company sent Christopher Gist to explore the lands while attempting to recruit settlers from Europe to populate the land grant. In 1754 the company began to build Fort Prince George at the forks of the Ohio River. However, the French also claimed the Ohio area. Before it was completed, Fort Prince George was seized by the French. The Indians in the area also claimed the Ohio Company lands and joined the French in seizing the fort and driving out the few settlers who had populated the company's lands. During the French and Indian War (1754–63), the company's land settlement and trade goals were halted.

After the war ended, the company was further hampered by the PROCLAMATION OF 1763, which prohibited settlement beyond the Appalachians. However, the company was encouraged by the TREATY OF FORT STANWIX in 1768, which adjusted the settlement line west. In the meantime, new land claims had overlapped the claims of the Ohio Company, prompting the company's representative, George Mercer, to exchange the Ohio Company land claims for shares in a new company called the Vandalia Company in 1770. Some of the Ohio Company's representatives continued to press their claims, but by 1779 the Ohio Company's land claims were overturned by the Virginia legislature. Since the Ohio Company had not surveyed their lands, their claims were ruled to be forfeited.

— Michael L. Cox

Old South Church

The Old South Church, also known as the Old South Meeting House, was constructed in Boston in 1729 as a place of worship for the Congregational Church. Since it was the largest building in the city in the 1760s and 1770s, it was used repeatedly for public meetings to discuss the issues of the imperial crisis and the RESISTANCE MOVEMENT (1764–75). Men like SAMUEL ADAMS and Dr. JOSEPH WARREN often spoke to large numbers of Bostonians, decrying British imperial regulation within its walls. The Old South Church is most noted as the location of the meeting immediately preceding the BOSTON TEA PARTY (December 16, 1773). On that occasion, 5,000 people packed the meetinghouse and listened to orators discuss the TEA ACT (1773). When Samuel Adams proclaimed that he did not see what else could be done to save the country, which may have been a prearranged signal, several in the crowd let out a whoop and began to march to Griffin's Wharf, where the "Mohawks" dumped tea into the harbor.

In subsequent months, as hostilities broke out into the REVOLUTIONARY WAR (1775–83), the British troops that occupied Boston tore out the pews and made the church into a riding school. After the war, the building returned to its previous function as a religious meetinghouse. It was turned into a museum celebrating American independence in 1877 and remains a highly visited historical landmark and museum today.

Olive Branch Petition (1775)

One of the most important documents of the AMERICAN REVOLUTION, the SECOND CONTINENTAL CONGRESS sent the Olive Branch Petition to King GEORGE III in July 1775. It was the most serious attempt by the American colonies to end hostilities and reconcile with Great Britain.

In the summer of 1774 the conflict between Great Britain and its North American colonies was intensifying, and colonists began to choose sides. Over the course of the next year, blood had been shed and the opponents had hardened their opinions. However, within the ranks of the revolutionaries there remained serious disagreements.

Radicals in the Continental Congress increasingly favored a complete break with Britain, but moderates like JOSEPH GALLOWAY, JOHN JAY, and JOHN DICKINSON still hoped for a peaceful solution. They continued to reject the idea of total independence for the American colonies. Dickinson, who wrote the Olive Branch Petition, was a Pennsylvania delegate and one of the outstanding writers of his generation. In the petition, Dickinson attempted to reassure the king that the colonists were loyal to the crown and pleaded with him to cease further hostilities and seek reconciliation. Despite the hopefulness of the moderates, the radical delegates believed that little good would come from such a gesture.

A few days after its adoption, congressional messengers departed for England with two original copies of the petition on separate ships. Arriving in London in mid-August, they promptly delivered a copy to Lord Dartmouth, the cabinet secretary in charge of colonial affairs. He, in turn, delivered a copy to the king, who by this time was so angry with the colonists that he refused even to read the document. A day later, on August 23, King George declared the colonies to be officially in rebellion. It is possible that had Congress offered the Olive Branch a year earlier, as many of the moderates had argued, it might have been more effective. Coming as it did after the BATTLES OF LEXINGTON AND CONCORD (April 19, 1775) and BUNKER HILL (June, 17, 1775), it was too late to do much good. The fact that the Olive Branch was adopted at the same time that Congress also adopted "A Declaration of the Causes and Necessity of Taking up Arms" reflects the divided mind of the delegates. The "Declaration" was a very different document that attempted to justify the colonists' defense of their homes and blamed the British for the outbreak of hostilities. Ironically, it was also partly written by John Dickinson.

Richard Penn and ARTHUR LEE, the Congressional messengers to London, reported the failure of their mission to the Continental Congress on September 2, 1775. While the hopes of moderate men were dashed, the outright refusal of the king to negotiate had the effect of unifying the various factions in Congress. That allowed the delegates to proceed with the drafting and adoption of the DECLARATION OF INDEPENDENCE (July 4, 1776) in unity of purpose and with clear conscience.

Further reading: Robert Middlekauff, *The Glorious Cause: The American Revolution, 1763–1789* (New York: Oxford University Press, 1982); Edmund S. Morgan, *The Birth of the Republic, 1763–1789* (Chicago: University of Chicago Press, 1992).

— Robert Lively

Oliver, Andrew (1706–1774)

Andrew Oliver was a British LOYALIST, hated by the American radicals for his continued support of British policies. Oliver was born in Boston to a prominent and wealthy colonial family. He graduated from Harvard in 1724, and 10 years later he married a sister of THOMAS HUTCHINSON. Throughout the remainder of his career, he would be closely linked with Hutchinson. Another of Hutchinson's sisters became Oliver's second wife, and he had a total of 17 children.

Oliver was a royal officeholder and ambitious politician, and he managed to work his way up the political ladder. He was the delegate from Boston to the Massachusetts General Court from 1743 to 1745. In 1746 Oliver was elected to the Massachusetts provincial council and held that position until 1765. He also served as the secretary of Massachusetts from 1756 until 1771. After the passage of the STAMP ACT (1765), Oliver agreed to act as a stamp agent, even though he knew how badly the public had received the act. As a result of his new job, his reputation sank even lower. On August 14, 1765, a mob hung Oliver in effigy beneath the LIBERTY TREE. They then marched to a building, situated on the Boston waterfront, owned by Oliver. Many colonists believed the government planned to use this building to store materials associated with the

Stamp Act. The mob attacked and destroyed the building and then turned and marched toward Oliver's house. Much to the shock and horror of Oliver and his family, the mob broke windows and destroyed expensive furniture, leaving the house in complete ruins. A few months later, Oliver resigned as a stamp agent and publicly renounced the Stamp Act. However, this event did not derail his political career.

In 1771 Oliver was appointed lieutenant governor of Massachusetts under the governorship of Thomas Hutchinson, making him the second-highest political official in Massachusetts. It was also during this time that Oliver formed *The Censor* with Hutchinson, a publication devoted to explaining the virtues and truths of the British constitution. It was not popular or profitable, and it ceased publication after a year of operation.

Oliver's position was not to last. He remained as the lieutenant governor of Massachusetts for only two years, until 1773. The reason for his decline dates back to the late 1760s. At that time, Oliver and Hutchinson had written several letters to Britain in which they criticized and apologized for the colony's outlandish behavior and recommended coercive solutions to these problems. BENJAMIN FRANKLIN, who was in London, managed to get possession of the private letters and forwarded them to Boston. When the letters were made public in 1773, a tremendous public outcry developed against Oliver. His already soiled reputation never recovered. Andrew Oliver died in 1774 before the start of the REVOLUTIONARY WAR (1775–83). During his funeral, a huge mob followed the carriage bearing his coffin, and they cheered as the casket was lowered into the grave.

See also RESISTANCE MOVEMENT.

Further reading: Bernard Bailyn, *The Ordeal of Thomas Hutchinson* (Cambridge, Mass.: Harvard University Press, 1974); Michael G. Kammen, *A Rope of Sand: The Colonial Agents, British Politics, and the American Revolution* (Ithaca, N.Y.: Cornell University Press, 1968).

— Brant Day

Orders in Council (1807–1812)

The British government issued a series of Orders in Council that, along with the Berlin and Milan Decrees of NAPOLEON BONAPARTE, severely restricted American TRADE. These measures became a major diplomatic irritant to Anglo-American relations and helped bring about the War of 1812 (1812–15).

With the war in Europe between France and Great Britain reaching a stalemate in 1806 and 1807, Napoleon decided to use commerce as a means of forcing the British to accept his domination of the Continent. On November 21, 1806, Napoleon issued his Berlin Decree, which proclaimed a blockade on Britain. The French did not have the navy to enforce this blockade, so Napoleon declared that any ship that stopped in a British port was forbidden access to the continent of Europe. Since his armies and allies controlled most of Europe, this decree made it impossible for a neutral power like the United States to trade with both England and Napoleonic Europe. In retaliation, the British government issued an Order in Council on January 7, 1807, that prohibited a ship belonging to a neutral power from trading between ports controlled by Napoleon. From the British perspective, this measure was relatively mild and was passed by a government controlled by the WHIG political party in England. While complicating American neutral trade, it did not prevent it. British Tories were unhappy with the order, and when they came into power later in 1807, they sought to strengthen it. Anglo-American relations also worsened in the wake of the CHESAPEAKE-LEOPARD affair (June 22, 1807). Starting on November 11, 1807, a Tory government in Great Britain issued several new Orders in Council. Although these regulations were confusing, they were intended to restrict further neutral trade with Napoleonic Europe. They did allow, however, a neutral ship to stop in a British port and then sail to a French or allied port with British goods. American neutral trade was to be limited, but not eliminated. Napoleon was not going to let the British have the last word, and on December 17, 1807, he issued the Milan Decree, which stated that any neutral ship that stopped at a British port or was searched by a British ship would be seized upon entering a European port controlled by France and its allies.

The British and French actions left the United States with few options. The American government sought a commercial policy that would compel both Great Britain and France to recognize its neutral rights. In response, the United States implemented the NON-IMPORTATION ACT (enacted in 1806) and passed the EMBARGO OF 1807, the NON-INTERCOURSE ACT (1809), and MACON'S BILL NO. 2 (1810). These laws appeared to have little effect on either belligerent. On April 26, 1809, the British adjusted their Orders of Council again, opening up trade to those countries, like Spain and Portugal, that had broken from the Napoleonic orbit. But this action was more in response to the changing European situation than an effort to appease American complaints. The same orders prohibited all trade with those areas still controlled by Napoleon. Finally, in the spring of 1812, Britain moved toward repealing the Orders in Council completely, since Napoleon had suggested he was canceling the Berlin and Milan Decrees, and the decline in American trade was having a stifling effect on the British economy. The British government made the removal of the trade restrictions official on June 23, 1812. Unfortunately, and unknown to anyone in Great Britain,

President JAMES MADISON had signed the Declaration of War on June 18, 1812.

See also ECONOMY; FOREIGN AFFAIRS; IMPRESSMENT.

Further reading: Reginald Horseman, *The Causes of the War of 1812* (Philadelphia: University of Pennsylvania Press, 1962); Bradford Perkins, *Prologue to War, 1805–1812* (Berkeley: University of California Press, 1968).

Otis, Harrison Gray (1765–1848)

Harrison Gray Otis was a leader of the FEDERALIST PARTY who opposed the DEMOCRATIC-REPUBLICAN PARTY's economic policies against French and English commercial measures during the administrations of THOMAS JEFFERSON and JAMES MADISON, and he was against fighting the War of 1812 (1812–15). Otis came from a prominent Massachusetts family; his uncle was JAMES OTIS. A Harvard graduate (1783) and a member of the Massachusetts bar, he held many political posts throughout his life, including seats in the Massachusetts House of Representatives, the United States House of Representatives, the Massachusetts Senate (where he served as president), and the United States Senate. He also was mayor of Boston. A vocal opponent of the War of 1812, he is most well-known for his sponsorship of the Hartford Convention, a meeting of delegates from the five New England states in December 1814 to protest the war with Great Britain and to debate proposals for secession from the union. The convention did not go so far as to vote for leaving the union, but it passed a resolution asserting that states had a right to oppose "unconstitutional" acts by the federal government. Although the Federalist Party fell out of favor after the Hartford Convention, Otis continued to defend his stance and the case for STATE'S RIGHTS.

Further reading: Samuel Elliot Morison, *Harrison Gray Otis, 1765–1848: The Urbane Federalist* (Boston: Houghton Mifflin, 1969).

— J. Brett Adams

Otis, James, Jr. (1725–1783)

A renowned legal scholar and active pamphleteer, James Otis contributed significantly to the debates surrounding law, parliamentary power, and sovereignty during the 1760s. Revered for his brilliance and impeccable attention to history and detail, Otis eventually lost popularity among radical WHIGS because his conciliatory views toward Great Britain appeared outdated as the colonies and Crown engaged in the debates that precipitated the REVOLUTIONARY WAR (1775–83).

Born in West Barnstable, Massachusetts, Otis graduated from Harvard in 1743, later studied law, and was admitted to the bar of Plymouth County in 1748. After moving to Boston, he married Ruth Cunningham and developed an expertise in common, civil, and admiralty law, as well as classical English political theory.

When in 1760 Great Britain sought to enforce the Sugar Act of 1733, Otis served as the king's advocate general of the vice admiralty court at Boston. The responsibility for issuing WRITS OF ASSISTANCE that would expedite the royal customs collectors' searches fell upon him. In a surprising move, Otis resigned from his post and argued the merchants' position against the writs of assistance. Although he lost his case in 1761, Otis provided a powerful rationale for the illegality of the issuance. Harking back to the 17th-century notion that Parliament could only enact laws consonant with natural law, he drew a definite line between the American and British ideas of parliamentary power.

Yet Otis did not heed the logical implications of his own argument. Rather, he grounded his polemics on the notion that Parliament was absolute but not arbitrary. Just and equitable laws derived from nature and reason, he argued, and only these could be codified by Parliament. If Parliament legislated an act that was unjust, it existed as only an aberration. And even in their opposition, the people were obligated to concede Parliament's absolute power until that body, recognizing its error, made the necessary corrections. This line of argumentation informed political tracts such as *A Vindication of the Conduct of the House of Representatives* (1762), *The Rights of the British Colonies Asserted and Proved* (1764), and *A Vindication of the British Colonies* (1765).

Between 1761 and 1769, Otis played an influential role in Massachusetts politics as a member of its General Court. But the RESISTANCE MOVEMENT (1764–75)—and colonial reaction to the SUGAR ACT (1764), the STAMP ACT (1765), the DECLARATORY ACT (1766), the TOWNSHEND DUTIES (1767), and the occupation of Boston—outpaced his political thought. His view of natural law and its relationship to parliamentary power proved anachronistic and satisfied neither the British nor the radical Whigs. The former argued that he sought to restrict the power of Parliament, while the latter accused him of countenancing passive obedience. The difficulty of maintaining such a position earned him tremendous scorn. Considered a traitor by the British administration, some Americans lambasted him as a "double-faced Jacobite Whig." In fact, Otis was neither a traitor nor an apologist. Rather, he remained wedded to the idea that laws—based on principles of equity and justice—derived from God and nature. Legal codification threatened to circumscribe these rights. Meanwhile, colonists came to redefine the debate over parliamentary power not in terms of justice, but of legislative authority. Each of the colonies had their own miniature parliaments in the form of their colonial legislatures, radicals contended, legitimated through their contractual relationships with the king. Whereas Otis continued to retain his faith in common law, the nation's founders set out to give fundamental rights a written form.

By the 1770s, most colonists had abandoned James Otis's cautious, conciliatory position. A brawl with customs officials in 1769 left him beaten and cut short his active political career. A supporter of the United States after its inception, he died on May 23, 1783.

Further reading: Bernard Bailyn, *The Ideological Origins of the American Revolution,* enlarged edition (Cambridge, Mass.: Harvard University Press, 1992); John J. Waters Jr., *The Otis Family, in Provincial and Revolutionary Massachusetts* (Chapel Hill: University of North Carolina Press, 1968).

— Daniel M. Cobb

P

Paine, Thomas (1737–1809)

Thomas Paine was the most influential pamphleteer of his time, and his essay COMMON SENSE (1776) profoundly influenced the course of the AMERICAN REVOLUTION. Thomas Paine was born in Thetford, England, the son of a QUAKER corset maker. His education was at best rudimentary, and he began his apprenticeship with his father at age 13. At 16 he ran away to join a PRIVATEER but was returned home by his father. At 19, Paine left home for good. Soon after he found himself in London, where he developed a passion for the natural sciences. Though he was not a practicing Quaker, his religious upbringing no doubt influenced his moral conscience and idealism, as did the inherent unfairness of his social station; his enthusiasm for Newtonian SCIENCE convinced him of the might of reason and helped shape his animosity toward the prerogatives of hereditary privilege.

For more than a decade and a half, Paine had little success in anything. His first marriage in 1759 to Mary Lambert ended a year later with her death in childbed. He gave up making corsets and began a new career as an excise-man (an official who collected internal taxes on liquor and tobacco). Paine was dismissed from his position twice, once for falsifying records and once for an extended absence from his post. (Paine was petitioning Parliament to raise the wages paid to excise-men; as a lobbyist in London, he met BENJAMIN FRANKLIN.) His second marriage, to Elizabeth Ollive in 1771, ended in a permanent separation three years later. Forced to declare bankruptcy, Paine decided to start afresh in North America.

Paine immigrated to Philadelphia in 1774, and with letters of introduction from Benjamin Franklin, he began to associate with supporters of political rebellion. Paine at first sought work as a teacher but soon was asked by the editor of *Pennsylvania Magazine* to try his hand at JOURNALISM. His interests were eclectic and he wrote on both science and politics. One of his early articles,"African Slavery in America," was a powerful condemnation of SLAVERY.

Paine arrived in the colonies when the quarrel with Britain was reaching a fever pitch. After the BATTLES OF LEXINGTON AND CONCORD (April 19, 1775), Paine began to articulate the idea that the colonies should free themselves from Britain. In January 1776 Paine anonymously published *Common Sense*, in which he argued for independence. Written in a plain and accessible style, the pamphlet was a huge success, selling more than 120,000 copies in its first year. In *Common Sense*, Paine argued for the virtues of a republic over a monarchy and the equality of rights among all citizens. During the course of the war that followed, Paine published 16 "Crisis" papers. The first issue opened with the stirring words, "These are the times that try men's souls."

With a talent for finding himself in the midst of major events, Paine returned to Europe in 1787 on the eve of the FRENCH REVOLUTION (1789–15). His goal was to secure the funding needed to build an iron bridge across the Schuylkill River, but he became distracted by the political events then raging. Incensed by EDMUND BURKE's attack on the French Jacobins in *Reflections on the Revolution in France* (1790), Paine published his *Rights of Man* in 1791. It was an even greater success than *Common Sense* had been. Paine's analysis of the fundamental causes for popular discontent promoted REPUBLICANISM and called for a break from the prison of heredity and privilege; indeed, it called for nothing less than the overthrow of the British monarchy and the establishment of a republic. Charged with seditious libel, Paine was forced to flee to the Continent. Paine was tried and convicted in absentia, and declared an outlaw in Britain.

Paine arrived in revolutionary France in 1792, was awarded French citizenship, and became one of the few foreign-born men elected to the National Convention. In the Convention, Paine voted for the formal abolition of the French monarchy, yet he deplored the terror being unleashed in France. Out of step with the radical Jacobins, Paine spoke to the Convention against the execution of the

Thomas Paine *(National Archives)*

Bourbon king and was arrested in late 1793. The American minister GOUVERNEUR MORRIS did little to secure his release, and Paine remained imprisoned until late 1794. With the overthrow and execution of Maximilian Robespierre and the end of the Terror, Paine was released and readmitted to the Convention.

While in prison, Paine wrote his last great pamphlet, *The Age of Reason* (1794;1796), which begins with the statement "I believe in one God, and no more; and I hope for happiness beyond this life." A tract on DEISM—Paine believed in a Supreme Being but opposed organized RELIGION—it attacked the tenets of traditional Christianity, including the idea that the Bible is divinely inspired. With this pamphlet, Paine offended the clergy and the pious on both sides of the Atlantic. Branded as an atheist by the devout, upon his return to the United States in 1802, he was not celebrated as of old. Furthermore, the country itself had changed. The ratification of the federal Constitution and the spread of FEDERALIST ideology had quelled the extreme enthusiasm of the Revolution. Though he continued his attacks on privilege and religion, Paine was

largely forgotten. At his death, only six mourners attended the funeral. His obituary read in part, "He had lived long, did some good and much harm." Recent scholarship has revised history's assessment of Paine's contribution; he is now regarded as "the English Voltaire."

See also FRENCH REVOLUTION.

Further reading: Eric Foner, *Tom Paine and Revolutionary America*; (New York: Oxford University Press, 1976); Philip S. Foner, ed., *The Complete Writings of Thomas Paine* (New York: Citadel Press, 1945); David Freeman Hawke, *Paine* (New York: Harper & Row, 1974).

— Robyn Davis McMillin

Panic of 1792

The first great financial panic of the new United States rocked New York City in March and April in 1792 and had ripple effects throughout the nation. The panic began with a wave of speculation led by William Duer and Alexander Macomb. Duer had been an active revolutionary, member of the CONTINENTAL CONGRESS, secretary to the board of treasury of the Confederation government, and an assistant to Secretary of the Treasury ALEXANDER HAMILTON. He was also a government supplier and speculator who repeatedly used insider information in his business deals. Unfortunately for Duer, he did not always succeed. He therefore was forever looking for the next scheme to recoup his losses.

Early in 1792 Duer and Macomb began speculating in the stock of the BANK OF THE UNITED STATES and the Bank of New York. They anticipated that the price would rise dramatically and borrowed extensively to corner the market. Speculative fever swept through New York. Rich and poor investors extended the two businessmen credit at high interest rates. When the stock failed to rise as quickly as Duer and Macomb expected, they began to default on their loans. The United States government made matters worse by suing Duer for $250,000 in unsettled accounts from his days with the treasury. Duer stopped payment on his loans on March 9, 1792, and two weeks later he went to debtors prison. Macomb joined him on April 12. In the meantime, countless New Yorkers lost money, prices collapsed, and many businesses went under.

The panic had an impact on the growing opposition to Alexander Hamilton's plans to strengthen the federal government. Duer had been president of the Society for the Encouragement of Manufacturers and may have embezzled some of its funds. Any effort for federal support for manufacturing now became tainted. Moreover, as far as THOMAS JEFFERSON and JAMES MADISON were concerned, Hamilton's close connection to Duer suggested that he, too, was enmeshed in corruption. On the economic front, however, the panic had less lasting effects. By the fall of 1792 prices had recovered and the ECONOMY continued to expand. Duer, however, spent the rest of his life in debtors prison.

Further reading: Stanley Elkins and Eric McKitrick, *The Age of Federalism: The Early American Republic, 1788–1800* (New York: Oxford University Press, 1993).

Paris, Treaty of (1783)

After their defeat at YORKTOWN (October 19, 1781), the British sought to make peace with their enemies—the Americans, the French, the Spanish, and the Dutch. The Treaty of Paris of 1783 between the United States and Great Britain provided full recognition of the independence of America and ended the REVOLUTIONARY WAR (1775–83).

When the CONTINENTAL CONGRESS appointed peace commissioners, it ordered them to consult fully with the French and follow any advice provided. Such instructions were not in the best interests of the United States. Peace commissioners JOHN ADAMS, BENJAMIN FRANKLIN, and JOHN JAY sidestepped the instructions and kept their negotiations secret from the French, thereby gaining several advantages for their country. Serious peace talks began in April 1782, and the preliminary articles of peace were agreed to on November 30, 1782. In deference to their allies, the peace negotiators stipulated that the final agreement would only be effective once all belligerents came to a settlement.

The treaty not only acknowledged independence but offered generous boundaries for the new nation. Instead of being confined to the coast east of the Appalachian Mountains, where most of the settlement in the colonies had occurred before 1776, the new country would have the Mississippi River as its western boundary. The treaty also guaranteed free navigation of that river and fishing rights off of the Grand Banks of Newfoundland and Nova Scotia. These were serious concessions on the part of the British. For its part, the United States promised not to put in place "lawful impediments" to the collection of debts and "to earnestly recommend" to the state legislatures "to provide restitution for all estate rights and properties which have been confiscated" from LOYALISTS. The United States also pledged not to seize any more property of the subjects of King GEORGE III. While the terms were generous, neither side fully lived up to them. The states did not return all confiscated property, and the huge debts run up by colonial Americans to British merchants often went unpaid. For their part, it was decades before the British abandoned all of their posts in the new western territories of the United States, and it was not until after the War of 1812 (1812–15)

that the British stopped contacts with Indians to undermine the American position in the territory they had ceded to the United States.

American allies did less well at the end of the war. Spain obtained FLORIDA and Minorca from the British but failed in its attempt to gain Gibraltar. France obtained little, other than humiliating its old enemy and a vicious debt. Holland, too, gained little of substance. The clear winner of the war was the United States of America.

See also FOREIGN AFFAIRS.

Further reading: Ronald Hoffman and Peter J. Albert, eds., *Peace and the Peacemakers: The Treaty of 1783* (Charlottesville: University Press of Virginia, 1986); Richard B. Morris, *The Peacemakers: The Great Powers and American Independence* (New York: Harper & Row, 1965).

Peale, Charles Willson (1741–1822)

Charles Willson Peale was one of the foremost portrait painters of his generation, and he was an active supporter of the revolutionary cause. Peale's interests were sweeping: He was also an inventor, taxonomist, politician, entrepreneur, showman, and reformer.

Peale stumbled into art shortly after he finished his apprenticeship as a saddler in his native Maryland. He had met an itinerant painter, was surprised anyone would pay for a portrait, and thought that since he could draw he could probably add painting to his repertoire for additional income. Unfortunately for Peale he began his career just as the colonial ECONOMY took a turn for the worst in 1762. He went into debt to purchase the tools of the saddler's trade along with the brushes, paint, and canvass for his artistic endeavors. He also entered politics—on the losing side in an election in 1765. He soon found himself sued for debt. Peale left Maryland and a pregnant wife and tried to paint himself out of debt. His travels took him to Boston, where he met JOHN SINGLETON COPLEY, and to London, where he studied in the studio of BENJAMIN WEST. Returning to the colonies in 1769, Peale became an extremely popular portrait painter. While he had plenty of work, payment was not always prompt or sufficient. He was able to relocate his family to Philadelphia in 1774, but he remained in debt.

The move placed Peale in a city that was about to assume the lead in revolutionary politics as the seat of the FIRST and SECOND CONTINENTAL CONGRESSES and as a hotbed of radicalism in the formation of the State of Pennsylvania. Peale became a "zealous advocate for the Liberties of his Country" and joined the local militia in August 1776. He soon found himself elected a lieutenant. Over the next couple of years Peale saw the REVOLUTIONARY WAR (1775–83) up close, watching the sufferings of the civilian population and experiencing the travail of the soldier. He

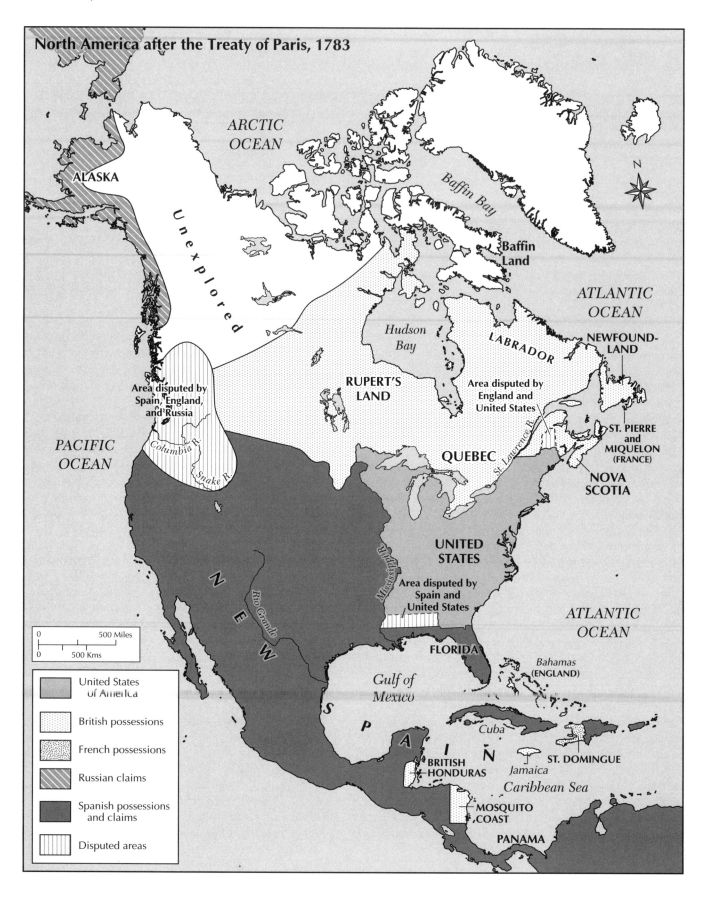

North America after the Treaty of Paris, 1783

ARCTIC OCEAN

ALASKA

Baffin Bay

Baffin Land

ATLANTIC OCEAN

U n e x p l o r e d

Hudson Bay

LABRADOR

NEWFOUND-LAND

Area disputed by Spain, England, and Russia

RUPERT'S LAND

Area disputed by England and United States

PACIFIC OCEAN

Columbia R.

Snake R.

QUEBEC

St. Lawrence R.

ST. PIERRE and MIQUELON (FRANCE)

NOVA SCOTIA

N
E
W

Rio Grande

UNITED STATES

Area disputed by Spain and United States

ATLANTIC OCEAN

FLORIDA

Bahamas (ENGLAND)

0   500 Miles
0   500 Kms

Gulf of Mexico

Cuba

S
P
A
I
N

BRITISH HONDURAS

Jamaica

ST. DOMINGUE

Caribbean Sea

MOSQUITO COAST

PANAMA

	United States of America
	British possessions
	French possessions
	Russian claims
	Spanish possessions and claims
	Disputed areas

also became increasingly politically active, being elected to the committees, and sometimes serving as chairman, that supervised the local government and economy of Philadelphia. As a member of the state assembly, Peale was an advocate of the democratic STATE CONSTITUTION of Pennsylvania, urged currency reform, and supported the gradual abolition of SLAVERY. His politics alienated potential patrons, since many of Pennsylvania's most affluent leaders opposed Peale's position on the constitution and in politics. Throughout his military service and political activities, he had never entirely given up the brush. But when he was defeated for reelection to the assembly in 1780, Peale decided to devote his energies more fully to his painting career.

Peale continued his commitment to the Revolution and sought to combine his republican ideals with his art. He had already begun "a collection of the portraits of characters distinguished from the American revolution," and he now worked to add to the collection as a way of chronicling what he saw as a great event in the history of humankind. However, he continued to have difficulty supporting himself and his family. One problem was that there were many who argued that artists were extraneous to a republican society; paintings were for societies steeped in luxury and were not appropriate for the simplicity and equality of a republican society. Another problem was more pragmatic: Peale had to constantly look for new clients, and he had to obtain payment from those for whom he had already painted portraits.

Peale's solution to both the ideological and practical dilemma was to try to create a form of public art—art that would be dependent upon the state and the people rather than rich patrons. He obtained support from state legislatures for portraits of GEORGE WASHINGTON, and Pennsylvania paid him to create a decorative arch for a public celebration. He also created a "moving picture" display that had several transparent pictures that could be manipulated to make them appear lifelike. Each of these efforts brought some income, but it was not dependable. People at first flocked to the "moving picture" exhibition in 1785, for instance, but soon lost interest. In 1788 Peale opened a museum that combined his paintings of American heroes with a variety of items reflecting North America's natural history, ranging from rattlesnake skins to stuffed buffalo. His hope was to establish a Smithsonian-like institution, including government support, that would educate the people about the richness of the North American natural world. Over the next several decades, Peale kept his museum open by adding new curiosities and even including staged shows to attract customers. Peale was thus far more than an artist, and his life can be seen, as scholar Joseph J. Ellis put it, "as a predecessor of Thomas Edison, Norman Rockwell, even P. T. Barnum."

See also ART; REPUBLICANISM.

Further reading: David R. Brigham, *Public Culture in the Early Republic: Peale's Museum and Its Audience* (Washington, D.C.: Smithsonian Institution Press, 1995); Joseph J. Ellis, *After the Revolution: Profiles of Early American Culture* (New York: W. W. Norton, 1979); Neil Harris, *The Artist in American Society: The Formative Years, 1790–1860* (New York: George Braziller, 1966); Charles Coleman Sellers, *Charles Willson Peale* (New York: Scribner's, 1969); Charles Coleman Sellers, *Mr. Peale's Museum: Charles Willson Peale and the First Popular Museum of Natural Science and Art* (New York: W. W. Norton, 1980); Kenneth Silverman, *A Cultural History of the American Revolution: Painting, Music, Literature, and Theatre in the Colonies and the United States from the Treaty of Paris to the Inauguration of George Washington, 1763–1789* (New York: Columbia University Press, 1976).

Phyfe, Duncan (1768–1854)

Duncan Phyfe was the foremost American cabinetmaker in an era of exceptional craftsmen. An immigrant from Scotland, Phyfe learned his craft in Albany before moving to New York in 1792. His business and reputation flourished as he opened and expanded a store at 35 Partition Street (later Fulton Street). He employed over 100 ARTISANS at the height of his popularity, overseeing all work along with two of his sons. A conservative Presbyterian mechanic and a FEDERALIST, he had very strict and methodical work and domestic habits. His furniture is known as the best of Federalist style. While he originally borrowed much of his work from Sheraton and his famed design books, he also borrowed from the French Empire style with its elegant curves that are so characteristic of his furniture. He is best known for the chairs and sofas produced before 1825, many having the lyre form or crossed-slat backs or republican eagle and acanthus carvings. He worked primarily in mahogany and later in rosewood and black walnut. He represented the classical (rather than the romantic) tradition in furniture and kept it alive in America well into the 19th century.

— Howard B. Rock

Pickering, Timothy (1745–1829)

Timothy Pickering was one of the leading politicians of his day, serving in several cabinet positions in the 1790s and in the Senate and House of Representatives in the early 1800s. Advocate of a strong national government when the FEDERALIST PARTY was in power, he became committed to STATE'S RIGHTS after the DEMOCRATIC-REPUBLICANS took control of the national government in 1801.

Pickering was born in Salem, Massachusetts, in 1745 and graduated from Harvard College in 1763 before turning to a career in law. He served in a few minor posts in Salem (selectman, town clerk, and representative in the general court) during the late 1760s and early 1770s. As the REVOLUTIONARY WAR (1775–83) approached, Pickering became a leading spokesman in favor of independence.

During the Revolutionary War he served in several prominent positions, including on the Board of War, as adjutant general and as quartermaster general. As quartermaster general, Pickering faced the financial problems of mobilizing a war. Despite shortages of funds and supplies, Pickering helped create an efficient CONTINENTAL ARMY. After the war ended, he speculated in land in the Wyoming Valley.

Still, Pickering aspired to political office. In 1790 President GEORGE WASHINGTON appointed Pickering to serve as a diplomat to the Seneca, with orders to prevent them from joining western Indian tribes in battles against the United States. Pickering's diplomatic successes did not go unnoticed by the president. In 1791 Washington named Pickering postmaster general, but he remained an active diplomat to the IROQUOIS until 1794. In 1795 Washington appointed Pickering secretary of war after HENRY KNOX resigned. The following year, Washington chose him to serve as secretary of state after Pickering revealed that former secretary of state EDMUND RANDOLPH had offered bribes to French officials. Pickering was instrumental in supporting the pro-British JAY'S TREATY (1794).

Pickering remained secretary of state under President JOHN ADAMS, which proved disastrous for the new president. Pickering and a cohort of Federalists, called the "High Federalists," went behind Adams's back and consulted with ALEXANDER HAMILTON on national issues. In 1798 Pickering opposed negotiations with France because he did not want the United States to be embroiled in European matters. Pickering, in fact, published the bribery demands of French diplomats, thus sparking the XYZ AFFAIR (1797–98). In 1799 Adams fired Pickering.

Pickering spent the rest of his life as a staunch Federalist and battled DEMOCRATIC-REPUBLICAN policies in the Senate (1803–11) and House of Representatives (1813–17). During his congressional career, he adamantly opposed the United States participation in the War of 1812 (1812–15) and supported a strong central government. In the 1810s, Pickering also supported secessionist causes in New England as a die-hard Federalist. After his term in the House of Representatives ended in 1817, Pickering retired to farm life and spent the remainder of his life attempting to improve agricultural productivity in New England. He died on January 29, 1829.

Further reading: Gerard H. Clarfield, *Timothy Pickering and the American Republic* (Pittsburgh, Pa.: University of Pittsburgh, 1980); Gerard H. Clarfield, *Timothy Pickering and American Diplomacy, 1795–1800* (Columbia: University of Missouri Press, 1969).

— William J. Bauer, Jr

Pinckney, Charles Cotesworth (1746–1825)

In his illustrious career as a soldier, statesman, and diplomat, Charles Cotesworth Pinckney served as an aide to GEORGE WASHINGTON during the REVOLUTIONARY WAR (1775–83), participated in the infamous XYZ AFFAIR, and twice ran for president of the United States. The eldest son of a prominent South Carolina family, Pinckney was born on February 25, 1746, in Charleston, South Carolina. At the age of seven he traveled with his family to Europe, where he remained until 1769. His European education included receiving private tutoring in London, attending various preparatory schools, and entering Oxford's Christ Church College in 1764. In early 1769 he followed up his formal educational training by studying botany, chemistry, and military science under the tutelage of leading experts in France.

Later that same year, he returned to America and began practicing law in South Carolina, passing the bar in 1770. Pinckney immediately embarked on a career in

Charles Cotesworth Pinckney. Engraving *(Library of Congress)*

public office. He was elected to the provincial assembly in 1769 and was made acting attorney general for three South Carolina towns in 1773. On September 28, 1773, he married Sarah Middleton. However, after her premature death in 1784, Pinckney married Mary Stead, the daughter of Benjamin Stead, on June 23, 1786. Although his wife bore three daughters, since two never married and the third had no children, no male heir emerged to carry on his name. Charles Cotesworth Pinckney was an active member of the Church of England, and he remained involved in both church work and bible study throughout his life. Committed to public service, Pinckney sat in the first South Carolina Provincial Congress in 1775 and later in both the lower and the upper houses of the South Carolina legislature.

During the Revolutionary War, he was a captain in the 1st South Carolina Regiment, moving quickly up the ranks as the war proceeded. In 1777 Pinckney traveled north and served as an aide to Washington's army at the BATTLES OF BRANDYWINE (September 11, 1777) and GERMANTOWN (October 4, 1777). After the war he resumed his career in public office, representing South Carolina in the CONSTITUTIONAL CONVENTION. At the Convention, he supported the idea of a strong national government and proposed that senators should serve without pay (although this proposal failed). In the new republic, Pinckney became a staunch FEDERALIST, consistent with his earlier advocacy of a strong national government.

Although he declined a number of prominent presidential appointments, including commanding the armed forces, serving as secretary of war, and sitting on the SUPREME COURT, he eventually accepted a diplomatic position to France in 1796. However, he was initially refused recognition as an emissary by the French Directory. A year later, Pinckney returned to France with a delegation that included JOHN MARSHALL and ELBRIDGE GERRY, a group that was implicated in the XYZ Affair. He unsuccessfully ran as a Federalist candidate for vice president in 1800 and for president in 1804 and 1808. In his later years, Pinckney practiced law in South Carolina and served on a number of philanthropic boards and societies. He died in Charleston on August 16, 1825.

Further reading: Marvin R. Zahniser, *Charles Cotesworth Pinckney, Founding Father* (Chapel Hill: University of North Carolina Press, 1967).

— Linda English

Pitt, William (1708–1778)

American colonists cheered William Pitt, a British politician, for opposing several policies of the British government directed toward the colonies. William Pitt is often referred to as the Elder because his son, William Pitt the Younger, was also an influential British politician. William Pitt was born in London to a prosperous family that made its fortune in colonial TRADE. He received a fine education at Eton and later at Oxford. After a short period of service in the army, he was elected to the House of Commons in 1735. Pitt was an eloquent speaker and soon became known as the "Great Commoner."

Pitt, through his rousing oratory and his opposition to Robert Walpole, soon rose through the parliamentary ranks. By 1746 he was postmaster general, and by 1756 he became secretary of state. In 1757, during the French and Indian War (1754–63), he formed a coalition government with the Duke of Newcastle. His expert handling of the government and army during the war earned him great respect. However, with the accession of King GEORGE III in 1760, Pitt was forced to resign from his position. He would never again obtain that level of power and influence. In 1763 he joined in attacking the government over the JOHN WILKES affair, and in 1765 he spoke out against the STAMP ACT (1765). Pitt opposed the Stamp Act because he believed only colonial assemblies should raise colonial taxes. These actions earned him the admiration of the American colonists.

In 1766 Pitt accepted the title of earl of Chatham and was elevated to the House of Lords. He became prime minister after forming another coalition government, but illness limited his effectiveness. He argued before Parliament for the withdrawal of troops from Boston, and later recommended that the SECOND CONTINENTAL CONGRESS be recognized as a lawful assembly with the responsibility of raising colonial taxes. However, the British government rejected his proposals.

Although he argued passionately against current British policy toward the colonies, he did not favor independence. Pitt was an imperialist and fully believed Britain's future lay abroad. In his plan, the colonial assemblies would have the right to levy taxes, but the British Parliament would have superiority in other matters. He saw no need for the American colonies to declare their independence, and he despised acts of violence or insurrection, like the BOSTON TEA PARTY (December 16, 1773), directed toward the British government.

The American colonists saw Pitt as a defender of their rights, and his name appeared in countless colonial newspapers, pamphlets, and broadsides. However, with his failing health he was unable to successfully oppose the measures taken by the British government toward the colonies. He resigned from his office in 1768. He continued to make appearances in Parliament and opposed granting the colonies their independence, wanting to keep the empire intact. In 1778, in typical Pitt fashion, he collapsed during a dramatic speech before Parliament. Pitt was taken home and died a few months later.

Further reading: Peter Douglas Brown, *William Pitt, Earl of Chatham, The Great Commoner* (London: Allen & Unwin, 1978); Marie Peters, *The Elder Pitt* (New York: Longman, 1998); O. A. Sherrard, *Lord Chatham and America* (London: Bodley Head, 1958).

— Brant Day

political parties

During the early republic, Americans' attitudes toward political parties underwent profound transformation from hostility to toleration, and finally to acceptance of party as a positive good. The terms party and faction were used interchangeably in the 18th and early 19th centuries. Slowly, party began to mean something positive, whereas faction retained its negative connotations. Despite their antiparty beliefs, Americans did form political parties. Unlike modern parties, however, these parties were temporary organizations formed to defeat a specific foe. Americans did not begin to accept the idea of a loyal opposition until the 1820s. Party theorists of the early 19th century came to believe that the biggest threat to the republic was not conflict but apathy. From this perspective, parties protected democracy and majority rule instead of threatening them.

English WHIG writers on politics, party, and faction greatly influenced American political leaders. The concept of a loyal opposition did not exist in England until the 1820s. It was not until 1826 that those who disagreed with the ruling party were called "His Majesty's Opposition." To oppose the king prior to the early 19th century was to invite charges of disloyalty and unpatriotic behavior. Thus there are important parallels between the United States and Great Britain regarding the attitudes towards parties and political opposition. Two good examples of British writers who had great influence upon Americans are Lord Bolingbroke and EDMUND BURKE. In first half of the 1730s, Bolingbroke published *Remarks on the History of England* (1700) and *A Dissertation upon Parties* (1735), in which he detailed the evils of faction. Bolingbroke and Burke defined party or faction as a group of men who sought office for personal gain. Thus parties were by definition corrupt and thwarted the general good.

After the 1760s, Burke began to modify his view of parties. He believed that a "party of principle" was needed to combat the evils of faction. A "party of principle" was not founded on the basis of self-interest; instead, it was built upon some agreed-to principle, and all members worked to promote the national interest "by their joint endeavors." Thus a "party of principle" would be a temporary expedient to defeat and eliminate corruption, after which the party would govern in the public interest.

Still, most Britons believed that factions and parties were symptoms of a troubled nation. In the ideal nation, there were no parties, since society and governance was based on consensus and harmony. The family was the most appropriate metaphor for the ideal state. The king was the father and his subjects his children. As one can define a common goal and interest of a family, one could do so for the nation as well. Opposition to the government was akin to disobeying one's father and betraying the family. Consequently, there was little room in the political culture for legitimate dissension. The king had a special responsibility to produce unity among his subjects. If he promoted one interest at the expense of the common good, he failed his family, and hence his nation. Bolingbroke's "patriot king" perhaps best illustrates what many thought made an ideal leader. The "patriot king" rose above partisanship and united the nation. He governed in the interest of the nation as a whole, and not one particular group or faction. For Americans in a republic, there was no king to which the people would pledge their filial loyalty, but once the Constitution was adopted, many believed that the president would fulfill the role of patriot king.

Bolingbroke's and Burke's ideas easily translated to colonial and revolutionary America. In colonial America, parties or factions largely conformed to this view. Factions were amorphous and changed in response to personal loyalty and issues. In some colonies, like New York, there were more or less permanent factions organized around the colony's most prominent families. In others, issues were more important, although personal patronage networks played a role everywhere. The revolution altered the political landscape by removing royal officials, but it did not change attitudes towards party or faction, and no permanent organizations developed. During the contest over the Constitution, FEDERALISTS and ANTI-FEDERALISTS mustered their forces in all of the states. Both groups expected that once the Constitution's fate had been decided these parties would cease to exist, and sure enough, these groups did formally disband. Although most proponents of the Constitution found themselves associated with the FEDERALIST PARTY in the 1790s, there is no direct correlation between the two federalist parties. One of the most famous Federalists in 1787 and 1788, JAMES MADISON, became a leader of the opposition party in the 1790s.

Many Americans believed that republics, especially one as extensive as the United States, were too fragile to withstand party competition. Thus the new United States had to be protected from parties. Madison tried to allay these fears in The *FEDERALIST PAPERS* (No. 10) by asserting that a large, diverse nation actually safeguarded a republic from the evils of party. He argued that multiple interest groups would in fact serve to preserve the republic because they would prevent one minority interest from dominating the government. In 1792 Madison further revised his view of party, only because he now believed that parties could not be prevented and thus should be steered into performing a purpose for the republic. Parties could check the excesses of each other. While Madison was eventually willing to tolerate parties, he did not celebrate them. His compatriots would not be so accepting of parties or faction, even as they acted as partisans themselves.

In his FAREWELL ADDRESS, President GEORGE WASHINGTON warned Americans against the "the baneful effects of the spirit of party." He cautioned that party contests served "always to distract the public councils and enfeeble the public administration." Although he believed divisions to be natural, he did not want to see parties in elective governments. Indeed, factions threatened the republic because they narrowed political motives and activities to the promotion of self-interest at the expense of the general good. Parties only created and exacerbated jealousies and disagreements and hence were "a spirit not to be encouraged." He called on Americans to be vigilant in order to defeat faction.

Two of Washington's former cabinet members, Secretary of the Treasury ALEXANDER HAMILTON and Secretary of State THOMAS JEFFERSON, certainly agreed with Washington even as they engaged in highly partisan activities. These two men led the Federalist and DEMOCRATIC-REPUBLICAN PARTIES, respectively. Even as they headed these parties and gave advice and direction to party activists, they saw no contradiction to their firmly held antiparty ideas. Each saw his party as a Burkean "party of principle" that would rescue government and the Constitution from special interests. Jefferson thought Hamilton's Federalist Party governed not in the interest of the whole people and endangered the republic, and Hamilton thought the same of Jefferson's Democratic-Republicans. Each believed that his party would vanquish the other and then unify the nation under his leadership. Jefferson hoped for suppression of parties and the return of harmony. He expressed this hope for a renewal of national unity when, in his first inaugural address, Jefferson declared that "we are all republicans, we are all federalists." Like Jefferson, JOHN TAYLOR OF CAROLINE, a leading Democratic-Republican Party theorist, continued to adhere to antipartyism. He believed that parties were part of the problems plaguing the young republic because they represented "a division of a whole" and not the solution. Despite and perhaps because of the party contests of the 1790s, many Americans persisted in their opposition to the idea of party.

Although Federalists continued to contest elections into the latter part of the 1810s, the War of 1812 (1812–15) marked the triumph of antiparty ideas and seemingly the end to party contests in the United States. Politicians celebrated the demise of party. In James Monroe's inaugural address, he praised the passing of party spirit, expressing his belief that without party strife, America could "soon attain the highest degree of perfection of which human institutions are capable. . ." Furthermore, the government and the nation would "exhibit such a degree of order and harmony as to command the admiration and respect of the civilized world." His successor, John Quincy Adams, shared Monroe's feelings. He quite self-consciously sought to banish party considerations from all his decisions whether they involved policy or appointments.

As Monroe and Adams maintained their classical ideas about party and celebrated the demise of party, others were starting to articulate new ideas about party as a positive good. These men, as typified by Martin Van Buren of New York, believed that the absence of parties posed more real danger to the republic because, without parties, sectional divisions could triumph. The "Era of Good Feelings"—a period honored by contemporaries and others for the absence of parties—was in fact a period in which many Americans were preoccupied with sectional conflict, as epitomized by the Missouri crises of 1819–21. Van Buren diagnosed the problem as the lack of national political parties. As early as 1817, Van Buren began to formulate a new theory of party in response to the personal rule of the Clinton family in the New York Democratic-Republican Party. His Albany Regency became one of the first organizations in America that was intended to be a permanent political party. Van Buren believed that parties could be a means of achieving principled goals. Whereas others argued that parties promoted self-interest, Van Buren claimed that the dominant antiparty rhetoric did so by allowing aristocratic elites to remain in control. Parties would open the highest public offices to all men because they would privilege principles over individuals. Van Buren's ideas paralleled the democratization of American civic culture and the expansion of the franchise to all adult white men. Vigorous national parties, according to Van Buren, would sustain the nation because they would combat apathy and encourage vigilance. As a United States senator in the early 1820s, Van Buren started to build bridges to like-minded men in other states to create a national party based upon these ideas. Van Buren's project culminated in the election of Andrew Jackson in 1828 and the creation of the Democratic Party.

The old antiparty consensus was replaced with a new proparty consensus. The changing ideas about political parties paralleled the process of democratization of American civic culture and the expansion of the electorate.

See also CORPORATISM; REPUBLICANISM.

Further reading: Lance Banning, *Sacred Fire of Liberty: James Madison and the Founding of the Federal Republic* (Ithaca, N.Y.: Cornell University Press, 1995); Ralph Ketcham, *Presidents above Party: The First American Presidency, 1789–1829* (Chapel Hill, N.C.: University of North Carolina Press, 1984); Jackson T. Main, *Political Parties before the Constitution.* (Chapel Hill: University of North Carolina Press, 1973).

— Terri Halperin

Pontiac's Rebellion (1763–1764)

After the close of the French and Indian War (1754–63), NATIVE AMERICANS rose up against the British Crown in a bloody war, called Pontiac's Rebellion, in the Ohio Valley and Great Lakes region. French officials had kept the peace in the area for more than a century. The governor at Quebec became a "father" to the tribes of the interior, taking care of his "children" by periodically distributing gifts of muskets, powder, blankets, and other trade goods. During the conflict between the French and English, many of the tribes fought for New France. When the British navy began intercepting French supply ships carrying the presents that the Indians now depended upon, New France could no longer ensure the well-being of her allies. As the war came to an end, and it became apparent that the French would not win, most of the Native Americans switched to the British side.

When Quebec and Montreal fell to the British and colonial armies, the Indians began to fear that they would soon have only Britain to supply them; no longer would they be able to play one European power against another. After the French surrendered CANADA to the British and gave Louisiana to Spain, Native American fears became reality. Moreover, the British commander, Lieutenant General Jeffrey Amherst, did not see the Native Americans as allies but as subjects. He thought that the Crown should not have to pay for its subjects' loyalty. He further believed that the Indians were lazy and poor fighters and that Britain had little to fear if the Native Americans were discontent. Amherst also had the problem of reducing the cost of occupying Canada and the lands between the Appalachi-

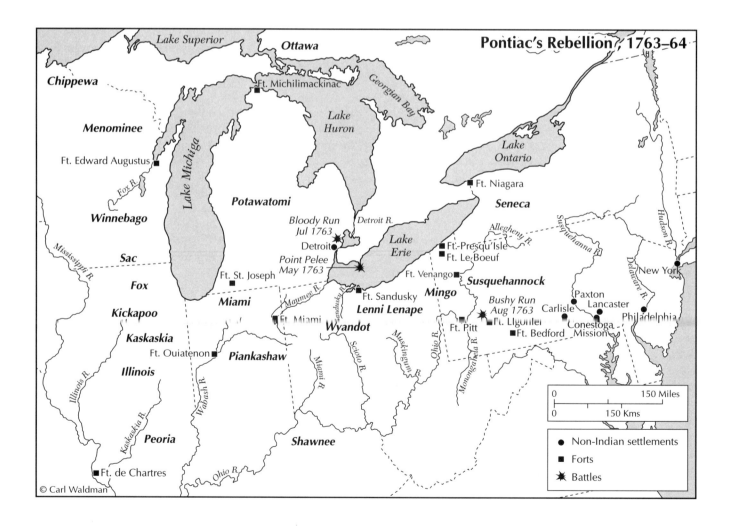

ans and the Mississippi. Soldiers and sailors were discharged and regiments disbanded. Against the advice of the king's experienced Indian agents like Sir William Johnson and John Stuart, Amherst cut the gifts to the Native Americans to a fraction of their former level. Without gunpowder and muskets, the Indians could not hunt.

In 1762 the Ottawa war chief Pontiac organized the tribes around Detroit in a bid to wrest control of the region from their new masters. The teachings of the Delaware visionary Neolin influenced Pontiac and many other Native Americans. Neolin preached that the Master of Life had told him that the Indians should abandon the corrupting liquor, trade goods, and firearms of the white man. He said that the Native Americans should rise up and drive out the European intruders from their lands. Pontiac planned to do just that. The British officials in North America had been hearing rumors of a rebellion for so long that they ignored them and lowered their guard.

Pontiac and his men attacked the fort at Detroit on May 9, 1763. The conflict soon spread throughout the entire backcountry from the Great Lakes to the outlying settlements of Pennsylvania and Virginia. The Indians hoped that the French army would return to help them. Pontiac and his allies achieved complete surprise due to British complacence. Men from the Shawnee, Miami, Potawatomi, Ottawa, Delaware, and Seneca Nations participated in the fighting. Nine military posts fell to Native American warriors, and they besieged Forts Pitt and Detroit. Major Henry Gladwin, Detroit's commander, had been warned of the impending assault and was ready. Since the fort could be supplied by water, it withstood the siege for five months. Once Amherst finally realized the danger, he sent relief columns to Forts Pitt and Detroit.

Diplomatic errors started the war, and diplomatic skill ended it. Sir William Johnson managed to keep five of the six IROQUOIS nations out of the struggle, and in 1764 he convinced the Seneca to withdraw from the conflict. Throughout that year, Johnson called the chiefs of the warring nations to his home at Johnson Hall in the Mohawk Valley. By giving presents and making masterful speeches, Sir William persuaded the Iroquois to stop fighting. In the South, John Stuart, the king's Indian agent for the CREEK and CHEROKEE, kept the war from spreading.

Pontiac's siege of Fort Detroit fell apart as summer turned to fall. Major Gladwin received men and equipment transported across Lake Erie, while smallpox raged through the Indian camps along the Detroit River. Pontiac lost his ability to lead as his popularity declined. News of the terms of the Treaty of Paris (1763) disheartened many of his warriors as a sign that the French king had abandoned them. By the fall of 1764, most of the fighting was over.

Further reading: Gregory Evans Dowd, *A Spirited Resistance: The North American Indian Struggle for Unity, 1745–1815* (Baltimore: Johns Hopkins University Press, 1992); William Nester, *"Haughty Conquerors": Amherst and the Great Indian Uprising of 1763* (Westport, Conn.: Praeger, 2000); Howard H. Peckham, *Pontiac and the Indian Uprising* (Detroit: Wayne State University Press, 1994).

— George Milne

popular culture

Although American popular culture varied from region to region and group to group, it is possible to venture a few generalizations concerning entertainment, holidays, and beliefs. Work and leisure were not as easily divided in the revolutionary and early national periods as they are today. Americans celebrated fewer holidays than their contemporaries in Europe, and their belief system was an odd mixture of the sacred and the secular.

The boundary between work time and personal time remained ambiguous for white revolutionary Americans. It was assumed that everyone would labor from sunrise to sundown. Work hours were often punctuated with breaks to drink beer or other alcohol. Most workers thought little of taking time off in the day to visit a dram shop, watch a parade or procession, or simply to congregate with friends. Every day was not a series of long interruptions, but life had a more fluid character with less concern for the clock.

The TAVERN remained a central community institution, where neighbors would gather to exchange pleasantries and information. Taverns also offered entertainment, including MUSIC, dancing, and even a form of stage production. THEATERS became increasingly popular, producing plays as well as featuring songs and short skits. Gambling was rampant. People bought lottery tickets, played cards and dice, and betted on a wide variety of objects. Blood sports like cock fighting were popular. Horse racing was not just limited to gentlemen. Even city cartmen were known for gathering at the edge of town to test their steeds against one another. Men also wrestled and fought with one another, sometimes as a test of strength and sometimes as the result of a quarrel. Men also often prided themselves on their rowdy behavior, disrupting bars and theaters, and harassing people on the street.

There was also more regular and less disruptive entertainment. In the countryside people gathered for corn huskings and barn raisings, activities that have since become the very image of the bucolic ideal of a world we have lost. Both urban and rural Americans joined VOLUNTARY ASSOCIATIONS in droves in this period. Some of these organizations were aimed at reform or the betterment of society. Others merely provided a vehicle for people of similar interests or

Engraving showing the last British troops leaving New York. New Yorkers began to observe Evacuation Day (November 25, 1783) as a holiday. *(Library of Congress)*

backgrounds to meet together. There were moral, library, tea, ethnic, journeymen, and religious societies, as well as a host of others.

Print culture became increasingly significant in the period. The revolutionary movement and the politics of the early 1790s depended heavily on the growing number of printing presses and newspapers to agitate and garner support. Beyond politics, with a European-American population that had a high degree of literacy, there was a great demand for a wide variety of printed material. Much of this reading matter was in the form of cheap books or broadsheets that might be sold by a street hawker or traveling salesman. These publications might include the confessions of a notorious criminal or a pirate at the gallows. Such stories would combine lurid personal details to pique the interest of the reader with a safe religious message on the dire consequences of a life of crime. Sensational novels like SUSANNA ROWSON's *Charlotte, a Tale of Truth* (1791) became best-sellers. Religious works also continued to be popular.

Americans did not celebrate many holidays; the religious calendar was almost devoid of any special day. Camp meetings offered an opportunity for people to gather in a holiday atmosphere to worship their God. The Sabbath was held sacred and was not a day for work. Those who attended religious services looked eagerly toward Sundays as a time to worship God and meet with friends. Sabbath breaking, however, also occurred, as some Americans viewed Sundays as their day to do what they pleased—often staying in a tavern all day or misbehaving in public. But beyond the weekly routine, the religious calender did not have a great deal of meaning for most Americans before 1820. Most Americans took almost no note at all of Easter, and New Englanders did not celebrate Christmas. For Americans elsewhere, Christmas and New Year's marked more of a carnival season with public drinking and disorderly behavior. Christmas as a family holiday did not begin to emerge until after 1820. New Englanders, and some others, commemorated the harvest with a Thanksgiving holiday, usually in early December.

Political holidays played a larger role in the popular culture than religious celebrations. Throughout the period, elections were days when men came together to vote and to drink. During the colonial period, the king's birthday, the arrival of a new governor, and Guy Fawkes Day were all observed with much hoopla and treating. The experience of the RESISTANCE MOVEMENT (1764–75) and the REVOLUTIONARY WAR (1775–83) led Americans to replace these days with a different set of festivities. Bostonians, for example, celebrated the anniversary of the British "massacre" of its citizens on March 5, 1770, and during the 1780s New Yorkers observed Evacuation Day (November 25, 1783), marking the date when the British finally left the city. In the 1790s DEMOCRATIC-REPUBLICANS took delight in holidays connected to the FRENCH REVOLUTION (1789–1815), much to the chagrin of the FEDERALIST PARTY. Two holidays quickly emerged that all Americans could agree upon: the Fourth of July and GEORGE WASHINGTON's birthday. But even their celebration became more partisan in the 1790s and early 1800s.

Perhaps the most difficult part of popular culture to understand is the belief system. European Americans in the revolutionary and early national period were overwhelmingly Protestant Christians. But this did not mean that they were also not superstitious. In fact, belief in white magic and witchcraft still existed, as attested by the number of horseshoes over doors and the attack of a Philadelphia mob in 1787 on a woman accused of being a witch. Americans held to the sanctity of a corpse. Rumors that medical students were paying grave robbers for cadavers in 1788 led to a riot in New York and an attack on the medical school.

On the more secular side, common folk had their own ideas about the meaning of the AMERICAN REVOLUTION.

When the founding fathers had met in the CONSTITU-TIONAL CONVENTION, they had hoped to create a balanced government that would filter out the immediate influence of the electorate. But the Revolution had awakened a popular faith in democracy and a concern with equality that could not be stifled. Rejecting any suggestion of hierarchy, Americans rallied to the Democratic-Republican Party because it promised to reverse the elitist policies of the Federalists. In short, we owe the egalitarian meaning of the American Revolution to developments in popular culture.

See also CITIES AND URBAN LIFE; JOURNALISM; POPU-LATION TRENDS; RELIGION; RIOTS; RURAL LIFE.

Further reading: Paul A. Gilje, *The Road to Mobocracy: Popular Disorder in New York City, 1763–1834* (Chapel Hill: University of North Carolina Press, 1987); Jack Larkin, *The Reshaping of Everyday Life, 1790–1830* (New York: Harper & Row, 1988); Simon P. Newman, *Parades and the Politics of the Street: Festive Culture in the Early American Republic* (Philadelphia: University of Pennsylvania Press, 1997); David Waldstreicher, *In the Midst of Perpetual Fetes: The Making of American Nationalism, 1776–1820* (Chapel Hill: University of North Carolina Press, 1997).

population trends

Between 1754 and 1820 the population grew at a rapid rate in what became the United States of America. Colonial statistics are not uniform, but in 1754 there were fewer than 1.5 million people in British North America; by 1776 the population was a little over 2.5 million; by 1790 the first federal census indicated that the population had reached almost 4 million; and by 1820 there were 9,638,453 people in the United States. This growth in population reflected approximately a 33 percent increase per decade.

While general numbers are useful, they obscure a few important details. First, this population increase was driven more by internal growth than IMMIGRATION. Second, there was tremendous geographical mobility. Third, although there was some urban expansion, the vast majority of the population remained in small towns or rural settings. Fourth, there was a dramatic change in AFRICAN-AMERICAN demographics; there emerged, especially in the North, a free black population. Finally, an important shift in the relative population of the North and the South began.

Immigration was not entirely absent from the period 1754 to 1820, but it was greatly reduced by war in North America and overseas. During the French and Indian War (1754–63), the REVOLUTIONARY WAR (1775–83), and the War of 1812 (1812–15), immigration came almost to a halt. Immigrants from Great Britain and Germany arrived in the 1760s and early 1770s in large numbers. Fewer immigrants came in the 1780s, but wars in Europe and the WEST INDIES convinced thousands of French, Irish, and others to come to the United States in the 1790s and early 1800s. After the EMBARGO OF 1807 and the economic downturn before the War of 1812, immigration again decreased, only to pick up again, especially among the Irish, after the Treaty of Ghent (1814). Besides affecting the number of people coming to North America, war had another important effect: In the wake of the Revolutionary War, as many as 100,000 LOYALISTS may have left the country.

This limited immigration and the outflow of Loyalists meant that the population growth depended principally upon natural increase. This fact had some important implications. The population remained youthful. Throughout most of this period, the average age of an American was about 16. Americans also married younger than Europeans, produced several children, and lived in larger households. Almost no one lived by themselves. Despite having large families, there was some decline in fertility in this period compared with the 17th century. A woman who married before 1800, but who continued to have children after that date, had an average of 6.4 children compared with 7.4 children in the 17th century. Ideas about family limitation were just beginning. Indeed, for women married between 1800 and 1849, the fertility rate dropped to 4.9. This pattern emerged first in the cities and the Northeast, thereafter spreading to the countryside and into the South and West.

The population increase fed the westward movement that began in earnest after the Revolutionary War. Settlement across the Appalachians occurred in both the North and the South. Kentucky, for example, had only a few scattered settlements in 1770. By 1790 there were 74,000 people living in Kentucky, spread out at 1.8 persons per square mile; in 1820 there were 564,000 Kentuckians living at 14.0 persons per square mile. The numbers are more dramatic for Ohio, since almost no European Americans lived in the region in 1790. However, 45,000 had moved there by 1800 and 581,000 by 1820 (at 14.5 persons per square mile). This mobility had an important impact on people. JAMES MADISON commented that when people moved into a new area, they no longer felt bound by the past; they did not recognize distinctions that may have been bred into a community of long standing. Washington Irving, describing the changed world Rip Van Winkle discovered after his nap through the AMERICAN REVOLUTION, declared that a whole new set of residents had moved into the town, which now had "a busy disputatious tone about it, instead of its accustomed phlegm and drowsy tranquility."

Cities partook in some of this growth. Before the Revolutionary War, the largest city—Philadelphia—had about 25,000 residents, with New York close behind. But many urban areas like Newport and Charleston had less than 10,000. Such numbers would hardly make a city today. We can consider these urban centers as cities because the residents lived in compact areas of less than a square mile with multifamily dwellings. During the early national period, a few colonial cities were left behind while many others grew rapidly. By 1820 New York City slightly outpaced Philadelphia, with 123,706 people to Philadelphia's 112,772. There also emerged some new population centers like Baltimore on the Chesapeake, which grew from a small town to a metropolis of over 62,000 by 1820. Cincinnati in Ohio went from nothing to having almost 10,000 inhabitants during the same period.

Despite all of this growth, the population remained rural in both the North and South. Most Americans continued to live on family farms in a world dictated by the agricultural rhythms of the seasons. But even in the countryside there were exceptions. The use of slave labor in the South meant that there were some households that included many slaves, with some plantations numbering into the hundreds. In the North, there was a slight decrease in the number of dependent nonfamily members in households during the period, since indentured servitude declined rapidly during this period and the North freed its slaves. But not everyone who lived in the region, especially in New England and the middle states, remained in AGRICULTURE. During the initial stages of the INDUSTRIAL REVOLUTION, factories were located in the countryside near convenient sources of water power.

Like the European-American population, the number of Africans Americans in the United States continued to grow, even though there were only a relatively limited number of imports of slaves from Africa or the West Indies. About one-fifth (325,806 out of 1,593,625 in 1760) of the British-American population in the 1750s was African or of African descent, almost all of them slaves. In 1790 there were 689,784 individuals listed as "Negro" in the first federal census; about 32,000 were free. In 1820, despite the closing of the SLAVE TRADE by most states before 1808 and the closing of the slave trade by federal law after 1808, there were 1,642,672 "Negroes," more than 133,000 free. While most of the free African Americans lived in the North, some lived in the South. Both free and enslaved blacks, with deepening roots in North America, developed a culture that became uniquely African American. Moreover, with a rough balance between the sexes, this population was able to continue to grow despite the evils of the institution of SLAVERY and the disadvantages of racism throughout the nation.

Beyond the fact that the majority of the African-American population remained slave and lived in the South, there was another important regional difference that emerged during the early republic. In 1790 there was a rough equality in the total number of inhabitants between the North and the South, with each region having about 1.96 million people. In 1820 the balance had shifted northward: The slave South had about 4.3 million; the North had 5.2 million. Within this statistic lay some significant individual state developments. On the eve of the Revolutionary War, Virginia was the most populous colony, with about 500,000 people. New York, with fewer than 200,000, had less population than Connecticut. By 1820 Virginia had increased to a little over a million inhabitants; New York, however, had become the most populous state with 1.3 million people. This differential between North and South—and states like New York and Virginia—continued to increase in the decades after 1820.

See also CITIES AND URBAN LIFE; LABOR AND LABOR MOVEMENTS; RURAL LIFE.

Further reading: U.S. Department of Commerce, *Historical Statistics of the United States, Colonial Times to 1957* (Washington, D.C.: U.S. Govt. Printing Office, 1957); Stella H. Sutherland, *Population Distribution in Colonial America* (New York: AMS Press, 1966); Robert V. Wells, *Revolutions in American's Lives: A Demographic Perspective on the History of Americans, Their Families, and Their Society* (Westport, Conn.: Greenwood Press, 1982).

poverty

While America remained an affluent society compared with anywhere else in the world, historians have detected an increasing level of poverty in the 18th and early 19th centuries. In the countryside, poverty evolved from the very success of Americans: As families grew, it became more difficult for parents to provide a sufficient patrimony to maintain the same level of wealth from generation to generation. There were several solutions to the problem. A family, or some of the adult children of a family, might move to the FRONTIER to obtain cheaper land. Life on the frontier, however, was often on the margins, and poverty might well continue. Difficulty in getting a clear title to land, conflicts with NATIVE AMERICANS, as well as government policies all might limit this type of opportunity. Second, a family might hire out some of its children as they reached working age, hoping to provide a career that was not bound to farming. However, many of the positions open to impoverished children, such as becoming a sailor or apprenticing in a poorly paid trade like shoemaking, were not particularly lucrative. In times of war, young men sought the bounties of the recruiter, hoping that it would help them to get established and buy land.

During the 18th century, greater disparities emerged between rich and poor in the cities. The most affluent resided in large brick homes with several rooms and fine furniture. The poor lived in wooden multifamily structures, often even sharing the room they rented with boarders.

These distinctions emerged as a function of the increased sophistication of the ECONOMY, but they were enhanced by war and upheaval. War broke families apart, leaving women either as widows or temporarily in charge of the household. In an era when women had limited economic opportunities, this development often left a family in difficult economic straits. Because of the compact nature of urban life, poverty was more visible in the cities. Civic leaders therefore had to develop strategies for dealing with the poor.

There were two forms of relief for the poor. The first, practiced in the cities and the countryside, was outdoor relief. In this system, the poor man or woman remained in the community and received aid to supplement their income. This assistance usually came in the form of wood or food during hard times to carry the individual or family until they could once again support themselves. The second was indoor relief—the creation of an institution to house and support the poor. Boston, New York, and Philadelphia each built an almshouse in the colonial period. But as the costs of such institutions expanded in the mid-18th century, civic leaders decided to emphasize the corrective features of the institutions. The almshouse became not just a place for the poor to live, but also a place where the poor would work. In the process, reformers believed that poor people would learn the value of work and become self-sufficient. Moreover, the money they generated would help cut the expenses of the institution, relieving the affluent tax payer of supporting the poor. This shift in the role of the almshouse represented a change in the understanding of poverty. In the 17th century, poverty had been seen simply as the work of God. The individual was not held at fault. In the 18th century, with of the rise of the Enlightenment, humans were held accountable for their actions. The poor therefore became capable of bettering themselves with the proper instruction. Unfortunately, the work provided in the almshouse was often menial and did not lead to the development of a skill.

By the early 19th century, most urban areas had institutions to help the poor. Outdoor relief, however, continued in many areas, especially during the winter season when work was difficult to find. Poor people often resented the almshouse and avoided it if they could. Private charity organizations also began to emerge as part of the rise of a middle class and their renewed concern with reform. Isabella Graham helped to organize one of the first of such organizations in New York City in 1797, called the Society for the Relief of Poor Widows with Small Children. This group identified what it considered worthy objects of charity, provided outdoor relief and encouraged habits of industry and independence. Sparked by evangelical reform, such groups expanded rapidly in the early 19th century.

See also CITIES AND URBAN LIFE; DISEASE AND EPIDEMICS; POPULATION TRENDS; RURAL LIFE.

Further reading: John K. Alexander, *Render Them Submissive: Responses to Poverty in Philadelphia, 1760–1800* (Amherst, Mass.: University of Massachusetts Press, 1980); Robert E. Cray Jr., *Paupers and Poor Relief in New York City and Its Rural Environs, 1700–1830* (Philadelphia: Temple University Press, 1988); Raymond A. Mohl, *Poverty in New York, 1783–1825* (New York: Oxford University Press, 1971); Gary B. Nash, *The Urban Crucible: Social Change, Political Consciousness and the Origins of the American Revolution* (Cambridge, Mass.: Harvard University Press, 1979); David J. Rothman, *The Discovery of the Asylum: Social Order and Disorder in the New Republic* (Boston: Little, Brown, 1971).

Priestley, Joseph (1733–1804)

For most of his career, Joseph Priestley resided in England as a dissenting minister, scientist, and writer of political theory. His position as a minister of an unestablished (non-Anglican) church, his republican sympathies, and his support of the FRENCH REVOLUTION (1789–1815) led to a mob attack on his house in Birmingham, England, on July 14, 1791. When the French Assembly made him a citizen of France in September 1792, he became even more unpopular in Great Britain. In 1794 he decided to move to the United States to escape persecution. Arriving in June, he was greeted with acclaim in New York and Philadelphia.

Priestley was famous, not only as a victim of a church and king mob, but as a man of SCIENCE who had isolated several gases in the laboratory. Although he was offered a position to teach chemistry in Philadelphia, he settled in Northumberland, Pennsylvania, where his son Joseph lived. Over the next several years Priestley remained active intellectually, presenting papers at the AMERICAN PHILOSOPHICAL SOCIETY. He also became identified with the DEMOCRATIC-REPUBLICAN PARTY and a friend of THOMAS JEFFERSON. He was attacked in the Federalist press and feared deportation under the Alien Act of 1798. He wrote extensively on RELIGION and was a proponent of the UNITARIAN church in the United States.

See also ALIEN AND SEDITION ACTS; FEDERALIST PARTY.

prisons

Punishment of criminals underwent a significant transformation in the revolutionary and early national eras. In the colonial period the emphasis had been on open display of punishment. Individual reformation was not the object; the idea was to demonstrate to the community the consequences of breaking the law. There were many offenses that led to capital punishment, and executions were in public. For lesser crimes, there was corporal punishment, usually in a place for all to see. Similarly, the stocks—the wooden shackles holding the feet or head and arms—exhibited an individual guilty of minor transgressions. Jails existed, but they were ordinarily used to hold a person awaiting trial or as a place to put vagrants, debtors, or other undesirables.

New modes of punishment emerged in the 1780s. Influenced by the ideas of the Enlightenment and the writings of Cesare Beccaria, reformers came to hold that the individual could be taught to change behavior—that humankind could be perfected. The focus shifted from the community to the individual. Capital and corporal punishment appeared barbaric and relics of an age gone by. In republican America, labor could teach virtue, and imprisonment could be an appropriate penalty for most crimes.

The state of Pennsylvania led the way in this reform effort. In 1786 the state legislature did away with many capital crimes and, as a step toward the new understanding of punishment, ordered that convicted criminals perform labor in public. This halfway measure did not satisfy men like BENJAMIN RUSH, who quickly emerged as spokesmen for further reform. Public labor was not punishment enough. Rush wanted the criminal to be removed from society until he had been transformed into a new being. Separation from the world would act as a deterrent to crime and facilitate discipline and the inculcation of proper values. The prison, in other words, was to be a "house of repentance" where "any signs of mirth, or even levity" were to be discouraged. Believing that treatment of the criminal should be determined based on the crime and the individual, Rush wrote that punishment should consist of some combination of "BODILY PAIN, LABOUR, WATCHFULNESS, SOLITUDE, AND SILENCE." It would also include "CLEANLINESS and A SIMPLE DIET." Rush published his ideas in 1787 and found a receptive audience; the Pennsylvania state legislature began to remove criminals from public view in 1789, and in 1790 the state established a system of private punishment and labor in the prison. The problem was that the facilities available were inadequate to the task. Philadelphia's Walnut Street Prison had been built in 1773 before imprisonment for crime had become standard punishment. During the 1790s conditions in the prison attracted further attention from reformers who decried the mingling of sexes and offenders and lamented the lack of private cells. The fact that debtors and vagrants were confined with criminals also created concern. Although the state instituted more reforms, separating the sexes and different categories of inmates, Walnut Street Prison became more crowded and never quite what the reformers had hoped. By 1820 Philadelphians had come to see the prison as a persistent problem for the city, and in 1823 the state began building

a new facility, Eastern State Penitentiary, that would take reform of prisoners to a new level.

Although the reality at the Walnut Street Prison never quite matched the ideal, other communities took the Pennsylvania effort to heart. Several states, including New York, Maryland, and Massachusetts, used the reforms at Walnut Street as a model, and THOMAS JEFFERSON designed the Richmond Penitentiary, which provided solitary confinement for each prisoner. But like their precursor, most of these institutions—and those in other states that did not reflect reform—proved inadequate. In 1816 New York began construction of the Auburn Penitentiary. New York's Auburn System would become a prototype for others, emphasizing the isolation of the convict into separate cells, strict regimen and discipline, and workshops to keep the prisoners busy and productive.

While state governments during the early republic struggled with how to reform the criminal, they did little to alleviate another form of prison inmate: the debtor. As late as 1816 there were 600 debtors held in New York City at any given time. This antiquated system of throwing an individual into jail for failing to meet his financial obligations was abandoned in the 1820s, 1830s, and 1840s.

See also REPUBLICANISM.

Further reading: Michael Meranze, *Laboratories of Virtue: Punishment, Revolution, and Authority in Philadelphia, 1760–1835* (Chapel Hill: University of North Carolina Press, 1996); David J. Rothman, *The Discovery of the Asylum: Social Order and Disorder in the New Republic* (Boston: Little, Brown, 1971); Alice Felt Tyler, *Freedom's Ferment: Phases of American Social History from the Colonial Period to the Outbreak of the Civil War* (Freeport, N.Y.: Books for Libraries Press, 1970).

privateering

Privateers were private armed vessels licensed to prey upon enemy commerce during wartime. In the 18th century, privateering was a legally sanctioned activity. It was recognized as legitimate and enshrined in custom, law, and diplomacy. Although the actions of privateers—often robbery on the high seas—seemed analogous to piracy, the two activities were distinct. Unlike piracy, privateering was government-sponsored, and it could only be conducted during wartime and against one's enemies. For sailors and shipowners, privateering was risky but attractive because captured vessels, "prizes," could be sold, with the proceeds or "prize money" to be split among the crew and owners according to an agreed formula.

Colonial Americans were prolific privateersmen in the various wars between Britain, France, and Spain. When the REVOLUTIONARY WAR (1775–83) commenced, many Americans continued the practice. The CONTINENTAL CONGRESS and the newly independent states licensed as many as 3,000 privateers. The British authorities licensed a smaller number of LOYALIST privateers in American and Canadian waters as well as the WEST INDIES. When the war spread to Europe, all of the belligerents, including France, Britain, Spain, and the Netherlands, authorized privateers to attack enemy shipping. American privateers also operated out of French ports.

After independence, privateering remained an important activity. Both the Americans and the French resorted to privateering, mainly in the West Indies, during the QUASI WAR (1798–1800). British privateers harassed American shipping during the prolonged maritime conflict with France (1793–1815). During the War of 1812 (1812–15), British and American privateers were active in the North Atlantic, the Caribbean, and in European waters.

Historians disagree as to the consequences of privateering. For example, some historians argue that privateering was a useful activity during the War of Independence. Because the Americans did not have a large naval force to rival Britain's Royal Navy, privateering offered a cheap and quick alternative to attack British shipping. The activities of privateers drove up insurance rates for British merchants who sought to engage in the Atlantic TRADE. It is unclear, however, how important this added cost was. Other historians argue that privateering undermined the effort to fill the embryonic Continental navy (as well as the state militias and CONTINENTAL ARMY) with experienced hands. Whether revolutionary or Loyalist, privateering provided many families in maritime communities with the funds to endure the wartime disruption of trade. This economic reality remained true in the conflicts that followed the Revolutionary War. For maritime communities and the families who lived in them, privateering was a natural adaptation to wartime conditions. Prior to the establishment of a large American navy, privateering provided an effective means of waging war at sea. Even established naval powers such as Britain, France, and Spain believed that privateering was a useful activity in a world of extensive maritime empires. As the Age of Sail gave way to the Age of Steam, privateering was gradually outlawed during the 19th century.

Further reading: Jerome R. Garitee, *The Republic's Private Navy: The American Privateering Business as Practiced by Baltimore During the War of 1812* (Middletown, Conn.: Wesleyan University Press, 1977); Edgar Stanton Maclay, *A History of American Privateers* (Freeport, N.Y.: Books for Library Press, 1970).

— Francis D. Cogliano

Proclamation of 1763 (October 7, 1763)

King GEORGE III issued the Proclamation of 1763 to prevent Anglo-American settlement west of the Appalachians. Often portrayed as a part of the new imperial regulations passed to control the colonies, the Proclamation of 1763 was a stopgap measure to deal with some real problems. Victory in the French and Indian War (1754–63) added all of CANADA, the area east of the Mississippi, and FLORIDA to the British Empire. Much of this region was unsettled by European Americans and was occupied by NATIVE AMERICANS. The British government had to develop a means to govern this area.

The Proclamation of 1763 was the initial step in what was thought to be an ongoing process. The proclamation created three new colonies in North America—Quebec, East Florida, and West Florida—and provided the means to establish representative government based on the model used in the other British colonies. The proclamation also extended the boundary of Georgia. But the most serious problem was preventing conflict between the Native Americans and the European Americans. PONTIAC'S REBELLION (1763) demonstrated how difficult and expensive it would be to protect colonists on the FRONTIER. The simplest thing to do would be to limit contact between European Americans and Native Americans. There was still plenty of unsettled land east of the Appalachians, especially in the colonies of the Floridas. The proclamation therefore ordered "all our loving subjects" from settling the area. Concerned, too, with the Native Americans who now also became King George's subjects, the proclamation prevented any land speculation in the area, since previously "great frauds and abuses have been committed in the purchasing lands of the Indians, to the great prejudice of our interest, and to the great dissatisfaction of the said Indians." The Proclamation of 1763 irritated rich and poor colonists, since it curtailed land speculation and prevented settlement. Its provisions remained in force until 1774 when the Quebec Act, sometimes considered one of the COERCIVE ACTS (1774), gave most of the western territory to Quebec.

See also RESISTANCE MOVEMENT.

Prophet, the Shawnee (Tenskwatawa) (1775–1836)

The Prophet was the brother of TECUMSEH and an important NATIVE AMERICAN religious leader in the early 19th century. He was born in present-day Ohio in 1775, one of a set of triplets born to Puckeshinwa and Methoataske. Unfortunately for the young Shawnee, his father, a war chief, was killed at the Battle of Point Pleasant in 1774. His mother, a CREEK, abandoned her children and fled the Ohio region during the turmoil of the REVOLUTIONARY WAR (1775–83). The young orphan and his brothers, including his elder brother Tecumseh, were raised by an

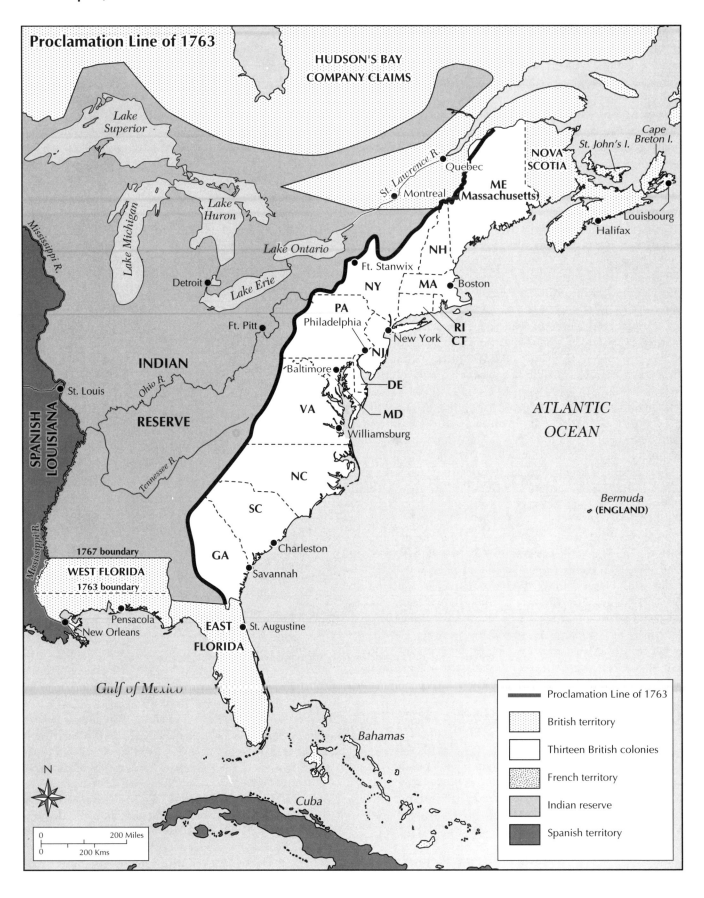

Proclamation Line of 1763

HUDSON'S BAY
COMPANY CLAIMS

Lake Superior

Lake Huron

Lake Michigan

Lake Ontario

St. Lawrence R.

Quebec

Montreal

NOVA SCOTIA

St. John's I.

Cape Breton I.

ME (Massachusetts)

Louisbourg

Halifax

NH

Ft. Stanwix

Lake Erie

Detroit

NY

MA

Boston

Mississippi R.

Ft. Pitt

PA

Philadelphia

New York

RI
CT

INDIAN

NJ

Ohio R.

Baltimore

DE

St. Louis

RESERVE

VA

MD

Williamsburg

ATLANTIC
OCEAN

Tennessee R.

NC

Mississippi R.

SC

Bermuda
• (ENGLAND)

SPANISH
LOUISIANA

1767 boundary

Charleston

WEST FLORIDA

1763 boundary

GA

Savannah

Pensacola

New Orleans

EAST

St. Augustine

FLORIDA

Gulf of Mexico

Bahamas

N

Cuba

		Proclamation Line of 1763
		British territory
		Thirteen British colonies
		French territory
		Indian reserve
		Spanish territory

0   200 Miles

0   200 Kms

older brother named Chiksika and an older sister named Tecumpease. These older siblings favored Tecumseh over his younger brothers because he showed signs of becoming an excellent hunter and warrior. The boy who would become the Prophet was never a good hunter and showed no prowess for war. He even gouged his eye out in a hunting accident. The young man attempted to compensate for his deficiencies by talking boldly, earning him the nickname Lalawethika, which meant the "Rattle" or "Noisemaker." As Lalawethika grew into adulthood, he became a notorious drunkard and underachiever. He followed his brother Tecumseh at the BATTLE OF FALLEN TIMBERS (August 20, 1794), but his performance was not meritorious.

His first 30 years passed without Lalawethika finding a role in Shawnee society. He attempted to become a healer with a little success, but most Shawnee considered him a failure. By 1804 Lalawethika had joined his brother Tecumseh and his followers in Indiana. In April 1805 Lalawethika lapsed into a comatose state and awakened a changed man. He said he had experienced a vision in which he had gone to the Master of Life, or Great Spirit, and seen the paradise of the spirit world. Lalawethika had been told by the Great Spirit that in order to go to the spirit world, the Indians had to adopt a stricter and more traditional way of life. No longer could the Indians drink alcohol, eat non-Indian food, or follow any of the practices of the white culture. In fact, the Indians had to restrict all contact with white people, Americans in particular. To reflect his newfound religious calling, Lalawethika adopted the name Tenskwatawa, or "The open door." He gave up drinking and became a holy figure known to European Americans as the Prophet.

Over the next several years, Tenskwatawa spread his message and attracted a large following. Americans such as William Henry Harrison, governor of the Indiana Territory, attempted to discredit Tenskwatawa and called him a fraud. Tenskwatawa accurately predicted a solar eclipse in 1806, solidifying his claim to be a prophet. Tenskwatawa and his followers moved to various locations in Ohio and Indiana, constantly facing supply problems and famine. In 1808 Tenskwatawa and his brother Tecumseh, who served as the organizer and everyday leader of the Prophet's followers, moved their village to Prophetstown on the Tippecanoe River in western Indiana. By 1811 Tecumseh was building a political alliance in unison with Tenskwatawa's religious movement. Tecumseh hoped to ally all of the tribes on the FRONTIER to resist further expansion by the United States. While Tecumseh was in the South recruiting allies, Governor Harrison formed an army and destroyed Prophetstown at the BATTLE OF TIPPECANOE (November 7, 1811). Much of the blame for the defeat fell on the shoulders of Tenskwatawa, who had promised the warriors that he could protect them from the American

bullets. As a result of his failure, Tenskwatawa lost most of his influence. During the War of 1812 (1812–15), he followed Tecumseh into CANADA, where Tecumseh died at the Battle of the Thames (October 5, 1813). After the war, Tenskwatawa and a few family members remained in Canada. He eventually returned to the United States in 1825 and assisted the government in removing many of the Shawnee to Missouri. He established a village near modern Kansas City, where he died in 1836.

Further reading: R. David Edmunds, *The Shawnee Prophet* (Lincoln: University of Nebraska Press, 1983).

— Michael L. Cox

Pulaski, Casimir (1748–1779)

A petulant and at times pretentious man, Casimir Pulaski fled Poland to serve in the CONTINENTAL ARMY. Despite his aristocratic heritage, he identified with the American cause and commanded the Legionary Corps of the Continental army. His intractability hindered his effectiveness as a leader, and his record in combat was mixed.

Pulaski was born the second child of an unusually wealthy family in Poland. During the late 1760s he fought alongside his father in the Knights of the Holy Cross in opposition to Russian control of Poland through King Stanislaw II. Although this movement crumbled in the wake of military defeat, Pulaski continued to lead periodic campaigns against the Russians. For a short time, he became the nation's most venerated hero. This fame came to a crashing halt, however, when he was framed for the attempted murder of the Polish king. Stigmatized and in terrible debt from his futile military campaigns, Pulaski fled to France only to be thrown into debtors prison. With virtually nowhere else to go, Pulaski appealed to the Americans and offered his services in their REVOLUTIONARY WAR (1775–83) in the summer of 1776.

In July 1777 Pulaski arrived in America, the beneficiary of a deal between representatives from the French and American governments. Armed with a letter of introduction from BENJAMIN FRANKLIN, Pulaski met with GEORGE WASHINGTON in August of that year. Although he had yet to receive his commission and had only volunteered to serve as an aid to Washington, he was pressed into service at the BATTLE OF BRANDYWINE (September 11, 1777). Pulaski led a dramatic counterattack on the British that, at the very least, afforded time for Washington's collapsing right flank to retreat.

Pulaski also led cavalry at Haddonsfield in support of General ANTHONY WAYNE's expedition to round up cattle to feed the troops in camp at VALLEY FORGE (1777–78). After resigning in protest of having to take orders from Wayne rather than Washington, he was reappointed on March 28,

1778, to lead Pulaski's Legion, a force composed of 68 dragoons and 200 foot soldiers. Pulaski's policy of recruiting German deserters from the British army, in violation of Washington's orders, proved disastrous. On October 14, 1778, at Little Egg Harbor in southern New Jersey, one of these men defected back to the British and led a devastating night attack on Pulaski's unsuspecting troops, killing 50 of his 200 infantrymen.

After a brief stint at the town of Minisink on the Delaware River, Pulaski was sent south to help meet the British invasion of Georgia. On May 11, 1779, during this southern campaign, Pulaski's legion was cut to pieces by a 900-man advance guard. Already in ill repute, Pulaski found himself involved in yet another bungled operation when the British, tipped off by a deserter, defeated the revolutionaries during their attack on Savannah on October 9, 1779. Pulaski suffered a fatal wound that day and died en route to a hospital on the American ship *Wasp*. He was buried at sea. Still a national hero in his native country, Pulaski remains a symbol of the bonds between Poland and the United States.

Further reading: Clarence A. Manning, *A Soldier of Liberty: Casimir Pulaski* (New York: Philosophical Library, 1945).

— Daniel M. Cobb

Putnam, Israel (Old Put) (1718–1790)

Israel Putnam, a famed soldier in the REVOLUTIONARY WAR (1775–83), was noted for his legendary military exploits.

Born in Salem (present-day Danvers), Massachusetts, Putnam moved to Pomfret, Connecticut, where he farmed for a living. He fought in the French and Indian War (1754–63), serving in campaigns at Montreal in 1760 and Havana in 1762 before commanding Connecticut forces during PONTIAC'S REBELLION (1763–64) at the siege of Detroit. He was also a member of the Connecticut general assembly and the SONS OF LIBERTY during the 1760s and 1770s. An outspoken critic of the British, legend has it that Putnam immediately abandoned his farm to join the war effort after hearing about fighting at LEXINGTON AND CONCORD (April 19, 1775). During the Revolutionary War he rose to the rank of major general in the CONTINENTAL ARMY. He played a key role in the BATTLE OF BUNKER HILL (June 17, 1775) but blundered in subsequent actions, suffering blame for losses in the BATTLE OF LONG ISLAND (August 27–30, 1776) and the loss of Forts Montgomery and Clinton (October 6, 1777). Court-martialed for negligence, he was exonerated, but he had lost the faith of GEORGE WASHINGTON. In 1779 Putnam succumbed to a paralytic stroke while on leave, thus bringing his military career to an end. He died 11 years later.

Further reading: William Farrand Livingston, *Israel Putnam: Pioneer, Ranger, and Major-General* (New York: G. P. Putnam's Sons, 1905).

— Sarah Eppler Janda

Q

Quakers (Society of Friends)

The Revolutionary era brought challenges and opportunities to American Quakers, members of the Religious Society of Friends founded in England in 1652. Advocating pacifism and a withdrawal from politics, Quakers, who first came to British America in 1656, found themselves in an awkward position during the REVOLUTIONARY WAR (1775–83), when the internecine nature of the conflict confronted every American with difficult choices. If their principles left Quakers susceptible to charges of disloyalty and even treason, those same principles also placed them in the forefront of the beginnings of reform movements, especially ANTISLAVERY AND ABOLITION.

During the RESISTANCE MOVEMENT (1764–75) many Quakers objected to British policies but offered only muted protests. In Pennsylvania this position was in part the result of the Quaker desire not to alienate the king in the hope that the British would do away with the proprietary government and make Pennsylvania a Crown colony. Quaker noninvolvement in the controversy also was the result of a movement begun in the 1750s to reform the Society of Friends, step away from political discourse, and focus efforts on aiding others through private means. While some Quakers participated in nonimportation movements, the sect as a whole sought to discourage its members from participating in COMMITTEES OF CORRESPONDENCE and any extra-legal body that opposed the royal government.

The onset of war divided the Quakers and left the reformists exposed to charges of being LOYALIST in sympathy and action. The Pennsylvania Yearly Meeting disowned almost 1,000 members for joining militias, serving in local committees, and actively supporting the revolutionary cause. By the end of the war, a separate group of expelled former Quakers organized themselves into the Free Quakers and unsuccessfully sought control of Society of Friends meetinghouses. Those who sought to remain neutral, or had Loyalist leanings, found themselves persecuted. Arguing that the payment of taxes to support the war or partici-

pating in the revolutionary government in any way was a violation of their pacifism, Quakers found themselves distrusted by many. Revolutionary committees levied heavy fines on pacifist Quakers, and when they did not pay, seized Quaker property by force. When Quakers crossed enemy lines for business or to attend their quarterly and yearly meetings, they provoked further animosity. Likewise, the Quakers sought to live under any government that was in place. If a British army occupied a city, the Quakers went about their business; if an American army occupied the same location, the Quakers attempted to live as they had under the British. In a brutal and long war, neutrality became increasingly difficult to maintain. In 1777 and 1778 the Revolutionary government in Pennsylvania arrested 17 leading Quakers and sent them to a harsh imprisonment in Winchester, Virginia. Two elderly and infirm Quakers died during their incarceration; a third died a year later, having never fully recovered from his confinement. Besides the loss of civil rights, Quakers also occasionally suffered mob harassment when crowds broke the windows of Quaker property and threatened further action.

If some Quakers suffered during the Revolutionary War, they also demonstrated an increasing commitment to reform. Since the 1750s Quakers had steadily moved against SLAVERY. By 1774 Philadelphia Quakers had provided for gradual emancipation and the education of slaves. In 1776 the Philadelphia Yearly Meeting resolved to disown any member who refused to manumit his slaves. Quakers helped organize manumission societies and supported legal action by the state governments against slavery. Quakers also reached out to aid NATIVE AMERICANS, sending missions to groups like the Seneca in the 1780s and 1790s. Quakers became active in other areas of reform, including changes in the punishment of criminals and seeking ways to help the poor. Although after the Revolutionary War Quakers no longer had a prominent role in politics, their involvement in philanthropy helped mold the future course of American HUMANITARIANISM.

Further reading: Jack D. Marietta, *The Reformation of American Quakerism, 1748–1783. Philadelphia.* (Philadelphia: University of Pennsylvania Press, 1984).

Quartering Act (May 3, 1765)

As a part of the effort to reorganize the British Empire, including the revenue bills called the SUGAR ACT (1764) and the STAMP ACT (1765), Parliament passed the Quartering Act to guarantee housing and supplies for troops stationed in colonial America. Although the act contributed to the tension created by the imperial crisis, it was not as offensive nor as onerous as the revenue regulations. In fact, BENJAMIN FRANKLIN, as a colonial agent in London, played a role in the final wording of the law. The Quartering Act had two key provisions: First, the law stipulated that the colony in which the troops were stationed had to find billeting in vacant buildings or barracks. This clause was considered a major concession to colonial Americans because it did not allow for the housing of soldiers in private houses. It also created problems for the British army, since it made it difficult to find housing for soldiers on the march. The second key provision, connected to the first, was that the act depended upon the colonial legislature to raise the money to support the soldiers. In essence, this clause gave the colony local control. There was no taxation without representation here. On the surface, it also made it appear easy to oppose the measure; a colonial assembly could nullify the law by refusing to fund the billeting of the troops.

Most colonies, however, complied with the law. When New York did not do so, it faced parliamentary wrath. In reaction to the New York assembly's noncompliance, Parliament enacted a law that prevented the assembly from passing any legislation until it met its obligations under the Quartering Act. New York's opposition to the Quartering Act also helped to convince Parliament to pass the TOWNSHEND DUTIES (1767). The New York assembly compromised and provided some money for British troops before the New York Suspending Act (July 2, 1767) went into effect.

Parliament renewed the Quartering Act several times during the 1760s and 1770s, since it always had an expiration date attached. In 1774 a slightly stiffer measure was added in reaction to the BOSTON TEA PARTY (1773)—and as part of the COERCIVE ACTS (1774)—indicating that the troop commander had the right to locate his troops geographically. The idea here was to prevent an assembly from offering to pay for quartering troops at a location away from where British officials felt they needed to have the troops stationed.

See also RESISTANCE MOVEMENT.

Further reading: John W. Shy, *Toward Lexington: The Role of the British Army in the Coming of the American Revolution* (Princeton, N.J.: Princeton University Press, 1965).

Quasi War (1798–1800)

The United States fought an undeclared naval war with France, 1798–1800, that is referred to as the Quasi War. The diplomatic rift began in 1796. France viewed JAY'S TREATY (1794), which gave Great Britain most-favored-nation trading status, as a repudiation of its treaties of commerce and alliance (1778) with the United States. In addition, victories in the WEST INDIES strengthened the French position in the Caribbean. In the spring of 1796, French privateers and warships began to seize American shipping in the West Indies, a policy that was made official by a French decree on July 2, 1796. Soon the French were even cruising off the coast of North America. Within two years over 330 American vessels were captured, driving insurance rates from less than 6 percent to as high as 40 percent. At such rates, American shipping was crippled. Efforts at negotiating a settlement ended in disaster when the French refused to begin discussion until the Americans paid a bribe. After this so-called XYZ AFFAIR (1797–98), hope for a peaceful settlement disappeared. Clamoring "millions for defense and not one cent for tribute," the United States prepared for war by expanding the army and creating a navy.

Fortunately for the United States, the construction of three frigates—the *Constellation, the United States,* and the *Constitution*—was almost complete after four years of work. Launched in the summer of 1798, these ships added some real punch to a newly organized naval department under Benjamin Stoddert. Other frigates and warships began to be built, and merchantmen were bought and converted to naval purposes. As early as July 7, 1798, when the newly commissioned *Delaware* captured the *Croyable* off the coast of New Jersey, American vessels began to strike back. While naval action could not drive every privateer from the sea, the Americans were able to punish the French for their depredations. Two frigate-size actions were also fought, both by the *Constellation*. On February 9, 1799, the *Constellation* met *L'Insurgente* off the island of Nevis and pounded it into surrender. Near Guadeloupe almost a year later, on February 1, 1800, the *Constellation* met a superior *La Vengeance* in an indecisive action that left both ships severely damaged. The Americans claimed that had *La Vengeance* not veered off in the dark of night, they would have captured or sunk the French ship.

The Quasi War had a dramatic impact within the United States. Riding a wave of war fever, the FEDERALIST PARTY gained in popularity over the DEMOCRATIC-REPUBLICANS. The Federalists then passed the ALIEN AND SEDITION ACTS (1798) to limit immigrant voting and stifle the opposition press. The navy and larger army needed money, so the Federalists increased taxes, leading to FRIES'S REBELLION (1799) in Pennsylvania. But the momentum could not be sustained, especially when President JOHN ADAMS opted to avoid outright war and reopened negotiations. The American peace commission found that conditions in France had shifted and that, with the rise of NAPOLEON BONAPARTE, a settlement was possible. The result was the Convention of 1800. This peace accord was not a diplomatic triumph. The French refused to pay any reparations for the seizures during the conflict, and they insisted on equal trading status with Great Britain. For the time being, however, they recognized American neutral rights and agreed to stop capturing American merchant vessels. Perhaps most importantly, Napoleon agreed that the FRENCH ALLIANCE (1778) with the United States no longer existed. The American Senate initially balked at these terms as conceding almost nothing, but eventually the Senate ratified the treaty. Napoleon's true aims remained hidden. Within days of his acceptance of the treaty, he had forced Spain to retrocede the Louisiana Territory to France and began dreaming of a French-American empire. The French failure to reconquer Saint-Domingue (HAITI), however, forced Napoleon to abandon these dreams in 1803 and agree to the LOUISIANA PURCHASE.

See also FOREIGN AFFAIRS.

Further reading: Alexander DeConde, *The Quasi-War: The Politics and Diplomacy of the Undeclared War, 1797–1801* (New York, Scribner, 1966); Stanley Elkins and Eric McKitrick, *The Age of Federalism* (New York: Oxford University Press, 1993).

Quebec, Battle of (December 31, 1775)

In an effort to drive the British out of North America and export their revolution, the Americans launched a two-pronged invasion of CANADA in the summer and fall of 1775. One prong was led by General Richard Montgomery, who attacked from New York and captured St. John's and Montreal. The other, headed by BENEDICT ARNOLD, had a difficult march through the Maine wilderness. Both expeditions started late in the campaign year. Arnold's forces had to cross swollen streams, deal with rainstorms and snow, and managed to get to the St. Lawrence River only by November 9. Over one-third of his force turned back. In early December, Arnold's 675 men were joined by Montgomery with about 300 men. They faced almost twice that many defenders in Quebec. Since many of the enlistments were about to expire with the coming of the new year, Montgomery and Arnold led an assault during a blizzard on December 31. Although the attack demonstrated daring

and bravery, it was also foolhardy. Montgomery was killed almost as soon as the battle began; Arnold suffered a serious wound to his leg. The Americans were beaten back and about 400 were taken prisoner. A small force remained to besiege the city, with some reinforcements added before spring. But with the thaw, British ships would sail up the unfrozen St. Lawrence to relieve Quebec. The Americans pulled back to Montreal, then retreated further to FORT TICONDEROGA, almost in complete rout. Although the campaign was a disaster, it demonstrated the ardor that some Americans had for the Revolution. Montgomery's death before Quebec, mirroring the great British hero General James Wolfe's death in 1759, became an important symbol for the cause of independence, and Montgomery was held up as a martyr.

Quincy, Josiah (1744–1775)

Josiah Quincy wrote a number of patriotic essays and played a key role in the events leading up to the REVOLUTIONARY WAR (1775–83). Born in Boston, Massachusetts, on February 23, 1744, to Josiah and Hannah Sturgis Quincy, he moved with his family to Braintree, Massachusetts, when he was 12. Members of the prominent Quincy family had lived in Braintree for several generations, and it was also home to such contemporary notables as JOHN HANCOCK, JOHN ADAMS, and ABIGAIL ADAMS. Quincy's father, a highly successful merchant, encouraged him to continue the family tradition of attending Harvard. After completing his B.A. in 1763 and his M.A. in 1766, he began practicing law in Boston and quickly rose to the top of his profession. On October 26, 1769, Quincy married Abigail Phillips and eventually fathered two children.

In 1770 the young and ambitious Quincy joined with John Adams in defending the British soldiers on trial for murder in what came to be called the BOSTON MASSACRE (March 5, 1770). Despite the concerns of his patriot father, who was flabbergasted by his son's involvement, Quincy's reputation grew even more after he and Adams successfully defended the British soldiers. In 1772 Quincy was appointed to the COMMITTEE OF CORRESPONDENCE, and in 1773 he began traveling extensively to meet with officials about the perceived English threat to local rights and liberty. In addition to his skills as a lawyer and orator, Quincy was also a gifted writer and made a number of key contributions to the discourse on liberty leading up to the Revolutionary War. He became one of the most vocal critics of Massachusetts governor THOMAS HUTCHINSON and wrote a defense of the BOSTON TEA PARTY (December 16, 1773) in the *Boston Gazette*. Described as passionate and fiery, Quincy wrote extensively on liberty and patriotism. His most influential work was *Observations on the Act of Parliament Commonly Called the Boston Port Bill with Thoughts on Civil Society and Standing Armies* (1774).

Quincy's life, though influential, proved to be brief. After a long bout with tuberculosis, he died on April 26, 1775, with the simple regret that he would be unable to serve his country any longer. Unbeknownst to him, his infant daughter had passed away just two weeks earlier, leaving his wife with only their son, also named Josiah Quincy, who went on to have a long and distinguished political career.

See also RESISTANCE MOVEMENT.

Further reading: Phillip McFarland, *The Brave Bostonians: Hutchinson, Quincy, Franklin, and the Coming of the American Revolution* (Boulder, Colo.: Westview Press, 1998).

— Sarah Eppler Janda

R

race and racial conflict

European Americans held race as an important element distinguishing one social group from another in the revolutionary and early national periods. Throughout this era, there were three major races identified in America: European Americans or whites, NATIVE AMERICANS or Indians, and AFRICAN AMERICANS or "Negroes." Most European Americans assumed an attitude of racial superiority over the other two races and enforced their ideas through war and repression.

Ideas concerning Native Americans remained mixed. On the one hand, most European Americans viewed the Native Americans as heathens; European Americans persisted on looking upon Indians as some less civilized group and created a mythology that the Native American relied almost entirely upon hunting and gathering. Since women did most of the labor in AGRICULTURE, European Americans did not think that farming was important to Indians. Many white Americans simply wanted to extinguish the remnants of the Native Americans that stood in the way of FRONTIER expansion. On the other hand, a few philanthropists argued against extermination, believing that the Indian was a doomed race and that it would be best to limit their contact with the European Americans. Ultimately, these ideas bore fruit in the removal policies of the Jacksonian period.

European-American attitudes toward African Americans, although challenged in the period, were less mixed. In 1754 most African Americans were slaves. Rationales existed for enslaving Africans—running the gamut from racial inferiority to captives in war—but not many European Americans worried enough about explaining the institution of SLAVERY to fully develop such ideas. The AMERICAN REVOLUTION changed the situation by emphasizing the ideal of liberty and leading to the freedom of tens of thousands of slaves. It now became necessary to articulate a more elaborate rationale for defending racial slavery. Although men like THOMAS JEFFERSON had held that Africans did not have the same intellectual capacities as European Americans, it was only in the early 19th century that white Americans, especially in the South, developed extensive scientific arguments for racial differences. Simultaneously, some Americans began to argue for the equality of all humankind, black or white. In particular, free African Americans seized upon the rhetoric of the AMERICAN REVOLUTION and turned it against the racist ideas of European Americans. Some whites also began to speak of the equality of all humans.

Racial conflict between white and black Americans assumed a variety of forms. The institution of slavery represented a form of racial conflict. On the one hand, white masters ultimately relied upon violence in order to subjugate slaves. On the other hand, slaves turned to intermittent violence—destruction of property, physical attacks, and occasional rebellion—to resist slavery. However, even in northern states where slavery was abolished or was in the process of being abolished, there was racism. White Americans occasionally used collective action to attack African Americans and their developing institutions.

See also GABRIEL'S REBELLION; RIOTS.

Further reading: David Brion Davis, *The Problem of Slavery in the Age of Revolution, 1770–1823* (Ithaca, N.Y.: Cornell University Press, 1975); Winthrop D. Jordan, *White over Black: American Attitudes toward the Negro, 1550–1812* (Chapel Hill: University of North Carolina Press, 1968); Gary B. Nash, *Race and Revolution* (Madison, Wis.: Madison House 1990); Bernard W. Sheehan, *Seeds of Extinction: Jeffersonian Philanthropy and the American Indian* (Chapel Hill: University of North Carolina Press, 1975).

Randolph, Edmund (1753–1813)

Edmund Randolph played a leading role in the CONSTITUTIONAL CONVENTION. Born into a wealthy Virginia planter family, Randolph studied law at the College of William and Mary. When the REVOLUTIONARY WAR (1775–83) broke out, father and son were torn apart by their opposing political views concerning the future of the colonies. Edmund's father, John Randolph, remained loyal to the Crown and followed the royal governor, JOHN MURRAY, LORD DUNMORE, to England in 1775. But his son Edmund embraced the revolutionary cause, and served as an aide-de-camp to General GEORGE WASHINGTON. Only 23 years old, Randolph became the youngest delegate in Virginia and was an ardent supporter of the adoption of Virginia's first STATE CONSTITUTION in 1776.

During the war Randolph continued to pursue an ambitious political career. He first became mayor of Williamsburg and then Virginia's attorney general. In 1779 he attended the CONTINENTAL CONGRESS and was finally elected governor of Virginia in 1785. His great moment in American history came when Randolph, the leader of the Virginia delegation, submitted the so-called Virginia Plan to the federal convention in Philadelphia in 1787. This bold plan called for the annulment of the ARTICLES OF CONFEDERATION and the creation of an entirely new constitution. The Virginia Plan proposed a strong central government with separate legislative, executive, and judicial branches enabling national legislation to veto state laws. The plan also called for a bicameral Congress, with the lower house (House of Representatives) elected by the people and an upper house (Senate) chosen by the lower house from nominees proposed by the state legislatures. After three days of furious debate and revision, the Virginia Plan became the basis of the United States Constitution.

By the time the Constitution was adopted, Randolph ironically declined to sign it because he worried about the increased power of the presidential office, which he saw as a "foetus of monarchy." When the constitution was submitted to the Virginia convention, however, Randolph urged the delegates to approve the constitution to prevent a breakup of the United States into a loose confederation. Under President Washington, Edmund Randolph became the attorney general of the United States and succeeded THOMAS JEFFERSON as secretary of state in 1794. The next year, the British minister to the United States released French diplomatic papers that falsely accused Randolph of seeking bribes from foreign diplomats for giving secret information. The compromised Randolph resigned from public office the same year, and his political career never recovered from this denunciation. He resumed his law practice but returned once again to the public arena when he became AARON BURR's major legal counsel in his trial for treason in 1807. Randolph's name was completely cleared after his death in 1813.

Further reading: Melvin E. Bradford, *Edmund Randolph: Lawyer, Political Leader of Virginia, and American Statesman* (Lawrence: University Press of Kansas, 1994);

John J. Reardon, *Edmund Randolph: A Biography* (New York: Macmillan, 1975).

— Dirk Voss

Randolph, John (1773–1833)

John Randolph was an independent-minded member of the DEMOCRATIC-REPUBLICAN PARTY. He was born on June 2, 1773, in Prince George County, Virginia. His formal education was sporadic, including stints at Princeton, Columbia, and William and Mary, none of which produced a completed degree. With the death of his mother in 1787 and his brothers in the 1790s (Randolph's father died in 1775), he settled down to manage the family estate. By 1799 he entered politics as a Democratic-Republican and a supporter of THOMAS JEFFERSON.

With Jefferson's election in 1800, Randolph exercised considerable power in Congress, serving as chair of the important Ways and Means Committee. He set aside his growing concern over centralized federal power to help Jefferson accomplish the LOUISIANA PURCHASE (1803).

Randolph believed in a strict-constructionist, STATE'S RIGHTS interpretation of the Constitution. He distrusted the modernizing democracy of early-19th-century America, a view he expressed succinctly when he said, "I am an aristocrat. . . . I love liberty; I hate equality." Randolph's political inflexibility would characterize his political career. Paradoxically, he grew to oppose Jefferson the man while espousing what he believed were the true, and betrayed, Jeffersonian principles.

Yet Randolph did not limit his opposition to Jefferson. He challenged JAMES MADISON and James Monroe even as he attacked the FEDERALIST PARTY. Speaking before Congress in 1806, Randolph declared himself a *tertium quid,* which is to say someone who cannot be defined. He led a failed attempt to impeach Justice SAMUEL CHASE, and the bungled case caused lasting damage to Randolph's reputation. He also opposed the Democratic-Republican administration's position on the YAZOO CLAIMS and the purchase of FLORIDA.

Randolph had been plagued by health problems his whole life, but in his later years heavy drinking and opium use accelerated the physical decline. He died on May 24, 1833. Even in death, Randolph proved defiant of convention. He was buried facing west, purportedly so he could "keep an eye on Henry Clay."

Further reading: Robert Dawidoff, *The Education of John Randolph* (New York: W. W. Norton, 1979).

— Jay R. Dew

Red Jacket (Sagoyewatha) (ca. 1750–1830)

After the REVOLUTIONARY WAR (1775–83), Red Jacket led the diplomatic struggle to keep the young American republic from swallowing all of the IROQUOIS territory. His arguments for resisting the ever-increasing pressure of the settlers were heard in numerous tribal conferences at the close of the 18th century.

Red Jacket first appeared in historical records as a courier for the British during the Revolutionary War. A British officer took a liking to the young man and gave him a red coat as a gift. Through the years, Sagoyewatha acquired similar coats and made them his trademark. He defended his homeland against the CONTINENTAL ARMY led by General JOHN SULLIVAN in 1779. There is little information to distinguish him as a warrior. Indeed, Red Jacket said that he considered himself an orator and not much of a fighter. He was reputed to be physically weak.

After the war, the state of New York was anxious to exert its authority over the western counties that made up the Iroquois Nation. Massachusetts claimed this same region as its own. Without a strong central government to resolve the disputes, New Yorkers decided the best way to solve the problem was to "extinguish" the NATIVE AMERICANS' property rights there.

The TREATY OF FORT STANWIX (1784) was the first of the agreements that whittled down the Iroquois holdings. Many of the Six Nations fled to CANADA, where the British gave them land. Red Jacket wanted to stay in his own country and did not want to sell any of it to the whites. He spoke out at Fort Stanwix and later at Buffalo Creek (1788) and Genesco (1797). At each of these conferences he tried to persuade the Iroquois not to part with any more land. Each time he lost.

Red Jacket thought that the Iroquois should protect their homes by force. He wanted the Six Nations to join the Miami confederacy and defended his views at the multi-tribal gathering at Au Glaize in 1792. CORNPLANTER, another Iroquois leader, thwarted his efforts. The Miami confederation suffered a catastrophic defeat at the BATTLE OF FALLEN TIMBERS (August 20, 1794) and soon broke up. Cornplanter and Red Jacket argued at several more council fires over the fate of the Iroquois land. Red Jacket always refused to sell more land. Cornplanter, on the other hand, believed that the Iroquois needed to face what he thought was the inevitable, arguing that the Iroquois needed to get the best deal they could while they were still strong.

By the War of 1812 (1812–15), the Iroquois had only a tiny reservation in New York State out of what had once been a vast empire. Red Jacket was too old to fight. He also now wanted to see the Americans win against the British and helped to raise Iroquois warriors to fight for the United States. His efforts enabled the Americans to win the Battle of the Chippewa (July 5, 1814). The government made him a lieutenant and awarded him a pension.

Red Jacket. Painting by Charles Bird King *(Library of Congress)*

Further reading: Anthony F. C. Wallace, *The Death and Rebirth of the Seneca* (New York: Knopf, 1969).

— George Milne

religion

Between 1750 and 1820, religion in what became the United States underwent a great transformation in the wake of the AMERICAN REVOLUTION. The Revolution freed Americans to make their own decisions concerning religious affiliation. For many ordinary people, this freedom was novel and exciting. In response, ministers learned to use new persuasive techniques to convince people to join their churches. This combination of freedom and persuasion proved very effective, and by 1820 more Americans had joined churches than ever before.

During the colonial period, religious diversity differed greatly from colony to colony. The middle colonies—Pennsylvania, New York, and New Jersey—were the most diverse. In each of these colonies, Presbyterians, BAPTISTS, Anglicans, and QUAKERS shared the stage with various other religious and ethnic groups, the most notable being German pietists. The southern colonies were also diverse, but less so. The Anglican Church was publicly supported, but Virginia's Anglicans were increasingly threatened by the growth of active Presbyterian and Baptist populations. Moreover, southern colonies had fewer religious institutions than their counterparts in the North. In New England, the Congregational Church remained supported by local taxes. Most churchgoers belonged to the Congregational Church, although there were significant populations of Quakers and Baptists.

In the middle of the 18th century, a revival now known as the First Great Awakening divided churches between New and Old Light congregations. These divisions affected Calvinist churches most deeply and were inspired in part by the English preacher George Whitefield. Whitefield first came to America in 1739 and introduced a more enthusiastic form of religion, gathering people into large groups and using emotional language to convince them to accept their dependence upon God. Similarly, Gilbert Tennent, a famous Presbyterian New Light minister, warned against the "danger of an unconverted ministry" in his 1740 sermon of the same name. Tennent believed that many Calvinist ministers were more interested in worldly ends than in bringing salvation to ordinary people. Despite their divisions, both New and Old Light churches remained committed to the central tenets of Calvinism, including

Many battle flags of the American Revolution carried religious inscriptions. *(Library of Congress)*

predestination and salvation by God's irresistible grace. As Tennent suggested, New Lights hoped to reinvigorate Calvinism by purifying it from any worldly influence.

Historians have sought to connect the divisions caused by the Great Awakening to the American Revolution. The causal relationship between the two events, however, remains uncertain. For starters, many of the founding fathers were more concerned with the political ideas of the Enlightenment than with religion, and some, such as THOMAS JEFFERSON and JOHN ADAMS, leaned toward DEISM. The Constitution itself makes no mention of God, except in the First Amendment. The First Amendment, however, was added to appease the Constitution's opponents, who worried that Congress might threaten RELIGIOUS LIBERTY. Moreover, it is important to note that the First Amendment applied only to Congress's powers over religion, not to the states. (Seven states maintained some aid to religion when the First Amendment was ratified.) On the other hand, New England ministers were central to securing popular support of the revolutionary cause. Most Americans, after all, organized their beliefs according to religion and not the Enlightenment. Many ministers worried that efforts to expand the Church of England (Anglicanism) in New England threatened their religious autonomy. For these ministers, Anglicanism was as serious a threat as the political machinations of king and Parliament. The revolution took its toll on Anglicanism even in strongholds like Virginia. Although most elite Virginians remained members of the Anglican church, the Revolution provided an opportunity for Baptists and other dissenters to vocalize their hostilities toward paying church taxes. Moreover, many Anglican ministers remained loyal to England and fled during the war. These two forces combined created a vacuum that new religious movements would fill.

Following the REVOLUTIONARY WAR (1775–83), each state guaranteed religious liberty to its citizens. In doing so, they cleared the space for the dramatic growth of new sects such as Baptists, METHODISTS, and Universalists, none of which had been major forces during the colonial period. In the absence of state support, religions developed the organizational structures that we now associate with denominationalism, including central committees and independent colleges. Denominationalism was a uniquely American invention, allowing each religious community to support its own institutions independent of the state. Moreover, the development of denominations enabled each religious group to control its own population across the extended space of an expanding America.

In the immediate postrevolutionary years, however, Methodists and Baptists benefited less from their nascent denominational structures than from their status as outsiders. Baptists were actually the least denominationally inclined of the primary religious sects. They strongly believed that each church should be locally governed. This localism was a great asset to democratic-minded Americans seeking to wrest control of their religious lives from established authorities. Methodism, on the other hand, was more centrally organized, but its theology embraced many aspects of popular religion, including supernaturalism and enthusiasm. Methodism's success had much to do with its openness to the religious beliefs of ordinary people. In addition, the educational and social backgrounds of Methodist, Baptist, and Universalist ministers were often much closer to those of ordinary people than the well-educated Presbyterians, Congregationalists, and Anglicans. By the middle of the 19th century, Methodists and Baptists would become the largest Protestant denominations in the country. In 1780 there were 400 Baptist and about 50 Methodist congregations; by 1820 Baptists and Methodists had about 2,700 congregations each. After 1820 these numbers would rise even faster.

In the South, Methodists welcomed free and enslaved AFRICAN AMERICANS to join their churches, making great inroads among this group in the postrevolutionary decades. Nonetheless, many white Methodists remained uncomfortable with the intermingling of races in worship, especially when African Americans brought their own spiritual traditions into Methodist churches. In 1816 African Americans established their own church, the African Methodist Episcopal Church. In part, the success of Methodists among black Americans was due to parallels between Methodist enthusiasm and African-American spiritual traditions. The Christianizing of the South's African-American population during this period was an important development in the larger history of American religion.

In the West, the ramifications of the Revolution can be seen most clearly. Following the Revolutionary War, thousands of settlers moved from the East into western New York, Vermont, and the Ohio Valley. While many brought their religious beliefs with them, the lack of existing institutions or a legal establishment made settlers open game for Congregationalists, Presbyterians, Methodists, Baptists, and other denominations competing for members. The result was a veritable battle for converts. Denominations established missionary societies in the East to send ministers and money to the FRONTIER. The battle for the West spurred denominations to organize more effectively, giving shape to the diverse, voluntary character of American religion.

The most successful western preachers employed emotional language and hosted large revivals during which many anxious souls could be converted. This Second Great Awakening created great outbursts of religiosity that churches and VOLUNTARY ASSOCIATIONS channeled into

denominational growth. The most famous Methodist revival took place in August 1801 in Cane Ridge, Kentucky. Over 10,000 persons were converted during a span of six intense days. To conservative eastern Presbyterians and Congregationalists, revivals posed a serious threat to Calvinism. Calvinists struggled to hold on to their predestinarian creed, arguing that western enthusiasts confused intensity of experience with the presence of divine grace. New Englanders, especially, debated the role of individuals in bringing about their own salvation, continuing conflicts that emerged during the First Great Awakening. Methodists understood, however, that on the frontier, individuals were in charge of their own religious choices. In the absence of an establishment, people would no longer defer to clerical authority. Despite their initial resistance, most Presbyterians and Congregationalists, such as the theologian Nathaniel Taylor, came to accept a greater role for the individual.

The combination of revivals, the growth of new denominations, and the desire of ordinary Americans to choose which church they joined resulted in tremendous growth for religious institutions. By 1820 Americans founded and attended more churches than ever before in their history. Success, however, led to millennial thinking. People started to believe that America was paving the way for the second coming of Christ. Protestants established bible, tract, and missionary societies to spread the gospel to all Americans. Millennial beliefs allowed Americans to conflate the purposes of the nation and of Protestantism. The tendency to combine religious and national identity led to deep conflicts over who belonged to a Christian America. To many in the North, the continuation of SLAVERY in the South was a gross violation of church doctrine. Northern Protestants also worried that CATHOLICS immigrating from Ireland would threaten their millennial hopes. In the early 19th century, anti-Catholicism was a central element of American Protestantism. In time, the belief that America was God's nation would legitimate America's imperial expansion across the continent.

See also EDUCATION.

Further reading: Jon Butler, *Awash in a Sea of Faith: Christianizing the American People* (Cambridge, Mass.: Harvard University Press, 1990); Sylvia R. Frey and Betty Wood, *Come Shouting to Zion: African American Protestantism in the American South and British Caribbean to 1830* (Chapel Hill: University of North Carolina Press, 1988); Nathan Hatch, *Democratization of American Christianity* (New Haven, Conn.: Yale University Press, 1989); William McLoughlin, *Revivals, Awakenings, and Reform* (Chicago: University of Chicago Press, 1978).

— Johann Neem

religious liberty

Since the Glorious Revolution in 1688–89, all Britons had been guaranteed religious liberty. Religious liberty in the 17th century, however, meant something very different than it did after the AMERICAN REVOLUTION, or today. For the most part, the goal of religious liberty was to limit social conflict. In Britain and in the colonies, office-holding could still be denied to persons of different faiths, most notably CATHOLICS and JEWS. Moreover, an established church was not seen as a violation of religious liberty. In England, the king and queen remained the heads of the Anglican Church. Similar institutions existed in America as well. In New England, each colony had a tax-supported church. In the South, the Anglican Church was also publicly supported. The only area in the British Empire that embraced religious diversity during the colonial era was the middle Atlantic. With the exception of the region surrounding New York City, neither New York, New Jersey, nor Pennsylvania had a state-sponsored church. Pennsylvania's founder, William Penn, was a QUAKER who believed strongly in the separation of church and state. Even more important, all three colonies had extremely diverse religious populations, including Quakers, Presbyterians, Lutherans, and Anglicans. New York had been settled originally by the Dutch, and Dutch Protestant churches remained prominent. On the eve of the REVOLUTIONARY WAR (1775–83), one-third of Pennsylvania's population was composed of German immigrants. In such an environment, it was impossible to establish any particular RELIGION.

Despite this diversity, residents of the middle colonies did not share our modern notion of religious liberty. Although they accepted religious diversity, most churchgoers never exercised choice about their religious affiliations. Instead, people were usually born into a church and belonged to it for the rest of their lives. Their notion of RELIGION was similar to the way we think about ethnicity today. The one major exception was the divisions inspired by the First Great Awakening in the middle of the 18th century. During the Great Awakening, churches split over doctrine and preaching styles. Many dissenters established their own churches. But the Great Awakening was deeply divisive because most churchgoers did not believe that ordinary individuals should be allowed to form their own churches. Instead, they considered the splitting of congregations abhorrent, and many divided churches strove to re-create unity.

The ways in which Americans thought about religious liberty were deeply affected by the Revolution. In Virginia, BAPTISTS, Presbyterians, and others were frustrated by the Anglican Church's official monopoly, and they supported disestablishment. THOMAS JEFFERSON actively feared the ministry, believing that ministers used religion to pursue their own interests over those of the people. Jefferson wrote the now-famous "Statute of Religious Freedom," passed in 1786 by the Virginia legislature. In the statute, Jefferson proclaimed that the state ought to play no part in religious affairs. Jefferson's goal was to free the state from religion, but for most ordinary Virginians, the statute enabled them to choose their own religious affiliations. Jefferson's statute, then, did not accomplish Jefferson's goals. Rather than diluting the role of religion in public life, the statute allowed ordinary people to become more active in their own religious destinies, and thus to strengthen the place of religion in the public sphere.

In New England, disestablishment was not as easily won. In Connecticut, Massachusetts, and New Hampshire, the clergy of the Congregational Church joined ranks with the FEDERALIST PARTY to maintain the establishment. Outsiders, such as Baptists, Universalists, and METHODISTS, had to struggle to earn legal recognition of their own churches. After 1800 these dissenters joined the DEMOCRATIC-REPUBLICAN PARTY (Jeffersonians) to challenge the Federalist-Congregational alliance. In 1811 in Massachusetts, Jeffersonians passed the Religious Freedom Act, granting all churches the same rights and seriously undermining the established church. In New Hampshire, Jeffersonians ended public support of religion in 1819. In Connecticut, conflict between the established ministry and Democratic-Republican dissenters was particularly intense. Connecticut's ministers struggled to retain control of the state's religious life, but they were eventually outnumbered by dissenters and, in 1818, the church was disestablished.

The First Amendment of the United States Constitution did not end state-supported religion in the United States. Instead, it eased fears among ANTI-FEDERALISTS that the new federal government would use its power to favor one religion over another at the national level. The establishment clause specifically prevented Congress from interfering with religious affairs, but it applied solely to Congress and not to the states. As seen above, most New England states maintained tax support for the Congregational Church well into the 19th century. While today we think of the First Amendment as protecting us from any state or federal support of religion, in the early republican era it also protected the rights of states to support the church of their choice.

The battle over disestablishment concerned the role of religion in society. To Federalists, the established church was the most effective means of providing all citizens with moral EDUCATION. Federalists feared that without an established church, citizens would lack the virtue necessary to live in a free society. Jeffersonians, joined by Baptists and other dissenters, suggested that voluntary religion was more effective at gaining adherents and teaching morality. Few Democratic-Republicans in New England accepted

The first prayer in Congress illustrates the complex relationship of religion and government in the United States. *(Billy Graham Center Museum)*

Jefferson's assertion that religion was a threat to the state. Instead, they believed that people were more inclined to support religion when they did so of their own free will. According to a delegate to Massachusetts's 1820 constitutional convention, religion would "be best promoted, by recognizing the inalienable right of every man to render that worship in the mode most consistent with the dictates of his own conscience." Disestablishment in New England, unlike in Virginia, was intended to increase the effectiveness of churches while accommodating the right and desire of people to choose their own religious affiliations.

By the second decade of the 19th century, most Americans faced new choices in their religious lives. Competing denominations arose in the place of the establishment, each with its own theology and its own benefits. With the growth of Baptists, Methodists, and other denominations, all of the United States became as diverse as the middle Atlantic. In all states, choice became the defining essence of religious liberty. No longer could a denomination take itself for granted; instead, each would have to struggle continuously to gain new adherents. Religious liberty did not

lead to the demise of religion in American life, but it made religious affiliations purely voluntary.

See also RELIGION.

Further reading: Christine Heyrman, *Southern Cross: The Beginnings of the Bible Belt* (Chapel Hill: University of North Carolina Press, 1997); William G. McLoughlin, *New England Dissent, 1680–1833: The Baptists and the Separation of Church and State,* 2 vols. (Cambridge, Mass.: Harvard University Press, 1971); Richard W. Pointer, *Protestant Pluralism and the New York Experience: A Study of Eighteenth-Century Religious Diversity* (Bloomington: Indiana University Press, 1988).

— Johann Neem

republicanism

"Republicanism" is the word historians use to describe the ideology of the American revolutionaries. The term derives from the Latin phrase *res publica*, which means the public thing or the commonwealth. Today we define a republic as any form of representative government. In the 18th century, at least before the independence of the United States, a republic could be any government for the common good. It was thus possible to have a monarchy that, since the king was guardian of the public good, was a republic. From this perspective the ideal form of government was one in which there was a balance among various elements in society: the one (monarch), the few (aristocrats), and the many (the demos, or the people). In theory the English government of the 18th century could be considered a republic because the king represented one element of society (monarchy), the House of Lords another (aristocracy), and the House of Commons the third (democracy). Of course this theory did not reflect the reality of English politics. The House of Commons was packed with aristocrats, but not nobility; the House of Lords was not that important; and government operated on a series of compromises between the Commons and the king that were worked out after the Glorious Revolution (1688–89). Many colonists believed that their own colonial governments mirrored this balance, with the governor representing the monarchy, the council representing the aristocracy, and the lower house representing the demos. But, as in England, this ideal was a pale reflection of reality.

Whatever the reality, the theory held that the balance between these various elements ensured that no one element would become corrupt and take away the liberty of the people. A corrupt monarchy would be despotism; a corrupt aristocracy would be an oligarchy; and a corrupt democracy would be a mobocracy and would lead to anarchy. Each of the corrupt forms would threaten the sanctity of property, which was closely connected in 18th-century minds to liberty.

Beyond balancing these various elements, a republic depended on the virtue of each element of society. Virtue in the 18th century could be defined as a willingness to put aside your interests for the public good. The opposite of virtue was corruption. In the 18th century, corruption was pursuing your own interests at the expense of the public interest. The best safeguard of a republic was having virtuous individuals at all levels of society. Since the 18th century was a period of intense study of the classics, republican thinkers cited the example of the Roman general Cincinnatus as the virtuous citizen par excellence. Cincinnatus lived in the early years of Roman history, when Rome was a small city-state. He was working in the field when a neighboring state invaded. Knowing his reputation as a great warrior and leader, the people of Rome came to Cincinnatus and asked him to beat back the invaders. Cincinnatus left the plow and, at the head of the Roman army, demolished their opponents. Upon his return the people hailed Cincinnatus and wanted to make him a king. But Cincinnatus put aside the riches and personal glory that the crown would provide—his own interest—and returned to his plow in his field. This image was extremely important to revolutionary Americans, and GEORGE WASHINGTON strove to live up to it.

Republicanism also entailed a cyclical view of history. All nations were seen as organic, that is, they were perceived as having a life cycle. In youth they were strong and vigorous; at maturity they were powerful and wise; and in old age they were decrepit and ready to die. This vision of history was sustained by example from antiquity. Israel, Greece, and Rome all were seen as following this basic cycle. The key, in each instance, was that when a state had become too large and too powerful, it was liable to corruption and the loss of virtue. Edward Gibbon demonstrated this progression in his *Decline and Fall of the Roman Empire* (1776).

The problem for American revolutionaries became determining where they as a society fit into this life cycle. Great Britain could be labeled as on the downswing; having conquered a huge empire, it had passed maturity and was entering its last stages before it collapsed. Colonial America, on the other hand, was a new country, with rigor and youth still before it. One of the arguments for independence held that the colonies should separate from Great Britain before its corrupting influence destroyed the virtue of the American people.

With republican ideas as a starting point, revolutionary Americans sought to establish new state governments, eventually creating the national government of the United States of America with the Constitution of 1787. In the process, many Americans came to believe that a republic could only exist without a king. This idea was best articulated by THOMAS PAINE in *COMMON SENSE* (1776). Paine and others believed that by its very nature, kingship was a corrupting influence and threatened virtue throughout society. Paine also attacked the idea of an aristocracy. Many revolutionaries ended up agreeing with him on this point as well. They argued that aristocrats depended on their title from the king and thus, by their intrinsic nature, were sycophants who pursued their own interests at the expense of the public good. Having rejected dependence upon the king and the aristocracy as a model for balance in government, revolutionaries had to find a new rationale for different branches of government. The idea that the revolutionaries ultimately hit upon, and which was used to defend the creation of the government under the United States Constitution, was that all elements of the government represented the people. The president was thus not akin to the king, who had represented the one; instead, regardless of the fact that he was chosen by the electoral college, he represented the people. Similarly, the Senate did not represent the aristocracy even though they too were not popularly elected under the procedures in the original

Constitution; as a body, the Senate represented the people. Finally, members of the House of Representatives were elected by the people (at least adult white male property holders) and represented the people (and three-fifths of each slave). With this logic underpinning the new form of government, a new understanding of the word *republic* began to emerge, equating it with a representative form of government.

With these changes there also occurred another important shift. Virtue was no longer seen as simply sacrificing one's own personal good for the public good. As Americans adjusted to the new republicanism and a new democratic egalitarian competitive society, virtue came to be seen as working hard for your own good. But since everyone was theoretically on the same playing field and competed as equals, out of this competition, as if guided by some unseen hand, the greater good of all in society would somehow be met. This shift was never complete, and Americans still debate how much restraint should be placed on open competition in the marketplace and in politics.

See also COMMONWEALTHMEN; CONSTITUTIONAL CONVENTION; CONSTITUTIONS, STATE.

Further reading: Bernard Bailyn, *Ideological Origins of the American Revolution* (Cambridge, Mass.: Harvard University Press, 1967, 1992); Gordon S. Wood, *The Radicalism of the American Revolution* (New York: Knopf, 1991).

resistance movement (1764–1775)

Although some colonists objected to the SUGAR ACT (1764), it was during the STAMP ACT (1765) controversy that a pattern of resistance emerged that was repeated, with some variations, in reaction to the TOWNSHEND DUTIES (1767) and the TEA ACT (1773). This resistance usually consisted of three parts. First, members of the colonial elite wrote pamphlets and newspaper articles articulating an ideological position opposed to imperial regulation, grounding their arguments on their understanding of the English constitution and the ideal of English liberty. Second, there was some effort at local and colonial organization through committees or congresses. Thus, in reaction to the Stamp Act, colonists formed the SONS OF LIBERTY to guide opposition, and there was a STAMP ACT CONGRESS (1765) to offer a petition and statement of grievances to the king. Although there were no large intercolonial meetings in response to the Townshend Duties, the Sons of Liberty and other committees organized on a local level and corresponded with each other. Local committees took the lead in the opposition to the Tea Act, but after the COERCIVE ACTS (1774), the FIRST CONTINENTAL CONGRESS (1774) met to coordinate activities. In all three cases opposition leaders called for a nonimportation movement to put economic pressure on Great Britain. Third, there were RIOTS in the street demonstrating against the imperial regulations and expressing some lower-class resentment against wealth. The committees, often recruited from the middle of society, sought to guide and limit the extent of this popular disorder. But without the mob in the street, it would have been impossible to sustain the resistance movement and enforce the resolutions passed by the committees and congresses.

Although from the perspective of July 4, 1776, it appears as if the resistance movement led inevitably to independence, it is important to remember that the process was long (over a decade) and never intended to break the colonies away from Great Britain. Resistance began in the name of English rights and traditions inherited from Great Britain: The arguments in the pamphlets and newspaper articles were all based on a reading of English political thinkers, and the traditions of popular disorder—belief that the people had a right to riot to express their grievances in the street—came from Great Britain. Similarly, the imperial crisis did not escalate with each new measure. Resistance was extremely intense in 1765 and 1766 but was defused by the repeal of the Stamp Act. Colonists had a difficult time speaking with a unified voice in reaction to the Townshend Duties, and opposition never gained the strength it had in 1765–66. The Tea Act itself also did not bring about a strong opposition everywhere. But once Parliament passed the Coercive Acts, many (but not all) colonial Americans felt compelled to resist.

Resistance, however, was not revolution. Few, even in 1774, saw the war on the horizon. Nor did they see independence and the renouncing of King GEORGE III. It would take the course of events at LEXINGTON AND CONCORD (April 19, 1775) and another year of conflict before many Americans were ready for the DECLARATION OF INDEPENDENCE (July 4, 1776). During that year, colonial Americans became a divided people. Some remained loyal to their king. Others were shocked that his majesty would wage war on them. On August 23, 1775, King GEORGE III declared his colonies to be in a state of rebellion and authorized the use of force, and even mercenaries, to put down the rebellion. In January 1776 THOMAS PAINE published his *COMMON SENSE* advocating not just independence but also a whole new social system without a monarchy. In July the SECOND CONTINENTAL CONGRESS declared that the king had sought to destroy American liberty and thereby abrogated the social contract. Only then did independence become an option pursued by many Americans.

See also REPUBLICANISM.

Further reading: Pauline Maier, *From Resistance to Revolution: Colonial Radicals and the Development of American Opposition to Britain, 1765–1776* (New York: Knopf,

1972); Robert Middlekauff, *The Glorious Cause: The American Revolution, 1763–1789* (New York: Oxford University Press, 1982); Edmund S. Morgan and Helen M. Morgan, *The Stamp Act Crisis: Prologue to Revolution* (Chapel Hill: University of North Carolina Press, 1953).

Revere, Paul (1734–1818)

Paul Revere was a skilled silversmith and astute businessman who has become a national icon thanks to Henry Wadsworth Longfellow's patriotic poem "Paul Revere's Ride" (written in 1860). Revere was the son of a French Huguenot immigrant who became a Boston silversmith. Paul Revere continued the family business when his father died, and he gained a reputation throughout the colonies as a master in his craft. Today, his creations are considered among the most outstanding achievements in American decorative arts.

Revere served as a second lieutenant in a failed campaign against the French fortifications on Lake Champlain at the beginning of the French and Indian War (1754–63). Returning to Boston in late 1756, Revere supplemented his family's income by engraving copper plates and dentistry. Revere was also very active in the St. Andrew's Lodge of Freemasons, along with JAMES OTIS and Dr. JOSEPH WARREN. Besides discussing business issues, members of the Lodge also discussed Enlightenment ideas that would later influence their reactions to events in Boston.

Revere joined the opposition to the STAMP ACT (1765), becoming a member of the SONS OF LIBERTY and the

Paul Revere's ride. Painting *(National Archives)*

North End Caucus. Revere also began engraving political cartoons for the *Boston Gazette.* After the BOSTON MASSACRE (March 5, 1770), Revere captured the scene in his engraving "The BLOODY MASSACRE perpetrated in King Street," which fueled colonial resentment. While no one knows if Revere participated directly in the BOSTON TEA PARTY (December 16, 1773), the Boston COMMITTEE OF CORRESPONDENCE sent him to New York bearing news of the incident. In 1774 Revere became the direct link between the Boston Committee of Correspondence and the CONTINENTAL CONGRESS in Philadelphia, transmitting information about the resistance in Massachusetts to the COERCIVE ACTS (1774). Revere not only served as a courier but also gathered intelligence concerning the movement of British troops, including the preparations of General THOMAS GAGE's troops in Boston in mid-April 1775. Dr. Joseph Warren commissioned Revere to warn SAMUEL ADAMS and JOHN HANCOCK in Lexington and others protecting the munitions in Concord, if the British troops left Boston. On the evening of April 18, spies observed British troops on the road to Concord, and Revere set out for Lexington. After warning Adams and Hancock, Revere and another rider, William Dawes, were intercepted by British officers. Dr. Samuel Prescott carried the warning on to Concord, and Revere, released by the British, returned to Lexington to retrieve Hancock's trunk full of papers and was there when the BATTLE OF LEXINGTON (April 19, 1775) began.

During the war, Revere served as lieutenant colonel in the Massachusetts militia, commanding the troops defending Castle Island in Boston Harbor. Revere also opened a powder mill where he cast musket balls and cannon for the army, and Congress commissioned him to design and print the first Continental currency and the first official seal. Revere's chances of advancement in the military ended with accusations of insubordination in the failed Penobscot campaign of 1779, although a court-martial acquitted Revere of all charges. Revere returned to Boston and his business interests, which by the end of the war included importation of European goods and a small hardware store. In 1801 Revere opened the first copper-rolling mill in America, which provided the copper sheeting for the hull of the USS *Constitution* and the dome of the Massachusetts State House. Revere turned all his business interests over to his sons and grandsons in 1810 and died in Boston on May 10, 1818.

Further reading: David Hackett Fisher, *Paul Revere's Ride* (New York: Oxford University Press, 1998); Jayne E. Triber, *A True Republican: The Life of Paul Revere* (Amherst, Mass.: University of Massachusetts Press, 1998).

— Heather Clemmer

Revolutionary War (1775–1783)

The Revolutionary War was the military conflict that achieved American independence. It began with the BATTLES OF LEXINGTON AND CONCORD on April 19, 1775, and lasted until the British evacuated New York City on November 25, 1783. The conflict engulfed all of the British mainland colonies and included battles of regular armies numbering into the thousands as well as partisan local warfare of bands of men numbering less than 100. While Americans today often view the war in cut-and-dry terms of the patriots versus the British, the actual conflict was a civil war that pitted one group of Anglo-Americans against another group of Anglo-Americans. For the people who lived through this long contest, the period was marked by difficulties and ambiguities.

Military historian John Shy suggests that the British strategy can be divided into three phases. At first the British believed that they were involved in a police action where their army was to put down a civil disturbance. When the British left Boston for Lexington and Concord on the night of April 18, 1775, they believed that the American rabble could not stand up to trained professional troops. They hoped a strong show of force would throw the colonists into confusion and convince them to obey the law. While this belief was sustained on Lexington Green, where the American forces quickly ran before the military might of the British, it did not hold as true at Concord Bridge or during the British troops' long retreat back to Boston. A similar understanding lay behind the frontal assault at BUNKER HILL on June 17, 1775. Thereafter, the British decided to retrench and engage in a more conventional form of war. They thus withdrew from Boston and sought a more strategic base for operations.

In conventional warfare of the 18th century, according to historian Shy's claims about the second phase of the war, the ideal was to outmaneuver the enemy and minimize casualties. In the 18th century it took time and money to train armies to march under fire, stand a few hundred yards from the enemy, and exchange volleys of musketry. When the British invaded New York in the summer of 1776, they succeeded brilliantly in outmaneuvering General GEORGE WASHINGTON and the CONTINENTAL ARMY. In battle after battle, Washington was forced to retreat, first from LONG ISLAND, then from Manhattan, then from WHITE PLAINS, across the Hudson, and out of New Jersey. The counterpunch that Washington launched at TRENTON AND PRINCETON on December 26, 1776, and January 3, 1777, hurt the British and compelled them to withdraw from most of New Jersey, but it did not change their strategy. The campaign of 1777 was also to be a war of maneuvers. The army under General WILLIAM HOWE may have taken the long route to Philadelphia via the Chesapeake Bay, but the British beat Washington at the BATTLE OF BRANDY-WINE (September 11, 1777) and captured Philadelphia. Unfortunately for the British, their larger strategic aims were not clearly defined. General JOHN BURGOYNE advanced south from CANADA throughout the summer of 1777, hoping to link up with Howe coming from New York City. Efforts of General HENRY CLINTON to do so with a smaller force were too little too late. Burgoyne had to surrender his army at SARATOGA (October 17, 1777), changing the complexion of the war.

With the defeat in Saratoga, and with the French entry into the war on the side of the United States, Great Britain had to reassess its position. This began a third phase of British strategy during the war, one that Shy calls pacification. The idea was for the British army to occupy an area of the southern colonies; solidify support with LOYALISTS; secure the southern colonies; and eventually work its way up to Virginia and the northern colonies. Simultaneously the army would hold onto strategic bases like New York and Newport. The British evacuated Philadelphia and centered an army on New York. In 1778 they captured Savannah. On May 12, 1780, they captured a large Continental force at CHARLESTON and began to move into the backcountry, but they overextended themselves. Although many Loyalists flocked to their cause, they had trouble controlling territory. Moreover, the British suffered serious setbacks at KING'S MOUNTAIN (October 7, 1780), where a large Loyalist force was wiped out, and at COWPENS (January 17, 1781), where Colonel BANASTRE TARLETON was lucky to escape with his life and a handful of soldiers. The commander of the southern army, CHARLES, LORD CORNWALLIS, seeking to punish the Americans for these defeats, pursued a Continental force under General NATHANAEL GREENE through North Carolina, abandoning his supply lines and the strategy of pacification. A pyrrhic victory at GUILFORD COURTHOUSE (March 15, 1781) left Cornwallis in no better position than he had been when he entered North Carolina. Eventually he made his way into Virginia, hoping to join British forces there and to connect with Clinton in New York. Unfortunately for the British, he found himself isolated at YORKTOWN and was forced to surrender to a Franco-American force on October 19, 1781. The war continued for two more years, but no major battles were fought.

Although much of the American strategy was reactive, it had four major components. First, there was an effort to drive the British off of the North American continent. Thus the forces that surrounded Boston in the spring and summer of 1775 hoped to see the British abandon the city and the colonies. In this they were partially successful. The British left Boston for Halifax, Nova Scotia, from which they launched a massive invasion of New York. Likewise, American forces attacked Canada, capturing Montreal on November 13, 1775. The Americans, however failed in

Major Battles of the Revolutionary War, 1775–83

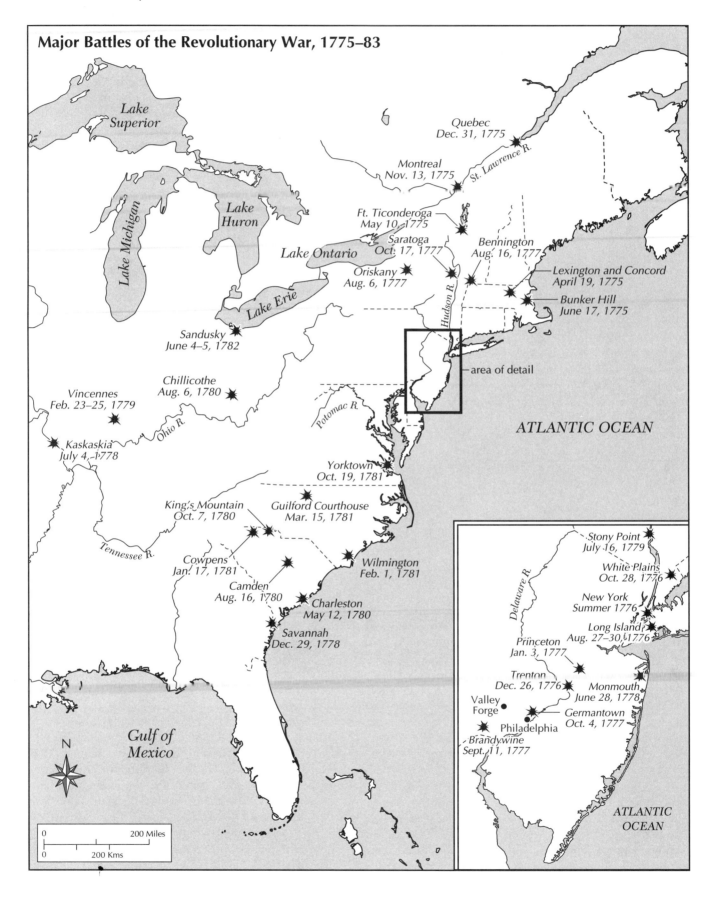

Lake Superior

Lake Michigan

Lake Huron

Lake Ontario

Lake Erie

Quebec
Dec. 31, 1775

Montreal
Nov. 13, 1775

St. Lawrence R.

Ft. Ticonderoga
May 10, 1775

Saratoga
Oct. 17, 1777

Bennington
Aug. 16, 1777

Oriskany
Aug. 6, 1777

Lexington and Concord
April 19, 1775

Bunker Hill
June 17, 1775

Hudson R.

Sandusky
June 4–5, 1782

Chillicothe
Aug. 6, 1780

Vincennes
Feb. 23–25, 1779

area of detail

Ohio R.

Potomac R.

ATLANTIC OCEAN

Kaskaskia
July 4, 1778

Yorktown
Oct. 19, 1781

King's Mountain
Oct. 7, 1780

Guilford Courthouse
Mar. 15, 1781

Tennessee R.

Cowpens
Jan. 17, 1781

Wilmington
Feb. 1, 1781

Camden
Aug. 16, 1780

Charleston
May 12, 1780

Savannah
Dec. 29, 1778

Gulf of
Mexico

N

0   200 Miles
0   200 Kms

Stony Point
July 16, 1779

White Plains
Oct. 28, 1776

Delaware R.

New York
Summer 1776

Long Island
Aug. 27–30, 1776

Princeton
Jan. 3, 1777

Trenton
Dec. 26, 1776

Monmouth
June 28, 1778

Valley
Forge

Germantown
Oct. 4, 1777

Philadelphia

Brandywine
Sept. 11, 1777

ATLANTIC
OCEAN

their assault on QUEBEC during a snowstorm on December 31, 1775. In early spring, the remnants of the American forces retreated back to New York.

After the effort to expel the British from the continent failed, the United States settled down to create a Continental army. The image of the embattled farmer defending his country against the British does not quite fit the reality of the Continental army. What General George Washington wanted was a professional army just like the army that the British had. Washington's genius was less on the battlefield—he lost most of the battles he fought—than in building and maintaining an army. Enlistments lengthened as the war continued, and mainly the poor filled its ranks. But the Continental army gave the new nation a focus and it provided a reason for the existence of a national government. As long as there was a Continental army, there was a United States. By the time the British surrendered at Yorktown, the army had a professional officer corps and well-trained men in the ranks.

The third major component to American strategy was to find allies. Colonial Americans had fought repeated wars against the French. They now sought support from their erstwhile enemy. Almost as soon as the rebellion began, France sent some aid to the colonists, hoping to weaken its longtime nemesis, Great Britain. The victory at Saratoga almost led to peace between Great Britain and the colonies, convincing the French to join the conflict. This alliance was crucial to American success. Without a French fleet off the Virginia capes, Cornwallis would have escaped the trap of Yorktown. Moreover, half the troops surrounding Cornwallis were French. The French supplied money, weapons, and uniforms throughout the war. American privateers and warships used French ports as bases. And the French extended the conflict to the WEST INDIES and beyond. The French also helped to bring in other allies, like the Spanish and the Dutch.

The fourth component of the American strategy involved the militia. These volunteer units were notoriously unreliable in battle. When confronted by the bright red uniforms of the British and the steel of their bayonets, the militia usually ran, exposing the flank of the Continental regulars. But the militia helped to win the war. At crucial times during the conflict, the militia filled the ranks of the army. Many of the men at Saratoga were militia. Similarly, in the guerrilla warfare that spread in the wake of the British invasion of the South, the militia played an important role. But perhaps the most significant contribution of the militia was local. Organized by committees of safety, in community after community, the militia were the means by which individuals were compelled to join the cause of independence. There was no better litmus test to measure the loyalty of an individual than to see if he showed up at the militia muster. If he did not come to the monthly drill, local leaders labeled him a Tory and declared him in opposition to Congress. Fines were then levied, and sometimes nonmilitia members were imprisoned and their property confiscated. This type of coercion helped to solidify support and raise money to fight the conflict. There were also some Loyalist militias. But by definition, the Tories relied on a regularly functioning government. During the revolution, that government broke down. In its place came the committees and WHIG (patriot) militia.

The Revolutionary War was sometimes a messy conflict. Armies marched across whole colonies, and regardless of allegiances, property might be seized by hungry soldiers. There were also zones between the camps of the contending forces where no law seemed to be in force. Similarly, the war saw neighbors fighting against each other and families divided. Local battles might be fought between contending groups of militias. Even if there were no invading army or battle fought locally, there was a constant drain of supplies and manpower. Continental currency was highly inflationary and TRADE was often disrupted. While some men joined the army for ideological reasons—either supporting independence or opposing it—others were mainly concerned with the recruitment bounty. Men switched sides during the war. They also deserted, leaving the army to return to their farms or civilian occupations. They would also desert to sign aboard a PRIVATEER—either American or British—hoping to make money in legalized piracy. While some men struck it rich, others were less fortunate. More than 10,000 Americans were captured at sea and imprisoned by the British. In this long drawn-out conflict, high-sounding ideas sometimes evaporated in the face of harsh realities.

The war took its toll among women as well as men. Often left behind when the men went off to fight, women had to expand their already extensive household duties to run farms and businesses. Some women joined the army as CAMP FOLLOWERS. It was their job to nurse the wounded, cook the food, and wash the clothes. Both the British and Continental armies included such women in their regimental account books. Whatever their sacrifices during the conflict, the men who created the new American government continued to exclude women from the political process.

Further reading: Francis D. Cogliano, *Revolutionary America, 1763–1815: A Political History* (London: Routledge, 2000); Don Higginbotham, *The War of American Independence: Military Attitudes, Policies, and Practices, 1763–1789* (New York: Macmillan, 1971); Robert Middlekauff, *The Glorious Cause: The American Revolution, 1763–1789* (New York: Oxford University Press, 1982); John Shy, *A People Numerous and Armed: Reflections on the Military Struggle for American Independence* (New York: Oxford University Press, 1970).

Rhode Island, Battle of (August 29, 1778)

The Battle of Rhode Island was the culmination of the first major effort of Franco-American cooperation after the FRENCH ALLIANCE (February 6, 1778) had been agreed upon. Despite a promising beginning, a combination of bad luck and misunderstandings almost led to disaster. As it was, the American army that was left behind to attack the British at Newport by itself managed a tactical victory, but it was ultimately forced to lift the siege and withdraw.

The British had occupied Aquidneck Island (the large island in Narragansett Bay sometimes called Rhode Island) almost unopposed on December 7, 1776. Newport, which was on the island, was to be used as a base of operations against New England and afforded one of the best harbors on the continent for the British navy. Until they withdrew from Newport on October 25, 1779, the British maintained a garrison of about 5,000 on the island. For most of this period, the occupation was marked by raid and counter-raid between the American forces on the mainland and the British forces on the island. But in the summer of 1778, when campaigns on the Delaware and in New York Harbor appeared unviable, a major Franco-American effort to dislodge the British was launched.

The plan was for the COMTE D'ESTAING to land the French troops he brought with him and, with his naval superiority, act in concert with a large force of the CONTINENTAL ARMY and New England militia to capture Newport. When the French arrived off Newport on July 29, the American forces were not quite ready. After some discussion, the American commander, General JOHN SULLIVAN, and d'Estaing agreed to a coordinated attack on August 10. But when General John Pigot, the British commander, withdrew from his advanced positions on the northern end of the island, Sullivan decided to move without the French. From a tactical standpoint he had little choice. From a diplomatic point of view, this was taking precedence over the French and injuring Gallic pride. The question became moot, however, when a British fleet arrived from New York on August 9. D'Estaing immediately put out to sea. The two fleets maneuvered for position, but before the battle could be closed a hurricane came up, scattering the ships of both nations. By August 14 the storm had ended. Both fleets were in need of repair. The British returned to New York. D'Estaing, following the advice of his captains, decided he needed to go to Boston to refit. The French sailed for Boston on August 22, leaving Sullivan to face the British alone. To make matters worse, thousands of militia had had enough of the campaign and went home.

Sullivan, enraged by the French withdrawal, had to lift the siege of Newport. He dug in with the remaining 7,000 troops on the northern end of Aquidneck Island. Pigot, sensing an advantage, decided to attack. An intense battle ensued in which the Americans repeatedly smashed the British advances. By the end of the day, the Americans had held their ground, with losses of 30 killed, 137 wounded, and 44 missing to the British losses of 38 killed, 210 wounded, and 44 missing. Both sides were too exhausted to continue the fight. Sullivan, recognizing that he was in danger of being cut off from the mainland by the British navy, successfully removed his troops from the island on the night of August 30. Two days later, 5,000 British reinforcements arrived. Had Pigot waited to attack, this addition might well have crushed Sullivan.

See also REVOLUTIONARY WAR.

riots

Riots were an important part of American society in the second half of the 18th and beginning of the 19th centuries. In the first part of this period, Americans resisted imperial regulation, expressed deep-felt grievances, and sought to manage their community through rioting. By the opening decades of the 19th century, riots increasingly represented divisions within the community. Thus rioting shifted from an almost legitimate activity to an increasingly illegitimate activity from 1750 to 1820.

A riot is a form of collective action taken by 12 or more individuals to effect their will immediately through the use of force, or the threat of the use of force, outside the normal channels of the legal process. A wide variety of types of crowd behavior can be included within this definition of rioting. Parading with an effigy, as was done during many STAMP ACT (1765) disturbances in an effort to threaten and coerce an individual, would be considered a riot. Similarly, the destruction of property, as in the attack on THOMAS HUTCHINSON's house on August 26, 1765, or in the BOSTON TEA PARTY (December 16, 1773), would also be a riot. So, too, would be an attack on an individual or a group of individuals, as occurred in Baltimore in the summer of 1812.

During the 18th century, many Americans believed that they had a legitimate right to riot when official channels of redress of grievances were closed to them or did not respond to their needs. This sense of legitimacy was directly connected to a belief in CORPORATISM—the idea that everyone within society shared a single interest. Ordinarily it was assumed that within the hierarchical structure of society, those on top would paternalistically protect those on the bottom of society. When for some reason this protection did not appear, then the people in the street believed that they had a right, almost a duty, to act in concert to defend the common interest. The crowd would seldom violently attack an individual; instead, it focused its attention on property. The classic case of this type of rioting in England, from where these principles were inherited, concerned the regulation of the price of bread. There was a common belief that there was a just price—one that was fair to both the baker and the purchaser—for bread. If prices rose too high, then the people could riot and compel the distribution or sale of the bread for a just price. This type of riot occurred infrequently in colonial America. However, during the REVOLUTIONARY WAR (1775–83), when goods sometimes became scarce and inflation forced the price of staples beyond the reach of the poor, there were scores of such riots.

Rioting was instrumental to the RESISTANCE MOVEMENT (1764–75). Colonial Americans demonstrated their opposition to the Stamp Act by rioting. Usually these disturbances, raised in the spirit of defending the community against outside intrusion, focused on an object that symbolized the immediate grievance. Thus anti–Stamp Act riots used effigies to intimidate stamp distributors into resigning. When Bostonians wanted to express their opposition to the Tea Act, they destroyed the tea by dumping it into the harbor. Colonial Americans did develop some more painful tactics. Applying a coat of tar and feathers to an individual, a practice begun in Massachusetts seaports in 1767, could inflict some personal harm. But its main intent was to hold the victim up to public ridicule, making him appear more an effigy of the devil than a real person. No one was ever killed by tar and feathers alone.

There were other riots going on in the same period. Most of them fit into the 18th-century pattern of disorder. Opposition to smallpox inoculation in Norfolk (1768 and 1769) and Marblehead (1774) led to disturbances centered on the destruction of property. In Marblehead the crowd broke some windows, burned a boat that transported the inoculated, and pulled down the hospital. Pulling down buildings was a favorite tactic of colonial crowds and occurred frequently in the many LAND RIOTS that took place in what is now Vermont, on Hudson River estates, in New Jersey, and in the Carolinas. These land riots, however, could sometimes turn more violent because they often pitted one segment of the community against another. Fatalities occurred in the WYOMING VALLEY WAR of Pennsylvania, and the regulator movements of the Carolinas (see NORTH CAROLINA REGULATION and SOUTH CAROLINA REGULATION).

Rioting shaded into outright warfare between supporters and opponents of independence during the Revolutionary War. But the community-based riot focusing on property persisted in the postwar years. New York City residents, for example, demonstrated their anger against grave robbing by destroying a hospital in 1788 in the Doctor's Riot; in other incidents, they tore down some bawdy houses in 1793 and 1799. The Shays rebels in 1786–88 limited most of their activity to closing courts and followed patterns of collective action established during the resistance movement. They quickly dispersed once confronted by armed troops representing the state. The

Whiskey rebels in 1794 generally confined themselves to tarring and feathering excise men, although they did engage in one gun battle. They, too, disbanded in the face of government opposition.

While similar disturbances continued to appear after 1800, rioting also began to change. In the democratic world created by the AMERICAN REVOLUTION, many argued that it was no longer necessary for people to riot, since they had a truly representative government and official channels for a redress of grievances. Moreover, with the rise of equality, people were cut off from a sense of dependence upon one another and began to associate more on political, racial, class, and ethnic lines. Along these fissures in society, the potential for personal physical violence grew. In the summer of 1812, as the United States entered a war with Great Britain, a wave of rioting swept over Baltimore that demonstrated this transition. In a riot reminiscent of the 18th century, Baltimore DEMOCRATIC-REPUBLICANS dismantled a FEDERALIST PARTY newspaper office on June 22. The action represented a standard attack on property like the pulling down of a house. Other riots followed that featured ethnic and racial attacks. Finally, on July 27–28, when some Federalists strove to reestablish the newspaper in the city, a bloody conflict ensued that saw the murder of two men and the brutal beating of several more. After 1820 riots increasingly included personal physical violence and fatalities.

See also SHAYS'S REBELLION; WHISKEY REBELLION.

Further reading: Paul A. Gilje, *Rioting in America* (Bloomington: University of Indiana Press, 1996); Paul A. Gilje, *The Road to Mobocracy: Popular Disorder in New York City, 1763–1834* (Chapel Hill: University of North Carolina Press, 1987); Pauline Maier, *From Resistance to Revolution: Colonial Radicals and the Development of American Opposition to Britain, 1765–1776* (New York: Knopf, 1972).

Rittenhouse, David (1732–1796)

Other than BENJAMIN FRANKLIN, David Rittenhouse was the most prominent American scientist in the 18th century. Rittenhouse had little formal education, growing up on a farm in rural Pennsylvania. But he had a natural penchant for mechanics and mathematics, and at an early age began studying on his own and developing his skills as an instrument maker. By the time he was 19 he had constructed a shop on his father's farm and made clocks and mathematical instruments. Starting in the 1750s, Rittenhouse's astronomical and surveying instruments became known as the best available in North America. Rittenhouse constantly strove to improve the mechanics of these instruments and thus became an inventor as well as a highly skilled ARTISAN.

Rittenhouse also put his technical knowledge to use. He was frequently hired as a surveyor; indeed, he was hired to fix the southwest boundary of Pennsylvania. In the 1770s and 1780s he surveyed the boundaries of several states, including New York, New Jersey, and Massachusetts. Rittenhouse also built his own observatory and helped to coordinate the North American observations of the transit of Venus in 1769. He built two orreries—working models of the solar system—one for the College of New Jersey (Princeton) and the other for the College of Philadelphia (University of Pennsylvania). He was granted several honorary degrees and published papers on mathematics and astronomy. Active in the AMERICAN PHILOSOPHICAL SOCIETY (APS) when Franklin died in 1791, Rittenhouse was named the second president of the APS. His fame as an astronomer and mathematician spread across the Atlantic, and he was appointed as a foreign member of the Royal Society of London in 1795.

Rittenhouse supported the AMERICAN REVOLUTION. He had moved to Philadelphia in 1770, where he served as the engineer for Philadelphia's Committee of Safety in 1775 and later was selected its vice president and president. He was also elected to the general assembly and participated in the writing of Pennsylvania's STATE CONSTITUTION in 1776. He was state treasurer from 1779 to 1787. During the REVOLUTIONARY WAR (1775–83) he helped to organize munitions in Philadelphia, even to the point of supervising the exchange of iron for lead in the city's clocks, since the lead was needed for bullets. After the war, he was on the committee that formed the BANK OF THE UNITED STATES. George Washington appointed him director of the United States Mint in 1792.

See also SCIENCE.

Further reading: Brooke Hindle, *David Rittenhouse* (Princeton, N.J.: Princeton University Press, 1964).

Rochambeau, Jean-Baptiste-Donatein de Vimeur, comte de (1725–1817)

Comte de Rochambeau was the commander of the French army in North America during the REVOLUTIONARY WAR (1775–83). Born into the French nobility at Vendome, France, he had already established a successful military career when the fighting in North America broke out, reaching the rank of brigadier general and inspector of the cavalry in 1761. In 1780 he was assigned the command of French land forces in the United States. Rochambeau and his troops arrived in Newport, Rhode Island, in July 1780, where the British navy bottled them up for nearly a year while Rochambeau waited in vain for French naval support. In June 1781, without naval support, he combined his troops with those of American general GEORGE WASH-

INGTON at WHITE PLAINS, New York, and slipped past the British and headed south to YORKTOWN. At Yorktown, the French and American armies—with support from the French navy under Admiral COMTE DE GRASSE—trapped CHARLES, LORD CORNWALLIS and a British army on a peninsula. Cornwallis surrendered on October 19, 1781, effectively ending the war.

Rochambeau stayed in the United States for another year, sailing home in January 1783. King Louis XVI rewarded him handsomely for his efforts in North America by appointing him to the position of commander of Calais. Back in France, Rochambeau supported the FRENCH REVOLUTION (1789–1815) from the outset. He was a successful commander of revolutionary forces—he commanded the northern army—and was made a field marshal in 1791. In time though, he became alarmed at the direction the revolution was taking and retired from his post in July 1792. He was arrested by the government of Maximilian Robespierre during the Reign of Terror, and only Robespierre's fall from power saved him from the guillotine. He was released from prison in 1794 and had his rank and lands restored by NAPOLEON BONAPARTE.

See also FRENCH ALLIANCE.

Further reading: Arnold Whitridge, *Rochambeau* (New York: Macmillan, 1965).

— J. Brett Adams

Ross, Betsy (1752–1836)

A seamstress in Philadelphia during the REVOLUTIONARY WAR (1775–83), Elizabeth "Betsy" Ross is the reputed creator of America's first national flag. Born into a QUAKER family as Elizabeth Griscom, Ross was the eighth child of 16. Apprenticed to a leading upholstery firm, Betsy was 21 when she married a fellow intern, John Ross, an Episcopalian. Because she had married outside her faith, the Society of Friends disowned Ross. The Rosses set up their own upholstery shop on Arch Street, but the partnership ended when a munitions explosion killed John in 1776. Undaunted, Ross kept the business going, applying her skill with a needle and thread to diverse projects. Records indicate she made flags for various naval vessels and, according to family legend, she embroidered ruffles on shirts belonging to General GEORGE WASHINGTON.

It was not until 1870 that word of her most famous commission came to light. At a meeting of the Historical Society of Pennsylvania, William Canby, one of Ross's grandsons, told of a meeting at her shop in June 1776 in which Washington and two members of the CONTINENTAL CONGRESS, ROBERT MORRIS and Colonel George Ross, her late husband's uncle, asked the seamstress to make the first flag for the United States. Ross recommended alterations to Washington's proposed design, and the finished banner incorporated her suggestion of five-pointed stars rather than those with six in the general's sketch. The American public embraced Canby's story, its purported authenticity bolstered by the facts of Ross's occasional employment as a flag maker and her acquaintance with Washington. Though no conclusive evidence has yet proven the validity of Ross's claim to fame, the Arch Street shop nevertheless stands as a shrine to the birthplace of the American flag. Still maintaining her upholstery business, Ross married John Ashburn in 1777 and had two children. Ashburn was captured by the British, however, and died in Old Mill Prison in 1782. A year later, Betsy took her third husband, John Claypoole, who had shared a prison cell with Ashburn. The Claypooles had five daughters. Betsy was widowed again in 1817. She lived in Philadelphia until her death in 1836 and is buried in Mt. Moriah Cemetery.

Further reading: Grace Humphrey, *Women in American History* (Indianapolis, Ind.: Bobbs-Merrill, 1919).

— Rita M. Broyles

Rowson, Susanna Haswell (1762–1824)

Most noted as the author of the best-selling *Charlotte, a Tale of Truth* (1791), Susanna Rowson wrote novels, poetry, and plays, as well as performed on stage. In later life, she operated a school for young females.

Although born in England, she spent much of her youth in Massachusetts. When the REVOLUTIONARY WAR (1775–83) broke out, she had to return to England because her father was a British officer. She remained in Great Britain until 1793, when she moved to the United States. By that time she was married and had become an author and actress. Her sentimental novel about Charlotte Temple, a woman seduced and abandoned by a British officer, was hugely successful in the United States, selling more copies than any other book until Harriet Beecher Stowe's *Uncle Tom's Cabin* (1851–52). Rowson's book was a morality tale that appealed to American sensibilities, demonstrating how a British officer could deceive even a virtuous young woman. Rowson and her husband had turned to the stage in 1792 to earn a living and were recruited to go to the United States and perform. Once in the United States, Rowson not only appeared in Philadelphia, Baltimore, Boston, and Annapolis, but she also wrote plays. She capitalized on American interest with the BARBARY PIRATES in 1795 by writing *Slaves in Algiers,* and she composed poetry with patriotic themes that was recited in THEATERS. In 1797 she decided to leave the stage to set up a school for young ladies in the Boston area. Rowson remained an educator for the rest of her life. She kept her pen active by writing textbooks, poetry, songs, essays, and additional novels.

See also EDUCATION.

Further reading: Cathy N. Davidson, *The Revolution and the Word: The Rise of the Novel in America* (New York: Oxford University Press, 1986).

rural life

Most Americans before 1820 lived in rural settings and worked on farms. While historical events sometimes intruded on this world and there were significant geographical differences, we can make some generalizations about the agrarian experience.

Life in the countryside was dictated by the seasons. This observation is logical when applied to the arena of work: For most of North America, sowing and harvesting follow a set rhythm come spring, summer, and autumn. But it also holds for other aspects of the agrarian world. Marriages usually occurred in March and April, as farmers prepared for the new growing year, or in November and December after harvest and before the darkest winter. Similarly, babies were born most frequently in late winter and early spring, indicating that conception often took place in late spring and early summer. Death and disease could strike at any time, but most deaths occurred in the winter when the weather was colder and nutrition was poorer, the result of a lack of work (thus less income) and a lack of fresh food.

People in the countryside lived in family units. Men married in their mid-20s, women a few years younger. Within a year of the wedding, a couple would likely have their first child and then average another pregnancy every two years. Few families did not experience serious illness and the death of some children. However large their family grew, housing was limited. Only the very wealthy could afford homes with several rooms. Instead, the landscape was littered with "indifferent," "poor and old," and "small and mean" dwellings of one or two rooms. Privacy hardly existed, as space served multiple purposes. In small houses there were no separate bedrooms, living rooms, or kitchens. Often all members of a family shared sleeping quarters. Chamber pots and nearby privies served their "necessary" function. Both the exteriors and the interiors were messy. One English traveler in 1818 wrote that there was "a sort of out-of-doors slovenliness. . . . You see bits of wood, timber, boards, chips, lying about, here and there, and pigs tramping about in a sort of confusion." Inside there was not much furniture—beds, a table and a few chairs—and little in the way of decoration. At night the open fireplace and a candle or two might serve for illumination. In the summertime there was no escape from the heat, and in winter there was only limited comfort from the cold in the fireplace or stove. Dirt was everywhere.

While these generalizations about rural life hold throughout the period and for most white Americans, there were some important variations. Many farm families suffered during war. Those who lived closest to the FRONTIER could experience depredations from NATIVE AMERICANS, but it is also important to remember that Indian warfare was not a constant and that European Americans and NATIVE AMERICANS frequently learned to deal with one another on a daily basis. The REVOLUTIONARY WAR (1775–83) had the most extensive and prolonged impact on people in the countryside. Both British and American military demands for manpower drained labor, leaving women to run the farm and labor in the fields (ordinarily white women worked mainly in the barnyard and household). Since the war sooner or later reached almost every community directly, with raiding militia units or marching armies, farms might suffer destruction, looting, or attacks on individuals—including rape. The QUASI WAR (1798–1800) had little effect on rural life, and the War of 1812 (1812–15) was not as much of a drain on manpower as the Revolutionary War and had a more limited geographical impact.

Regionally, the biggest difference was between the North and South. The northern states had never relied heavily on SLAVERY for LABOR, although some slaves had worked on farms. The emancipation of slaves therefore made little difference on the agrarian scene, except that many rural AFRICAN AMERICANS left the countryside for the city once they were freed. The southern states remained committed to slavery. Not every southerner owned slaves. Many people in the South farmed and lived in the same manner as those in the North. But the presence of slavery in the region provided a whole other standard of living that was lower than the white farmstead—the slave quarter. It also provided examples of affluence to aspire to—the plantation house.

The family farm was never entirely self-sufficient and had always participated in the market to some extent. During the revolutionary and early national periods, profit became even more important. With this development there was also a growing consumerism, first in the northeast and spreading south and west. With increased income from surplus production, people began to replace wooden bowls with porcelain plates, purchase more furniture, and decorate their homes. By 1820 rural Americans had started to notice the dirt and buy brooms.

See also AGRICULTURE; POPULAR CULTURE; POPULATION TRENDS.

Further reading: Allan Kulikoff, *From British Peasants to Colonial American Farmers* (Chapel Hill: University of North Carolina Press, 2000); Jack Larkin, *The Shaping of Everyday Life, 1789–1840* (New York: Harper & Row, 1988).

Rush, Benjamin (1746–1813)

Benjamin Rush exemplified the ideals of the Age of Enlightenment and earned his well-deserved place in history due to his contributions to both SCIENCE and the founding of the United States of America.

Rush was born in Byberry, Pennsylvania, on January 4, 1746, to John and Susanna Rush, and he died in Philadelphia on April 19, 1813. Rush's early education and devout religious views grew together first in a private school and then at the College of New Jersey at Princeton, where he graduated in 1760. Following a six-year medical apprenticeship and formal education in MEDICINE and chemistry, he enrolled in the medical program at the University of Edinburgh. After completing his education at Edinburgh in 1768, Rush investigated the use of chemical reactions in factories in England. Upon his return to America in 1769, Rush was appointed professor of chemistry at the College of Philadelphia. In 1770 he published *Syllabus of a Course of Lectures on Chemistry,* a slim volume of lectures on chemistry presented in a medical context. Rush's appointment as a chemistry professor and his subsequent publications marked the formalization of chemistry as an academic discipline in America.

Throughout Rush's career he taught over 3,000 students in chemistry and medicine, instilling in them a methodology of clinical interpretation of disease. Rush's belief that all diseases stemmed from one cause that could be cured by debilitating methods such as bloodletting and purging, while not unusual in his time, has led to excessive condemnation by historians. During the yellow fever outbreak in Philadelphia in 1793, Rush's cures were feared by some more than the disease itself.

Rush served as surgeon and physician general of the Middle Department of the CONTINENTAL ARMY during the REVOLUTIONARY WAR (1775–83), but he resigned in 1778, believing that his superior mismanaged military hospitals. His superior, however, was supported by General GEORGE WASHINGTON, and this eventually led to Rush's questioning Washington's judgment on many things, including military matters. Rush later regretted his criticism of Washington.

In addition to his work in chemistry and medicine, Rush was considered the father of psychiatry in America. His belief in the connection between the body and the mind led to an unorthodox approach to treating the insane. His lectures and discussions on the operation of the mind, along with his practical experience, culminated in 1812 in his book *Medical Inquiries and Observations Upon the Diseases of the Mind.*

Aside from his medical influence, Rush's political influence in a turbulent era is equally impressive. In 1776 Rush was a member of the CONTINENTAL CONGRESS and a signer of the DECLARATION OF INDEPENDENCE (July 4, 1776). He supported greater education for women, helped found Dickinson College, and served as a trustee for that institution. Rush differed from many politicians of his day in his outspoken opposition to SLAVERY and capital punishment. He also called for both penal and educational reform, the latter in the form of a network of colleges, eventually leading to a national university. President JOHN ADAMS appointed him to the duties of the treasurer of the United States Mint, a post he held until his death in 1813.

Further reading: Nathan G. Goodman, *Benjamin Rush: Physician and Citizen, 1746–1813* (Philadelphia: University of Pennsylvania Press, 1934); David Freeman Hawke, *Benjamin Rush: Revolutionary Gadfly* (Indianapolis, Ind.: Bobbs-Merrill, 1971).

— Susan Jorgenson

S

Sacagawea (Sacajawea) (1790?–1884?)

While only in her teens, Sacagawea saved the LEWIS AND CLARK EXPEDITION (1803–06). Without the horses she helped them obtain, the "Corps of Discovery" under MERIWETHER LEWIS and WILLIAM CLARK would have been unable to cross the Continental Divide and find the headwaters of the Columbia River. Their hope was to find the Shoshone and persuade them to sell ponies to the Americans. The negotiations between Lewis and Clark and that tribe took place in the foothills of the Bitterroot Range in what is now Idaho. The more than 60 Shoshone warriors could have easily overwhelmed the small exploring party and taken more trade goods and rifles than they had ever seen before. The NATIVE AMERICANS were cautious until Sacagawea recognized one of the chiefs as her older brother, Cameahwait. The young woman acted as a translator and secured the horses necessary for the rest of the trip.

Historians have few hard facts about Sacagawea. Most of what we know comes form the records left by Lewis and Clark. The rest of her life is shrouded in legend. Even the date of her death is a mystery. There are some things that historians do know: Sacagawea was a Shoshone born around 1790 somewhere near the source of the Missouri River. At a young age, Hidatsa warriors captured and enslaved her. During this time she learned to speak their language. The Hidatsas ranged the vast length of the Missouri River, trading furs, slaves, and hides with the Mandan for guns and other goods. Toussaint Charbonneau, a trader of French descent, met with a Hidatsa band in a Mandan village in what is now North Dakota. One story says he won her and another Native-American woman in a bet; an alternative version says that he merely bought her. The two married, and in February 1805 she gave birth to Jean Baptiste Charbonneau.

Lewis and Clark wintered in the same village in 1804–05. They thought that the Charbonneaus might help them by acting as translators because Toussaint Charbonneau spoke Hidatsa and French, while Sacagawea was flu-ent in Shoshone and Hidatsa. In April 1805 the couple and their newborn baby accompanied the Corps of Discovery into the interior of the continent that was at that time unknown to the Americans. When she acted as a translator, she interpreted the speeches of her Shoshone kinsmen into Hidatsa, her husband translated the Hidatsa into French, and a French-speaking American officer delivered them in English to Lewis or Clark. It is surprising that such a complex system appears to have worked so well.

The journals left by the two officers mention only one incident in which they asked Sacagawea for help: pointing out which fork of the river to take to reach her people. Scholars believe that she helped at other times and in other ways. When the couple returned to St. Louis, Captain Clark offered their son an education, and the Charbonneaus agreed. They later had a daughter named Lizette. Some sources record Sacagawea's death from fever in 1812, but Shoshone tradition says she lived on the Wind River Reservation until 1884.

Further reading: Stephen E. Ambrose, *Undaunted Courage: Meriwether Lewis, Thomas Jefferson and the Opening of the American West* (New York: Simon & Schuster, 1996); Ella E. Clark and Margot Edmonds Clark, *Sacagawea of the Lewis and Clark Expedition* (Berkeley: University of California Press, 1979).

— George Milne

St. Clair, Arthur (1736–1818)

Arthur St. Clair was an able but not always successful officer in the REVOLUTIONARY WAR (1775–83) who became the first governor of the Northwest Territory. St. Clair was born in Scotland and joined the British forces to fight in CANADA during the French and Indian War (1754–63). He married into the wealthy Boston family of Governor James Bowdoin in 1760. Two year later he resigned form the British army with a commission of a lieutenant and bought a large estate of 1,000 acres in western Pennsylvania. Governor John Penn made him the official agent of the colonial administration on the FRONTIER. As justice of the county court he tried to stay out of the conflicts between Virginia and the Shawnee, thus preventing a NATIVE AMERICAN invasion of Pennsylvania.

Soon after the outbreak of the Revolutionary War, the CONTINENTAL CONGRESS appointed him colonel. He personally raised the best regiment in Pennsylvania in only six weeks. "Be the sacrifice ever so great," he wrote to a friend, "it must be yielded upon the altar of patriotism." His troops arrived in Canada in 1776, just in time to cover the retreat of the American army. In the winter of 1776–77, Congress appointed him brigadier general and he participated in the BATTLES OF TRENTON (December 26, 1776) and PRINCETON (January 3, 1777). In the spring of 1777, now promoted to major general, Congress ordered him to defend FORT TICONDEROGA to prevent any British invasions from the north. When a superior British force marched on Fort Ticonderoga, St. Clair's decision to evacuate the fort created an uproar, since public opinion thought the fort to be impregnable. A court-martial under Benjamin Lincoln exonerated St. Clair, but he was never put in command again. He worked as aide-de-camp to GEORGE WASHINGTON at the BATTLE OF BRANDYWINE (September 11, 1777), organized exchanges of prisoners, and recruited soldiers in Pennsylvania.

After the war, he became Pennsylvania's delegate to the Continental Congress from 1785 to 1787. In his last year of office Congress elected him its president and governor of the Northwest Territory, a position he held for 15 years. As governor, he defended the treaties made in 1784 and 1785 that had deprived the tribes of most of their land. Tribal leaders complained that military compulsion and fraud had coerced them to sign the treaties. In a grand council at Fort Harmar in 1789, St. Clair tried to play the different tribes against each other, but his manipulation backfired and led to war. A small confederated Indian army surprised and defeated the larger American forces under the personal command of St. Clair. Again, a congressional committee and George Washington exonerated St. Clair of any guilt for this humiliating defeat, but his political career began to stall. In the following years, Governor St. Clair tried to prevent the creation of new states in the Northwest Territory. When St. Clair tried to nullify the newly created state of Ohio, President THOMAS JEFFERSON removed him from office in 1802. St. Clair died impoverished in 1818.

Further reading: Frazer E. Wilson, *Arthur St. Clair, Rugged Ruler of the Old Northwest: An Epic of the American Frontier* (1944; reprint, Greenville, Ohio: Windmill Publications 1990).

— Dirk Voss

Sampson, Deborah (1760–1827)

An adventurous young woman from Massachusetts, Deborah Sampson is the only woman who, disguised as a man, officially served as a soldier during the REVOLUTIONARY WAR (1775–83). One of eight children her father abandoned, Sampson was not yet six when her mother began boarding her outside the home. At 10, Sampson became an indentured servant on a Middleborough farm. There she acquired domestic skills, becoming an excellent spinner and weaver. She also tended the garden and livestock; learned to hunt, shoot, and to wield farm implements as adeptly as her master's eight sons; was taught to read and write, a privilege not accorded to all young women at the time.

The Revolutionary War was into its fourth year when Sampson turned 18 and her indentured servitude ended. She taught school for a time but primarily earned her board with various families in the community by spinning and weaving their cloth. As she moved from house to house, Sampson listened to discussions of politics and war, which fanned the desire to participate actively in her country's defense. Not content with a woman's secondary and largely domestic role in the patriarchal society of the 18th century, Sampson resolved to serve in the army as a man. A tall woman for the period—five feet, nine inches—with a sturdy figure and plain features, she acquired men's clothes, bound her breasts, cut her hair, and went to the local TAVERN to enlist. She was accepted as a recruit named Timothy Thayer, but she got drunk afterward and failed to show up for assembly. People questioned the identity of the delinquent soldier, and soon Sampson's hoax was exposed. She claimed she had meant it as a joke.

On her next attempt, Sampson left the familiarity of Middleborough and successfully enlisted at Worcester on May 20, 1782, for a three-year term in the Fourth Massachusetts Regiment of the CONTINENTAL ARMY. She called herself Robert Shurtliff, taking the first and middle names of a dead elder brother. Her compatriots accepted her guise and teased her for being too young to shave. Fearful of discovery, she became adept at tending to her personal hygiene and laundry needs while almost constantly in the company of men. Even when wounded in action, she managed to extract the musket ball from her thigh and dress the wound herself, avoiding the need for a doctor to undress her. Throughout her service, Sampson performed the tasks put to her as Shurtliff and endured every hardship. No one suspected her true sex. Falling victim to a fever epidemic (see DISEASE AND EPIDEMICS) while in Philadelphia in 1783 proved to be her undoing. Trying to check Sampson's heartbeat, a doctor unwound the binding around her breasts and discovered her secret. It was not until after her recovery, however, that her true

An engraving showing Deborah Sampson, disguised as a man, delivering a message to George Washington *(Library of Congress)*

identify was discretely revealed. She had promised her sympathetic Philadelphia physician that, upon returning to her regiment, she would personally deliver his letter to her commanding officer. All who knew Private Shurtliff were amazed to learn the truth, and most applauded Sampson's efforts.

Having served 18 months, Deborah Sampson received an honorable discharge at WEST POINT on October 25, 1783. She returned to Massachusetts and to a woman's life, marrying Benjamin Gannett in 1785 and having three children. A 1797 book of her exploits preceded Sampson-Gannett's 1802–03 lecture tour regarding her service in the Continental army. In 1792 she petitioned Massachusetts for her unpaid wages, and in 1818 the United States Congress for a veteran's pension. She was successful in both cases. When she died in 1827 at age 63, her husband asked Congress to continue his wife's allotment. Though Benjamin Gannet did not live to see it, he was the first man awarded a United States government pension for military service performed by his wife.

See also WOMEN'S RIGHTS AND STATUS.

Further reading: Lucy Freeman and Alma Bond, *America's First Woman Warrior: The Courage of Deborah Sampson* (New York: Paragon House, 1992).

— Rita M. Broyles

San Lorenzo, Treaty of (October 27, 1795)

Sometimes known as the Pinckney Treaty, named for the American negotiator Thomas Pinckney, this agreement in 1795 settled three key issues between Spain and the United States. First, the Spanish agreed to the 31st parallel as the boundary between West FLORIDA and the United States, an issue that had been in dispute since the TREATY OF PARIS (1783) ending the REVOLUTIONARY WAR (1775–83). Second, the Spanish granted Americans free navigation on the Mississippi River. The Spanish had officially prohibited such navigation, but the level of illicit shipping on the river had been growing with the American population west of the Appalachian Mountains. Finally, also in part as a recognition of the inability to stop illegal transfer of goods, the Spanish granted the right of free deposit in New Orleans. This privilege permitted Americans to store goods in New Orleans before shipping without paying customs duties. Although this last provision was for three years only, it allowed for an extension at New Orleans or some other port.

The terms of the treaty were a diplomatic triumph for the United States, granting tremendous advantages without conceding very much. South Carolinian Thomas Pinckney, who had diplomatic experience as minister to Great Britain, was partially responsible for this success. He refused a defensive alliance with Spain as a condition of the treaty. Much of the success, however, was also due to larger geopolitical circumstances. The FRENCH REVOLUTION (1789–1815) had pushed Spain into a costly war and an alliance with Great Britain. In 1795 Spain sought a way out of the war but feared that withdrawal could lead to conflict with the British. With the Senate approval of the JAY'S TREATY (1794), rapprochement between the Americans and British would leave the Spanish exposed in its North American territories of Florida and Louisiana. Spain also began to recognize that it needed the TRADE of the United States to help sustain New Orleans. Finally, Spain realized that the American population expanding into the West provided the Americans with a strength in numbers that it could not begin to match.

See also FOREIGN AFFAIRS.

Saratoga, surrender at (October 17, 1777)

The surrender of General JOHN BURGOYNE's army at Saratoga changed the course of the REVOLUTIONARY WAR (1775–83). It was the first great victory in the war for Americans, and it convinced the French that they had better join the conflict before the British made peace with their rebellious colonists. It also culminated a campaign that had the potential to seriously harm the cause of American independence.

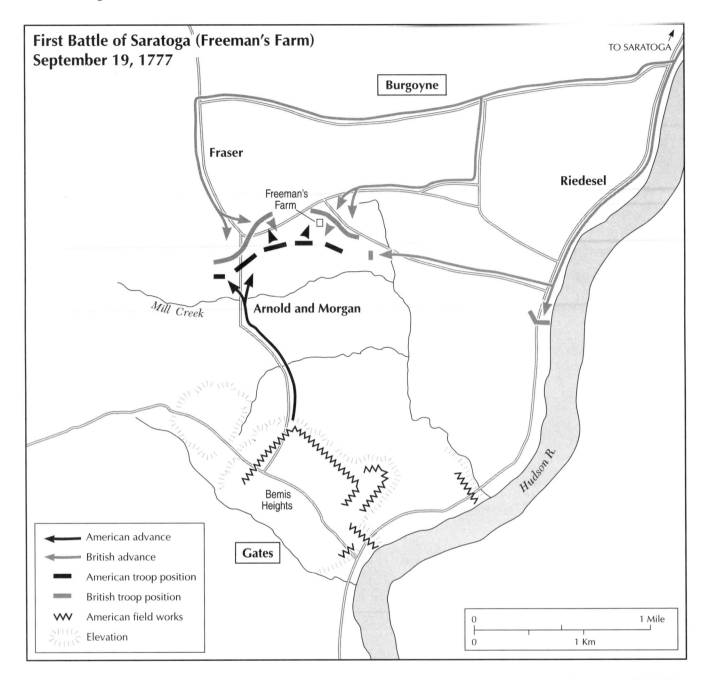

**First Battle of Saratoga (Freeman's Farm)
September 19, 1777**

TO SARATOGA

Burgoyne

Fraser

Riedesel

Freeman's
Farm

Arnold and Morgan

Mill Creek

Hudson R.

Bemis
Heights

Gates

◄━━ American advance

◄━━ British advance

▬▬ American troop position

▬▬ British troop position

WW American field works

)))) Elevation

0		1 Mile
0	1 Km	

Historians have long debated the failure of the British to coordinate their activities in the summer of 1777. As Burgoyne launched an invasion from CANADA, General Sir WILLIAM HOWE headed in the opposite direction, leaving New York City by sea to attack Philadelphia from the Chesapeake. Lieutenant Colonel Barry St. Leger's thrust from the Great Lakes did not have enough punch to be of much help to Burgoyne either. Criticism of the British for not acting in concert misses an important point: When Burgoyne left Canada with a well-trained and well-led army, no one thought he needed help. His force of close to 9,000 men was expected to defeat the Americans.

Burgoyne easily captured FORT TICONDEROGA (July 6, 1777) at the foot of Lake Champlain, and his troops defeated retreating Americans at the Battle of Hubbardton on July 7, 1777. At this point, his army began to get bogged down by the terrain and American delaying tactics of obstructing the road from Lake Champlain to the Hudson River. Had the British immediately after these victories managed to engage the American forces under General

PHILIP SCHUYLER, they might have won the day, since Schuyler had only a few thousand men under his command at the time. But Burgoyne did not reach the Hudson until July 30, and his supplies began to run low. To remedy this deficit, he sent a raiding party into Vermont. That unit was almost wiped out at the Battle of Bennington (August 16, 1777). In the meantime, the American command fell to HORATIO GATES, and reinforcements began to pour into the American lines by the thousands.

Gates decided to dig his troops in on Bemis Heights, south of Saratoga on the west side of the Hudson River. For Burgoyne to advance on Albany, he would have to attack Gates, who now held fortified high ground in the British path. Two battles ensued: The first was the Battle of Freeman's Farm (September 19, 1777). Burgoyne divided his army into three columns and advanced toward the Americans. This might have provided a wonderful opportunity to defeat the British detail, since the columns remained separated for most of the battle. Instead, Gates kept the majority of his troops in their entrenchments, allowing only some of his regiments to advance and meet the British attack. Even so, on the scene of the battle, the Americans out-

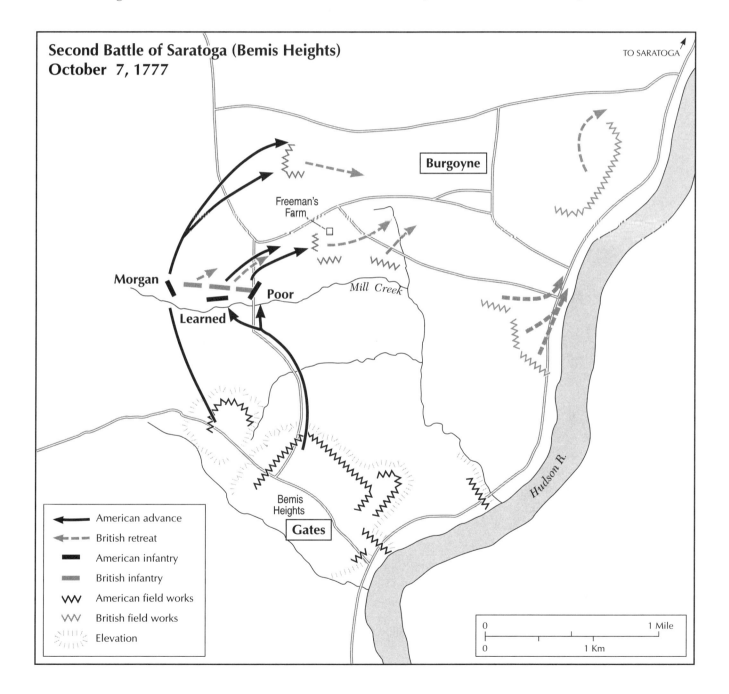

Second Battle of Saratoga (Bemis Heights)
October 7, 1777

TO SARATOGA

Burgoyne

Freeman's Farm

Morgan

Poor

Learned

Mill Creek

Bemis Heights

Gates

Hudson R.

American advance
British retreat
American infantry
British infantry
American field works
British field works
Elevation

0   1 Mile
0   1 Km

numbered the British by a two to one margin. The fighting was intense, with the frontline American units led by DANIEL MORGAN and BENEDICT ARNOLD. In the evening, the column of German mercenaries that had advanced along the Hudson River joined the battle and swept the American right. As a result, the Americans withdrew to the safety of Gate's entrenched position. Exhausted, the British occupied the battlefield they had won at the cost of 600 casualties. The Americans still were in front of them on Bemis Heights.

Burgoyne's position was desperate by the time of the Battle of Bemis Heights (October 7, 1777). He had only about 5,000 men left in his army; the Americans numbered over 10,000. General HENRY CLINTON's expedition up the Hudson had captured some forts below Albany, but he could not relieve Burgoyne. Faced with retreat through hostile territory, followed by a large enemy army, and the possible onslaught of winter, Burgoyne decided that his only hope was to smash the enemy in front of him. He ordered a large reconnaissance force of about 1,500 men to the American right flank. The move was also to cover a foraging party. When Gates saw the movement, he ordered an attack. The British line had been strung out too long, and the Americans drove them back into their own entrenchments. Excited by their victory and led by Benedict Arnold, who had been dismissed from active duty but had joined the battle on his own, the Americans assaulted the British position. This effort soon fell apart and both armies separated. Burgoyne's army was shattered, and he retreated to Saratoga, where he surrendered his entire force on October 17, 1777.

Further reading: Richard M. Ketchum, *Saratoga: Turning Point of America's Revolutionary War* (New York: Holt, 1997); Max M. Mintz, *The Generals at Saratoga: John Burgoyne and Horatio Gates* (New Haven, Conn.: Yale University Press, 1990).

Schuyler, Philip John (1733–1804)

Philip John Schuyler was an accomplished soldier, statesman, and patriot. He first rose to prominence as a member of the Albany city council in 1756. His land holdings and political career grew, securing a place for Schuyler among the provincial gentry.

Credited with distinguished service in the French and Indian War (1754–63), Schuyler was elected in 1768 to the New York colonial assembly. In the revolutionary atmosphere of the 1770s, he was selected to be a delegate to the SECOND CONTINENTAL CONGRESS. In June 1775 GEORGE WASHINGTON named Schuyler one of four major generals, assigning him command of the Northern Department of New York. While planning the campaign of 1775–76 in CANADA, recurring attacks of rheumatism forced Schuyler to delegate operational command to General Richard Montgomery, who went on to capture Montreal. Montgomery's defeat at QUEBEC (December 31, 1775), coupled with the loss of FORT TICONDEROGA (July 6, 1777), discredited Schuyler. He was replaced by HORATIO GATES. Schuyler's personal loss was compounded at SARATOGA (October 17, 1777), where British forces sacked his New York estate before surrendering. Schuyler wanted to clear his name and in October 1778 demanded a court-martial. Although acquitted with honor, Schuyler resigned from the military.

After the war he held a series of public offices, including intermittent service in the New York State Senate and the United States Senate. He advised the FEDERALISTS in their drive to ratify the Constitution and remained a close friend to Washington. Schuyler and his wife, Catharine Van Rensselaer, had 15 children; eight survived childhood, including one daughter who later married ALEXANDER HAMILTON. Schuyler died in 1804.

Further reading: Don R. Gerlach, *Philip Schuyler and the American Revolution in New York, 1733–1777* (Lincoln: University of Nebraska Press, 1964); Don R. Gerlach, *Proud Patriot: Philip Schuyler and the War of Independence, 1775–1783* (Syracuse, N.Y.: Syracuse University Press, 1987).

— Jay R. Dew

science

The expansion of new areas of settlement, the preoccupation with fighting the REVOLUTIONARY WAR (1775–83), and the creation of a new nation left little room for purely theoretical science in America. Practical science—called natural philosophy at the time—became dominant and included biology, botany, invention, and the physical sciences.

There were two kinds of pure scientists in this period: Those who had the money and leisure to pursue their investigations independently, and those who taught at colleges. Because of the religious orientation of most institutions of higher learning before the Revolutionary War, science was not initially an important part of the curriculum. Thus most scientists were independent scholars. After the war, the number of colleges expanded, and science became regularly taught. Despite the addition of science to the curriculum, the universities were still only training undergraduates, not postgraduate scientists.

The pursuit of science also depended upon communicating the results of study. Before the 1760s there were no major scientific societies in America. Therefore, most of the publications by colonial scientists appeared in the *Philosophical Transactions of the Royal Society*, a journal produced by the Royal Society of London. This participation in an English scientific society diminished in the decade preceding the Revolutionary War, due mostly to hostilities but also to the rise of two important American societies. The first appeared in Philadelphia and was called the AMERICAN PHILOSOPHICAL SOCIETY (1769). BENJAMIN FRANKLIN helped to attract scientific interest in the City of Brotherly Love with his experiments and lectures on electricity. The second major society was the American Academy of Arts and Sciences (1780) established in Boston.

Government provided little support for science. A survey of the active scientists of the time and their work illustrates the crucial role that individual men played in the foundations of American science. In the realm of theory, mathematician Robert Adrian independently proved the law of least squares, and Theodore Strong proved Stewart's circle theorem in 1814. Born in colonial America, Benjamin Thompson, Count Rumford, went into exile after the Revolutionary War because of his work as a spy for the British. He was, however, an important physicist whose investigations on heat were the foundation for the modern theory on the mechanical nature of heat.

Most science in this period was not theoretical; instead, it was practical and observable. DAVID RITTENHOUSE was an important Philadelphian astronomer and inventor, proficient in practical and observational astronomy. In 1769 he built the first astronomical telescope in British North America and in 1793 he discovered a comet. Another important astronomer was W. C. Bond, an untrained instrument- and clock-maker who later became the director of Harvard College Observatory. In 1811 he discovered a comet using the telescope he had set up in the parlor of his home. Robert Hare was a professor of chemistry who invented two important tools for chemical analysis: the oxy-hydrogen blowpipe, in 1801, and the deflagrator, a device that created a powerful electric arc, in 1820. In geology, Amos Eaton published his famous work, *Index to the Geology of the Northern States,* in 1818.

Americans were active in botany and zoology. Scientists in Europe were interested in North American flora and fauna for comparative study. In the early colonial period the emphasis was on collecting plants and animals to be shipped back to Europe for study and analysis. In the late colonial and revolutionary periods, American scientists began to do their own study and publish their own collections of data. The foremost American botanist of America was John Bartram, who traveled extensively throughout the East Coast collecting plants and seeds. He exchanged information, as well as specimens, with the many of the leading European botanists of the time. He published two books: one on the area from Lake Ontario to Pennsylvania, in 1751, and one on FLORIDA, in 1766.

David Rittenhouse, a self-educated scientist, designed and constructed clocks and telescopes. Rittenhouse constructed the first working model of the solar system in 1767 and built an observatory to watch the movement of Venus. He succeeded Benjamin Franklin as the president of the American Philosophical Society in 1791. Engraving *(Library of Congress)*

Benjamin Smith Barton, W. P. C. Barton, Jacob Bigelow, Thomas Nuttall, and John Terry all published important botanical works in the early 19th century. The two Bartons were an uncle and nephew who worked as professors at the University of Pennsylvania. Bigelow and Nuttall were both students of Benjamin Smith Barton, and Terry was a doctor who worked as a professor at WEST POINT, Princeton, and Columbia. For zoology, the work of Alexander Wilson was the most important of this time. Born in Scotland, he moved to Philadelphia in 1794. In 1802 he met the son of John Bartram, WILLIAM BARTRAM, who stimulated his interest in ornithology. From 1808 to 1813 he publish the seven volumes of his work *American Ornithology.*

Practical inventors and tinkerers had the greatest impact on American society. While not trained scientists, such men pushed technological innovation in important directions. SAMUEL SLATER left England in 1789 with the blueprints of textile machinery in his head. He built the first successful textile factory in the United States and began the American INDUSTRIAL REVOLUTION. ROBERT

FULTON experimented with the steam engine as a means of driving boats on rivers. His steamboat, the *Clermont*, transformed American communications and transportation within a decade of its first appearance on the Hudson River in 1807. And ELI WHITNEY's cotton gin altered the course of AGRICULTURE in the South and allowed for the establishment of the Cotton Kingdom.

Further reading: Silvio Bedini, *Thinkers and Tinkers: Early American Men of Science* (New York: Scribner's, 1975); John C. Greene, *American Science in the Age of Jefferson* (Ames: Iowa State University Press, 1984); Brooke Hindle, *The Pursuit of Science in Revolutionary America, 1735–1789* (Chapel Hill: University of North Carolina Press, 1956); Raymond P. Stearns, *Science in the British Colonies of America* (Urbana: University of Illinois Press, 1970).

— Susan Jorgenson

Scotch-Irish

More properly called Ulster Scots, these 18th-century immigrants were one of the largest and most important minorities in the British North American colonies. Their hostility to English rule and their antiauthoritarian attitudes made them an important factor in the events of the revolutionary era, especially on the FRONTIER where they were often in the majority.

The Ulster Scots were part of a large migration from Scotland to Northern Ireland in the early 17th century. The English intended to pacify the Irish CATHOLICS of the north by introducing a loyal population of Protestant landowners. They enticed the Presbyterian Scots with land grants and other incentives, but the arrangement was never a satisfactory one. The Scotch-Irish experience in Ireland only served to intensify their hatred of the English. By the 18th century they had become objects of ethnic, religious, and economic discrimination. Irish Catholics hated them, and the Anglo-Irish considered them inferior. As Presbyterians they were religious nonconformists, and laws such as the Test Act of 1704 excluded them from government jobs and attendance at universities. Making matters worse, the British Navigation Acts gave English industries preference over those in Ireland, and unfair taxation further magnified the sense of grievance.

Poor harvests and an economic depression in the early 18th century made conditions unbearable for many Ulster Scots. Beginning around 1717 there was an exodus to the American colonies. This was part of a broader migration of "border Britons," including the Scots, Welsh, Irish, Cornish, and the Scotch-Irish from the periphery of the British Isles to the colonies. Between 1717 and 1775 over 250,000 Scotch-Irish crossed the Atlantic to settle in British North America. At the beginning of the REVOLUTIONARY WAR (1775–83) the Scotch-Irish were roughly 10 percent of the colonial population.

On arriving in the colonies, many Scotch-Irish moved into the backcountry. The move to the frontier was partly the result of POVERTY and the need for cheap land. It also reflected a desire to settle as far away as possible from the English who dominated the coastal areas. By the mid-18th century the Scotch-Irish could be found in the western portions of all 13 colonies. The largest number settled in the lands to the west of Pennsylvania, the Carolinas, and Georgia. By the last quarter of the 18th century they were moving west across the Appalachians.

In many respects the Scotch-Irish were ideal frontierspeople. They were tough people, hardened by years of bad fortune and worse treatment. On the frontier they often lived in isolated settlements and under trying conditions. Celtic tribal values governed these frontier communities. The Scotch-Irish were proud and protective of their honor and took their religion seriously, but drinking and violence were also part of the Scotch-Irish heritage. However, rich traditions of hospitality, MUSIC, and storytelling softened the rigors of frontier life.

Their toughness was sometimes a disadvantage. As settlements moved westward, the Scotch-Irish increasingly came into contact with NATIVE AMERICANS, for whom they had only disdain. The resulting violence threatened settlements and upset trading patterns between the tribes and eastern merchants. This conflict forced colonial governments to bear the expense of sending troops to protect the frontier. Further complicating matters, the backcountry folk were frequently at odds with their own colonial governments concerning issues of unfair taxation and lack of representation.

The years from 1740 to 1765 were full of tension and conflict in the colonies. The Scotch-Irish were often involved in such backcountry disturbances as the Paxton Boys revolt in Pennsylvania (1763) and the regulator movements in the Carolinas (1766–70) (see NORTH CAROLINA REGULATION and SOUTH CAROLINA REGULATION). Many resisted the PROCLAMATION OF 1763, which was intended to limit access to the country west of the Appalachians.

The large Scotch-Irish population guaranteed the importance of Presbyterianism, and when evangelical revivals swept the colonies in the 1730s, the Irish evangelist William Tennant and his sons found a ready harvest among the Scotch-Irish in the middle colonies. This Great Awakening was in many respects a precursor to the AMERICAN REVOLUTION, encouraging sectarianism, individualism, and antiauthoritarianism, attitudes that were common among the Scotch-Irish. Concern that an Anglican bishop would be appointed for the colonies at times drove them to cooperate with QUAKERS and other groups who shared their fear.

During the early national era, the Scotch-Irish continued to be an important factor on the frontier, spearheading westward expansion and playing an increasingly active role in the politics of the new republic. Scotch-Irish culture was particularly influential in the South and the West, where its values formed part of the core of those emerging regional cultures.

Further reading: David Hackett Fischer, *Albion's Seed: Four British Folkways in America* (New York: Oxford University Press, 1989); James Leyburn, *The Scotch-Irish: A Social History* (Chapel Hill: University of North Carolina Press, 1962).

— Robert Lively

Seabury, Samuel (1729–1796)

LOYALIST spokesman and a founder of the Protestant Episcopal Church, Samuel Seabury was born in Groton, Connecticut, on November 30, 1729. He was the son of wealthy parents who encouraged him to pursue an advanced education. Graduating from Yale College in 1748, he became a doctor shortly after studying MEDICINE at the University of Edinburgh between 1752 and 1753 and was ordained in the Anglican Church before returning to New England.

After being made a missionary by the Society for the Propagation of the Gospel, Seabury preached to followers in New Brunswick, New Jersey, between 1753 and 1757. He then moved to Jamaica, New York, to serve as a parish rector. In 1766 he moved yet again, this time to Westchester, New York, where he became a leading figure in the community.

A devout Loyalist, Seabury noted with alarm the drift toward revolution in British North America after 1770. In 1774–75 he wrote pamphlets opposing the formation of the FIRST CONTINENTAL CONGRESS under the name A. W. Farmer, and his activities in support of the Crown eventually led to his arrest and brief imprisonment by supporters of the Revolution. He escaped from prison and fled to New York City and the protection of British forces in 1776, living there for the duration of the REVOLUTIONARY WAR (1775–83) as a doctor, political essayist, and cleric.

Seabury led the Loyalist exodus to Nova Scotia when the war ended in 1783, but his widely admired work in the church spurred Connecticut's Anglican clergy to name him a bishop in spite of his opposition to the creation of the United States. Church officials in England refused to consecrate him for fear of meddling in internal American affairs, but the Scottish Episcopal Church did, and Seabury returned to the United States as the rector of St. James's Church and the Bishop of Connecticut. He quickly organized a diocese centered on New London, and in 1789 he helped form the American Protestant Episcopal Church.

In 1793 he published a collection of sermons entitled *Discourses on Several Subjects,* and in 1798 (two years after his death) supporters revised and added to the collection, publishing it as *Discourses on Several Important Subjects.* Seabury died in New London on February 25, 1796, and left behind a formidable legacy as a defender of New England's High Church.

See also RELIGION.

Further reading: Bruce E. Steiner, *Samuel Seabury, 1729–1796: A Study in the High Church Tradition* (Athens, Ohio: Ohio University Press, 1971).

— Lance Janda

Shakers

The United Society of Believers in Christ's Second Appearing—more commonly known as the Shakers—established religious communities in the United States in the last decades of the 18th century. Members of this millenarian sect practiced celibacy, publicly professed their sins, and engaged in hard labor, in addition to creating a unique style of ARCHITECTURE, furniture, and handicraft that was distinct in its functional simplicity and fine workmanship.

The founder of the American Shakers was ANN LEE, a Manchester-born woman who moved from England to Colonial America in 1774. Lee, known to her followers as Mother Ann, was perceived as the female embodiment of Christ's dual nature. Her early influences derived from the Wardley Society, a radical offshoot of the QUAKERS, which she joined in Manchester in 1758. The members of the Wardley Society distinguished themselves by their unique form of worship, which included shaking, trembling, dancing, shouting, and generally moving their bodies in a chaotic manner, thus earning them the name "Shaking Quakers." Lee led a group of eight across the ocean to North America, landing in New York in 1774. They established a community near Albany, New York, called Niskeyuna (now Watervliet) in 1776, although through revivals and preaching tours their influence extended well beyond their modest community.

The Shaker movement was deeply influenced by the prevalent millennial beliefs of the late 18th century. Many millenarian sects believed that "judgment day" was near and, through their devout faith and practices, they would ultimately be saved. Shakers established celibacy as a principle tenet of their sect; since the end was near, there was no need to procreate. New members came from either conversions or adoptions. Further, Mother Ann believed that sexual relations impeded one's relationship with God. Between their "shaking" ritual and their celibacy, the Shakers were ridiculed and scorned by other religious denominations of the period. However, they garnered admiration from their contemporaries for the order, simplicity, and prosperity of their farming communities. Their labor and ingenuity produced a number of unpatented inventions and led to a distinct design of architecture (usually barns) and furniture. Shakers designed furniture without needless decoration, reflecting their conviction that the appearance of an item should follow its function. Since the process of constructing goods was considered to be an act of prayer, the austerity of Shaker furniture reflected the piety and fine workmanship of its creator.

Mother Ann died in 1784 and, shortly thereafter, elders in the sect structured their followers into a communal pattern that served as the model for Shaker communities throughout the early national period. The first Shaker community, established on this model in 1787, was located at New Lebanon, New York. It served as the center for the Shaker RELIGION as the movement gradually spread to New England, Kentucky, Ohio, and Indiana. The period between 1774 and 1820 represents the building stage for Shakerism in the United States; by 1826 there were 18 Shaker villages in eight states. By the end of the 19th century, membership steadily declined, and today there are very few surviving Shakers.

Further reading: Edward Deming Andrews, *People Called Shakers: A Search for the Perfect Society* (New York: Oxford University Press, 1953); Stephen J. Stein, *The Shaker Experience in America: A History of the United Society of Belivers* (New Haven, Conn.: Yale University Press, 1992).

— Linda English

Shays's Rebellion

In 1786 and 1787 farmers in western Massachusetts, following patterns of crowd behavior practiced in the RESISTANCE MOVEMENT (1764–75), closed courts, freed men imprisoned for debt, and fought with government forces. Daniel Shays, a former revolutionary army captain, led some of this action, and this insurrection became known as Shays's Rebellion. FEDERALISTS cited this uprising, which occurred shortly before the meeting of the CONSTITUTIONAL CONVENTION in Philadelphia in the summer of 1787, as an argument for the creation of a stronger national government.

The postwar years of the 1780s were a period of economic turmoil. When British creditors demanded payment from eastern New England merchants in the mid-1780s, these businessmen had little choice but to shift the burden onto their debtors—those who lived in the countryside. But with low prices for their products and almost no cash, the rural debtors could not meet their obligations. Compounding these difficulties, the government of Massachusetts had

imposed high taxes to pay the state debt from the REVOLUTIONARY WAR (1775–83). This policy to repay the debt favored eastern speculators who had purchased state notes at a discount—often from soldiers and farmers—and now expected the state to pay full value. Pressed by creditors and tax collectors, farmers in western Massachusetts sought tax relief from the legislature, asking to pay their debts with paper money or commodities instead of specie. These pleas were rejected by the upper house, which was more sympathetic to eastern creditors and merchants.

Faced with the threat of losing their property and livelihood to pay taxes and debts, poor farmers in the West formed committees and held conventions to condemn the government, and they began closing courts in the summer and fall of 1786. Many of these men had been in the forefront of the revolutionary movement, having served in the CONTINENTAL ARMY or WHIG militia. They wondered how the government could forget their sacrifices in the name of "liberty." With a force that numbered as high as 2,000 men, the rebels reached a turning point that winter when they tried to capture the arsenal at Springfield, Massachusetts. Fearing a large-scale uprising, nervous eastern merchants contributed money and lobbied state officials to recruit an army to put down the rebellion. The state government ordered 600 men, led by General William Shepard, to Springfield. Confronted by armed rebels under the leadership of Shays on January 25, 1787, a nervous Shepard fired cannon into the crowd, killing four and wounding at least a score of others. Over the next few weeks, the state militia from the East, led by General Benjamin Lincoln, defeated the rebels in several encounters. Daniel Shays and other rebel leaders had to flee the state, first to Rhode Island and finally seeking refuge in Vermont.

While this movement for debtor relief was most intense in Massachusetts, similar actions occurred elsewhere in 1786 and 1787. In New Hampshire, angry farmers surrounded the legislature in the state capital in an effort to have their grievances redressed. Crowds also closed courts in Rhode Island, Maryland, and South Carolina to prevent legal action against debtors. Governor GEORGE CLINTON of New York was so concerned with the spread of the disorder that he ordered the apprehension of any Shaysites who sought to escape to his state. Once the authorities in Massachusetts had regained control in the western part of the state, they were relatively lenient, pardoning all but Shays and three other leaders almost immediately, and then pardoning the rest after they were arrested, tried, and convicted of treason. Ironically, too, the next round of elections swept debt-relief supporters into the legislature, which then passed measures to ease the situation.

Although the rebellion did not seriously threaten the stability of the state or national government, Federalists argued that the Shaysites had exposed a flaw in the structure of the national government. The government under the ARTICLES OF CONFEDERATION had been ineffectual in suppressing the uprising. Similarly, the Federalists claimed that the insurrection revealed the impotence of the national government in dealing with the economic problems. Both positions ignored the fact that the state government had successfully suppressed the rebels and eventually dealt with the economic distress of its citizens. Regardless of the ability of Massachusetts to solve its own difficulties, the aftermath of Shays's Rebellion played a significant role in the framing and ratification of the Constitution.

See also LAND RIOTERS; RIOTS.

Further reading: Robert A. Gross, ed., *In Debt to Daniel Shays: The Bicentennial of an Agrarian Rebellion* (Charlottesville: University Press of Virginia, 1993); David P. Szatmary, *Shays' Rebellion: The Making of an Agrarian Insurrection* (Amherst: University of Massachusetts Press, 1980).

— Jeffrey Davis

Sherman, Roger (1721–1793)

A leading figure in the CONTINENTAL CONGRESS and author of the Connecticut Compromise at the CONSTITUTIONAL CONVENTION, Roger Sherman is perhaps Connecticut's most prominent revolutionary hero. The third of seven children raised by William Sherman and his second wife Mehetabel, he was born in Newton, Massachusetts, on April 19, 1721. Sherman moved to Connecticut when he was a young man and worked as a shoe cobbler and county surveyor before being admitted to the bar in 1754. After he became a lawyer, he then threw himself into colonial politics.

He was elected to the Connecticut general assembly in 1755, served as a justice of the peace for Litchfield County between 1755 and 1761, and then moved to New Haven to become a successful retail merchant. Sherman was a judge in New Haven in 1765–66 and a superior court judge between 1766 and 1789. During those years he became an ardent supporter of independence, attending the Continental Congress from 1774 to 1781, and from 1783 to 1784. He agreed to the cession of Connecticut's western land claims, helped codify Connecticut laws in 1783, and was elected mayor of New Haven in 1784.

Three years later he was one of Connecticut's delegates to the Constitutional Convention, where he proposed the Connecticut Compromise to break a deadlock between large and small states regarding the manner in which congressional seats were apportioned. States with large populations argued for representation based on the number of voters in each state, while states with smaller populations feared political obscurity in such an arrangement and pushed for equal representation for every state. Sherman proposed a bicameral Congress in which representation in the upper house (the Senate) was the same for every state, while in the lower house (the House of Representatives) it was based on population. The compromise appeased parties on all sides and proved one of the key building blocks on which the Constitution was based.

A devout Christian, a committed FEDERALIST, and the father of 15 children via two wives, Sherman was a member of the House of Representatives from 1789 to 1791 and of the Senate from 1791 until his death in 1793. He is famous for having signed each of the key documents associated with the creation of the United States: the Articles of Association (1774), the DECLARATION OF INDEPENDENCE (July 4, 1776), the ARTICLES OF CONFEDERATION (1781), and the Constitution of the United States (1787). No one else signed all four.

Further reading: Christopher Collier, *Roger Sherman's Connecticut: Yankee Politics and the American Revolution* (Middletown, Conn.: Wesleyan University Press, 1971); John G. Rommel, *Connecticut's Yankee Patriot: Roger Sherman* (Hartford, Conn.: American Revolution Bicentennial Commission of Connecticut, 1980).

— Lance Janda

Slater, Samuel (1768–1835)

Samuel Slater was a British immigrant to the United States who developed the first mechanized cotton textile mill in the United States. Slater grew up in Belper, England, and began an apprenticeship to Jedediah Strutt, a local textile mill operator, in 1783. As Strutt's apprentice, Slater learned the mechanics, finance, and labor organization of a typical English textile mill. In 1789 Slater immigrated to the United States. Soon after his arrival, he met Moses Brown and William Almy, two textile entrepreneurs from Providence, Rhode Island. Almy and Brown had attempted to build a textile factory, but they needed the expertise of an experienced mill operator. Slater, Brown, and Almy formed a business partnership for which Brown and Almy would provide funds for Slater to build and run a textile mill in Pawtucket in exchange for a half-share in the venture.

The mill was driven by waterpower and Slater developed a special labor system. By 1792 whole families found employment in the mill, including children aged seven to 12. Slater sometimes ran into opposition from fathers who resented the paternal authority he expressed toward the child workers. These difficulties led Slater to strive to form meaningful partnerships with families and prompted him to allow a high degree of family autonomy in the mills. More significantly, he found himself caught between the profit-driven Almy and Brown and the worker families when conditions deteriorated and pay was too low to feed the children adequately. He tried in vain to convince Almy and Brown to improve conditions and provide more pay. Consequently, the families struck the mill in 1795 and 1796.

The partnership between Almy, Brown, and Slater broke down after a decade, with the two venture capitalists losing faith in the determined Slater. Meanwhile, Slater found other partners in Providence and set about replicating the Pawtucket mill in other New England states, New York, and Pennsylvania. By 1810 approximately 15 mills operated in the northeastern states, with Slater holding financial interest in three. Slater personally put up funds to build more textile mills in New England between 1810 and 1830. Other Slater-style mills appeared; by 1820 there were literally hundreds of mill towns in the Northeast. The Slater mill system also provided a partial model for entrepreneur Francis Cabot Lowell and others who built a large textile operation around Waltham, Massachusetts, beginning in 1813. Lowell and his partners developed an alternative system known as the Waltham or Lowell system, in which girls and young women were recruited to leave their families to work in the mills. Slater's mill operations continued well into the 19th century, under the name Slater and Sons.

See also INDUSTRIAL REVOLUTION.

Further reading: Barbara M. Tucker, *Samuel Slater and the Origins of the American Textile Industry, 1790–1860* (Ithaca, N.Y.: Cornell University Press, 1984).

— James R. Karmel

slavery

Although North American slavery accounted for a relatively small proportion of New World slaves, it assumed increasing importance worldwide during the 19th century. Of the 12–15 million African people forcibly transported to the New World between the 1500s and 1800s, fewer than 1 million became slaves in North America. Still, North American slavery became a focal point of debates over justice and humanity by the time of the American Civil War. In part, this had to do with the paradox of slavery in the world's leading democratic republic; it also stemmed from the increasingly public debates over slavery and abolition (see ANTISLAVERY AND ABOLITION) waged in American politics and social life, debates that dated to the American revolutionary era.

Slavery's roots on American soil date to the early 1600s, when British colonists began importing slaves as laborers. For a century prior to this time, the colonial powers of Portugal and Spain had dominated the international SLAVE TRADE. Nevertheless, from 1619, when a ship landed at Jamestown with 20 "Negroes," through the 1860s, slavery became a definitive part of British colonial and then American culture. North American slave systems diverged from Old World bondage in two ways: First, slavery existed in perpetuity. This meant that all descendants of the enslaved person—usually following the mother's status—were themselves enslaved. The only way to attain freedom was to run away or to be freed by a private manumission (which might require special permission from the colonial legislature). Second, North American slave laws defined bondage in racial terms. In Virginia during the 1660s, new slave laws differentiated between white indentured servitude and black slavery: The former was a temporary status, the latter permanent. By the early 1700s, every American colony sanctioned slavery in such a statutory manner. In short, slavery and race became intertwined in British North America.

Slavery's growth paralleled that of the American colonies. Planters in Virginia and Maryland turned to slave labor to cultivate tobacco during the 1600s. By the time of the REVOLUTIONARY WAR (1775–83), Chesapeake slaveholders held the largest number of slaves in the new nation. Beginning in the early 1700s, South Carolina slaveholders utilized slaves for rice production. Labor needs and racial attitudes combined to make slavery an integral part of colonial American life. In southern colonies, enslaved people often worked on plantations but, particularly in the middle colonies and Delaware, Maryland, and Virginia, they might also work on smaller farms and in urban settings. In Massachusetts and Connecticut, where the overall population of enslaved persons remained relatively small, slaves worked as household servants and did other menial tasks. In New York and Pennsylvania, slaves tilled various crops (wheat and corn, for example) in addition to serving as butlers, drivers, and general laborers.

Slavery was a significant part of the American ECONOMY. Cash crops such as tobacco and rice commanded worldwide markets for American slaveholders, not to mention wealth for colonial merchants and British agents. Slavery also indirectly shaped American enterprise. It has been estimated that one-seventh of the New England shipbuilding business was engaged in the overseas slave trade before 1800. Indeed, in the 1790s Pennsylvania abolitionists tracked dozens of slave-trading voyages from the United States, the majority of which had New England origins.

Slavery grew for both technological and ideological reasons during the early republic. The development of the cotton gin in 1793 rejuvenated slavery by making cotton production more efficient and profitable. During the 1780s, as tobacco prices sagged and some Chesapeake slaveholders began embracing antislavery ideas, planters in the Deep South saw a possible future in cotton production and started experimenting with cotton machinery to separate seeds from cotton. ELI WHITNEY's invention merely improved upon this machinery. At the same time, slaveholders in South Carolina, Georgia, and North Carolina expressed proslavery sentiments that were aimed squarely at undercutting the early abolition movement. When Pennsylvania QUAKERS presented a petition seeking an end to the overseas slave trade to the First (federal) Congress in 1790, representatives from both Georgia and South Carolina harshly criticized them. White-American society relied on AFRICAN-AMERICAN bondage, these men argued. Without slaves to clear fields, drain swamps, plant and harvest crops, and to engage in other forms of backbreaking labor, they claimed that their economy and society would be hampered. The petition was accepted but not acted upon.

During the second half of the 18th century and the first few decades of the 19th century, the institution of slavery underwent a number of important transformations. For the first time in Anglo-American culture, an abolitionist movement emerged to put slavery on the defensive. Until about the 1750s, most of the major religious institutions in Anglo-American culture sanctioned bondage. The Society of Friends, better known as the QUAKERS, initiated the first attack on slavery during the 1750s and 1760s when it forced slaveholders from their ranks. During the revolutionary era, many guilt-ridden slave masters emancipated slaves by private deed. And abolition gained a foothold in politics and law. Pennsylvania became the first state in the new union to adopt a gradual-abolition statute by which newly born slaves would be slowly freed over the next several decades. Between the 1780s and early 1800s, every other northern state would banish bondage in similar fashion (the Massachusetts Supreme Court declared slavery unconstitutional in 1783, the only such decision of the time).

But the institution of slavery also grew from the close of the 18th century through the American Civil War. In 1790 the first federal census (which despite some errors remains a reliable gauge of slavery at the time) counted over 700,000 bondspeople and over 60,000 free people of color. By 1830, according to the census, the number of slaves had more than doubled. By the Civil War, the number of slaves would total 3.5 million. Moreover, the geographic shape of slavery had shifted during the early national period. From along the Atlantic seaboard, slavery declined north of the Chesapeake but spread into many new states in the American South and Southwest: Kentucky and Tennessee in the 1790s; Alabama, Arkansas, FLORIDA, Mississippi, and Missouri during the next few decades. By the 1820s, slavery was a completely sectional institution, albeit one that still had national standing as well as national economic ramifications. (Early New England factories utilized raw materials such as cotton produced by slaves, turn-

ing out finished goods such as shirts and shoes destined for southern markets and plantations.)

The study of slavery has changed significantly over the past 30 years, emphasizing more than ever the lives, struggles, and world views of the enslaved. Enslaved people created many defensive mechanisms to survive bondage. Resistance included running away, to achieve freedom or to escape particularly harsh treatment; sabotage and work slowdowns; and outright rebellion. The revolutionary era saw a substantial number of runaways, in large measure due to the REVOLUTIONARY WAR (1775–83). Britain's JOHN MURRAY, EARL OF DUNMORE issued a proclamation promising freedom to all slaves fleeing the owners involved in the rebellion. Whether or not they knew of Dunmore's offer, several thousand African Americans ran to the British-controlled territory, especially New York City and Charleston. For decades after the Revolutionary War, slave rebellions occurred in southern states: In 1794 a slave rebellion was planned and foiled in Southampton County, Virginia; in 1800 one of the most famous slave plots (GABRIEL'S REBELLION) was uncovered outside of Richmond, Virginia, but torrential rains and betrayals wiped out the conspiracy before it started; in 1811 a large uprising occurred outside Natchez, Mississippi; and in 1822 Denmark Vesey planned a slave revolt in Charleston, South Carolina, that was eventually discovered and put down before getting off the ground. In the cases of Gabriel's Rebellion and Denmark Vesey's plot, details about revolutionary ideology remain sketchy. However, it is safe to argue that both of these slave rebels and their supporters sought to use violence to close the contradictions between American slavery and American freedom, believing that slaveholders would never emancipate enslaved people of their own volition.

Most of the founding fathers from the southern colonies, including Thomas Jefferson and George Washington, owned slaves. Washington is depicted here with slaves on his estate in Mount Vernon. Lithograph by Currier & Ives *(Library of Congress)*

The formation of a solidified slave culture was also an important mechanism of survival for bondspeople. Generally defined as a melding of African and Western religious principles and customs under slavery, slave culture was much more than that. Slave culture represented the beginning of a black nationalist ethos with direct connections to African custom and belief. It also took the more practical form of community values shaped from a common experience of oppression—a web of relationships and ideas that offered black families strength in the face of constant threats of violence and separation. Finally, slave culture was an autonomous space apart from oppressive white-American society, where enslaved people might simply carry on certain religious practices and celebrate in a particular manner. Slave culture might include transcendent customs such as the ring shout, a dance derived from African religious ceremonies. It might also include such things as naming practices: While slaveholders often insisted on naming slave children (as a means of control), African Americans renamed them in honor of ancestors, parents, and African customs.

Slave culture was not uniform throughout the United States, however. The type of slave system, as well as geography, influenced the formation and deeper meaning of slave culture. In South Carolina, for example, rice cultivation occurred through the task system: Slaves were assigned certain tasks (such as the clearing of a field, or working on an irrigation ditch) which, when completed, allowed bondspeople to engage in other activities such as tending to a garden to supplement food rations. In addition, South Carolina slave masters often lived apart from their slaves during the hottest summer months, leaving bondspeople under the eye of white overseers and black slave drivers. Thus, while South Carolina bondage was one of the most brutal slave systems on the North American continent, it also ironically offered the most distance from white authority. African-derived cultural patterns and linguistic systems developed more fully in South Carolina than anywhere else, and some still survive (such as Gullah). Finally, South Carolinians probably learned rice cultivation techniques from enslaved people forcibly removed from rice-growing regions of Western Africa, such as modern-day Angola. At the beginning of the 18th century and extending through the early 1800s, South Carolina slave masters prized African rice cultivators. Their traditions survived the horrors of the middle passage and took root in South Carolina.

In the Chesapeake states of Virginia and Maryland, however, the relatively smaller size of plantations dictated a different path for development of slave culture. Slave masters often lived in closer proximity to bondspeople, and they sought to influence their daily lives to a much greater extent. Evangelical Christianity spread more rapidly among slaves in the Chesapeake during the late 18th and early 19th centuries, because slaves were less isolated from European-American institutions. In addition, Virginia and Maryland slaveholders preferred to import slaves from the Caribbean, not directly from African shores as did South Carolinians. By the revolutionary era, moreover, lagging tobacco fortunes created a surplus of slave labor in Virginia and Maryland. Many Chesapeake planters even supported calls to end the overseas slave trade. On the other hand, South Carolinians brought in 40,000 slaves before a congressional ban of the trade took effect in 1808, ironically rejuvenating the African presence on South Carolina plantations in the early 19th century.

To be sure, African traditions survived and even thrived among Chesapeake slaves, as they did even in northern locations. Still, regional variations proved telling in the formation and development of slave culture in North America.

See also RACE AND RACIAL CONFLICT.

Further reading: Ira Berlin, *Many Thousand Gone: The First Two Hundred Years of Slavery in North America* (Cambridge, Mass.: Harvard University Press, 1998); David Brion Davis, *Slavery in the Age of Revolution, 1770–1823* (Ithaca, N.Y.: Cornell University Press, 1975); Norrece Jones, *Born a Child of Freedom, Yet a Slave: Mechanisms of Control and Strategies of Resistance in Antebellum South Carolina* (Middletown, Conn.: Wesleyan University Press, 1990); Jean Soderlund, *Quakers and Slavery: A Divided Spirit* (Princeton, N.J.: Princeton University Press, 1985); Sterling Stuckey, *Slave Culture: Nationalist Theory and the Foundations of Black America* (New York: Oxford University Press, 1982).

— Richard Newman

slave trade

Although the overseas slave trade in North America accounted for a relatively small percentage of slaves exported from Africa, it became a focal point for American reformers in the final decades of the 18th century. According to the most recent scholarly estimates, the slave trade forcibly removed 12–15 million Africans between the 16th and 19th centuries, with many Africans being sent to Latin American locales such as Brazil or to the Caribbean. Less than 5 percent of enslaved Africans came to North America. Between 1700 and the 1780s, roughly 250,000 Africans arrived in North America via the slave trade. Routes of the slave trade to America differed according to the needs and predilections of slave owners. Colonial Virginians imported slaves from the WEST INDIES, preferring that they be "seasoned," or worked in; South Carolinians, on the other hand, purchased slaves directly from African shores, favoring ethnic groups who had cultivated rice and could transfer their skills to New World plantations. Northern colonies imported slaves as well, although in fewer numbers. Between 1757 and 1766, Philadelphians brought about 1,300 slaves to the city's port, much fewer than either Virginians or South Carolinians might import in a given year. But even though northern colonies were not the largest slave importers, northern ports and ships directed much of the overseas slave trade to North America, particularly following the REVOLUTIONARY WAR (1775–83). During the 1790s, for example, Pennsylvania abolitionists tracked dozens of cases in which captains from New England ports imported slaves destined for southern plantations.

The slave trade came under intense public attack during the revolutionary era. The concern for human rights and self-determination that accompanied the AMERICAN REVOLUTION led many ministers, statesman, and even slaveholders to view the slave trade as a violation of both natural rights and religious dictates. THOMAS JEFFERSON's initial draft of the DECLARATION OF INDEPENDENCE chastised King GEORGE III for forcing the slave trade upon Americans. Celebrated Philadelphia physician and reformer BENJAMIN RUSH issued one of the most stirring attacks on the slave trade: a 1773 pamphlet, *An Address to the Inhabitants of the British Settlements in America, upon Slave-Keeping*. New England clergyman ISAAC BACKUS, Virginia politician GEORGE MASON, and President GEORGE WASHINGTON were some of the other figures who similarly came to oppose the slave trade. In fact, the slave trade was halted in every state except South Carolina and Georgia. But the new federal Constitution of 1787 did not ban the slave trade nationally.

Indeed, the slave trade became one of the first points of sectional conflict in early congressional politics. The Constitution declared that Congress could not ban the trade until 1807—"20 years hence" from the CONSTITUTIONAL CONVENTION of 1787. In the First Congress in 1790, early abolitionists petitioned the government to curtail African imports before the 1807 date. Proslavery advocates in South Carolina and Georgia threatened disunion if any slave trade ban occurred before the constitutional deadline. Congress backed away from the issue but revisited it briefly in 1794 by passing a law banning American ships from visiting foreign ports for the purposes of carrying out the slave trade. Between 1800 and 1807, when Congress ultimately passed a slave trading ban (to take effect on January 1, 1808), South Carolinians imported 40,000 slaves. Nonetheless, January 1, 1808, became "a day of public thanksgiving," as Philadelphian ABSALOM JONES put it, for free black communities, marking the end of the slave trade.

See also AFRICAN AMERICANS; ANTISLAVERY AND ABOLITION; SLAVERY.

Further reading: Ira Berlin, *Many Thousand Gone: The First Two Centuries of Slavery in North America* (Cam-

A 1780s broadside advertising a slave auction *(Library of Congress)*

bridge, Mass.: Harvard University Press, 1998); Gary B. Nash, *Red, White and Black: The Peoples of Early America*, 4th ed. (Upper Saddle River, N.J.: Prentice Hall, 2000); Hugh Thomas, *The Slave Trade: The Story of the Atlantic Slave Trade, 1440–1870* (New York: Simon & Schuster, 1997).

— Richard Newman

Society of Friends   See Quakers

Sons of Liberty

Although the term "Sons of Liberty" came to represent almost anyone who opposed imperial regulation in the 1760s and was extended to those who fought for independence after 1776, it originally referred to the committee in each community that organized the opposition to the STAMP ACT (1765). The size and social standing of these committees varied from town to town. Boston's committee, originally called the LOYAL NINE, did not have many members, and most came from the middling ranks of society. New York City had either 10 or 18 members, depending on what list is used, but it had more merchants and LAWYERS represented among the number. Charleston, South Carolina, had 26 members, including Christopher Gadsden, a wealthy merchant, and many ARTISANS. Albany had over 90 Sons of Liberty, while other groups had over 100.

Whatever their number and social standing, the Sons of Liberty played a central role in the resistance to the Stamp Act by placing themselves between the colonial leadership and the mob in the street. The Sons of Liberty thereby added muscle to nonimportation agreements and declarations in opposition to imperial regulation while striving to restrain crowd behavior. Without rioting to coerce stamp distributors into resigning, to close courts, and to ensure noncompliance with the Stamp Act, all the petitions and pamphlets in the world would have been meaningless. But if the RIOTS went too far, then the political message of the anti-Stamp Act forces would be muted. The Sons of Liberty engaged in a precarious balancing act by organizing crowd demonstrations, developing contacts with mob leaders, and interceding at crucial moments to mute the full impact of the mob. They were not always successful, but they managed to control or guide the situation often enough to sustain the opposition to imperial regulation and nullify the effects of the Stamp Act.

The Sons of Liberty was a local association within each community; there was no pan-colonial group called Sons of Liberty. However, as the crisis wore on, the various Sons of Liberty groups began to correspond with each other to coordinate positions, and some groups even sent delegations to visit one another.

Once the Stamp Act was repealed, the Sons of Liberty disbanded in some communities and continued in others. The experience of organizing resistance, contacting other communities, and working with both the mob and colonial leadership had two long-lasting results. First, the Sons of Liberty gave additional political voice to men from the middle of society. Second, in reaction to other imperial measures, many of the same men either reasserted the Sons of Liberty or organized new committees to coordinate resistance. When rebellion turned to revolution, these committees even began to take over the functions of government.

See also COMMITTEES OF CORRESPONDENCE.

Further reading: Paul A. Gilje, *The Road to Mobocracy: Popular Disorder in New York City, 1763–1834* (Chapel Hill: University of North Carolina Press, 1987); Pauline Maier, *From Resistance to Revolution: Colonial Radicals and the Development of American Opposition to Britain, 1765–1776* (New York: Knopf, 1972); Edmund S. Morgan and Helen M. Morgan, *The Stamp Act Crisis: Prologue to Revolution* (Chapel Hill: University of North Carolina Press, 1953).

South Carolina Regulation (1767–1769).
During the late 1760s the South Carolina Regulation—an elite-led social-reform movement employing vigilante methods—erupted on the southern FRONTIER. This movement had its origin in the unique history of the southern backcountry. The defeat of powerful coastal Indians in the Yamassee War early in the 18th century allowed European hunters and Indian traders to move into the fertile South Carolina backcountry. Colonists did not settle the region in large numbers until the 1740s, when they began pouring into the area from colonies to the north. Despite prolonged conflicts with the CHEROKEE that lasted until the mid-1760s, backcountry settlers rapidly developed the region's ECONOMY. Initially, most farmers concentrated on feeding their families through hunting and growing a little corn, but many quickly began to take advantage of commercial crops such as grain, cotton, indigo, and tobacco. The most ambitious invested in enslaved workers to help them expand production. Forced black laborers provided aspiring planters with wealth and status. The problem for these backcountry elites was the absence of government institutions and laws to deal with discontented Indians, rebellious slaves, greedy bandits, and squatters who lived by hunting and gathering. All of these people threatened the sanctity of property and the needs of a commercial economy based on SLAVERY.

While the area expanded economically and the number of colonists grew exponentially, the infrastructure did not keep pace. Government institutions—civil and criminal courts, jails, even a land office—did not exist in the backcountry. The lack of courts and jails made debts difficult to collect and attracted horse thieves and bandits. When planters wanted to collect debts, bring criminals to justice, or patent land, they had to travel to Charleston, which could take two weeks. The South Carolina assembly, overwhelmingly made up of easterners eager to protect their own interests, did little to rectify the situation.

Responding to a wave of crimes in the mid-1760s, property holders, led by slave owners, took the law into their own hands. Outraged over their lack of success in getting bandits and horse thieves convicted in the Charleston court, they began in the fall of 1767 to attack outlaw communities, burning houses, taking property, and flogging suspects. Adopting the name Regulators, they sent a petition to the governor and the assembly calling for the establishment of courts in the backcountry, legal reforms, changes in the poor law, and the creation of new laws to force people without visible means of subsistence, such as hunters, to work. While the assembly set about obtaining the Crown's approval of a circuit-court act, it legitimated the vigilante actions of the Regulators by appointing two companies of Rangers, made up largely of Regulators, to suppress outlaw gangs. These Rangers tracked outlaws even in North Carolina, Virginia, and Georgia. They killed large numbers of outlaws and took others to Charleston to stand trial. By March 1768, the campaign was deemed a success.

But rather than end their activities, the Regulators turned their attention to such marginal people as squatters, vagrants, and hunters, who either could not, or would not, make AGRICULTURE and land ownership their main goals in life. Such people were flogged, expelled from their communities, or forced to work. Women who transgressed traditional sexual norms were whipped or dunked. Emboldened by their successes, the Regulators defied authorities by preventing them from serving all warrants or writs, except writs of debt, in the backcountry. The governor and the assembly, aware of how much they needed the support of Regulators in case of slave uprisings or renewed conflict with NATIVE AMERICANS, did little to suppress the vigilante movement, which was soon in complete control of the backcountry. However, opposition developed among backcountry inhabitants who abhorred the violence and the choice of victims. Their resistance, in some instances itself violent, and the eventual passage of a circuit-court act ended the Regulator movement in 1769. In late 1771 the governor issued pardons for Regulators facing damage suits brought by their victims. Unlike the North Carolina Regulators who demanded a more equitable economic system for free farmers, the South Carolina Regulators enabled elite men to consolidate their power and push the backcountry several steps closer to becoming a well-ordered slave society

See also NORTH CAROLINA REGULATION; RIOTS.

Further reading: Richard Maxwell Brown, *The South Carolina Regulators: The Story of the First American Vigilante Movement* (Cambridge, Mass.: Harvard University Press, 1963); Rachel N. Klein, *Unification of a Slave State: The Rise of the Planter Class in the South Carolina Backcountry, 1760–1808* (Chapel Hill: University of North Carolina Press, 1990); Charles Woodmason, *The Carolina Backcountry on the Eve of the Revolution . . .* , edited and introduced by Richard J. Hooker (Chapel Hill: University of North Carolina Press, 1953).

— Marjoleine Kars

Stamp Act (March 22, 1765)
Along with the SUGAR ACT (1764), the Stamp Act was intended to raise revenue in the colonies explicitly for paying part of "the expenses of defending, protecting, and securing" the colonies from NATIVE AMERICAN and foreign threats. Since Great Britain had accumulated a debt over £120 million, the British first minister, GEORGE GRENVILLE, thought it only appropriate that the colonies contribute to their own defense. Maintaining an army in North America would cost about £200 thousand per year. The Sugar and Stamp Acts together were to raise about half that sum, with the rest of the money provided by Parliament. The British believed that Stamp duties were an innocuous tax and would be self-enforceable. Great Britain already had a stamp tax, and since the duty would be levied on all legal and commercial papers—liquor licenses, land instruments, indentures, cards, dice, newspapers, pamphlets, advertisements, academic degrees, and appointments to office—colonists could not undertake any business without the stamped paper. Anyone interested in any transaction—whether it was buying a piece of property, sailing a ship, or exchanging goods—would use the stamped paper to ensure the transaction was legal. To make the law more acceptable, the British government chose local politicians within the colonies as stamp agents.

The law, however, was not acceptable to most colonists. The Stamp Act created a crisis in the relationship between Great Britain and the colonies. The opposition took many forms and established a pattern that would be followed throughout the RESISTANCE MOVEMENT

An angry mob protests against the Stamp Act by throwing stamped documents onto a bonfire in Boston, August 1764 *(Hulton/Archive)*

(1764–75). On one level was the reaction of the elite. The Virginia House of Burgesses and eight other colonial houses of assembly passed resolves asserting that only representatives elected by the colonists had the right to tax the colonies. Nine colonies also sent representatives to a STAMP ACT CONGRESS in New York in October 1765 that declared that Parliament had no right to tax the colonies. Men like DANIEL DULANY wrote pamphlets exploring the constitutional issues. Dulany, for instance, denied the idea that colonial Americans were virtually represented in Parliament, and asserted the right of the colonists to be taxed only by actual representatives that they voted into office. Other colonial Americans struggled to distinguish between internal taxation (to raise revenue within the colonies) and external taxation (to regulate the empire), declaring that Parliament had a right to the second form of taxation, but not the first. In addition, groups of merchants in several seaports passed agreements against importing goods from Great Britain in an effort to put economic pressure on their British counterparts to have the measure repealed.

On another level was the reaction of the people in the street. The Stamp Act led to a wave of rioting that swept through the colonies. Mobs in Boston marched through town with an effigy of stamp distributor ANDREW OLIVER and tore down a building he had constructed on the waterfront on August 14, 1765. Twelve days later, another Boston mob gutted the house of Lieutenant Governor THOMAS HUTCHINSON. Similar disturbances occurred in several seaports, forcing stamp distributors to resign and making the law a dead letter. The mob seemed to rule the streets in community after community. The Stamp Act was to take effect on November 1, 1765. That day came and went with, after some coercion by the people in the streets, business continuing as usual. Crowds also added muscle to the nonimportation agreements by coercing those who imported goods from Great Britain. The mob made a self-enforceable law unenforceable.

Local leaders formed a series of loose associations to coordinate the crowd action and the resolves of the elite. In Boston the group at first called itself the LOYAL NINE, later taking the name that was used elsewhere—SONS OF LIBERTY. These groups strove to guide the mob, to correspond between towns and colonies to coordinate their positions, and to enforce resolves against the use of stamped paper. In most colonies it was the Sons of Liberty, with mobs close by, who saw to it that ships sailed without stamped paper and that all judicial proceedings were stopped. They even sought to put additional pressures on merchants who did not comply with nonimportation agreements.

All of these measures had some impact on Great Britain. British merchants, unable to collect debts in closed colonial courts and suffering a decline in TRADE, petitioned Parliament to repeal the law. Oddly, what made the most difference in Parliament was neither the colonial opposition nor the merchant's petitions. Instead, the crucial factor in the repeal of the Stamp Act was the fact that there was a change in government. Grenville, who was never popular with King GEORGE III, was forced from office in the summer of 1765 over issues unrelated to colonial policy. In Grenville's place the king appointed a new administration headed by Lord Charles Rockingham, who had opposed the Stamp Act in the first place. Given the colonial opposition and the pressure of British merchants, Rockingham had the act repealed (March 18, 1766). However, to placate his opposition and to avoid giving in on the constitutional issues, he also had Parliament pass the DECLARATORY ACT (1766), which stated that Parliament had the right to legislate for the colonies in all cases whatsoever.

Further reading: Paul A. Gilje, *The Road to Mobocracy: Popular Disorder in New York City, 1763–1834* (Chapel Hill: University of North Carolina Press, 1987); Pauline Maier, *From Resistance to Revolution: Colonial Radicals and the Development of American Opposition to Britain, 1765–1776* (New York: Knopf, 1972); Edmund S. Morgan and Helen M. Morgan, *The Stamp Act Crisis: Prologue to Revolution* (Chapel Hill: University of North Carolina Press, 1953).

Stamp Act Congress (October 1765)

In reaction to the STAMP ACT (1765), the Massachusetts assembly circulated a letter to the other colonies in North America suggesting that they meet in a congress in New York City to discuss how they should oppose the tax measure. Nine colonies responded to the invitation. Virginia, North Carolina, and Georgia could not send delegates because their governors refused to call the assemblies to choose delegates. New Hampshire did not send a delegate but approved the proceedings.

Twenty-seven delegates attended the meeting, and although they chose conservative Timothy Ruggles to preside over the congress, they drew up a strongly worded petition against the Stamp Act. Like most petitions of the 18th century, the congress began with a statement of loyalty to the king, proclaiming that they were "sincerely devoted" and had "the warmest Sentiments of Affection and Duty to His Majesty's Person and Government." However, they also asserted "that his Majesty's Subjects in these Colonies, are entitled to all the inherent Rights and Liberties of his Natural born Subjects, within the Kingdom of *Great Britain*" and "that it is inseparably essential to the Freedom of a People, and the undoubted Right of *Englishmen*, that no Taxes be imposed on them, but with their own Consent, given personally, or by their Representatives." Besides protesting the Stamp Act, the delegates also officially objected to the SUGAR ACT (1764).

The delegates believed that Parliament had the right to pass laws regulating the empire, but they held that Parliament did not have the right to raise taxes within the colonies. They hotly debated whether to include an explicit statement affirming Parliament's right to legislate external affairs in their petition, but decided not to do so. The congress also did not advocate any overt resistance to the law. While neither too radical nor too conservative, the Stamp Act Congress represented an important early effort at intercolonial cooperation.

Further reading: Edmund S. Morgan and Helen M. Morgan, *The Stamp Act Crisis: Prologue to a Revolution* (Chapel Hill: University of North Carolina Press, 1953).

state's rights

The issue of state's rights—the idea that a state had the right to resist federal intrusion on its laws—arose almost as soon as the United States first became a nation. Americans fought the REVOLUTIONARY WAR (1775–83) in part as a means to guarantee that a central government, in this case Parliament, could not dictate taxes to each colony. When the revolutionaries established their first form of government under the ARTICLES OF CONFEDERATION, they asserted that "each state retains its sovereignty, freedom and independence," and that all powers not expressly granted in the Articles were left to the states. Taxes were to be levied in proportion to the population of each state and raised by each state on its own.

The members of the Philadelphia CONSTITUTIONAL CONVENTION found these restrictions too limiting and therefore created a more powerful government, dependent on simple majorities (or two-thirds majority to override a presidential veto) and capable of raising and collecting its own taxes. The founding fathers also inserted a loophole into the Constitution: Article 1, Section 8 included a statement that Congress had the power "to make all Laws which shall be necessary and proper for carrying into Execution the foregoing powers, and all other Powers vested by this Constitution in the Government of the United States. . ."

ANTI-FEDERALISTS had many objections to the Constitution, including the belief that the new government destroyed the rights of individual states. As a result of anti-Federalist complaints, supporters of the Constitution agreed to pass a BILL OF RIGHTS. The last and tenth of this list of rights, and amended unto the Constitution, stated: "The powers not delegated to the United States by the Constitution, nor prohibited by it to the States, are reserved to the States, or to the people." Between this article and the "necessary and proper" clause there was a great deal of room for debate over the relative power of the federal and state governments.

That debate was joined as the first party system emerged in the 1790s. ALEXANDER HAMILTON and the FEDERALIST PARTY used the "necessary and proper" clause to expand the powers of government and create institutions like the FIRST BANK OF THE UNITED STATES. The DEMOCRATIC-REPUBLICAN opposition, led by THOMAS JEFFERSON and JAMES MADISON, held that this was too broad of an interpretation of the Constitution and drained power from the states. While each side jockeyed for position during the mid-1790s, it was only when the Federalist government passed the ALIEN AND SEDITION ACTS (1798) that Jefferson and Madison fully articulated a state's rights argument. Writing the VIRGINIA AND KENTUCKY RESOLUTIONS (1798), Madison and Jefferson asserted that "whensoever the general government assumes undelegated powers, its acts are unauthoritative, void, and of no force." While staking out an extreme state's rights position, the Virginia and Kentucky Resolutions did not have a big impact on the rest of the nation. The ELECTION OF 1800 and Jefferson's victory left the repressive measures of the Alien and Sedition Act moot.

As the Democratic-Republicans gained power in the early 1800s, the Federalists had to turn to state's rights arguments. Some Federalists opposed the LOUISIANA PURCHASE because they believed there was no constitutional provision to permit the acquisition of territory and because any new states that might result would weaken the political voice of the existing states. Similarly, Federalists argued against the EMBARGO OF 1807 and provisions to support the trade ban because it hurt the interests of the New England states, the stronghold of the Federalists. The most extreme statement of state's rights by Federalists occurred in opposition to the War of 1812 (1812–15). In their resolutions passed at the Hartford Convention, the Federalists asked the New England state legislators to protect their citizens from forcible enlistment into the militia, army, or navy—in effect nullifying the American war effort. With the war over even before the Hartford Convention adjourned, the resolutions had little real impact beyond further discrediting the Federalist Party.

In the years after 1820, state's rights would emerge repeatedly as a divisive issue concerning Internal Improvements, TARIFFS, BANKS, and SLAVERY. Ultimately, the issue would contribute to the origins of the Civil War.

See also POLITICAL PARTIES.

Further reading: Saul Cornell, *The Other Founders: Anti-Federalism and the Dissenting Tradition in America, 1788–1828* (Chapel Hill: University of North Carolina Press, 1999).

Steuben, Frederick, baron von (1730–1794)

A relatively obscure foreign officer who arrived at VALLEY FORGE in the bleak winter of 1778, Baron Frederick von Steuben became a crucial element in the CONTINENTAL ARMY's development and success as a fighting unit. Born into a Prussian military family in 1730, Steuben entered the officer corps of the Prussian army while still in his teens. He attained the rank of captain while serving in the Seven Year's War and was attached for a time to the general staff of Frederick the Great, Europe's foremost military genius. When peace came in 1763, Steuben left the army. For the next 12 years he was court chamberlain to the prince of Hohenzollern-Hechingen, during which time he supposedly acquired the title of baron. Heavily in debt when he left that situation in 1775, he sought various military and civilian posts in Europe. Finally, in 1777, he came to BENJAMIN FRANKLIN's attention in Paris. After securing an endorsement and a loan, Steuben was soon on his way to America.

Upon his arrival, Steuben wrote to the CONTINENTAL CONGRESS and offered his services to the fledgling nation, asking only payment of his expenses. Satisfied that this military expert was flexible enough to adapt his training methods to the raw American troops, GEORGE WASHINGTON welcomed Steuben into the fold. The baron's robust personality and military expertise had an energizing effect on the ragtag volunteer army he found wintering at Valley Forge. Unable to speak English, Steuben worked through interpreters as he undertook to transform the demoralized, disorganized men into confident, efficient soldiers. He began by composing a uniform code of drill, writing his instructions in French, which were then translated into English. The drill regulations were transcribed daily and passed along to all levels of command, so that eventually every officer and drill instructor could make his own copy. Steuben formed a model company of 100 specially chosen men; wishing to train them personally for maximum effect, he learned the English words for his instructions and delivered them by rote. The men from the model company would then become drill sergeants for their own units. As the soldiers became more proficient under Steuben's demanding yet good-humored tutelage, enthusiasm for precision drilling spread throughout the army and morale increased. Washington recognized Steuben's remarkable achievement by recommending him for the post of inspector general with the rank of major general. When the Continental army marched out of Valley Forge in June 1778, it had attained a level of discipline comparable with that of the professional British regulars. Steuben's drill manual grew into the *Regulations for the Order and Discipline of the Troops of the United States*, which remained the official guide for military training and procedure until 1812.

In 1780 Washington granted Steuben's wish for a field command, and he served as a division commander during the siege at YORKTOWN (October 19, 1781). After the Revolution, Steuben became a citizen of the United States and resided in upstate New York. Rising debts almost forced him into bankruptcy in 1790, but the federal government awarded him an annual pension of $2,500 for his wartime services. Baron Steuben died on November 28, 1794.

Further reading: Page Smith, *A New Age Now Begins*, vol. 2 of; *A People's History of the American Revolution*, (New York: McGraw Hill, 1989); *Frederick William Baron von Steuben, Baron Von Steuben's Revolutionary War Drill Manual: A Facsimile Reprint of the 1794 Edition* (New York: Dover Publications, 1985).

— Rita M. Broyles

Story, Joseph (1779–1845)

Joseph Story was the leading academic on the early SUPREME COURT of the United States. Born in Massachusetts on September 18, 1779, and educated at Harvard, Story studied law in the office of Samuel Sewall, later chief justice of the Supreme Court of Massachusetts. In 1801 he began practicing law and was soon elected to the Massachusetts legislature. An avowed DEMOCRATIC-REPUBLICAN (Jeffersonian), in 1808–09 he represented Massachusetts in the United States House of Representatives, where he opposed the EMBARGO OF 1807, thus earning the distrust of many leading Democratic-Republicans, including THOMAS JEFFERSON. He then returned to Massachusetts, where he served again in the legislature.

On November 18, 1811, President JAMES MADISON appointed Story an associate justice of the Supreme Court of the United States. At age 32, he was the youngest person ever appointed to the Supreme Court, and he remained on the Court for 34 years. As a justice, Story quickly allied himself with Chief Justice JOHN MARSHALL. Perhaps the most important majority opinion he wrote was in *Martin v. Hunter's Lessee* (1816), upholding the Supreme Court's jurisdiction over the state courts. Story also wrote the Court's opinion in the case of the *Amistad*, directing that the alleged slaves who seized that vessel be freed and returned to their homes in Africa. In 1835, when John Marshall died, Story was widely thought to be the most capable successor as chief justice, but President Andrew Jackson opted not to make the appointment, largely because he considered Story dangerous to the cause of STATE'S RIGHTS.

Story was extraordinarily productive. His position as a Supreme Court justice allowed him some free time, and in 1829 he decided to occupy this time by teaching law at Harvard Law School. Between 1832 and 1845 he published a series of commentaries covering such diverse subjects as the Constitution, equity jurisprudence and pleading, and bailments. These gained Story an international reputation and a fairly large income. He died on September 10, 1845.

Further reading: R. Kent Newmyer, *Supreme Court Justice Joseph Story: Statesman of the Old Republic* (Chapel Hill: University of North Carolina Press, 1985); William Wetmore Story, *Life and Letters of Joseph Story* (Boston: Little, Brown, 1851).

— Lindsay Robertson

Stuart, Gilbert (1755–1828)

Gilbert Stuart, a provincial artist in the 1770s, became the leading portraitist in the new nation, especially renowned for his paintings of the Revolutionary hero and president GEORGE WASHINGTON. His father operated a snuff mill in North Kingston, Rhode Island, where he was born in 1755. The family moved to Newport when he was a young boy, where he met the traveling artist Cosmo Alexander, who provided the young Stuart with lessons and employment as his assistant on his travels to Pennsylvania, Virginia, and Scotland, where his unexpected death in 1772 left Stuart stranded. After making his way back to Newport, he continued his portrait work. When his LOYALIST father moved to Nova Scotia in 1775 to avoid the revolutionary crisis, the young patriot artist departed for London, where he struggled for work until BENJAMIN WEST helped him with lessons and employment. His "self portrait" of 1778 shows his increasing knowledge of English and European styles and models. He began to achieve success and commissions from prominent people but was forced to flee London in 1787 to escape his creditors.

Stuart arrived in New York in 1793 to seek the patronage of the new nation's merchants, politicians, and REVOLUTIONARY WAR (1775–83) heroes. Armed with a letter from Chief Justice JOHN JAY, he secured a sitting of President George Washington in Philadelphia in 1795, the first of several Stuart paintings of the first president. MARTHA WASHINGTON commissioned another likeness, the "George Washington Athenaeum Portrait" (1796, National Portrait Gallery). He worked in Philadelphia for nine years before moving briefly to the new capital, WASHINGTON D.C., in 1803, then leaving for Boston in 1805, where he remained for the rest of his life.

Stuart's cosmopolitan painterly technique used rapid and facile brushwork along with subtle blending of color to create an atmospheric style. However, the artist had difficulty finishing his sittings and often was perilously in debt. He died insolvent in Boston in 1828.

See also ART.

Further reading: James Tomas Flexner, *Gilbert Stuart: A Great Life in Brief* (New York: Knopf, 1955).

— David Jaffe

Stuart, John   See Bute, John Stuart, earl of

Suffolk Resolves (September 9, 1774)

In an effort to provide a course of action to resist further imperial regulation, SAMUEL ADAMS had the county convention in Suffolk, Massachusetts, draw up a series of resolves opposing the changes in Massachusetts government dictated by the COERCIVE ACTS (1774). Written by JOSEPH WARREN, the resolves were delivered to the FIRST CONTINENTAL CONGRESS by PAUL REVERE on September 16, 1774. As its first official action, the Continental Congress endorsed the Suffolk Resolves, thus assuming a supervisory role over the resistance to the Coercive Acts in Massachusetts.

The resolves began with a fiery preamble that referred to Lord FREDERICK NORTH as having "the arbitrary will of a licentious minister" and decried the British soldiers in Boston as "military executioners." The Coercive Acts were labeled "murderous." The resolves also outlined a series of measures intended to circumvent or nullify the British legislation. Tax collectors were not to send their receipts to the treasury. The colony's councillors, now appointed by the governor instead of elected, were urged to resign. Everyone was to ignore the action of judges appointed with new commissions, and all judicial orders were not to be followed. The Suffolk Resolves also called for a nonimportation movement. As radical as these steps appeared, many in the Continental Congress saw them as following a moderate course. All measures were viewed as defensive, and the resolves reasserted the colonial "affection for his majesty." There was no call to drive the British troops out of Boston, and there was no unilateral assumption of the previous colonial government. The Suffolk Resolves were an important first step in the Continental Congress's emergence as a guiding force in the crisis caused by the Coercive Acts, and they helped to prepare the way for THE ASSOCIATION, which led to a nonimportation movement that further aggravated the imperial crisis.

Further reading: Jack N. Rakove, *The Beginnings of National Politics: An Interpretive History of the Continental Congress* (New York: Knopf, 1979).

suffrage

Americans took the broad right to vote that had existed during the colonial period and expanded it during the

AMERICAN REVOLUTION. In England the franchise was based on property. The standard requirement was a 40-shilling freehold, which meant that the right to vote was given to adult males who owned property that was worth 40 shillings annually in income or rent. In the 18th century this limited those who voted in England to about one-fifth of the adult male population. Property qualifications in colonial America had a less restrictive effect because property ownership was much more widespread. Some colonies, like Massachusetts and Rhode Island, simply adopted the 40-shilling freehold. In other colonies, like Virginia and North Carolina, the right to vote was restricted to those who owned a certain amount of acreage. Taken as a whole, over 50 percent of the adult white males in the colonies had the right to vote.

The RESISTANCE MOVEMENT (1764–75) and the REVOLUTIONARY WAR (1775–83) compelled Americans to rethink suffrage. Because revolutionary Americans made an issue of the relationship between taxation and representation and because large numbers of men were called upon to fight the war for independence, there was a clamor for including more people in the political process. The writing of new state constitutions provided the opportunity to do so. Only Vermont in 1777, which was not yet recognized as a legitimate entity by the other states, provided for universal manhood suffrage. Other states came close. Pennsylvania granted the right to vote to all adult male taxpayers and their adult sons. New York and Maryland reduced the property qualification by about half. New York even allowed tenants to vote if they rented sufficient property and paid taxes. Several states detached voting requirements from owning property to paying taxes, a move that generally increased those eligible to vote and altered the rationale behind the franchise. Traditionally, WHIG theory held that a voter should own a permanent stake in society—property—to ensure his independent judgement. Now, just the fact that a person was taxed meant that he should have some say in government. The new requirements became so inclusive that in some states free AFRICAN AMERICANS, if they met the other requirements, were allowed to vote and until 1807 propertied women could vote in New Jersey.

Not everyone was pleased with these developments. Men like JOHN ADAMS wanted property to be more broadly distributed, but he also still clung to the stake-in-society ideal. Adams wished that more people owned land so that they could "take Care of Liberty, Virtue, and Interest of the Multitude in all Acts of Government." But he also held that giving propertyless men the right to vote would corrupt the republic. "Such is the Frailty of the human Heart," Adams wrote, "that very few Men, who have no Property, have any Judgement of their own." Instead of being independent, the propertyless will be "directed by Some Man of property, who has attached their Minds to his Interest."

Adams, however, never understood the full force of the democratic movement. Over the course of the next few decades, state after state abandoned property qualifications for voting. Leading the way were the new states admitted into the union. Vermont, when it finally became a state in 1791, and Kentucky in 1792 both wrote universal manhood suffrage into their constitutions. Most other new states did the same. By the early 1800s the more established eastern states followed suit. Often, however, this expansion of the franchise came with some cost. When New York State removed its property qualifications for adult white men in 1821, it retained them for African Americans. By 1824 every state but Louisiana, Virginia, and Rhode Island had universal white manhood suffrage.

See also CONSTITUTIONS, STATE; REPUBLICANISM.

Further reading: Marc W. Kruman, *Between Authority and Liberty: State Constitution Making in Revolutionary America* (Chapel Hill: University of North Carolina Press, 1997); J. R. Pole, *Political Representation in England and the Origins of the American Republic* (New York: St. Martin's Press, 1966).

Sugar Act (April 5, 1764)

Confronted with the need to raise revenue to help support an army to defend the colonies, the British government under the leadership of GEORGE GRENVILLE passed the Sugar Act (1764) to lower the tax on imported sugar to North America. From the British perspective, this measure was logical. Under the previous legislation, the Molasses Act of 1733, colonists were to pay six pence per gallon on foreign molasses. This duty was prohibitive and was intended to help British WEST INDIES planters. Before the new law, it was assumed that if the colonists could not afford to buy the foreign product, they would be compelled to buy molasses produced in the British West Indies. The reduction in the tax therefore reduced the price of imported molasses and represented a net gain in customs collections, since little or no duties were paid at the higher tax rate. To help enforce this measure, the Grenville government, which had already begun to tighten up customs enforcement, added provisions to further assist the customs agency.

In particular, the Sugar Act allowed customs agents to take their court cases to an Admiralty court away from the immediate neighborhood of the customs violation. Prior to this provision, it was very difficult for a customs officer to gain a conviction when a merchant violated the law because the trial would be held before a local jury that would side with the merchant. The new Vice Admiralty Court, to be located in Halifax, Nova Scotia, would not have a jury and it would not be under local influence. The measure also added some items to the list of enumerated goods, items that could only be exported to Great Britain. The new enumerated goods included hides, whale fins, and iron.

Many colonists objected to this law. Merchants had long-established procedures to sidestep imperial measures and had developed smuggling into an art form. Thus, even during the French and Indian War (1754–63), they had illegally imported molasses from the French and other foreign West Indies colonies. The Sugar Act threatened to disrupt their business and hurt their profits. Moreover, it was passed at a time when the colonies were struggling economically in a postwar recession. Merchants in several colonies therefore organized to express their discontent with the measure. For the most part, they concentrated on economic arguments, saying that the measure would hurt their ability to pay their debts to British merchants. In a few instances, the merchants also addressed the ideological issues, expressing concern over being taxed without being represented and declaring their disapproval of the arbitrary nature of the new customs laws. These protests had little impact in the colonies or in Great Britain. The Sugar Act remained in force, but to make it more acceptable, the British government in 1766 reduced the duty to one pence per gallon. It would take other imperial regulations, especially the STAMP ACT (1765), to galvanize American resistance further.

See also RESISTANCE MOVEMENT.

Further reading: Edmund S. Morgan and Helen M. Morgan, *The Stamp Act Crisis: Prologue to Revolution* (Chapel Hill: University of North Carolina Press, 1953).

Sullivan, John (1740–1795)

John Sullivan was a capable but controversial general of the REVOLUTIONARY WAR (1775–83). He later helped to put down SHAYS'S REBELLION (1786–87). A lawyer and major in the New Hampshire militia, Sullivan was a delegate to the FIRST CONTINENTAL CONGRESS in 1774. In 1775 he became a member of the SECOND CONTINENTAL CONGRESS, which appointed him a brigadier general. He helped General GEORGE WASHINGTON's troops lay siege to Boston until the British evacuated the city (March 17, 1776).

After promotion to major general in 1776, Sullivan was captured by the British in the BATTLE OF LONG ISLAND (August 27–30, 1776). The British admiral LORD RICHARD HOWE released Sullivan as a sign of goodwill for peace negotiations and exchanged him for the British general Richard Prescott. Sullivan immediately rejoined the CONTINENTAL ARMY, participating in the retreat in New Jersey, commanding the right flank in the BATTLE OF TRENTON (December 26, 1776), and fighting the British at PRINCETON (January 3, 1777).

Sullivan's failed attack on the British on Staten Island and growing criticism of his conduct at the BATTLE OF BRANDYWINE (September 11, 1777) caused members of Congress to question his competence and to propose suspending Sullivan from active duty. Washington, however, supported Sullivan, and further investigations cleared his name from any wrongdoings. Sullivan hurriedly rejoined Washington in an effort to reconquer Philadelphia in the BATTLE OF GERMANTOWN (October 4, 1777). Although the British repulsed the American attack, Sullivan achieved his assigned task, restoring his reputation.

Sullivan spent the winter with Washington in VALLEY FORGE (1777–78) and took command of the troops in Rhode Island in the spring of 1778 in an attempt to drive the British forces from Newport. The siege of the coastal town depended on the close cooperation of the French fleet under COUNT D'ESTAING. D'Estaing, however, withdrew his forces after a hurricane scattered his ships. The British counterattacked at the BATTLE OF RHODE ISLAND (August 29, 1778). However, thanks to Sullivan, the American land forces withdrew in good order, preventing many casualties and loss of supplies.

In 1779 Congress ordered John Sullivan to wage a scorched-earth campaign against the IROQUOIS in New York. Under Sullivan, joined by General GEORGE CLINTON, the Americans burned 18 Iroquois towns, destroyed 160,000 bushels of corn, and laid waste to the Indians' fruit and vegetable gardens, depriving the Iroquois of their economic resources. Feeling ill from his campaign in the wilderness and still harassed by critics, he resigned in November 1779.

Sullivan continued his political career as a member of the Continental Congress for two more years. In 1782 he became a member of the New Hampshire constitutional convention and served until 1786 as attorney general and as speaker of the state assembly (in 1785). In 1786 he was elected president (governor) of New Hampshire and helped to put down Shays's Rebellion (1786–87). He was reelected two more times and ended his political career as a United States district judge, a position he held until his death in 1795.

See also NATIVE AMERICANS.

Further reading: Charles P. Whittemore, *A General of the Revolution, John Sullivan of New Hampshire* (New York: Columbia University Press, 1961).

— Dirk Voss

Supreme Court

The Supreme Court of the United States was established by Article III of the United States Constitution. Article III contains far less detail than Article I (establishing the

Congress) and Article II (establishing the Executive), and much of the operation of the judiciary was worked out over ensuing decades by the Supreme Court itself and by Congress. Article III contains three sections. Section 1 vests the "judicial power of the United States" in "one supreme Court, and in such inferior Courts as the Congress may from time to time ordain and establish." The Supreme Court was thus created directly by the Constitution; all lower federal courts were created by Congress. Section 1 also provides that the justices (and all other federal judges) "shall hold their Offices during good Behaviour," which means they are not subject to removal from office except by IMPEACHMENT. Section 2 lists those cases in which the Supreme Court has appellate jurisdiction and those in which it has original jurisdiction—where it can act as a trial court. Section 3 deals with the crime of treason. Nothing in Article III gave the Supreme Court the power to say what the Constitution meant and to invalidate the acts of the other branches (or the states) if it found them unconstitutional. Power over state legislation was given to the Supreme Court by Congress in the JUDICIARY ACT OF 1789. Power over federal acts was claimed by the Court in *MARBURY V. MADISON* (1803). The march to claim and keep this power—which is called the power of judicial review—defines the history of the Court during the early republican period.

Dispute persists over whether the framers intended the Court to exercise the power of judicial review. ALEXANDER HAMILTON, in the *FEDERALIST PAPERS*, urged that while the federal courts would be "beyond comparison the weakest of the three departments of power," it would "belong" to the federal courts to "ascertain" the meaning of the Constitution "as well as the meaning of any particular act proceeding from the legislative body." As history has demonstrated, it is hard to reconcile these two statements.

Whatever the case, the first two Supreme Courts declined to assert the power to invalidate legislation. GEORGE WASHINGTON named as the first chief justice JOHN JAY of New York, who had coauthored the *Federalist Papers*. Joining him as associate justices were John Rutledge of South Carolina, John Blair of Virginia, JAMES WILSON of Pennsylvania, William Cushing of Massachusetts, and James Iredell of North Carolina. The Supreme Court met for the first time in the then-capital, New York, on February 1, 1790. Three years passed before the Supreme Court heard a case of consequence. Finally, in 1793 *Chisholm v. Georgia* arrived on the docket. Alexander Chisholm was a South Carolinian who had brought a federal lawsuit against Georgia for failing to pay him under a state bond. Georgia claimed that as a sovereign state it could not be sued in federal court. The Supreme Court held otherwise. The states and Congress balked at the decision, and within five years the Eleventh Amendment to

the Constitution was ratified, overturning the decision. In 1794 Chief Justice John Jay accepted an appointment as special ambassador to England, where he negotiated what came to be known as JAY'S TREATY (1794). On his return to the United States in 1795, he resigned from the Supreme Court to become governor of New York. Washington appointed as his successor Oliver Ellsworth of Connecticut, principal author of the JUDICIARY ACT OF 1789, which established the lower federal courts. Other justices also joined the Supreme Court. Justice Rutledge had resigned in 1791, and he was replaced by Thomas Johnson of Maryland. Johnson resigned a year later, and he was replaced by William Paterson of New Jersey. Justice Blair resigned in 1796, and his place was filled by SAMUEL CHASE of Maryland, who would later be impeached. Justice James Wilson, a notorious speculator, died in 1798 in North Carolina, to which he had fled from New Jersey creditors. Justice James Iredell died in 1799. President JOHN ADAMS named successors to the latter two. To replace Wilson, Adams nominated Bushrod Washington, the nephew and heir of President George Washington. Adams named Alfred Moore of North Carolina to Iredell's seat.

In 1800 the capital moved from Philadelphia to WASHINGTON, D.C., and the FEDERALIST PARTY lost the presidency. Immediately before Adams turned power over to the incoming Jefferson administration, Chief Justice Oliver Ellsworth tendered his resignation, and Adams hurriedly appointed his secretary of state, JOHN MARSHALL, to fill his place. Marshall's appointment was the single most important event in the history of the Supreme Court.

John Marshall revolutionized the Supreme Court. During the course of his 34-year tenure as chief justice, he abolished (for the most part) the justices' practice of writing separate (*seriatim*) opinions, forged the members of the Supreme Court into a unified whole under his command, and established the power of judicial review, thereby fixing the Supreme Court as the central player in the definition of constitutional rights and responsibilities. His tenure began with the landmark case of *Marbury v. Madison*, in which for the first time the Supreme Court invalidated a federal act as unconstitutional. There followed a series of decisions (including *Fletcher v. Peck*, *McCulloch v. Maryland*, and *Trustees of Dartmouth College v. Woodward*) in which the Supreme Court invalidated as unconstitutional acts of various states. The centralizing tendency of his constitutional opinions was controversial, and Marshall won many enemies, particularly in the South. Nevertheless, his legacy persists.

The political and constitutional impact of the Marshall Court is well known. Less well known is the structure of the institution over which he presided. The Supreme Court itself, as noted, was established directly by the Constitution. The lower federal courts—the federal district and circuit courts—were established by the Judiciary Act of 1789, then briefly reformed by the JUDICIARY ACT OF 1801, then reestablished along the lines set forth in the Judiciary Act of 1789 when the 1801 Judiciary Act was repealed in 1802. From the justices' vantage, the worst part of the structure established by the 1789 act was the circuit court. The circuit courts acted both as appellate courts over the district courts and as trial courts. The circuit courts comprised the district judge for the district in which the court sat and the Supreme Court justice(s) assigned to that circuit. This meant that for most of the working year, the justices were not hearing cases in the capital; instead, they were riding around the country, presiding over appeals from district court decisions and trials. The circuit responsibility was removed temporarily by the Judiciary Act of 1801 and then reinstated when that act was repealed the following year. Circuit riding continued to occupy the major part of the justices' time during most of the 19th century.

Where did the Supreme Court meet? Perhaps surprisingly, the Supreme Court lacked its own building until the 1930s. During its first two decades, when the capital was in New York, Philadelphia, and then Washington, D.C., the Supreme Court met in a variety of places, from state courtrooms to congressional committee rooms. In 1810 the justices were finally given a courtroom of their own in the basement of the United States Capitol. It was there that most of the major landmark cases of the Marshall Court were heard and decided, and there that our modern constitutional order was largely fashioned.

Further reading: Robert Shnayerson, *The Illustrated History of the Supreme Court of the United States* (New York: Harry N. Abrahms, 1986).

— Lindsay Robertson

T

Talleyrand-Périgord, Charles-Maurice, prince de Bénévent (1754–1838)

The nimble politician and diplomat Charles-Maurice de Talleyrand-Périgord (usually called Prince Talleyrand) served in seven different governments in France. He is most noted for his role in the Congress of Vienna, where he managed to ensure that France, even though defeated, would still be considered a power in Europe. As French foreign minister in the late 1790s and early 1800s, he was involved in the XYZ AFFAIR (1797–98) and the LOUISIANA PURCHASE (1803).

The second son of a minor French noble family, Talleyrand was trained as a priest. By the beginning of the FRENCH REVOLUTION (1789–1815), he was a bishop. Supporting moderate reform, he advocated the surrender of all church lands to the French state and government support for the clergy. For his position on the church he was excommunicated. During the most radical phase of the French Revolution, he was sent to England on a diplomatic mission. Rather than return to France, where he might have been guillotined, he went to the United States. In 1796, after a more conservative regime had seized power in France, he returned to his native country and was appointed foreign minister. It was from this position that he had his agents, labeled X, Y, and Z, demand bribes from American negotiators. This mistake led to the QUASI WAR (1798–1800) between France and the United States. But it was also Talleyrand, after NAPOLEON BONAPARTE had seized power, who orchestrated the negotiations that ended the undeclared war. Similarly, Talleyrand played a key role in the discussions leading up to the American purchase of Louisiana, insisting that if France gave up New Orleans, it would have little use for the entire territory. Although he was made a prince by Napoleon, he disagreed with the emperor's ambition to dominate Europe and retired in 1807. He came out of retirement for the Congress of Vienna, representing the restored Bourbon kings of France. He retired again in 1815, subsequently serving the July Monarchy (1830–48) of King Louis-Philippe as ambassador to Great Britain.

See also FOREIGN AFFAIRS.

Tammany Society

The Tammany Society, or Columbian Order, was founded in 1786 in New York City as a fraternal organization. Centering on the figure of the legendary Delaware chief Tamanend, members developed a ritual based on NATIVE AMERICAN symbols: The leaders were sachems, the members braves; Tammanyites wore native costume at celebrations; and they called their meeting place a wigwam. Although the Tammany Society had some more affluent members, it attracted a disproportionate number of ARTISANS. Initially, its aim was "to cherish . . . the great principles of civil liberty . . . to cultivate political information . . . to give exercise to the divine emotions of charity – and finally . . . to enjoy without restraint the generous effusions of national enthusiasm." Given its membership, the Tammany Society quickly took on an egalitarian and democratic caste.

In the early 1790s Tammany centered its activities on celebrating various patriotic holidays, but the controversies of 1793 and 1794 brought it into politics, supporting the DEMOCRATIC-REPUBLICANS and THOMAS JEFFERSON. With almost 500 members, Tammany played a key role in artisan support for Jefferson in the ELECTION OF 1800. By that time, Tammany was a political bastion of AARON BURR. After Burr's fall from grace, Tammany continued to be important in Democratic-Republican politics. Representing worker interests, Tammany supported a number of democratic causes, including ending imprisonment for debt and universal manhood SUFFRAGE. Tammany became part of the political organization of Martin Van Buren and the Democratic Party. By the 1830s Tammany had become a political machine that many viewed as the epitome of corrupt urban politics.

Further reading: Alfred F. Young, *The Democratic Republicans of New York: The Origins, 1763–1797* (Chapel Hill: University of North Carolina Press, 1967).

tariffs

Taxes on imported goods are called tariffs. Such taxes have played an important role in the political controversies in American history, from colonial complaints over imperial policy to debates over the use of tariffs to raise revenue and protect industry in the United States.

Although imperial trade regulations passed by Parliament are not often considered tariffs, these measures often functioned just like the tariffs of the national period. Laws such as the Molasses Act (1733) that taxed imported sugar were meant to encourage agricultural production in the British WEST INDIES at the expense of France and other foreign powers. Both the SUGAR ACT (1764), which decreased the tax on sugar but provided for better enforcement, and the TOWNSHEND DUTIES (1767) were taxes on imports intended to raise revenue. While such measures led to the RESISTANCE MOVEMENT (1764–75) and contributed to the outbreak of the REVOLUTIONARY WAR (1775–83), Americans had to rely on customs duties once they achieved independence. The CONTINENTAL CONGRESS failed to successfully impose such regulations, while several states, such as Massachusetts and Pennsylvania, collected tariffs in the 1780s to protect production of manufactured items and raise revenue.

Almost as soon as the new congress under the Constitution of the United States met, it passed a tariff. The Tariff Act of 1789 placed a 5 percent duty on all imported items and added extra duties to certain items. Carriages, for example, carried a 15 percent duty. Although ALEXANDER HAMILTON sought further protection for American manufacturers in the 1790s, he was not successful. The only legislative encouragement for industry before the War of 1812 (1812–15) came from measures like the EMBARGO OF 1807. The decline of TRADE that occurred after 1808 through the War of 1812 helped to spur American industry. Recognizing this growth as a positive development, DEMOCRATIC-REPUBLICANS passed a protective tariff in 1816. Imports on items like cotton and woolen goods had to pay a 25 percent tax until 1819. In 1818 the tariff deadline was extended to 1826. By that time, tariffs had become a central political issue, separating the developing POLITICAL PARTIES and dividing the nation into sections.

Further reading: F. W. Taussig, *The Tariff History of the United States* (New York: G. P. Putnam's Sons, 1892).

Tarleton, Banastre (1754–1833)

A brilliant cavalry officer, renowned for his tactics of relentless pursuit, sudden appearance, and swift assault with sabers and bayonets, Banastre Tarleton became one of the most hated men of the REVOLUTIONARY WAR (1775–83). Born in Liverpool, England, on August 21, 1754, he was the third of seven children in a wealthy merchant family whose money came from sugar and slaves. He attended Oxford for two years and briefly studied law at the prestigious Middle Temple. When he was 19 his father died and left him a sizeable fortune, which Tarleton quickly squandered. In April 1775 he purchased a commission as a cornet in the king's cavalry, the lowest and cheapest commissioned officer rank one could buy.

With rebellion underway in America, he took leave of his regiment the following year and crossed the Atlantic with CHARLES, LORD CORNWALLIS's force and participated in the failed attack upon Charleston. When the expedition returned to New York in August 1776, Tarleton volunteered to serve in the 16th Light Dragoons. He found his niche in the cavalry, and his rise as an officer was rapid. In January 1778 Tarleton was promoted to captain, skipping over the rank of lieutenant, and by August he was a lieutenant colonel in the British Legion, a regiment of cavalry

Bostonians paying the exciseman *(National Archives)*

and infantry recruited from among New York LOYALISTS. He was not yet 24 years old. Generally described as a short, well-proportioned, and powerful man, Tarleton fought in many prominent actions during the Revolutionary War.

While serving in New Jersey, he was in the raiding party that captured General CHARLES LEE at Basking Ridge, but his notoriety is largely due to his service in the South. A rigid commander on the march and during battle, Tarleton was often indifferent to the actions of his troops in the aftermath. At Monck's Corner (April 14, 1780) and at the Waxhaws (May 29, 1780) in South Carolina, Tarleton and his men reportedly refused to give quarter to surrendering American soldiers and massacred them. More than once, Tarleton's British Legion drew criticism for its brutal behavior, earning its leader the epithets "Bloody Tarleton" and "Bloody Ban." In retaliation for his actions, victorious American soldiers at KING'S MOUNTAIN (October 7, 1780) shouted "Tarleton's Quarter" as they slaughtered surrendering Loyalists. Until the end of the war, the British Legion served primarily in the Carolinas, participating in the successes at CAMDEN (August 16, 1780) and GUILFORD COURTHOUSE (March 15, 1781), where Tarleton lost two fingers on his right hand, and in the disastrous defeat at COWPENS (January 17, 1781), where he narrowly escaped but lost most of his men. While keeping British supply lines open in South Carolina, the legion combed the swamps in a fruitless attempt to capture guerrilla leader FRANCIS MARION. By referring to his elusive quarry as "this damned old fox," Tarleton became responsible for General Marion's enduring nickname of "Swamp Fox."

Tarleton's fighting days in the war ended at YORKTOWN (October 19, 1781), but the hostility toward the cavalryman did not cease. His reputation was such that, in the round of dinner parties that followed the surrender among officers of the American, French, and British armies, Tarleton was the only British officer not invited. He was outraged, feared for his life, and sought protection from the French, though COMTE DE ROCHAMBEAU remarked that he, too, viewed the outcast as a butcher and a barbarian. Nevertheless, Tarleton returned to adulation in England in 1782 and to a life of dissipation within the circle of friends surrounding the Prince of Wales. In 1787 Tarleton drew fierce criticism for a published attack on his former mentor, Cornwallis and wrote his own chronicle of the southern campaigns in America during 1780 and 1781, omitting reference to the disaster at Cowpens, for which he had always denied blame. Tarleton represented Liverpool in the House of Commons for seven terms between 1790 and 1812, but his military career languished. Though he attained the rank of general in 1812, he served only in domestic backwaters and never saw action again. In 1816 he asked for and received a baronetcy, and when his old friend ascended to the throne as George IV, Tarleton became a knight of the Order of Bath. Infirm and ailing from gout, he died at home in 1833.

Further reading: Robert D. Bass, *The Green Dragoon: The Lives of Banastre Tarleton and Mary Robinson* (New York: Redman, 1957); John Buchanan, *The Road to Guilford Courthouse: The American Revolution in the Carolinas* (New York: John Wiley, 1997).

— Rita M. Broyles

taverns

Taverns were important institutions in the late 18th and early 19th centuries. Food, drink, and sometimes lodging could be found at a tavern. They were also a prominent locus of sociability. Whether in the city or in the country, whole communities depended on taverns to gather people together to exchange gossip and news. Taverns had economic functions as well. Deals were made in taverns and jobs could be found. Taverns along the waterfront were often rendezvous houses for recruiting sailors. Illicit activity also occurred in some taverns, including gambling and prostitution.

Before the REVOLUTIONARY WAR (1775–83), a wide spectrum of society patronized the same tavern in cities; rich and poor sat in the same room and interacted. Political discussion flowed as freely as alcohol. During the RESISTANCE MOVEMENT (1764–75), groups like the SONS OF LIBERTY often met in taverns. In New York City, for example, Montagne's Tavern was the center of organization activity in the LIBERTY POLE/TREE controversies. At the same time there was growing social stratification in tavern going. Philadelphia's City Tavern, founded in 1773, was more expensive than others and catered to LAWYERS and merchants. Because of this stratification, some members of the elite argued against using taverns for political discussion; the first Pennsylvania STATE CONSTITUTION, which provided that all laws had to be published and presented before the public, was accused of encouraging tavern government. Regardless of this charge, taverns remained important in politics. During the 1790s and early 1800s, different political organizations, like the DEMOCRATIC-REPUBLICAN SOCIETIES, met in taverns.

Beyond politics, all kinds of associations met at taverns as a convenient and public location for people to congregate, including ethnic societies and early labor organizations. Within a community, a tavern owner often exerted influence on his customers, and sometimes acted as an informal banker to people who lived on the margins.

See also TEMPERANCE.

Further reading: David W. Conroy, *In Public Houses: Drink and the Revolution in Colonial Authority* (Chapel

Hill: University of North Carolina Press, 1995); Jack Larkin, *The Reshaping of Everyday Life, 1790–1840* (New York: Harper & Row, 1988); Peter Thompson, *Rum Punch and Revolution: Tavern Going and Public Life in Eighteenth-Century Philadelphia* (Philadelphia: University of Pennsylvania Press, 1999).

Taylor, John, of Caroline (1753–1824)

During the early national period, John Taylor of Caroline was a leading political theorist and advocate of the type of liberal democratic thought known as Jeffersonian democracy. Born in Caroline County, Virginia, Taylor was still a child when his parents died. His uncle Edmund Pendleton took him in and gave him a good education. After attending the College of William and Mary, he studied law with his uncle and was admitted to the Virginia bar in 1774. During the REVOLUTIONARY WAR (1775–83), Taylor served in the CONTINENTAL ARMY where he attained the rank of colonel. He resigned in 1779 to serve with the Virginia militia.

Taylor was elected to the Virginia House of Delegates from 1779 to 1781, 1783 to 1785, and 1796 to 1800. As a legislator, his libertarian and democratic leanings were obvious from the beginning. He was most interested in such democratic issues as RELIGIOUS LIBERTY, voting rights, and fair representation. Taylor filled two unexpired terms in the United States Senate and was elected to the Senate twice in his own right. In 1797 he served as a presidential elector.

A leading ANTI-FEDERALIST, Taylor's opposition to the new Constitution reflected his concern that a strong central government would fail to respect individual rights. He believed that the freedom of the individual was much more secure under state governments. Taylor particularly disagreed with the ideas of nationalists like JOHN ADAMS and ALEXANDER HAMILTON, and throughout his life he remained a strong supporter of THOMAS JEFFERSON. However, he objected to President Jefferson's willingness to compromise. During a third term in the house of delegates, his STATE'S RIGHTS convictions led him to introduce JAMES MADISON's Virginia Resolution (part of the VIRGINIA AND KENTUCKY RESOLUTIONS, 1798) In his later years he was associated with a dissident group of old DEMOCRATIC-REPUBLICANS led by JOHN RANDOLPH and sometimes called the *Tertium Quid*.

Despite his active political life, John Taylor thought of himself as a gentleman farmer and author. His writings, although long and difficult, provide one of the best examples of the mixture of classical republican and more modern laissez-faire ideals that characterized Jeffersonian political thought. Taylor produced his most important works during the last decade of his life. *An Inquiry into the Principle and Policy of the United States Government* (1814) was Taylor's long-delayed response to John Adams's *Defense of the Constitutions of Government of the United States* (1787). His *Construction Construed and Constitutions Vindicated* (1820) contained strong arguments in favor of state's rights and a strict interpretation of the Constitution. The *Arator*, a book of essays on scientific AGRICULTURE published in 1813, provides the best examples of his agricultural ideas. As a southern planter and a slaveholder, Taylor was typical of his class in his belief that Congress could not restrict the expansion of SLAVERY into the territories. John Taylor died at Hazelwood, his plantation in Caroline County, Virginia, in 1824 while filling another unexpired Senate term.

See also REPUBLICANISM.

Further reading: Charles William Hill, Jr., *The Political Theory of John Taylor of Caroline* (Rutherford, N.J.: Fairleigh Dickinson University Press, 1976); Robert E. Shalhope, *John Taylor of Caroline* (Columbia: University of South Carolina Press, 1980).

— Robert Lively

Tea Act (May 10, 1773)

Parliament passed the Tea Act in 1773 to aid the British East India Company, which was on the verge of bankruptcy, by allowing it to sell its tea directly to the North American colonies. There was nothing sinister in the plan, and it was not intended to corrupt American liberty. Colonial appetite for luxury items like tea had been growing in the second half of the 18th century, and much of the colonial demand for tea was met by smuggling tea from the Dutch. Before the Tea Act, British East India tea had to be shipped to England, sold on the wholesale market there, pay an English tax, and then be reshipped to the colonies, where it paid another tax since it was the only item still taxed under the TOWNSHEND DUTIES (1767) after 1770. The Tea Act did away with the reselling process and the tax in England, making it less expensive than smuggled tea. To facilitate the process further, the East India Company would contract the selling of tea to specific firms in each colony. Theoretically, everyone would win from this measure: The East India Company would make some money. Colonists would have a cheaper product. And Great Britain would gain revenue from the Townshend Duties.

Many colonists, however, objected to the Tea Act. Smugglers and merchants who were not given the tea contracts saw their livelihood jeopardized. Others believed that the measure would corrupt American society by establishing a monopoly and was a subtle way to compel compliance with the Townshend Duties. Besides protesting and petitioning the measure, colonists in Boston staged the BOSTON TEA PARTY (December 16, 1773). Other colonies also destroyed the imported tea. This led to an escalating conflict with Great Britain, which passed the COERCIVE ACTS (1774), and the eventual opening of hostilities in the battles of LEXINGTON AND CONCORD on April 19, 1775.

See also REPUBLICANISM; RESISTANCE MOVEMENT.

Further reading: Benjamin Woods Labaree, *The Boston Tea Party* (New York: Oxford University Press, 1966).

Tecumseh (1768–1813)

Tecumseh tried to unite all NATIVE AMERICANS to defend against the expansion of the United States into territories beyond the Appalachian Mountains after American independence. The movement he led marked the last serious opposition of Native Americans east of the Mississippi against the relentless American demands for more land. With his death, most eastern tribes accepted that they could not defeat the invaders through armed resistance.

Tecumseh was born in a village on the Mad River in what is now Ohio. His father died fighting British and Virginians in LORD DUNMORE's War (1774). Soon after, Tecumseh's mother gave birth to triplets. One of the babies died, but the surviving boy and girl grew into adulthood. The baby boy, Tenskwatawa (1775–1836), became an important religious leader known as THE SHAWNEE PROPHET.

The REVOLUTIONARY WAR (1774–83) ended before Tecumseh could join the fighting. The Shawnee, like most tribes, sided with the British against their rebelling subjects. The Crown promised to stop the American settlers that threatened to overrun Shawnee hunting grounds. Each year more colonists streamed over the mountains and established farms and villages on land they bought from tribal members who had no authority to sell it. Other times the Americans simply took the land and killed any Native Americans who tried to stop them. Allying themselves with the English king seemed to be the only way to protect themselves and their homes. When the war ended, the British turned over to the Americans the entire country east of the Mississippi River. The British tried to assure their Native-Americans allies that the United States merely had jurisdiction over the area and that the land itself still belonged to the tribes.

The United States government said it wanted the land sales to be fair and legal, but this rarely happened. Moreover, the authorities did not have enough soldiers or even the desire to keep the settlers off Native American domains. The tribes defeated American military expeditions into the region in the early 1790s, but the Indians lost at the BATTLE OF FALLEN TIMBERS (August 20, 1794). After this battle, the United States took over most of the Ohio Territory under the terms of the TREATY OF GREENVILLE (1795).

Tecumseh joined in some of the fighting to protect his people's homes. Tenskwatawa could not fight because he lost an eye in an accident and drank heavily. However, in April 1805 Tenskwatawa had a vision that changed his life. He told his friends and neighbors that they must return to the old ways, to give up drinking, and to avoid relying on the manufactured goods brought in by the traders. Tecumseh listened to his brother's vision and believed that his message might unite the various tribes to resist the advancing Americans. He also learned an important lesson from the Americans: The colonies had banded together and defeated the mighty British Empire. Tecumseh believed if he and Tenskwatawa could convince the tribes to put aside their disputes and fight for their homes as one nation, they might win against the United States.

For the next few years, the two brothers spread their ideas from Alabama to Wisconsin. Tenskwatawa settled at Prophetstown on the Tippecanoe River in what is now western Indiana, where his followers could live far from the corrupting Americans. Tecumseh traveled to many different tribes in the hopes of convincing them to join together to protect their lands. This mission was difficult, since many of tribes were bitter enemies. Moreover, some of the southern tribes now lived in cabins and farmed like their white neighbors. They showed little interest in Tecumseh's confederation and Tenskwatawa's plea to return to simple life.

The territorial governor of Indiana, William Henry Harrison, saw the movement as a direct threat. Harrison suspected that the British in CANADA were helping Tecumseh with weapons and supplies. Tecumseh and the governor met several times in the first decade of the 1800s but never reached a final agreement. During one conference in Vincennes (1810), they became so angry at each other they drew weapons and almost started fighting.

Harrison marched on Prophetstown with an army of about 1,000 men while Tecumseh was traveling and Tenskwatawa was in charge. The Prophet foolishly attacked the American camp against his brother's orders and suffered a major defeat in the BATTLE OF TIPPECANOE (November 7, 1811). After the battle, many warriors lost faith in the movement and left. Tecumseh and his followers retreated into British Canada. When the War of 1812 (1812–15) broke out, Harrison invaded Canada and defeated a mixed force of Native Americans and British soldiers at the Battle of the Thames (October 5, 1813). Tecumseh died in the fighting. Within two decades, the American government forced the eastern tribes to leave their ancient homelands and move west across the Mississippi.

Further reading: R. David Edmunds, *Tecumseh and the Quest for Indian Leadership* (Boston: Little, Brown, 1984).

— George Milne

temperance

Temperance, the drive to restrict alcohol consumption, was the longest-running social-reform movement in the United States, beginning in the 1740s and culminating with the Eighteenth Amendment. From 1756 to 1820, Americans for the first time began to express concerns about alcohol consumption and to envision a world in which alcohol was not permitted.

American colonists drank large amounts of alcohol, in part because they did not have much else to drink. Water was tainted with the stigma of POVERTY, and it could be unhealthy, often carrying refuse and excrement and teeming with disease. Those families that had cows reserved the milk to make butter and cheese. In addition, before refrigeration and pasteurization, there was no way to prevent fruit juices from fermenting. Naturally occurring airborne yeast entered any fruit juice and caused fermentation. Coffee was unfamiliar to most colonists until the late 18th century. Tea remained an expensive luxury until tea duties were lowered in 1745. And so, when colonists drank, they drank alcohol.

Alcohol was an important part of early modern culture. Colonists drank for religious and secular celebrations, weddings, birthings, funerals, MEDICINE, beauty, and with meals. Early modern men and women believed that alcohol was salubrious. Employers and employees shared morning toddies and afternoon drinks to cement their relationships.

The first concerns about alcohol in colonial America arose in the medical community in the 1740s. Physicians, particularly Philadelphian BENJAMIN RUSH, noted a new disease, then called the WEST INDIES dry gripes, which caused a painful death in those who drank rum (later discovered to be lead poisoning from the West Indies lead stills). Rush's experiences during the REVOLUTIONARY WAR (1775–83), when he worked for the CONTINENTAL ARMY, furthered his concerns regarding alcohol and led him to publish pamphlets detailing the dangers of hard liquors. For example, in Rush's 1784 booklet "Inquiry into the Effects of Spirituous Liquors on the Human Body and Mind," he asserted that spirits transformed a person into something less than human: "in fetor, a skunk; in filthiness, a hog; in obesity, a he-goat."

Rush's recommendations went mostly unheeded until the early 19th century. Instead, in the late 18th century colonists began to drink more alcohol than ever when the price of whiskey dropped dramatically. In order to purchase larger farms, Americans had begun heading west where they grew corn. The country's poor roads meant, however, that farmers could not get their corn to market while it was still edible. Western farmers realized that if they distilled their corn into whiskey they would have a profitable product that would not spoil before it could be sold. Soon the price of whiskey dropped and colonists could afford to drink more than ever.

The increasing consumption of whiskey and resulting drunkenness led to anxiety about the moral rectitude of the newborn republic at the start of the 19th century. When a doctor named William Clark read Rush's pamphlet about the evils of drunkenness, he showed it to his minister, who in turn shared it with influential members of their small New York town. These citizens banded together on April 30, 1808, to establish the first formal temperance group in the United States, the Union Temperance Society of Moreau and Northumberland. In 1813 Reverend Lyman Beecher also read Rush's pamphlet and helped to found the Connecticut Society for the Reformation of Morals, a group focused on temperance. Other clergy soon founded similar organizations.

The success of ministers in founding temperance groups is partly explained by the worry of the developing middle class about finding sober workers. Businessmen also feared that increased alcohol consumption would disrupt social relationships, particularly as employer-employee relationships changed during the 1820s. Until the 1820s employees generally lived with their employers, and employers were responsible for the welfare of their workers. The new emphasis on family privacy and on the home as a refuge from the workplace in the early 19th century led employers to remove workers from their homes. Businessmen, especially in New England, may have felt guilty about leaving workers to fend for themselves and fearful of the workers over whom they exercised less and less control. When Presbyterian and Congregationalist ministers began preaching about self-discipline and sobriety, the new business class, perhaps in order to relieve their guilt, agreed with this message enthusiastically.

Employers discovered that the ministers' message released them from responsibility for their workers. Employers' wives found the new message exciting because it gave them an important role in instilling self-discipline in the republic. Women founded hundreds of organizations to curb prostitution, reform asylums and orphanages, help widows with young children, and reduce drinking. Women's temperance efforts were more successful than their other social-reform labors. Their exertions were aided by improvements in water sanitation that made water safe to drink.

While temperance was not as effective as its advocates hoped, it was popular among the business class, and the movement became increasingly powerful. Already by the mid-1830s the American Temperance Society had 2,000 chapters, and average annual consumption rates of spirits dropped from five gallons per capita in 1830 to two gallons per capita in 1845, where it remains today.

See also MARRIAGE AND FAMILY LIFE; RELIGION; VOLUNTARY ASSOCIATIONS; WOMEN'S RIGHTS AND STATUS.

Further reading: Nathan O. Hatch, *Democratization of American Christianity* (New Haven, Conn.: Yale University Press, 1989); Paul E. Johnson, *A Shopkeeper's Millennium: Society and Revival in Rochester, New York, 1815–1837* (New York: Hill & Wang, 1978); W. J. Rorabaugh, *The Alcoholic Republic: An American Tradition* (New York: Oxford University Press, 1979).

— Sarah Hand Meacham

theater

American theater underwent a dramatic transformation from 1754 to 1820. In the colonial period theaters had a difficult time sustaining themselves, and performances were usually in barns or a building that had been adopted temporarily for stage production. By 1820 almost every city had a theater of its own.

During the 1750s theatrical troupes traveled to New York, Philadelphia, Williamsburg, and other locations, but could not find a permanent home. Part of the problem was that the cities and towns were too small to sustain permanent establishments, and part of the problem was that there were moral objections to the theater. During the STAMP ACT (1765) crisis, for example, New York's theater closed its doors. When the theater opened again in the spring of 1766, a crowd shouting "liberty, liberty" stormed into the building, attacked the patrons, and tore the place apart because the theater seemed an inappropriate extravagance at the time. During the REVOLUTIONARY WAR (1775–83), WHIGS continued to oppose theaters as a violation of their REPUBLICANISM. Many British officers, however, loved the theater and often organized their own performances. Major JOHN ANDRE was known for this type of activity.

Although the debate over theater continued in the United States after the war was over, opposition was not so strong as to prevent performances. GEORGE WASHINGTON enjoyed the theater and believed that it could be a means to inculcate morality. It was in this spirit that ROYALL TYLER wrote his play *The Contrast* (1787). Opponents, however, viewed theaters as a symbol of corrupt aristocracy and a place of immorality. As theaters developed in the 1790s and early 1800s in several cities, the antitheater adherents had an argument: Prostitutes used the theater as a place to rendezvous with customers, and audiences became rowdy and disorderly.

Regardless of their morality of lack of morality, theaters spread throughout the United States in the early national period. Philadelphia's Chestnut Street Theater opened in 1793, followed by New York's Park Theater in 1765. Other cities and towns built theaters as well. Productions were varied. Sometimes the theater would include Shakespeare or a more contemporary play. Often, the theater production would contain greater variety, with differ-

Philadelphia's Chestnut Street Theater was modeled after the Theatre Royal in Bath, England. Opened in 1794, the theater was destroyed by fire in 1820, but a new theater with the same name opened in 1822. Engraving *(Library of Congress)*

ent skits, short plays, and musical performances. Theater managers, like WILLIAM DUNLAP, strove to hire popular talent from England to draw in an audience, but American actors became increasingly popular on their own. Further development of competitive theaters and theaters that appealed to different classes would not occur until the 1820s and 1830s.

Further reading: Robert E. Shalhope, *The Roots of Democracy: American Thought and Culture, 1760–1800* (Boston: Twayne, 1990).

Tippecanoe, Battle of (November 7, 1811)

The American victory at Tippecanoe (in today's western Indiana) disrupted TECUMSEH's federation of NATIVE AMERICAN tribes in the Old Northwest, allowing the Americans to strengthen their hold on the region. After the battle, Tecumseh and his followers relied even more heavily on British aid and sanctuary in CANADA, unable to mount effective resistance in the United States. The engagement also brought the territorial governor of Indiana, William Henry Harrison, to national prominence.

The Tippecanoe River ran near the village of Prophetstown, named for Tecumseh's brother, THE SHAWNEE PROPHET, Tenskwatawa. The settlement thrived during the end of the first decade of the 1800s, with members of many different tribes answering Tecumseh's call for a united effort against the encroachments of the Americans in the area. They met at Prophetstown in order to organize safely beyond the reach of the white settlers and soldiers. There, the villagers could return to the traditional lifestyles of their ancestors, avoiding whiskey and other European-American goods that the Prophet saw as corrupting. The site also offered access to Canada, so the inhabitants could draw upon supplies and weapons from the British.

The United States government looked upon the settlement with alarm. A short distance from the FRONTIER stood the headquarters of a highly organized resistance movement led by two capable men. Harrison received permission from President JAMES MADISON to move against the settlement. The governor had little trouble raising volunteers to strengthen his force of regular army troops. In late September 1811 he carefully marched his men toward the town.

The governor knew he would face his enemies without their best leader. Tecumseh was on one of his missions to neighboring tribes to make alliances, having left Tenskwatawa in charge with orders to avoid a fight. The Indian confederation did not have enough strength yet to stand up to the Americans, and Tecumseh needed time to unite all the Native Americans. The Prophet did not listen to his brother and prepared for battle. In the early morning hours of November 7, 1811, the warriors of Prophetstown silently surrounded the American campsite a few miles away from the village. They planned to slip some men into the camp to confuse the soldiers and kill Harrison. The rest of the Indi-

ans outside the defenses were to fire into the startled camp as soon as the signal was given. Harrison had prepared for just such a surprise attack. The men slept with their muskets and the encampment stood in an easily defended area. A sentry sounded the alarm around four in the morning when he saw the warriors trying to sneak into the base. The Americans took some heavy casualties at first, but then rallied and beat back their attackers. When the sun came up, most of the Prophet's men had returned to the town to pack and flee with their families. An American patrol found the village deserted and Harrison ordered it burned along with any supplies they found.

Although Harrison lost more men then Tenskwatawa, the battle ruined the Prophet's reputation. The movement to unite all the Native Americans against the United States never recovered from the blow.

Further reading: R. David Edmunds, *Tecumseh and the Quest for Indian Leadership* (Boston: Little, Brown, 1984).
— George Milne

Townshend Duties (June 29, 1767)

Led by Charles Townshend, the British Parliament passed customs duties in 1767, called the Townshend Duties, to raise revenue from the North American colonies. This measure triggered a new wave of conflict between the colonies and Great Britain.

The Rockingham administration that had repealed the STAMP ACT (1765; repealed 1766) and had appeared so favorable to the colonies did not last through the summer of 1766. In its place WILLIAM PITT, now Lord Chatham, organized a new government. Chatham, however, was not the same energetic man who had led Britain to victory in the French and Indian War (1754–63). The leadership of his administration soon fell into drift, and Charles Townshend ended up playing a leading role in molding policy by the spring of 1767. A £500,000 tax cut in Great Britain, combined with continued colonial expenses, convinced Townshend to raise revenue in North America. News that the colonial assembly in New York had refused to comply with the QUARTERING ACT of 1765 further aggravated the situation. Some colonial Americans had distinguished between internal and external taxation, including BENJAMIN FRANKLIN in testimony before Parliament, during the Stamp Act crisis. Internal taxes like the Stamp Act were intended to raise revenue within the colonies and were by right, so colonial Americans claimed, the province of their own assemblies. External taxes were duties and regulations that governed imperial relations and were within the powers of Parliament to manage the empire. Townshend decided to use this distinction and have Parliament pass duties on glass, lead, painter's colors, paper, and tea

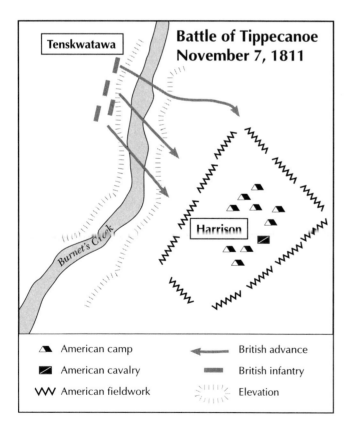

**Battle of Tippecanoe
November 7, 1811**

Tenskwatawa

Burnet's Creek

Harrison

▲	American camp	←	British advance
◨	American cavalry	▬	British infantry
WWW	American fieldwork	⑊	Elevation

imported into the colonies. These "external" taxes would raise about £40,000. This money was to be used to pay royal officials in the colonies and make them independent of the colonial assemblies. In addition, Townshend also had passed a series of rules and regulations to make customs collection more efficient, including the expansion of the Admiralty Court system.

Colonial Americans were unsure of how to respond to the Townshend Duties, and the RESISTANCE MOVEMENT (1764–75) never assumed the full proportions it had against the Stamp Act. Some Americans acknowledged that Parliament may have acted within its proper bounds by passing the customs regulations, even if the intent was to raise revenue. Others began to argue that the distinction between internal and external taxes was invalid if the external tax was not to regulate the empire, but to raise money. This point gained popularity after it appeared in JOHN DICKINSON's *Letters from a Pennsylvanian Farmer* (1767–68). Still, efforts at setting up nonimportation agreements had difficulty getting started, as merchants in some seaports refused to join, undercutting the efforts of merchants in other seaports. The Massachusetts legislature strove to take the lead, issuing a Circular Letter (February 11, 1768) admitting the right of Parliament to be "the supreme legislative Power over the whole Empire," but asserting that it was one of the "fundamental Rules of the British Constitution" that an individual could not have his property taken away from him without his own consent—in other words, only the direct representatives of the colonists could tax the colonies. Since only a few colonial assemblies were in session, the response to this letter was not great.

In 1768 and 1769, however, tensions between the colonies and Great Britain increased, especially in Boston. The Massachusetts Circular had alienated Governor FRANCIS BERNARD from the assembly. Simultaneously, conflicts erupted in the street between newly appointed customs officials and the people of Boston. Several RIOTS ensued, especially after customs agents seized JOHN HANCOCK's sloop the *Liberty* (June 10, 1768). To help control the situation, the British government ordered troops to Boston. Against this backdrop, resistance began to spread. Customs officials were harassed in several ports, and some crowds began to use tar and feathers as a means to humiliate a few lower officials. By 1769 a nonimportation movement finally started to take hold across the colonies. Animosity between the British troops and citizens in Boston and New York City, which was as much over the competition for jobs as imperial problems, led to confrontations known as the BATTLE OF GOLDEN HILL in New York (January 18, 1770) and the BOSTON MASSACRE (March 5, 1770) in New England's leading port.

By the time those two conflict took place, the leaders of Parliament had decided to abandon the Townshend Duties. Recognizing the unpopularity of the measures in the colonies realizing that the hoped-for revenue was not forthcoming, a new set of ministers decided to abandon the regulations. The government under LORD FREDERICK NORTH in April 1770 repealed all the duties, except the tax on tea. Like the DECLARATORY ACT (1766), the one remaining duty on tea was meant as a symbolic gesture to assert Parliamentary supremacy. The repeal effectively defused the imperial crisis until 1773.

Further reading: Robert Middlekauff, *The Glorious Cause: The American Revolution, 1763–1789* (New York: Oxford University Press, 1982).

trade

In the revolutionary era, trade became increasingly important as Americans sought more market opportunity through commercial transactions with each other and with peoples from around the world. Inland or domestic trade began to increase in the years before the REVOLUTIONARY WAR (1775–83). Colonial farming families produced a variety of items, including cloth, hats, deerskin, beaver pelts, barrels, rum, cider, and whiskey, to supplement incomes. Towns such as Lancaster, Pennsylvania, and Elizabeth, New Jersey, became important centers for this trade. By the 1770s more and more Americans focused on buying, selling, and making profits. The trade expansion of the mid- and late 18th century also produced an increased demand for paper money, which was restricted by British mercantile regulations.

While in many ways the Revolutionary War disrupted these developments, the conflict also created new opportunities. Warships and privateers threatened the overseas trade of both sides. But independence also allowed Americans to seek new markets. Similarly, marching armies and military depredations by British and American forces might cut off some trade, but the goods required to wage war increased the demand for domestic trade. Equipping the British, American, and French armies meant big business for farmers now preoccupied with the market. They produced foodstuffs and supplies for armies on the move, and by doing so they contributed to an expanding domestic trade. Increased inland trade during the war and just after led to many political efforts to create a ready supply of paper money in various states in the 1780s.

An economic downturn took place between 1784 and 1788 that severely depressed all manner of commercial exchange in the nation, underscoring the need for more available and stable paper currency. Also, various commercial policies of the states served to depress trade. The United States Constitution addressed these problems by creating a uniform trade policy (inland and foreign) for

Painting showing dock workers unloading sugar and cotton from the *John,* a merchant trade vessel, at a busy Salem, Massachusetts, wharf *(Library of Congress)*

Americans. The men at the CONSTITUTIONAL CONVENTION (1787) also addressed currency problems affecting traders by barring states from issuing their own currencies and creating a legal tender that was exclusively national. However, individual BANKS continued to issue banknotes to be used as currency well into the 19th century, both facilitating and complicating domestic trade.

After a slow start due to colonial restrictions, the war, and depression, foreign trade increased significantly between 1793 and 1807. Foreign mercantile trade created thriving coastal communities that took advantage of nearly constant war between England and France from 1793 until 1815. Merchants attained unprecedented wealth by shipping goods from French and British colonies through a reexport market to the United States and then to Europe. For the most part, American ships did not face interception because of their neutral status, as long as they stopped at an American port before heading to Europe. Some products of this reexport trade passing from the East and WEST INDIES via American ships included coffee, sugar, cocoa, silk, spices, and dyes. Other trade products included whale oil, wheat, tobacco, cotton, and fish. The American CHINA TRADE began in 1784, with an American ship completing a round-trip voyage from New York to Canton, China, and returning with tea, silk, and porcelain. The mercantile boom was especially good for port cities such as Baltimore, Salem, Boston, Philadelphia, Portsmouth, Charleston, New York, and Savannah. New opportunities arose for ARTISANS, sailors, shipbuilders, bankers, insurers, investors, and others sharing in the commercial wealth. For example, Baltimore's population grew by 156 percent between 1790 and 1810 as the city became a center of trade through the reexport market and by exporting flour milled from Susquehanna and Chesapeake wheat.

Some merchants amassed huge fortunes, such as STEPHEN GIRARD of Philadelphia, Robert Oliver of Baltimore, and Thomas Boylston of Salem. Merchants made money via the overseas trade in two ways: First, they earned commissions from the products of American planters and manufacturers that they sold. Second, they bought and sold cargos, often reaping large profits from the resale of rare imports. American exports grew from $20.2 million in 1790 to $108.3 million in 1807. Imports grew at a similar rate. Large commercial banks prospered by providing merchants with credit and capital to sustain operations. Examples of these commercial banks include the

BANK OF THE UNITED STATES (Philadelphia), BANK OF NORTH AMERICA (Philadelphia), and the Bank of New York (New York).

In general, government policy facilitated the expansion of the foreign trade throughout the period. This situation changed between 1807 and 1815 with a long disruption in overseas commerce caused by the EMBARGO OF 1807 and the War of 1812 (1812–15). After the war, overseas commerce resumed, but not with the same intensity due to new protectionist legislation passed in 1816 and renewed competition from European traders.

Inland trade steadily expanded in the 1790s as foreign trade increased. Gradually, more and more farmers and artisans earned profits from AGRICULTURE and manufacturing. Inland villages grew into towns as centers of specialized production for sale in regional markets. One example of this phenomenon was Franklin, Massachusetts, which produced 6,000 hats annually by 1810. Gettysburg and Carlisle, Pennsylvania, are two more villages that expanded into market towns between 1790 and 1810. Inland trade in textiles, leather goods, beer, bricks, wheat, iron, paper, vegetables, meats, iron tools, wagons, shoes, and other products increased throughout the period

A boom in domestic manufacturing caused by the suspension in foreign commerce between 1807 and 1814 led to even more inland trade. With greater manufacturing came the demand for roads, bridges, and canals to facilitate trade between towns, cities, and states. The period between 1810 and 1830 is noteworthy for efforts by individual states to charter companies to build privately operated turnpikes, bridges, and canals. Numerous companies received state charters for the construction and operation of these internal improvements, and merchants benefitted by reduced shipping costs and shorter transport times. The most famous example of an internal improvement is the Erie Canal, which was completed in 1825 and connected the East Coast with the Great Lakes and northwest.

The state and national governments pursued policies that encouraged these developments. Expanded inland trade contributed to the chartering of numerous state banks, which often provided capital for internal-improvements efforts meant to spur local market activity. In Pennsylvania alone, the state assembly chartered 41 new banks in 1814. In 1816 the federal government acted successfully to spur ever greater inland trade by passing a high protective TARIFF for goods such as wool and cotton textiles, iron, leather, hats, paper, and sugar. Along with the second Bank of the United States, the tariff became an important component of the American System of economic development instituted in the postwar years. The Panic of 1819 substantially set back inland trade. This economic depression was caused by excessive land speculation, banknote devaluation, and severe credit curtailment. Congress acted again to

facilitate domestic trade by raising the tariff in 1824. By 1825 inland trade was in full recovery from the panic and about to enter a new boom with the rise of railroad transport in the 1830s and 1840s.

See also FOREIGN AFFAIRS; INDUSTRIAL REVOLUTION.

Further reading: Stuart Bruchey, *Enterprise: The Dynamic Economy of A Free People* (Cambridge, Mass.: Harvard University Press, 1991); Diane Lindstrom, *Economic Development in the Philadelphia Region, 1810–1850* (New York: Columbia University Press, 1978); George Rogers Taylor, *The Transportation Revolution* (New York: Harper & Row, 1951); Charles Sellers, *The Market Revolution: Jacksonian America, 1815–1846* (New York: Oxford University Press, 1991); Gordon S. Wood, *The Radicalism of the American Revolution* (New York: Knopf, 1991).

— James R. Karmel

Trenton and Princeton, Battles of (December 26, 1776, and January 3, 1777)

After the disastrous campaign of the summer and fall of 1776, General GEORGE WASHINGTON gained two crucial victories by attacking outposts at Trenton and Princeton in New Jersey and forcing a British withdrawal to the area immediately surrounding New York City. While these victories did not significantly impair the British army, they represented a major political coup, rallying the supporters of independence and gaining international attention.

Washington's army had experienced a string of defeats starting with the BATTLE OF LONG ISLAND (August 27–30, 1776) that compelled him to abandon New York City, the lower Hudson River Valley, and most of New Jersey. Indeed, he was lucky to escape the British war machine with any troops. By the beginning of December he had been driven into Pennsylvania and had only a few thousand men, many of whom would soon go home as their enlistments ran out. In this circumstance, he planned something daring.

Flush with victory, General WILLIAM HOWE ordered his army into winter quarters on December 14. Not expecting an attack, he strung out his forces along a line in New Jersey that ran from the Delaware near Trenton to New Brunswick in the east. Howe knew he was vulnerable, but having issued a proclamation offering a pardon to all who signed a loyalty oath to the king, he sought to defend His Majesty's newly identified subjects. Winter weather and the dispirited morale of the CONTINENTAL ARMY, he believed, would help protect his exposed forces.

Washington devised a multipronged attack across the Delaware for late December. He crossed the river on Christmas night, but conditions prevented one wing of the attack to the south from doing the same. Washington went ahead with his assault on Trenton the next morning and surprised the HESSIAN garrison. Despite the element of shock and the completeness of the victory, 500 Hessians escaped from Trenton. With other British forces nearby to the south at Mt. Holly and to the north at Princeton, Washington recrossed the Delaware into Pennsylvania. During the next couple of days, Washington began to realize the effectiveness of his attack, as the Hessians withdrew from all of their advanced positions. He crossed the Delaware again, and by December 31, 1776, had concentrated 5,000 men and 40 howitzers at Trenton.

The British, however, wanted to reverse the loss of Trenton. CHARLES, LORD CORNWALLIS and 5,500 regulars advanced on Washington's position. By January 2, 1777, Cornwallis believed that he had Washington trapped at Trenton, pinned down between a superior British force and the Delaware River. Running into some difficulties in getting his own troops across a creek, Cornwallis decided to wait until the next day to finish Washington and end the rebellion. That night, Washington slipped the trap. Keeping a small force in Trenton to maintain campfires and to make noise digging entrenchments, the Continental army used a new road to the south to advance on Princeton. On the morning of January 3, 1777, the Continentals attacked. An intense battle ensued, and the Americans were almost driven back before Washington rallied his men and captured the outpost. Again, however, many of the British soldiers escaped, some to join Cornwallis at Trenton and others retreating to the major British depot at New Brunswick. Regardless of this shortcoming, Washington's victories were complete. The British decided to abandon most of New Jersey, maintaining posts only at Amboy and New Brunswick. Washington took his army to a winter encampment at MORRISTOWN, NEW JERSEY, and both armies awaited the spring of 1777 to renew the campaign.

See also. REVOLUTIONARY WAR.

Further reading: Don Higginbotham, *The War of American Independence: Military Attitudes, Policies, and Practices, 1763–1789* (New York: Macmillan, 1971); Robert Middlekauff, *The Glorious Cause: The American Revolution, 1783–1789* (New York: Oxford University Press, 1982).

Trumbull, John (1756–1843)

More than any other artist, John Trumbull is responsible for our image of the REVOLUTIONARY WAR (1775–83). His 250–300 historical paintings of battles and events, like the signing of the DECLARATION OF INDEPENDENCE (July 4, 1776), faithfully represent the people and the scenes that made the United States.

The son of Governor Jonathan Trumbull of Connecticut, a young John Trumbull wanted to study art with JOHN SINGLETON COPLEY. His father packed him off to Harvard instead. Shortly after he graduated, the Revolutionary War broke out and Trumbull obtained a commission in the CONTINENTAL ARMY. He saw action at DORCHESTER HEIGHTS (March 4–5, 1776) and was in high demand as an aide because of his ability to draw. He left the army in 1777, serving briefly again as a volunteer in the Rhode Island campaign in 1778. He tried his hand in several speculative ventures during the war, but in 1780 he obtained special permission to go to England where he studied with BENJAMIN WEST. On November 19, 1780, the British government arrested him for treason, possibly in retaliation for the execution of Major JOHN ANDRE. Trumbull was quickly released and left for the Continent.

He returned to the United States in 1783. Over the next decade Trumbull traveled a great deal in Europe and the United States. It was also his most productive period as an artist, during which he painted some of his best-known historical works, like the *Battle of Bunker Hill* and the *Death of General Montgomery in the Attack on Quebec*. He began his most famous painting *The Declaration of Independence* by 1789 but took eight years to complete it. He painted 36 of the 48 individuals in the work from life. He also used a sketch of the arrangement of the room by THOMAS JEFFERSON to capture the surrounding detail. Between 1794 and 1800 he served as secretary to JOHN JAY. After 1800 he relied on his painting to earn a living. Unfortunately this line of work became increasingly difficult for him, and most critics believe that his best work was behind him. He painted large, if imperfect, copies of some of his historical paintings for the new Capitol building in 1816 and 1817. Yale set up a gallery for his work in 1832 and provided Trumbull with a stipend for the remainder of his life.

See also ART.

Further reading: Irma B. Jaffe, *John Trumbull, Patriot-Artist of the American Revolution* (Boston: New York Graphic Society, 1975).

Tyler, Royall (1757–1826)

Even with a successful career as a jurist, Royall Tyler's greatest accomplishments were in LITERATURE and the early American THEATER. Tyler wrote *The Contrast* in 1787, a comic play that satirizes social pretensions. In the wake of the REVOLUTIONARY WAR (1775–83), Tyler became a literary voice of the AMERICAN REVOLUTION.

Tyler was born in 1757 to a prominent Boston family. With his inheritance, Tyler attended Harvard College, earning a B.A. in 1776. He continued his legal studies, receiving a Harvard M.A. in 1778 and admission to the bar in 1780. Tyler practiced law in Maine for two years before returning to Boston.

After an unsuccessful courtship of Abigail Adams, daughter of JOHN ADAMS, Tyler sought to mend his broken heart by joining the campaign against SHAYS'S REBELLION (1786–87) in western Massachusetts. Despite Tyler's limited success in the campaign, his efforts caught the attention of Governor James Bowdoin. Tyler was sent to New York City in March 1787. It was his first encounter with New York City and its theater. In just over a month, Tyler wrote *The Contrast* and saw it performed by the American Company at the John Street Theater. The play was the first professionally produced American comedy.

Influenced by Richard Sheridan's *The School for Scandal* (1777), Tyler's *The Contrast* highlights the differences between American and British values and manners. In the end, the play champions blunt American pragmatism over duplicitous British formalism. One character, Brother Jonathan, stands out as a no-nonsense, honest fellow. This character developed a life of its own in American folklore and literature. Some scholars have even claimed that the character is the prototype for Uncle Sam, the personification of the United States government.

A successful essayist and author, Tyler continued to practice law, eventually serving as chief justice of the Vermont Supreme Court. As the initially unsigned playwright of *The Contrast,* however, he captured elements of his era in a comedy of manners.

Further reading: G. Thomas Tanselle, *Royall Tyler* (Cambridge, Mass.: Harvard University Press, 1967).

— Jay R. Dew

U

Unitarianism

American Unitarianism developed in Boston and eastern Massachusetts during the decades following the REVOLUTIONARY WAR (1775–83). Unitarians questioned many of the central tenets of orthodox Calvinism. They downplayed original sin, arguing instead that humans were capable of both good and bad acts and that they were responsible for their own moral decisions. Moreover, Unitarianism was greatly influenced by the historicism of German biblical criticism. Although Unitarians agreed with their orthodox counterparts that the Bible was the final authority in all matters of theology, they also believed that the Bible was a historical product written by humans. Thus the Bible could not be taken at face value but must be interpreted through scholarship and the use of reason. For some Unitarians, this approach—a tradition that dated back to 17th-century radical Protestantism—offered the possibility to access the "true" Bible without the corruptions of subsequent writers and theologians. To orthodox thinkers, however, any questioning of the Bible was tantamount to heresy.

The roots of Unitarianism can be traced into the 18th century. In America, many proto-Unitarian ministers, such as Charles Chauncy, were critical of the enthusiasm associated with the revivals of the First Great Awakening. More importantly, Unitarianism owed much to the Enlightenment. Unitarians valued the application of reason over faith and were therefore more willing to question the Bible when it challenged common sense or the laws of nature. A central contention of Unitarians was that the Trinity was unjustified both by Scripture and by reason. They believed that Jesus was the subordinate son of God and not his equal, hence the term "unitarian." God was a single entity and not a composite of three disparate parts.

The most famous moment in American Unitarianism is no doubt the "Unitarian Controversy" of 1805. The controversy was caused by the decision of Harvard to appoint Henry Ware to the Hollis Professor of Divinity. A known liberal, Ware's appointment was seen as an affront to orthodox Congregationalists. Moreover, the controversy exposed a class division within Massachusetts Congregationalism, with many members of the eastern political elite aligning themselves with Unitarianism's liberal theology, even though they were a minority within the state. Orthodox minister JEDIDIAH MORSE launched a vitriolic campaign against Ware, and by 1807 many orthodox ministers deemed Harvard unfit to prepare ministers. They turned instead to Williams College and the newly established Andover Seminary.

The 1805 controversy brought divisions between liberals and orthodoxy into the open, making it more difficult for the two camps to exist peaceably within the same parish churches. In 1812 a prominent orthodox minister refused to share pulpits with liberal clergymen. Throughout the 1810s and 1820s, parishes divided between liberal and orthodox elements, making the establishment ineffective and unwieldy. In the context of these divisions, Unitarian leader Reverend William Ellery Channing's 1819 speech "Unitarian Christianity" laid the groundwork for a complete break between liberal and orthodox Congregationalists. In this speech, Channing made clear that reason and science must mediate the truths within the Bible. In 1825 Channing and others founded the American Unitarian Association, thus making their separation from orthodox Congregationalism official.

See also DEISM; RELIGION.

Further reading: Daniel Walker Howe, *The Unitarian Conscience: Harvard Moral Philosophy, 1805–1861* (Cambridge, Mass.: Harvard University Press, 1970); Conrad Wright, ed., *A Stream of Light: A Short History of American Unitarianism* (Boston: Skinner House Books, 1975); Conrad Wright, *The Beginnings of Unitarianism in America* (Boston: Beacon Press, 1955).

— Johann Neem

Valcour Island, Battle of (October 11, 1776)
Although the British won the Battle of Valcour Island on
Lake Champlain, the fact that they had to build a fleet of
ships to fight an American flotilla delayed an invasion from
CANADA for a year. That extra year was vital to American
success. When General JOHN BURGOYNE finally advanced
south from Canada in 1777, he ultimately met a huge
American army and was compelled to surrender at
SARATOGA (October 17, 1777).

Between the autumn of 1775 and the summer of 1776,
the Americans managed to gain control of Lake Champlain
and create a small fleet of vessels to prevent any British invasion from Canada. The Americans also built several gunboats
and galleys at a shipyard at Skenesborough, below FORT
TICONDEROGA. The Americans succeeded almost in spite of

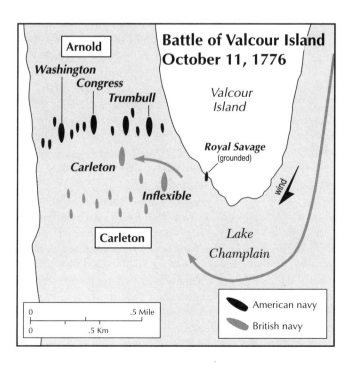

themselves, as petty squabbles between the military leaders
and between the states hampered military activity. Ultimately, command of the lake forces fell to BENEDICT
ARNOLD, who combined his experience at sea with his
energy as a leader. The British, who held St. Johns on the
northern shore of the lake, built a more powerful fleet of
their own. Arnold sailed up the lake to Valcour Island,
anchoring his vessels in a defensive line, hoping that his stationary vessels could outgun the heavier British vessels as
they tacked to get into position to fire. The idea was to have
the British sail south of Valcour Island and attack them from
the weather gauge. The British spotted the Americans as
they cleared the southern end of the island, and with their
superior seamanship and firepower they pummeled Arnold's
forces. By nightfall, Arnold was lucky to escape south along
the lakeshore past the British ships. Pursued the next day,
the Americans ran the vessels that had not been captured
ashore and set them afire. Arnold then led the remnants of
his men to Fort Ticonderoga, just ahead of pursuing Indians.
The American naval forces on Lake Champlain had been
destroyed or captured and the path for invasion cleared. But
with winter coming on, the British would have to wait until
the spring of the next year to push much farther.

Further reading: Don Higginbotham, *The War of American Independence: Military Attitudes, Policies, and Practices, 1763–1789* (New York: Macmillan, 1971); Robert
Middlekauff, *The Glorious Cause: The American Revolution, 1783–1789* (New York: Oxford University Press,
1982).

Valley Forge, encampment of (1777–1778)
On December 19, 1777, with the campaign season at an
end and the British in control of Philadelphia, GEORGE
WASHINGTON took his ragged CONTINENTAL ARMY into
winter quarters at Valley Forge, Pennsylvania, about 20
miles northwest of the occupied capital. It was a hilly,

Baron von Steuben at Valley Forge, 1777 *(National Archives)*

wooded site at the junction of the Schuylkill River and Valley Creek, far enough from the city so the British could not approach unnoticed and a secure base from which the Americans could counter enemy expeditions into the area. With the implementation of a skillfully planned system of entrenchments, fortifications, and artillery placements, Valley Forge was virtually impregnable by late winter. Battling deep snow and freezing temperatures was another matter, however. That winter, of the approximately 11,000 soldiers that constituted Washington's army, almost 3,000 were unfit for duty due to lack of shoes and clothing. Adequate shelter became their first priority, and the men immediately began felling trees and building log huts. Washington offered cash prizes for the best and fastest built and for the best roofing material they could concoct. Over 1,000 huts were built, most being completed by the end of the year. Once his men were adequately housed, Washington moved out of his own tent and into rented quarters in the village, the Isaac Potts house.

The general's troubles were many that winter. Aware of factions within the army and CONTINENTAL CONGRESS who doubted his leadership abilities and wanted him removed as commander in chief, Washington weathered the CONWAY CABAL while at Valley Forge. Despite the fact that Pennsylvania and the other colonies were not destitute of supplies, procuring and issuing provisions to the army through official channels was a continual problem. Meat and bread were often unavailable for days at a time.

Medicines, bedding straw, blankets, drinking water, salt, and alcohol (an integral part of the 18th-century diet) were also severely limited. Much of the army was virtually naked, forcing men to borrow clothes from one another when called upon to stand guard duty. Those without shoes stood on their hats to protect their feet from the snow. And when the various states did send provisions for their Continental regiments, they were for their own state troops only, resulting in an uneven distribution of goods, with units from the larger and wealthier states being the best supplied. Nor was the want limited to the army's human contingent. Horses, used as cavalry mounts and to pull wagons and artillery pieces, also faced starvation. To ease the demands on what fodder was available, Washington sent a detachment of cavalry to Trenton for the winter. Nevertheless, over 1,500 horses died at Valley Forge.

Not surprisingly, such drastic shortages of food and supplies—not to mention back wages—kept the men on the verge of mutiny, though somehow many persevered with wry good humor. Officers and men alike, however, indulged in brawling, drinking, and gambling. Hunger drove many marauding bands of soldiers into the surrounding countryside, prompting Washington to institute punishment for unauthorized absences and looting. Desertion among the men was rampant, and those caught routinely received 100 lashes as punishment, though two extreme cases resulted in hanging. The officers, who paid most of their own expenses while in the field, were also not immune to the lure of home and family and better conditions outside the army. They began resigning by the dozen in December, one division alone losing 50 of its leaders. Those not resigning requested furloughs in such numbers that Washington was compelled to reserve approval for those above the rank of captain. Chronic absences among his senior staff forced much of the burden of command onto Washington alone.

Within the camp, problems of boredom and cleanliness needed to be addressed. Soldiers were put to work making cartridges and spittoons. Latrines were dug in the frozen turf, filled in, and redug as necessary. Huts needed inspection for repairs, and dead horses and rotting garbage had to be buried. Although the worst of the sick cases were sent to hospitals in outlying areas, illness seriously depleted the ranks of the men in camp. Exposure and overcrowding made colds endemic among the troops, with the colds often turning to pneumonia. Severe frostbite required amputation, with shock and infection the resultant dangers. Unsanitary conditions contributed to dysentery, typhoid, and typhus, as well as to the proliferation of lice and bedbugs. Cases of insanity were also noted among the men. Smallpox was a major threat to the health of the army, and with the end of the campaign season, inoculation was ordered for those who had not already had the disease. Of the 4,000 men who were inoculated against smallpox throughout the winter, only 10 died.

The bleakness of the situation at Valley Forge was brightened, however, by the arrival of Baron FREDERICK VON STEUBEN, a Prussian army officer who volunteered his services to Washington and instituted a uniform system of drill. As various units were intermixed in the training process, a new sense of belonging to a truly Continental army developed, and the precision and skill the men acquired in the maneuvers on the field increased their morale and self-confidence. In February MARTHA WASHINGTON arrived from Virginia and set to work organizing the officers' wives for darning, mending, and nursing duties, as well as overseeing various social activities. The onset of spring still found the army near starvation, and Washington organized foraging parties that particularly targeted LOYALIST sympathizers. The soldiers took all they could find, but most of the surrounding farms had already been picked clean by scavengers from both armies. The sense of desperation finally began to ease in March, when a herd of 500 cattle was expected at the end of the month, and in April as the shad began running in the Schuylkill, providing fish for immediate consumption and, once salted and preserved, for later use. The weather was variable but gradually progressed from warm to hot. When the Continental army left its winter encampment on June 19, 1778, the conditions were a far cry from those that had greeted its arrival. The attitude of the men had changed as well. No longer the

starved, naked, ill-trained disparate force they had been six months earlier, the soldiers who emerged from Valley Forge were a confident, cohesive unit with a renewed commitment to the war effort.

See also REVOLUTIONARY WAR.

Further reading: Page Smith, *A New Age Now Begins: A People's History of the American Revolution,* vol. 2 (New York: McGraw Hill, 1989); John B. B. Trussell Jr., *Birthplace of an Army: A Study of the Valley Forge Encampment* (Harrisburg: Commonwealth of Pennsylvania, Pennsylvania Historical and Museum Commission, 1983).

— Rita M. Broyles

Vergennes, Charles Gravier, comte de
(1717–1787)

An experienced diplomat, Charles Gravier, comte de Vergennes served as French foreign minister from 1774 to 1787 and was the architect behind France's support of the Americans in the REVOLUTIONARY WAR (1775–83). Concerned with both the humiliation suffered by France in the French and Indian War (1754–63) and the balance of power in Europe, Vergennes saw the American rebellion as an opportunity to weaken Great Britain. His position was pragmatic, not ideological; if the American colonies became independent, he believed Britain's commercial power would be crushed. In early 1776 he persuaded King Louis XVI to begin secret preparations for war and encouraged Spain to do the same. On May 2, 1776, the French government began clandestine financial aid to the United States, providing 1 million livres to buy arms and supplies. After the American victory at SARATOGA (October 17, 1777), Vergennes sought a greater commitment to the United States to prevent an accommodation between the Americans and the British. On February 6, 1778, he concluded two treaties with the United States: one for commerce and the other a military alliance. War broke out openly between France and Great Britain on June 17, 1778.

The support of Vergennes was crucial to the winning of independence by the United States. France provided money, supplies, armies, and a navy, all of which played a major role in the victory at YORKTOWN (October 19, 1781). France also helped to bring Spain and the Netherlands into the war as allies of the United States. Although the war was popular in France, it did not have the long-term effects Vergennes had hoped. The United States, violating its agreement with France, negotiated separately and gained a highly favorable peace in the TREATY OF PARIS (1783). Vergennes accepted this agreement because the conflict had pushed France to the brink of bankruptcy. The war thus led to a financial crisis in France that precipitated the FRENCH REVOLUTION (1789–1815). Although Great Britain lost the jewel in its imperial crown, it quickly recovered its commercial prowess and expanded its empire into other domains.

See also FOREIGN AFFAIRS; FRENCH ALLIANCE.

Further reading: Ronald Hoffman and Peter J. Albert, eds., *Diplomacy and the Revolution: The Franco-American Alliance of 1778* (Charlottesville: University Press of Virginia, 1981); Richard B. Morris, *The Peacemakers: The Great Powers and American Independence* (Syracuse, N.Y.: Syracuse University Press, 1985); William C. Stinchcombe, *The American Revolution and the French Alliance* (New York: Harper & Row, 1969).

Vice Admiralty Courts

When the British Parliament decided to strengthen its imperial control over the colonies in the early 1760s, it turned to the Vice Admiralty Courts to enforce customs regulations. Colonial Americans had developed customs evasion to a fine art. Customs officials had found that it was almost impossible to gain a conviction in a colonial court because the juries would be sympathetic to the accused customs evaders. Vice Admiralty Courts were originally an arm of the Admiralty to determine lawful prizes during war, disputes between masters and seamen, and violations of the Acts of Trade. These courts did not use juries and would therefore be immune to local pressure. From the British perspective, they were the perfect tool to guarantee that customs regulations would be followed. As a part of the SUGAR ACT (1764), a new Vice Admiralty Court was established in Halifax, Nova Scotia. The act also permitted the customs officials to choose the court that they wished to prosecute the case and placed the burden of proof on the accused customs offender. The idea was to have such customs cases moved to the Vice Admiralty Court in Halifax. The accused smuggler would also have to bear the extra costs of a legal defense away from his own port, and there would be no jury packed with his friends and relatives. Believing that trial by a jury of one's peers was the right of every Englishperson, Colonial Americans saw this measure as an effort to destroy American liberty.

See also RESISTANCE MOVEMENT.

Further reading: Carl Ubbelohde, *The Vice Admiralty Courts and the American Revolution* (Chapel Hill: University of North Carolina Press, 1960).

Virginia and Kentucky Resolutions (1798)

The Virginia and Kentucky Resolutions were passed in 1798 by the state legislatures of Virginia and Kentucky to protest the ALIEN AND SEDITION ACTS (1798). The resolutions addressed STATE'S RIGHTS, nullification, and the question of arbitration between the federal government and state governments. Both documents recalled the themes of the AMERICAN REVOLUTION, arguing that tyranny and corruption were not necessarily imposed by external forces but could also develop internally, thus threatening a government from within.

JAMES MADISON secretly authored the Virginia Resolution, passed by the Virginia legislature on December 24, 1798. Madison argued that an individual state had the right to challenge any use of federal power it deemed unconstitutional. When the federal government exceeded its power and broke the compact that formed government, Madison wrote that "the states, who are parties thereto, have the right and are in duty bound to interpose for arresting the progress of the evil."

The Kentucky state legislature passed two resolutions, each anonymously written by THOMAS JEFFERSON, then the vice president of the United States. Jefferson could have been charged with violating the Sedition Act, making the need for secrecy all the more compelling. The first Kentucky Resolution, passed on November 16, 1798, said that each state "has an equal right to judge for itself" the validity of any federal activity that extended beyond the delegated powers. Echoing the rhetoric of the Revolution, Jefferson also argued that each state had the right to determine its own "measure of redress." The Kentucky legislature passed a second resolution on November 22, 1799, further sharpening the case for nullification. The Kentucky Resolutions presented the most aggressive argument for state's rights.

The Virginia and Kentucky Resolutions clearly stated that the federal government should operate only with the consent of the individual states. The central government could not be trusted to police itself, Madison and Jefferson contended, so the states had a duty to restrict the federal government to its delegated powers. When passed along to the other states for approval, however, the Virginia and Kentucky Resolutions were for the most part dismissed. The arguments for nullification were resurrected by southern slaveholders during the sectional crisis leading to the Civil War. John C. Calhoun especially leaned on the words of Madison and Jefferson to support his justification of state's rights. Madison vigorously opposed Calhoun, claiming that his arguments were taken out of context. The Virginia and Kentucky Resolutions were a reaction to the Alien and Sedition Acts in particular and an outgrowth of the struggle between the FEDERALIST PARTY and DEMOCRATIC-REPUBLICANS.

Further reading: James Morton Smith, *Freedom's Fetters: The Alien and Sedition Laws and American Civil Liberties* (Ithaca, N.Y.: Cornell University Press, 1966).

— Jay R. Dew

Virginia dynasty

Four of the first five presidents of the United States, for a total of eight of nine terms, came from the same state—Virginia. This early trend has been called the Virginia dynasty. At the time of the CONSTITUTIONAL CONVENTION, Virginia was the largest and most populous state. Excluding its claim to the Northwest Territories, Virginia comprised the present states of Virginia, West Virginia, and Kentucky. Perhaps equally important was the fact that Virginia had developed an articulate and outstanding group of leaders drawn from the ranks of LAWYERS and slaveholding plantation owners. Given this leadership and the size and population of Virginia, it appeared only natural that the state would provide prominent national leaders.

Foremost among these men was GEORGE WASHINGTON, who during the convention in Philadelphia was expected to become the first president. Washington chose to serve only two terms. His immediate successor was JOHN ADAMS from Massachusetts. Adams, however, served only one term and was defeated in the ELECTION OF 1800 by THOMAS JEFFERSON. While Jefferson had come to oppose many of the FEDERALIST PARTY policies of Washington and Adams, he had been Washington's first secretary of state and was a Virginian. His two terms were followed by his protégé, secretary of state, and fellow Virginian, JAMES MADISON. By this time, Federalists were complaining that there ought to be a constitutional amendment against having two individuals from the same state elected in succession. Madison's political success led to the complete dominance of the DEMOCRATIC-REPUBLICAN PARTY and the election of James Monroe in 1816. Monroe was also from Virginia and had been Madison's secretary of state. The Virginia dynasty was finally broken by the election of John Quincy Adams in 1824.

Virginia Resolves (May 30, 1765)

At the instigation of PATRICK HENRY, the Virginia House of Burgesses—its lower house of assembly—passed a set of resolutions in May 1765 declaring opposition to the STAMP ACT (1765). Henry was a relatively new member of the Burgesses, but he had already earned something of a reputation as a firebrand. He introduced the resolutions after the majority of members had left and as the burgesses were about to adjourn—only 39 of 117 members were in attendance. While the resolves merely echoed the message of previous petitions against imperial regulation agreed to by the Virginia legislature, the language and tone of these resolves was more intense. The first two resolves traced the rights of Virginians to the earliest settlements and the charters for colonial government issued by the kings of England. The next two resolves asserted that "the distinguishing Characteristick of *British* Freedom, without which the ancient Constitution cannot exist" is that taxation could only be exacted by "the People themselves, or by Persons chosen by themselves," and that the right to be governed and taxed by laws of their own choosing "hath been constantly recognized by the Kings and People of *Great Britain.*"

There remains some confusion over the exact process by which these resolutions were passed. On May 30, 1765, the Burgesses agreed to five resolutions. The next day it rescinded the fifth resolution, which declared that only the Virginia general assembly had the right to tax the colonists and that any challenge to this right "has a manifest Tendency to destroy British as well as American Freedom." When newspapers throughout the colonies printed the Virginia Resolves, however, they included the fifth and one or two others. Historians are unsure how the newspapers obtained the sixth and seventh resolves. The additional resolutions were highly inflammatory, declaring that colonists "are not bound to yield Obedience" to any taxes other than those imposed by the colonial legislature, and that anyone speaking or writing that Parliament had the right to tax the colony would be deemed "AN ENEMY TO THIS HIS MAJESTY'S COLONY." The seven resolves together had a tremendous impact on the other colonies, and when eight other colonial assemblies passed their own resolutions, they used the more provocative seven resolutions as a model.

See also RESISTANCE MOVEMENT.

Further reading: Pauline Maier, *From Resistance to Revolution: Colonial Radicals and the Development of American Opposition to Britain, 1765–1776* (New York: Knopf, 1972); Edmund S. Morgan and Helen M. Morgan, *The Stamp Act Crisis: Prologue to Revolution* (Chapel Hill: University of North Carolina Press, 1953).

voluntary associations

Between 1750 and 1820, the number and type of voluntary associations increased dramatically. The colonial period had few voluntary associations. The most important voluntary association was the church. New England Calvinists believed that all churches should be independent congregations. While each church was voluntary, every New England state except Rhode Island taxed residents to support Congregational ministers. In the South the Anglican Church was established by law, but dissenting sects had the same right to organize separate churches as they did in England. In the middle colonies, where religious affiliations were extremely diverse, there was no established church. Only in the middle colonies did a truly voluntary system of churches exist during the colonial period. There were a few other types of voluntary associations during the colonial era. The FREEMASONS had a limited presence in some urban areas. Voluntary fire companies were prevalent in cities where wooden buildings built in close proximity made fires a serious threat. There were also some self-improvement societies, such as BENJAMIN FRANKLIN's Philadelphia "Junto," but these would remain rare until after independence.

The REVOLUTIONARY WAR (1775–83) dramatically increased the number of voluntary associations, as citizens mobilized to fight the British. In town after town, people formed COMMITTEES OF CORRESPONDENCE and of safety and joined militia units. These associations lacked any legal basis, and their existence was a testament to their revolutionary character. In the absence of British rule, voluntary associations replaced legitimate governments as the source of political authority and stability. THOMAS HUTCHINSON, the royal governor of Massachusetts, referred to these committees and town meetings as "mock" assemblies, reinforcing their illegitimate status. Even the provincial congresses and the CONTINENTAL CONGRESS were, to a degree, voluntary associations; they lacked any legitimate powers except those accepted by the people of the states.

When peace replaced war, the new nation's leaders resisted the spread of voluntary associations. While they appreciated the important role that voluntary associations had played in winning the war, they also understood that these associations could be employed to topple the new state governments. According to THOMAS JEFFERSON, voluntary associations were useful "for revolutionary purposes," but when revolution was not desired they were "dangerous machines."

Despite such warnings, the postrevolutionary period saw a dramatic increase in the number and type of voluntary associations. The most notable increase was among the Freemasons, who spread throughout the nation. This group provided opportunities for men to gather on a social basis while making important economic and political connections. In addition to the Masons, Revolutionary elites established lyceums, libraries, agricultural and mechanics' societies, and academies. Most of these associations aimed to instill wholesome morals and values in citizens. Revolutionary leaders believed that without properly educating its citizens, a republic was at risk of losing its liberty.

Ordinary people demanded greater access to the rights of association. Although most states abolished the established church after the Revolution, Connecticut, New Hampshire, and Massachusetts did not. Growing denominations such as BAPTISTS and METHODISTS argued that all churches should be placed on an equal footing and that no particular denomination should benefit from state support. Baptists and Methodists believed that voluntarism was the best way to organize a church, and the growth in their denominations following the Revolutionary War proved them to be correct. During the Second Great Awakening of the postrevolutionary decades, the number of churches in the nation skyrocketed.

Evangelical RELIGION emphasized a Christian's duty to do good to others, and people in towns all over the country established charitable and moral societies to act on this mandate. Evangelical Christians greatly expanded the scope of voluntary associations. Before, most associations had been limited to elites and used for private purposes. Evangelicals, however, democratized membership and employed voluntary associations to change the behavior of others. TEMPERANCE societies sought to end drunkenness; moral societies hoped to reform the manners of individuals; and missionary societies encouraged religiosity among all Americans.

Despite the increase in voluntary associations, one particular type of voluntary association found its rights greatly limited. Journeymen's associations, which were early unions, discovered that state courts refused to allow them to bargain collectively. In the colonial days, master and journeyman ARTISANS usually shared a single interest and masters would work for the good of an entire trade. After independence, however, journeymen sought control over their own fortunes, especially as artisanal trades moved from small shops to larger factories. In New York, Pennsylvania, and Massachusetts, courts explicitly limited the rights of journeymen's associations. Voluntary associations, state courts explained, were free to develop, but they should not use their collective power to affect the rights of others. Judges argued that by seeking collective bargaining rights, journeymen trampled on the right of masters to hire any person they chose at any agreeable wage. As the states became more accepting of the rights of voluntary associations, they also established boundaries on their actions. Journeymen's associations tested these boundaries, which would be challenged even more adamantly by ANTISLAVERY associations in the antebellum era.

See also EDUCATION; LABOR AND LABOR MOVEMENTS; RELIGION.

Further reading: Richard D. Brown, "The Emergence of Urban Society in Rural Massachusetts, 1760–1820" *Journal of American History* 51 (1974): 29–51; Lori Ginzberg, *Women and the Work of Benevolence: Morality, Politics, and Class in the Nineteenth-Century United States* (New Haven, Conn.: Yale University Press, 1990); Peter Dobkin Hall, *The Organization of American Culture, 1700–1900: Private Institutions, Elites, and the Origins of American Nationality* (New York: New York University Press, 1982); Conrad Edick Wright, *The Transformation of Charity in Postrevolutionary New England* (Boston: Northeastern University Press, 1992).

— Johann Neem

Warren, Joseph (1741–1775)

A spokesman in the RESISTANCE MOVEMENT (1764–75) to imperial regulation, Joseph Warren died at the beginning of the REVOLUTIONARY WAR (1775–83).

Warren was born in Roxbury, Massachusetts, in 1741. In 1755, the same year his father died, Warren entered Harvard College. After graduation, he apprenticed with Dr. James Lloyd and became an established physician. During a smallpox epidemic (see DISEASE AND EPIDEMICS) in Boston in 1763, the new doctor quickly became known as a successful innoculator. Indeed, Warren became friends with a patient named JOHN ADAMS as a result of the epidemic. By 1769 he had emerged as one of Boston's most celebrated physicians.

Warren also became active in politics, giving numerous speeches at Faneuil Hall alongside men like JOHN HANCOCK and SAMUEL ADAMS. In the aftermath of the BOSTON MASSACRE (March 5, 1770), he became a skilled propagandist, frequently urging military strength and preparation. The BOSTON TEA PARTY (December 16, 1773) increased his standing in the anti-British movement. In 1774 Warren led the committee that drafted the SUFFOLK RESOLVES, and on April 18, 1775, he dispatched PAUL REVERE and William Dawes on their famous journeys. Warren served in three provincial congresses in Massachusetts, rising to president of the third.

On June 14, 1775, Warren was named a major general in the provincial army. Three days later, acting as a volunteer because his commission had not yet arrived, Warren was swept up in the BATTLE OF BUNKER HILL (June 17, 1775), where he moved to hold the colonial position on Breed's Hill. Though resisting two waves of attack, he was caught in the third British charge. Among the last of the American forces left on Breed's Hill, Warren was shot in the head and killed.

Further reading: John Cary, *Joseph Warren: Physician, Politician, Patriot* (Urbana: University of Illinois Press, 1961).

— Jay R. Dew

Warren, Mercy Otis (1728–1814)

As a historian, poet, and dramatist, Mercy Otis Warren provided both fascinating political commentary and a valuable insider's look at the events surrounding the AMERICAN REVOLUTION. Born in Barnstable, Massachusetts, in 1728, Mercy received little formal education, except what she gleaned from her brothers' tutoring sessions. Mercy's brother, JAMES OTIS, was a leading political activist during the RESISTANCE MOVEMENT (1764–75) who publicly opposed various English measures, including the STAMP ACT (1765). Relationships to prominent revolutionary figures such as James Warren, ABIGAIL ADAMS, and JOHN ADAMS gave Mercy expert knowledge of the turbulent events surrounding the American Revolution, which she subsequently applied to her creative works.

On November 14, 1754, Mercy Otis married James Warren, a Massachusetts political leader, and the couple resided mainly in Plymouth, Massachusetts, except for the 10 years when they lived in Milton in the house once owned by Governor THOMAS HUTCHINSON. They had five sons, compelling Warren to juggle motherhood with her writing career. Warren held strong views on women's roles in society. Although she believed in the importance of motherhood, she felt that women had the right to pursue other career interests. Women needed to manage their time wisely, thus allowing them to live in both the world of intellect and the world of domesticity. In letters she wrote to her friend Abigail Adams, Warren asserted that a good education proved critical to sharpening women's minds and distracting them from frivolous pursuits. She recognized that domestic responsibilities often hindered a woman's ability to challenge herself intellectually, but she asserted that it was worth the effort.

Warren applied her intellectual skills toward writing plays and recording the experiences of the revolutionary period. Her major works include *The Adulateur* (1773), *The Group* (1775), *Poems, Dramatic and Miscellaneous* (1790), and *A History of the Rise, Progress, and Termination of the*

American Revolution (3 volumes, 1805). In the political satires *The Adulateur* and *The Group,* Warren directed her political attacks at the increasingly unpopular Governor Thomas Hutchinson. She also predicted that a war against England would inevitably occur. The playwright maintained strong republican convictions and criticized those who exhibited "aristocratic" tendencies. Through personal correspondence, Warren offered her opinions on political matters to a number of major political figures, including John Adams, SAMUEL ADAMS, James Winthrop, JOHN DICKINSON, THOMAS JEFFERSON, GEORGE WASHINGTON, ELBRIDGE GERRY, and HENRY KNOX.

In her history of the Revolution, few people escaped Warren's biting political commentary, including the second president of the United States, John Adams. For example, Warren questioned Adams's ability to keep his passions and prejudices intact, and she noted, as well, his excessive "pride of talents" and ambition. Adams objected to Warren's depiction of him, and a rift consequently developed in their friendship that lasted for almost five years. Mercy Otis Warren's influence waned as a new generation of politicians came into power in the early 19th century. However, through her literary contribution, her imprint on the Revolution remains firm. She died in Plymouth, Massachusetts, on October 19, 1814.

See also REPUBLICANISM; WOMEN'S RIGHTS AND STATUS.

Further reading: Jeffrey H. Richards, *Mercy Otis Warren* (New York: Twayne, 1995); Rosemarie Zagarri, *A Woman's Dilemma: Mercy Otis Warren and the American Revolution* (Arlington Heights, Ill.: Harlan Davidson, 1995).

— Linda English

Washington, District of Columbia

Washington, D.C., is the first planned capital of a modern nation and one of the few founded solely for the purpose of government. Established in 1791 as the District of Columbia, Washington became the seat of power after a "dinner table bargain" was reached between THOMAS JEFFERSON and ALEXANDER HAMILTON. Both men served in GEORGE WASHINGTON's cabinet, Jefferson as secretary of state and Hamilton as secretary of the treasury, and they often disagreed on matters of federal policy. To forge a compromise, JAMES MADISON brokered a deal over a private dinner wherein Jefferson accepted Hamilton's arrangement for the federal assumption of state debts, a cornerstone of his financial plan; in return, the nation's capital would be moved to the South. The southern states generally opposed Hamilton's plan because it increased their dependence upon the federal government. The proposal to move the national capital to the South was intended to appease their concerns. Jefferson accepted

The White House as it appeared in 1807 *(Library of Congress)*

and later regretted the bargain; the area selected was swampy, hot, and devoid of culture. However, the capital perfectly represented the new country: They were both full of expectation for the future. Jefferson was the first president to be inaugurated in Washington, which he dubbed the "republican city."

Washington, D.C., derives its compound name from George Washington and Christopher Columbus. Independent of any state, the nation's capital functions as a sovereign municipality. The city itself is a marvel in municipal planning, largely the work of Frenchman PIERRE L'EN-FANT, who planned the city in the 1790s. Bordered by the Potomac and Anacostia Rivers, the Capitol—the building housing Congress—lies at the heart of the city, where four unequal quadrants intersect. Two grids of thoroughfares overlap, creating open traffic circles and broad avenues. From the Capitol, the National Mall extends west past the Washington Monument, presently ending at the Lincoln Memorial. The executive residence faces the Washington Monument across the Ellipse. Constructed almost entirely of marble, the architecture of the city is modeled after classical antiquity, resembling monuments to Athenian democracy and Roman republicanism.

However, Washington, D.C., did not develop into the present-day metropolitan area until the early 20th century. L'Enfant originally intended for the Mall to showcase the institutions of the three branches of government: the executive mansion, Capitol building, and SUPREME COURT. In 1901 the Commission of Fine Arts, headed by Frederick Law Olmstead, proposed a revival of L'Enfant's original plans. Industrialization and the Civil War had taken their toll upon the capital; railroad tracks actually crossed the Mall. The residents agreed to implement the beautification project, which culminated in the completion of the Lincoln Memorial in 1922. The original plans were slightly altered in 1935, when the Supreme Court building was erected across from the Capitol between the Library of Congress and Union Station. L'Enfant had originally envisioned the three leading institutions of government lining the Mall; however, this was not possible due to limited space. Yet, for the most part, the city that exists today can be directly traced to the plans laid out two centuries earlier. The capital grew larger, keeping pace with the nation as a whole. President Franklin Roosevelt's New Deal programs produced significant government expansion after 1933, and by the end of World War II, Washington had become the center of power in world politics.

Further reading: James Sterling Young, *The Washington Community, 1800–1828* (New York: Columbia University Press, 1966).

— Lauren Held

Washington, George (1732–1799)

No one looms larger in the pantheon of American heroes than George Washington, whose service in the REVOLUTIONARY WAR (1775–83) and as the first president of the United States earned him adulation bordering on worship from contemporaries and future generations alike. ABIGAIL ADAMS said Washington was made of "majestick fabric," and upon his death in 1799 the House of Representatives proclaimed him "first in war, first in peace, and first in the hearts of his countrymen." In the 19th century, Americans named the national capital, an imposing monument, and a state in his honor, while towns like Stoughtonham Township in Massachusetts paid their respects by changing their name to Washington as well. Some did so as early as 1776, while Washington was alive and the outcome of the Revolutionary War remained uncertain, and families rushed to name their children after him years before and long after he became president.

The larger than life popular image of Washington as father of the country has made his more human side difficult to understand. The first president seems cold and aloof to our skeptical age, and we look past his imposing visage on the one-dollar bill for cracks in his Olympian legend. Our collective cynicism is fueled by the knowledge that writers like "PARSON" MASON LOCKE WEEMS fabricated stories about Washington, including the famous (and completely fictional) account in which a young Washington confesses his role in destroying a family cherry tree by proclaiming to his father, "I can't tell a lie Pa; you know I can't tell a lie. I did cut it with my hatchet." Similar myths remain prevalent even today, and they combine with facts regarding Washington's virtues to create a portrait of a man so seemingly great that few Americans can relate to him. This is unfortunate, for the real Washington was both more and less heroic than his legend suggests.

He was born on February 22, 1732, at Wakefield, a country home in Westmoreland County, Virginia, near the Potomac River. His father Augustine was a successful farmer and land speculator, and he trained George in the ways of a Virginia planter prior to his death in 1743. Washington learned to ride and shoot, traveled with his father on business, and developed a strong ambition to become a wealthy and successful landowner is his own right. One of seven children, and the oldest son of Augustine's second marriage, Washington became a land surveyor in 1749 after his mother blocked his plan to join the Royal Navy. He surveyed much of Virginia's vast western land claims until he inherited Mount Vernon following the death of his half brother Lawrence in 1752. Thereafter he lived as a country gentleman.

Yet financial success as a planter could not satisfy Washington's desire for renown, and he joined the Virginia militia as a lieutenant colonel in 1754 with the hope of find-

George Washington. Painting by Charles Willson Peale *(West Point Museum Collections, United States Military Academy)*

ing fame on the battlefield. His actions on the FRONTIER helped to bring on the French and Indian War (1754–63). At the head of a small force of Virginians and Indians, Washington beat a smaller French force in what is now western Pennsylvania. He also had his men build Fort Necessity in the same area, but he was forced to surrender the outpost to the French after a brief siege (July 3, 1754). The debacle marked the opening round of the French and Indian War and clouded Washington's reputation. He subsequently left the militia rather than accept a demotion in rank. Yet Washington quickly sought to redeem himself, volunteering to accompany a British army led by General Edward Braddock in an attack on French and NATIVE AMERICAN forces west of the Appalachians. The ponderous expedition suffered ambush and virtual annihilation (July 9, 1755), but Washington fought bravely and had two horses shot out from under him. He emerged from the battle a

hero, and Virginia governor Robert Dinwiddie rewarded him with promotion to full colonel and command of the Virginia regiment. Washington fought in the ensuing war for 40 frustrating months, pleading for reinforcements and gradually losing one-third of his men. He failed in attempts to gain a commission in the British army, but he accompanied a column commanded by General John Forbes that finally captured Fort Duquesne in 1758. With the French threat to Virginia's western frontier eliminated, Washington retired from the militia and married a fabulously wealthy widow named Martha Dandridge Custis (see WASHINGTON, MARTHA DANDRIDGE CUSTIS), who owned hundreds of slaves and almost 18,000 acres of land. By 1759 Martha and George were among the most celebrated families in Virginia.

They embraced a comfortable life during the 1760s, hosting countless parties and successfully winning a seat for George in the Virginia House of Burgesses. Washington excelled as a horseman and dancer, loved hosting parties and wearing fine clothes, and worked hard as a land speculator and wheat farmer. While expanding Mount Vernon he devoted himself to his two stepchildren, John and Martha, and served as a justice of the peace even as he acquired more than 20,000 acres of land near the Great Kanawha River as a reward for his service in the French and Indian War. Critics accused him of impropriety for scheming to have the House of Burgesses name a good friend as surveyor of the land and for buying territory at low prices from other veterans granted land by Virginia, but his reputation remained strong enough that he commissioned CHARLES WILLSON PEALE to paint his portrait in 1772. Washington characteristically posed for the painting wearing his militia uniform; whatever his financial successes, he wanted to be remembered as a soldier.

Washington grew increasingly frustrated with British policy in North America, which blocked westward expansion and prevented him from selling his lucrative western land to settlers. He also believed that the Crown was denying Americans their rights as English subjects, and he supported the RESISTANCE MOVEMENT (1764–75), serving as a delegate to both the FIRST and SECOND CONTINENTAL CONGRESSES. After war began at LEXINGTON AND CONCORD (April 10, 1775), he wore his militia uniform to meetings as a not-so-subtle reminder that he deserved command of the new CONTINENTAL ARMY, and when JOHN ADAMS nominated him for the post, his peers quickly assented. They recognized his military experience, dignified bearing, sense of command, and his reputation as a man of character and high principles.

Washington assumed command of American forces in June and maintained a land blockade of Boston, which compelled British forces to withdraw in the spring of 1776. In August the British landed an army of 34,000 men commanded by General WILLIAM HOWE near New York City.

In a series of contests, beginning with the BATTLE OF LONG ISLAND (August 27–30, 1776), Howe battered Washington's army time and again. Jeering British troops blew fox horns while pursuing the broken American army, and only Howe's tentative advance, the intervention of bad weather, and the onset of winter saved American forces from outright destruction. Washington's inexperience as a field commander led to most of the defeats. In his defense, he learned his lessons well; Washington never again risked his entire army in a general engagement, adopting instead a cautious Fabian approach to warfare designed to keep his army intact.

He won important early victories at TRENTON AND PRINCETON (December 26, 1776, and January 3, 1777, respectively) and spent the duration of the war with his tiny army. In eight and a half years in the field, he slept only three nights at Mount Vernon. He also refused a salary and supported civilian rule over his army, even when Congress seemed to have forgotten about his starving and ill-equipped men. Washington confronted mutinies among his men and conspiracies among his officers to have him replaced, and he struggled with chronic shortages of men and supplies. But he never abandoned hope. Conditions slowly improved after the British general JOHN BURGOYNE surrendered at SARATOGA (October 17, 1777) and France entered the war alongside the United States.

In 1781 Washington made the most brilliant decision of the war when he marched his army south from New York to join combined French and American forces besieging a British army commanded by General CHARLES, LORD CORNWALLIS at Yorktown, Virginia. When a French fleet blocked Cornwallis's seaward escape, a great victory was assured, and the British surrendered on October 19th. Triumph at Yorktown led directly to the end of the war and the signing of the TREATY OF PARIS (1783), which recognized the independence of the United States. After the British evacuated New York City in November 1783, Washington stunned the world by resigning his commission and returning to Mount Vernon.

His resignation became the most admired act of his life, for it demonstrated civic virtue and an unselfish sense of duty that awed his generation. Washington knew the way in which his resignation would be received, and he acted in large measure to enhance his reputation. Yet he could have been a king or a dictator in America and used the army for his own ends, or demanded vast rewards for his service to his country. Instead he went home and expected to live the remainder of his days at Mount Vernon as a modern-day Cincinnatus (a general in ancient Rome who returned to his farm after winning a war and saving the Republic).

To his dismay, Washington found that his fame precluded isolation from public life. He emerged from retirement to serve as president of the CONSTITUTIONAL CONVENTION (1787) and then served two terms as the first president of the United States between 1789 and 1797. In each case he left Mount Vernon reluctantly, wary of damaging his reputation through association with political endeavors that might have failed, and in each case his role proved vital. His prestige gave credibility to the Constitutional Convention, and it is difficult to imagine the delegates reaching any sort of consensus without his leadership. Moreover, many of them approved the strong, centralized powers of the new federal government only because they believed Washington would be the first president and that only he could be trusted not to abuse those powers. Washington acceded to popular pressure and became the first president of the United States in April of 1789.

As president he oversaw the creation of the first federal government, sided with ALEXANDER HAMILTON in disputes over the Constitution, and noted with dismay the increasing factionalism of his countrymen. He wanted to retire following his first term but was persuaded to stay by supporters and was unanimously reelected. Washington crushed the WHISKEY REBELLION in 1794, kept the United States neutral after the outbreak of the FRENCH REVOLUTION (1789–1815) and the ensuing wars between Britain and France, and sent an army led by ANTHONY WAYNE to defeat Native Americans in the Ohio River Valley in 1794.

He declined a third term in office in 1796; peacefully transferred power to his successor, John Adams, in 1797; and established the tradition that no president should serve more than two terms. In his FAREWELL ADDRESS he warned Americans to avoid permanent alliances with foreign countries and to be wary of POLITICAL PARTIES. He died two years later on December 14, 1799.

Washington left behind a compelling record of military and political achievement. He almost single-handedly held the Continental army together for eight years, battling the British, mutinies, conspiracies, and supply shortages that would have broken more ordinary leaders. He was not a great field commander, but he learned from his mistakes and bided his time until conditions were ripe for the masterstroke at Yorktown. Politically, he proved remarkably astute at discerning the will of Congress and at creating an image of himself that strongly appealed to his generation. Less politically experienced and intellectually gifted than founders like THOMAS JEFFERSON or John Adams, he retained a sense of pragmatism and virtue as president that encouraged popular faith in the government and kept the United States out of war in the early years of the republic. Most importantly, he oversaw the creation of the Constitution, which provided a foundation on which a new and distinctly American form of government could be built.

As a human being, Washington's legacy is more complex. He treated his slaves harshly yet provided for their emancipation following his death. He proved a loving husband and stepfather yet nurtured an abiding affection for Sally Fairfax, the wife of a good friend, for almost all of his life. He was vain, hot-tempered, and ambitious, but he balanced these qualities with a zealous self-discipline that made him a model of civil and gentlemanly behavior. Less educated than any of the galaxy of great minds that crowd the revolutionary era, he earned the universal admiration of his peers through force of will and devotion to principle. And though popular to the point of deification in many parts of the country, he struggled to maintain a relationship with his LOYALIST mother, who opposed the Revolution all of her life.

What all this effort—24 years of service following his nomination to command the Continental army in 1775—cost him can never be known. If his popular epitaph as the "father of his country" is well deserved, so too is the one he unwittingly wrote for himself in a letter to the MARQUIS DE LAFAYETTE in 1784. Faced with old age and the prospect of death, Washington said he would not repine, for "I have had my day."

Further reading: John Ferling, *Setting the World Ablaze: Washington, Adams, Jefferson, and the American Revolution* (New York: Oxford University Press, 2000); James Thomas Flexner, *Washington: The Indispensable Man* (New York: New American Library, 1984); Willard Sterne Randall, *George Washington: A Life* (New York: Henry Holt, 1997).

— Lance Janda

Washington, Martha Dandridge Custis
(1731–1802)

Martha Dandridge Custis Washington was the wife of GEORGE WASHINGTON, the first president of the United States and commander in chief of the CONTINENTAL ARMY during the REVOLUTIONARY WAR (1775–83). Although she had no role model to follow, Martha diligently and graciously served her country in her capacity as America's first "first lady." Embracing her domestic responsibilities, she proved to be a dutiful wife and attentive mother to both her children and her grandchildren.

Martha Dandridge was born at Chestnut Grove in New Kent County, Virginia, on June 2, 1731. She received a traditional education for young women in the 18th century, which emphasized such domestic skills as sewing, housekeeping, cooking, as well as reading, writing, dancing, and MUSIC. At the age of 18, Martha married Daniel Parke Custis, a wealthy plantation owner who was 20 years her senior. The couple had four children, although two died in infancy. In 1757 Custis died, leaving Martha with a substantial estate and two small children, John Parke (Jacky) and Martha (Patsy).

On January 6, 1759, after a short courtship, Martha married George Washington, a young colonel in the Virginia militia who had served in the French and Indian War (1754–63). The couple and Martha's two small children moved to Washington's plantation, Mount Vernon, in April 1759. Although Mount Vernon remained the Washington's family home, future events dictated that the couple spend a number of years living elsewhere. During the Revolutionary War, Martha joined her husband at VALLEY FORGE (1777–78). She also joined him on some of his later campaigns in New Jersey, New York, and Pennsylvania, living simply and doing all she could to support the war effort. When her last surviving son, John Parke died of "camp fever" in 1781, Martha and George adopted his two youngest children, Eleanor Parke Custis (Nelly) and George Washington Parke Custis (Wash or Tub).

After the inauguration of her husband as president on April 30, 1789, Martha and her grandchildren uprooted themselves from their home in Mount Vernon and moved to New York, then the national capital. Shortly thereafter, the family moved to the new capital in Philadelphia, staying there until the end of George's presidency. While in Philadelphia, Martha, or "Lady Washington" as she came to be known, diligently performed her duties as a hostess for the weekly receptions held by the first couple. Although cast in a very public role, Martha confided to friends her preference for a more private life. She gladly returned home to Mount Vernon with her family on March 15, 1797, after the completion of George's second term. The couple enjoyed two short years surrounded by their loved ones at Mount Vernon before George's death in 1799. Martha burned all but two of the letters written between the couple over the course of their courtship and marriage, again reaffirming her desire for privacy. Martha Dandridge Custis Washington died on May 22, 1802, in the presence of her beloved granddaughter Nelly. Fittingly, she was buried next to her husband at Mount Vernon in a family tomb.

Further reading: Joseph E. Fields, *"Worthy Partner:" The Papers of Martha Washington* (Westport, Conn.: Greenwood Press, 1994).

— Linda English

Washington Benevolent Societies

Second-generation FEDERALIST PARTY founded Washington Benevolent Societies in an effort to revive their party's flagging political fortunes during the first decades of the 19th century. Although older party leaders instinctively mistrusted grassroots politics, young Federalists believed that such efforts were the only way to sustain the party. Thus the societies epitomized belated FEDERALIST PARTY efforts to adapt to the changing political culture of the early republic and embrace popular politics. The first society appeared shortly after GEORGE WASHINGTON's death in 1799, and although most societies disappeared by 1824, the Philadelphia society remained active through the 1830s.

The first society, named the Washington Society of Alexandria, began as an effort to honor George Washington. Founded in January 1800 by a group of Washington's friends and acquaintances, the society pledged to support charities that Washington favored as well as sponsoring celebrations on Washington's birthday, February 22. Membership was by invitation only and dues were prohibitively high to restrict membership. Unlike its successors, the Alexandria group did not have an explicitly political agenda.

President THOMAS JEFFERSON's EMBARGO OF 1807 hastened the creation of other Washington Societies. In 1808 young Federalists founded societies in Philadelphia, New York, and Boston, eventually creating more than 200 such organizations. The New York group was the first to call itself the Washington Benevolent Society. Like the original Alexandria society, these societies engaged in charitable activities, although the extent and commitment varied widely from society to society. These activities included direct grants to the needy, employment training, legal advice, firewood, clothing, and support for free schools. Charitable activities, however, were secondary to politics.

In contrast to the Alexandria club, these newer groups opened their membership, with some qualification, to all voters. The societies still required annual dues, but these dues were nominal and the president could waive them based on need. Members were required to be American citizens, have good moral character, and be firmly attached to the Constitution. In practice, these requirements meant that members had to support the Federalist Party.

The societies' political activities fell into two categories. The societies served as auxiliaries to the local Federalist Party organizations and, in areas where there was no local committee, they performed the responsibilities of nominating candidates and conducting campaigns. In addition, societies sponsored celebrations, orations, parades on Washington's birthday, and festivities on July 4 and the anniversary of Washington's first inauguration.

With the irreversible decline of the Federalist Party after the Hartford Convention and the Treaty of Ghent in 1814, Washington Benevolent Societies also lost their relevance. No more new societies were founded, and eventually the others faded away.

See also POLITICAL PARTIES; VOLUNTARY ASSOCIATIONS.

Further reading: David Hackett Fischer, *The Revolution in American Conservatism: The Federalist Party in the Era of Jeffersonian Democracy* (New York: Harper & Row, 1965).

— Terri Halperin

Wayne, Anthony (1745–1796)

Nicknamed "Mad Anthony" because of his rash decisions in battle, Anthony Wayne was born in 1745 in Pennsylvania into a prosperous farming family. On March 25, 1766, Wayne married Mary Penrose, the daughter of a Pennsylvania merchant.

Wayne entered public life in 1774 when he was elected to the Provincial Convention to discuss the COERCIVE ACTS (1774). In 1776 the Pennsylvania Committee of Safety nominated Wayne to serve as a colonel in the CONTINENTAL ARMY, and later that year he assumed command of FORT TICONDEROGA. Wayne disliked his time at Fort Ticonderoga, but he impressed higher officials with his discipline, orderliness, and military successes in CANADA, earning a promotion to brigadier general in 1777. On September 20 and 21, 1777, Wayne suffered a disastrous defeat at the hands of the British army at Paoli, Pennsylvania. General WILLIAM HOWE's army killed 200 and injured 100 more colonial troops under Wayne during the Paoli "massacre." A court-martial investigating the affair acquitted Wayne of any misconduct. In 1781 GEORGE WASHINGTON ordered Wayne to accompany the MARQUIS DE LAFAYETTE to Virginia. He conducted successful campaigns in Virginia and Georgia until the REVOLUTIONARY WAR (1775–83) ended.

After the war, Wayne entered private life. Sickness weakened his constitution, and he wanted to devote time to the rice plantation in Georgia he acquired during the war. However, his plantation endeavor failed and Wayne returned to Pennsylvania, where he was elected to the House of Representatives. His political career was short-lived, but he used his time to expand the military and pressed for settler claims against NATIVE AMERICANS in the South. In 1792 President George Washington appointed Wayne commander of the Legion army. The United States had experienced problems with Native American tribes in the Old Northwest since the conclusion of the Revolutionary War. Native American groups in the Ohio River Valley did not recognize land cessions that occurred after the Revolutionary War and actively resisted Americans settling on the FRONTIER. Federal efforts to quell resistance failed. In 1790 a pan-Indian army (mostly Miami and Shawnee) ambushed Josiah Harmar's army, and two years later another pan-Indian army routed ARTHUR ST. CLAIR on the Wabash River.

Battling health problems, Wayne marched against the Native Americans in the Old Northwest in 1793. In 1794 he led an army of more than 4,000 troops that defeated

Miami Little Turtle's pan-Indian army at the BATTLE OF FALLEN TIMBERS (August 20, 1794). To assure peace between United States settlers and Native Americans, Wayne presided over the TREATY OF GREENVILLE (1795) that ceded the present-day state of Ohio to the United States and established two forts to prevent Indians and settlers from attacking each other. Wayne's expedition crushed overt Indian military resistance in the Old Northwest for nearly two decades. Wayne did not live long after his military successes in the Old Northwest. He died on December 15, 1796, on Presque Isle, Pennsylvania.

Further reading: David Paul Nelson, *Anthony Wayne: Soldier of the Early Republic* (Bloomington: Indiana University Press, 1985); John Preston, *A Gentleman Rebel: Mad Anthony Wayne* (Garden City, N.Y.: Garden City Publishing, 1930).

— William J. Bauer, Jr.

Webster, Noah (1758–1843)

Long a proponent of a national culture, Noah Webster standardized a distinctly American form of the English language. In his spellers, readers, and grammar books, Webster provided a more uniform means of spelling, pronunciation, and writing. In early titles such as *The American Spelling Book* (1783) and *An American Selection of Lessons in Reading and Speaking* (1804), Webster evoked the nationalist fervor that infused life during the early republic. In addition to authoring *An American Dictionary of the English Language* (1828), Webster also assisted in the founding of Massachusetts's Amherst College. Like many of his generation, Webster looked upon the masses as crude and potentially destructive. He considered religious and educational training essential to the formation of a virtuous and moral citizenry.

Born in West Hartford, Connecticut, Noah Webster showed an early proclivity for higher learning. After graduating from Yale College in 1778, he worked as both a teacher and clerk before beginning a short career in law. Webster published the first part of his *A Grammatical Institute of the English Language,* in 1783 and followed it with a grammar and reader over the course of the next two years. Aimed at an elementary audience, his speller proved a surprising success. By the end of the 1830s, some 15 million copies were in print; the number quadrupled by the turn of the century. The goal of these and later works was nothing short of establishing a national linguistic standard.

An ardent FEDERALIST who supported a strong central government and advocated the ratification of the Constitution, Webster also invested tremendous time, energy, and money into securing copyright legislation. To do so, he traveled throughout the country, visiting the state capitals and forming close connections with political leaders from South Carolina to Connecticut. He counted BENJAMIN FRANKLIN as an ally in his effort to formalize and simplify English spelling. Despite the fact that some of his spelling reforms took hold, Webster did make a lasting impression in the realm of orthography.

Webster married Rebecca Greenleaf on October 26, 1789, and soon moved to New York to begin work as an editor for two Federalist newspapers, the *Minerva* and the *Herald.* Ten years passed before he and his family relocated to New Haven. The political climate changed, however, as the FEDERALIST PARTY suffered from internal division during the 1790s and was defeated by THOMAS JEFFERSON in 1800. Already alienated by the divisiveness, Webster left his editorship in 1803.

Webster then returned to a life devoted to learning. He published works on reading, epidemics (see DISEASE AND EPIDEMICS), economics, and SCIENCE throughout the latter years of his life. His lexicographical triumph came with the 1806 publication of *A Compendious Dictionary of the English Language.* In this short volume, Webster recorded words that had yet to be incorporated into other dictionaries. During the next 20 years he continued to build on this work, publishing the stunning *An American Dictionary of the English Language* in 1828. Webster's dictionary incorporated words from both LITERATURE and everyday speech, provided primary as well as secondary and tertiary definitions, and included etymologies. In retrospect, many of his definitions were flawed and his etymologies lagged behind the work of more advanced linguists. Nonetheless, Webster gained renown both within and outside the Unites States through his many publications, particularly his dictionaries.

Further reading: V. P. Bynack, "Noah Webster's Linguistic Thought and the Idea of an American National Culture" *Journal of the History of Ideas* 45 (1984): 99–114; Harlan Giles Unger, *Noah Webster: The Life and Times of an American Patriot* (New York: John Wiley, 1998).

Daniel M. Cobb

Weems, "Parson" Mason Locke (1759–1825)

Mason Locke Weems was a priest, book agent, traveling salesman, and author. Born in 1759 near Herring Bay, Anne Arundel County, Maryland, little is known about his childhood. It is believed that at around the age of 14 he traveled abroad for an education in London and at the University of Edinburgh. With the onset of the REVOLUTIONARY WAR (1775–83), Weems returned to Maryland. There is some evidence that he and his brother became blockade runners to supply the revolutionary effort during the war, but this is not firmly established.

Weems's life after the war is better documented. He studied theology, hoping eventually to be ordained into the ministry. He encountered great difficulty in securing ordination, however. With the colonies detached from England, there was no Anglican bishop available for Weems in North America. Weems and Edward Gantt, a friend in the same predicament, turned to BENJAMIN FRANKLIN and JOHN ADAMS for help. Franklin offered little advice other than scorn and the suggestion that Weems and Gantt simply not worry about official ordination. Adams recommended seeking ordination from the Church of Denmark. Weems and Gantt were saved by a new act of Parliament that relaxed the allegiance requirements for ordination, and Weems entered the ministry in 1784.

He served for seven years as rector in Anne Arundel County and began publishing and reprinting books. By 1792 Weems had stepped down from his parish to become a traveling bookseller for publisher MATHEW CAREY of Philadelphia. He continued selling books and Bibles for three decades, bringing the written word to cities and farm communities along the Atlantic seaboard.

Weems also began to write his own stories. In 1800 he wrote and published his most influential work, a biography of GEORGE WASHINGTON. It is worth noting the extended title: *A History of the Life and Death, Virtues and Exploits of General George Washington, and Containing a Great Many Curious and Valuable Anecdotes, Tending to Throw Much Light on the Private as Well as Public Life and Character of That Very Extraordinary Man, the Whole Happily Calculated to Furnish a Feat of True Washingtonian Entertainment and Improvement Both to Ourselves and Our Children*. Because Weems occasionally preached at the Pohick Church, he could advertise himself as Parson Weems, "Formerly Rector of Mt. Vernon Parish," thus lending an air of credibility to his book.

The Life of Washington is hardly an objective biography of Washington. On the contrary, it is a fictionalized tale of heroism, portraying Washington as a Moses-like character sent from God to deliver the American people from the bondage of the British Empire. The fifth edition, appearing in 1806, featured the story of the honest boy Washington, the hatchet, and the cherry tree. Weems's "biography" was widely successful, achieving publication in over 70 editions and in a variety of languages. The book told the story of the Revolutionary War in an exciting, dramatic, and personal way that appealed to readers of all ages. Weems went on to write similar biographies of Benjamin Franklin, General FRANCIS MARION, and William Penn.

Established as a successful moralizer, Weems penned one of the first TEMPERANCE books published in America, *The Drunkard's Looking Glass: Reflecting a Faithful Likeness of the Drunkard* (1812). He turned his attention to other sins as well, including *God's Revenge Against Murder* (ca. 1807), *God's Revenge Against Gambling* (ca. 1810), *God's Revenge Against Adultery* (1815), *God's Revenge Against Dueling* (1820), and *The Bad Wife's Looking Glass* (1823).

These books sold and appealed to a certain audience, though none reached the success of the Washington biography. Weems died in Beaufort, South Carolina, in 1825. His version of the Revolutionary War lived on, shaping the myths and collective memory of countless readers.

Further reading: Harold Kellock, *Parson Weems of the Cherry Tree* (New York: Century Co., 1928); Lewis Leary, *The Book-Peddling Parson* (Chapel Hill, N.C.: Algonquin Books, 1984).

— Jay R. Dew

West, Benjamin (1738–1820)

Beginning as a provincial artist in colonial British American, Benjamin West ended up as the court painter of King GEORGE III and president of the Royal Academy in London. Along the way he painted over 700 paintings, and his London studio became the center of influence and training for the generation of aspiring American artists who returned to chronicle the revolutionary era in the new nation. West, however, remained in Europe.

West was born in 1738 in the QUAKER community of Springfield, Pennsylvania, outside Philadelphia. His training came from a series of the European and American itinerant artists who traveled through the colonies painting portraits of the colonial gentry. West's early work in portraiture drew upon English mezzotints for models; he also expanded into paintings of historical events and landscapes. Several significant Pennsylvanians provided patronage to the young artist. One, the Reverend William Smith, provost of the University of Pennsylvania, made possible a trip to Italy, where West could study the Old Masters and immerse himself in the contemporary European art world. These European travels to Italy and France, eventually took West to London in 1763, where exhibitions of his work brought him notice and success. His fiancée Elizabeth Shewell joined him there along with her cousin Matthew Pratt, who became the first of West's American pupils. West would correspond with JOHN SINGLETON COPLEY and welcome to his studio CHARLES WILLSON PEALE, GILBERT STUART, RALPH EARLE, JOHN TRUMBULL, and Washington Allston.

Increasingly, West turned toward history paintings after the 1760s. He used a neoclassical style and drew on topics from Roman antiquity for such works as *Agrippina Landing at Brundisium with the Ashes of Germanicus*

(1768, Yale University Art Gallery). This painting brought West his first commission from George III of an eventual 60 portraits and history paintings for the British monarch, along with an ambitious and uncompleted project to decorate the royal chapel at Windsor with religious paintings. By 1780 West was receiving a royal stipend of £1,000 per year and took for himself the title of "historical painter to the king of England."

See also ART.

Further reading: Robert C. Alberts, *Benjamin West: A Biography* (Boston: Houghton Mifflin, 1978); Helmut von Erffa and Allen Staley, *The Paintings of Benjamin West* (New Haven, Conn.: Yale University Press, 1986); Dorinda Evans, *Benjamin West and His American Students* (Washington, D.C.: Smithsonian Institution Press, 1980).

— David Jaffe

West Indies

The term "West Indies" refers to the region of the Caribbean Sea. The islands of the West Indies exerted an important influence on Americans in the revolutionary and early republican eras. The West Indies and North America were tied through TRADE, shared the institution of SLAVERY, and were politically and diplomatically interconnected.

During the colonial period, from the British perspective, the West Indies colonies of Jamaica and Barbados were their most important colonies in the Americas. Great profits could be earned from plantations growing sugar on these islands. The North American colonies fit into this equation as suppliers of food and carriers of slaves from Africa. Not content with this role for the British colonies, Americans also engaged in illicit trade with the French, Dutch, and Spanish of the region. It was in response to this illicit trade that Great Britain began to tighten imperial regulations in the 1760s, including passage of the SUGAR ACT (1764). After the REVOLUTIONARY WAR (1775–83), much of the West Indies trade was closed to the United States. The wars between France and Great Britain (1793–1815) helped to reinvigorate West Indies trade, especially with the French colonies and the newly independent HAITI. The revolutions in the Spanish colonies following the Napoleonic Wars also increased trade with the region, although contact with the British colonies remained restricted.

Throughout this period, slavery tied North America and the West Indies together. Most colonies in the Caribbean had a more extensively developed plantation economy than the mainland colonies. But there were many similarities between slavery in the two areas, especially in coastal South Carolina and tidewater Virginia, both densely populated with slaves. Elsewhere, merchant connections, slave traders, and even the slaves themselves (many of whom had Caribbean roots) had direct personal knowledge of the West Indies slave system. During the 1790s and early 1800s, the great slave revolt in the French colony of Saint-Domingue (Haiti) had a searing impact on American slaveholders, suggesting to them their own fate if they did not fully control their chattel workers. In turn, the movement to free slaves in some parts of the United States had an influence on slaves throughout the West Indies.

The West Indies were often the centerpiece for contests over empire. During the French and Indian War (1754–63) the British were as much concerned with controlling the West Indies as North America. During the peace negotiation, France gave up CANADA so that it could retain possessions in the Caribbean. The West Indies were also an important locus of action during the Revolutionary War. Naval control of the region was vital to both the French and the British, and it contributed directly to the victory at YORKTOWN (October 19, 1781). The French disaster at the Battle of the Saintes (April 12, 1782)—a naval engagement fought in the straits between Dominica and Guadeloupe—helped to bring both Great Britain and France to the peace table to end the conflict. During the 1790s and early 1800s the West Indies became the center of much of the conflict over neutral rights, with British and French navies seizing American merchant ships.

Although the West Indies had played a central role in American history into the beginning of the 19th century, it decreased in importance thereafter as the nation turned inward and expanded over a continent.

See also FOREIGN AFFAIRS.

West Point

West Point, New York, is where the United States Military Academy was established in 1802. This former fort is located at a curve in the Hudson River that was the most defensible point in the Hudson Highlands. During the REVOLUTIONARY WAR (1775–83), this New York fort became a strategic base connecting New England with the rest of the states. BENEDICT ARNOLD, the commander of West Point, plotted to surrender the fortifications to the British but was foiled in his treason by the capture of Major JOHN ANDRE. After the war the United States government maintained an outpost at West Point, purchasing the land in the 1790s.

A military academy had been a dream of GEORGE WASHINGTON and the FEDERALIST PARTY, but they never successfully put one into place. However, the academy was finally established under the administration of THOMAS JEFFERSON. Unlike the Federalists, Jefferson and the

DEMOCRATIC-REPUBLICANS did not see the academy as the training ground for the children of the well-born. Instead, they viewed it as a republican institution, and Jefferson insisted that West Point be open to the sons of all citizens. His hope was to replace the Federalist army officer corps, where appointments had often been based on personal connections, with a more republican officer corps, where talent and ability would be crucial. For Jefferson, establishing the military academy became another way for him to counter what he saw as the aristocratic pretensions of the Federalists.

Further reading: Theodore J. Crackel, *Mr. Jefferson's Army: Political and Social Reform of the Military Establishment, 1801–1809* (New York: New York University Press, 1987); Theodore J. Crackel, *The Illustrated History of West Point* (West Point, N.Y.: Harry. N. Abrams, 1991).

Whately, Thomas (?–1772)

Although a minor official in Great Britain, Thomas Whately played a significant role in the developing imperial crisis of the 1760s and 1770s. As a secretary for GEORGE GRENVILLE in the treasury office, Whately drew up the STAMP ACT (1765). In the process he solicited the opinion of as many experts on colonial affairs as possible, including THOMAS HUTCHINSON. Ignoring most of this advice, which indicated that colonists would oppose the measure, Whately drafted a reasonable law that the British thought would be self-enforceable.

Whately also wrote the pamphlet *The Regulations Lately Made concerning the Colonies and the Taxes Imposed Upon Them, Considered* (London, 1765), which not only defended the SUGAR ACT (1764) but also elaborated upon the idea of virtual representation. Whately admitted that it was a violation of liberty to impose taxes without the consent of representatives of the taxed. However, he argued that the colonists were represented in Parliament in the same manner that all British subjects were represented: "for every Member of Parliament sits in the House not as a Representative of his own Constituents, but as one of that August Assembly by which all the Commons of *Great Britain* are represented." In other words, each member of Parliament protects the "rights and interests" of the whole empire. This was a powerful argument in the 18th century and was taken seriously by many colonists. DANIEL DULANY responded by arguing that since Parliament could pass taxes on the colonists that had no impact on the people of Great Britain, even by the standards of virtual representation, Parliament did not represent the colonists.

Whately remained an active politician and member of Parliament until his death in 1772. But even from the grave, he exerted some influence on the imperial crisis. BENJAMIN FRANKLIN had gained possession of a series of letters to Whately written by Thomas Hutchinson in which the Massachusetts official had decried the course of events in Boston in the late 1760s. Franklin forwarded them to Boston, where they were made public in 1773, destroying the last vestiges of Hutchinson's popularity and leading to his recall as governor.

See also CORPORATISM; RESISTANCE MOVEMENT.

Further reading: Bernard Bailyn, *The Ordeal of Thomas Hutchinson* (Cambridge, Mass.: Harvard University Press, 1974); Robert Middlekauff, *The Glorious Cause: The American Revolution, 1763–1789* (New York: Oxford University Press, 1882); Edmund S. Morgan and Helen M. Morgan, *The Stamp Act Crisis: Prologue to Revolution* (Chapel Hill: University of North Carolina Press, 1953).

Wheatley, Phillis (1753?–1784)

This prodigy surprised Americans of the revolutionary generation with her ability to command language and write poetry. Phillis Wheatley was born in Africa and captured by slave traders when she was about eight years old. She was fortunate in that she was brought to Boston and sold to an affluent family—the Wheatleys—as a household slave. Susanna Wheatley treated young Phillis kindly, teaching her to read and write English. Phillis's extraordinary talents soon became apparent, and she even learned enough Latin to translate Ovid. Still only a teenager, she began to write poetry on religious themes that astonished her white patrons. By 1772 several of her poems had been published, and her fame spread across the Atlantic. The Wheatleys sent Phillis to England in 1773, where she impressed a new round of patrons. A volume of her poetry was published in England, *Poems on Various Subjects, Religious and Moral* (1773), but the illness of her American patroness, Susanna Wheatley, compelled her to return to Boston. Soon after arriving in Boston, Phillis received her manumission papers. For the next few years, Wheatley continued to write poetry, some of which supported the resistance to Great Britain. In 1778 she married a free black named John Peters, but their life together was a struggle. She had three children, but two died in early infancy. Never of a strong constitution, Wheatley died in poverty and obscurity in 1784 at about age 30.

The first AFRICAN-AMERICAN writer to be published, Phillis Wheatley was an important symbol for her time. In an age when men like THOMAS JEFFERSON denied the intellectual equality of blacks, the achievements of Phillis Wheatley came to be a powerful ANTISLAVERY argument. While much of her work was religious, she also wrote some patriotic poetry and explored issues of race. In her 1773

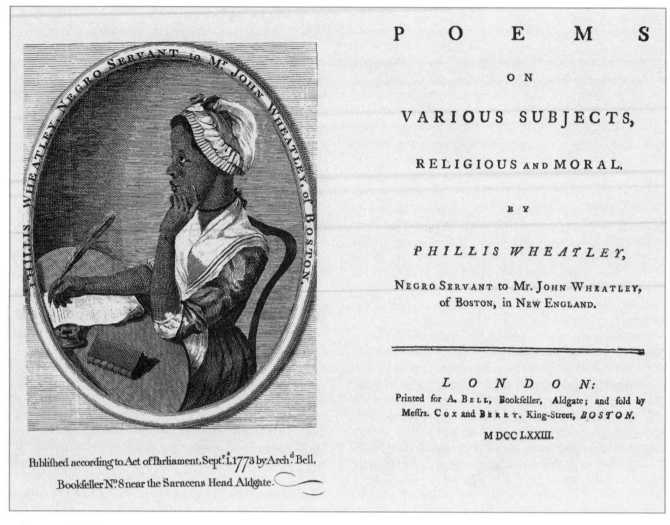

Title page of Phillis Wheatley's most famous work, *Poems on Various Subjects, Religious and Moral* (1773) *(Library of Congress)*

poem "On Being Brought from Africa to America" she wrote:

> 'Twas mercy brought me from my *Pagan* land,
> Taught my benighted soul to understand
> That there's a God, that there's a *Savior* too:
> Once I redemption neither sought nor knew.
> Some view our sable race with scornful eye,
> "Their colour is a diabolic die."
> Remember *Christians*, *Negroes*, black as *Cain*,
> May be refin'd, and join th' angelic trian.

See also SLAVERY; SLAVE TRADE.

Further reading: William H. Robinson, *Phillis Wheatley and Her Writings* (New York: Garland, 1984).

Whigs

The term "Whig" has several different meanings, depending on the historical context. The term emerged in the second half of the 17the century in Great Britain as a derogatory word to describe those who opposed James, the Duke of York, inheriting the crown of his brother Charles II. Supporters of the Stuart monarchy derived the word from "whigamore," which had been applied to Scottish covenanters (Presbyterians who helped to bring on the English civil wars of the 1640s) as an insult. Whigs supported parliamentary supremacy and the Protestant succession. They thus became the prime movers behind the Glorious Revolution (1688–89) that drove the CATHOLIC James II from the throne and enhanced the role of Parliament in government. The Whigs then coalesced into a political party, opposed by the Tories who supported a stronger monarchy. With the Hanoverian succession in 1714, the Whigs emerged as the dominant political force, and in one form or another they controlled the government for most of the rest of the 18th century.

However, in the 18th century there also emerged important divisions among the Whigs. While the political party became entrenched under leaders like Sir Robert Walpole (sometimes this group is referred to as the Whig oligarchy), another group, referred to as COMMONWEALTHMEN or the real or true Whigs, began to criticize Walpole and his supporters for abandoning Whig principles and amassing too much power at the expense of the liberty of the people. The individuals who would later become the leaders of the AMERICAN REVOLUTION became avid readers of the pamphlets and articles written by the true Whigs. Throughout the 1760s and 1770s, opposition to imperial regulation was often defended in the name of Whig principles. In fact, once the REVOLUTIONARY WAR (1775–83) broke out, the supporters of the resistance movement called themselves Whigs and their opponents Tories.

There are two other important uses of the word Whig: First, an American Whig political party, advocating a more active government, emerged in the 1830s and 1840s. Second, historians sometimes use the phrase "Whig history" to describe an interpretation of either the English or the American past that de-emphasizes conflict among social groups and centers on the inevitable unfolding of the triumph of liberty and democracy. Critics of this interpretation do not see that triumph as inevitable or complete. They also believe that Whig history tends to focus on the stories of great white men while ignoring the history of race, class, and gender.

See also REPUBLICANISM.

Further reading: Gordon S. Wood, *The Creation of the American Republic, 1776–1787* (Chapel Hill: University of North Carolina Press, 1969).

Whiskey Rebellion (1794)

Armed rebellion broke out in 1794 in western Pennsylvania when federal tax collectors attempted to serve court summonses on farmers and distillers who failed to pay an excise tax on whiskey. This came to be called the Whiskey Rebellion.

In 1791 Secretary of the Treasury ALEXANDER HAMILTON proposed a series of excise taxes to raise revenue for the new federal government. The most controversial of these taxes fell on distilled spirits, with a 25 percent tax on all whiskey production. This new excise tax was particularly burdensome on farmers in the West, where whiskey was used as a form of barter and was an integral part of the ECONOMY.

The excise tax met with widespread opposition, especially in the FRONTIER areas of Pennsylvania, and its collection was difficult. Resistance to the excise tax in western Pennsylvania stemmed from several factors. That region, and the frontier as a whole, suffered from a lack of hard currency that was required to pay the taxes. Without ready cash, farmers became increasingly frustrated at what they perceived to be an unresponsive government that did not understand the hardships they faced due to a lack of specie. Moreover, citizens in the West resented having to travel to distant courts in Philadelphia to plead their cases rather than using local courts.

Throughout 1792 and 1793, local resistance to the tax oftentimes led to violence. After several meetings denouncing the law, farmers took matters into their own hands. A group of individuals calling themselves the "whiskey boys" attacked federal tax collectors, shaving their heads, stripping them naked, tarring and feathering them, and leaving them tied to trees deep in the woods. Even the nonviolent protest became heated as DEMOCRATIC-REPUBLICAN SOCIETIES (anti-Washington administration political clubs) in the East as well as the West called for a repeal of the tax.

Failed efforts to collect the tax only strengthened the federal government's resolve. In the summer of 1794, at the urging of Alexander Hamilton, Marshal David Lennox and Supervisor of Collection John Neville tried to serve writs to western Pennsylvanians to appear in Philadelphia courts to answer for noncompliance with the tax law. In response to these efforts by the government, some 50 armed local men assembled at the Mingo Creek Church in Washington County. Word spread quickly, and soon an even larger group gathered to confront the marshal and Neville. On the morning of July 16, these men surrounded John Neville's house on Bower Hill, believing that they would find David Lennox there. Their plan was to demand the surrender of both the writs and Neville's commission as tax collector. However, only Neville, his wife, and granddaughter were in the house. In a brief skirmish, Neville repulsed the attackers, wounding several and killing one. The next day, after Neville left his house in the hands of a military guard, the whiskey rebels renewed the assault. During this exchange of gunfire at Bower Hill, several men were wounded and at least two were killed before the government forces surrendered and the rebels destroyed the house. Among the dead was insurgent leader James McFarland, a REVOLUTIONARY WAR (1775–83) hero and militia captain who became a martyr to the insurrectionists and a regional symbol of the anti-excise cause.

Events moved faster after the violence at Bower Hill. At a meeting on July 23, David Bradford, a DEMOCRATIC-REPUBLICAN politician and the county's attorney general, emerged as a spokesman for the more radical insurgents. Bradford called for the raising of a militia as well as confiscating the federal mails to identify government sympathizers. Angered by what he found in the captured mail, Bradford threatened to march the local militia on Pittsburgh as a show of force. Moderates managed to convince the whiskey rebels not to follow Bradford's call to occupy Pittsburgh. In the meantime, the federal government sent a commission to western Pennsylvania to assess the situation, and they determined that it was impossible to resolve the conflict peacefully. Approximately 12,000 troops were then mustered from Pennsylvania, Maryland, Virginia, and New Jersey to quell the rebellion by order of the administration of GEORGE WASHINGTON. With Washington in the lead, the army marched to Fort Cumberland, where Washington turned command of the army over to General HENRY LEE. By the time the federal army reached Pittsburgh, the rebel leaders, including David Bradford, had already fled the region. Still, the army arrested about 150 insurgents. Many of these individuals were released, but about 20 men were marched back to Philadelphia to stand trial. Only two were found guilty, and they were later pardoned by President Washington.

The suppression of the Whiskey Rebellion strengthened the power and legitimacy of the federal government to enforce law. It also allowed the president to lay the blame for the rebellion squarely on the Democratic-Republican Societies, thus discrediting and permanently damaging their effectiveness in criticizing the Washington administration.

See also HUGH HENRY BRACKENRIDGE.

Further reading: Leland D. Baldwin, *Whiskey Rebels: The Story of a Frontier Uprising* (Pittsburgh, Pa.: University of Pittsburgh Press, 1939); Thomas P. Slaughter, *The Whiskey Rebellion: Frontier Epilogue to the American Revolution* (New York: Oxford University Press, 1986).

— Jeffrey A. Davis

White Plains, Battle of (October 28, 1776)

At the Battle of White Plains, General WILLIAM HOWE's superior British forces outmaneuvered and outfought the CONTINENTAL ARMY under General GEORGE WASHINGTON but failed to crush the Americans. Howe had compelled Washington to move most of his army out of the northern part of Manhattan by landing in Westchester County, threatening to cut Washington off from the mainland. The Continental army, numbering as many as 14,000, dug in along a series of hills at the village of White Plains. While the entrenchments presented a formidable obstacle, Washington initially failed to recognize that they were dominated by Chatterton Hill across the Bronx River and on the American right. Just before the battle, Washington recognized his mistake and quickly sent troops to fortify the position.

The Americans began the battle by sending several regiments (about 1,500 men) against the British, but this force was driven back by repeated flanking movements. Although Howe planned a frontal assault against the American line, it was never carried out. Instead, he sent British and HESSIAN units against the hastily constructed position on Chatterton Hill. The first assault was beaten back, but ultimately the Hessians and some British dragoons swung around the far American right, routed the militia units in front of them, and swept the Americans off the hill. With a few hours of daylight left, the British hesitated and failed to take advantage of their position to roll up the entire American line. The British suffered 231 casualties. The American numbers are less certain; they lost anywhere from 150 to 350 men.

A second attack on October 30 was canceled because of a heavy rainstorm. Washington used the cover of the weather to withdraw a few miles further to stronger positions. But this move also allowed Howe to cut back toward Manhattan, surround FORT WASHINGTON, and capture 3,000 Americans.

See also REVOLUTIONARY WAR.

Further reading: Robert Middlekauff, *The Glorious Cause: The American Revolution, 1763–1789* (New York: Oxford University Press, 1982).

Whitney, Eli (1765–1825)

Eli Whitney not only invented the cotton gin, but he also pioneered the use of interchangeable parts in the production of firearms. Whitney grew up on a small farm in Westboro, Massachusetts. At age 17 he left home to attend Yale College. After graduating in 1792 he headed south to pursue a teaching career, accepting a job as a tutor in Savannah, Georgia, where he made the acquaintance of Catherine Greene, widow of the REVOLUTIONARY WAR (1775–83) general NATHANAEL GREENE. While visiting her plantation, Whitney saw the need for a machine that could separate the sticky seeds from the cotton lint in green-seed, short-staple cotton. Demand for cotton to feed English mills was high, and a cheap way to clean cotton was needed to make large-scale production possible in the South. Whitney produced a workable cotton gin in 1793 and patented it 1794. However, he was unable to protect his patent, and he and his partner, Phineas Miller, made very little money from the invention. Because he could not protect his patent, unlicensed copies of Whitney's cotton gin spread throughout the South, helping cotton to become the region's most valuable crop. More ominously, the cotton boom breathed new life into the institution of southern SLAVERY.

Whitney found his way to financial success in the firearms industry while making an important contribution to the development of mass production and industrialization. In 1797, when the United States faced a possible war with France, Whitney won a contract from the federal government to produce 10,000 muskets for the army. Whitney promised to produce the muskets in two years. He built a factory in Hamden, Connecticut, and designed a system of manufacturing parts in standard sizes that could be used interchangeably to build complete muskets. This was a revolutionary concept, since guns at that time were made separately by individual gunsmiths, which meant that if a part broke, it had to be remade by hand to fit that particular gun. Whitney's method of making standardized individual parts was ultimately successful, although it took him 10 years instead of the promised two. Whitney convinced many who doubted his methods in 1801 when he arranged a demonstration for incoming president THOMAS JEFFERSON. At that demonstration in WASHINGTON D.C., witnesses picked random parts from scattered piles and then were able to use those parts to assemble complete working muskets. Whitney's method marked an important step in the development of techniques of mass production.

Whitney married Henrietta Edwards in 1817. They had four children, three of whom survived into adulthood. His son, Eli Whitney Jr., continued to manufacture arms in the Hamden plant after his father's death in 1825.

Further reading: Constance McLaughlin Green, *Eli Whitney and the Birth of American Technology* (Boston: Little, Brown, 1956); Jeannette Mirsky and Allen Nevins, *The World of Eli Whitney* (New York: Macmillan, 1952).

— J. Brett Adams

THE FIRST COTTON-GIN.—Drawn by William L. Sheppard.—[See Page 814.]

Engraving showing slaves operating a cotton gin while owners inspect the cotton *(Library of Congress)*

Wilderness Road

The land-speculating Transylvania Company hired DANIEL BOONE to establish a path to the territory west of the Appalachian Mountains that would allow new settlers to reach the firm's lands in what is now Kentucky. Before the creation of the new route—the Wilderness Road—travel to the lands south of the Ohio River was tedious and fraught with danger. One route started in Pittsburgh and continued down the Ohio to present-day Louisville. However, boats were easy targets for NATIVE AMERICANS who wanted to stop the intruders from settling on their hunting grounds. The Wilderness Road made the western passage safer. People could travel in large groups, and if they were attacked they could seek shelter in the woods and hills that lined the way. The Wilderness Road ultimately stretched from the southern reaches of Pennsylvania through the Cumberland Gap in western Virginia to the banks of the Ohio River at Louisville. Parts of the trail branched off to Boonesborough and Lexington.

On March 10, 1775, Daniel Boone and about 30 men set out to blaze a trail to the rich farmlands to the west. The pioneers soon ran into trouble. Immediately to the south lay the Chickamaugans, a confederation of refugees from the CHEROKEE, Shawnee, and other Native American. tribes. Their leader DRAGGING CANOE promised that Kentucky would be "a dark and bloody ground." He believed that the Native Americans who had sold the lands to the Transylvania Company and other European Americans had no right to do so. Boone and those who followed behind him quickly learned that the Native Americans meant to defend what they believed was still their home. On March 24, 1775, a war party attacked the advance elements of the road builders, killing one of the leaders and his slave. The main group withstood a second attack by quickly building a fort of logs. After beating back the assault, they continued with the road. In May 1775 the men arrived at the lush bluegrass country of western Kentucky, where they built Boonesborough. The site had many of the essentials for a thriving town: water, fertile soil, and access to the salt licks for their livestock.

The outbreak of the REVOLUTIONARY WAR (1775–83) threw Kentucky into turmoil. Britain allied itself with the Native Americans of the region, and warriors attacked settlements throughout the territory. Americans retaliated by hunting down and killing Indians, often without bothering to find out if they were friendly or not. After the war, the road was a pathway for a flood of new immigrants from the East seeking cheap land.

Further reading: Hazel Dickens-Garcia, *To Western Woods: The Breckenridge Family Moves to Kentucky in 1793* (Rutherford, N.J.: Fairleigh Dickinson University Press, 1991); Otis Rice, *Frontier Kentucky* (Lexington: University Press of Kentucky, 1975).

— George Milne

Wilkes, John (1725–1797)

In the eyes of many American colonists, the Englishman John Wilkes was a champion for liberty and justice who fought for these rights against a dishonest government. Born into a modest family—his father, a member of the middle class, was a successful distiller—Wilkes was an energetic man, well educated, witty, and exuberant. He attended school in Europe and, after returning to Britain, won election to Parliament in 1757. In his early political career, he was a close friend and supporter of WILLIAM PITT.

In 1763 Wilkes started publication of the satirical journal *The North Briton.* This journal was published in direct opposition to *The Briton,* a journal financed and backed by the British government. In the infamous No. 45 issue of *The North Briton,* Wilkes overstepped his bounds and aggressively attacked the integrity of the British government, accusing British politicians of putting lies into the mouth of the king. The government labeled his attack as seditious libel, a serious charge that required a trial. In 1764 the king and his ministers dismissed Wilkes form his seat in Parliament, and Wilkes fled across the English Channel to France to avoid a libel suit. However, after running out of funds in 1768, he had no choice but to return to his home country. The government had not forgotten his attack and forced him to stand trial. He was found guilty and sentenced to several months of light probation.

During his trial, Wilkes again ran for election to Parliament. Although he won the election, the government barred Wilkes from his seat and called for a new election. Wilkes won election to Parliament again, not once, not twice, but four times. Each time he was prevented from taking his proper place. The American colonists followed the struggle between Wilkes and Parliament with great interest. Many colonists felt that Parliament had treated Wilkes unjustly, and they adopted him as a symbol of liberty who was fighting for the rights of all Englishmen. Fearing that if the British could crush liberties at home they would do the same in the colonies, the colonists actively sought to help Wilkes in his plight. Virginia sent him tobacco, and South Carolina sent money to pay down his debts. The phrase "Wilkes and Liberty" became commonplace throughout the colonies. The number "45," for the *North Briton No. 45,* also became symbolically important to Americans. (Both Wilkes and Americans knew that the number also suggested a challenge to the House of Hanover, since the last invasion of the Stuart heir to the throne—the so-called "pretender"—occurred in Scotland in 1745.) In 1774 Wilkes finally took his proper seat in the House of Commons.

While in Parliament during the REVOLUTIONARY WAR (1775–83), Wilkes often spoke in favor of American independence. He believed that the war was unreasonable and brutal and that the colonies could not be regained by force, a viewpoint that only increased his popularity among the American colonists. He, along with Isaac Barre, is the namesake for the city of Wilkes-Barre, Pennsylvania.

Further reading: Louis Kronenberger, *The Extraordinary Mr. Wilkes, His Life and Times* (New York: Doubleday, 1974); Peter D. G. Thomas, *John Wilkes, A Friend to Liberty* (Oxford: Oxford University Press, 1996).

— Brant Day

Wilkinson, James (1757–1825)

EDMUND RANDOLPH once remarked that James Wilkinson was "the only man that I ever saw who was from bark to the very core a villain." Wilkinson was born in 1757 in Maryland, the son of a merchant-planter. In 1773 Wilkinson traveled to Pennsylvania, where he studied to be a doctor. MEDICINE did not seem to be his calling, however, and Wilkinson's peripatetic spirit soon led him north to Boston, where he lived until the beginning of the REVOLUTIONARY WAR (1775–83).

In 1775 he served as an aide to General NATHANAEL GREENE and supplied the Revolutionary army with information about the maneuvers of the British troops in Boston. Wilkinson moved up the ranks of the CONTINENTAL ARMY and participated in the BATTLES OF TRENTON (December 26, 1776) AND PRINCETON (January 3, 1777). He rose to the rank of brigadier general and, between 1777 and 1781, served as secretary of the Board of War. Wilkinson's personality—he had a tendency to self-promotion—led to disputes with other officers and he even fought a bloodless duel with General HORATIO GATES. On November 12, 1778, he married Ann Biddle, the daughter of a Pennsylvania businessman.

After the war ended, Wilkinson moved to Pennsylvania and picked up farming. In 1784 he moved to Kentucky and exploited the dissident FRONTIER conditions. Beginning in 1787, while still in the army's pay, he sold information to Spanish officials who wanted to discover if residents of western Pennsylvania would be agreeable to Spanish rule. Wilkinson used the opportunity to attempt, unsuccessfully, to organize the area into a new state. In 1792 military service swept Wilkinson to the Old Northwest, where he served under General ANTHONY WAYNE at the BATTLE OF FALLEN TIMBERS (August 20, 1794). Four years later, he was the commander of Fort Detroit.

After the LOUISIANA PURCHASE (1803), President THOMAS JEFFERSON appointed Wilkinson to serve as military governor of the new territory. During his time in Louisiana, Wilkinson plotted to erect his own empire in Mexico and the West. Wilkinson proposed to Vice President AARON BURR that they should seize Louisiana, parts of northern Mexico, and possibly annex all of Mexico. However, when Burr began to put his plan into motion, Wilkinson backed out and informed Jefferson that Burr proposed to attack New Orleans. In 1808 Jefferson sent Wilkinson to New York to put down opposition to the EMBARGO OF 1807.

Wilkinson's duplicitous actions finally began to catch up with him in 1809, when Daniel Clark accused Wilkinson of engineering Burr's scheme in the South. Wilkinson was court-martialed twice, but both times the military courts acquitted him. In 1810 Wilkinson wedded for the second time, marrying Celestine Laveau Trudeau. They had three children. Between 1821 and 1825 Wilkinson entered land speculation schemes in Texas and Mexico. He died on December 28, 1825, in Mexico City and is buried at Iglesia de San Miguel Archangel.

Further reading: Thomas Hay and M.R. Werner, *The Admirable Trumpeter: A Biography of James Wilkinson* (Garden City, N.Y.: Doubleday, 1941); James Jacobs, *Tarnished Warrior: Major-General James Wilkinson* (New York: Macmillan, 1938).

— William J. Bauer, Jr.

Wilson, James (1742–1798)

James Wilson was a progressive legal thinker, a signer of the DECLARATION OF INDEPENDENCE (July 4, 1776), and an important member of the CONSTITUTIONAL CONVENTION. Born in Carskerdo, near St. Andrews, Scotland, Wilson's farmer parents, intending him perhaps for the Presbyterian ministry, provided him with a superior education. He studied at the University of St. Andrews, the University of Glasgow, and at the divinity school attached to St. Mary's College, an important seat for the ideas of the Scottish Enlightenment. Wilson, however, did not complete his theological studies and, with an eye toward secular advancement, sailed in 1765 for America. Once in Pennsylvania, he applied to and was accepted at the law offices of JOHN DICKINSON, where he studied for the bar and to which he was admitted in late 1767. In 1771 Wilson married the heiress Rachel Bird. In July 1774 he was elected to the Cumberland County COMMITTEE OF CORRESPONDENCE and to the first Pennsylvania provincial convention. That year Wilson amended a manuscript he wrote as a law student in 1768 and had it published under the title *Considerations on the Nature and Extent of the Legislative*

Authority of the British Parliament. In this pamphlet, distributed to the members of the FIRST CONTINENTAL CONGRESS, Wilson asserted that the British Parliament had no authority whatsoever over the colonies and stated his political conviction that "all power is derived from the people." Though Wilson originally opposed the colonists' drive for independence (his interest was to preserve Pennsylvania's balanced government), in the end he voted for it and signed the Declaration of Independence.

While Wilson held that government rested on the consent of the governed, he sought to impede what he feared was the unchecked will of the majority. At heart he was a conservative revolutionary. He was disgusted at the state's radical and democratic 1776 constitution that abolished the office of governor and placed all political power in a unicameral legislature. Though he continued in his support of the independence movement, his legal defenses of LOYALISTS, his position on the state constitution (see CONSTITUTIONS, STATE), and his opposition to price controls generated popular animosity against him. In what would be labeled the "Fort Wilson" riot, shots were exchanged between militiamen in the street and a group of Wilson's supporters at his home on October 4, 1779. Several men in the street, and one person in Wilson's house, were killed before an elite troop of cavalry dispersed the crowd.

Political conservatives regained control of Pennsylvania in 1782 and sent Wilson to the Continental Congress, where he served in 1782–83 and again in 1785–87. At the Constitutional Convention, Wilson strongly supported the creation of a national government. He helped draft the Constitution and then led the efforts to have it ratified in Pennsylvania.

Seeking to be named as the first chief justice of the SUPREME COURT, Wilson in 1789 wrote to President GEORGE WASHINGTON expressly to ask for the post. Washington instead invited JOHN JAY to become chief justice and he appointed Wilson as an associate justice. Wilson supported judicial review (the power of American courts to decide if government acts adhere to the Constitution) and believed in the inherent importance of the Supreme Court. In the end, Wilson's financial problems stemming from land speculation and entrepreneurial ventures ruined him and cast a shadow on his reputation. He died insolvent.

Further reading: Charles Page Smith, *James Wilson, Founding Father: 1742–1798* (Chapel Hill: University of North Carolina Press, 1956).

— Robyn Davis Mcmillin

Witherspoon, John (1723–1794)

John Witherspoon was an educator, Presbyterian clergyman, and a signer of the DECLARATION OF INDEPENDENCE (July 4, 1776). He was born and educated in Scotland, where he entered the University of Edinburgh at he age of 13 to study theology. After serving as pastor at several Presbyterian churches in Scotland, he was offered the presidency of the College of New Jersey (later Princeton University). Witherspoon moved to Princeton in 1768.

As a college president, Witherspoon brought the ideals of the Enlightenment to the American classroom. Under his leadership, Princeton attendance rivaled that of Yale, and the financial endowment blossomed. He raised teaching standards and expanded the curriculum to emphasize instruction through lecture. Library holdings increased in quantity as well as quality. Some scholars have credited Witherspoon with inventing the word "Americanism," based on a 1781 article that explored the differences between the language as spoken in America and in England.

As a clergyman, Witherspoon's theology was evangelical but moderate, appealing to Old Side (opponents of the Great Awakening) and New Side Presbyterians (supporters of the Great Awakening) alike. Witherspoon's theology also connected Christianity to REPUBLICANISM, emphasizing what he called "the rights of private judgement . . . universal and unalienable." In Scotland, Witherspoon had defended the right of people to choose their own ministers. Building on these ideas in America, Witherspoon supported the ideology of popular rights and resistance to arbitrary power.

In June 1776 Witherspoon was a delegate to the CONTINENTAL CONGRESS in Philadelphia. He became the only clergyman to sign the Declaration of Independence. Witherspoon continued to work in Congress, laboring on more than 100 committees and contributing to the construction of the ARTICLES OF CONFEDERATION. In 1787 he attended the New Jersey convention that ratified the Constitution.

Witherspoon's final years were a struggle. His wife, Elizabeth, died in 1789, and he remarried at the age of 68. His second wife, Ann Dill, was a 24-year-old widow; the age difference caused a minor scandal in the halls of Princeton. After two years of suffering from blindness, Witherspoon died in 1794. He was buried on the grounds of the university he had guided since his arrival in America.

Further reading: Henry F. May, *The Enlightenment in America* (New York: Oxford University Press, 1976); Douglas Sloan, *The Scottish Enlightenment and the American College Ideal* (New York: Teacher's College Press, Columbia University, 1971).

— Jay R. Dew

women's rights and status

Prior to the AMERICAN REVOLUTION, most Anglo-American women identified themselves primarily as members of

This drawing of women voting in New Jersey depicts the sole instance in Revolutionary America when property qualifications for suffrage were defined without regard to sex, from 1790 to 1807. *(Howard Pyle Collection, Delaware Art Museum)*

households and families, deriving their status less from their own abilities and ambitions than from the statuses of their fathers and husbands. Women's work focused largely on the household, including cleaning, child rearing, making clothing, processing and preserving food, and managing the dairy and the kitchen garden. The small number of women who managed businesses, farms, or plantations typically did so following a husband's death (and even then this was exceptional). In New England, married women could serve as "deputy husbands," an informal status allowing them to make legally recognized business decisions when their husbands were absent or ill. But a woman assumed the role of deputy husband as a temporary addition to her primary responsibilities, which remained centered in households. Even very wealthy women did not escape housework, although after mid-century they were increasingly valued as loving wives and mothers rather than as productive household managers. The economic value of Anglo-American women's household labor was widely recognized, for few households could survive without the services that women provided. Nevertheless, gender relations within

households were hierarchical, subordinating women to their fathers and husbands.

Anglo-American women's precise legal rights varied from colony to colony, although the shared British common-law tradition made most practices fairly similar throughout the 13 colonies. Coverture was the most important legal principle in determining women's rights and status. Under coverture, a woman's legal and political identity was absorbed by her husband, who assumed control over his wife along with her property, earnings, and children. Coverture could be mitigated by antenuptial contracts, which allowed women to maintain control over property they inherited or acquired after marriage. But antenuptial contracts required the prospective husband's consent and were signed only by a minority of wealthy couples. Women whose husbands were absent for extended periods or whose husbands had deserted them or gone bankrupt could petition for "feme sole" status, allowing them to engage in TRADE and control property. Widows were typically guaranteed of receiving a "dower right," one-third of the husband's property; even so, they lacked total control over their inheritances. For example, in most colonies a widow could not sell inherited land without permission from the court; similarly, a husband might choose to make his wife's inheritance contingent on her remaining single after his death. Access to divorce was extraordinarily limited, requiring a legislative act in most colonies. Although the New England colonies permitted "absolute divorce," which allowed both parties to remarry, these divorces were granted rarely and mostly to men.

The development of colonial economic and legal systems affected enslaved women and NATIVE AMERICAN women differently. By mid-century, the expansion of SLAVERY had dramatically increased the total number of slaves in the Chesapeake and the coastal South, enabling enslaved women to find partners and establish families and kin networks. And although most enslaved women continued to work in the fields, a small percentage worked as house servants, nurses, or midwives. Although these changes improved the quality of women's lives, they did not mitigate the legal constraints of slavery. Slave marriages were not recognized by law; all children born to enslaved women followed the condition of their mother, regardless of the father's status, and enslaved parents had no legal authority over their children. Native American women saw their status deteriorate over the course of the 18th century, as the growing reliance on European trade upset the balance of power between women and men in Indian communities. European traders sought goods like skins and furs, commodities that were produced by hunting and trapping—work that was traditionally performed by Native American men. In return, the traders offered European weapons, clothing, and cooking utensils. When Indian communities became dependent on European goods, women were devalued because their work did not produce tradeable commodities. Women in many tribes, including the CHEROKEE and IROQUOIS, also appear to have lost political power during this period, partly because of men's new economic dominance and partly because Indian-European diplomacy, which was conducted almost exclusively by men, played an increasingly pivotal role in political decision making.

The RESISTANCE MOVEMENT (1764–75) and the REVOLUTIONARY WAR (1775–83) changed women's status both within their households and in the larger public sphere. Much of the agitation during the imperial crisis was aimed at encouraging Americans to resist taxation and undermine parliamentary authority by boycotting the imported goods that Parliament had taxed. Because many of these goods, especially tea and cloth, were purchased by women for use in households, Anglo-American women's work became politicized. A woman's decision to buy tea for her family or boycott it was no longer private and personal; instead, it was a political choice with repercussions that affected her community and even the thirteen colonies. Similarly, in order to avoid purchasing British cloth, women began spinning and weaving, tasks that many had abandoned by the 1760s. In the South, slave women were removed from the fields and set to spinning and weaving. In northern urban areas, many women and children began making cloth at home for sale. Compared with British goods, "homespun" cloth was rough and coarse, and wearing homespun became a visible badge of patriotism. During the war, homespun was used not only for regular clothing but also for soldiers' shirts and blankets. Domestic textile manufacture became even more explicitly politicized when women formed associations, often calling themselves "Daughters of Liberty," to spin, weave, and sew. With the outbreak of the Revolutionary War, many WHIG and LOYALIST women faced new challenges. The absence of their husbands, sons, and fathers left them responsible for managing farms, plantations, and businesses under uncertain and dangerous conditions. Other women became CAMP FOLLOWERS, traveling with the CONTINENTAL ARMY to provide laundry, cooking, and sewing. Elite urban women formed associations to raise money in support of the Revolution. While some women saw these new responsibilities as burdens, others clearly saw them as opportunities. All these activities enlarged women's interests, turning many into passionate political advocates, broadening their vision of the world, and changing their understanding of themselves. Many women no longer identified themselves only as members of families and communities. Instead, women and men alike began to see themselves as patriots, as participants in a political process that extended far beyond their households and communities.

Revolutionary agitation and a deepening commitment to REPUBLICANISM also politicized Anglo-American households in more abstract ways. Political thinkers had long drawn analogies between political and family structures, arguing, for example, that a king's right to rule his subjects was analogous to a man's right to rule his wife and children. In the revolutionary context, the tyranny of the Crown and Parliament seemed to parallel the tyranny of an unequal marriage. Revolutionaries aspiring to create a society based upon virtue, in which citizens were bound by affection and respect rather than duty, invoked more egalitarian marriages as the model for a republic. This less hierarchical vision of marriage celebrated husbands and wives as each other's companions and gave Anglo-American women new stature. Sermons, periodicals, and fiction trumpeted the republican woman for her virtue, patience, and industry, qualities that had been valued long before the war. But this literature also singled out new qualities for praise, including reason, EDUCATION and civic-mindedness. By emphasizing the virtue and importance of the abstract, idealized wife, politicians and writers necessarily raised the status of real Anglo-American women.

Although the American Revolution did not abolish slavery, enslaved AFRICAN-AMERICAN women and men took advantage of the war to pursue freedom. In peacetime, both before and after the Revolutionary War, runaway slaves were disproportionately male; women's ties to children made escape especially difficult. During the war, however, the British army offered enslaved women and men protection and freedom in return for abandoning their Whig masters, enabling entire families to escape together. And the chaos of war made it possible for groups of slaves to escape regardless of the presence of the British army. THOMAS JEFFERSON later estimated that some 30,000 Virginia slaves ran away over the course of the war, many of them women. Of the 23 slaves who escaped from Jefferson himself, more than half were female. In Massachusetts, groups of slaves, including women, joined together to petition the legislature for freedom. Immediately after the war, a small flurry of voluntary manumissions helped create a free black community in the upper South. Both during and after the war, slaves throughout the colonies and states pointed out the contradiction between the defense of slavery and the revolutionary ideal of self-determination.

Just as the Revolution did not abolish slavery, it did not change Anglo-American women's legal status. Nevertheless, the creation of a republic did lead to subtle changes in white women's status. Although the founders never considered granting women SUFFRAGE, they did consider them to be citizens of the nation. Thus, women were entitled to civil rights, which included representation in the lower house of Congress, where legislators were apportioned by a state's population, male and female alike. From the founders' perspective, not all citizens were entitled to the same rights; suffrage depended not on citizenship, but on a combination of factors, including gender, race, and property ownership, that excluded many men as well as women from voting. Men who could vote were expected to represent the interests of their dependents, including women, children, and slaves, at the polls. Anglo-American women were thus excluded from full political rights but entitled to civil rights such as representation and legal protection. Significantly, this ambiguous status did nothing to challenge the fundamental legal principle of coverture, which continued to restrict married women's property rights and structure their relationship to the state.

As nonvoting citizens, European-American women were expected to serve the state primarily through their families as "Republican wives" and "Republican mothers." The ideology of republican wife- and motherhood incorporated the notions of female virtue that had emerged during the Revolution into a broad program for producing virtuous citizens. The republican wife inspired and encouraged her husband, the voting citizen, to adhere to the highest moral standards both at home and in the public sphere.

The republican mother was charged with inculcating republican virtues in her children, especially her sons, from early infancy. Americans thus imbued traditional female roles with new political significance. This new valuation of wife- and motherhood appears to have changed expectations of marriage, at least among the middle and upper classes. Diaries and letters suggest that both women and men began to view marriage as a source of emotional fulfillment and personal happiness rather than as only Christian duty and economic strategy.

These new expectations manifested themselves in divorce proceedings and in new educational opportunities. Following the Revolutionary War, several states enacted legislation to make divorce more accessible, allowing "loss of affection" to be cited as grounds for divorce. Moreover, although divorce remained rare, a greater percentage of divorces were sought and received by women. Indeed, access to divorce was women's clearest legal gain in the early republic. But these changes did not benefit poor women, who could not afford legal costs, nor did they apply to women of any class in the South. There, state legislatures retained the right to grant divorce through individual acts of law until well into the 19th century.

Ideals of republican womanhood contributed to a dramatic expansion of educational institutions that benefitted middle-class and wealthy women throughout the nation. Because republican virtue demanded reason and intellect as well as affection, increasing numbers of Americans committed family resources to finance education for their daughters. Hundreds of private female academies opened throughout the nation, offering young women an unprecedented curriculum in reading, composition and rhetoric, math, history, the sciences, ART, MUSIC, and, less frequently, Greek and Latin. But these gains did not extend to poor women or African-American women.

Further reading: Nancy F. Cott, *The Bonds of Womanhood: "Woman's Sphere in New England, 1778–1835* (New Haven, Conn.: Yale University Press, 1977); Linda K. Kerber, *Women of the Republic: Intellect and Ideology in Revolutionary America* (Chapel Hill: University of North Carolina Press, 1980); Mary Beth Norton, *Liberty's Daughters: The Revolutionary Experience of the American Woman, 1750–1800* (New York: Little, Brown, 1980); Marylynn Salmon, *Women and the Law of Property in Early America* (Chapel Hill: University of North Carolina Press, 1986).

— Catherine E. Kelly

writs of assistance

In 1761 a famous legal case came before the Supreme Court of Massachusetts that challenged the general search warrants—writs of assistance—issued to customs officials. This case is often cited as the opening salvo in the imperial crisis that led to the AMERICAN REVOLUTION. Over a half-century later, JOHN ADAMS, who watched the court case and was entranced with the brilliant oratory of JAMES OTIS JR. attacking the writs, proclaimed, "Then and there the Child of Independence was born."

Writs of assistance had long been issued in both the colonies and in Great Britain as an efficient and effective means of customs enforcement. These writs allowed a customs official to search property without obtaining a specific court order. Without this power, it would be possible for smugglers to move goods while the customs official searched for a judge to issue a specific search warrant. There is little question that within the confines of Anglo-American law as practiced in the 18th century, the writs of assistance were legal. However, they were irksome to many Boston merchants who made money smuggling and trading with the enemy during the French and Indian War (1754–63). The ascension of King GEORGE III to the throne in England in 1760 compelled the Massachusetts Supreme Court, headed by THOMAS HUTCHINSON, to reissue the writs. Whenever a new monarch became king, standard legal orders had to be reissued.

Massachusetts politics was at the time fiercely contested between a faction led by the Otis family on one side and the Hutchinson family on the other. James Otis Jr. seized the opportunity of the reissuing of the writs to embarrass Thomas Hutchinson and to gain both merchant and popular support. Although law and precedent were on the side of the writs and Hutchinson, Otis made his case by applying to a higher ideal. He declared that the writ "is against the fundamental principles of law. The privilege of house. A man who is quiet is as secure in his house as a prince in his castle." Otis turned this basic assertion into a challenge to Parliament by contending that "An act against the constitution is void, an act against natural equity is void." Otis thus put the constitution, nature, and equity above Parliament and precedent. The implications of this position, as Adams later stated, were revolutionary. In 1761, however, few were willing to pursue those implications, since the British constitution was little more than a series of laws and unwritten precedents, and no one knew for sure what nature and equity would dictate. In the next two decades Americans would return to this challenge and explore the meaning of the principles articulated by Otis. Hutchinson and the four other judges on the supreme court, of course, decided that the writs of assistance were legal.

See also RESISTANCE MOVEMENT.

Further reading: Bernard Bailyn, *The Ordeal of Thomas Hutchinson* (Cambridge, Mass.: Harvard University Press, 1974); John J. Waters, *The Otis Family in Provincial and Revolutionary Massachusetts* (Chapel Hill: University of North Carolina Press, 1968).

Wyoming Valley War

Between 1769 and 1807, a series of land wars broke out among Connecticut and Pennsylvania settlers in the Wyoming Valley in Pennsylvania. As IMMIGRATION increased into the American colonies during the 18th century, the need for land prompted many people to move to the western FRONTIER. This migration alleviated overcrowding in eastern communities and offered new opportunities for settlers, but it also sparked heated disputes over western land titles.

In the 1750s a group of Connecticut settlers formed the Susquehannah Company and laid claim to lands in the Wyoming Valley region of Pennsylvania. The settlers argued that the company had a legal right to the land based on a 1662 royal charter, which outlined Connecticut's borders as extending to the Pacific Ocean. On the other side of the dispute was the Penn family, who also claimed the lands based on a 1681 royal charter, which laid out the family's land rights. The Pennsylvania Assembly endorsed the Penns' claims and supported Pennsylvania settlers who had claims in the same region. Soon sporadic fighting broke out. Pennsylvania and Connecticut farmers raided and burned each other's barns and fields. These confrontations lasted on and off until 1807, when a statute was finally passed that endorsed the Connecticut claims and reimbursed the Pennsylvania claimants in cash for the loss of their lands.

Nearly a century of migration had opened new lands and created opportunities for settlers in America, but at the same time colonial and later state legislatures, as well as proprietors and landlords, struggled for legal control over land. Oftentimes, this sparked violence among settlers as they sought to protect and secure their property claims.

See also LAND RIOTS; RIOTS.

— Jeffrey A. Davis

X

XYZ affair (1797–1798)

The XYZ affair was an incident between the United States and France that almost led to war. Diplomatic relations between the two nations were first strained when the United States refused to aid France in its war with Great Britain, as the Franco-American Treaty of 1778 seemed to require. The situation was further aggravated with the signing of JAY'S TREATY (1794), under which the United States appeared to accept the British definition of "neutrality." President JOHN ADAMS sought to relieve the diplomatic tensions and sent CHARLES C. PINCKNEY, JOHN MARSHALL, and ELBRIDGE GERRY to France as envoys.

By the time Pinckney, Marshall, and Gerry arrived in Paris in October 1797, the French legislature had been ejected from power. Out of this coup d'état a new French government emerged, the "Directory." CHARLES-MAURICE DE TALLEYRAND-PÉRIGORD (usually referred to as Talleyrand, and, later, Prince Talleyrand), the French foreign minister, believed he could exploit the political feuds and divisions within the United States to French advantage. He met with Adams's envoys briefly and unofficially, promising that a more thorough discussion would follow. Weeks passed before the American delegation was contacted again, and even then only by three agents of Talleyrand, not the minister himself. The agents said that the Directory would not engage in diplomatic discussion with the United States without a "gift" of about $10 million to the government, plus another $250,000 for Talleyrand himself. Pinckney, Marshall, and Gerry balked at the French demand for a bribe. Out of these "negotiations" developed the FEDERALIST PARTY slogan, "Millions for defense, but not a cent for tribute."

The envoys reported the incident to President Adams, who in turn reported it to Congress. By the spring of 1798, the communication from the American delegation had been made public. The names of the three French agents were substituted with the letters X, Y, and Z, adding to the sense of intrigue. The incident stirred up public outrage, anger, and indignation. Congress suspended all relations with France and began to strengthen military forces.

The two nations skirmished on the seas in the QUASI WAR (1798–1800) but avoided a full declaration of war. The French government denounced the X, Y, and Z agents as rogue elements that did not speak for the Directory. Adams sent another commission to France in 1799 to resolve the growing hostility. Before this new commission reached Paris, however, NAPOLEON BONAPARTE had taken control of France. By the fall of 1800, France and the United States had reestablished friendly terms.

See also FOREIGN AFFAIRS; FRENCH REVOLUTION.

Further reading: Alexander DeConde, *The Quasi-War: The Politics and Diplomacy of the Undeclared War with France, 1797–1801* (New York: Scribner, 1966); William Stinchcombe, *The XYZ Affair* (Westport, Conn.: Greenwood, 1980).

— Jay R. Dew

"Yankee Doodle"

This popular song came to symbolize the American character during the REVOLUTIONARY WAR (1775–83). It emphasized the rural nature of the new United States and demonstrated pride in the American lack of sophistication and the flouting of authority. At one time the song was believed to have been composed by a British officer to deride colonials during the French and Indian War (1754–63). Subsequently, scholars have discovered that the song originated in the colonies, reflecting provincial satire and self-mocking humor. British soldiers used the song in both the French and Indian War and the Revolutionary War to make fun of their American cousins. Americans, in turn, seized upon the tune, added stanzas, and made it their own. Soldiers in the CONTINENTAL ARMY sang "Yankee Doodle" when celebrating victories, and the song was played as the British stacked their arms during the surrender at SARATOGA (October 17, 1777). In the FRENCH REVOLUTION (1789–1815), the Paris Guard played the song after the surrender of the Bastille. Ever since the Revolutionary War, Yankee Doodle has remained popular with Americans and is still taught to children across the nation.

See also MUSIC.

Yates, Abraham, Jr. (1724–1796)

Abraham Yates, a civil servant most of his life, supported the rights of the common man and gave voice to the ANTI-FEDERALIST viewpoint during the 1780s. Yates's father, a blacksmith, apprenticed young Abraham as a cobbler, but Yates yearned for more. By his late 20s, Yates was working at the law office of Peter Silvester, where he read for the bar and discovered the writings of John Locke and other members of the English Enlightenment. With the support of Robert Livingston, Jr., Yates won appointment as sheriff of Albany County, New York, in 1754. During his five years in this position, Yates became increasingly aware of the disparity between colonists and British subjects back in England and of the inequalities that existed between the colonists themselves. Having to remove poor squatters from land held, but not used, by wealthy titleholders forced Yates to question the rights of the poor. Yates also served as sheriff during the early years of the French and Indian War (1754–63), giving him plenty of opportunities to witness how British officers treated colonists. While serving as sheriff, Yates won election to Albany's common council in 1753. As a man who had worked hard to obtain his economic and political status in the community, Yates found many supporters in Albany who reelected him every year to the council until 1773. From 1774 to 1776 he was a member and chairman of the Albany COMMITTEE OF CORRESPONDENCE.

With the start of the REVOLUTIONARY WAR (1775–83), Yates's political fortunes grew beyond city and county positions to statewide prominence. In 1775 he was elected to represent Albany at New York's provincial congress and continued in that capacity until the congress's dissolution in 1777, serving as president pro tem in 1775 and 1776. While in the provincial congress, Yates also was a member of the council of safety. He chaired the convention committee that produced the first New York State constitution, a document ratified by state convention in April 1777. Yates was in the New York State Senate from 1778 to 1790, where he supported Governor GEORGE CLINTON's legislative program. In 1783 Yates was also given the distinction of becoming the first postmaster of Albany.

During the 1780s, Yates's concern for the equitable rights of all Americans increased, especially after the cessation of war with Great Britain. Yates opposed what he saw as a privileged elite trying to gain control of the CONTINENTAL CONGRESS and attempting to centralize governmental power. Writing under the pseudonyms "Cato," "Sydney," and "Rough Hewer," Yates defended the sovereignty of the thirteen states and clearly represented the anti-Federalist point of view. He served in the Continental Congress in 1787–88 and wrote several unpublished manuscripts on New York history, highlighting examples of instances when aristocrats had repressed the common individual. In 1790 Yates was elected mayor of Albany, a position he held until his death in 1796.

Further reading: Stefan Bielinski, *Abraham Yates, Jr., and the New Political Order in Revolutionary New York* (Albany: New York State American Revolution Bicentennial Commission, 1975).

— Heather Clemmer

Yazoo claims

The Yazoo claims arose from perhaps the grandest land speculation effort in the early republic. The story of the Yazoo claims is rife with corruption and intrigue, and their resolution set the course for the expansion of federal judicial power in the era of the Marshall Court.

In 1795 the Georgia Mississippi Company and three other land-speculation concerns purchased from the state of Georgia 35 million acres of land in the region centered on the Yazoo River in what became the Mississippi Territory for $500,000. The act authorizing the sale was the product of widespread corruption. When a preliminary sale bill passed in December 1794, for example, only one of the legislators voting for it had not been bribed. In 1796 the Georgia Mississippi Company sold its stake in the Yazoo lands to the New England Mississippi Land Company for $1,138,000. On the very day this deal closed, all of the Yazoo grants were repudiated by the succeeding Georgia legislature. So complete was this repudiation that all records of the grants were ordered excised from Georgia's public records, and the original act of sale was burned in the public square at Louisville, where the legislature had convened, by a REVOLUTIONARY WAR (1775–83) veteran holding a magnifying glass and bringing the destroying fire down "from God."

The ensuing battle over title carried over to Congress when the United States acquired Georgia's western land claims in 1802. Opposition to the claims of the Yazoo transferees was focused on the circumstances of the passage of the original act of sale. On the floor of Congress, pro- and anti-Yazooists incessantly debated the legitimacy of the original grants and the validity of the subsequent repeal. The Yazooists were aggressive in pressing their claims, regularly employing numerous high-ranking agents—including soon-to-be Associate Justice JOSEPH STORY—as Capitol Hill lobbyists, yet despite their efforts, they had no luck at forcing a compromise. The anti-Yazooists refused to recognize the land titles of speculators whose claims traced to widespread bribery and the corruption of public officials.

After failing in Congress, the speculators opted to look to the SUPREME COURT for relief. In 1803 the New England Mississippi Land Company engineered a lawsuit that ultimately reached the Supreme Court as *Fletcher v. Peck.* The speculators argued that the repeal act was unconstitutional because it violated the contracts clause of the Constitution, which provided that "[n]o State shall . . . pass any . . . Law impairing the Obligation of Contracts. . . ." The Supreme Court, under Chief Justice JOHN MARSHALL, agreed, issuing an opinion in 1810 holding that the Yazoo speculators did indeed have a valid claim, as the act of the Georgia legislature repealing the act of sale was unconstitutional. This marked the Supreme Court's first exercise of the judicial review power to invalidate the legislative act of a state. Anti-Yazooists in Congress were furious. Some even proposed sending federal troops into the Yazoo territory to keep the speculators out, and Congress debated whether the Supreme Court had to be obeyed. Ultimately, the federal legislature decided to abide by the Supreme Court's decision. In 1814 Congress implemented a plan for providing compensation to the Yazoo speculators.

Further reading: C. Peter Magrath, *Yazoo: Law and Politics in the New Republic: The Case of Fletcher v. Peck* (Providence, R.I.: Brown University Press, 1966).

— Lindsay Robertson

Yorktown, surrender at (October 19, 1781)

The British surrender at Yorktown marked the end of the last major campaign of the REVOLUTIONARY WAR (1775–83) and ensured American independence. The campaign was marked by confusion, poor choices, and misfortune on the part of the British, and superb planning, coordination between the French and CONTINENTAL ARMIES, and good luck on the part of the Americans.

The campaign began with General CHARLES, LORD CORNWALLIS's decision to march into Virginia after his efforts in North Carolina brought few tangible results. Leaving Wilmington, North Carolina, on April 25, 1781, Cornwallis reached Petersburg, Virginia, by May 20. Once in Virginia he met BENEDICT ARNOLD and another British army. With about 7,000 men under his command, he unleashed a devastating series of raids that sacked the state's capital and almost captured Governor THOMAS JEFFERSON. Continental troops under the command of the MARQUIS DE LAFAYETTE were no match for Cornwallis and could do little more than keep their distance and shadow his movements. In July, the British commander in chief, Sir HENRY CLINTON, began to send a series of contradictory orders to Cornwallis. Clinton and Cornwallis had for some time had difficulty working together. Now Clinton sent Cornwallis reinforcements, then asked for them back, then told him to prepare to march north to coordinate an attack on Philadelphia, then told him to occupy a town on the sea-

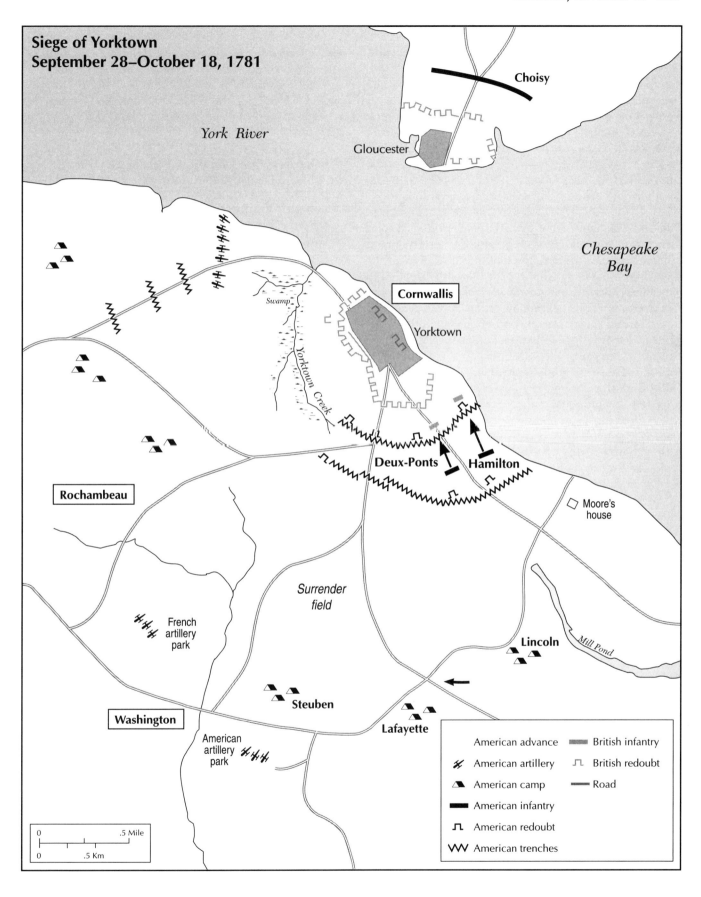

**Siege of Yorktown
September 28–October 18, 1781**

Choisy

York River

Gloucester

Chesapeake Bay

Swamp

Cornwallis

Yorktown

Yorktown Creek

Deux-Ponts   **Hamilton**

Rochambeau

Moore's house

Surrender field

Mill Pond

Lincoln

French artillery park

Steuben

Washington

Lafayette

American artillery park

American advance	British infantry
American artillery	British redoubt
American camp	Road
American infantry	
American redoubt	
American trenches	

0   .5 Mile

0   .5 Km

coast that could harbor the British navy. Cornwallis himself waffled, finally deciding to fortify a small tobacco port called Yorktown in August.

In the meantime General GEORGE WASHINGTON and the French commander General COMTE DE ROCHAMBEAU were planning an allied attack on New York City. That task began to look increasingly impossible in the summer of 1781. Then, on August 14, word arrived that the French fleet in the WEST INDIES under the command of Admiral DE GRASSE was going to sail to the Chesapeake. With the possibility of obtaining, however briefly, naval superiority, Washington decided to try to trap Cornwallis at Yorktown. The American and French armies then undertook a complex maneuver, marching and sailing their combined armies 400 miles south to the mouth of the Chesapeake Bay while convincing Clinton that they still intended to attack New York. Washington in particular played a central role in planning this delicate operation. As the combined American and French armies concentrated in southern Virginia in the first half of September, there was still the British fleet to worry about. A British fleet from the West Indies had anticipated de Grasse's move and had joined with the ships stationed in New York. This British naval force was roughly equal to that of the French. The British navy sallied forth and met de Grasse in the Battle of the Capes (September 5, 1781), an indecisive contest. Although undefeated, the British ships returned to New York. The French continued on to the Chesapeake, sealing the fate of Cornwallis in Yorktown.

With half as many ground troops as the Franco-American armies, and boxed in by the French navy, Cornwallis was trapped. He did little to help himself. The British did not attack the Americans as they approached Yorktown. Then, confronted with an overwhelming force, Cornwallis withdrew his men from their first line of entrenchments, ceding the earthworks to the Americans and French and thereby simplifying the siege process. Beginning on October 7, the allied troops began to build their first parallel— a series of trenches parallel to the British position. When that was completed, a second parallel was begun on October 11 and completed on October 14. The Franco-American lines were then 300 yards from the British. To complete the parallel, two redoubts had to be taken: The Americans, under Colonel ALEXANDER HAMILTON, captured Redoubt No. 10, while the French seized Redoubt No. 9. Throughout the siege the attackers poured a devastating artillery fire into the British. Cornwallis launched one counterattack on October 16 with little success. On the same night he attempted to cross the York River and escape, but bad weather forced him to abandon this last effort to save his army. On October 17 he asked for a parley, and the next day he agreed to terms, surrendering about 8,000 men on October 19, 1781.

Further reading: Don Higginbotham, *The War of American Independence: Military Attitudes, Policies, and Practices, 1763–1789* (New York: Macmillan, 1971).

Young, Thomas (1731–1777)

Emerging from obscure origins in the colony of New York, Thomas Young was a strident revolutionary who had a major impact on the RESISTANCE MOVEMENT (1764–75) in Albany and Boston. He also played a leading role in the radical politics of Pennsylvania and Vermont in the opening years of the REVOLUTIONARY WAR (1775–83).

Young managed to gain a medical education and set himself up as a physician in Dutchess County, New York, by 1753. He bought land in what is now Vermont sometime around 1760 but lost the investment because of a faulty title. He moved to Albany in the mid-1760s and became involved in the opposition to the STAMP ACT (1765). He then moved to Boston and again became a leader against British imperial regulation. He delivered the first oration commemorating the anniversary of the BOSTON MASSACRE (March 5, 1770) and was active in Boston's COMMITTEE OF CORRESPONDENCE. He also spoke at the OLD SOUTH CHURCH shortly before the BOSTON TEA PARTY (December 16, 1773) and joined in the dumping of tea into the harbor. He left Boston in September 1774 for Newport and then moved to Philadelphia in April 1775. In Philadelphia he became one of the radical party, helped to draw up the Pennsylvania state constitution (see CONSTITUTIONS, STATE), and in the spring of 1777 supported Vermont's bid for status as a state. As a part of his efforts on behalf of the GREEN MOUNTAIN BOYS, he provided a copy of the Pennsylvania Constitution to the representatives from Vermont, who then used the democratic document as a model for their own constitution. Serving as a doctor and tending to sick American soldiers, Young caught a fever and died almost impoverished on June 22, 1777.

Chronology

1761

Boston attorney James Otis writes a legal argument denouncing the use of writs of assistance, which allow British customs officials to search property without obtaining a specific court order.

1763

The Treaty of Paris ends the French and Indian War. France cedes Canada and virtually all territory east of the Mississippi River in North America to Great Britain.

Chief Pontiac and his warriors attack Fort Detroit in a failed attempt to drive out the British; the campaign becomes known as Pontiac's Rebellion.

King George III issues the Proclamation of 1763 to establish British colonies Quebec, East Florida, and West Florida and to protect Indian land west of the Appalachians from British settlement.

1764

Britain enacts the Sugar Act, which reduces the tax on British sugar imports but provides for better enforcement of tax collection. Colonists object to the law.

James Otis's *The Rights of the British Colonies Asserted and Proved* is published. The pamphlet asserts that the Sugar Act is inconsistent with natural law.

The British Currency Act of 1764 prohibits the printing and distribution of paper money in any of the thirteen colonies.

1765

English law professor William Blackstone begins publishing *Commentaries on the Laws of England.* These lucid, widely available volumes lead to a democratization of the legal profession in the United States.

The British Parliament enacts the Stamp Act of 1765 in order to raise revenue to pay the costs of governing and protecting the American colonies; mobs in more than 40 American communities demonstrate against the tax, often compelling stamp masters to resign.

The Quartering Act of 1765 compels American colonists to provide housing for British soldiers where barracks are unavailable.

Daniel Dulany's pamphlet *Considerations on the Propriety of Imposing Taxes in the British Colonies* attacks the claim that colonial Americans are virtually represented in Parliament.

Led by Patrick Henry, the Virginia House of Burgesses passes the Virginia Resolves, which declare opposition to the Stamp Act and assert colonists' right to be governed and taxed by laws of their own choosing.

The Loyal Nine, a group of men from the middle ranks of Boston society, organize street resistance to the Stamp Act.

Representatives from nine American colonies participate in the Stamp Act Congress; the congress issues a petition to the king to voice colonist disapproval of the Stamp Act of 1765.

1766

Parliament repeals the Stamp Act but reserves the right to levy future taxes on British colonies.

1767

Daniel Boone begins to explore Kentucky.

Parliament imposes the Townshend Duties of 1767 to raise revenues from the North American colonies.

John Dickinson's *Letters from a Farmer in Pennsylvania* is published to object to the Townshend Duties.

Property holders in the frontier west of South Carolina respond to the region's lawlessness by organizing as the Regulators. This vigilante group attacks bandit encampments in the backcountry.

1768

Customs officials impound the *Liberty,* a sloop owned by Boston merchant John Hancock. Riots result and the British government decides to send troops to Boston.

The Massachusetts legislature issues a circular letter, written by Samuel Adams, to urge other American colonies to join in petitioning Parliament opposing the Townshend Duties.

British officials purchase lands in what will become West Virginia, Kentucky, and western Pennsylvania from the Iroquois Confederacy through the 1768 Treaty of Fort Stanwix.

1769

A nonimportation movement begins to take hold in the colonies in defiance of the Townshend Duties of 1767.

The American Philosophical Society is founded in Philadelphia.

1770

A series of confrontations between New York civilians and British soldiers culminates in a riot popularly known as the Battle of Golden Hill.

The Green Mountain Boys organize under Ethan Allen to resist New York authorities' efforts to enforce their land claims in Vermont territory.

Benjamin Rush publishes *Syllabus of a Course of Lectures in Chemistry,* a textbook that begins to formalize chemistry as an academic discipline.

Parliament rescinds the Townshend Duties except for the tax on tea.

British troops fire on a Boston crowd, killing five. The incident, known as the Boston Massacre, was a result of the tensions between soldiers and civilians over jobs and between the British Parliament and the American colonists following the passage of the Townshend Duties of 1767. Following the "massacre," Samuel Adams organizes the successful movement demanding the removal of British troops from Boston.

John Adams and Josiah Quincy serve as attorneys for the British soldiers accused of participating in the so-called Boston Massacre.

1771

At the behest of the North Carolina assembly, Governor William Tryon's troops crush the North Carolina Regulators, farmers who had been sporadically rioting since 1766 to protest oppressive local and colonial authorities, in the Battle of Alamance.

1772

A group of Providence merchants burn the British customs-enforcement schooner *Gaspee.*

Samuel Adams calls for the creation of committees of correspondence to coordinate anti-British resistance in Massachusetts and, ultimately, throughout the colonies.

1773

The Tea Act of 1773 permits the British East India Company to bypass middlemen and sell tea directly to colonial distributors in America, undermining the colonies' thriving traffic in smuggling. The act reduces the price on tea while leaving the Townshend Duties on tea intact.

The Boston Tea Party takes place: Citizens dump British tea into Boston Harbor to protest the Tea Act.

The poems of Phillis Wheatley are published in England.

1774

The Transylvania Company buys a large tract in Kentucky from the Cherokee Nation; Cherokee warrior Dragging Canoe refuses to recognize the sale and vows to kill any whites who settle the claim.

Religious leader Ann Lee migrates to the American colonies, where she founds Shaker societies.

Parliament passes the Coercive Acts in an effort to force colonists to recognize Parliament's sovereignty. Known in the colonies as the "Intolerable Acts," they consist of the Boston Port Bill, which closes the port; the Massachusetts Government Act, which curtails colonists' participation in local government; the Administration of Justice Act, which permits the Crown to choose the location of trials; and the Quartering Act, which compels colonists to pay for the housing of British soldiers enforcing these laws.

The Quebec Act of 1774 grants territory west of the Appalachians to Canada.

The First Continental Congress meets in Philadelphia to form a unified response to the Coercive Acts and assumes a supervisory role in Massachusetts's resistance.

Continental Congress unanimously endorses the Suffolk Resolves, which declare the Coercive Acts "murderous" and recommend economic sanctions against Great Britain.

Continental Congress unanimously approves an economic boycott of Great Britain, Ireland, and the West

Indies. The congress forms the Continental Association to execute this "non-importation, non-consumption, and non-exportation agreement."

Continental Congress debates and approves a petition to King George III declaring colonists' rights and grievances.

Virginia royal governor John Murray, Lord Dunmore defeats the Shawnee in Ohio Territory in Lord Dunmore's War.

Pennsylvania Quakers found the Pennsylvania Abolition Society, the first antislavery society in the colonies.

1775

As an agent of the Transylvania Company, Daniel Boone blazes the Wilderness Road and establishes the frontier community of Boonesborough.

Patrick Henry delivers his "Give Me Liberty" speech to members of the Second Virginia Convention.

Paul Revere, William Dawes, and others ride through the countryside around Boston to warn colonial minutemen of the approach of British troops.

The Revolutionary War begins as British soldiers clash with colonial minutemen at Lexington and Concord, Massachusetts.

The Committee of One Hundred organizes a provisional government for New York.

The Second Continental Congress, or Confederation Congress, convenes on May 10.

Benedict Arnold and Ethan Allen capture the British fort at Ticonderoga, New York.

Continental Congress names Virginian George Washington commander in chief of the Continental army.

Colonial forces resist British efforts to break the siege of Boston in the Battle of Bunker Hill.

King George III declares that the American colonies are in a state of open rebellion and authorizes the use of force to restore order.

Continental Congress founds the American navy.

The royal governor of Virginia, John Murray, Lord Dunmore, issues the Dunmore Proclamation, offering freedom for all slaves and servants who rally to the king's cause.

Benedict Arnold and General Richard Montgomery launch an attack on Montreal on December 31; a blizzard impedes their efforts and Montgomery is killed.

1776

Thomas Paine's *Common Sense,* an influential radical pamphlet against monarchy and tyranny, is published. It urges independence and formation of a republic.

Henry Knox brings cannons that were captured at Ticonderoga to Boston.

Faced with entrenched American forces on Dorchester Heights, the British evacuate Boston.

Captain John Barry's *Lexington* captures the United States's first British prize, the HMS *Edward.*

The Virginia Constitutional Convention adopts the Virginia Bill of Rights, which later serves as the foundation of the United States Bill of Rights.

Continental Congress appoints a committee to draft the Declaration of Independence; it consists of Thomas Jefferson (writer), John Adams, Benjamin Franklin, Robert Livingston, and Roger Sherman. The Declaration is debated and signed. It asserts that the thirteen colonies are now "free and independent states."

The Second Continental Congress appoints a committee to draft a plan of perpetual union; the result, the Articles of Confederation, is to be the new nation's first constitution.

The British win a resounding victory at the Battle of Long Island, nearly entrapping Washington's army.

Tadeusz Kościuszko, a Polish military engineer, joins the Continental army, lending his expertise to the American cause.

Washington crosses the Delaware River and captures a force composed of Hessian soldiers at the Battle of Trenton.

1777

Washington's army defeats British forces at the Battle of Princeton.

Benjamin Franklin goes to France to negotiate for a French alliance.

British forces under General William Howe defeat American forces under George Washington at the Battle of Brandywine. The British march into Philadelphia.

Iroquois forces under Chief Joseph Brant allied with the English attack frontier settlers.

British general John Burgoyne surrenders at Saratoga, New York.

The Second Continental Congress sends a draft of the first constitution of the United States, the Articles of Confederation, to each of the 13 original states.

Washington and his army endure a brutal winter at Valley Forge, Pennsylvania; Baron Frederick von Steuben arrives in America and helps train the Continental army.

1778

France becomes a formal ally of the United States.

General William Howe resigns command of the British armies in North America; General Henry Clinton becomes commander in chief.

Continental forces strike General Clinton's army at the indecisive Battle of Monmouth Courthouse. Mary Hays McCauly, or "Molly Pitcher," performs services for the Revolutionary cause and enters American legend.

U.S. lieutenant colonel George Rogers Clark captures two British forts, neutralizing the British in the West and establishing a U.S. claim to the Northwest Territory.

1779

John Adams helps draft the Massachusetts state constitution, which later serves among James Madison's models in drafting the U.S. Constitution.

American forces under General John Sullivan invade Iroquois territory, burning crops and villages to destroy Iroquoia's ability to make war.

Captain John Paul Jones, aboard the *Bonhomme Richard,* captures the British warship *Serapis.*

1780

The American Academy of Arts and Sciences is founded in Boston.

British forces under General Henry Clinton capture Charleston, South Carolina, costing Americans virtually the entire southern army.

The marquis de Lafayette convinces the French government to send 12 additional battalions to fight with Washington's army.

The plot of U.S. general Benedict Arnold to surrender West Point to the British is uncovered; he escapes to British lines.

Pennsylvania becomes the first state in the new union to adopt a gradual emancipation statute.

Robert Morris organizes the Bank of Pennsylvania with private investments to support the Continental army.

African-American Paul Cuffe and six other men petition the Massachusetts Legislature against taxing them without their consent.

Benedict Arnold, now allied with the British, attacks Virginia, capturing Richmond and destroy American supplies.

1781

American troops under General Daniel Morgan decisively defeat British forces under Colonel Banastre Tarleton at the Battle of Cowpens.

British general Charles, Lord Cornwallis defeats American forces at the Battle of Guilford Courthouse but sustains heavy casualties.

By June all thirteen former colonies have ratified the first constitution of the United States, the Articles of Confederation.

Continental Congress charters the Bank of North America, directed by Robert Morris.

An estimated 16,000 Continental and French troops lay Siege to the British army under General Charles Cornwallis, numbering 7,250, at Yorktown, Virginia. Lord Cornwallis surrenders on October 19.

1782

Large numbers of British loyalists begin abandoning their homes in the United States for Canada and England; some 100,000 eventually leave the United States.

J. Hector St. John de Crèvecoeur publishes *Letters from an American Farmer.*

1783

Noah Webster publishes *The American Spelling Book.*

The Treaty of Paris of 1783, which officially ends the Revolutionary War, is signed. John Adams, John Jay, and Benjamin Franklin are the principal American negotiators. The treaty cedes all Iroquois land to the United States; returns Florida, in British hands since 1763, to Spain; expands American territory to the Mississippi River and assures free Mississippi navigation; and promises fishing rights to Newfoundland and Nova Scotia.

The last British troops evacuate New York City, ending British occupation of its former colonies. George Washington stuns the world by resigning his commission and returning home to Mount Vernon.

John Trumbull embarks on his most productive period as an artist, painting more than 250 historical pictures commemorating the defining events of the Revolutionary War.

1784

Continental Congress selects New York City as the temporary capital of the United States.

The New York Manumission Society is founded.

Iroquois Indians surrender their lands west of Pennsylvania to the United States in the Treaty of Fort Stanwix of 1784.

1785

Thomas Jefferson replaces Benjamin Franklin as minister to France. John Adams is named minister to Britain.

Continental Congress passes the Land Ordinance of 1785 to outline a framework for the settlement of the Northwest Territory.

Barbary pirates seize several U.S. merchant ships in the Mediterranean Sea.

1786

Thomas Jefferson pens the Virginia Statute of Religious Freedom, which is the first attempt to guarantee absolute religious liberty in the United States.

Daniel Shays leads a rebellion in Massachusetts when the state refuses to help debt-ridden farmers. The uprising is put down within a year.

Delegates from five states convene in Annapolis, Maryland, to consider federal regulation of commerce; Alexander Hamilton calls for a constitutional convention to be attended by all the states to amend the Articles of Confederation.

The Tammany Society is founded in New York City as a fraternal organization.

1787

Continental Congress passes the Northwest Ordinance of 1787, which states that the Northwest Territory will be divided into no fewer than three but no more than five new states. It prohibits slavery in the territory and establishes the process by which a territory becomes a state.

Royall Taylor's *The Contrast,* the first professionally produced American comedy, opens in New York City.

Meeting in Philadelphia to revise the Articles of Confederation, the delegates at the Constitutional Convention instead vote to create an entirely new form of government.

The New Jersey Plan advocates a national government that does not infringe on the rights of individual states, with all states represented equally regardless of population.

Edmund Randolph of Virginia presents the Virginia Plan, which places power into the hands of a strong centralized federal government, with representation proportional to each state's population.

Roger Sherman's "Connecticut Compromise" resolves the differences between the New Jersey Plan and the Virginia Plan.

The Great Compromise of 1787 counts five slaves as three voters for the purpose of congressional representation.

The Constitutional Convention approves the Constitution of the United States.

Benjamin Franklin's influential essay "On the Constitution" is released to promote the recently drafted Constitution.

The *Federalist Papers,* 85 political essays written in support of the Constitution by Alexander Hamilton, John Jay, and James Madison, begin to appear in a New York newspaper under the pseudonym "Publius."

The Free African Society is founded.

1788

By summer nine of the 13 states have ratified the U.S. Constitution, giving it legal force.

1789

The Constitution takes effect on March 4, 1789; ballots of presidential electors are announced when the U.S. Congress formally convenes in April.

George Washington is inaugurated as the first president of the United States at Federal Hall in New York City on April 30. John Adams is sworn in as vice president.

Former slave Olaudah Equiano publishes his memoir *The Interesting Life of Olaudah Equiano.* It is the first published American slave narrative.

John Fenno publishes the pro-Federalist Party *Gazette of the United States,* the first U.S. newspaper founded solely as an organ of one political faction.

The Judiciary Act of 1789 establishes the structure of the judiciary branch.

1790

Maryland grants a 10-mile square of land on the Potomac River to the federal government to be designated the District of Columbia, the new capital city.

Rhode Island merchant Moses Brown backs Samuel Slater's textile mill in Rhode Island; Slater's mill brings the Industrial Revolution to the United States.

The first federal census counts a population of nearly 4 million people.

1791

Benjamin Banneker, a black mathematician and astronomer, publishes his *Almanack and Ephemeris.*

A confederation of tribes under the leadership of Miami chief Little Turtle defeats General Arthur St. Clair in the Northwest Territory

Benjamin Franklin's autobiography is published.

The United States admits Vermont as a state.

The First Bank of the United States begins operations, assuming and guaranteeing the national debt of the United States. Democratic-Republicans oppose the bank, holding that the ability to charter corporations such as banks is exclusively a state's right.

William Bartram publishes his *Travels,* an illustrated naturalist study of the flora and fauna of North America.

Pierre L'Enfant designs the street plan and public buildings of the District of Columbia.

The first 10 amendments to the Constitution, known as the Bill of Rights, are adopted; they guarantee U.S. citizens certain basic freedoms.

1792

Stock speculation creates the first great financial panic to rock the new nation.

George Washington is elected to his second term as president of the United States.

1793

Britain declares war on France.

"Citizen" Edmond Genet, ambassador of France, comes to the United States seeking American support for France in its war against Britain.

President Washington's Neutrality Proclamation declares the intent of the United States to maintain friendly relations with both Britain and France while the two countries are at war.

Eli Whitney invents the cotton gin; the machine makes it profitable to grow short-staple cotton, spurring the growth of slavery in the South.

The U.S. Supreme Court decision *Chisholm v. Georgia* upholds the right of a citizen to sue a state government in federal court.

The Fugitive Slave Law of 1793 permits the owner of a runaway slave or his agent to arrest and return the slave to captivity.

Benjamin Rush performs valuable services during a yellow fever epidemic in Philadelphia.

A group of Philadelphia citizens founds the first Democratic-Republican Society, and dozens of similar clubs soon begin around the country; these grassroots organizations are the first to oppose President Washington.

1794

Methodist preacher Richard Allen forms the first separate African-American congregation.

The federal government commissions a series of super frigates to protect American merchant ships.

Settlement of the Northwest Territory (now the states of Ohio and Indiana) increases.

General Anthony Wayne defeats the Northwest Indian Confederation in the Battle of Fallen Timbers.

Richard Allen and Absalom Jones publish *A Narrative of the Proceedings of the Black People During the late Awful Calamity in Philadelphia* to admonish Philadelphia leadership for rumormongering against blacks.

Settlers in Pennsylvania wage the Whiskey Rebellion to protest the federal excise tax on liquor. President Washington musters 12,000 militiamen to quell the uprising.

Special envoy John Jay and British foreign minister William Grenville negotiate Jay's Treaty of 1794 to resolve tensions between the United States and Great Britain. Britain agrees to remove troops from America's western territories, pay reparations to American merchants, and permit limited American trade in the West Indies, while the United States grants the British trading rights and permission to intercept American ships trading with France and French colonies.

1795

In the Greenville Treaty of 1795 the Native Americans of Ohio end their war against the United States, cede most of what is now Ohio to the U.S. government, and agree to move westward.

In the Treaty of San Lorenzo, Spain grants the United States free navigation of the Mississippi River, access to New Orleans, and a favorable Florida boundary.

The Naturalization Act of 1795 allows free white immigrants to apply for U.S. citizenship after five years of residence.

1796

English physician Edward Jenner improves inoculation against smallpox using a weakened form of cowpox.

Gilbert Stuart paints his most famous portrait of George Washington.

Philadelphia's *American Daily Advertiser* prints President Washington's farewell address. This influential speech recommends a policy of political isolation from Europe and warns Americans to be wary of political parties.

Federalist John Adams is elected as the nation's second president.

1797

French anger over the fluctuation of U.S. treaties between France and Great Britain leads to an undeclared naval war known as the Quasi War of 1798–1800. The situation is further complicated by an implied request by France for cash bribes to accept U.S. diplomatic officials. The incident becomes known as the XYZ affair.

John Trumbull completes his most famous painting, "The Declaration of Independence."

1798

U.S. Congress passes the Eleventh Amendment to the U.S. Constitution, prohibiting citizens of one state from suing the government of another.

The Naturalization Act of 1798 changes the necessary period of residence before citizenship is granted from five to 14 years.

Federalists in U.S. Congress enact the Alien Act of 1798, the Alien Enemies Act of 1798, and the Sedition Act of 1798, all of which give the U.S. government broad abilities to punish treasonable activities and deport foreigners.

The Democratic-Republican led legislatures of Kentucky and Virginia react to the Alien and Sedition Acts by declaring that federal legislation operate only with the consent of the states.

1799

The federal government's direct tax on land prompts violent protest in eastern Pennsylvania, culminating in Fries's Rebellion.

Leading free black Philadelphians, including Absalom Jones, Richard Allen, and James Forten, unsuccessfully petition Congress to halt the slave trade.

1800

Gabriel's Rebellion, a planned uprising of 1,000 blacks in Richmond, is foiled by informers and a massive rainstorm.

The Franco-American Convention of 1800 ends the undeclared naval war (the Quasi War) precipitated by French attacks on U.S. commercial vessels. There, Napoleon agrees that the French alliance of 1778 is no longer binding.

Washington, D.C., becomes the capital of the United States.

The Democratic-Republican candidate, Thomas Jefferson, defeats the incumbent Federalist candidate, John Adams, in the presidential election. Political parties dominate a presidential contest for the first time; the result is the first peaceful transfer of power from one party to another.

1801

John Marshall becomes chief justice of the U.S. Supreme Court.

The Judiciary Act of 1801 reorganizes the federal court system, giving President Adams the power to appoint 16 new federal judges, including the infamous "midnight judges," before Thomas Jefferson is inaugurated.

At a demonstration of Eli Whitney's mass production techniques for incoming president Thomas Jefferson, witnesses are able to assemble working muskets from random parts.

After the United States refuses to increase its tribute for protection from the Barbary pirates, Tripoli declares war on the United States.

Tent revivals inspire thousands of Americans in remote frontier regions to commit to Protestant faiths.

1803

The U.S. Supreme Court decides *Marbury v. Madison,* establishing the precedent of judicial review.

Thomas Jefferson signs the Louisiana Purchase Treaty, acquiring millions of acres of land from the French and putting a large population of Indians, including the Plains tribes, under American jurisdiction.

William Clark and Meriwether Lewis begin a three-year expedition to explore the western territories that have been added to the United States; they are guided by Sacagawea for much of their journey.

The United States blockades Tripoli.

1804

Absalom Jones becomes the first black priest ordained by the Episcopal Church.

The Twelfth Amendment, which requires separate votes for president and vice president, is ratified.

The House of Representatives impeaches Supreme Court Justice Samuel Chase, a Federalist, for making partisan comments from the bench, but the Senate acquits him.

Barbary pirates capture the grounded USS *Philadelphia;* American sailors burn the ship in Tripoli harbor.

Aaron Burr and Alexander Hamilton duel at Weehawken, New Jersey, over Hamilton's attacks on Burr's reputation; Hamilton is mortally wounded.

Democratic-Republican Thomas Jefferson is reelected president over Federalist Charles Cotesworth Pinckney.

Following the Haitian slave revolt, Haiti becomes the first independent black republic in the Western Hemisphere. President Jefferson refuses diplomatic recognition of the nation.

1805

In the *Essex* decision, the British Admiralty Court rules that American merchant ships must prove their neutrality to British maritime authorities.

A final peace treaty between Tripoli and the United States is signed aboard the USS *Constitution.*

Lewis and Clark's "Corps of Discovery" reaches the Pacific Ocean.

1806

The Non-Importation Act of 1806 prohibits certain British goods.

Lewis and Clark reach St. Louis, Missouri, after a 28-month journey of exploration.

1807

The first commercially successful American steamboat, later known as the *Clermont,* travels up the Hudson River from New York City to Albany. It was built by Robert Fulton.

U.S. Congress passes the Slave Trade Abolition Act of 1807, which outlaws the African slave trade.

The British ship HMS *Leopard* fires on the USS *Chesapeake* just outside Chesapeake Bay.

Scandal erupts when the plan of former U.S. vice president Aaron Burr to either form an independent republic in the Southwest or invade Spanish territory becomes public. He is accused of treason but acquitted by Chief Justice John Marshall.

The Embargo Act of 1807 prohibits all international trade from U.S. ports. Intended to counteract British and French legislation that is disrupting U.S. commercial activity, the act proves devastating to the American economy.

1808

The fur trading industry flourishes; John Jacob Astor establishes the American Fur Company Inc., which expands to the West.

Helped by his brother Tecumseh, Tenskwatawa, known as the Shawnee Prophet, establishes Prophetstown in Indiana Territory as a traditionalist spiritual enclave for Native Americans.

The Union Temperance Society of Moreau and Northumberland is founded. It is the first formal temperance group in the United States.

Democratic-Republican James Madison wins the presidential race against Federalist Charles Cotesworth Pinckney.

1809

The Non-Intercourse Act of 1809 repeals the Embargo Act of 1807 and restores international trade with all nations except France and Great Britain.

1810

The Macon Act of 1810, or Macon's Bill No. 2, restores U.S. trade with France and Great Britain but promises to resume nonintercourse with one power if the other lifts its trade constraints.

Fletcher v. Peck declares a Georgia state law void under the U.S. Constitution. It is the first ruling to nullify a state law.

Elkanah Watson organizes the first agricultural fair, beginning the rural American tradition of the county fair.

1811

Construction of the National Road begins in Cumberland, Maryland. The road will facilitate American settlement west of the Appalachians.

Tecumseh calls for a confederation of Native American tribes to forcibly resist white settlement of western lands.

William Henry Harrison defeats a confederation of Native American forces led by Tenskwatawa in the Battle of Tippecanoe in Indiana Territory.

By a narrow margin, Congress votes against rechartering the First Bank of the United States.

1812

In response to British attacks on American shipping, the United States declares war on Britain; the conflict is known as the War of 1812.

Indian leaders Tecumseh and Black Hawk ally their forces with the British, conducting raids on American settlements.

James Madison is reelected to the presidency.

On President Madison's orders, General William Hull attempts an invasion of Canada; the attack fails and Hull surrenders Detroit to the British.

Documents

The Declaration of Independence
(A Transcription from the National Archives)

IN CONGRESS, July 4, 1776.

The unanimous Declaration of the thirteen united States of America,

When in the Course of human events, it becomes necessary for one people to dissolve the political bands which have connected them with another, and to assume among the Powers of the earth, the separate and equal station to which the Laws of Nature and of Nature's God entitle them, a decent respect to the opinions of mankind requires that they should declare the causes which impel them to the separation.

We hold these truths to be self-evident, that all men are created equal, that they are endowed by their Creator with certain unalienable Rights, that among these are Life, Liberty and the pursuit of Happiness.—That to secure these rights, Governments are instituted among Men, deriving their just powers from the consent of the governed,—That whenever any Form of Government becomes destructive of these ends, it is the Right of the People to alter or to abolish it, and to institute new Government, laying its foundation on such principles and organizing its powers in such form, as to them shall seem most likely to effect their Safety and Happiness. Prudence, indeed, will dictate that Governments long established should not be changed for light and transient causes; and accordingly all experience hath shewn, that mankind are more disposed to suffer, while evils are sufferable, than to right themselves by abolishing the forms to which they are accustomed. But when a long train of abuses and usurpations, pursuing invariably the same Object evinces a design to reduce them under absolute Despotism, it is their right, it is their duty, to throw off such Government, and to provide new Guards for their future security.—Such

has been the patient sufferance of these Colonies; and such is now the necessity which constrains them to alter their former Systems of Government. The history of the present King of Great Britain is a history of repeated injuries and usurpations, all having in direct object the establishment of an absolute Tyranny over these States. To prove this, let Facts be submitted to a candid world.

He has refused his Assent to Laws, the most wholesome and necessary for the public good.

He has forbidden his Governors to pass Laws of immediate and pressing importance, unless suspended in their operation till his Assent should be obtained; and when so suspended, he has utterly neglected to attend to them.

He has refused to pass other Laws for the accommodation of large districts of people, unless those people would relinquish the right of Representation in the Legislature, a right inestimable to them and formidable to tyrants only.

He has called together legislative bodies at places unusual, uncomfortable, and distant from the depository of their public Records, for the sole purpose of fatiguing them into compliance with his measures.

He has dissolved Representative Houses repeatedly, for opposing with manly firmness his invasions on the rights of the people.

He has refused for a long time, after such dissolutions, to cause others to be elected; whereby the Legislative powers, incapable of Annihilation, have returned to the People at large for their exercise; the State remaining in the mean time exposed to all the dangers of invasion from without, and convulsions within.

He has endeavoured to prevent the population of these States; for that purpose obstructing the Laws for Naturalization of Foreigners; refusing to pass others to encourage their migrations hither, and raising the conditions of new Appropriations of Lands.

He has obstructed the Administration of Justice, by refusing his Assent to Laws for establishing Judiciary powers.

He has made Judges dependent on his Will alone, for the tenure of their offices, and the amount and payment of their salaries.

He has erected a multitude of New Offices, and sent hither swarms of Officers to harrass our people, and eat out their substance.

He has kept among us, in times of peace, Standing Armies without the Consent of our legislatures.

He has affected to render the Military independent of and superior to the Civil power.

He has combined with others to subject us to a jurisdiction foreign to our constitution, and unacknowledged by our laws; giving his Assent to their Acts of pretended Legislation:

For Quartering large bodies of armed troops among us:

For protecting them, by a mock Trial, from punishment for any Murders which they should commit on the Inhabitants of these States:

For cutting off our Trade with all parts of the world:

For imposing Taxes on us without our Consent:

For depriving us in many cases, of the benefits of Trial by Jury:

For transporting us beyond Seas to be tried for pretended offences.

For abolishing the free System of English Laws in a neighbouring Province, establishing therein an Arbitrary government, and enlarging its Boundaries so as to render it at once an example and fit instrument for introducing the same absolute rule into these Colonies:

For taking away our Charters, abolishing our most valuable Laws, and altering fundamentally the Forms of our Governments:

For suspending our own Legislatures, and declaring themselves invested with power to legislate for us in all cases whatsoever.

He has abdicated Government here, by declaring us out of his Protection and waging War against us.

He has plundered our seas, ravaged our Coasts, burnt our towns, and destroyed the lives of our people.

He is at this time transporting large Armies of foreign Mercenaries to compleat the works of death, desolation and tyranny, already begun with circumstances of Cruelty & perfidy scarcely paralleled in the most barbarous ages, and totally unworthy the Head of a civilized nation.

He has constrained our fellow Citizens taken Captive on the high Seas to bear Arms against their Country, to become the executioners of their friends and Brethren, or to fall themselves by their Hands.

He has excited domestic insurrections amongst us, and has endeavoured to bring on the inhabitants of our frontiers, the merciless Indian Savages, whose known rule of warfare, is an undistinguished destruction of all ages, sexes and conditions.

In every stage of these Oppressions We have Petitioned for Redress in the most humble terms: Our repeated Petitions have been answered only by repeated injury. A Prince whose character is thus marked by every act which may define a Tyrant, is unfit to be the ruler of a free people.

Nor have We been wanting in attentions to our British brethren. We have warned them from time to time of attempts by their legislature to extend an unwarrantable jurisdiction over us. We have reminded them of the circumstances of our emigration and settlement here. We have appealed to their native justice and magnanimity, and we have conjured them by the ties of our common kindred to disavow these usurpations, which, would inevitably interrupt our connections and correspondence. They too have been deaf to the voice of justice and of consanguinity. We must, therefore, acquiesce in the necessity, which denounces our Separation, and hold them, as we hold the rest of mankind, Enemies in War, in Peace Friends.

We, therefore, the Representatives of the united States of America, in General Congress, Assembled, appealing to the Supreme Judge of the world for the rectitude of our intentions, do, in the Name, and by Authority of the good People of these Colonies, solemnly publish and declare, That these United Colonies are, and of Right ought to be

Free and Independent States; that they are Absolved from all Allegiance to the British Crown, and that all political connection between them and the State of Great Britain, is and ought to be totally dissolved; and that as Free and Independent States, they have full Power to levy War, conclude Peace, contract Alliances, establish Commerce, and to do all other Acts and Things which Independent States may of right do. And for the support of this Declaration, with a firm reliance on the protection of divine Providence, we mutually pledge to each other our Lives, our Fortunes and our sacred Honor.

Georgia:
   Button Gwinnett
   Lyman Hall
   George Walton
North Carolina:
   William Hooper
   Joseph Hewes
   John Penn
South Carolina:
   Edward Rutledge
   Thomas Heyward, Jr.
   Thomas Lynch, Jr.
   Arthur Middleton
Massachusetts:
   John Hancock
Maryland:
   Samuel Chase
   William Paca
   Thomas Stone
   Charles Carroll of Carrollton
Virginia:
   George Wythe
   Richard Henry Lee
   Thomas Jefferson
   Benjamin Harrison
   Thomas Nelson, Jr.
   Francis Lightfoot Lee
   Carter Braxton
Pennsylvania:
   Robert Morris
   Benjamin Rush
   Benjamin Franklin
   John Morton
   George Clymer
   James Smith
   George Taylor
   James Wilson
   George Ross
Delaware:
   Caesar Rodney

   George Read
   Thomas McKean
New York:
   William Floyd
   Philip Livingston
   Francis Lewis
   Lewis Morris
New Jersey:
   Richard Stockton
   John Witherspoon
   Francis Hopkinson
   John Hart
   Abraham Clark
New Hampshire:
   Josiah Bartlett
   William Whipple
Massachusetts:
   Samuel Adams
   John Adams
   Robert Treat Paine
   Elbridge Gerry
Rhode Island:
   Stephen Hopkins
   William Ellery
Connecticut:
   Roger Sherman
   Samuel Huntington
   William Williams
   Oliver Wolcott
New Hampshire:
   Matthew Thornton

The Articles of Confederation
Agreed to by Congress November 15, 1777; ratified and in force, March 1, 1781

James D. Richardson, ed. *A Compilation of the Messages and Papers of the Presidents*, 1789–1897. Vol. 1 (Washington, D.C.: 1898), p. 9 ff.

To ALL TO WHOM these Presents shall come, we the undersigned Delegates to the States affixed to our Names send greeting. Whereas the Delegates of the United States of American in Congress assembled did on the fifteenth day of November in the Year of our Lord One Thousand Seven Hundred and Seventy seven, and in the Second Year of the Independence of America agree to certain articles of Confederation and perpetual Union between the States of Newhampshire, Massachusetts-bay, Rhodeisland and Providence Plantations, Connecticut, New York, New Jersey, Pennsylvania, Delaware, Maryland, Virginia, North-Carolina, South-Carolina and Georgia in the Words following, viz. "Articles of Confederation and perpetual Union between the states of New-hampshire, Massachusetts-bay, Rhodeisland and Providence Plantations, Connecticut, New-York, New-Jersey, Pennsylvania, Delaware, Maryland, Virginia, North-Carolina, South-Carolina and Georgia.

Art. I. The Stile of this confederacy shall be "The United States of America."

Art. II. Each state retains its sovereignty, freedom and independence, and every Power, Jurisdiction and right, which is not by this confederation expressly delegated to the United States, in Congress assembled.

Art. III. The said states hereby severally enter into a firm league of friendship with each other, for their common defence, the security of their Liberties, and their mutual and general welfare, binding themselves to assist each other, against all force offered to, or attacks made upon them, or any of them, on account of religion, sovereignty, trade, or any other pretence whatever.

Art. IV. The better to secure and perpetuate mutual friendship and intercourse among the people of the different states in this union, the free inhabitants of each of these states, paupers, vagabonds and fugitives from Justice excepted, shall be entitled to all privileges and immunities of free citizens in the several states; and the people of each state shall have free ingress and regress to and from any other state, and shall enjoy therein all the privileges of trade and commerce, subject to the same duties, impositions and restrictions as the inhabitants thereof respectively, provided that such restriction shall not extend so far as to prevent the removal of property imported into any state, to any other state of which the Owner is an inhabitant; provided also that no imposition, duties or restriction shall be laid by any state, on the property of the united states, or either of them.

If any Person guilty of, or charged with treason, felony, or other high misdemeanor in any state, shall flee from Justice, and be found in any of the united states, he shall upon demand of the Governor or executive power, of the state from which he fled, be delivered up and removed to the state having jurisdiction of his offence.

Full faith and credit shall be given in each of these states to the records, acts and judicial proceedings of the courts and magistrates of every other state.

Art. V. For the more convenient management of the general interests of the united states, delegates shall be annually appointed in such manner as the legislature of each state shall direct, to meet in Congress on the first Monday in November, in every year, with a power reserved to each state, to recal its delegates, or any of them, at any time within the year, and to send others in their stead, for the remainder of the Year.

No state shall be represented in Congress by less than two, nor by more than seven Members; and no person shall be capable of being a delegate for more than three years in any term of six years; nor shall any person, being a delegate, be capable of holding any office under the united states, for which he, or another for his benefit receives any salary, fees or emolument of any kind.

Each state shall maintain its own delegates in a meeting of the states, and while they act as members of the committee of the states.

In determining questions in the united states, in Congress assembled, each state shall have one vote.

Freedom of speech and debate in Congress shall not be impeached or questioned in any Court, or place out of Congress, and the members of congress shall be protected in their persons from arrests and imprisonments, during the time of their going to and from, and attendance on congress, except for treason, felony, or breach of the peace.

Art. VI. No state without the Consent of the united states in congress assembled, shall send any embassy to, or receive any embassy from, or enter into any conference, agreement, or alliance or treaty with any King, prince or state; nor shall any person holding any office of profit or trust under the united states, or any of them, accept of any present, emolument, office or title of any kind whatever from any king, prince or foreign state; nor shall the united states in congress assembled, or any of them, grant any title of nobility.

No two or more states shall enter into any treaty, confederation or alliance whatever between them, without the consent of the united states in congress assembled, specifying accurately the purposes for which the same is to be entered into, and how long it shall continue.

No state shall lay any imposts or duties, which may interfere with any stipulations in treaties, entered into by the united states in congress assembled, with any king, prince or state, in pursuance of any treaties already proposed by congress, to the courts of France and Spain.

No vessels of war shall be kept up in time of peace by any state, except such number only, as shall be deemed necessary by the united states in congress assembled, for the defence of such state, or its trade; nor shall any body of forces be kept up by any state, in time of peace, except such number only, as in the judgment of the united states, in congress assembled, shall be deemed requisite to garrison the forts necessary for the defence of such state; but every state shall always keep up a well regulated and disciplined militia, sufficiently armed and accoutred, and shall provide and constantly have ready for use, in public stores, a due number of field pieces and tents, and a proper quantity of arms, ammunition and camp equipage.

No state shall engage in any war without the consent of the united states in congress assembled, unless such state be actually invaded by enemies, or shall have received certain advice of a resolution being formed by some nation of

Indians to invade such state, and the danger is so imminent as not to admit of a delay, till the united states in congress assembled can be consulted: nor shall any state grant commissions to any ships or vessels of war, nor letters of marque or reprisal, except it be after a declaration of war by the united states in congress assembled, and then only against the kingdom or state and the subjects thereof, against which war has been so declared, and under such regulations as shall be established by the united states in congress assembled, unless such state be infested by pirates, in which case vessels of war may be fitted out for that occasion, and kept so long as the danger shall continue, or until the united states in congress assembled shall determine otherwise.

Art. VII. When land-forces are raised by any state for the common defence, all officers of or under the rank of colonel, shall be appointed by the legislature of each state respectively by whom such forces shall be raised, or in such manner as such state shall direct, and all vacancies shall be filled up by the state which first made the appointment.

Art. VIII. All charges of war, and all other expences that shall be incurred for the common defence or general welfare, and allowed by the united states in congress assembled, shall be defrayed out of a common treasury, which shall be supplied by the several states, in proportion to the value of all land within each state, granted to or surveyed for any Person, as such land and the buildings and improvements thereon shall be estimated according to such mode as the united states in congress assembled, shall from time to time direct and appoint. The taxes for paying that proportion shall be laid and levied by the authority and direction of the legislatures of the several states within the time agreed upon by the united states in congress assembled.

Art. IX. The united states in congress assembled, shall have the sole and exclusive right and power of determining on peace and war, except in the cases mentioned in the sixth article—of sending and receiving ambassadors—entering into treaties and alliances, provided that no treaty of commerce shall be made whereby the legislative power of the respective states shall be restrained from imposing such imposts and duties on foreigners, as their own people are subjected to, or from prohibiting the exportation or importation of any species of goods or commodities whatsoever—of establishing rules for deciding in all cases, what captures on land or water shall be legal, and in what manner prizes taken by land or naval forces in the service of the united states shall be divided or appropriated—of granting letters of marque and reprisal in times of peace—appointing courts for the trial of piracies and felonies committed on the high seas and establishing courts for receiving and determining finally appeals in all cases of captures, provided that no member of congress shall be appointed a judge of any of the said courts.

The united states in congress assembled shall also be the last resort on appeal in all disputes and differences now subsisting or that hereafter may arise between two or more states concerning boundary, jurisdiction or any other cause whatever; which authority shall always be exercised in the manner following. Whenever the legislative or executive authority or lawful agent of any state in controversy with another shall present a petition to congress, stating the matter in question and praying for a hearing, notice thereof shall be given by order of congress to the legislative or executive authority of the other state in controversy, and a day assigned for the appearance of the parties by their lawful agents, who shall then be directed to appoint by joint consent, commissioners or judges to constitute a court for hearing and determining the matter in question: but if they cannot agree, congress shall name three persons out of each of the united states, and from the list of such persons each party shall alternately strike out one, the petitioners beginning, until the number shall be reduced to thirteen; and from that number not less than seven, nor more than nine names as congress shall direct, shall in the presence of congress be drawn out by lot, and the persons whose names shall be commissioners or judges, to hear and finally determine the controversy, so always as a major part of the judges who shall hear the cause shall agree in the determination: and if either party shall neglect to attend at the day appointed, without shewing reasons, which congress shall judge sufficient, or being present shall refuse to strike, the congress shall proceed to nominate three persons out of each state, and the secretary of congress shall strike in behalf of such party absent or refusing; and the judgment and sentence of the court to be appointed, in the manner before prescribed, shall be final and conclusive; and if any of the parties shall refuse to submit to the authority of such court, or to appear to defend their claim or cause, the court shall nevertheless proceed to pronounce sentence, or judgment, which shall in like manner be final and decisive, the judgment or sentence and other proceedings being in either case transmitted to congress, and lodged among the acts of congress for the security of the parties concerned: provided that every commissioner, before he sits in judgment, shall take an oath to be administered by one of the judges of the supreme or superior court of the state, where the cause shall be tried, "well and truly to hear and determine the matter in question, according to the best of his judgment, without favour, affection or hope of reward:" provided also that no states shall be deprived of territory for the benefit of the united states.

All controversies concerning the private right of soil claimed under different grants of two or more states, whose jurisdictions as they may respect such lands, and the states which passed such grants are adjusted, the said grants or either of them being at the same time claimed to have originated antecedent to such settlement of jurisdiction, shall on the petition of either party to the congress of the united states, be finally determined as near as may be in the same manner as is before prescribed for deciding disputes respecting territorial jurisdiction between different states.

The united states in congress assembled shall also have the sole and exclusive right and power of regulating the alloy and value of coin struck by their own authority, or by that of the respective states—fixing the standard of weights and measures throughout the united states—regulating the trade and managing all affairs with the Indians, not members of any of the states, provided that the legislative right of any state within its own limits be not infringed or violated—establishing and regulating post-offices from one state to another, throughout all the united states, and exacting such postage on the papers passing thro' the same as may be requisite to defray the expenses of the said office—appointing all officers of the land forces, in the service of the united states, excepting regimental officers—appointing all the officers of the naval forces, and commissioning all officers whatever in the service of the united states.—making rules for the government and regulation of the said land and naval forces, and directing their operations.

The united states in congress assembled shall have authority to appoint a committee, to sit in the recess of congress, to be denominated "A Committee of the States," and to consist of one delegate from each state; and to appoint such other committees and civil officers as may be necessary for managing the general affairs of the united states under their direction—to appoint one of their number to preside, provided that no person be allowed to serve in the office of president more than one year in any term of three years; to ascertain the necessary sums of Money to be raised for the service of the united states, and to appropriate and apply the same for defraying the public expences—to borrow money, or emit bills on the credit of the united states, transmitting every half year to the respective states an account of the sums of money so borrowed or emitted—to build and equip a navy—to agree upon the number of land forces, and to make requisitions from each state for its quota, in proportion to the number of white inhabitants in such state; which requisition shall be binding, and thereupon the legislature of each state shall appoint the regimental officers, raise the men and cloath, arm and equip them in a soldier like manner, at the expence of the united states, and the officers and men so cloathed, armed and equipped shall march to the place appointed, and within the time agreed on by the united states in congress assembled: But if the united states in congress assembled shall, on consideration of circumstances judge proper that any state should not raise men, or should raise a smaller number than its quota, and that any other state should raise a greater number of men than the

quota thereof, such extra number shall be raised, officered, cloathed, armed and equipped in the same manner as the quota of such state, unless the legislature of such state shall judge that such extra number cannot be safely spared out of the same, in which case they shall raise officer, cloath, arm and equip as many of such extra number as they judge can be safely spared. And the officers and men so cloathed, armed and equipped, shall march to the place appointed, and within the time agreed on by the united states in congress assembled.

The united states in congress assembled shall never engage in a war, nor grant letters of marque and reprisal in time of peace, nor enter into any treaties or alliances, nor coin money, nor regulate the value thereof, nor ascertain the sums and expences necessary for the defence and welfare of the united states, or any of them, nor emit bills, nor borrow money on the credit of the united states, nor appropriate money, nor agree upon the number of vessels of war, to be built or purchased, or the number of land or sea forces to be raised, nor appoint a commander in chief of the army or navy, unless nine states assent to the same: nor shall a question on any other point, except for adjourning from day to day be determined, unless by the votes of a majority of the united states in congress assembled.

The congress of the united states shall have power to adjourn to any time within the year, and to any place within the united states, so that no period of adjournment be for a longer duration than the space of six Months, and shall publish the Journal of their proceedings monthly, except such parts thereof relating to treaties, alliances or military operations as in their judgment require secresy; and the yeas and nays of the delegates of each state on any question shall be entered on the Journal, when it is desired by any delegate; and the delegates of a state, or any of them, at his or their request shall be furnished with a transcript of the said Journal, except such parts as are above excepted, to lay before the legislatures of the several states.

Art. X. The committee of the states, or any nine of them, shall be authorised to execute, in the recess of congress, such of the powers of congress as the united states in congress assembled, by the consent of nine states, shall from time to time think expedient to vest them with; provided that no power be delegated to the said committee, for the exercise of which, by the articles of confederation, the voice of nine states in the congress of the united states assembled is requisite.

Art. XI. Canada acceding to this confederation, and joining in the measures of the united states, shall be admitted into, and entitled to all the advantages of this union: but no other colony shall be admitted into the same, unless such admission be agreed to by nine states.

Art. XII. All bills of credit emitted, monies borrowed and debts contracted by, or under the authority of congress, before the assembling of the united states, in pursuance of the present confederation, shall be deemed and considered as a charge against the united states, for payment and satisfaction whereof the said united states, and the public faith are hereby solemnly pledged.

Art. XIII. Every state shall abide by the determinations of the united states in congress assembled, on all questions which by this confederation are submitted to them. And the Articles of this confederation shall be inviolably observed by every state, and the union shall be perpetual; nor shall any alteration at any time hereafter be made in any of them; unless such alteration be agreed to in a congress of the united states, and be afterwards confirmed by the legislatures of every state.

AND WHEREAS it hath pleased the Great Governor of the World to incline the hearts of the legislatures we respectively represent in congress, to approve of, and to authorize us to ratify the said articles of confederation and perpetual union. KNOW YE that we the under-signed delegates, by virtue of the power and authority to us given for that purpose, do by these presents, in the name and in behalf of our respective constituents, fully and entirely ratify and confirm each and every of the said articles of confederation and perpetual union, and all and singular the matters and things therein contained: And we do further solemnly plight and engage the faith of our respective constituents, that they shall abide by the determinations of the united states in congress assembled, on all questions, which by the said confederation are submitted to them. And that the articles thereof shall be inviolably observed by the states we respectively represent, and that the union shall be perpetual. In Witness whereof we have hereunto set our hands in Congress. Done at Philadelphia in the state of Pennsylvania the ninth Day of July in the Year of our Lord one Thousand seven Hundred and Seventy-eight, and in the third year of the independence of America.

JOSIAH BARTLETT
JOHN WENTWORTH JUN^r
AUGUST 8th 1778
} On the part and behalf of the State of New Hampshire

JOHN HANCOCK
SAMUEL ADAMS
ELBRIDGE GERRY
FRANCIS DANA
JAMES LOVELL
SAMUEL HOLTEN
} On the part and behalf of the State of Massachusetts Bay

WILLIAM ELLERY
HENRY MARCHANT
JOHN COLLINS
} On the part and behalf of the State of Rhode-Island and Providence Plantations

ROGER SHERMAN
SAMUEL HUNTINGTON
OLIVER WOLCOTT
TITUS HOSMER
ANDREW ADAMS
} On the part and behalf of the State of Connecticut

JA^S DUANE
FRA^S LEWIS
W^M DUER
GOUV MORRIS
} On the Part and Behalf of the State of New York

JNO WITHERSPOON
NATH^L SCUDDER
} On the Part and in Behalf of the State of New Jersey. Novr 26, 1778. —

ROB^T MORRIS
DANIEL ROBERDEAU
JON^A BAYARD SMITH.
WILLIAM CLINGAN
JOSEPH REED 22d July 1778
} On the part and behalf of the State of Pennsylvania

THO M:KEAN
    Feby 12 1779
JOHN DICKINSON
    May 5th 1779
NICHOLAS VAN DYKE,
} On the part & behalf of the State of Delaware

JOHN HANSON
    March 1 1781
DANIEL CARROLL d^o
} On the Part and behalf of the State of Maryland

RICHARD HENRY LEE
JOHN BANISTER
THOMAS ADAMS
JN^O HARVIE
FRANCIS LIGHTFOOT LEE
} On the Part and Behalf of the State of Virginia

JOHN PENN
    July 21st 1778
CORN^S HARNETT
JN^O WILLIAMS
} On the part and Behalf of the State of N^o Carolina

HENRY LAURENS
WILLIAM HENRY DRAYTON
JN^O MATHEWS
RICH^D HUTSON
THO^S HEYWARD Junr
} On the part & behalf of the State of South-Carolina

JN^O WALTON
    24th July 1778
EDW^D TELFAIR
EDW^D LANGWORTHY
} On the part of & behalf of the State of Georgia

The Constitution of the United States

James D. Richardson, ed. *A Compilation of the Messages and Papers of the Presidents, 1789–1897*, Vol. 1, (Washington, D.C., 1898–1906), p. 21 ff.

WE THE PEOPLE of the United States, in Order to form a more perfect Union, establish Justice, insure domestic Tranquility, provide for the common defence, promote the general Welfare, and secure the Blessings of Liberty to ourselves and our Posterity, do ordain and establish this Constitution for the United States of America.

Art. I

Sec. 1. All legislative Powers herein granted shall be vested in a Congress of the United States, which shall consist of a Senate and House of Representatives.

Sec. 2. The House of Representatives shall be composed of Members chosen every second Year by the People of the several States, and the Electors in each State shall have the Qualifications requisite for Electors of the most numerous Branch of the State Legislature.

No Person shall be a Representative who shall not have attained to the Age of twenty five Years, and been seven Years a Citizen of the United States, and who shall not, when elected, be an Inhabitant of that State in which he shall be chosen.

Representatives and direct Taxes shall be apportioned among the several States which may be included within this Union, according to their respective Numbers, which shall be determined by adding to the whole Number of free Persons, including those bound to Service for a Term of Years, and excluding Indians not taxed, three fifths of all other Persons. The actual Enumeration shall be made within three Years after the first Meeting of the Congress of the United States, and within every subsequent Term of ten Years, in such Manner as they shall by Law direct. The Number of Representatives shall not exceed one for every thirty Thousand, but each State shall have at Least one Representative; and until such enumeration shall be made, the State of New Hampshire shall be entitled to chuse three, Massachusetts eight, Rhode-Island and Providence Plantations one, Connecticut five, New-York six, New Jersey four, Pennsylvania eight, Delaware one, Maryland six, Virginia ten, North Carolina five, South Carolina five, and Georgia three.

When vacancies happen in the Representation from any State, the Executive Authority thereof shall issue Writs of Election to fill such Vacancies.

The House of Representatives shall chuse their Speaker and other Officers; and shall have the sole Power of Impeachment.

Sec. 3. The Senate of the United States shall be composed of two Senators from each State, chosen by the Legislature thereof, for six Years; and each Senator shall have one Vote.

Immediately after they shall be assembled in Consequence of the first Election, they shall be divided as equally as may be into three Classes. The Seats of the Senators of the first Class shall be vacated at the Expiration of the second Year, of the second Class at the Expiration of the fourth Year, and of the third Class at the Expiration of the sixth Year, so that one third may be chosen every second Year; and if Vacancies happen by Resignation, or otherwise, during the Recess of the Legislature of any State, the Executive thereof may make temporary Appointments until the next Meeting of the Legislature, which shall then fill such Vacancies.

No Person shall be a Senator who shall not have attained to the Age of thirty Years, and been nine Years a Citizens of the United States, and who shall not, when elected, be an Inhabitant of that State for which he shall be chosen.

The Vice President of the United States shall be President of the Senate, but shall have no Vote, unless they be equally divided.

The Senate shall chuse their other Officers, and also a President pro tempore, in the Absence of the Vice President, or when he shall exercise the Office of President of the United States.

The Senate shall have the sole Power to try all Impeachments. When sitting for that Purpose, they shall be on Oath or Affirmation. When the President of the United States is tried, the Chief Justice shall preside: And no Person shall be convicted without the Concurrence of two thirds of the Members present.

Judgment in Cases of Impeachment shall not extend further than to removal from Office, and disqualification to hold and enjoy any Office of honor, Trust or Profit under the United States: but the Party convicted shall nevertheless be liable and subject to Indictment, Trial, Judgment and Punishment, according to Law.

Sec. 4. The Times, Places and Manner of holding Elections for Senators and Representatives, shall be prescribed in each State by the Legislature thereof; but the Congress may at any time by Law make or alter such Regulations, except as to the Places of chusing Senators.

The Congress shall assemble at least once in every Year, and such Meeting shall be on the first Monday in December, unless they shall by Law appoint a different Day.

Sec. 5. Each House shall be the Judge of the Elections, Returns and Qualifications of its own Members, and a Majority of each shall constitute a Quorum to do Business; but a smaller Number may adjourn from day to day, and may be authorized to compel the Attendance of absent Members, in such Manner, and under such Penalties as each House may provide.

Each House may determine the Rules of its Proceedings, punish its Members for disorderly Behaviour, and, with the Concurrence of two thirds, expel a Member.

Each House shall keep a Journal of its Proceedings, and from time to time publish the same, excepting such Parts as may in their Judgment require Secrecy; and the Yeas and Nays of the Members of either House on any question shall, at the Desire of one fifth of those Present, be entered on the Journal.

Neither House, during the Session of Congress, shall, without the Consent of the other, adjourn for more than three days, nor to any other Place than that in which the two Houses shall be sitting.

Sec. 6. The Senators and Representatives shall receive a Compensation for their Services, to be ascertained by Law, and paid out of the Treasury of the United States. They shall in all Cases, except Treason, Felony and Breach of the Peace, be privileged from Arrest during their Attendance at the Session of their respective Houses, and in going to and returning from the same; and for any Speech or Debate in either House, they shall not be questioned in any other Place.

No Senator or Representative shall, during the Time for which he was elected, be appointed to any civil Office under the Authority of the United States which shall have been created, or the Emoluments whereof shall have been encreased during such time; and no Person holding any Office under the United States, shall be a Member of either House during his Continuance in Office.

Sec. 7. All Bills for raising Revenue shall originate in the House of Representatives; but the Senate may propose or concur with Amendments as on other Bills.

Every Bill which shall have passed the House of Representatives and the Senate, shall, before it become a Law, be presented to the President of the United States; If he approve he shall sign it, but if not he shall return it, with his Objections to that House in which it shall have originated, who shall enter the Objections at large on their Journal, and proceed to reconsider it. If after such Reconsideration two thirds of that House shall agree to pass the Bill, it shall be sent, together with the Objections, to the other House, by which it shall likewise be reconsidered, and if approved by two thirds of that House, it shall become a Law. But in all such Cases the Votes of both Houses shall be determined by yeas and Nays, and the Names of the Persons voting for and against the Bill shall be entered on the Journal of each House respectively. If any Bill shall not be returned by the President within ten Days (Sundays excepted) after it shall have

been presented to him, the Same shall be a Law, in like Manner as if he had signed it, unless the Congress by their Adjournment prevent its Return, in which Case it shall not be a Law.

Every Order, Resolution, or Vote to which the Concurrence of the Senate and House of Representatives may be necessary (except on a question of Adjournment) shall be presented to the President of the United States; and before the Same shall take Effect, shall be approved by him, or being disapproved by him, shall be repassed by two thirds of the Senate and House of Representatives, according to the Rules and Limitations prescribed in the Case of a Bill.

Sec. 8. The Congress shall have Power To lay and collect Taxes, Duties, Imposts and Excises, to pay the Debts and provide for the common Defence and general Welfare of the United States; but all Duties, Imposts and Excises shall be uniform throughout the United States;

To borrow Money on the credit of the United States;

To regulate Commerce with foreign Nations, and among the several States, and with the Indian Tribes;

To establish an uniform Rule of Naturalization, and uniform Laws on the subject of Bankruptcies throughout the United States;

To coin Money, regulate the Value thereof, and of foreign Coin, and fix the Standard of Weights and Measures;

To provide for the Punishment of counterfeiting the Securities and current Coin of the United States;

To establish Post Offices and post Roads;

To promote the Progress of Science and useful Arts, by securing for limited Times to Authors and Inventors the exclusive Right to their respective Writings and Discoveries;

To constitute Tribunals inferior to the supreme Court;

To define and punish Piracies and Felonies committed on the high Seas, and Offences against the Law of Nations;

To declare War, grant Letters of Marque and Reprisal, and make Rules concerning Captures on Land and Water;

To raise and support Armies, but no Appropriation of Money to that Use shall be for a longer Term than two Years;

To provide and maintain a Navy;

To make Rules for the Government and Regulation of the land and naval Forces;

To provide for calling forth the Militia to execute the Laws of the Union, suppress Insurrections and repel Invasions;

To provide for organizing, arming, and disciplining, the Militia, and for governing such Part of them as may be employed in the Service of the United States, reserving to the States respectively, the Appointment of the Officers, and the Authority of training the Militia according to the discipline prescribed by Congress;

To exercise exclusive Legislation in all Cases whatsoever, over such District (not exceeding ten Miles square) as may, by Cession of particular States, and the Acceptance of Congress, become the Seat of the Government of the United States, and to exercise like Authority over all Places purchased by the Consent of the Legislature of the State in which the Same shall be, for the Erection of Forts, Magazines, Arsenals, dock-Yards, and other needful Buildings;—And

To make all Laws which shall be necessary and proper for carrying into Execution the foregoing Powers, and all other Powers vested by this Constitution in the Government of the United States, or in any Department or Officer thereof.

Sec. 9. The Migration or Importation of such Persons as any of the States now existing shall think proper to admit, shall not be prohibited by the Congress prior to the Year one thousand eight hundred and eight, but a Tax or duty may be imposed on such Importation, not exceeding ten dollars for each Person.

The Privilege of the Writ of Habeas Corpus shall not be suspended, unless when in Cases of Rebellion or Invasion the public Safety may require it.

No Bill of Attainder or ex post facto Law shall be passed.

No Capitation, or other direct, Tax shall be laid, unless in Proportion to the Census or Enumeration herein before directed to be taken.

No Tax or Duty shall be laid on Articles exported from any State.

No Preference shall be given by any Regulation of Commerce or Revenue to the Ports of one State over those of another: nor shall Vessels bound to, or from, one State, be obliged to enter, clear, or pay Duties in another.

No Money shall be drawn from the Treasury, but in Consequence of Appropriations made by Law; and a regular Statement and Account of the Receipts and Expenditures of all public Money shall be published from time to time.

No Title of Nobility shall be granted by the United States. And no Person holding any Office of Profit or Trust under them, shall, without the Consent of the Congress, accept of any present, Emolument, Office, or Title, of any kind whatever, from any King, Prince or foreign State.

Sec. 10. No State shall enter into any Treaty, Alliance, or Confederation; grant Letters of Marque and Reprisal; coin Money; emit Bills of Credit; make any Thing but gold and silver Coin a Tender in Payment of Debts; pass any Bill of Attainder, ex post facto Law, or Law impairing the Obligation of Contracts, or grant any Title of Nobility.

No State shall, without the Consent of the Congress, lay any Imposts or Duties on Imports or Exports, except what may be absolutely necessary for executing its inspection Laws: and the net Produce of all Duties and Imposts, laid by any State on Imports or Exports, shall be for the Use of the Treasury of the United States; and all such Laws shall be subject to the Revision and Controul of the Congress.

No State shall, without the Consent of Congress, lay any Duty of Tonnage, keep Troops, or Ships of War in time of Peace, enter into any Agreement or Compact with another State, or with a foreign Power, or engage in War, unless actually invaded, or in such imminent Danger as will not admit of delay.

Art. II

Sec. 1. The executive Power shall be vested in a President of the United States of America. He shall hold his Office during the Term of four Years, and, together with the Vice President, chosen for the same Term, be elected, as follows

Each State shall appoint, in such Manner as the Legislature thereof may direct, a Number of Electors, equal to the whole Number of Senators and Representatives to which the State may be entitled in the Congress: but no Senator or Representative, or Person holding an Office of Trust or Profit under the United States, shall be appointed an Elector.

The Electors shall meet in their respective States, and vote by Ballot for two Persons, of whom one at least shall not be an Inhabitant of the same State with themselves. And they shall make a List of all the Persons voted for, and of the Number of Votes for each; which List they shall sign and certify, and transmit sealed to the Seat of the Government of the United States, directed to the President of the Senate. The President of the Senate shall, in the Presence of the Senate and House of Representatives, open all the Certificates, and the Votes shall then be counted. The Person having the greatest Number of Votes shall be the President, if such Number be a Majority of the whole Number of Electors appointed; and if there be more than one who have such Majority, and have an equal Number of Votes, then the House of Representatives shall immediately chuse by Ballot one of them for President; and if no person have a Majority, then from the five highest on the List the said House shall in like Manner chuse the President. But in chusing the President, the Votes shall be taken by States, the Representation from each State having one Vote; A quorum for this Purpose shall consist of a Member or Members from two thirds of the States, and a Majority of all the States shall be necessary to a Choice. In every Case, after the Choice of the President, the Person having the greatest Number of Votes of the Electors shall be the Vice President. But if there should remain two or more who have equal Votes, the Senate shall chuse from them by Ballot the Vice President.

The Congress may determine the Time of chusing the Electors, and the Day on which they shall give their Votes; which Day shall be the same throughout the United States.

No Person except a natural born Citizen, or a Citizen of the United States, at the time of the Adoption of this Constitution, shall be eligible to the Office of President; neither shall any Person be eligible to that Office who shall not have attained to the Age of thirty five Years, and been fourteen Years a Resident within the United States.

In Case of the Removal of the President from Office, or of his Death, Resignation, or Inability to discharge the Powers and Duties of the said Office, the Same shall devolve on the Vice President, and the Congress may by Law provide for the Case of Removal, Death, Resignation or Inability, both of the President and Vice President, declaring what Officer shall then act as President, and such Officer shall act accordingly, until the Disability be removed, or a President shall be elected.

The President shall, at stated Times, receive for his Services, a Compensation, which shall neither be encreased nor diminished during the Period for which he shall have been elected, and he shall not receive within that Period any other Emolument from the United States, or any of them.

Before he enter on the Execution of his Office, he shall take the following Oath or Affirmation:—"I do solemnly swear (or affirm) that I will faithfully execute the Office of President of the United States, and will to the best of my Ability, preserve, protect and defend the Constitution of the United States."

Sec. 2. The President shall be Commander in Chief of the Army and Navy of the United States, and of the Militia of the several States, when called into the actual Service of the United States; he may require the Opinion, in writing, of the principal Officer in each of the executive Departments, upon any Subject relating to the Duties of their respective Offices, and he shall have Power to grant Reprieves and Pardons for Offences against the United States, except in Cases of Impeachment.

He shall have Power, by and with the Advice and Consent of the Senate, to make Treaties, provided two thirds of the Senators present concur; and he shall nominate, and by and with the Advice and Consent of the Senate, shall appoint Ambassadors, other public Ministers and Consuls, Judges of the supreme Court, and all other Officers of the United States, whose Appointments are not herein otherwise provided for, and which shall be established by Law: but the Congress may by Law vest the Appointment of such inferior Officers, as they think proper, in the President alone, in the Courts of Law, or in the Heads of Departments.

The President shall have Power to fill up all Vacancies that may happen during the Recess of the Senate, by granting Commissions which shall expire at the End of their next Session.

Sec. 3. He shall from time to time give to the Congress Information of the State of the Union, and recommend to their Consideration such Measures as he shall judge necessary and expedient; he may, on extraordinary Occasions, convene both Houses, or either of them, and in Case of Disagreement between them, with Respect to the Time of Adjournment, he may adjourn them to such Time as he shall think proper; he shall receive Ambassadors and other public Ministers; he shall take Care that the Laws be faithfully executed, and shall Commission all the Officers of the United States.

Sec. 4. The President, Vice President and all civil Officers of the United States, shall be removed from Office on Impeachment for, and Conviction of, Treason, Bribery, or other high Crimes and Misdemeanors.

Art. III

Sec. 1. The judicial Power of the United States, shall be vested in one supreme Court, and in such inferior Courts as the Congress may from time to time ordain and establish. The Judges, both of the supreme and inferior Courts, shall hold their Offices during good Behaviour, and shall, at stated Times, receive for their Services, a Compensation, which shall not be diminished during their Continuance in Office.

Sec. 2. The judicial Power shall extend to all Cases, in Law and Equity, arising under this Constitution, the Laws of the United States, and Treaties made, or which shall be made, under their Authority;—to all Cases affecting Ambassadors, other public Ministers and Consuls;—to all Cases of admiralty and maritime Jurisdiction;—to Controversies to which the United States shall be a Party;—to Controversies between two or more States;—between a State and Citizens of another State;—between Citizens of different States,—between Citizens of the same State claiming Lands under Grants of different States, and between a State, or the Citizens thereof, and foreign States, Citizens or Subjects.

In all Cases affecting Ambassadors, other public Ministers and Consuls, and those in which a State shall be Party, the supreme Court shall have original Jurisdiction. In all the other Cases before mentioned, the supreme Court shall have appellate Jurisdiction, both as to Law and Fact, with such Exceptions, and under such Regulations as the Congress shall make.

The Trial of all Crimes, except in Cases of Impeachment, shall be by Jury; and such Trial shall be held in the State where the said Crimes shall have been committed; but when not committed within any State, the Trial shall be at such Place or Places as the Congress may by Law have directed.

Sec. 3. Treason against the United States, shall consist only in levying War against them, or in adhering to their Enemies, giving them Aid and Comfort. No Person shall be convicted of Treason unless on the Testimony of two Witnesses to the same overt Act, or on confession in open Court.

The Congress shall have Power to declare the Punishment of Treason, but no Attainder of Treason shall work Corruption of Blood, or Forfeiture except during the Life of the Person attainted.

Art. IV

Sec. 1. Full Faith and Credit shall be given in each State to the Public Acts, Records, and judicial Proceedings of every other State. And the Congress may by general Laws prescribe the Manner in which such Acts, Records and Proceedings shall be proved, and the Effect thereof.

Sec. 2. The Citizens of each State shall be entitled to all Privileges and Immunities of Citizens in the several States.

A Person charged in any State with Treason, Felony, or other Crime, who shall flee from Justice, and be found in another State, shall on Demand of the executive Authority of the State from which he fled, be delivered up, to be removed to the State having Jurisdiction of the Crime.

No Person held to Service or Labour in one State, under the Laws thereof, escaping into another, shall, in Consequence of any Law or Regulation therein, be discharged from such Service or Labour, but shall be delivered up on Claim of the Party to whom such Service or Labour may be due.

Sec. 3. New States may be admitted by the Congress into this Union; but no new States shall be formed or erected within the Jurisdiction of any other State; nor any State be formed by the Junction of two or more States, or Parts of States, without the Consent of the Legislatures of the States concerned as well as of the Congress.

The Congress shall have Power to dispose of and make all needful Rules and Regulations respecting the Territory or other Property belonging to the United States; and nothing in this Constitution shall be so construed as to Prejudice any Claims of the United States, or of any particular State.

Sec. 4. The United States shall guarantee to every State in this Union a Republican Form of Government, and shall protect each of them against Invasion; and on Application of the Legislature, or of the Executive (when the Legislature cannot be convened) against domestic Violence.

Art. V

The Congress, whenever two thirds of both Houses shall deem it necessary, shall propose Amendments to this Constitution, or, on the Application of the Legislatures of two thirds of the several States, shall call a Convention for proposing Amendments, which, in either Case, shall be valid to all Intents and Purposes, as Part of this Constitution, when ratified by the Legislatures of three fourths of the several States, or by Conventions in three fourths thereof, as the one or the other Mode of Ratification may be proposed by the Congress; Provided that no Amendment which may be made prior to the Year One thousand eight hundred and eight shall in any Manner affect the first and fourth Clauses in the Ninth Section of the first Article; and that no State, without its Consent, shall be deprived of its equal Suffrage in the Senate.

Art. VI

All Debts contracted and Engagements entered into, before the Adoption of this Constitution, shall be as valid against the United States under this Constitution, as under the Confederation.

This Constitution, and the Laws of the United States which shall be made in Pursuance thereof; and all Treaties made, or which shall be made, under the Authority of the United States, shall be the supreme Law of the Land; and the Judges in every State shall be bound thereby, any Thing in the Constitution or Laws of any State to the Contrary notwithstanding.

The Senators and Representatives before mentioned, and the Members of the several State Legislatures, and all executive and judicial Officers, both of the United States and of the several States, shall be bound by Oath or Affirmation, to support this Constitution; but no religious Test shall ever be required as a Qualification to any Office or public Trust under the United States.

Art. VII

The Ratification of the Conventions of nine States, shall be sufficient for the Establishment of this Constitution between the States so ratifying the Same.

Done in Convention by the Unanimous Consent of the States present the Seventeenth Day of September in the Year of our Lord one thousand seven hundred and Eighty seven and of the Independence of the United States of America the Twelfth. In witness whereof We have hereunto subscribed our Names,

G° WASHINGTON—Presid^t
and deputy from Virginia

New Hampshire	{ JOHN LANGDON NICHOLAS GILMAN		Delaware	{ GEO: READ GUNNING BEDFORD jun JOHN DICKINSON RICHARD BASSETT JACO: BROOM
Massachusetts	{ NATHANIEL GORHAM RUFUS KING		Maryland	{ JAMES McHENRY DAN OF ST THOS JENIFER DANL CARROLL
Connecticut	{ WM SAML JOHNSON ROGER SHERMAN		Virginia	{ JOHN BLAIR — JAMES MADISON, JR.
New York	ALEXANDER HAMILTON		North Carolina	{ WM BLOUNT RICHD DOBBS SPAIGHT HU WILLIAMSON
New Jersey	{ WIL: LIVINGSTON DAVID BREARLEY WM PATERSON JONA: DAYTON		South Carolina	{ J. RUTLEDGE CHARLES COTESWORTH PINCKNEY CHARLES PINCKNEY PIERCE BUTLER
Pennsylvania	{ B FRANKLIN THOMAS MIFFLIN ROBT MORRIS GEO. CLYMER THOS FITZSIMONS JARED INGERSOLL JAMES WILSON GOUV MORRIS		Georgia	{ WILLIAM FEW ABR BALDWIN

Articles in addition to, and Amendment of the Constitution of the United States of America, proposed by Congress, and ratified by the Legislatures of the several States, pursuant to the fifth Article of the original Constitution.

[The first 10 amendments went into effect November 3, 1791.]

Art. I

Congress shall make no law respecting an establishment of religion, or prohibiting the free exercise thereof; or abridging the freedom of speech, or of the press; or the right of the people peaceably to assemble, and to petition the government for a redress of grievances.

Art. II

A well regulated Militia, being necessary to the security of a free State, the right of the people to keep and bear Arms, shall not be infringed.

Art. III

No Soldier shall, in time of peace be quartered in any house, without the consent of the Owner, nor in time of war, but in a manner to be prescribed by law.

Art. IV

The right of the people to be secure in their persons, houses, papers, and effects, against unreasonable searches and seizures, shall not be violated, and no Warrants shall issue, but upon probable cause, supported by Oath or affirmation, and particularly describing the place to be searched, and the persons or things to be seized.

Art. V

No person shall be held to answer for a capital, or otherwise infamous crime, unless on a presentment or indictment of a Grand Jury, except in cases arising in the land or naval forces, or in the Militia, when in actual service in time of War or public danger; nor shall any person be subject for the same offence to be twice put in jeopardy of life or limb; nor shall be compelled in any criminal case to be a witness against himself, nor be deprived of life, liberty, or property, without due process of law; nor shall private property be taken for public use, without just compensation.

Art. VI

In all criminal prosecutions, the accused shall enjoy the right to a speedy and public trial, by an impartial jury of the State and district wherein the crime shall have been committed, which district shall have been previously ascertained by law, and to be informed of the nature and cause of the accusation; to be confronted with the witnesses against him; to have compulsory process for obtaining witnesses in his favor, and to have the Assistance of Counsel for his defence.

Art. VII

In Suits at common law, where the value in controversy shall exceed twenty dollars the right of trial by jury shall be preserved and no fact tried by a jury, shall be otherwise re-examined in any Court of the United States, than according to the rules of the common law.

Art. VIII

Excessive bail shall not be required, nor excessive fines imposed, nor cruel and unusual punishments inflicted.

Art. IX

The enumeration in the Constitution, of certain rights, shall not be construed to deny or disparage others retained by the people.

Art. X

The powers not delegated to the United States by the Constitution, nor prohibited by it to the States, are reserved to the States respectively, or to the people.

Art. XI

Jan. 8, 1798

The Judicial power of the United States shall not be construed to extend to any suit in law or equity, commenced or prosecuted against one of the United States by Citizens of another State, or by Citizens or subjects of any Foreign State.

Art. XII

Sept. 25, 1804

The Electors shall meet in their respective states, and vote by ballot for President and Vice-President, one of whom, at least, shall not be an inhabitant of the same state with themselves; they shall name in their ballots the person voted for as President, and in distinct ballots the person voted for as Vice-President, and they shall make distinct lists of all persons voted for as President, and of all persons voted for as Vice-President, and of the number of votes for each, which lists they shall sign and certify, and transmit sealed to the seat of the government of the United States, directed to the President of the Senate;—The President of the Senate shall, in the presence of the Senate and House of Representatives, open all the certificates and the votes shall then be counted;—The person having the greatest number of votes for President, shall be the President, if such number be a majority of the whole number of Electors appointed; and if no person have such majority, then from the persons having the highest numbers not exceeding three on the list of those voted for as President, the House of Representatives shall choose immediately, by ballot, the President. But in choosing the President, the votes shall be taken by states, the representation from each state having one vote; a quorum for this purpose shall consist of a member or members from two-thirds of the states, and a majority of all the states shall be necessary to a choice. And if the House of Representatives shall not choose a President whenever the right of choice shall devolve upon them, before the fourth day of March next following, then the Vice-President shall act as President, as in the case of the death or other constitutional disability of the President.—The person having the greatest number of votes as Vice-President, shall be the Vice-President, if such number be a majority of the whole number of Electors appointed, and if no person have a majority, then from the two highest numbers on the list, the Senate shall choose the Vice-President; a quorum for the purpose shall consist of two-thirds of the whole number of Senators, and a majority of the whole number shall be necessary to a choice. But no person constitutionally ineligible to the office of President shall be eligible to that of Vice-President of the United States.

Bibliography

Anderson, Fred. *Crucible of War: The Seven Years' War and the Fate of Empire in British North America, 1754–1766.* New York: Alfred A, Knopf, 2000.

Appleby, Joyce. *Capitalism and the New Social Order: The Republican Vision of the 1790s.* New York: New York University Press, 1984.

Bailyn, Bernard. *The Ideological Origins of the American Revolution.* rev. ed. Cambridge, Mass.: Harvard University Press, 1992.

———. *The Ordeal of Thomas Hutchinson.* Cambridge, Mass.: Harvard University Press, 1974.

Banning, Lance. *The Jeffersonian Persuasion: The Evolution of a Party Ideology.* Ithaca, N.Y.: Cornell University Press, 1978.

———. *The Sacred Fire of Liberty: James Madison and the Founding of the Federal Republic.* Ithaca, N.Y.: Cornell University Press, 1995.

Boydston, Jeanne. *Home and Work: Housework, Wages, and the Ideology of Labor in the Early Republic.* New York: Oxford University Press, 1990.

Buel, Joy Day, and Richard Buel Jr. *The Way of Duty: A Woman and Her Family in Revolutionary America.* New York: W. W. Norton, 1995.

Bushman, Richard L. *King and People in Provincial Massachusetts.* Chapel Hill: University of North Carolina Press, 1985.

———. *The Refinement of America: Persons, Houses, Cities.* New York: Alfred A. Knopf, 1992.

Calloway, Colin. *The American Revolution in Indian Country: Crisis and Diversity in Native American Communities.* Cambridge, U.K.: Cambridge University Press, 1995.

Cayton, Andrew. *The Frontier Republic: Ideology and Politics in the Ohio Country, 1780–1825.* Kent, Ohio: Kent State University Press, 1986.

Christie, Ian R. *Crisis of Empire: Great Britain and the American Colonies, 1754–1783* New York: W. W. Norton, 1966.

Clark, Christopher. *The Roots of Rural Capitalism: Western Massachusetts, 1780–1860.* Ithaca, N.Y.: Cornell University Press, 1990.

Countryman, Edward. *A People in Revolution.* New York: Hill and Wang, 1981.

Davis, David B. *The Problem of Slavery in the Age of the Democratic Revolution.* Ithaca, N.Y.: Cornell University Press, 1975.

Dowd, Gregory. *A Spirited Resistance: The North American Indian Struggle for Unity, 1745–1815.* Baltimore: Johns Hopkins University Press, 1992.

Edmunds, R. David. *Tecumseh and the Quest for Indian Leadership.* Boston: Little, Brown, 1984.

Elkins, Stanley, and Eric McKitrick. *The Age of Federalism.* New York: Oxford University Press, 1993.

Ellis, Joseph. *The American Sphinx: The Character of Thomas Jefferson.* New York: Random House, 1997.

———. *The Passionate Sage: The Character and Legacy of John Adams.* New York: W. W. Norton, 1993.

Ellis, Richard. *The Jeffersonian Crisis: Courts and Politics in the Young Republic.* New York: Oxford University Press, 1971.

Faragher, John Mack. *Daniel Boone: The Life and Legend of an American Pioneer.* New York: Holt, 1992.

Fischer, David Hackett. *Paul Revere's Ride.* New York: Oxford University Press, 1994.

Flexner, James Thomas. *Washington: The Indispensable Man.* Boston: Little, Brown, 1969.

Foner, Eric. *Tom Paine and Revolutionary America.* New York: Oxford University Press, 1976.

Frey, Sylvia. *Water from the Rock: Black Resistance in a Revolutionary Age.* Princeton, N.J.: Princeton University Press, 1991.

Gilje, Paul A. *The Road to Mobocracy: Popular Disorder in New York City, 1763–1834.* Chapel Hill: University of North Carolina Press, 1987.

Gordon-Reed, Annette. *Thomas Jefferson and Sally Hemings: An American Controversy.* Charlottesville: University Press of Virginia, 1997.

Greene, John C. *American Science in the Age of Jefferson.* Ames: Iowa State University Press, 1984.

Gross, Robert. *The Minutemen and Their World.* New York: Hill and Wang, 1976.

Hatch, Nathan O. *The Democratization of Christianity.* New Haven, Conn.: Yale University Press, 1989.

———. *The Sacred Cause of Liberty: Republican Thought and the Millennium in Revolutionary New England.* New Haven, Conn.: Yale University Press, 1977.

Hatley, Tom. *Dividing Paths: Cherokees and South Carolina through the Era of the Revolution.* New York: Oxford University Press, 1995.

Heyrman, Christine Leigh. *Southern Cross: The Beginnings of the Bible Belt.* Chapel Hill: University of North Carolina Press, 1997.

Hickey, Donald R. *The War of 1812: A Forgotten Conflict.* Urbana: University of Illinois Press, 1989.

Higginbotham, Don. *The War of Independence: Military Attitudes, Policies, and Practice, 1763–1789.* New York: Macmillan, 1983.

Hoerder, Dirk. *Crowd Action in Revolutionary Massachusetts, 1765–1780.* New York: Academic Press, 1977.

Holton, Woody. *Forced Founders: Indians, Debtors, Slaves, and the Making of the American Revolution in Virginia.* Chapel Hill: University of North Carolina Press, 1999.

Horsman, Reginald. *Diplomacy of the New Republic, 1775–1815.* Arlington Heights, Ill.: Harlan Davidson, 1985.

Isaac, Rhys. *The Transformation of Virginia, 1740–1790.* Chapel Hill: University of North Carolina Press, 1982.

Jensen, Joan. *Loosening the Bonds: Mid-Atlantic Farm Women, 1750–1850.* New Haven, Conn.: Yale University Press, 1986.

Jensen, Merrill. *The New Nation: A History of the United States during the Confederation, 1781–1789.* New York: Alfred A. Knopf, 1950.

Juster, Susan. *Disorderly Women: Sexual Politics and Evangelicalism in Revolutionary New England.* Ithaca, N.Y.: Cornell University Press, 1994.

Kaplan, Lawrence S. *"Entangling Alliances With None": American Foreign Policy in the Age of Jefferson.* Kent, Ohio: Kent State University Press, 1987.

Kelley, Catherine E. *In the New England Fashion: Reshaping Women's Lives in the Nineteenth Century.* Ithaca, N.Y.: Cornell University Press, 1999.

Kerber, Linda K. *Women of the Republic: Intellect and Ideology in Revolutionary America.* Chapel Hill: University of North Carolina Press, 1980.

Klein, Rachel N. *The Unification of a Slave State: The Rise of the Planter Class in the South Carolina Backcountry, 1760–1808.* Chapel Hill: University of North Carolina Press, 1990.

Kohn, Richard. *Eagle and Sword: The Federalist Creation of a Military Establishment in America, 1783–1802.* New York: Macmillan, 1975.

Larkin, Jack. *The Reshaping of Everyday Life, 1700–1940.* New York: Harper & Row, 1988.

Lewis, Jan. *The Pursuit of Happiness: Family and Values in Jefferson's Virginia.* Cambridge: Cambridge University Press, 1983.

Maier, Pauline. *From Resistance to Revolution: Colonial Radicals and the Development of American Opposition to Britain, 1765–1776.* New York: Alfred A. Knopf, 1972.

Main, Jackson Turner. *Political Parties before the Constitution.* Chapel Hill: University of North Carolina Press, 1973.

Mayer, Holly. *Belonging to the Army: Camp Followers and Community in the American Revolution.* Columbia: University of South Carolina Press, 1996.

McCoy, Drew. *The Elusive Republic: Political Economy in Jeffersonian America.* Chapel Hill: University of North Carolina Press, 1980.

McDonald, Forrest. *Novus Ordo Secolorum: The Intellectual Origins of the Constitution.* Lawrence: University Press of Kansas, 1985.

Meranze, Michael. *Laboratories of Virtue: Punishment, Revolution, and Authority in Philadelphia, 1760–1835.* Chapel Hill: University of North Carolina Press, 1996.

Middlekauf, Robert. *The Glorious Cause: The American Revolution, 1763–1789.* New York: Oxford University Press, 1982.

Morgan, Edmund S., and Helen M. Morgan. *The Stamp Act Crisis: Prologue to Revolution.* Chapel Hill: University of North Carolina Press, 1953.

Nash, Gary B. *Forging Freedom: The Formation of Philadelphia's Black Community, 1720–1840.* Cambridge, Mass.: Harvard University Press, 1988.

———. *Race and Revolution.* Madison, Wis.: Madison House, 1990.

———. *The Urban Crucible: Social Change, Political Consciousness and the Origins of the American Revolution.* Cambridge, Mass.: Harvard University Press, 1979.

Nelson, William E. *The Americanization of the Common Law: The Impact of Legal Change on Massachusetts Society, 1760–1830.* Cambridge, Mass.: Harvard University Press, 1975.

Norton, Mary Beth. *Liberty's Daughters: The Revolutionary Experience of American Women, 1750–1800.* Boston: Little, Brown, 1980.

Onuf, Peter. *The Origins of the Federal Republic: Jurisdictional Controversies in the United States, 1775–1787.* Philadelphia: University of Pennsylvania Press, 1983.

———. *Statehood and Union: A History of the Northwest Ordinance.* Bloomington: Indiana University Press, 1987.

Peterson, Merrill. *Thomas Jefferson and the New Nation.* New York: Oxford University Press, 1970.

Potter, Janice. *Liberty We Seek: Loyalist Ideology in Colonial New York and Massachusetts.* Cambridge, Mass.: Harvard University Press, 1983.

Quarles, Benjamin. *The Negro in the American Revolution.* Chapel Hill: University of North Carolina Press, 1961.

Rakove, Jack. *The Beginnings of National Politics: An Interpretive History of the Continental Congress.* New York: Alfred A. Knopf, 1979.

———. *Original Meanings: Politics and Ideas in the Making of the Constitution.* New York: Alfred A. Knopf, 1996.

Rohrbough, Malcolm J. *The Trans-Appalachian Frontier: People, Societies, and Institutions, 1775–1850.* New York: Oxford University Press, 1978.

Ronda, James P. *Lewis and Clark among the Indians.* Lincoln: University of Nebraska Press, 1984.

Royster, Charles. *A Revolutionary People at War: The Continental Army and the American Character, 1775–1783.* Chapel Hill: University of North Carolina Press, 1979.

Rutland, Robert. *The Birth of the Bill of Rights, 1776–1791.* Boston: Northeastern University Press, 1991.

Schultz, Ronald. *The Republic of Labor: Philadelphia Artisans and the Politics of Class, 1720–1830.* New York: Oxford University Press, 1983.

Slaughter, Thomas. *The Whiskey Rebellion.* New York: Oxford University Press, 1986.

Smith, Barbara Clark. *After the Revolution: The Smithsonian History of Everyday Life in the Eighteenth Century.* New York: Random House, 1985.

Szatmary, David P. *Shays's Rebellion: The Making of an Agrarian Rebellion.* Amherst: University of Massachusetts Press, 1980.

Taylor, Alan. *William Cooper's Town: Power and Persuasion on the Frontier in the Early American Republic.* New York: Alfred A. Knopf, 1995.

Travers, Len. *Celebrating the Fourth: Independence Day and the Rites of Nationalism in the Early Republic.* Amherst: University of Massachusetts Press, 1997.

Ulrich, Laurel Thatcher. *A Midwife's Tale: The Life of Martha Ballard, Based on Her Diary, 1785–1812.* New York: Alfred A. Knopf, 1990.

Waldsteicher, David. *In the Midst of Perpetual Feasts: The Making of American Nationalism, 1776–1820.* Chapel Hill: University of North Carolina Press, 1997.

Watts, Steven. *The Republic Reborn: War and the Making of Liberal America, 1790–1820.* Baltimore: Johns Hopkins University Press, 1987.

Wood, Gordon S. *The Creation of the American Republic, 1776–1787.* Chapel Hill: University of North Carolina Press, 1967.

———. *The Radicalism of the American Revolution.* New York: Alfred A. Knopf, 1992.

Young, Alfred F. *The Shoemaker and the Tea Party: Memory and the American Revolution.* Boston: Beacon Press, 1999.

Index

Boldface page numbers denote extensive treatment of a topic. *Italic* page numbers refer to illustrations; *c* refers to the Chronology; and *m* indicates a map.